GUIDE TO
THE HOUSE
OF
COMMONS
2019

THE TIMES

GUIDE TO

THE HOUSE

OF

COMMONS

2019

TIMES BOOKS
LONDON

First published in 2020 by Times Books

An imprint of HarperCollins Publishers
Westerhill Road
Bishopbriggs
Glasgow G64 2QT
www.harpercollins.co.uk

A catalogue record for this book is available from the
British Library

ISBN 978-0-00-839258-1

10 9 8 7 6 5 4 3 2 1

Printed and bound by CPI Group (UK) Ltd.,
Croydon, CR0 4YY

Editor: Ian Brunskill
Deputy Editor: Matthew Lyons
Assistant Editors: Ben Dilks, Eugene Smith
Researchers: Liana Bravo Balsa, Myfanwy Craigie,
Adeola Eribake, Tali Fraser, Sam Hall, Liam Hill,
Fin Kavanagh, Ali Mitib, Hannah Smith, Noah Vickers

Design: Andrew Keys, Stephen Petch
Picture research: Charles Bowden
Graphics: Phil Slatter

Thanks to: Ian Amis, Claire Bishop, Gerry Breslin,
Rebecca Callanan, Anthony Coates, Sonia Dawkins,
Eleanor Eve, Alice Foster, Kerry Grainger, Rana Greig,
Jeremy Griffin, Tim Hames, Robert Hands,
Romina Hopkins, Alan Hunter, Dennis Kavanagh,
Jethro Lennox, Lord Lexden, Ailsa McNeil,
Karen Midgley, Karen Newton, Claire Patchett,
Angela Patrick, Peter Riddell, Hannah Rock, Pia Sarma,
Tim Shearring, Sam Stewart, Matthew Swift and the
Times graphics team, Craig Tregurtha, Emma Tucker,
John Witherow, Sarah Woods, Max Young

Contents

General election 2019

THE CAMPAIGN TO END A HUNG PARLIAMENT

by Francis Elliott

The hung parliament elected in 2017 collapsed itself with a rare display of brio. All stages of the Early Parliamentary General Election Act 2019 passed in a single day on October 29. Boris Johnson had tried three times previously to force the country to the polls but, needing a two-thirds majority under the provisions of the Fixed-term Parliaments Act (FTPA), had failed on each occasion as the opposition parties had resisted.

It was not hard to see why Labour MPs were not keen. The party had suffered a bad defeat at the European parliamentary elections in May required by the extension of the original Brexit deadline of March 28, 2019. It was true that the Conservatives had suffered an even worse humiliation but the governing party had since replaced the unpopular Theresa May with Mr Johnson. Jeremy Corbyn insisted that he wanted the election on offer but lacked the authority to force Labour MPs to vote for it. His chief whip, Nick Brown, repeatedly warned the Labour leader that he would face a potentially fatal revolt if he tried to whip in favour of an early election.

Better by far, thought many opposition MPs, to keep the new prime minister trapped in a parliament that he could not control than give him what he wanted: the chance to appeal to voters to give him the mandate to finally resolve the issue that had roiled the country for more than three years. Until mid-October it seemed that most other opposition parties held the same view. The Lib Dems and SNP co-operated with Labour and a group of Tory MPs to ensure that Mr Johnson was forced to break a "no ifs or buts" pledge to take the UK out of the EU, deal or no deal, on October 31, a deadline set after Mrs May failed to avoid the May European elections.

No sooner had the Benn Act, named after its main sponsor the Labour MP Hilary Benn, come into force, however, than the calculations of political advantage shifted again. Mr Johnson, shorn of a credible threat of a no-deal exit, took an agreement from the EU that Mrs May had previously rejected, in effect agreeing to customs and regulatory checks between Great Britain and Northern Ireland. The sacrifice of the Democratic Unionist Party (DUP) as allies, in going back on his word on these checks, made his parliamentary position even more untenable but he could offer voters an agreed departure on January 31, 2020, rather than a chaotic crash-out.

Calculations in Edinburgh were also evolving. Nicola Sturgeon started to press hard for an election that the SNP wanted to fight before the trial of the party's former leader Alex Salmond on 14 charges of indecent and sexual assault relating to his time as Scotland's first minister. The party's leader in Westminster, Ian Blackford, initially resisted the pressure from Bute House, arguing that it should not repeat the error of 1979 when it had voted with the Conservatives to precipitate an election that ushered in Margaret Thatcher. If it was going to be a handmaiden to Mr Johnson the SNP needed cover.

When Jo Swinson was elected Lib Dem leader on July 22 it looked as if she had inherited a winning hand. The party had cleaned up in the European elections as Remain voters responded to its unambiguous message on Brexit. A victory in the Brecon & Radnorshire by-election on August 1 swelled a sense of momentum behind a party that began to believe that it could be the big beneficiary of a significant political realignment. In an attempt to outflank Labour as the main advocates of Remain, Ms Swinson said that a Lib Dem government would revoke Article 50, in effect cancelling the result of the 2016 referendum.

On October 26 *The Observer* broke the story that the Lib Dems and the SNP would back a bill that circumvented the FTPA for an election to be held on December 12. Crucially it needed only a simple Commons majority. Labour MPs, no longer confident that they could prevent the election, were now anxious not to be seen to have been dragged to the voters against their will. The dam had burst.

For Mr Johnson an election was the least bad option but it was still freighted with risk. The UK had not had a December general election for almost a century. The scars of the 2017 poll were still fresh. His deal with the EU had meant betraying the DUP so only an outright majority would do: there were no other parties that would be willing to serve as partners. That meant that falling even one seat short of the 326 finishing post would mean that he was out of Downing Street. Loss would mean that he would go down as one of Britain's shortest-serving prime ministers, not an outcome easily countenanced by any politician and especially not one who had declared as a child that he wanted to be "world king".

Success depended in large part on neutralising the Brexit Party led by Nigel Farage. Mr Farage's new outfit, launched just before the European elections, offered an outlet to Leave voters to vent their frustration at the failure to implement the result of the 2016 referendum. An analysis of its success in the May poll suggested that it was drawing two former Tory voters to every one who had backed Labour in 2017. The dangers it posed to the prospects of a Conservative majority were obvious.

Mr Johnson's vulnerability to Mr Farage gave him little choice but to adopt a hard line on Brexit. Although rarely explicit, Tory MPs had understood his pitch in the leadership election as being the candidate best placed to fight an early election and void the threat posed by the Brexit Party. The series of controversial steps he took in his early months in charge — the prorogation of parliament, the expulsion of MPs who had facilitated the Benn Act, the ramping up of no-deal threats to Brussels — were all understood by his party in the context of the overwhelming imperative to convince Leave voters that Mr Johnson was committed to their cause. Nevertheless, a YouGov poll published on October 30, the day after MPs finally voted for the election, showed the Brexit Party to be on 13 per cent, far too high for Mr Johnson to be confident of success.

The question was whether the Conservatives should seek to do a deal with Mr Farage or hold their nerve and trust the dynamics of a campaign around a binary question of EU membership to squeeze him and his party out of contention. Lynton Crosby, the veteran strategist who had masterminded Mr Johnson's two London mayoral election victories, had advocated the latter course since early summer. Mr Crosby, while not himself directly involved in the Tory campaign, had suggested his protégé Isaac Levido to oversee it. Mr Levido, spotted in Mr Johnson's leadership HQ in July the day before his victory in the leadership election was announced, had been quietly preparing through the autumn at Conservative Campaign HQ and agreed with his mentor. Mr Johnson formally announced the start of the campaign on November 6 in a brief statement in Downing Street. He opened by saying he did not want an early election but had no choice because parliament was paralysed. He insisted that the country was "so nearly there" with an "oven-ready" deal in place. The deal delivered everything he had wanted from Brexit, he said: it would enable more money for public services like the NHS, allow for a "Australian points-based" immigration system and "take back control of our laws". Examples of things that the UK would do differently were the creation of freeports, the banning of live exports of animals and the removal of VAT on sanitary goods. He asserted that the deal would enable the UK to leave the EU "whole and entire and perfect as we promised". Further delay would be bad for democracy and the economy. He finished by saying that if elected he would govern as a compassionate, moderate leader.

It took Mr Johnson a little under four minutes to deliver all the elements of a core script that did not change for the next five weeks. The brevity was in contrast to Mr Corbyn's prolix launch six days earlier in Battersea Arts Centre, southwest London. It would, he said, be the "most ambitious and radical campaign this country has ever seen". A Labour government would transform Britain by taking on "the few who run a corrupt system". He identified "tax dodgers, dodgy landlords, bad bosses and big polluters". Named targets included "billionaire media barons like Rupert Murdoch" in a rogues gallery that included Crispin Odey, Mike Ashley, Jim Ratcliffe and the Duke of Westminster. There were references to Royal Mail, water companies, rail firms, tuition fees, homelessness, food banks, universal credit and climate change. On Brexit he said "we have to get this issue sorted" and promised that Labour would do so in six months. "We'll let the people decide whether to leave with a sensible deal or remain." He insisted: "That really isn't complicated."

He added that the NHS was "not for sale" and that any post-Brexit trade deal with the US should not involve giving American firms greater access to it, telegraphing his main line of attack. "The prime minister wants you to believe that we're having this election because Brexit is being blocked by an establishment elite," he said in a statement that tried to move the debate on to his favoured ground. "People aren't fooled so easily. They know the Conservatives are the establishment elite." He ended the 1,700-word pitch by saying that Labour would bring "real change for the many not the few ... even if the rivers freeze over."

In framing the election as a battle against an uncaring elite the Labour leader had been helped by two members of Mr Johnson's cabinet: Jacob Rees-Mogg and Alan Cairns. Mr Rees-Mogg, the Commons leader, unwisely suggested in a radio interview that Grenfell Tower victims had lacked common sense in listening to official advice to stay in their flats despite the blaze. Meanwhile, Mr Cairns, the Welsh secretary, denied knowledge of the circumstances of a collapsed rape trial involving two of his former aides only to be confronted with evidence that seriously undermined the denial. Mr Cairns was sacked pending an official investigation. Mr Rees-Mogg was banished from the airwaves by CCHQ and spent the remainder of the campaign confined to his own constituency of Somerset North East.

One of the many unhappy consequences of the FTPA was the advent of the five-week election campaign and although not actually held under that legislation it informed the date of the 2019 poll. The period between the dissolution of parliament on November 6 and polling day broke down into three phases: initial skirmishing up to the date of the close of candidate nominations on November 14; the parties' policy reveal culminating in the Conservatives' manifesto publication on November 24; and the final run-in, interrupted by a Nato meeting that included a two-day visit by Donald Trump from December 2.

In the first phase there was the now traditional parade of candidates outed by their opponents or the media for various political infelicities and then for the most part dropped by their parties. There was also a rush to fill vacancies left by MPs who at the last minute declared that they were standing down. Among them was Tom Watson, the former deputy leader of the Labour Party, and many of the expelled pro-European Tories, including Ken Clarke and Sir Oliver Letwin. (A handful of the Tory refuseniks ran, unsuccessfully, as independent candidates, most notably Dominic Grieve in Beaconsfield and David Gauke in Hertfordshire South West.)

While Mr Corbyn's team endeavoured to ensure that plum vacancies were filled by members of his faction, Mr Johnson made fealty to his deal an absolute condition of all Tory candidates, not only the newly selected ones. Mr Johnson and Ben Elliott, the Conservative Party co-chairman, were as ruthless as Mr Corbyn in ensuring that favoured sons and daughters were given sure-bet seats ensuring the usual influx of former special advisers and other well-connected Westminster operators.

Mr Farage and the Brexit Party were the dominant story of the opening phase, however, as they faced up to the reality that Mr Johnson had shot their fox. Mr Farage and his main money-man, Richard Tice, had been seeking an electoral pact with the Tories ever since Mr Johnson was elected. Their initial bid was high: the Brexit Party would not stand against "committed Brexiteer" Tories and a further 60 seats on two conditions: firstly, the party would be given a free run in the Labour-held seats where it believed it was best placed to win; secondly, Mr Johnson would drop any attempt to renegotiate the Withdrawal Agreement. "If they go down the withdrawal agreement route we will be their deadliest enemies. We can be their best friends, or their worst enemies," Mr Farage had said on September 13. "I very much hope that at some point Boris Johnson will simply look at the numbers and say [working together] is unavoidable.

We have to do something here. It's the only way we can win. If we stand against them they cannot win a majority. We end up with another hung parliament." Referring to seats such as Bolsover and Bassetlaw, he added: "If Boris Johnson really thinks he can win in those seats I don't know what he's smoking … it just isn't going to happen."

Mr Johnson did, however, think he could win in those seats and in dozens of Labour-held Leave-voting constituencies like them: indeed his whole strategy was predicated on him doing so. His analysis of the 2017 disaster, and that of his chief adviser Dominic Cummings, was not that Mrs May's strategy was wrong but that it was delivered so badly and that the timing was off. Mr Cummings had been a peripheral figure in British politics since the 2016 referendum, during which he led the Vote Leave campaign. The implosion of first Mr Johnson and then Michael Gove, his former boss, during the 2016 Tory leadership election had left him marooned. As Mrs May took over the job of delivering Brexit Mr Cummings had drifted away from a project that he feared was doomed.

Anticipating that Brexit would need another political mandate to be completed, however, he had started to re-engage early in 2019. He commissioned a series of focus groups in the Midlands to test the attitudes of voters he thought critical to delivering that mandate. At the time Mr Cummings had thought that it might require a new party to rescue Brexit but the fall of Mrs May and the election of Mr Johnson offered a more established vehicle. From the start of his premiership Mr Johnson stuck to a strategy crafted by the former Vote Leave director that echoed some of that campaign's theme: more cash for the NHS and an "Australian-style points-based immigration system" (a formulation whose meaninglessness is its greatest political virtue) allied to new insights from the Cummings focus groups that voters in Labour heartland seats were considerably more hardline on crime than the Westminster consensus.

The Tories would need more than Brexit to drive a wedge between voters and Mr Corbyn in Labour heartlands but it could be done. As the media awoke to the scale of the ambition so it latched on to a report by the right-leaning think tank Onward that identified towns such as Workington, with a strong rugby league tradition, as having a high proportion of voters likely to respond to the renewed Tory seduction. The unbroken swathe of Labour-held seats from north Wales across to the coast of northeast England allowed phrase-makers to borrow from the US and coin the Red Wall as a convenient catch-all for the Tories' target list.

Mr Farage, just as in 2016, was a fly in the ointment. As the days ticked down towards the close of nominations the Brexit Party leader came under intense pressure from other Brexiteers to withdraw and not split the Leave vote. Among those urging him to pack up were Arron Banks, who had bankrolled the Leave.EU outfit in 2016. Finally on November 12 Mr Farage announced a messy compromise: the Brexit Party would not stand in the 317 seats won by the Tories in 2017 but would contest 274 mostly Labour-held seats. Although not ideal — the Brexit Party would end up costing the Tories victory in at least a dozen seats — Mr Farage's partial capitulation shored up the Conservative position in the party's own heartlands, where the main threat was posed by the Liberal Democrats. Conservative pessimists had feared that a hardline Brexit position would put off Tory voters in seats, mainly in the south of England, that had voted heavily to remain in the EU in 2016. What was the point of winning from Labour only to see those gains wiped out by losses to the Lib Dems and SNP elsewhere? In not contesting the Tories' 2017 seats Mr Farage lifted much of this danger.

The decision had a secondary important effect: it removed his status as a national campaigner. Broadcasters no longer had to give the Brexit Party equal weight and Farage found himself bracketed with the leaders of the Green Party and Plaid Cymru in negotiations over TV debates. These, just as in the previous three general elections, became one of the more predictable and sometimes outright tedious stories of the campaign. The most important outcome, the advent of the first ever head-to-head debates between the two potential prime ministers, received the least coverage, presented as it was as a fait accompli by the two main parties and the hosts, ITV and the BBC. Faced with such a coincidence of interest from the parties and broadcasters, protests from the Lib Dems and others were futile. Despite the novelty neither debate changed the narrative of the campaign and neither Mr Johnson nor Mr Corbyn made any serious gaffes either in the ITV debate on November 19 nor on the BBC one on December 6. They helped, however, to foster the impression that the contest was essentially binary and none of the other formats offered to appease Ms Swinson and the other smaller parties gave them anything like an equivalent opportunity to challenge that impression.

On November 22 Mr Corbyn launched Labour's manifesto. Loaded with more policies and more spending commitments than two years previously the party had trailed many of the most eye-catching promises already, including a commitment to provide free broadband to every home and business in the UK within a decade. The manifesto reflected Mr Corbyn's analysis that the party had been too timid in 2017 both in prospectus and in the seats it targeted. He and some of his allies blamed Labour Party staffers inherited from earlier regimes for falling short. Given a second chance he was determined not to allow his ambitions to be curtailed again. There was no denying the scale of the programme laid out in the 105-page manifesto. At its heart was a promise to bring about "a green transformation" aiming to put the UK on track for net-zero carbon by 2030. Other notable policies included a promise to build 150,000 new council and social homes a year within five years at a cost of £75 billion; an immediate 5 per cent pay rise for public sector workers, with year-on-year above-inflation pay rises to follow, together with the introduction of a "real living wage" of at least £10 an hour; and five nationalisation programmes putting rail, water, gas, electricity and broadband providers under state control. New taxes on second homes, reversing inheritance tax cuts and imposing VAT on private school fees were intended as crowd-pleasing punitive measures against an elite to contrast, and supposedly help to pay for, giveaways such as free personal at-home care for the over-65s, scrapping tuition fees and reduced primary school class sizes.

The most expensive handout was held back for the Sunday newspapers: a pledge to scrap a planned increase in the state retirement pension age for women and compensate those affected. Perhaps unsurprisingly this £50 billion pledge was kept separate from Labour's costing document, which claimed to balance current spending with revenue raisers including higher taxes on companies and higher earners. Even without the pension policy the figure totalled £83 billion, a sum that had it been delivered would have had the state grow to its highest level since the war and match that of Germany, although remaining well short of French levels.

The Conservative manifesto, produced a week later, was an altogether more modest affair. After the trauma of Mrs May's disastrous social care policy, announced without warning or consultation in the middle of an election campaign two years previously, it was no surprise that Mr Johnson took a safety-first approach. The two most eye-catching promises were a pledge for an "extra" 5,000 nurses and a promise to cut the starting rate for national insurance payments. The first was problematic because it relied on improving retention rates as well as recruitment and the second was at best modest. Although it allowed the party to claim that it was cutting the taxes of 31 million workers, its value was only about £100 a year. Once experts were able to crunch the numbers the difference between the Tory and Labour spending programmes was stark. For every additional £1 the Conservatives were committed to spending by the end of the next parliament Labour was offering £28.

Paul Johnson, director of the Institute for Fiscal Studies, said: "If a single budget had contained all these tax and spending proposals we would have been calling it modest. As a blueprint for five years in government the lack of significant policy action is remarkable."

The scale of spending commitments was the subject of one of the few internal splits affecting the Conservative campaign. Figures such as Mr Cummings and Lee Cain, Mr Johnson's director of communications, fretted at being so vastly outspent by Labour but Mr Levido and Sajid Javid, the chancellor, insisted that the party had to resist undermining its own reputation for fiscal responsibility. The dividing line with Labour on economic credibility was worth preserving even at the risk that it limited the claims that Mr Johnson could make about bringing to a close the age of austerity. Mr Levido advanced one other argument that helped to win the day: the Tories, he said, had made a mistake in 2017 by responding every time Mr Corbyn made a retail offers to voters. It gave Labour's plans more profile and by repeatedly saying that they were unaffordable Mrs May irritated voters tired of a decade of cuts. Better, he said, to simply ignore Mr Corbyn's shop window and leave voters to draw their own conclusions over the validity of Labour's advertising.

The Lib Dems, as in so much else, fell awkwardly in the middle when it came to spending promises. In an inverse of the Conservative claims for Brexit, the Lib Dems claimed that their policy would provide a £50 billion "Remain bonus" for the economy. Individual promises included 20,000 more teachers and 35 hours a week of free childcare for all two to four-year-olds for 48 weeks of the year. The 96-page document included some old favourites, such as legalising cannabis and a penny on income tax to pay for increases in NHS spending, that again fell between Labour and Tory promises. A pledge to tax frequent flyers attracted most publicity, especially after Ms Swinson was forced to admit that she herself routinely flew from Scotland to London as she sought to balance her family life, constituency and Westminster responsibilities.

The SNP, meanwhile, kept it simple: a vote for the party would add to the pressure for a second independence referendum and to scrap Trident.

Since Labour had already said that it would consider granting another plebiscite if a majority of MSPs elected in Holyrood elections in 2021 wanted one, the party's manifesto was in effect the opening of a negotiation with Mr Corbyn to form a coalition in the event that Mr Johnson was denied an outright majority. While it was false to claim, as Mr Johnson repeatedly did, that a Labour government would inflict two more referendums in a year Mr Corbyn could not definitively rule out another independence vote because he needed to keep the SNP in play.

On November 26 the Labour leader was hit by a problem very much of his own making, however, when the chief rabbi made an attack in *The Times* on his record on antisemitism. Ephraim Mirvis said that Mr Corbyn's claims to have tackled the issue were a "mendacious fiction". He wrote: "A new poison, sanctioned from the very top, has taken root in the Labour Party." Although he stopped short of asking voters not to back Labour explicitly he wrote: "When December 12 arrives I ask every person to vote with their conscience. Be in no doubt, the very soul of our nation is at stake."

By ill-chance the article appeared just as Mr Corbyn was due to publish Labour's faith manifesto. His failure to address the chief rabbi directly at that event, as well as when he was interviewed by Andrew Neil on the BBC, marked a low point for the Labour leader. In 2017 he had largely shrugged off attacks on his past support for the IRA and Hamas and had seen his personal ratings rise, albeit from a low base and never into net positive. Labour's poll ratings again rose over the course of the campaign but the leader's scores remained dire. The head-to-head debates provided slight upticks but not nearly enough to change the picture. Although he referenced his opponent's support for the IRA in the BBC debate Mr Johnson largely left it to others to make the most direct attacks on Mr Corbyn's past associations and his worldview. Among the most devastating were the assessments of former Labour MPs such as Ian Austin, John Mann and John Woodcock. Their claim that Mr Corbyn would be a danger in No 10 helped to explain why he failed to make more of Mr Trump's visit for a scheduled Nato leaders' meeting a week before polling day. Labour's central attack on Mr Johnson's Brexit plan was that it would leave the UK as a whole, and the NHS in particular, vulnerable to US predation in trade talks with Mr Trump. Yet the visit came and went without major incident. The US president observed an uncharacteristically diplomatic silence on the UK election. Asked about his previous claim that in trade talks "everything" had to be on the table, he said he would not want the NHS even if it was offered on a "silver platter".

For as long as Mr Corbyn's ratings, particularly with former Labour voters, remained so negative it mattered less to the Tory campaign that the electorate was far from enamoured with Mr Johnson. In particular polls highlighted a lack of trust in the prime minister. His refusal to submit to media scrutiny, meanwhile, was becoming a campaign theme. With little to say beyond all-too-few key messages by the final weeks, Mr Johnson's tactics were becoming obvious. His willingness to mug for the cameras, and newspapers' willingness to publish images of the prime minister with that day's prop, had for weeks filled space that might otherwise have been given over to a more searching examination of his claims. After stringing the BBC along for weeks Mr Cain finally informed them that the Tory leader would not, after all, submit to the same grilling by Neill as that endured by Mr Corbyn. The resulting media storm was just that, however: a storm in and about the media that blew itself out.

More serious for Johnson was an image of a seriously ill four-year-old boy forced to sleep on a chair in the A&E waiting room of Leeds General Infirmary because of a lack of suitable beds. His refusal to look at the picture when shown it by the ITV reporter Joe Pike on his phone, and the bizarre confiscation of the device, gave the Tories their most torrid day.

The fundamentals of the campaign had been set, however, as soon as Mr Farage had withdrawn more than half the Brexit Party candidates. The Tories had done a better job of rallying Leave voters behind them than Labour had in squeezing the Lib Dems and other Remain voters. Mr Corbyn's unpopularity in the party's traditional heartlands had softened the Labour vote sufficiently for the Tories to drive in a series of wedges — of which Brexit was only the largest — to separate the opposition party from its former base. A game-plan that Mrs May had failed so badly to execute two years previously came good for Mr Johnson.

Francis Elliott is political editor of The Times

BEHIND THE UPS AND DOWNS OF THE POLLS

by Anthony Wells

Opinion polling went into the 2019 election under a cloud. The perception was that the polls had got the 2015 general election wrong, the 2016 EU referendum wrong and the 2017 general election wrong. In some cases this was unfair — while the polls were almost universally wrong in 2015, they had a far more mixed record in 2016 and 2017 — but nevertheless the reputation of the industry had rarely been lower. People who wanted to dismiss opinion polling as "always wrong" had an excuse to do so and media reporting of polling numbers was often heavily caveated.

The difficulties faced by the polling industry did not translate into any shortage of pollsters. Ten companies produced regular voting intention polls throughout the campaign and another three — ORB, Number Cruncher Politics and Qriously — produced single polls.

YouGov continued its long-term relationship with *The Times* and *The Sunday Times* but also conducted polling for Sky. Ipsos Mori continued to poll for the *Evening Standard*, BMG for *The Independent* and Opinium for *The Observer*. The *Telegraph* published regular polls by Savanta Com Res and *The Mail on Sunday* from Deltapoll (a new company set up by the former heads of political polling at ICM and YouGov). Survation conducted weekly polls for *Good Morning Britain* and ICM, whose long-term relationship with *The Guardian* petered out in 2018, instead provided polls for Reuters. Kantar published regular voting intention figures without a media partner.

The poll lead during the 2019 campaign, unlike the excitement of 2017, was largely static. The Conservatives began the race with a large lead and although Labour did pick up support during the campaign so did the frontrunners. Labour increased its support by squeezing the Liberal Democrats; the Conservatives added to theirs through the withdrawal and subsequent squeezing of the Brexit Party. The end result was that the Tory lead remained largely steady. Labour's hopes that Jeremy Corbyn would repeat his feat of 2017 were dashed: he began the campaign with poor leadership ratings and they remained negative during the campaign.

POLLING METHODS

The methodological challenges faced by the polling industry go back before the faults of the last election to the debacle of 2015, when the polls systemically understated the Tory lead. The official inquiry under Professor Patrick Sturgis had ruled out causes such as shy Tories, late swing or faulty turnout models and instead concluded that the people being interviewed in polls were not representative enough. Samples simply had too many Labour voters. In practice the problem appeared to be that samples contained too many politically engaged, Labour-voting young people.

In 2017 the polling industry took aggressive measures to try to correct this failing. There had been some improvements in the representativeness of samples, companies having added sampling quotas or weights based on education (to reduce over-representation of graduates) or political interest, but there were much more radical changes aimed more directly at reducing the pro-Labour error. Companies added grand demographic models that weighted down those (Labour-voting) groups that traditionally have lower turnout and "don't knows" were re-allocated in ways favourable to the Tories. The result was that the 2017 polls ended up overstating Conservative support, in some cases quite significantly.

For the 2019 elections the polling companies stripped away the more enthusiastic innovations that had backfired in 2017. There were none of the great overhauls that had characterised the previous election. Turnout models mostly went back to simply asking people how likely they were to vote. In most cases pollsters were using similar methods to the ones they used in 2015, with a few tweaks or additions to their weights to improve the samples.

During the campaign itself the biggest cause of variation in the polls of 2019 appeared to be past vote-weighting. It is normal practice for all polls to use weighting by demographics to fine-tune their samples. We know from the census, for example, that British adults are 51 per cent women and 49 per cent men, so if a raw sample is 45 per cent women the polling company "weights" the female respondents up to their correct proportion.

Since the 1990s the overwhelming majority of polling companies have also weighted their samples by how people voted at the previous election. On the whole this has worked well: we know what the actual result was at the previous election, so comparing how respondents voted with the actual election result is a good way of making sure that samples are politically representative as well as demographically representative. It all depends, however, on people accurately reporting their past vote to polling companies.

In the run-up to the 2019 election it appeared that people did not. Based on panel studies (that is, asking people in 2017 how they had just voted and then asking the same people again in 2019) people who voted Labour in 2017 seemed to be much less likely to admit it to pollsters than people who voted Tory. This risked upsetting polling companies' approaches to weighting. If 30 per cent of a sample were people who said they voted Labour in 2017, how could a pollster tell if it was because the sample contained too few former Labour voters — in which case, weighting it to the actual share would make the poll more accurate — or because some people were not admitting it (in which case, weighting it to the actual share would risk overstating Labour)?

The different approaches that polling companies took to this dilemma led to some variation in terms of results. Some companies relying on simple past-vote weighting tended to show smaller Tory leads. Companies who factored in a level of false recall, such as Kantar; had the ability to use data collected contemporaneously with the 2017 election, such as Opinium or YouGov; or avoided past-vote weighting on principle, such as Ipsos Mori, showed larger Conservative leads.

FINAL EVE-OF-ELECTION POLLS *(excludes Northern Ireland, except *)*

	C	Lab	LD	Green	Brexit	Lead
Opinium	45	33	12	2	2	12
Ipsos Mori	44	33	12	3	2	11
NCPolitics	43	33	12	3	3	10
Kantar	44	32	13	3	3	12
YouGov (MRP)	43	34	12	3	3	9
Qriously*	43	30	12	4	3	13
Panelbase	43	34	11	3	4	9
Survation	45	34	9	3	3	11
Deltapoll	45	35	10	3	4	10
BMG	41	32	12	3	4	9
ICM	42	36	12	2	3	6
Savanta Com Res	41	36	12	2	3	5

ACTUAL RESULT

	C	Lab	LD	Green	Brexit	Lead
Excluding NI	44.7	33	11.8	2.8	2.1	11.7
Including NI	43.6	32.1	11.6	2.7	2	11.5

Twelve companies produced polls in the final few days of the election campaign. The vast majority of them were within two points of the actual level of support for all the main parties; Ipsos Mori and Opinium were almost spot on. What errors there were tended to be understatements of the Conservative lead; Savanta Com Res and ICM both notably understated the margin of victory.

Less important statistically, but perhaps more so for the reputation of the polling industry, the polls got the story right. They showed a large lead for the Conservative Party and the actual result was a large lead for the Conservative Party.

MRP AND CONSTITUENCY POLLS

One of the few success stories in polling at the 2017 election was the YouGov MRP model (or multi-level regression and post-stratification). MRP is a technique for projecting data from a large national survey on to smaller geographical areas, in this case parliamentary constituencies. Where normal polls produce only national vote shares, an MRP model produces projected shares for each individual seat. In 2017 this had correctly predicted a hung parliament when the majority of traditional polls had been pointing towards a Tory majority. Consequently at the 2019 election there was great expectation around YouGov's MRP model and a number of other MRP models trying to replicate the technique's success.

In practice it performed less well at this election. YouGov's initial release of the 2019 model showed a Conservative lead of 11 points and a parliamentary majority of 68 seats. The updated version just before the election was further from the result, showing a Tory majority of only 28 seats. While the totals were out, the actual pattern of swings in the YouGov model was accurate: it correctly showed the Conservatives making great progress in Leave-voting traditionally Labour seats in the North and Midlands but performing less well in London, including the only Labour gain in Putney. It underlined the value of MRP in translating vote shares into seats, but showed that it was still reliant upon getting the right shares to begin with.

After being largely absent in 2017 the emphasis on tactical voting and the number of seats with unusual factors in play also led to a re-emergence of constituency polling in 2019, with Survation and Deltapoll conducting regular constituency polls for different clients.

Survation's constituency polls for *The Economist* focused on mainstream Labour-versus-Conservative seats such as Great Grimsby, Gedling and Wrexham. These were the exception, though, and most of the constituency polls focused on Liberal Democrat target seats, many commissioned by the Liberal Democrats themselves, on those seats where the question of which party was best placed to beat the Tories was unclear, or on those contested by high-profile defectors or independents such as Luciana Berger, Sam Gyimah or David Gauke. Most of these were commissioned by Peter Kellner on behalf of an "independent", but presumably pro-European and pro-tactical voting, donor. Few of the polls were late enough in the campaign to allow a direct comparison to the results (the polls commissioned by the Liberal Democrats were conducted when the party was polling higher overall) but those few performed well in general.

Overall the 2019 election was a successful one for the pollsters and a huge relief for the industry after previous misses. Given that most polling companies make little actual money from political polling and run it primarily for the positive publicity it gives them, there would be an inevitable question over the future of the industry if the only publicity it ever delivered was the reputational damage of getting it wrong.

This time round, however, most of the industry appears to have learnt from the mistakes of the last two elections. In 2015 the samples had been too Labour, in 2017 the adjustments had been too Conservative. The hope was that 2019 would get it just right. In the event, it looks as though it worked.

Anthony Wells is research director for YouGov

STATISTICAL ANALYSIS: LABOUR'S STRUGGLE

by Colin Rallings and Michael Thrasher

At the third time of asking in little more than four years the electorate delivered the Conservatives a decisive 80-seat majority in the House of Commons. It was the party's most clear-cut victory since Margaret Thatcher's second landslide over three decades ago in 1987. As then, the electoral system helped to exaggerate the scale of the party's superiority against a divided opposition, but that will bother Boris Johnson not one jot as he seeks to "get Brexit done".

The Conservatives increased their share of the vote for an unprecedented sixth election in succession and polled the second largest number of votes of any party at any general election in British history (the record was set by John Major in 1992 with 14.09 million) but many of their 57 seat gains owed more to the plummeting Labour vote than to an upsurge in their own support. Across the UK the Conservative share rose by just over 1 percentage point to 43.6 per cent, their best performance since 1979, whereas Labour fell back 8 points compared to the last contest in 2017 and lost 60 seats. As a result Labour now has 202 MPs, 163 fewer than the Conservatives. Nonetheless its 32.1 per cent share of the vote was higher than it managed in either 2010 or 2015.

In crude terms the slack was taken up by an uptick for the Liberal Democrats, by the Brexit Party polling rather better than Ukip did in 2017 and by an increase in support for both the Scottish National Party in Scotland and the Greens. The number and proportion of people voting Liberal Democrat rose by half but despite that the party had one fewer seat in the new parliament, 11, than in the old. Some small consolation for the party can be had from an increase in its second places from 38 in 2017 to 91 now, the vast majority in Conservative-held constituencies.

The SNP went some way to matching its astonishing result in 2015 when it won all the seats in Scotland bar three with a 50 per cent share of the total vote there. This time the party made 13 gains and took 48 of the country's 59 seats (coming second in the other 11) with a 45 per cent share. It has by far the largest bloc of MPs outside the two main parties. Plaid

Cymru in Wales retained its four seats but came nowhere close to adding to that tally.

The Brexit Party eclipsed Ukip both in numbers of candidates and in votes attracted. Its share of the vote only just topped 2 per cent, however, and it achieved its best position, second place, in only three constituencies. The Greens easily held on to their one seat but their modest rise in vote share was insufficient to threaten any further breakthrough.

In Northern Ireland there was a clear decline in support for the Democratic Unionist Party (DUP) and Sinn Fein. The DUP also lost seats, so that for the first time ever unionist parties in the province did not return the larger number of members to Westminster.

Although this election marked a modest move away from the two-party domination of 2017, with the combined Conservative and Labour share of the vote falling from 83.3 per cent to 75.7 per cent, those two parties still have nine in ten of all British MPs and, excluding the Speaker, all bar 12 of the 573 seats in England and Wales. Moreover, Labour is in second place in three quarters of Conservative-held seats and the Conservatives are the nearest challengers in more than 90 per cent of Labour territory.

Distribution of first and second places

	C	Lab	LD	SNP	Grn	Brex	Ind	SF	DUP	APNI	SDLP	UUP	Total 1st
C		275	80	6			4						365
Lab	186		9	1	2	3	1						202
LD	7			4									11
SNP	20	26	2										48
PC	3	1											4
Green		1											1
Speaker							1						1
SF							1		4		1	1	7
DUP								1		4	1	2	8
APNI									1				1
SDLP								1	1				2
Total 2nd	216	303	91	11	2	3	7	2	6	4	2	3	650

A record 47.6 million electors were eligible to vote on December 12, three quarters of a million more than in 2017. With turnout down in every country except Scotland, however, 200,000 fewer votes were cast. That had an impact on the level of representativeness that each party could claim. The Conservatives were endorsed by just under three in ten electors, a bare fraction more than Mrs May had secured two years earlier. By contrast, Labour's support among the whole electorate fell back from 28.3 per cent in 2017 to 21.6 per cent. With a UK-wide turnout of 67.3 per cent, the 32.7 per cent of electors who abstained were once again in the majority. Not since 1979 has any winning party won the votes of a third or more of all electors.

A total of 3,320 candidates contested the election, similar to the number in 2017. The Conservatives and Labour contested every seat in Great Britain except that of the Speaker. The Conservatives' sister party in Northern Ireland also fielded four candidates. The Liberal Democrats did not contest the Speaker's seat, nor did they put up a candidate in another 20 seats. This was usually as a result of the Unite to Remain alliance created with the Greens and Plaid Cymru, whereby the parties agreed on a single candidate.

The Greens had 497 candidates (30 more than in 2017) and the Brexit Party put up 275, following the decision by its leader, Nigel Farage, that it would not compete in any Conservative-held seat. Ukip, which as recently as 2015 had fought every constituency in England and Wales, this time fielded only 44 candidates, with none polling more than 2.4 per cent of the vote. In all, 1,275 candidates lost their deposit by failing to poll 5 per cent or more of the valid vote in their constituency.

There was a record proportion of women candidates: 33.8 per cent compared with 29.4 per cent in 2017, and for the first time a major party, Labour, had more female than male candidates. After the 2019 election Labour and the Liberal Democrats also had a majority of women MPs: 104 out of 202 in Labour's case; 7 out of 11 for the Liberal Democrats. The overall number of women MPs, 220, is the highest ever. Five candidates declared themselves "non-binary". It is difficult to precisely determine the number of candidates drawn from a black, Asian or other minority ethnic group but 65 members of these groups were elected in 2019 (10 per cent of all MPs) compared with the previous record of 52 in 2017. They comprised 22 Conservatives, 41 Labour and 2 Liberal Democrats.

THE BATTLE FOR VOTES

The analysis that follows concentrates on Great Britain, with Northern Ireland discussed separately alongside country-specific analyses for the other nations of the UK.

The Conservatives polled 44.7 per cent of the popular vote in Britain, an increase of 1.3 points on 2017, and won 365 seats. It was the party's highest share since 1979 and its largest number of seats since 1987. It gained 57 seats and lost ten: seven to the SNP, two to the Liberal Democrats and one to Labour. The Conservative vote in Scotland declined but the gap between them and Labour in third place widened significantly. In Wales, where the party gained six seats, the Conservatives recorded their highest share of the vote for more than a century and equalled the largest number of seats they had won there at any election since 1859.

As in 2017 the Conservatives performed best in seats that had strongly voted to leave the EU and/or that had voted heavily for Ukip in 2015. Their vote in such places was up by more than 6 points on average following a double-figure increase last time. This pattern applied in their own and in Labour-held constituencies. Indeed the party gained 16 of the 34 previously Labour seats where the Leave vote in 2016 was 65 per cent or more.

The Conservatives did noticeably less well in their own Remain-voting, more affluent seats in the south of England. Here their vote share was often down by 3 percentage points or more. With Labour falling by an even larger amount, however, and the Liberal Democrats having to make up substantial ground to have any chance, Conservative possession was rarely threatened.

In 2017 Labour activists had argued that, although the election was lost, the momentum of the campaign in terms of increases in both votes and seats was theirs. There could be no such claim this time. The party fell back sharply in every part of the country and in every type of seat. And although its 32.9 per cent vote share was above the level of either 2010 or 2015, its return of only 202 MPs was the worst since taking on the Stanley Baldwin-led National Government in 1935.

The party did especially badly in several parts of the country once seen as its own heartlands. It was down by more than 8 percentage points to an all-time low in Scotland and, as in 2015, won but a single seat there. In the Yorkshire and the Humber region a double-digit drop in share put Labour behind the Conservatives in votes for the first time since 1983 and it lost nine seats. In the North East, the one region where it had advanced less than the Conservatives two years ago, the outcome was even worse: Labour's share fell by almost 13 points with the Conservatives winning more seats than at any time since at least 1959.

Nor was there much comfort in London and other constituencies in England and Wales notable for a young, ethnically diverse population, where the party had done so well in 2017. In London and in those seats with the largest number of ethnic minority voters Labour's vote was down by more than 6 percentage points; in student-heavy seats the drop was of the order of 5 points.

With the Conservatives also failing to make headway in such areas it was often the Liberal Democrats who benefited. Even though they polled in excess of a million more votes and had a vote share 4 percentage points higher than in 2017 they continued to languish in post-coalition doldrums. Their 11.8 per cent share of the vote in Great Britain was worse than at any election between February 1974 and 2010. They again failed to have any MPs elected in Wales and both lost and gained a seat in Scotland to remain on four. In England they gained one seat but lost two to finish one down overall on seven MPs.

The party's best performances came in strongly Remain-voting Conservative-held seats where they enjoyed a double-figure increase in share of the vote. In London and the South East their vote rose by 6 points or more. Nonetheless in only 15 of the 91 seats where they were in second place were they 10 points or less behind the winner. Returning to the level of representation they had between 1997 and 2015 still seems a distant prospect. And this despite them being given a clear run in forty seats in England and three in Wales, including several of the ones they held, as part of the Unite to Remain alliance. Of the seven sitting MPs who defected to the Liberal Democrats, four finished in a respectable second place, two came third and one did not stand.

The Greens were unopposed by their alliance colleagues in a total of nine constituencies, including Brighton Pavilion, where Caroline Lucas has been the MP since 2010. She further increased her majority but elsewhere the party struggled to make an impact. Its vote share rose by 1 percentage point to nearly 3 per cent, but its candidates lost their deposit in all but 31 of the constituencies it contested and polled above 10 per cent of the vote in only five of them.

The nationalist parties experienced mixed fortunes. The SNP markedly increased both its vote share and seats won and reduced the number of seats where its tenure was only marginal. Indeed in 2019 it was also within 10 points of being the victor in nine of the eleven it did not win. Plaid Cymru were beneficiaries of the Remain alliance in seven seats in Wales including three of the four they had held going into the election. Although they retained third place overall their vote share was down slightly and nowhere did they finish in second place.

The Brexit Party's performance must be interpreted in the context of its decision not to challenge the Conservatives. Its 2.1 per cent share of the total vote in Britain in fact equated to 5.1 per cent in those seats it fought. The performance of its 15 candidates in Scotland and of those in the southern half of England was derisory. In the north and in parts of Wales, though, it frequently scored above 10 per cent of the vote, perhaps saving Labour from even greater losses.

Excluding the Speaker there were 461 independent and small party candidates in Britain who together polled more than 350,000 votes. The largest single group was Ukip's 44 candidates, followed by the Christian People's Alliance with 29, the Yorkshire Party with 28 and the Monster Raving Loony Party with 24. They all lost their deposits.

Much attention was focused on the 18 ex-MPs who had either resigned or been deprived of their party's whip and decided to stand again for a different party or as independents. None of the 11 who in effect stood as independents came close to winning: three came a usually rather distant second and another three lost their deposits. The former Conservative Dominic Grieve polled nearly 30 per cent of the total vote in Beaconsfield but still finished more than 15,000 votes behind his successor.

In two other cases an independent candidate polled significantly well against a full range of party competition. In Ashfield the council leader Jason Zadrozny helped to push Labour from first to third place. In Devon East, Claire Wright finished second for the third time running, polling more than 40 per cent of the vote.

ENGLAND

The pattern of the election in England is neatly summed up by the fact that the Conservatives made 48 gains from Labour yet lost only a single seat to it: Putney. Granted, this was only about half the number of gains that David Cameron achieved in 2010 but the Labour share of the vote fell by more than it did then and the 4.9 per cent swing to the Conservatives was greater than for any sitting government in modern times.

The Conservatives' 47.2 per cent share of the vote matched that at Mrs Thatcher's first election victory in 1979; Labour's 33.9 per cent was far from an historic low, though, and it won more seats in England itself, 179, than it had in either 1983 or 1987. Indeed, although the two-party share dropped back from 2017's near-fifty-year high of 87.3 per cent, in 2019 only 8 of the 532 English MPs elected on a party ticket were not drawn from either the Conservative or Labour parties.

The increase of almost 5 percentage points in the Liberal Democrat vote was insufficient to bring widespread gains; the Greens retained their single seat but came close nowhere else; neither the Brexit Party nor the array of independent and smaller party candidates could do better than an occasional second place.

The real change in England took place in the five regions of the Midlands and the North where the Conservatives registered 44 of their gains. The party had already served notice of its threat to Labour in the so-called Red Wall by making six gains from Labour against the run of play two years ealier. Constituencies such as Derbyshire North East and Stoke on Trent South that had been safely Labour for decades had been trending Conservative since 2010 before falling two years ago. There was a range of other seats, such as Bishop Auckland, Great Grimsby and Tony Blair's old seat of Sedgefield, where a similar change had left Labour's position increasingly precarious. This time the swing to the Conservatives was greatest in the North East (8.4 per cent) and smallest in London (2.7 per cent). As in 2017 London was the only region where the Conservative share declined.

In seats that the Conservatives already held and where there had been sizeable support for Leave and for Ukip they often motored ahead. The party's share was up by almost 20 per cent in Thurrock (the one seat where Ukip polled more than 10,000 votes in 2017) and jumped by more than Labour's fell in Boston & Skegness as well as in Mansfield and Walsall North (two of their other 2017 gains). There can be little doubt that the Brexit Party's decision not to contest such constituencies gave the Conservatives a much easier run.

The Conservative gains can crudely be divided into two types. In about a dozen cases they were simply winning back seats that they had held under David Cameron. In seats such as High Peak, Keighley and Warrington South the swing to the Conservatives was below average and the Brexit Party polled poorly. To these could be added constituencies such as Bolton North East, Bury South and Darlington, which had been Conservative through the Thatcher years until at least 1992. The Brexit Party lost its deposit in those seats too.

Some of their other gains were truly historic, including Bolsover and the two other Stoke-on-Trent seats (Labour since their creation in 1950), Don Valley (since 1922), Leigh (also 1922), Bassetlaw (1929), Wakefield (1931) and Sedgefield (1935). In each case the Labour share of the vote plunged by at least twice as much as the Conservatives' rose, with the Brexit Party being the other beneficiary. A similar pattern has left some Labour seats such as Hemsworth, Stockton North and Wansbeck as unlikely new marginals.

For all the anecdotal and polling evidence about the toxicity of the Labour leadership and the public perception of its trustworthiness and competence, there can be little doubt that Brexit and its delivery shaped the outcome. Post-election polling by Lord Ashcroft suggests that more than 70 per cent of 2016 Leave voters supported the Conservatives (many for the first time), whereas Remainers spread their votes more widely and therefore less effectively in a first-past-the-post electoral system.

In Labour seats that had voted Leave by 65 per cent or more in 2016 the party's vote share dropped by an average of almost a third and its support in pro-Leave seats declined more heavily when there was a Brexit Party candidate than when there was not. Brexit's two second places in England were both in Barnsley, where the Conservative vote hardly shifted, and it also polled more than a quarter of the vote in Hartlepool where both the biggest parties lost ground. It is arguable that these seats, and perhaps a handful of others, could have been won by the Conservatives if there had been no Brexit presence.

It is also important to note the demographic changes that characterise many of the constituencies that have newly rejected Labour. Their populations have been ageing and the rapid building of private housing estates has introduced a different type of voter. The patterns of employment have shifted too. Where there was once highly unionised heavy industry there is now a proliferation of light industrial units and often insecure service sector jobs. This is no longer traditional Labour territory.

Labour's sole gain of Putney, one of only 13 seats where its share of the vote increased, neatly encapsulates how the electoral battleground is changing from the other side too. Heavily pro-Remain and with a young, middle-class and highly educated electorate, it was one of the few types of seat where Labour woes were at least attenuated. The party's share also increased in Canterbury, Leeds North West and Portsmouth South, where there are large numbers of students. Those are three of the 27 seats in England that Labour gained from either the Conservatives or the Liberal Democrats in 2017. Altogether it retained as many as 14 of them, sometimes with an increased majority. Labour was not down and out everywhere.

The Liberal Democrats put their faith in committed Remainers or, at the least, attracting the tactical votes of those who wanted to keep the Conservatives out. A similar pitch had yielded dividends in 1997; it did not work this time. They did increase their share by 10 percentage points or more in 44 seats that tended to be either Remain voting and/ or subject to particular local circumstances. Their sharpest increase was in the Conservative leadership contender Jeremy Hunt's Surrey South West seat (28.9 points) closely followed by Esher & Walton (27.7 per cent) where a vigorous campaign was mounted against Dominic Raab, the foreign secretary. They ran the sitting MP to within a thousand votes in Cheltenham, Wimbledon and Winchester, but gained only the very marginal Richmond Park and more impressively St Albans, where their vote share was up nearly 18 percentage points at Labour's expense. It is interesting to note that the Liberal Democrat vote rose by almost as much in the constituency that the former Labour MP Chuka Umunna vacated (Streatham) as in the one to which he decamped (Cities of London & Westminster).

After the election there were only 14 seats in England where the Liberal Democrats were within 10 points of victory. They did just fail to win back Sir Nick Clegg's old seat of Sheffield Hallam but were squeezed by Labour and the Conservatives in Leeds North West, which they also lost in 2017 and where they are now far behind in third place. They face a similar predicament some of their other former strongholds. In 2005 the party won all five seats in Cornwall; in the duchy's now six constituencies it is in a distant third place in four and seriously challenges the Conservatives in St Ives alone. In Norfolk North, where Norman Lamb stood down after 18 years as MP, the Liberal Democrat share of the vote fell by more than a third and the seat was easily surrendered. They also lost Carshalton & Wallington (theirs since 1997) and Eastbourne, which has bounced back and forth between them and the Conservatives for 30 years.

SCOTLAND

The SNP fell back in the 2017 election from the dizzy heights it had reached two years earlier when it won 56 of Scotland's 59 constituencies. It lost a quarter of its vote and 21 seats as the Conservatives, Labour and the Liberal Democrats all made gains. The Ruth Davidson-led Conservative revival was especially impressive, the party winning 12 additional seats and beating Labour in the popular vote for the first time since 1959. In fully 46 of Scotland's seats, though, the majority of the first-placed party over its nearest rival was less than 10 per cent — the conventional definition of a marginal — and it was against that background that the 2019 election was fought. A swing in the SNP's favour from both Labour and the Conservatives since 2017 enabled the party to make 13 net gains. An 8-point increase in its vote share contrasted with a drop of 3.5 points for the Conservatives and a slump of more than 8 points for Labour. Predictably it was those parties' marginal seats that fell.

The Conservatives lost ground but did retain six of their previous thirteen seats. They appeared to be cushioned by two factors: in the three constituencies running coast to coast across the south of Scotland pro-union electors and relatively large majorities proved sufficient to thwart the SNP challenge. In parts of the rural northeast, characterised by greater-than-average scepticism about both nationalism and EU membership, the SNP underperformed. In Banff & Buchan, the only Scottish constituency to vote Leave in 2016, the Conservatives increased their majority.

All six Labour gains in 2017 had been by a margin of 6 percentage points or less and all six fell again this time. The party's sole representative remains Ian Murray in Edinburgh South, who reprised the rather lonely role he had from 2015 to 2017. "The cockroach who survived Labour's nuclear holocaust," as he put it himself. Indeed Labour's 18.6 per cent share of the vote in Scotland marked the first occasion on which it had fallen below 20 per cent since it first started fielding a significant number of candidates there back in 1918. After 2019 it appeared to be marooned as the third party in Scotland, a very long way from being able to make a decisive contribution to a future Labour general election victory.

The Liberal Democrats retained four seats overall and had the distinction of bringing about the SNP's single loss, in Fife North East. The most marginal seat in the UK, with an SNP majority of only two votes, it had previously been in Liberal Democrat hands for nearly 30 years until 2015. Of more significance, though, was the party's own defeat in Dunbartonshire East, the constituency of Jo Swinson, the party leader. It was one of only 17 across Britain where the party's vote share declined by 3 percentage points or more and the SNP nudged ahead by fewer than 150 votes. Ms Swinson, no longer an MP, felt obliged to resign the leadership immediately.

The 56 candidates from other parties had no impact in Scotland. They all lost their deposits, including the 22 Greens and 15 Brexit Party representatives.

The political landscape in Scotland looked only a little less precarious after the election than it did before. For whereas the number of SNP-held marginal seats has dropped from 30 to 13, all but two of the 11 held by other parties fall into that category.

WALES

As in 2015 and 2017 the overall pattern of results in Wales closely resembled that in England. The Conservative share rose by more than 2 percentage points to 36.1 per cent, its highest level since the 19th century. Labour, on the other hand, was down 8 points to 40.9 per cent, which nonetheless was better than in either 2010 or 2015. The swing from Labour to the Conservatives was 5.2 percentage points, compared with 4.9 in England.

Six seats in Wales changed hands directly between Labour and the Conservatives. The latter matched their 1983 performance by winning 14; Labour held on in 22, its lowest total since representation in Wales was expanded to 40 constituencies in 1997.

The Conservatives gained five of the seven most marginal seats in Wales, including a swathe in the northeast of the country that clearly voted Leave in the 2016 referendum. One of them, Wrexham, had been Labour since 1935. Their wild card victory was in Ynys Mon (the Isle of Anglesey), which had been touted to fall to Plaid Cymru after the retirement of Albert Owen, the sitting Labour MP. The two marginals they failed to win — Gower and Cardiff North — were both relatively middle-class, Remain-voting Labour gains in 2017.

Eleven seats in Wales were subject to the electoral pact between the Greens, the Liberal Democrats and Plaid Cymru. In truth it made little difference to the outcome. The Liberal Democrat vote did rise, if only to 6 per cent, but the party failed by some distance to hang on to its August 2019 by-election victory in Brecon & Radnorshire. After the December general election it once again had no representation in Wales. The other two parties stood aside for the Greens in the Vale of Glamorgan, but the impact there simply enabled them to save their deposit.

Plaid's vote slipped a little to fractionally under 10 per cent but it retained all four of its seats. The electoral pact did it no harm in three of them, but there was no such co-operation in Ceredigion. Plaid had gained this from the Liberal Democrats by only 104 votes in 2017; this time they surged ahead to leave the erstwhile Liberal Democrat MP in a humiliating third place.

The Brexit Party fielded candidates in all 32 non-Conservative seats in Wales, saving their deposit in 21 of them and polling an average of 7.3 per cent of the vote in those they contested. A second place in Blaenau Gwent was their best showing, but they polled above 10 per cent in a handful of other safe Labour "valleys" constituencies too.

NORTHERN IRELAND

Whereas in the 2017 general election there was a significant increase in support for the two main parties in the province, the Democratic Unionist Party and Sinn Fein, this time they both lost vote share and the DUP lost seats as well. The main beneficiary was the non-sectarian Alliance party, whose share more than doubled to nearly 17 per cent, establishing it firmly in third place. The Social Democratic and Labour Party also increased its share by more than 3 percentage points and so reversed a run of five elections where it had fallen back.

The DUP's most embarrassing loss was in Belfast North, where its Westminster leader Nigel Dodds fell to Sinn Fein at least partly because the SDLP chose not to stand to avoid splitting the nationalist vote. Sinn Fein returned the favour in Belfast South, where the SDLP, which had held the seat for a dozen years until 2017, defeated the DUP's only female MP in the last parliament, Emma Little Pengelly, after a swing of more than 18 percentage points.

There was no such co-operation in Foyle. Here, another 18-point swing let the SDLP regain the seat from Sinn Fein. Foyle had been an SDLP stronghold for more than 30 years until 2017, including more than two decades as the seat for the Nobel Peace Prize winner John Hume, one of the architects of the 1998 Good Friday Agreement.

The Ulster Unionist Party, which has become something of the bridesmaid of Northern Ireland electoral politics in recent years, again failed to win a seat, albeit with a vote share that crept up a little to 11.7 per cent. As in 2017 it came closest in the perpetual marginal of Fermanagh & South Tyrone, where the DUP again stood aside. This time Michelle Gildernew's majority for Sinn Fein was only 57 votes and it is worth reflecting that more than 300 ballot papers in the constituency were deemed invalid at the count.

The decision of the independent MP Lady Sylvia Hermon to stand aside in Down North paved the way for a more traditional battle. Both the SDLP and Sinn Fein decided not to contest the seat in favour of the Alliance party, whereas there was competition between the DUP, the UUP and the Conservatives in this middle-class Protestant-majority constituency. In the end the pact was crucial and the Alliance came out on top with 45 per cent of the vote, despite the three avowedly unionist parties together polling more than half the total.

Of the total 102 candidates in Northern Ireland, 21 were drawn from outside the main five parties. The Northern Ireland Conservatives fielded only four candidates, down from seven in 2017 and sixteen in 2015, who together polled little more than 5,000 votes and who all lost their deposits. The only case of a smaller party exceeding 5 per cent of the constituency-wide vote was People Before Profit, who came second to Sinn Fein in Belfast West.

TURNOUT

Before the election there was much speculation about the impact of the time of year on people's willingness to turn out and vote. Some academic research cited clear evidence that voters were more reluctant to go to the polls in the winter. Other sources pointed to the very high turnout at the last winter election in February 1974 and countered that the perceived closeness or significance of a contest was the defining factor. It was also the case that the proportion of electors with a postal vote and thus able to vote at their own convenience had risen from 2 per cent in 1974 to nearly 20 per cent in 2019.

In the event turnout was down everywhere except in Scotland where, ironically, the days are even shorter than elsewhere. The UK turnout of 67.3 per cent was 1.5 percentage points lower than in 2017, although still higher than at any general election between 2001 and 2015. The decline was greatest in Northern Ireland, where it was down 3.6 points to 61.8 per cent; in Scotland there was a 1.7 point increase to 68.1 per cent. In England it was down 1.6 points to 67.5 per cent and in Wales by 2.0 to 66.6 per cent.

The large number of marginal seats in Scotland may have helped to boost the rise, although the general relationship between marginality and turnout was once again rather weak. In those constituencies in England and Wales where a party was defending a majority of less than 5 per cent turnout fell on average by just less than 1 percentage point. In places where the majority going into the election was 20 points or more, turnout fell a little more but only by an average of 1.9 points.

Sharper differences could be found in seats with large numbers of black,

Asian and other ethnic minority voters, where average turnout was down by almost 4 points (in 2017 it had risen strongly in the self-same areas), and in Labour-held constituencies that had recorded a large Leave vote at the 2016 referendum (down 3.4 points). Many of these now non-voters are likely to have been former Labour supporters.

A total of 219 constituencies had turnouts in excess of 70 per cent (there were 274 in 2017 and 181 in 2015) and it fell below 60 per cent in 83 cases (33 in 2017 and 96 in 2015). The highest turnouts in England were in Richmond Park (78.7 per cent), which the Liberal Democrats gained, and in Kenneth Clarke's former Nottinghamshire seat of Rushcliffe (78.5 per cent). The highest in Wales was in Cardiff North (77.0 per cent) as it had been at both previous elections. In Scotland, Dunbartonshire East (80.1 per cent) registered the highest turnout anywhere in the UK as it sealed Jo Swinson's fate. In Northern Ireland, Fermanagh & South Tyrone (69.7 per cent) again topped the table.

At the other extreme Hull East was the only constituency where fewer than half the eligible electorate participated (49.3 per cent) with scarcely more turning out in the city's other two seats. In Chorley, where the new Speaker Sir Lindsey Hoyle sought re-election with no major party challengers, the 51.2 per cent turnout was down by more than 20 points compared with 2017.

THE TASK NOW FACING LABOUR

The near 12-point gap in vote share and the gulf of 163 in parliamentary seats between Labour and the Conservatives make it very difficult for the party to contemplate winning back power at a single general election. Labour would need to gain 124 seats at that election to secure a majority of two. Only on three occasions in the past hundred years has it achieved such an advance: 1929 (+136), 1945 (+139) and 1997 (+147). In 1929 it fielded many more candidates than at the previous election; in both 1945 and 1997 its gains were sufficient to win a landslide, not simply creep over the line.

The task looks even harder in terms of swing. A direct swing from Conservative to Labour of 7 percentage points would make Labour simply the largest party. The key seats for this target are Pendle and Northampton North, both Labour until 2010 but where the Conservatives polled over half the total vote in December 2019. A swing of 12 points is needed to claim even the narrowest overall majority. The pivotal seat here is Bromley & Chislehurst, which has a Conservative majority in excess of 10,000 votes.

The record postwar national swing for either party is the 10.2 per cent Tony Blair achieved in 1997. It would be slightly easier for Labour if it took significant votes from the SNP in Scotland, but the results in 2019 give few indications of that happening.

It is also likely that the government will use its majority to enact the long delayed redrawing of constituency boundaries. Whether that is on the basis of 600 MPs, which David Cameron was keen to pursue, or by retaining a 650-seat House of Commons, the levelling up of electorates is almost certain to provide a further boost for the Conservatives' chances of re-election without a single vote being cast.

Yet with an ever-more volatile electorate, and with an unpredictable post-Brexit future ahead, Labour should not be completely written off. The old maxim — oppositions don't win elections; governments lose them — could yet apply if Boris Johnson's tenure as prime minster goes awry.

Swing required for Labour

Outcome	% Swing from from C to Lab	Pivotal seat
Lab and C tie (279 seats)	6.96	Pendle
Labour largest party	6.97	Northampton North
Labour majority of 2 (326 seats)	12.0	Bromley & Chislehurst
Lab majority of 30 (340 seats)	13.6	Airdrie & Shotts
Lab majority of 50 (350 seats)	14.3	Aylesbury

Colin Rallings and Michael Thrasher are emeritus professors at the University of Plymouth and associate members of Nuffield College, Oxford

Concise summary results by country

	VOTES	VOTES %	% CHANGE	CANDIDATES	ELECTED	LOST DEP
ENGLAND						
C	12,710,848	47.2	1.8	532	345	0
Lab	9,125,178	33.9	-8.0	532	179	5
LD	3,340,840	12.4	4.6	520	7	108
Green	819,769	3.0	1.2	454	1	424
Brexit	547,106	2.0	2.0	228	0	138
Others	367,925	1.4	-1.6	444	1	426
Total Vote	26,911,666			2,710	533	1,101
Electorate	39,897,593					
Turnout	67.5%					
SCOTLAND						
C	692,939	25.1	-3.5	59	6	0
Lab	511,838	18.6	-8.5	59	1	7
LD	263,417	9.5	2.8	59	4	13
SNP	1,242,380	45.0	8.1	59	48	0
Green	28,122	1.0	0.8	22	0	22
Brexit	13,243	0.5	0.5	15	0	15
Others	7,122	0.3	-0.2	19	0	19
Total Vote	2,759,061			292	59	76
Electorate	4,053,050					
Turnout	68.1%					
WALES						
C	557,234	36.1	2.5	40	14	0
Lab	632,035	40.9	-8.0	40	22	0
LD	92,171	6.0	1.5	32	0	15
PC	153,265	9.9	-0.5	36	4	10
Brexit	83,908	5.4	5.4	32	0	11
Green	15,828	1.0	0.7	18	0	17
Others	9,916	0.6	-1.6	18	0	17
Total Vote	1,544,357			216	40	70
Electorate	2,319,374					
Turnout	66.6%					

The performance of Labour and Labour Co-op candidates is aggregated under the heading Labour

	VOTES	VOTES %	% CHANGE	CANDIDATES	ELECTED	LOST DEP
NORTHERN IRELAND						
DUP	244,128	30.6	-5.4	17	8	0
SF	181,853	22.8	-6.7	15	7	2
Alliance	134,115	16.8	8.8	18	1	2
SDLP	118,737	14.9	3.1	15	2	2
UUP	93,123	11.7	1.4	16	0	2
Others	19,650	2.5	-0.8	14	0	13
C	5,433	0.7	0.2	4	0	4
Green	1,996	0.2	-0.7	3	0	3
Total Vote	799,035			102	18	28
Electorate	1,293,971					
Turnout	61.8%					
GREAT BRITAIN						
C	13,961,021	44.7	1.3	631	365	0
Lab	10,269,051	32.9	-8.1	631	202	12
LD	3,696,428	11.8	4.3	611	11	136
SNP	1,242,380	4.0	0.9	59	48	0
Green	863,719	2.8	1.1	494	1	463
Brexit	644,257	2.1		275	0	164
PC	153,265	0.5	0.0	36	4	10
Others	384,963	1.2	-1.5	481	1	462
Total Vote	31,215,084			3,218	632	1,247
Electorate	46,270,017					
Turnout	67.5%					
UNITED KINGDOM						
C	13,966,454	43.6	1.3	635	365	4
Lab	10,269,051	32.1	-7.9	631	202	12
LD	3,696,428	11.5	4.2	611	11	136
SNP	1,242,380	3.9	0.8	59	48	0
Green	865,715	2.7	1.1	497	1	466
Brexit	644,257	2.0		275	0	164
DUP	244,128	0.8	-0.1	17	8	0
SF	181,853	0.6	-0.2	15	7	2
PC	153,265	0.5	0.0	36	4	10
Alliance	134,115	0.4	0.2	18	1	2
SDLP	118,737	0.4	0.1	15	2	2
UUP	93,123	0.3	0.0	16	0	2
Others	404,613	1.3	-1.5	495	1	475
Total Vote	32,014,119			3,320	650	1,275
Electorate	47,563,988					
Turnout	67.3%					

Voting in the English regions

	C	LAB	LD	GREEN	BREXIT	OTHERS	TOTAL
EAST MIDLANDS							
votes	1,280,724	740,975	182,665	60,067	35,344	38,677	2,338,452
votes %	54.8	31.7	7.8	2.6	1.5	1.7	100.0
2017 votes %	50.7	40.5	4.3	1.5		3.0	100.0
change	4.0	-8.8	3.5	1.1	1.5	-1.4	
seats	38	8	0	0	0	0	46
2017 seats	31	15	0	0		0	46
electorate							3,482,370
turnout %							67.2
2017 turnout %							69.0
change							-1.9
EASTERN							
votes	1,754,091	749,906	410,849	90,965	11,707	50,751	3,068,269
votes %	57.2	24.4	13.4	3.0	0.4	1.7	100.0
2017 votes %	54.6	32.7	7.9	1.9		2.9	100.0
change	2.5	-8.3	5.5	1.1	0.4	-1.2	
seats	52	5	1	0	0	0	58
2017 seats	50	7	1	0		0	58
electorate							4,495,684
turnout %							68.2
2017 turnout %							69.8
change							-1.6
LONDON							
votes	1,205,129	1,812,810	562,564	115,527	51,735	18,355	3,766,120
votes %	32.0	48.1	14.9	3.1	1.4	0.5	100.0
2017 votes %	33.1	54.5	8.8	1.8		1.8	100.0
change	-1.1	-6.4	6.1	1.3	1.4	-1.3	
seats	21	49	3	0	0	0	73
2017 seats	21	49	3	0		0	73
electorate							5,580,660
turnout %							67.5
2017 turnout %							70.1
change							-2.6
NORTH EAST							
votes	478,208	532,127	85,243	29,732	100,910	23,872	1,250,092
votes %	38.3	42.6	6.8	2.4	8.1	1.9	100.0
2017 votes %	34.4	55.4	4.6	1.3		4.3	100.0
change	3.8	-12.9	2.3	1.1	8.1	-2.4	
seats	10	19	0	0	0	0	29
2017 seats	3	26	0	0		0	29
electorate							1,946,976
turnout %							64.2
2017 turnout %							66.0
change							-1.8

	C	LAB	LD	GREEN	BREXIT	OTHERS	TOTAL
NORTH WEST							
votes	1,321,072	1,638,258	277,505	86,815	136,196	63,838	3,523,684
votes %	37.5	46.5	7.9	2.5	3.9	1.8	100.0
2017 votes %	36.2	54.9	5.4	1.1		2.5	100.0
change	1.3	-8.4	2.5	1.4	3.9	-0.7	
seats	32	41	1	0	0	1	75
2017 seats	20	54	1	0		0	75
electorate							5,368,857
turnout %							65.6
2017 turnout %							67.8
change							-2.2
SOUTH EAST							
votes	2,512,869	1,029,966	848,382	183,724	12,868	64,917	4,652,726
votes %	54.0	22.1	18.2	3.9	0.3	1.4	100.0
2017 votes %	53.8	28.6	10.5	3.1		3.9	100.0
change	0.2	-6.5	7.7	0.8	0.3	-2.6	
seats	74	8	1	1	0	0	84
2017 seats	72	8	2	1		1	84
electorate							6,628,228
turnout %							70.2
2017 turnout %							71.2
change							-1.0
SOUTH WEST							
votes	1,612,090	713,226	554,504	115,021	11,139	47,474	3,053,454
votes %	52.8	23.4	18.2	3.8	0.4	1.6	100.0
2017 votes %	51.4	29.1	14.9	2.3		2.3	100.0
change	1.4	-5.8	3.2	1.5	0.4	-0.7	
seats	48	6	1	0	0	0	55
2017 seats	47	7	1	0		0	55
electorate							4,242,610
turnout %							72.0
2017 turnout %							71.8
change							0.2
WEST MIDLANDS							
votes	1,449,289	918,123	213,903	80,556	36,646	13,437	2,711,954
votes %	53.4	33.9	7.9	3.0	1.4	0.5	100.0
2017 votes %	49.0	42.5	4.4	1.7		2.4	100.0
change	4.4	-8.6	3.5	1.3	1.4	-1.9	
seats	44	15	0	0	0	0	59
2017 seats	35	24	0	0		0	59
electorate							4,194,172
turnout %							64.7
2017 turnout %							66.9
change							-2.3

	C	LAB	LD	GREEN	BREXIT	OTHERS	TOTAL
YORKSHIRE AND THE HUMBER							
votes	1,097,376	989,787	205,225	57,362	150,561	46,604	2,546,915
votes %	43.1	38.9	8.1	2.3	5.9	1.8	100.0
2017 votes %	40.5	49.0	5.0	1.3		4.3	100.0
change	2.6	-10.1	3.1	1.0	5.9	-2.5	
seats	26	28	0	0	0	0	54
2017 seats	17	37	0	0		0	54
electorate							3,958,036
% turnout							64.3
2017 turnout %							66.4
change							-2.0

Seats that changed hands 2017–19

CONSERVATIVE GAINS

From Labour
Ashfield
Barrow & Furness
Bassetlaw
Birmingham Northfield
Bishop Auckland
Blackpool South
Blyth Valley
Bolsover
Bolton North East
Bridgend
Burnley
Bury North
Bury South
Clwyd South
Colne Valley
Crewe & Nantwich
Darlington
Delyn
Derby North
Dewsbury
Don Valley
Dudley North
Durham North West
Gedling
Great Grimsby
Heywood & Middleton
High Peak
Hyndburn
Ipswich

Keighley
Kensington
Leigh
Lincoln
Newcastle-under-Lyme
Penistone & Stocksbridge
Peterborough
Redcar
Rother Valley
Scunthorpe
Sedgefield
Stockton South
Stoke-on-Trent Central
Stoke-on-Trent North
Stroud
Vale of Clwyd
Wakefield
Warrington South
West Bromwich East
West Bromwich West
Wolverhampton
  North East
Wolverhampton
  South West
Workington
Wrexham
Ynys Mon

From Liberal Democrats
Carshalton & Wallington
Eastbourne
Norfolk North

LABOUR GAINS

From Conservatives
Putney

LIBERAL DEMOCRAT GAINS

From Conservatives
Richmond Park
St Albans

From SNP
Fife North East

SNP GAINS

From Conservatives
Aberdeen South
Angus
Ayr, Carrick & Cumnock
Gordon
Ochil & South Perthshire
Renfrewshire East
Stirling

From Labour
Coatbridge, Chryston
  & Bellshill
East Lothian

Glasgow North East
Kirkcaldy &
  Cowdenbeath
Midlothian
Rutherglen &
  Hamilton West

From Liberal Democrats
Dunbartonshire East

ALLIANCE GAINS

From Independent
Down North

SDLP GAINS

From DUP
Belfast South

From Sinn Fein
Foyle

SINN FEIN GAINS

From DUP
Belfast North

Three-way marginal seats

CONSTITUENCY	1ST	% MAJ 1ST OVER 2ND	2ND	% MAJ 1ST OVER 3RD	3RD
Ynys Mon	C	5.4	Lab	7.0	PC
Sheffield Hallam	Lab	1.3	LD	8.8	C
East Lothian	SNP	6.6	Lab	9.6	C
Barnsley East	Lab	8.5	Brexit	10.4	C
Hartlepool	Lab	8.8	C	11.8	Brexit
Cities of London & Westminster	C	9.3	LD	12.7	Lab
Wimbledon	C	1.2	LD	14.8	Lab
Ashfield	C	11.7	Ash	14.8	Lab
Kirkcaldy & Cowdenbeath	SNP	2.6	Lab	15.1	C
Antrim South	DUP	6.3	UUP	16.2	APNI
Kensington	C	0.3	Lab	17.0	LD
Down South	SF	3.3	SDLP	17.1	DUP
Carmarthen East & Dinefwr	PC	4.4	C	17.8	Lab
Doncaster North	Lab	5.8	C	18.3	Brexit
Barnsley Central	Lab	9.7	Brexit	18.7	C
Finchley & Golders Green	C	11.9	LD	19.6	Lab
Midlothian	SNP	11.8	Lab	19.8	C

Seats in rank order of % turnout

Top and bottom 20 constituencies only

	CONSTITUENCY	% TURNOUT	1ST		CONSTITUENCY	% TURNOUT	1ST
1	Dunbartonshire East	80.3	SNP	631	Birmingham Ladywood	56.2	Lab
2	Richmond Park	78.7	LD	632	Middlesbrough	56.1	Lab
3	Rushcliffe	78.5	C	633	Strangford	56.0	DUP
4	Sheffield Hallam	78.2	Lab	634	Wentworth & Dearne	55.8	Lab
5	St Albans	78.1	LD	635	Wolverhampton North East	55.6	C
6	Stroud	78.0	C	636	Glasgow North East	55.5	SNP
7	Winchester	77.9	C	637	Barnsley East	54.8	Lab
8	Westmorland & Lonsdale	77.8	LD	638	Walsall North	54.4	C
9	Wimbledon	77.7	C	639	Leeds Central	54.2	Lab
10	Esher & Walton	77.7	C	640	Great Grimsby	53.9	C
11	Devon Central	77.5	C	641	Leicester West	53.6	Lab
12	Somerset North	77.4	C	642	West Bromwich West	53.4	C
13	Wirral West	77.3	Lab	643	Birmingham Erdington	53.3	Lab
14	Kenilworth & Southam	77.2	C	644	Wolverhampton South East	53.2	Lab
15	Truro & Falmouth	77.2	C	645	Nottingham North	53.1	Lab
16	Hitchin & Harpenden	77.1	C	646	Blackley & Broughton	52.6	Lab
17	Putney	77.0	Lab	647	Hull North	52.2	Lab
18	Cardiff North	77.0	Lab	648	Hull West & Hessle	52.1	Lab
19	Bath	76.9	LD	649	Chorley	51.2	Speaker
20	Derbyshire Dales	76.9	C	650	Hull East	49.3	Lab

Seats in rank order of % majority

CONSTITUENCY	% MAJ	MAJ	2ND
Conservative seats			
1 Bury North	0.22	105	Lab
2 Kensington	0.34	150	Lab
3 Bury South	0.80	402	Lab
4 Bolton North East	0.87	378	Lab
5 Moray	1.05	513	SNP
6 High Peak	1.09	590	Lab
7 Wimbledon	1.18	628	LD
8 Carshalton & Wallington	1.28	629	LD
9 Gedling	1.36	679	Lab
10 Heywood & Middleton	1.40	663	Lab
11 Aberdeenshire West & Kincardine	1.58	843	SNP
12 Cheltenham	1.65	981	LD
13 Winchester	1.67	985	LD
14 Blyth Valley	1.74	712	Lab
15 Stoke-on-Trent Central	2.09	670	Lab
16 Chipping Barnet	2.11	1,212	Lab
17 Delyn	2.25	865	Lab
18 Durham North West	2.40	1,144	Lab
19 Chingford & Woodford Green	2.61	1,262	Lab
20 Bridgend	2.74	1,157	Lab
21 Dewsbury	2.77	1,561	Lab
22 Warrington South	3.25	2,010	Lab
23 Clwyd South	3.41	1,239	Lab
24 Burnley	3.47	1,352	Lab
25 Dumfries & Galloway	3.51	1,805	SNP
26 Birmingham Northfield	3.81	1,640	Lab
27 Wolverhampton South West	4.04	1,661	Lab
28 Cheadle	4.18	2,336	LD
29 Leigh	4.18	1,965	Lab
30 Keighley	4.22	2,218	Lab
31 Cambridgeshire South	4.34	2,904	LD
32 Esher & Walton	4.35	2,743	LD
33 West Bromwich East	4.43	1,593	Lab
34 Lewes	4.48	2,457	LD
35 Vale of Clwyd	4.91	1,827	Lab
36 Ynys Mon	5.38	1,968	Lab
37 Peterborough	5.40	2,580	Lab
38 Derby North	5.40	2,540	Lab
39 Guildford	5.69	3,337	LD
40 Stroud	5.82	3,840	Lab
41 Wrexham	6.36	2,131	Lab
42 Aberconwy	6.38	2,034	Lab
43 Pudsey	6.49	3,517	Lab

CONSTITUENCY	% MAJ	MAJ	2ND
Conservative seats			
44 Vale of Glamorgan	6.50	3,562	Lab
45 Lincoln	6.94	3,514	Lab
46 Hyndburn	6.96	2,951	Lab
47 Hastings & Rye	7.45	4,043	Lab
48 Wakefield	7.46	3,358	Lab
49 Darlington	7.57	3,294	Lab
50 Watford	7.63	4,433	Lab
51 Hendon	7.68	4,230	Lab
52 Dumfriesshire, Clydesdale & Tweeddale	7.69	3,781	SNP
53 Wycombe	7.70	4,214	Lab
54 Truro & Falmouth	7.71	4,561	Lab
55 Eastbourne	7.86	4,331	LD
56 Don Valley	7.99	3,630	Lab
57 Reading West	8.17	4,117	Lab
58 St Ives	8.32	4,280	LD
59 Colne Valley	8.38	5,103	Lab
60 Southport	8.61	4,147	Lab
61 Redcar	8.64	3,527	Lab
62 Cities of London & Westminster	9.25	3,953	LD
63 Southampton Itchen	9.49	4,498	Lab
64 Stockton South	9.60	5,260	Lab
65 Broxtowe	9.65	5,331	Lab
66 Berwickshire, Roxburgh & Selkirk	9.69	5,148	SNP
67 Banff & Buchan	9.74	4,118	SNP
68 Calder Valley	9.99	5,774	Lab
69 Hazel Grove	9.99	4,423	LD
70 Milton Keynes North	10.00	6,255	Lab
71 Workington	10.04	4,176	Lab
72 Norwich North	10.24	4,738	Lab
73 Devon East	10.47	6,708	Ind
74 Filton & Bradley Stoke	10.50	5,646	Lab
75 Milton Keynes South	10.85	6,944	Lab
76 Sedgefield	10.86	4,513	Lab
77 West Bromwich West	11.02	3,799	Lab
78 Ipswich	11.05	5,479	Lab
79 Altrincham & Sale West	11.21	6,139	Lab
80 Blackpool South	11.27	3,690	Lab
81 Northampton South	11.50	4,697	Lab
82 Bolsover	11.54	5,299	Lab
83 Shipley	11.56	6,242	Lab
84 Ashfield	11.70	5,733	Ash
85 Hitchin & Harpenden	11.71	6,895	LD

CONSTITUENCY	% MAJ	MAJ	2ND
Conservative seats			
86 Wolverhampton North East	11.90	4,080	Lab
87 Finchley & Golders Green	11.91	6,562	LD
88 Wokingham	11.91	7,383	LD
89 Preseli Pembrokeshire	11.93	5,062	Lab
90 Barrow & Furness	12.57	5,789	Lab
91 Rushcliffe	12.63	7,643	Lab
92 Rother Valley	12.97	6,318	Lab
93 Swindon South	13.06	6,625	Lab
94 Loughborough	13.12	7,169	Lab
95 Worcester	13.28	6,758	Lab
96 Copeland	13.74	5,842	Lab
97 Pendle	13.91	6,186	Lab
98 Northampton North	13.93	5,507	Lab
99 Morecambe & Lunesdale	14.02	6,354	Lab
100 Worthing East & Shoreham	14.07	7,474	Lab
101 Penistone & Stocksbridge	14.56	7,210	Lab
102 Surrey South West	14.61	8,817	LD
103 Uxbridge & Ruislip South	14.96	7,210	Lab
104 Stoke-on-Trent North	15.66	6,286	Lab
105 Crewe & Nantwich	15.75	8,508	Lab
106 Wells	16.21	9,991	LD
107 Harrow East	16.51	8,170	Lab
108 Sutton & Cheam	16.54	8,351	LD
109 Newcastle-under-Lyme	16.64	7,446	Lab
110 Crawley	16.75	8,360	Lab
111 Clwyd West	16.78	6,747	Lab
112 Corby	16.98	10,268	Lab
113 Harrogate & Knaresborough	16.99	9,675	LD
114 Scunthorpe	17.09	6,451	Lab
115 Brecon & Radnorshire	17.26	7,131	LD
116 Camborne & Redruth	17.27	8,700	Lab
117 Colchester	17.65	9,423	Lab
118 Bishop Auckland	17.77	7,962	Lab
119 Cambridgeshire South East	17.85	11,490	LD
120 Bournemouth East	17.87	8,806	Lab
121 Stevenage	17.96	8,562	Lab
122 Bolton West	17.96	8,855	Lab
123 York Outer	18.04	9,985	Lab
124 Woking	18.11	9,767	LD
125 Taunton Deane	18.36	11,700	LD
126 Carmarthen West & Pembrokeshire South	18.39	7,745	Lab

CONSTITUENCY	% MAJ	MAJ	2ND
Conservative seats			
127 Wantage	18.84	12,653	LD
128 Shrewsbury & Atcham	18.99	11,217	Lab
129 Gloucester	19.12	10,277	Lab
130 Carlisle	19.40	8,319	Lab
131 Rossendale & Darwen	19.50	9,522	Lab
132 Chippenham	19.77	11,288	LD
133 Monmouth	19.88	9,982	Lab
134 Macclesfield	19.88	10,711	Lab
135 Scarborough & Whitby	20.65	10,270	Lab
136 Croydon South	20.79	12,339	Lab
137 South Ribble	20.82	11,199	Lab
138 Welwyn Hatfield	21.05	10,955	Lab
139 Mole Valley	21.08	12,041	LD
140 Romsey & Southampton North	21.16	10,872	LD
141 Morley & Outwood	21.70	11,267	Lab
142 Erewash	21.73	10,606	Lab
143 Thanet South	21.94	10,587	Lab
144 Bournemouth West	22.08	10,150	Lab
145 Blackpool North & Cleveleys	22.15	8,596	Lab
146 Great Grimsby	22.16	7,331	Lab
147 Kingswood	22.75	11,220	Lab
148 Hexham	22.86	10,549	Lab
149 Dorset West	23.15	14,106	LD
150 Hertfordshire South West	23.55	14,408	Ind
151 Thornbury & Yate	23.68	12,369	LD
152 Bromley & Chislehurst	23.90	10,891	Lab
153 Henley	23.92	14,053	LD
154 Chelsea & Fulham	24.01	11,241	LD
155 Thurrock	24.19	11,482	Lab
156 Dover	24.22	12,278	Lab
157 Middlesbrough South & Cleveland East	24.31	11,626	Lab
158 Totnes	24.38	12,724	LD
159 Witney	24.76	15,177	LD
160 Telford	25.55	10,941	Lab
161 Basingstoke	25.95	14,198	Lab
162 Somerset North East	26.16	14,729	Lab
163 Derbyshire North East	26.16	12,876	Lab
164 Rugby	26.46	13,447	Lab
165 Eastleigh	26.47	15,607	LD
166 Rochford & Southend East	26.63	12,286	Lab
167 Devon North	26.65	14,813	LD
168 Banbury	26.72	16,813	Lab
169 Newbury	26.75	16,047	LD
170 Tunbridge Wells	26.80	14,645	LD

CONSTITUENCY	% MAJ	MAJ	2ND	CONSTITUENCY	% MAJ	MAJ	2ND
Conservative seats				**Conservative seats**			
171 Worthing West	27.12	14,823	Lab	217 Huntingdon	32.77	19,383	Lab
172 Beaconsfield	27.15	15,712	Ind	218 Hertfordshire North East	32.88	18,189	Lab
173 Yeovil	27.31	16,181	LD				
174 Bassetlaw	27.56	14,013	Lab	219 Rochester & Strood	32.88	17,072	Lab
175 Stafford	28.11	14,377	Lab	220 Gillingham & Rainham	32.90	15,119	Lab
176 Beckenham	28.20	14,258	Lab	221 The Cotswolds	33.04	20,214	LD
177 Somerset North	28.26	17,536	Lab	222 Mansfield	33.09	16,306	Lab
178 Norfolk North	28.32	14,395	LD	223 Newton Abbot	33.30	17,501	LD
179 Hemel Hempstead	28.40	14,563	Lab	224 Ribble Valley	33.35	18,439	Lab
180 Stoke-on-Trent South	28.46	11,271	Lab	225 Maidenhead	33.36	18,846	LD
181 Halesowen & Rowley Regis	28.51	12,074	Lab	226 Horsham	33.41	21,127	LD
				227 Dorset South	33.60	17,153	Lab
182 Cornwall North	28.55	14,752	LD	228 Kettering	33.96	16,765	Lab
183 Aylesbury	28.68	17,373	Lab	229 Norfolk South	34.05	21,275	Lab
184 Sussex Mid	28.99	18,197	LD	230 Hampshire North East	34.10	20,211	LD
185 Nuneaton	29.09	13,144	Lab	231 Runnymede & Weybridge	34.28	18,270	Lab
186 Chesham & Amersham	29.13	16,223	LD				
187 Plymouth Moor View	29.15	12,897	Lab	232 Portsmouth North	34.37	15,780	Lab
188 Swindon North	29.34	16,171	Lab	233 Reigate	34.45	18,310	Lab
189 Somerton & Frome	29.61	19,213	LD	234 Hampshire East	34.62	19,696	LD
190 St Austell & Newquay	29.63	16,526	Lab	235 Derbyshire Dales	34.75	17,381	Lab
191 Stourbridge	29.70	13,571	Lab	236 Eddisbury	34.82	18,443	Lab
192 Burton	29.74	14,496	Lab	237 Aldershot	34.84	16,698	Lab
193 Elmet & Rothwell	29.80	17,353	Lab	238 Bedfordshire South West	34.86	18,583	Lab
194 Epsom & Ewell	30.06	17,873	LD	239 Chichester	35.09	21,490	LD
195 Harborough	30.14	17,278	Lab	240 Torbay	35.20	17,749	LD
196 Bexleyheath & Crayford	30.30	13,103	Lab	241 Waveney	35.21	18,002	Lab
197 Dorset Mid & Poole North	30.45	14,898	LD	242 Suffolk Coastal	35.21	20,533	Lab
				243 Berwick-upon-Tweed	35.23	14,835	Lab
198 Devon Central	30.52	17,721	Lab	244 Dartford	35.47	19,160	Lab
199 Sherwood	30.71	16,186	Lab	245 Montgomeryshire	35.48	12,138	LD
200 Weston-Super-Mare	30.79	17,121	Lab	246 Tatton	35.51	17,387	Lab
201 Forest of Dean	30.83	15,869	Lab	247 Fylde	35.60	16,611	Lab
202 Chelmsford	30.85	17,621	LD	248 Thanet North	35.68	17,189	Lab
203 Ruislip, Northwood & Pinner	30.99	16,394	Lab	249 Selby & Ainsty	35.69	20,137	Lab
				250 Wellingborough	35.71	18,540	Lab
204 Southend West	31.07	14,459	Lab	251 Folkestone & Hythe	36.16	21,337	Lab
205 Derbyshire Mid	31.17	15,385	Lab	252 Derbyshire South	36.22	19,335	Lab
206 Surrey Heath	31.28	18,349	LD	253 Stratford-on-Avon	36.28	19,972	LD
207 Dudley North	31.44	11,533	Lab	254 Redditch	36.39	16,036	Lab
208 Wyre & Preston North	31.71	16,781	Lab	255 Bracknell	36.48	19,829	Lab
209 Isle of Wight	31.89	23,737	Lab	256 Tewkesbury	36.65	22,410	LD
210 Buckingham	32.16	20,411	LD	257 Arundel & South Downs	36.67	22,521	LD
211 Wiltshire North	32.19	17,626	LD	258 Salisbury	36.73	19,736	LD
212 Congleton	32.43	18,561	Lab	259 Sutton Coldfield	36.83	19,272	Lab
213 Harlow	32.44	14,063	Lab	260 Amber Valley	37.06	16,886	Lab
214 Hertford & Stortford	32.65	19,620	Lab	261 Spelthorne	37.15	18,393	Lab
215 Walsall North	32.73	11,965	Lab	262 Bedfordshire North East	37.35	24,283	Lab
216 Gravesham	32.76	15,581	Lab	263 Windsor	37.36	20,079	LD

CONSTITUENCY	% MAJ	MAJ	2ND	CONSTITUENCY	% MAJ	MAJ	2ND
Conservative seats				**Conservative seats**			
264 Staffordshire Moorlands	37.63	16,428	Lab	308 Bromsgrove	42.57	23,106	Lab
265 Romford	37.88	17,893	Lab	309 Worcestershire West	42.58	24,499	LD
266 Poole	37.89	19,116	Lab	310 Tamworth	42.63	19,634	Lab
267 Leicestershire North West	37.90	20,400	Lab	311 Norfolk North West	42.75	19,922	Lab
				312 Chatham & Aylesford	42.78	18,540	Lab
268 Bedfordshire Mid	38.11	24,664	Lab	313 Suffolk South	42.81	22,897	Lab
269 Beverley & Holderness	38.19	20,448	Lab	314 Cannock Chase	42.92	19,879	Lab
270 The Wrekin	38.30	18,726	Lab	315 Meon Valley	42.96	23,555	LD
271 Broadland	38.37	21,861	Lab	316 Yorkshire East	43.18	22,787	Lab
272 Solihull	38.44	21,273	Lab	317 Hornchurch & Upminster	43.18	23,308	Lab
273 Kenilworth & Southam	38.70	20,353	LD				
274 Penrith & The Border	38.72	18,519	Lab	318 Dorset North	43.31	24,301	LD
275 Harwich & Essex North	38.84	20,182	Lab	319 Faversham & Kent Mid	43.61	21,976	Lab
276 Cornwall South East	39.08	20,971	Lab	320 Saffron Walden	43.74	27,594	LD
277 Warwickshire North	39.11	17,956	Lab	321 Lichfield	43.78	23,638	Lab
278 Wiltshire South West	39.40	21,630	Lab	322 Bognor Regis & Littlehampton	43.93	22,503	Lab
279 Hereford & Herefordshire South	39.65	19,686	Lab	323 Basildon South & Thurrock East	43.98	19,922	Lab
280 Newark	39.84	21,816	Lab	324 Bexhill & Battle	44.10	26,059	Lab
281 Ashford	40.01	24,029	Lab	325 Epping Forest	44.11	22,173	Lab
282 Stone	40.02	19,945	Lab	326 Thirsk & Malton	44.45	25,154	Lab
283 Devon South West	40.16	21,430	Lab	327 Hampshire North West	44.65	26,308	LD
284 Norfolk Mid	40.21	22,594	Lab	328 Gainsborough	44.99	22,967	Lab
285 Cambridgeshire North West	40.26	25,983	Lab	329 Suffolk West	45.09	23,194	Lab
286 Surrey East	40.27	24,040	LD	330 Daventry	45.43	26,080	Lab
287 Bury St Edmunds	40.33	24,988	Lab	331 Fareham	45.57	26,086	Lab
288 Skipton & Ripon	40.35	23,694	Lab	332 Orpington	45.93	22,378	Lab
289 Charnwood	40.45	22,397	Lab	333 Rutland & Melton	46.17	26,924	Lab
290 Shropshire North	40.61	22,949	Lab	334 Cleethorpes	46.22	21,418	Lab
291 Great Yarmouth	40.64	17,663	Lab	335 Basildon & Billericay	46.26	20,412	Lab
292 Tiverton & Honiton	40.66	24,239	Lab	336 Grantham & Stamford	46.43	26,003	Lab
293 Hertsmere	40.83	21,313	Lab	337 Bosworth	46.57	26,278	Lab
294 Haltemprice & Howden	40.84	20,329	Lab	338 Ludlow	47.08	23,648	LD
295 Sevenoaks	40.85	20,818	LD	339 Devizes	47.09	23,993	LD
296 Old Bexley & Sidcup	41.07	18,952	Lab	340 Richmond (Yorks)	47.16	27,210	Lab
297 Northamptonshire South	41.49	27,761	Lab	341 Tonbridge & Malling	47.26	26,941	LD
298 Suffolk Central & Ipswich North	41.58	23,391	Lab	342 Christchurch	47.39	24,617	LD
				343 Havant	47.42	21,792	Lab
299 Leicestershire South	41.77	24,004	Lab	344 Sittingbourne & Sheppey	47.63	24,479	Lab
300 Devon West & Torridge	41.84	24,992	LD	345 Gosport	48.04	23,278	Lab
301 Wealden	42.12	25,655	LD	346 New Forest West	48.51	24,403	LD
302 Maidstone & The Weald	42.13	21,772	Lab	347 Herefordshire North	48.71	24,856	LD
303 Meriden	42.16	22,836	Lab	348 Witham	48.80	24,082	Lab
304 Wyre Forest	42.35	21,413	Lab	349 Braintree	48.86	24,673	Lab
305 Bridgwater & Somerset West	42.39	24,439	Lab	350 Sleaford & North Hykeham	48.93	32,565	Lab
306 Broxbourne	42.41	19,807	Lab	351 New Forest East	49.72	25,251	Lab
307 Dudley South	42.56	15,565	Lab	352 Worcestershire Mid	49.92	28,018	Lab

CONSTITUENCY	% MAJ	MAJ	2ND	CONSTITUENCY	% MAJ	MAJ	2ND
Conservative seats				**Labour seats**			
353 Aldridge-Brownhills	50.42	19,836	Lab	30 Stalybridge & Hyde	6.95	2,946	C
354 Brigg & Goole	50.55	21,941	Lab	31 Wirral West	7.00	3,003	C
355 Norfolk South West	50.90	26,195	Lab	32 Worsley & Eccles South	7.20	3,219	C
356 Brentwood & Ongar	54.89	29,065	Lab	33 Eltham	7.32	3,197	C
357 Louth & Horncastle	55.16	28,868	Lab	34 Houghton &	7.82	3,115	C
358 Rayleigh & Wickford	56.47	31,000	Lab	Sunderland South			
359 Staffordshire South	56.49	28,250	Lab	35 Walsall South	8.14	3,456	C
360 Cambridgeshire	56.63	29,993	Lab	36 Barnsley East	8.45	3,217	Brexit
North East				37 Tynemouth	8.67	4,857	C
361 Clacton	56.78	24,702	Lab	38 Rotherham	8.75	3,121	C
362 Maldon	59.60	30,041	Lab	39 Hartlepool	8.76	3,595	C
363 Castle Point	60.15	26,634	Lab	40 Plymouth Sutton &	8.95	4,757	C
364 Boston & Skegness	61.45	25,621	Lab	Devonport			
365 South Holland &	62.71	30,838	Lab	41 Erith & Thamesmead	9.08	3,758	C
The Deepings				42 Hull West & Hessle	9.11	2,856	C
				43 Enfield Southgate	9.41	4,450	C
Labour seats				44 Battersea	9.45	5,668	C
1 Bedford	0.31	145	C	45 Putney	9.46	4,774	C
2 Coventry North West	0.44	208	C	46 Barnsley Central	9.68	3,571	Brexit
3 Alyn & Deeside	0.50	213	C	47 Washington &	9.92	3,723	C
4 Dagenham & Rainham	0.67	293	C	Sunderland West			
5 Coventry South	0.89	401	C	48 Torfaen	10.07	3,742	C
6 Weaver Vale	1.11	562	C	49 Bristol North West	10.19	5,692	C
7 Sheffield Hallam	1.25	712	LD	50 Sheffield South East	10.21	4,289	C
8 Warwick & Leamington	1.46	789	C	51 Birmingham Erdington	10.22	3,601	C
9 Wansbeck	2.01	814	C	52 Durham	10.28	5,025	C
10 Newport West	2.08	902	C	53 Ilford North	10.41	5,218	C
11 Stockton North	2.50	1,027	C	54 Reading East	10.59	5,924	C
12 Normanton, Pontefract	2.64	1,276	C	55 Makerfield	10.71	4,740	C
& Castleford				56 Croydon Central	11.01	5,949	C
13 Hemsworth	2.69	1,180	C	57 Ashton-under-Lyne	11.05	4,263	C
14 Canterbury	3.05	1,836	C	58 Durham North	11.24	4,742	C
15 Chesterfield	3.21	1,451	C	59 Chester	11.30	6,164	C
16 Warrington North	3.23	1,509	C	60 Portsmouth South	11.31	5,363	C
17 Oldham East &	3.25	1,499	C	61 Huddersfield	11.79	4,937	C
Saddleworth				62 Blaydon	12.11	5,531	C
18 Wolverhampton	3.69	1,235	C	63 Leicester West	12.11	4,212	C
South East				64 Leicester East	12.18	6,019	C
19 Hull East	3.82	1,239	C	65 Llanelli	12.21	4,670	C
20 Gower	4.13	1,837	C	66 Newcastle upon Tyne	12.27	5,765	C
21 Wentworth & Dearne	5.21	2,165	C	North			
22 Lancaster & Fleetwood	5.26	2,380	C	67 Nottingham North	12.71	4,490	C
23 Doncaster Central	5.48	2,278	C	68 Cardiff North	13.26	6,982	C
24 Newport East	5.49	1,992	C	69 Birmingham Edgbaston	13.26	5,614	C
25 Halifax	5.53	2,569	C	70 Southampton Test	13.81	6,213	C
26 Doncaster North	5.82	2,370	C	71 Wirral South	14.02	6,105	C
27 Bradford South	5.90	2,346	C	72 Leeds East	14.16	5,531	C
28 Batley & Spen	6.66	3,525	C	73 Derby South	14.18	6,019	C
29 Sunderland Central	6.82	2,964	C	74 Enfield North	14.41	6,492	C

CONSTITUENCY	% MAJ	MAJ	2ND	CONSTITUENCY	% MAJ	MAJ	2ND
Labour seats				**Labour seats**			
75 Wigan	14.94	6,728	C	123 South Shields	25.30	9,585	C
76 Pontypridd	15.07	5,887	C	124 St Helens North	25.67	12,209	C
77 Neath	15.34	5,637	C	125 Nottingham South	26.11	12,568	C
78 Brent North	15.57	8,079	C	126 Leeds West	26.23	10,564	C
79 Lancashire West	15.83	8,336	C	127 Slough	26.73	13,640	C
80 Islwyn	15.91	5,464	C	128 York Central	27.36	13,545	C
81 Denton & Reddish	16.00	6,175	C	129 Bermondsey &	27.51	16,126	LD
82 Feltham & Heston	16.44	7,859	C	Old Southwark			
83 Brighton Kemptown	16.61	8,061	C	130 Blaenau Gwent	28.61	8,647	Brexit
84 Caerphilly	17.03	6,833	C	131 Cynon Valley	29.18	8,822	C
85 Coventry North East	17.31	7,692	C	132 Sefton Central	29.72	15,122	C
86 Jarrow	17.48	7,120	C	133 Hove	30.22	17,044	C
87 Bristol South	17.86	9,859	C	134 Warley	30.91	11,511	C
88 Cambridge	17.94	9,639	LD	135 Sheffield Brightside &	30.99	12,274	C
89 Ellesmere Port & Neston	17.98	8,764	C	Hillsborough			
90 Brentford & Isleworth	18.03	10,514	C	136 Streatham	31.30	17,690	LD
91 Harrow West	18.14	8,692	C	137 Hornsey & Wood Green	31.49	19,242	LD
92 Exeter	18.51	10,403	C	138 Salford & Eccles	32.25	16,327	C
93 Bolton South East	18.71	7,598	C	139 Newcastle upon Tyne	32.76	12,278	C
94 Gateshead	18.88	7,200	C	Central			
95 Tyneside North	18.96	9,561	C	140 Stretford & Urmston	32.79	16,417	C
96 Easington	19.03	6,581	C	141 Merthyr Tydfil &	32.89	10,606	C
97 Sheffield Heeley	19.96	8,520	C	Rhymney			
98 Rochdale	20.38	9,668	C	142 Aberavon	33.20	10,490	C
99 Bristol East	20.70	10,794	C	143 Leeds North East	33.84	17,089	C
100 Luton South	20.82	8,756	C	144 Hammersmith	34.34	17,847	C
101 Hayes & Harlington	21.05	9,261	C	145 Barking	34.67	15,427	C
102 Luton North	21.71	9,247	C	146 Greenwich & Woolwich	34.76	18,464	C
103 Leeds North West	21.81	10,749	C	147 Vauxhall	34.81	19,612	LD
104 Ogmore	22.05	7,805	C	148 Newcastle upon Tyne	35.66	15,463	C
105 Hull North	22.20	7,593	C	East			
106 Edinburgh South	22.31	11,095	SNP	149 Preston	35.95	12,146	C
107 Swansea West	22.65	8,116	C	150 Mitcham & Morden	36.03	16,482	C
108 Wythenshawe &	23.23	10,396	C	151 Oxford East	36.13	17,832	C
Sale East				152 Islington South &	36.24	17,328	LD
109 Swansea East	23.74	7,970	C	Finsbury			
110 Cardiff West	23.79	10,986	C	153 Birmingham Perry Barr	36.34	15,317	C
111 Stockport	24.07	10,039	C	154 Blackley & Broughton	37.29	14,402	C
112 Ealing Central & Acton	24.27	13,300	C	155 Bristol West	37.36	28,219	Green
113 Tooting	24.47	14,307	C	156 Lewisham East	37.95	17,008	C
114 Middlesbrough	24.62	8,395	C	157 St Helens South &	38.01	19,122	C
115 Norwich South	24.69	12,760	C	Whiston			
116 Ealing North	24.72	12,269	C	158 Ealing Southall	38.10	16,084	C
117 Hampstead & Kilburn	24.72	14,188	C	159 Rhondda	38.59	11,440	C
118 Birmingham Yardley	24.98	10,659	C	160 Leeds Central	39.10	19,270	C
119 Oldham West & Royton	25.04	11,127	C	161 Wallasey	39.41	18,322	C
120 Westminster North	25.07	10,759	C	162 Edmonton	39.70	16,015	C
121 Birmingham Selly Oak	25.10	12,414	C	163 Blackburn	40.92	18,304	C
122 Cardiff South & Penarth	25.18	12,737	C	164 Bradford East	41.06	18,144	C

CONSTITUENCY	% MAJ	MAJ	2ND	CONSTITUENCY	% MAJ	MAJ	2ND
Labour seats				**Liberal Democrat seats**			
165 Halton	41.07	18,975	C	6 St Albans	10.93	6,293	C
166 Cardiff Central	41.08	17,179	C	7 Richmond Park	11.94	7,766	C
167 Lewisham West & Penge	41.35	21,543	C	8 Oxford West &	15.20	8,943	C
168 Birkenhead	41.83	17,705	BSJP	Abingdon			
169 Brent Central	42.48	20,870	C	9 Kingston & Surbiton	17.24	10,489	C
170 Nottingham East	43.48	17,393	C	10 Twickenham	21.89	14,121	C
171 Croydon North	44.37	24,673	C	11 Bath	23.63	12,322	C
172 Ilford South	45.07	24,101	C				
173 Leicester South	45.22	22,675	C	**Scottish National seats**			
174 Leyton & Wanstead	46.71	20,808	C	1 Dunbartonshire East	0.28	149	LD
175 Poplar & Limehouse	47.17	28,904	C	2 Gordon	1.46	819	C
176 Islington North	48.67	26,188	LD	3 Kirkcaldy &	2.64	1,243	Lab
177 Holborn & St Pancras	48.89	27,763	C	Cowdenbeath			
178 Dulwich &	48.96	27,310	Green	4 Ayr, Carrick & Cumnock	5.00	2,329	C
West Norwood				5 East Lothian	6.64	3,886	Lab
179 Manchester Withington	52.66	27,905	LD	6 Glasgow North East	7.51	2,548	Lab
180 Sheffield Central	53.57	27,273	C	7 Ochil & South Perthshire	7.78	4,498	C
181 West Ham	53.80	32,388	C	8 Argyll & Bute	8.55	4,110	C
182 Birmingham Hall Green	53.88	28,508	C	9 Aberdeen South	8.74	3,990	C
183 Manchester Central	55.63	29,089	C	10 Angus	8.79	3,795	C
184 Hackney North &	58.36	33,188	C	11 Rutherglen &	9.72	5,230	Lab
Stoke Newington				Hamilton West			
185 Garston & Halewood	59.30	31,624	C	12 Lanark & Hamilton East	9.77	5,187	C
186 Lewisham Deptford	59.44	32,913	C	13 Renfrewshire East	9.80	5,426	C
187 Camberwell & Peckham	59.80	33,780	C	14 Ayrshire Central	11.40	5,304	C
188 East Ham	60.73	33,176	C	15 Coatbridge, Chryston &	11.66	5,624	Lab
189 Bradford West	61.04	27,019	C	Bellshill			
190 Bethnal Green & Bow	61.96	37,524	C	16 Midlothian	11.83	5,705	Lab
191 Hackney South &	62.43	33,985	C	17 Airdrie & Shotts	13.08	5,201	Lab
Shoreditch				18 Glasgow South West	13.30	4,900	Lab
192 Liverpool Wavertree	62.44	27,085	C	19 Perth &	13.96	7,550	C
193 Birmingham Hodge Hill	63.67	28,655	C	North Perthshire			
194 Walthamstow	63.85	30,862	C	20 Motherwell & Wishaw	14.11	6,268	Lab
195 Tottenham	64.40	30,175	C	21 Glasgow East	14.46	5,566	Lab
196 Birmingham Ladywood	67.86	28,582	C	22 Glasgow North	15.48	5,601	Lab
197 Manchester Gorton	68.11	30,339	C	23 Glasgow Central	16.14	6,474	Lab
198 Liverpool West Derby	68.16	29,984	C	24 Na h-Eileanan an Iar	16.84	2,438	Lab
199 Liverpool Riverside	70.17	37,043	C	(Western Isles)			
200 Bootle	70.27	34,556	C	25 Stirling	17.59	9,254	C
201 Knowsley	72.70	39,942	C	26 Ayrshire North & Arran	17.70	8,521	C
202 Liverpool Walton	74.83	30,520	C	27 Inverclyde	18.83	7,512	Lab
				28 Glasgow South	18.98	9,005	Lab
Liberal Democrat seats				29 Inverness, Nairn,	19.05	10,440	C
1 Caithness, Sutherland &	0.65	204	SNP	Badenoch & Strathspey			
Easter Ross				30 Linlithgow &	19.50	11,266	C
2 Fife North East	2.87	1,316	SNP	Falkirk East			
3 Westmorland & Lonsdale	3.67	1,934	C	31 Dunfermline &	20.00	10,699	Lab
4 Edinburgh West	6.91	3,769	SNP	Fife West			
5 Orkney & Shetland	10.82	2,507	SNP	32 Glasgow North West	21.04	8,359	Lab

CONSTITUENCY		% MAJ	MAJ	2ND
Scottish National seats				
33	Dunbartonshire West	21.16	9,553	Lab
34	Edinburgh North & Leith	21.58	12,808	Lab
35	Edinburgh East	21.79	10,417	Lab
36	Edinburgh South West	22.98	11,982	C
37	East Kilbride, Strathaven & Lesmahagow	23.65	13,322	Lab
38	Ross, Skye & Lochaber	23.69	9,443	LD
39	Paisley & Renfrewshire North	23.96	11,902	Lab
40	Livingston	24.61	13,435	C
41	Paisley & Renfrewshire South	24.79	10,679	Lab
42	Kilmarnock & Loudoun	26.58	12,659	C
43	Falkirk	26.75	14,948	C
44	Glenrothes	28.30	11,757	Lab
45	Cumbernauld, Kilsyth & Kirkintilloch East	28.40	12,976	Lab
46	Dundee West	29.48	12,259	Lab
47	Dundee East	29.54	13,375	C
48	Aberdeen North	33.87	12,670	C
Plaid Cymru seats				
1	Carmarthen East & Dinefwr	4.41	1,809	C
2	Arfon	9.57	2,781	Lab
3	Ceredigion	15.78	6,329	C
4	Dwyfor Meirionnydd	15.84	4,740	C
Green seat				
1	Brighton Pavilion	34.38	19,940	Lab

CONSTITUENCY		% MAJ	MAJ	2ND
Speaker				
1	Chorley	43.62	17,392	Ind
Sinn Fein seats				
1	Fermanagh & South Tyrone	0.11	57	UUP
2	Down South	3.26	1,620	SDLP
3	Belfast North	3.96	1,943	DUP
4	Tyrone West	18.16	7,478	DUP
5	Newry & Armagh	18.29	9,287	DUP
6	Ulster Mid	21.37	9,537	DUP
7	Belfast West	37.83	14,672	PBP
Democratic Unionist seats				
1	Belfast East	4.29	1,819	APNI
2	Antrim South	6.26	2,689	UUP
3	Lagan Valley	14.31	6,499	APNI
4	Upper Bann	16.41	8,210	SF
5	Antrim East	18.00	6,706	APNI
6	Strangford	18.86	7,071	APNI
7	Londonderry East	24.44	9,607	SDLP
8	Antrim North	28.88	12,721	UUP
Alliance seat				
1	Down North	7.30	2,968	DUP
SDLP seats				
1	Belfast South	32.52	15,401	DUP
2	Foyle	36.29	17,110	SF

Vote share change since 2017 by party

CONSTITUENCY	% CHANGE	1ST		CONSTITUENCY	% CHANGE	1ST
Conservative				45 Blackpool North & Cleveleys	8.2	C
Top and bottom 50 constituencies only				46 Carmarthen East & Dinefwr	8.2	PC
1 Thurrock	19.1	C		47 Cambridgeshire North East	8.1	C
2 Mansfield	17.3	C		48 The Wrekin	8.0	C
3 Norfolk North	16.9	C		49 Hyndburn	8.0	C
4 Dudley North	16.6	C		50 Wolverhampton South East	8.0	Lab
5 Leicester East	14.4	Lab				
6 Walsall North	14.2	C		585 Tooting	-4.8	Lab
7 Cannock Chase	13.3	C		586 Hampshire East	-4.9	C
8 Stoke-on-Trent South	13.1	C		587 Renfrewshire East	-4.9	SNP
9 Boston & Skegness	13.1	C		588 Edinburgh East	-4.9	SNP
10 Redcar	12.8	C		589 Edinburgh West	-4.9	LD
11 Great Grimsby	12.7	C		590 Bath	-4.9	LD
12 Bassetlaw	11.9	C		591 Paisley & Renfrewshire North	-5.0	SNP
13 Cleethorpes	11.9	C		592 Woking	-5.2	C
14 Great Yarmouth	11.6	C		593 Aberdeenshire West & Kincardine	-5.2	C
15 Dudley South	11.5	C		594 Chesham & Amersham	-5.3	C
16 Wolverhampton North East	11.4	C		595 Sefton Central	-5.3	Lab
17 Clacton	11.0	C		596 Hartlepool	-5.3	Lab
18 Redditch	11.0	C		597 Birkenhead	-5.3	Lab
19 Telford	10.9	C		598 Streatham	-5.3	Lab
20 Brigg & Goole	10.9	C		599 Beckenham	-5.4	C
21 West Bromwich West	10.9	C		600 Berwickshire, Roxburgh & Selkirk	-5.4	C
22 Devon North	10.8	C		601 Cambridgeshire South	-5.5	C
23 Gateshead	10.8	Lab		602 Brentford & Isleworth	-5.5	Lab
24 Scunthorpe	10.3	C		603 Battersea	-5.5	Lab
25 Birmingham Yardley	10.0	Lab		604 Airdrie & Shotts	-5.6	SNP
26 Rochford & Southend East	10.0	C		605 Surrey Heath	-5.6	C
27 Chatham & Aylesford	9.6	C		606 South Shields	-5.6	Lab
28 Derbyshire North East	9.5	C		607 Perth & North Perthshire	-5.6	SNP
29 Castle Point	9.5	C		608 Windsor	-5.8	C
30 Leigh	9.4	C		609 Inverclyde	-5.8	SNP
31 Harlow	9.4	C		610 Cardiff North	-5.9	Lab
32 Burnley	9.4	C		611 Glasgow South	-5.9	SNP
33 Sherwood	9.3	C		612 Hitchin & Harpenden	-6.0	C
34 Basildon South & Thurrock East	9.3	C		613 Hampshire North East	-6.0	C
35 Middlesbrough South & Cleveland East	9.2	C		614 Runnymede & Weybridge	-6.0	C
36 Nuneaton	9.0	C		615 Epsom & Ewell	-6.1	C
37 Warwickshire North	8.9	C		616 Caithness, Sutherland & Easter Ross	-6.2	LD
38 Southport	8.9	C		617 Aberdeen South	-6.2	SNP
39 Plymouth Moor View	8.8	C		618 Mole Valley	-6.4	C
40 Louth & Horncastle	8.7	C		619 Cities of London & Westminster	-6.7	C
41 Cornwall North	8.6	C		620 Maidenhead	-7.0	C
42 Halesowen & Rowley Regis	8.6	C		621 Wokingham	-7.1	C
43 West Bromwich East	8.5	C		622 Leeds North East	-7.4	Lab
44 Sedgefield	8.4	C		623 Ross, Skye & Lochaber	-7.6	SNP

CONSTITUENCY	% CHANGE	1ST	CONSTITUENCY	% CHANGE	1ST
624 Ealing Central & Acton	-7.7	Lab	37 Bradford East	-2.4	Lab
625 Wimbledon	-8.1	C	38 Cornwall South East	-2.4	C
626 Hampstead & Kilburn	-8.2	Lab	39 Hexham	-2.5	C
627 Hertfordshire South West	-8.4	C	40 Colchester	-2.5	C
628 Putney	-8.4	Lab	41 St Austell & Newquay	-2.5	C
629 Edinburgh North & Leith	-8.7	SNP	42 Keighley	-2.6	C
630 Edinburgh South West	-8.7	SNP	43 Bournemouth East	-2.8	C
631 Beaconsfield	-9.1	C	44 Aberconwy	-2.9	C
632 Esher & Walton	-9.3	C	45 Warwick & Leamington	-2.9	Lab
633 Guildford	-9.7	C	46 Berwick-upon-Tweed	-2.9	C
634 Fife North East	-11.1	LD	47 Glasgow North	-3.0	SNP
			48 Rutherglen & Hamilton West	-3.1	SNP
Labour			49 Chipping Barnet	-3.1	C
Top and bottom 50 constituencies only			50 Reading West	-3.1	C
1 Bradford West	11.5	Lab			
2 Portsmouth South	7.6	Lab	581 Aberavon	-14.3	Lab
3 Southport	6.4	C	582 Stoke-on-Trent North	-14.3	C
4 Leeds North West	4.5	Lab	583 Renfrewshire East	-14.3	SNP
5 Putney	4.4	Lab	584 Merthyr Tydfil & Rhymney	-14.3	Lab
6 Canterbury	3.3	Lab	585 St Albans	-14.4	LD
7 Chingford & Woodford Green	1.9	C	586 Chesterfield	-14.6	Lab
8 Isle of Wight	1.3	C	587 Wokingham	-14.7	C
9 Manchester Gorton	1.3	Lab	588 Tyneside North	-14.8	Lab
10 Bethnal Green & Bow	0.9	Lab	589 Hartlepool	-14.8	Lab
11 Bermondsey & Old Southwark	0.9	Lab	590 Dudley North	-14.9	C
12 Truro & Falmouth	0.7	C	591 Blyth Valley	-15.0	C
13 Montgomeryshire	0.4	C	592 Wansbeck	-15.1	Lab
14 Vale of Glamorgan	-0.1	C	593 Makerfield	-15.1	Lab
15 Wycombe	-0.2	C	594 Rotherham	-15.1	Lab
16 Battersea	-0.4	Lab	595 Leigh	-15.1	C
17 Reading East	-0.6	Lab	596 Esher & Walton	-15.2	C
18 Cardiff North	-0.6	Lab	597 Middlesbrough	-15.2	Lab
19 Twickenham	-0.7	LD	598 Scunthorpe	-15.3	C
20 Liverpool Walton	-1.0	Lab	599 Wigan	-15.5	Lab
21 Eastbourne	-1.2	C	600 Cambridgeshire South	-15.6	C
22 Cardiff Central	-1.2	Lab	601 Hitchin & Harpenden	-15.7	C
23 Vauxhall	-1.2	Lab	602 West Bromwich East	-15.7	C
24 Bristol North West	-1.7	Lab	603 Durham North	-15.7	Lab
25 Solihull	-1.9	C	604 Torfaen	-15.8	Lab
26 Bath	-1.9	LD	605 South Shields	-15.9	Lab
27 Altrincham & Sale West	-2.0	C	606 Rother Valley	-16.0	C
28 Somerset North	-2.0	C	607 Bolsover	-16.0	C
29 Croydon Central	-2.1	Lab	608 Leicester East	-16.2	Lab
30 Hereford & Herefordshire South	-2.2	C	609 Great Grimsby	-16.7	C
31 Devon Central	-2.2	C	610 Aberdeen North	-16.8	SNP
32 Norfolk North	-2.3	C	611 Sedgefield	-17.1	C
33 Birmingham Yardley	-2.3	Lab	612 Don Valley	-17.8	C
34 Worthing East & Shoreham	-2.4	C	613 Birkenhead	-17.8	Lab
35 Uxbridge & Ruislip South	-2.4	C	614 Doncaster Central	-17.9	Lab
36 Birmingham Hodge Hill	-2.4	Lab	615 Redcar	-18.1	C

#	CONSTITUENCY	% CHANGE	1ST
616	Ashfield	-18.1	C
617	Easington	-18.2	Lab
618	Washington & Sunderland West	-18.2	Lab
619	Hemsworth	-18.5	Lab
620	Falkirk	-18.6	SNP
621	Houghton & Sunderland South	-18.7	Lab
622	Hull East	-19.1	Lab
623	Finchley & Golders Green	-19.6	C
624	Jarrow	-20.0	Lab
625	Normanton, Pontefract & Castleford	-21.6	Lab
626	Barnsley East	-21.9	Lab
627	Doncaster North	-22.1	Lab
628	Barnsley Central	-23.8	Lab
629	Wentworth & Dearne	-24.7	Lab
630	Bassetlaw	-24.9	C

Liberal Democrat

Top and bottom 50 constituencies only

#	CONSTITUENCY	% CHANGE	1ST
1	Surrey South West	28.9	C
2	Esher & Walton	27.7	C
3	Finchley & Golders Green	25.3	C
4	Hitchin & Harpenden	24.8	C
5	Cambridgeshire South	23.4	C
6	Wimbledon	22.7	C
7	Wokingham	21.7	C
8	Cities of London & Westminster	19.6	C
9	Tunbridge Wells	18.4	C
10	St Albans	17.7	LD
11	Wantage	17.4	C
12	Streatham	17.0	Lab
13	Surrey Heath	16.4	C
14	Henley	16.0	C
15	Totnes	15.9	C
16	Hampstead & Kilburn	15.8	Lab
17	Guildford	15.3	C
18	Mole Valley	15.0	C
19	Chelsea & Fulham	14.9	C
20	Somerset North East	13.8	C
21	Arundel & South Downs	13.3	C
22	Hampshire North East	13.3	C
23	Chesham & Amersham	13.3	C
24	Woking	13.3	C
25	Cambridgeshire South East	13.2	C
26	Maidenhead	13.2	C
27	Chelmsford	12.9	C
28	Eddisbury	12.6	C
29	Stratford-on-Avon	12.4	C
30	Harrogate & Knaresborough	12.2	C
31	Winchester	12.1	C
32	Romsey & Southampton North	11.9	C

#	CONSTITUENCY	% CHANGE	1ST
33	Ealing Central & Acton	11.7	Lab
34	Sussex Mid	11.6	C
35	Sevenoaks	11.5	C
36	Chichester	11.5	C
37	Windsor	11.2	C
38	Rushcliffe	11.1	C
39	Horsham	11.0	C
40	Epsom & Ewell	11.0	C
41	Meon Valley	10.5	C
42	Fife North East	10.2	LD
43	Runnymede & Weybridge	10.0	C
44	Witney	10.0	C
45	Hornsey & Wood Green	9.9	Lab
46	Christchurch	9.9	C
47	Spelthorne	9.6	C
48	Oxford West & Abingdon	9.5	LD
49	Kenilworth & Southam	9.4	C
50	Newbury	9.2	C
560	Blyth Valley	0.7	C
561	Devon West & Torridge	0.6	C
562	Great Grimsby	0.5	C
563	Liverpool Walton	0.3	Lab
564	Wentworth & Dearne	0.3	Lab
565	Devon East	0.3	C
566	Leicestershire North West	0.3	C
567	Ashfield	0.3	C
568	Wells	0.2	C
569	High Peak	0.1	C
570	Carshalton & Wallington	0.1	C
571	Maidstone & The Weald	0.1	C
572	Birmingham Hodge Hill	0.0	Lab
573	Knowsley	-0.1	Lab
574	Manchester Gorton	-0.2	Lab
575	New Forest East	-0.6	C
576	Hull West & Hessle	-0.8	Lab
577	Manchester Withington	-0.9	Lab
578	Blaydon	-1.0	Lab
579	Gordon	-1.0	SNP
580	Rochdale	-1.1	Lab
581	Torbay	-1.1	C
582	Durham North West	-1.2	C
583	Bosworth	-1.2	C
584	Sheffield Hallam	-1.3	Lab
585	Hertfordshire South West	-1.5	C
586	St Ives	-1.6	C
587	Inverness, Nairn, Badenoch & Strathspey	-1.6	SNP
588	Redcar	-1.8	C
589	Montgomeryshire	-2.2	C

CONSTITUENCY	% CHANGE	1ST		CONSTITUENCY	% CHANGE	1ST
590 Canterbury	-2.4	Lab		Tweeddale		
591 Truro & Falmouth	-2.9	C	28	Ross, Skye & Lochaber	8.1	SNP
592 Berwick-upon-Tweed	-2.9	C	29	Inverness, Nairn, Badenoch &	8.0	SNP
593 Colchester	-3.0	C		Strathspey		
594 Cornwall South East	-3.3	C	30	Coatbridge, Chryston & Bellshill	7.9	SNP
595 Dunbartonshire East	-3.8	SNP	31	Motherwell & Wishaw	7.9	SNP
596 Orkney & Shetland	-3.8	LD	32	Linlithgow & Falkirk East	7.9	SNP
597 Argyll & Bute	-4.0	SNP	33	Argyll & Bute	7.8	SNP
598 Bermondsey & Old Southwark	-4.5	Lab	34	East Kilbride, Strathaven &	7.5	SNP
599 Cornwall North	-5.8	C		Lesmahagow		
600 Portsmouth South	-5.9	Lab	35	Airdrie & Shotts	7.5	SNP
601 Eastbourne	-5.9	C	36	Caithness, Sutherland & Easter Ross	7.4	LD
602 Burnley	-6.0	C	37	Fife North East	7.3	LD
603 Devon North	-8.0	C	38	Glasgow South West	7.2	SNP
604 Birmingham Yardley	-9.1	Lab	39	Rutherglen & Hamilton West	7.2	SNP
605 St Austell & Newquay	-11.0	C	40	Midlothian	7.1	SNP
606 Ceredigion	-11.6	PC	41	Dundee West	7.1	SNP
607 Southport	-12.9	C	42	Glasgow North West	7.0	SNP
608 Leeds North West	-15.9	Lab	43	Glasgow South	7.0	SNP
609 Norfolk North	-18.1	C	44	Livingston	6.9	SNP
			45	Gordon	6.9	SNP
Scottish National			46	Dunbartonshire East	6.8	SNP
1 Stirling	14.4	SNP	47	Dunbartonshire West	6.8	SNP
2 Renfrewshire East	13.7	SNP	48	Berwickshire, Roxburgh & Selkirk	6.0	C
3 Falkirk	13.6	SNP	49	Edinburgh East	5.9	SNP
4 Aberdeen South	13.2	SNP	50	East Lothian	5.6	SNP
5 Aberdeen North	12.7	SNP	51	Moray	5.4	C
6 Edinburgh South West	12.0	SNP	52	Orkney & Shetland	5.0	LD
7 Ochil & South Perthshire	11.2	SNP	53	Glasgow North East	4.7	SNP
8 Dundee East	11.0	SNP	54	Na h-Eileanan an Iar	4.5	SNP
9 Angus	10.6	SNP	55	Glasgow Central	4.5	SNP
10 Inverclyde	9.9	SNP	56	Edinburgh West	4.4	LD
11 Edinburgh North & Leith	9.7	SNP	57	Edinburgh South	3.0	Lab
12 Ayrshire North & Arran	9.6	SNP	58	Banff & Buchan	1.3	C
13 Paisley & Renfrewshire North	9.6	SNP	59	Kirkcaldy & Cowdenbeath	-1.0	SNP
14 Paisley & Renfrewshire South	9.6	SNP				
15 Ayr, Carrick & Cumnock	9.4	SNP	**Plaid Cymru**			
16 Lanark & Hamilton East	9.3	SNP	1	Ceredigion	8.7	PC
17 Glasgow North	9.3	SNP	2	Arfon	4.3	PC
18 Cumbernauld, Kilsyth &	9.3	SNP	3	Dwyfor Meirionnydd	3.2	PC
Kirkintilloch East			4	Pontypridd	2.5	Lab
19 Ayrshire Central	9.0	SNP	5	Caerphilly	1.6	Lab
20 Glasgow East	8.9	SNP	6	Gower	1.5	Lab
21 Dunfermline & Fife West	8.8	SNP	7	Swansea West	1.4	Lab
22 Aberdeenshire West & Kincardine	8.6	C	8	Wrexham	1.4	C
23 Kilmarnock & Loudoun	8.5	SNP	9	Ynys Mon	1.1	C
24 Glenrothes	8.3	SNP	10	Swansea East	0.9	Lab
25 Perth & North Perthshire	8.3	SNP	11	Alyn & Deeside	0.8	Lab
26 Dumfries & Galloway	8.2	C	12	Ogmore	0.7	Lab
27 Dumfriesshire, Clydesdale &	8.2	C	13	Bridgend	0.6	C

CONSTITUENCY		% CHANGE	1ST	CONSTITUENCY		% CHANGE	1ST
14	Cardiff South & Penarth	0.5	Lab	26	Carmarthen East & Dinefwr	-0.4	PC
15	Aberavon	0.3	Lab	27	Merthyr Tydfil & Rhymney	-0.6	Lab
16	Newport West	0.3	Lab	28	Carmarthen West &	-0.7	C
17	Llanelli	0.2	Lab		Pembrokeshire South		
18	Vale of Clwyd	0.2	C	29	Islwyn	-0.9	Lab
19	Preseli Pembrokeshire	0.1	C	30	Cardiff West	-1.1	Lab
20	Clwyd West	0.1	C	31	Aberconwy	-1.4	C
21	Newport East	0.0	Lab	32	Torfaen	-1.5	Lab
22	Delyn	-0.1	C	33	Neath	-1.7	Lab
23	Clwyd South	-0.2	C	34	Cynon Valley	-5.3	Lab
24	Cardiff North	-0.3	Lab	35	Rhondda	-8.6	Lab
25	Monmouth	-0.3	C	36	Blaenau Gwent	-15.5	Lab

Top targets by rank order of required swing

CONSTITUENCY		1ST PARTY	% SWING REQUIRED	CONSTITUENCY		1ST PARTY	% SWING REQUIRED
Conservative targets				29	Doncaster North	Lab	2.9
1	Bedford	Lab	0.20	30	Bradford South	Lab	3.0
2	Coventry North West	Lab	0.20	31	Batley & Spen	Lab	3.3
3	Alyn & Deeside	Lab	0.20	32	Sunderland Central	Lab	3.4
4	Dagenham & Rainham	Lab	0.30	33	Stalybridge & Hyde	Lab	3.5
5	Coventry South	Lab	0.40	34	Wirral West	Lab	3.5
6	Weaver Vale	Lab	0.6	35	Worsley & Eccles South	Lab	3.6
7	Warwick & Leamington	Lab	0.7	36	Eltham	Lab	3.7
8	Gordon	SNP	0.7	37	Ochil & South Perthshire	SNP	3.9
9	Wansbeck	Lab	1.0	38	Houghton &	Lab	3.9
10	Newport West	Lab	1.0		Sunderland South		
11	Stockton North	Lab	1.2	39	Walsall South	Lab	4.1
12	Normanton, Pontefract &	Lab	1.3	40	Argyll & Bute	SNP	4.3
	Castleford			41	Tynemouth	Lab	4.3
13	Hemsworth	Lab	1.3	42	Aberdeen South	SNP	4.4
14	Canterbury	Lab	1.5	43	Rotherham	Lab	4.4
15	Chesterfield	Lab	1.6	44	Hartlepool	Lab	4.4
16	Warrington North	Lab	1.6	45	Angus	SNP	4.4
17	Oldham East &	Lab	1.6	46	Plymouth Sutton &	Lab	4.5
	Saddleworth				Devonport		
18	Westmorland & Lonsdale	LD	1.8	47	Erith & Thamesmead	Lab	4.5
19	Wolverhampton South East	Lab	1.8	48	Hull West & Hessle	Lab	4.6
20	Hull East	Lab	1.9	49	Enfield Southgate	Lab	4.7
21	Gower	Lab	2.1	50	Battersea	Lab	4.7
22	Carmarthen East & Dinefwr	PC	2.2	51	Putney	Lab	4.7
23	Ayr, Carrick & Cumnock	SNP	2.5	52	East Lothian	SNP	4.8
24	Wentworth & Dearne	Lab	2.6	53	Lanark & Hamilton East	SNP	4.9
25	Lancaster & Fleetwood	Lab	2.6	54	Renfrewshire East	SNP	4.9
26	Doncaster Central	Lab	2.7	55	Washington &	Lab	5.0
27	Newport East	Lab	2.7		Sunderland West		
28	Halifax	Lab	2.8	56	Torfaen	Lab	5.0

CONSTITUENCY	1ST PARTY	% SWING REQUIRED
Labour targets		
1 Bury North	C	0.1
2 Kensington	C	0.2
3 Bury South	C	0.4
4 Bolton North East	C	0.4
5 High Peak	C	0.5
6 Gedling	C	0.7
7 Heywood & Middleton	C	0.7
8 Blyth Valley	C	0.9
9 Stoke-on-Trent Central	C	1.0
10 Chipping Barnet	C	1.1
11 Delyn	C	1.1
12 Durham North West	C	1.2
13 Chingford & Woodford Green	C	1.3
14 Kirkcaldy & Cowdenbeath	SNP	1.3
15 Bridgend	C	1.4
16 Dewsbury	C	1.4
17 Warrington South	C	1.6
18 Clwyd South	C	1.7
19 Burnley	C	1.7
20 Birmingham Northfield	C	1.9
21 Wolverhampton South West	C	2.0
22 Leigh	C	2.1
23 Keighley	C	2.1
24 West Bromwich East	C	2.2
25 Vale of Clwyd	C	2.5
26 Ynys Mon	C	2.7
27 Peterborough	C	2.7
28 Derby North	C	2.7
29 Stroud	C	2.9
30 Wrexham	C	3.2
31 Aberconwy	C	3.2
32 Pudsey	C	3.2
33 Vale of Glamorgan	C	3.2
34 East Lothian	SNP	3.3
35 Lincoln	C	3.5
36 Hyndburn	C	3.5
37 Hastings & Rye	C	3.7
38 Wakefield	C	3.7
39 Glasgow North East	SNP	3.8
40 Darlington	C	3.8
41 Watford	C	3.8
42 Hendon	C	3.8
43 Wycombe	C	3.8
44 Truro & Falmouth	C	3.9
45 Don Valley	C	4.0
46 Reading West	C	4.1
47 Colne Valley	C	4.2
48 Southport	C	4.3
49 Redcar	C	4.3
50 Southampton Itchen	C	4.7
51 Arfon	PC	4.8
52 Stockton South	C	4.8
53 Broxtowe	C	4.8
54 Rutherglen & Hamilton West	SNP	4.9
55 Calder Valley	C	5.0
56 Milton Keynes North	C	5.0
57 Workington	C	5.0
Liberal Democrat targets		
1 Dunbartonshire East	SNP	0.1
2 Wimbledon	C	0.6
3 Sheffield Hallam	Lab	0.6
4 Carshalton & Wallington	C	0.6
5 Cheltenham	C	0.8
6 Winchester	C	0.8
7 Cheadle	C	2.1
8 Cambridgeshire South	C	2.2
9 Esher & Walton	C	2.2
10 Lewes	C	2.2
11 Guildford	C	2.8
12 Eastbourne	C	3.9
13 St Ives	C	4.2
14 Cities of London & Westminster	C	4.6
15 Hazel Grove	C	5.0
Scottish National targets		
1 Caithness, Sutherland & Easter Ross	LD	0.3
2 Moray	C	0.5
3 Aberdeenshire West & Kincardine	C	0.8
4 Fife North East	LD	1.4
5 Dumfries & Galloway	C	1.8
6 Edinburgh West	LD	3.5
7 Dumfriesshire, Clydesdale & Tweeddale	C	3.8
8 Berwickshire, Roxburgh & Selkirk	C	4.8
9 Banff & Buchan	C	4.9
Plaid Cymru target		
1 Ynys Mon	C	3.5
Brexit targets		
1 Barnsley East	Lab	4.2
2 Barnsley Central	Lab	4.8

MPs who stood down before the election

CONSERVATIVE

* **Bebb, Guto** Aberconwy
Bellingham, Sir Henry Norfolk North West
Benyon, Richard Newbury
* **Boles, Nick** Grantham & Stamford
Burt, Alistair Bedfordshire North East
+ **Clarke, Kenneth** Rushcliffe
Davies, Glyn Montgomeryshire
Duncan, Sir Alan Rutland & Melton
++ **Elphicke, Charlie** Dover
Fallon, Sir Michael Sevenoaks
Field, Mark Cities of London & Westminster
Grant, Bill Ayr, Carrick & Cumnock
+ **Greening, Justine** Putney
Griffiths, Andrew Burton
+ **Hammond, Philip** Runnymede & Weybridge
Harrington, Richard Watford
Heaton-Jones, Peter North Devon
Herbert, Nick Arundel & South Downs
Hollingbery, Sir George Meon Valley
Hurd, Nick Ruislip, Northwood & Pinner
James, Margot Stourbridge
Johnson, Joseph Orpington
Kennedy, Seema South Ribble
Lancaster, Mark Milton Keynes North
Lefroy, Jeremy Stafford
+ **Letwin, Sir Oliver** Dorset West

Lidington, Sir David Aylesbury
McLoughlin, Sir Patrick Derbyshire Dales
Morgan, Nicky Loughborough
Newton, Sarah Truro & Falmouth
Perry, Claire Devizes
Prisk, Mark Hertford & Stortford
* **Rudd, Amber** Hastings & Rye
Simpson, Keith Broadland
Soames, Sir Nicholas Mid Sussex
Spelman, Dame Caroline Meriden
+ **Stewart, Rory** Penrith & The Border
Swire, Sir Hugo East Devon
Thomson, Ross Aberdeen South
Tredinnick, David Bosworth
Vaizey, Edward Wantage

LABOUR

* **Austin, Ian** Dudley North
Bailey, Adrian West Bromwich West
Barron, Sir Kevin Rother Valley
Blackman-Woods, Dr Roberta City of Durham
Campbell, Ronnie Blyth Valley
Clwyd, Ann Cynon Valley
Cunningham, Jim Coventry South
De Piero, Gloria Ashfield
* **Ellman, Dame Louise** Liverpool Riverside
Farrelly, Paul Newcastle-under-Lyme
Fitzpatrick, Jim Poplar & Limehouse
++ **Hepburn, Stephen** Jarrow
Hoey, Kate Vauxhall
++ **Hopkins, Kelvin** Luton North

Jones, Helen Warrington North
Lucas, Ian Wrexham
++ **O'Mara, Jared** Sheffield, Hallam
Owen, Albert Ynys Môn
Pearce, Teresa Erith & Thamesmead
Pound, Stephen Ealing North
Robinson, Geoffrey Coventry North West
Smith, Owen Pontypridd
Twigg, Stephen Liverpool West Derby
Vaz, Keith Leicester East
Watson, Tom West Bromwich East
+ **Woodcock, John** Barrow & Furness

LIBERAL DEMOCRAT

Allen, Heidi Cambridgeshire South (*elected for Conservatives in 2017*)
Cable, Sir Vince Twickenham
Lamb, Norman Norfolk North

INDEPENDENT GROUP FOR CHANGE

Coffey, Ann Stockport (*elected for Labour in 2017*)
Ryan, Joan Enfield North (*elected for Labour in 2017*)

INDEPENDENT

Hermon, Lady Down North

DEMOCRATIC UNIONIST

Simpson, David Upper Bann

* *Sat as independent after resigning party whip*
+ *Sat as independent after party whip was withdrawn*
++ *Sat as independent after suspension from party*

Defeated MPs

BIRKENHEAD SOCIAL JUSTICE
* **Field, Frank** Birkenhead

CONSERVATIVE
Clark, Colin Gordon
Goldsmith, Zac Richmond Park
Graham, Luke Ochil &
   Perthshire South
Hair, Kirstene Angus
Kerr, Stephen Stirling
Main, Anne St Albans
Masterton, Paul Renfrewshire
   East

DEMOCRATIC UNIONIST
Dodds, Nigel Belfast North
Little Pengelly, Emma
   Belfast South

INDEPENDENT
\+ **Gauke, David** Hertfordshire
   South West
* **Godsiff, Roger** Birmingham
   Hall Green
\+ **Grieve, Dominic** Beaconsfield
* **Lewis, Ivan** Bury South
\+ **Milton, Anne** Guildford
* **Shuker, Gavin** Luton South
* **Williamson, Chris** Derby North

INDEPENDENT GROUP
FOR CHANGE
* **Gapes, Mike** Ilford South
* **Leslie, Chris** Nottingham East
\+ **Soubry, Anna** Broxtowe

LABOUR
Burden, Richard
   Birmingham Northfield
Chapman, Jenny Darlington
Coaker, Vernon Gedling
Cooper, Julie Burnley

Crausby, Sir David Bolton
   North East
Creagh, Mary Wakefield
Dakin, Nic Scunthorpe
Dent Coad, Emma Kensington
Drew, David Stroud
Flint, Caroline Don Valley
Forbes, Lisa Peterborough
Frith, James Bury North
Gaffney, Hugh Coatbridge,
   Chryston & Bellshill
George, Ruth High Peak
Goodman, Helen Bishop Auckland
Grogan, John Keighley
Hanson, David Delyn
Hayman, Susan Workington
Jones, Susan Clwyd South
Jones, Graham Hyndburn
Killen, Gerard Rutherglen &
   Hamilton West
Laird, Lesley Kirkcaldy &
   Cowdenbeath
Lee, Karen Lincoln
Marsden, Gordon Blackpool South
Martin, Sandy Ipswich
McInnes, Liz Heywood
   & Middleton
Moon, Madeleine Bridgend
Onn, Melanie Great Grimsby
Pidcock, Laura Durham
   North West
Platt, Joanne Leigh
Rashid, Faisal Warrington South
Reynolds, Emma Wolverhampton
   North East
Rowley, Danielle Midlothian
Ruane, Christopher Vale of Clwyd
Sherriff, Paula Dewsbury
Skinner, Dennis Bolsover
Smeeth, Ruth Stoke-on-Trent
   North
Smith, Laura Crewe & Nantwich

Smith, Eleanor Wolverhampton
   South West
Snell, Gareth Stoke-on-Trent
   Central
Sweeney, Paul Glasgow North East
Turley, Anna Redcar
Walker, Thelma Colne Valley
Whitfield, Martin East Lothian
Williams, Paul Stockton South
Wilson, Phil Sedgefield

LIBERAL DEMOCRAT
Berger, Luciana Finchley &
   Golders Green (*elected Labour
   MP for Liverpool Wavertree in
   2017*)
\+ **Brake, Thomas** Carshalton
   & Wallington
Dodds, Jane Brecon
   & Radnorshire
Gyimah, Samuel Kensington
   (*elected Conservative MP for
   Surrey East in 2017*)
Lee, Phillip Wokingham (*elected
   Conservative MP for Bracknell
   in 2017*)
Lloyd, Stephen Eastbourne
\+ **Sandbach, Antoinette** Eddisbury
Smith, Angela Altrincham & Sale
   West (*elected Labour MP for
   Pensitone & Stocksbridge in 2017*)
Swinson, Jo Dunbartonshire East
Umunna, Chuka Cities of London
   & Westminster (*elected Labour
   MP for Streatham in 2017*)
\+ **Wollaston, Sarah** Totnes

SCOTTISH NATIONAL
Gethins, Stephen Fife North East

SINN FEIN
McCallion, Elisha Foyle

* elected for Labour in 2017
\+ elected for Conservatives in 2017

By-elections 2017-19

West Tyrone

Held on May 3, 2018. Caused by resignation of Barry McElduff.

	Electorate	Share %	Change from 2017 %
	64,101	54.6	
Órfhlaith Begley SF	16,346	46.7	-4.1
Thomas Buchanan DUP	8,390	24.0	-3.0
Daniel McCrossan SDLP	6,254	17.9	4.9
Chris Smyth UUP	2,909	8.3	3.1
Stephen Donnelly Alliance	1,130	3.2	0.9
Majority	7,956	22.7	

Lewisham East

Held on June 14, 2018. Caused by resignation of Heidi Alexander.

	Electorate	Share %	Change from 2017 %
	66,140	33.2	
Janet Daby Lab	11,033	50.2	-17.7
Lucy Salek LD	5,404	24.6	20.2
Ross Archer C	3,161	14.4	-8.6
Rosamund Adoo-Kissi-Debrah Green	788	3.6	1.9
Mandu Reid Women	506	2.3	-
David Kurten Ukip	380	1.7	0.0
Anne Waters FBM	266	1.2	-
Maureen Martin CPA	168	0.8	0.3
Majority	5,629	25.6	

Source: House of Commons Library

Newport West

Held on February 17, 2019. Caused by death of Paul Flynn.

	Electorate	Share %	Change from 2017 %
	63,623	37.0	
Ruth Jones Lab	9,308	39.6	-12.7
Matthew Evans C	7,357	31.3	-8.0
Neil Hamilton Ukip	2,023	8.6	6.1
Jonathan Clark PC	1,185	5.0	2.6
Ryan Jones LD	1,088	4.6	2.4
Amelia Womack Green	924	3.9	2.8
June Davies Renew	879	3.7	-
Richard Suchorzewski Assembly	205	0.9	-
Ian Mclean Soc Dem	202	0.9	-
Philip Taylor DVP	185	0.8	-
Hugh Nicklin FBM	159	0.7	-
Majority	1,951	8.3	

- Results omit candidates who polled fewer than 100 votes
- Key to abbreviations is on page 74

Peterborough

Held on June 6, 2019. Caused by successful recall petition against Fiona Onasanya.

	Electorate	Share %	Change from 2017 %
	70,199	48.3	
Lisa Forbes Lab	10,484	30.9	-17.2
Mike Greene Brexit	9,801	28.9	-
Paul Bristow C	7,243	21.4	-25.5
Beki Sellick LD	4,159	12.3	8.9
Joseph Wells Green	1,035	3.1	1.3
John Whitby Ukip	400	1.2	-
Tom Rodgers CPA	162	0.5	-
Stephen Goldspink Eng Dem	153	0.5	-
Patrick O'Flynn Soc Dem	135	0.4	-
Howling Laud Hope Loony	112	0.3	-
Andrew Moore Ind	101	0.3	-
Majority	683	2.0	

Brecon & Radnorshire

Held on August 1, 2019. Caused by recall petition against Chris Davies.

	Electorate	Share %	Change from 2017 %
	53,393	59.0	
Jane Dodds LD	13,826	43.9	14.8
Chris Davies C	12,401	39.4	-9.2
Des Parkinson Brexit	3,331	10.6	-
Tomas Davies Lab	1,680	5.3	-12.4
Lady Lily The Pink Loony	334	1.1	-
Liz Philips UKIP	242	0.8	-0.6
Majority	1,425	4.5	

The new
parliament

WE MUST LEARN FROM TWO YEARS OF CHAOS

by Robert Lisvane

Over the centuries parliaments have acquired nicknames reflecting their different characters. In 1388 there was the Wonder-Working Parliament; in 1404 the Unlearned or Dunces' Parliament (because on the instructions of King Henry IV it contained no lawyers); and in 1614 the Addled Parliament, so called because it passed no legislation.

The parliament elected in 2017 might well go down in history as the Gridlocked Parliament; for although it was the scene of extraordinary parliamentary events it found itself virtually unable to legislate on any matter of contention, which, during those years, meant anything to do with Brexit. The government was repeatedly defeated on the central plank of Theresa May's policy, which led to her resignation. Not only that but the Supreme Court found that her successor had acted unlawfully in the high duty of advising his sovereign on the prorogation of parliament; and, in the Commons, the explicit wording of standing orders was imaginatively re-interpreted by the Speaker, providing opportunities for coalitions of backbenchers to take control of the business of the house away from the government in order to pass legislation giving instructions to the government about the Brexit process.

An overwhelming Conservative majority in the new parliament has all but removed the risk of gridlock, but there are lessons to be learnt from the chaos of the past two years.

On April 18, 2017, Mrs May, then riding high in the opinion polls, with a lead over the Labour opposition of up to 20 points, proposed a general election. The Fixed-term Parliaments Act 2011 meant that she could not simply seek a dissolution from the Queen but had instead to secure a two-thirds majority from the House of Commons for the motion "that there shall be an early general election". She succeeded by 522 votes to 13, the opposition parties finding it difficult, despite her poll lead, to back away from their own calls for a general election.

The outcome of the election was hubristic, to say the least, for Mrs May. She had inherited the small majority achieved by David Cameron in 2015:

330 seats from 36.9 per cent of the vote, giving an overall working majority of 12, taking into account that the Sinn Fein MPs take no part. On June 8 the electorate took away her working majority, giving the Conservatives 317 seats despite a higher percentage of the popular vote (42.3 per cent), a loss of 13 seats. By contrast Labour's performance had strengthened throughout the campaign and they secured 262 seats on 40.0 per cent of the vote, with the Scottish National Party (SNP) at 35 seats, the Liberal Democrats at 12 and, crucially, the Democratic Unionist Party (DUP) with 10 seats.

Mrs May might have been better advised to soldier on with a minority government but she came to a "confidence and supply" arrangement with the DUP (sweetened by a considerable package of financial support for Northern Ireland). It is arguable that the DUP would in any event have voted for much of what was covered by the agreement and, despite their undertaking to support the government on "legislation pertaining to the United Kingdom's exit from the European Union", this aspect of the deal was by no means trouble-free.

The loss of Mrs May's majority was not her only difficulty. Her authority within government was much diminished, as was collective responsibility (and confidentiality) within her cabinet. In the parliamentary party the new situation emboldened factions, notably the European Research Group, which consisted of MPs who took the hardest line on Brexit, including advocacy of departure with no deal "if necessary". Julian Smith, the chief whip for much of the 2017 parliament (he was appointed in November 2017) found himself fighting a losing battle.

If the 2017 general election had set the stage for two years of gridlock, the European Union (Withdrawal) Bill began to write the script. Mrs May needed the legislation to deal with the mechanics of withdrawal, not least in order to ensure that there was a functioning statute book on the day of departure. But on December 13, 2017, the government was defeated by 309 votes to 305 on an amendment to give parliament a "meaningful vote" on the final Brexit deal. The draft Withdrawal Agreement governing the UK's departure from the EU was published on November 14, 2018. The "meaningful vote" was to have taken place on December 11 but (undoubtedly correctly) foreseeing a heavy defeat the government decided the day before the vote to withdraw its motion.

The first "meaningful vote" took place on January 15, 2019, and the government, losing by 432 votes to 202, crashed to the heaviest defeat suffered by a government in modern times. The litany of defeat continued:

on the UK not leaving the EU without an agreement (January 29), 318-310; on support for the government's approach to leaving (February 14), 303-258. On March 12 Mrs May tried a second "meaningful vote"; this was defeated by 391 votes to 242, a majority of 149. On March 29 there was a third "meaningful vote", which rejected the Withdrawal Agreement once more, this time by a majority of 58.

The defeats on the three meaningful votes demonstrate the way in which the Fixed-term Parliaments Act had put Mrs May into a straitjacket and turned at least a couple of centuries of constitutional expectation on its head. In order to be able to form an administration, generations of students have been told, a party must be able to command a majority of the House of Commons. When that majority is clearly lost, or is lost on a significant matter, then either the government resigns and a different administration is formed on the basis that it can command the confidence of the Commons, or the prime minister of the day seeks a dissolution of parliament and there is a general election and a fresh start.

Fixed-term parliaments had actually been in the 2010 manifestos of both the Conservative Party and the Liberal Democrats, but with the formation of the Conservative/Lib Dem coalition they assumed greater importance. The 2011 act provides two ways of ending a parliament: either the government loses, by a simple majority, a motion "that this house has no confidence in Her Majesty's government" and no motion expressing confidence in the administration is passed within 14 days, or a motion "that there shall be an early general election" is passed by a two-thirds majority. One effect of the act was of course that it prevented the Tories, as the senior partner in the coalition government, pulling the rug from under the Liberal Democrats. It also meant, however, that in the absence of either of the two prescribed ways of ending a parliament the incumbent government is trapped: however important the matters upon which it loses votes and so demonstrates that it does not have the confidence of the Commons (and the "meaningful votes" could hardly have been more important) it remains swinging in the wind, unable to escape. So it was with the May administration.

At the same time, and for the remainder of the parliament, the government's troubles were greatly increased by the Speaker's readiness to ignore both firm parliamentary convention and precedent, and indeed the explicit wording of some standing orders.

Thus the amendments that were both allowed and selected for debate and decision included those to programme motions (December 4, 2018; January 9, 2019, the "Grieve amendment" that required Mrs May to respond within three days with an alternative plan if the Commons did not accept the Withdrawal Agreement); to business motions allowing backbenchers to take control of the house's business and stage a series of "indicative votes" (March 27, 2019, and again on April 1, 2019); to give precedence over other business to the European Union (Withdrawal) (No 5) Bill, also known as the "Cooper-Letwin Bill" (April 3, 2019); and to allow substantive proposals to be put forward under the "emergency debate" standing order No 24, which provides that the house may decide only that it "has considered" a matter. To those who thought that John Bercow, the Speaker, favoured (and had always favoured) the opposition over the government, and to those who saw him as a firm if not publicly avowed supporter of the Remainer cause, these decisions perhaps came as no surprise. They nevertheless fuelled a debate as to the extent of a Speaker's discretion in interpreting the standing orders and practice of the house.

In Mr Bercow's defence it is possible to point to the actions of his predecessor Sir Henry Brand in refusing further debate on the motion to bring in the Protection of Property and Person (Ireland) Bill in February 1881. In Brand's judgment the house was at a stand. The obstruction provided by the Irish nationalist MPs meant that no progress could be made. On his own authority he introduced what became known as the closure, in other words moving directly to deciding the question before the house without further debate. When the house has no other recourse, so the case for the defence runs, it is permissible for its presiding officer to facilitate ways in which its will may be done. Mr Bercow's retirement and the substantial government majority in the new parliament may mean that these issues remain academic.

On May 24, 2019, Mrs May gave up the unequal struggle and announced that she would resign as leader of the Conservative Party on June 7 and as prime minister once a successor had been elected. Boris Johnson became that successor on July 23, 2019, but the parliamentary arithmetic meant that he had no greater freedom of action than had Mrs May.

In many respects it was the mixture as before. The Johnson government lost its working majority on its first sitting day as a result of defections by Conservative MPs and was defeated on its very first division (Mr Johnson became the first prime minister to achieve this since Lord Rosebery in 1894) and on 11 more votes. The government was forced to seek a further extension to the two-year Article 50 period before Britain's exit from the EU; it was forced to publish documents about no-deal preparations; it lost the motion for a parliamentary recess during the Conservative Party conference; it lost on the arrangements for a Saturday sitting to debate the Brexit Withdrawal Agreement; it was forced to allow more time for the Commons to debate the Withdrawal Agreement Bill; and through amendments to the Northern Ireland (Executive Formation) Bill it had to provide fortnightly statements on progress towards the formation of an executive, with the Commons sitting for five days after any such statement.

The new prime minister tried three times to use the provisions in the Fixed-term Parliaments Act for "an early general election", which would have required 434 MPs to vote in favour, but failed on all three occasions, with 298 votes in favour (September 4, 2019), 293 votes in favour (September 9) and 299 votes in favour (October 28).

On the return of parliament from the summer recess on September 3 the House of Commons again passed a motion allowing MPs to take control of the order paper. The result was the European Union (Withdrawal) (No 2) Act 2019, which received royal assent on September 9 and which required the prime minister to seek an extension of three months to exit day unless by that time parliament had either approved an exit deal or had approved leaving without one.

For some time beforehand there had been growing concern that parliament might be lengthily prorogued in the run-up to exit day so as to prevent it calling the government to account. So it proved. At a meeting of the Privy Council at Balmoral on August 28 an Order in Council was made proroguing parliament from no later than September 12 to October 14. The pro-EU campaigner Gina Miller sought a declaration that the prime minister's advice upon which this was done was unlawful. The divisional court dismissed the claim on the grounds that the issue was not justiciable, but gave leave for the matter to be decided by the Supreme Court.

On September 24 that court decided that the issue was justiciable; that Article IX of the Bill of Rights 1689 (excluding the courts from considering proceedings in parliament) did not apply; that prorogation with the effect of frustrating parliament from carrying out its constitutional functions would be unlawful; and that the prime minister's advice was thus unlawful. The prorogation was declared void and parliament resumed its business. It was lawfully prorogued on October 8 after the longest parliamentary session since the English Civil War. The State Opening took place on October 14 and a further government defeat, on the European Union (Withdrawal) (No 6) Bill, which denied parliamentary approval for the agreement until the passage of legislation to ratify it, followed on October 19.

Finally, Boris Johnson sidestepped the Fixed-term Parliaments Act entirely with the Early Parliamentary General Election Bill, requiring only simple majorities, which passed through all its stages in both houses on October 29 and 30 and provided that there should be a general election on December 12, 2019.

The election gave the Conservatives a landslide victory with an overall majority of 80 seats. Labour were hammered, losing 60 seats, and the Liberal Democrats won only 11 seats (also losing that of their leader, Jo Swinson). Despite the SNP advance in Scotland, where a gain of 13 seats took them to a total of 48, the parliamentary landscape had changed out of all recognition and Mr Johnson could set about governing with very little parliamentary restriction.

The implications became clear with the publication of a new European Union (Withdrawal Agreement) Bill on December 19, 2019, which considerably reduced the degree of parliamentary involvement in the Brexit process. The European Union (Withdrawal) Act 2018 had made ratification of the Withdrawal Agreement subject to the approval of the House of Commons; the new bill would repeal that requirement. Moreover, the parliamentary scrutiny of international treaties, introduced by the Constitutional Reform and Governance Act 2005, was in the case of the Withdrawal Agreement to be disapplied. In addition the UK/EU joint committee of ministers overseeing the implementation and application of the Withdrawal Agreement was to have no parliamentary oversight.

The years 2017-19 were testing times for the United Kingdom's constitutional arrangements. So what is the outlook for our constitution? The starting point for most commentators is page 48 of the Conservative Party's manifesto for the 2019 general election. That manifesto promises repeal of the Fixed-term Parliaments Act 2011. The act will go unlamented to its legislative grave, but there is one problem that will need to be solved. The act removed by statute the power of the sovereign to dissolve parliament. If the procedures set out in the act are to be repealed then the previous prerogative power will need to be re-instated. It will be interesting to see the terms in which this is done and the possible implications for the wider royal prerogative.

Also promised is a Constitution, Democracy and Rights Commission.

There is general agreement that, after the turbulence of the past two or three years, there needs to be a calm and informed examination of our constitutional arrangements, but there are also considerable concerns about how the government proposes to go about this. A royal commission on the criminal justice system is promised. Why is the constitution commission not to be a royal commission? How independent will it be? How far will it be asked to consider only those matters that the government wishes to bring forward? And given the huge range of its proposed responsibilities, what chance is there of it reaching conclusions in any realistic timeframe? The uncertainties of the 2017 parliament may provide ammunition for those who wish to see a written constitution; and the continuing disproportionate numbers required to elect each MP of different parties will ensure that the first-past-the-post system continues to have its critics; but the Conservative manifesto rules out any change to the voting system.

"We will ensure," the manifesto says, "that judicial review is available to protect the rights of the individuals against an overbearing state, while ensuring that it is not abused to conduct politics by other means or create needless delays." As yet there is no indication of what this might mean in practice, although it is suggested that judicial review might be limited to those cases in which a ministerial decision is so unreasonable that no person acting reasonably could have made it (known as Wednesbury unreasonableness). To those who see the current availability of judicial review as something that tilts the balance of the constitution towards the interests of the individual citizen, this is potentially concerning.

The decision of the Supreme Court in finding the prorogation of parliament unlawful clearly still rankles with the government, although as yet there is no indication as to how it might proceed.

Moving away from the government's manifesto proposals, it has been suggested that the House of Commons standing orders need to be reviewed in order to put them beyond the reach of re-interpretation in the style of Mr Bercow. Such an exercise would be wholly wrong-headed. It is not possible to draft standing orders that are immune to deliberate misinterpretation, and in any event the common sense and judgment demonstrated by the new Speaker, Sir Lindsay Hoyle, in his first weeks in office show that parliamentary expectations have returned to pre-Bercow settings.

Early in the new parliament the possibility of merging government departments and so reducing the number of cabinet ministers was canvassed. Such a change might make parliamentary scrutiny and calling the government to account in detail more difficult to achieve, but at least for the moment the prospect has receded. So too, for the time being, has that of a huge increase in the number of special advisers in order to provide a source of policy formation and advice parallel to that of the civil service.

The 2013 review of boundary changes (which would reduce the size of the Commons from 650 to 600 MPs) has still not been implemented and the 2019 general election took place within 2010 constituency boundaries. The Conservative manifesto promised "updated and equal parliamentary boundaries" but the new government's intentions are not yet clear.

The role of the House of Lords will be much reduced in the 2019 parliament. When the government was in an embattled minority in the House of Commons, the Lords could give the Commons a second bite at amendments that it had turned down and the numbers in that house might well produce a different answer second time round. Now the Lords will have to rely on the strength of their arguments in the knowledge that, in almost all circumstances, the government will be confident of reversing Lords amendments in the Commons.

The future of the Union will be a growing problem, made worse by the fact that Scotland and Northern Ireland voted differently from England and Wales in the EU referendum; by the resurgence of the SNP in the 2019 election; and by the feeling in some English regions that they are disadvantaged. The Holyrood elections in 2021 may increase the centrifugal forces in the Union and the pressure for a second Scottish independence referendum (against which Mr Johnson has set his face) may be a complicating factor.

Finally there is the UK's departure from the European Union. Despite winning the general election on the simplistic slogan of Get Brexit Done, the really tough negotiations lie ahead for the new government and there is nothing to suggest that they will be any easier than what has gone before.

The turbulence of the last parliament may encourage some to rush headlong to reform of our constitution. That would be unwise: the problems of 2017-19 were primarily political rather than constitutional and recent experience has taught us the importance of respect for conventions and reasonable expectations. If the constitution is treated with respect it will serve us well; if it is not, then we are in unknown territory.

Lord Lisvane was the clerk of the House of Commons 2011-14 and now sits as a

The cabinet

Prime minister, first lord of the Treasury and minister for the civil service	**Boris Johnson**
Chancellor of the exchequer	**Rishi Sunak**
Secretary of state for the Home Department	**Priti Patel**
Secretary of state for foreign and commonwealth affairs and first secretary of state	**Dominic Raab**
Secretary of state for defence	**Ben Wallace**
Lord chancellor and secretary of state for justice	**Robert Buckland**
Secretary of state for education	**Gavin Williamson**
Secretary of state for international trade, president of the Board of Trade and minister for women and equalities	**Elizabeth Truss**
Secretary of state for business, energy and industrial strategy and minister for Cop26	**Alok Sharma**
Secretary of state for health and social care	**Matt Hancock**
Secretary of state for work and pensions	**Thérèse Coffey**
Secretary of state for transport	**Grant Shapps**
Secretary of state for housing, communities and local government	**Robert Jenrick**
Lord privy seal and leader of the House of Lords	**Baroness Evans of Bowes Park**
Secretary of state for Scotland	**Alister Jack**
Secretary of state for Wales	**Simon Hart**
Secretary of state for Northern Ireland	**Brandon Lewis**
Secretary of state for environment, food and rural affairs	**George Eustice**
Secretary of state for international development	**Anne-Marie Trevelyan**
Secretary of state for digital, culture, media and sport	**Oliver Dowden**
Chancellor of the duchy of Lancaster and minister for the Cabinet Office	**Michael Gove**
Minister without portfolio	**Amanda Milling**

ALSO ATTENDING CABINET

Chief secretary to the Treasury	**Steve Barclay**
Attorney general	**Suella Braverman**
Parliamentary secretary to the Treasury (chief whip)	**Mark Spencer**
Lord president of the council and leader of the House of Commons	**Jacob Rees-Mogg**

February 2020

General election 2019: results by constituency

EU REFERENDUM RESULT
The estimates of how each constituency in England, Scotland and Wales voted in the EU referendum were provided by Chris
Hanretty, professor of politics at Royal Holloway, University of London. The referendum was counted at local authority level, rather
than at constituency level, except in Northern Ireland. Although some local authorities have released more detailed information,
not all have done so. For full details of the estimates see "A real interpolation and the UK's referendum on EU membership" by Chris
Hanretty, in the *Journal Of Elections, Public Opinion And Parties.*

Aberavon

MAJORITY 10,490 (33.20%)   LABOUR HOLD   TURNOUT 62.27%

STEPHEN KINNOCK
BORN Jan 1, 1970
MP 2015-

Son of the former Labour leader Neil Kinnock and husband of Helle Thorning-Schmidt, the prime minister of Denmark between 2011 and 2015. Jeremy Corbyn critic. Backed Lisa Nandy for leader, 2020; supported Yvette Cooper and Owen Smith in 2015 and 2016. Select cttees: Brexit, 2017-; European scrutiny, 2015-. Champions local steel-making: member of the APPG on steel and metal-related industries, and chairman of its steel 2020 sub-cttee. Campaigned for Remain; supported passing Theresa May's withdrawal agreement

	Electorate	Share %	Change from 2017 %
	50,747		
*S Kinnock Lab	17,008	53.83	-14.29
C Lang C	6,518	20.63	+2.89
G Davies Brexit	3,108	9.84	
N Hunt PC	2,711	8.58	+0.28
S Kingston-Jones LD	1,072	3.39	+1.59
C Beany Ind	731	2.31	
G Finney Green	450	1.42	

in September 2019 to avert no-deal. Director, World Economic Forum, 2009-12; British Council, 2005-08. Member, Consensus. Honorary associate, National Secular Society. Ed: Drayton Manor HS; Queens' Coll, Cambridge (BA modern languages); Coll of Europe.

CHALLENGERS
Charlotte Lang (C) Lobbyist in healthcare, financial services and

energy sectors. **Glenda Davies** (Brexit) Nurse and teacher. **Nigel Hunt** (PC) Owner, clothing label. Cllr, Neath Port Talbot C, 2017-. **Sheila Kingston-Jones** (LD) Former NHS dietician.

CONSTITUENCY PROFILE
This south Wales constituency has been represented by Labour since 1922, including by Ramsay MacDonald, the party's first prime minister, between 1922 and 1929. Labour typically achieves a comfortable absolute majority. A working-class, industrial area that contains the huge Tata steelworks in Port Talbot.

EU REFERENDUM RESULT
60.1% Leave   Remain 39.9%

Aberconwy

MAJORITY 2,034 (6.38%)   CONSERVATIVE HOLD   TURNOUT 71.29%

ROBIN MILLAR
BORN Oct 15, 1968
MP 2019-

Engineer. Replaced Guto Bebb, the MP for this seat since 2010 and a former Conservative minister. Mr Bebb had the whip removed for rebelling over Brexit, meaning that he ended his time in parliament as an independent. Cllr, Suffolk CC, 2015-19. Father was chairman of the Bangor branch of the old Conwy Association. Still carries a rosette given to him by Lord Roberts of Conwy, the former Plaid Cymru MP for Conwy, for helping his campaign in 1974. Contested Arfon, 2010. Ed: Ysgol Friars; University of Manchester (BEng engineering).

	Electorate	Share %	Change from 2017 %
	44,699		
R Millar C	14,687	46.09	+1.50
E Owen Lab	12,653	39.71	-2.91
L Goodier PC	2,704	8.49	-1.37
J Edwards LD	1,821	5.71	+2.79

CHALLENGERS
Emily Owen (Lab) Information and support officer, MS Society. Cllr, Conwy County BC, 2016-17. Said in 2019 that she had been drugged and raped in a "politically motivated attack". Contested this seat, 2017. **Lisa Goodier** (PC) Senior project manager, flood risk. Former business development manager. Cllr, Penmaenmawr TC, 2019-. **Jason Edwards** (LD) Director of a social media enterprise providing training to young people in film and TV. Speaks

Welsh as first language. Cllr, Penmaenmawr TC, 2017-.

CONSTITUENCY PROFILE
A coastal north Wales seat held by the Conservatives since 2010, although Labour came within 700 votes of taking it in 2017. Mixture of Welsh and English-speaking areas, with a high proportion of Welsh speakers. Boundary changes before 2010 removed the university city of Bangor from the seat, making it more favourable to the Conservatives, Labour having held it during the New Labour years. Contains the seaside resort of Llandudno. About a quarter of residents are retired.

EU REFERENDUM RESULT
52.2% Leave   Remain 47.8%

Aberdeen North

MAJORITY 12,670 (33.87%) SNP HOLD TURNOUT 59.87%

KIRSTY BLACKMAN
BORN Mar 20, 1986
MP 2015-

Deputy leader of the SNP in Westminster, 2017-. Party spokeswoman: economy, 2017-; House of Lords, 2015-17. Former parliamentary assistant to three MSPs. Select cttees: procedure, 2019-; European statutory instruments, 2018-19; Ipsa and the electoral commission, 2017-19; Scottish affairs, 2015-16. APPGs: offshore oil and gas industry; corporate governance; infant feeding; inequalities. Censured by Commons clerks for bringing children to a committee meeting, 2016. Champions gender equality and working mothers. Yet to

	Electorate	Share %	Change from 2017 %
	62,489		
*K Blackman SNP	20,205	54.01	+12.73
R Houghton C	7,535	20.14	-2.55
N Ali Lab	4,939	13.20	-16.81
I Davidson LD	2,846	7.61	+3.00
S Leslie Brexit	1,008	2.69	
G Ingerson Green	880	2.35	

rebel against party whip. Cllr, Aberdeen CC, 2007-15. Ed: Robert Gordon's Coll.

CHALLENGERS
Ryan Houghton (C) Suspended a month before election for controversial tweets. Seven years in RAF. Cllr, Aberdeen CC, 2017-. **Nurul Ali** (Lab) Oil and gas consultant. Cllr, Newham LBC, 1998-2002. Ed: University of Leeds (BEng chemical engineering); Cass

Business School (MBA). **Isobel Davidson** (LD) Wildlife consultant. Cllr, Aberdeenshire C, 2007-. Contested this seat in 2017. **Seb Leslie** (Brexit) Cllr, Aberdeenshire C, 2017-. Father of the *Game of Thrones* actress Rose Leslie.

CONSTITUENCY PROFILE
Elected Labour MPs from 1922 until 2015, except when the Unionist John Burnett won in 1931. The seat contains Aberdeen University, making for a substantial student vote. It also has many EU citizens. In the 2014 referendum on Scottish independence 59 per cent in Aberdeen voted No.

EU REFERENDUM RESULT
43.1% Leave   Remain 56.9%

Aberdeen South

MAJORITY 3,982 (8.74%) SNP GAIN FROM CONSERVATIVE TURNOUT 69.43%

STEPHEN FLYNN
BORN Oct 13, 1988
MP 2019-

Career politician who described the election campaign as "nerve-racking" because his wife was due to give birth two days after polling day. Replaced a Conservative MP who only gained the seat in 2017. Cllr, Aberdeen CC, 2015-; group leader, 2016. Was a part-time office manager for Maureen Watt, a member of the Scottish parliament. Also worked as an office manager and senior parliamentary assistant to Callum McCaig, who was the Aberdeen South MP from 2015 until 2017. Voted Remain and supported a second Brexit

	Electorate	Share %	Change from 2017 %
	65,719		
S Flynn SNP	20,380	44.66	+13.20
D Lumsden C	16,398	35.94	-6.21
I Yuill LD	5,018	11.00	+5.15
S Simpson Lab	3,834	8.40	-12.15

referendum. Ed: University of Dundee (MA history and politics; MLitt international politics).

CHALLENGERS
Douglas Lumsden (C) IT consultant. Cllr, Aberdeen CC, 2017-. Voted Remain, but opposed second referendums on both Brexit and Scottish independence. **Ian Yuill** (LD) Chartered marketer. Cllr, Aberdeen CC, 1994-. Contested: this seat, 2001; Scottish parliament, 1999; Dundee East,

1992. **Shona Simpson** (Lab) Wife of Barney Crockett, the lord provost of Aberdeen City C.

CONSTITUENCY PROFILE
Conservative or Unionist for most of the second half of the 20th century. Labour held the seat for only one term between 1966 and 1987, before winning it from 1997 until 2015. The Conservative Ross Thomson took the seat in 2017, but stepped down after a fellow MP accused him of sexual assault, a claim that he denied. Mostly affluent and suburban, the constituency contains more rural areas than the neighbouring seat of Aberdeen North.

EU REFERENDUM RESULT
32.1% Leave   Remain 67.9%

Aberdeenshire West & Kincardine

MAJORITY 843 (1.58%)   **CONSERVATIVE HOLD**   **TURNOUT 73.44%**

ANDREW BOWIE
BORN May 28, 1987
MP 2017-

	Electorate	Share %	Change from 2017 %
	72,640		
*A Bowie C	22,752	42.65	-5.20
F Mutch SNP	21,909	41.07	+8.62
J Waddell LD	6,253	11.72	+3.08
P Coffield Lab	2,431	4.56	-6.50

Vice-chairman, Conservative Party, 2019-. PPS to: Theresa May, 2019; Matt Hancock, Jeremy Wright, 2018. Office manager, Liam Kerr MSP, 2016-17. Parliamentary assistant and rural affairs adviser to Ian Duncan MEP, 2015-16. Northeast Scotland campaign manager, 2015 general election. Work and pensions select cttee, 2017-18. APPGs: democracy in the world; farming; Scottish sport. Toed the government line on withdrawal agreement and indicative votes. Backed Boris Johnson in the 2019 Conservative leadership contest. Junior warfare officer in the navy, 2007-10. Ed: Inverurie Academy; University of Aberdeen (MA history and politics; vice-president, Conservative and Unionist Association).

CHALLENGERS
Fergus Mutch (SNP) Party's head of communications and research, 2015-. Parliamentary assistant to Alex Salmond in the Scottish parliament, 2012-15. Plays the bagpipes. Contested Scottish parliament, 2016. **John Waddell** (LD) Former public affairs manager, Law Society of Scotland. Contested: this seat, 2017; Aberdeen City C, 2017; Scottish parliament, 2016. **Paddy Coffield** (Lab) Former maths teacher and IT specialist.

CONSTITUENCY PROFILE
Predecessors of this seat were Conservative for most of the postwar period, although under the most recent boundaries the constituency was held by the Liberal Democrats from 1997 to 2015. Sparse and rural. The population is about 98 per cent white and home ownership is common. Like the other Aberdeen constituencies, there is high employment in oil and gas.

EU REFERENDUM RESULT

38.5% Leave   Remain 61.5%

Airdrie & Shotts

MAJORITY 5,201 (13.08%)   **SNP HOLD**   **TURNOUT 62.14%**

NEIL GRAY
BORN Mar 16, 1986
MP 2015-

	Electorate	Share %	Change from 2017 %
	64,008		
*N Gray SNP	17,929	45.08	+7.47
H McFarlane Lab	12,728	32.00	-5.09
L Nolan C	7,011	17.63	-5.56
W Crossman LD	1,419	3.57	+1.46
R McGowan Green	685	1.72	

Athlete who represented Scotland in the 400m. Worked as a journalist on local newspapers and for BBC Radio Orkney. Aide to Alex Neil MSP: campaign manager, 2011; constituency office manager, 2008-15. Campaigned to Remain; supported a second EU referendum and soft Brexit options. SNP spokesman: fair work and employment, 2015-17; social justice, 2017-18; work and pensions, 2018-19. Finance select cttee, 2015-. APPG vice-chairman: children who need palliative care; Scottish sport; women and work; youth employment. APPG member: sport; poverty. Ed: Kirkwall GS; University of Stirling (BA politics and journalism).

CHALLENGERS
Helen McFarlane (Lab) Programme director, NHS Education for Scotland, 2006-. Trade unionist; served on executive council of Unite. Contested this seat in 2017. **Lorraine Nolan** (C) Contested North Lanarkshire C in 2019, 2018 and 2017.

CONSTITUENCY PROFILE
This working-class north Lanarkshire seat was held by Labour until 2015. From 2005 to 2010 it was represented by John Reid, who served as home secretary and in several other cabinet posts under Tony Blair. John Smith, the Labour Party leader from 1992 to 1994, held Monklands East, the seat's predecessor, from 1983 until his death in 1994. Labour came within 150 votes of winning in 2017. The constituency is predominantly urban and contains the towns of Calderbank, Chapelhall and Glenmavis. Airdrie is Gaelic for "high hill pasture".

EU REFERENDUM RESULT

39.8% Leave   Remain 60.2%

Aldershot

LEO DOCHERTY
BORN Oct 4, 1976
MP 2017-

Army veteran who served in Iraq and Afghanistan from 2001 to 2007. Wrote *Desert of Death*, a book about his time in the armed forces, in 2007. Backed Boris Johnson for leader, 2019. Selected to defend his seat despite local activists lobbying for the prominent Eurosceptic Daniel Hannan to be considered. PPS to: James Brokenshire, 2018-19; Jeremy Wright, 2019; Nicky Morgan, 2019. Assistant whip, 2019-. Select cttees: defence, 2017-19; arms export controls, 2017-19. APPGs: aerospace; Kuwait; UAE. Director, Conservative Middle

	Electorate	Share %	from 2017 % Change
	72,617		
*L Docherty C	27,980	58.37	+3.31
H Kaye Lab	11,282	23.54	-8.08
A Hilliar LD	6,920	14.44	+7.01
D Wallace Green	1,750	3.65	+1.42

East Council, 2010-17. Contested Caerphilly, 2015. Cllr, South Oxfordshire DC, 2011-15. Ed: School of Oriental and African Studies, University of London; RMA, Sandhurst.

CHALLENGERS
Howard Kaye (Lab) Train driver; on executive committee of Aslef, the train drivers' union. Contested: Surrey South West, 2015; Waverley BC, 2019; Surrey police and crime commissioner, 2016. **Alan Hilliar** (LD) Business technology consultant.

Contested this seat in the previous two elections.

CONSTITUENCY PROFILE
A safe Conservative seat held by the party since 1918. Contains the northeast Hampshire military town after which it is named, and Farnborough, both in the London commuter belt. The Liberal Democrats often came second in the New Labour era, squeezing the Tory majority to less than 6,000. Aldershot barracks is home to 4,000 troops. It is the residence of former Ghurkhas and thus has the largest proportion of Buddhists in the country, at 3.1 per cent of the population.

EU REFERENDUM RESULT
57.9% Leave   Remain 42.1%

Aldridge-Brownhills

WENDY MORTON
BORN Nov 9, 1967
MP 2015-

Businesswoman who ran a small electronics firm from 1992 to 2015. Brought forward a successful private member's bill in 2016 to ensure that Great Ormond Street Hospital would receive the royalties from JM Barrie's *Peter Pan* in perpetuity. Campaigned to Remain but voted for withdrawal agreement each time and for no-deal; backed Jeremy Hunt, 2019. Parly under-sec: Foreign Office, 2020-; justice, 2019-20. Rebelled three times while assistant whip, 2018-19. PPS to Jo Johnson, 2016. Select cttees: international development,

	Electorate	Share %	from 2017 % Change
	60,138		
*W Morton C	27,850	70.79	+5.38
D Morgan Lab	8,014	20.37	-9.48
I Garrett LD	2,371	6.03	+2.69
B McComish Green	771	1.96	
M Beech Loony	336	0.85	-0.55

2015-17; arms export controls, 2016-17. Cllr, Richmondshire DC, 2001-06; resigned after she and other councillors were accused of bullying an officer but a Standards Board inquiry subsequently cleared them. Contested: Tynemouth, 2010; Newcastle Central, 2005. Ed: Open University (MBA).

CHALLENGERS
David Morgan (Lab) IT technician and union official, GMB. Contested Walsall C, 2019,

2018. **Ian Garrett** (LD) History teacher. Cllr, Sandwell MBC, 1994-2002. Contested: this seat, 2017, 2015; West Bromwich East 2010, 2005, 2001.

CONSTITUENCY PROFILE
A suburban and rural West Midlands seat held by the Conservatives since 1979, having been won by Labour in 1974 after the constituency was split from Walsall. Aldridge is an affluent suburb of Walsall to the west, and Brownhills is a former mining community. Residents tend to be older than average and there is a substantial Sikh community. About 75 per cent of homes are owner-occupied.

EU REFERENDUM RESULT
67.7% Leave   Remain 32.3%

Altrincham & Sale West

SIR GRAHAM BRADY
BORN May 20, 1967
MP 1997-

Chairman of the 1922 committee from 2010 to 2019; resigned to consider standing for party leader before ruling himself out. Joined the Conservatives aged 16 to save grammar schools. Eurosceptic; successfully lobbied to ensure Conservatives had a neutral stance during the Brexit referendum campaign. Rebelled on Theresa May's EU withdrawal bill in first meaningful vote before backing it in all subsequent votes. Previously rebelled on Europe, HS2 and constitutional issues. Shadow ministerial and PPS roles, 1999-2007. Resigned from

	Electorate	Share %	from 2017 %	Change
	73,096			
*G Brady C	26,311	48.05	-2.97	
A Western Lab	20,172	36.84	-2.01	
+A Smith LD	6,036	11.02	+3.35	
G Coggins Green	1,566	2.86	+0.97	
N Taylor Lib	454	0.83	+0.26	
I Kiani Ind	224	0.41		

the front bench over grammar schools. Youngest Conservative MP in 1997. Deputy chairman, Centre for Policy Studies, 2016-. Knighted in 2018. Previously worked in PR. Ed: Altrincham GS; Durham University (LLB).

CHALLENGERS
Andrew Western (Lab) Former civil engineering consultant. Cllr, Trafford MBC, 2011-; council leader, 2018-. **Angela Smith** (LD) Labour MP, Penistone &

Stocksbridge, 2010-19; Sheffield Hillsborough, 2005-10. Resigned from Labour in February 2019 in protest at Jeremy Corbyn's leadership and co-founded The Independent Group; joined Lib Dems in September 2019. Shadow environment minister, 2014-15; shadow deputy leader of the Commons, 2011-14.

CONSTITUENCY PROFILE
Safe Conservative seat since 1924, in south of Greater Manchester. Affluent, with high home ownership. More than 40 per cent of residents have a degree. Significant Jewish community and a surviving grammar school system.

EU REFERENDUM RESULT

38.5% Leave	Remain 61.5%

Alyn & Deeside

MARK TAMI
BORN Oct 3, 1962
MP 2001-

Only Labour MP in north Wales not to lose their seat. Leaked Labour papers listed him as hostile to Jeremy Corbyn in 2016; he made no leadership nominations in 2015 or 2016 but backed Sir Keir Starmer in 2020. Campaigned to Remain; said he could not vote for a Brexit deal unless it included a second referendum. Chairman, APPG on stem-cell transplantation; his eldest son, Max, survived leukaemia in 2007 aged 9. Long-serving trade unionist before parliament; former head of policy at the engineering union Amicus. Supported the

	Electorate	Share %	from 2017 %	Change
	62,783			
*M Tami Lab	18,271	42.48	-9.61	
S Sen C	18,058	41.99	+1.59	
S Wall Brexit	2,678	6.23		
D Lalek LD	2,548	5.92	+3.52	
S Hills PC	1,453	3.38	+0.76	

introduction of compulsory voting. Treasury whip, 2007-10. Ed: Enfield GS; University of Wales, Swansea (BA history).

CHALLENGERS
Sanjoy Sen (C) Chemical engineer in North Sea oil. Semi-finalist on *Mastermind*, 2019. Contested: Aberdeen North, 2015; Camden C, 2018. **Simon Wall** (Brexit) Qualified teacher and independent training consultant. **Donna Lalek** (LD) Barrister; bank employee and

former teacher. Cllr, Broughton and Bretton CC, 2017-.

CONSTITUENCY PROFILE
Part of the industrial hinterland north of Wrexham and west of Cheshire. Boundaries changed in 1983; its predecessors consistently returned Labour MPs from 1950, but with slim majorities in elections in which the party did badly nationally, such as in 1983 and 2010. The southern part of the seat is more rural, with the largest towns, Connah's Quay and Buckley, in the north. A significant proportion of employment is in manufacturing, with Tata Steel and Toyota in the constituency.

EU REFERENDUM RESULT

58.1% Leave	Remain 41.9%

Amber Valley

NIGEL MILLS
BORN Oct 28, 1974
MP 2010-

Backbench Brexiteer. Worked as a tax adviser and chartered accountant. ERG member; backed Boris Johnson for leader, 2019. Apologised for playing *Candy Crush* during a committee meeting on pension reform in 2014. Frequent rebel during coalition years, including over launching airstrikes on Islamic State in Iraq and plain cigarette packaging. Endured two recounts before winning the seat in 2010. Select cttees: public accounts, 2015-; backbench business, 2018-; work and pensions, 2018-, 2012-15; Northern Ireland, 2017-.

	Electorate	Share %	Change from 2017 %
	69,976		
*N Mills C	29,096	63.85	+7.31
A Thompson Lab	12,210	26.80	-11.63
K Smith LD	2,873	6.31	+3.90
L Pizzey Green	1,388	3.05	+1.63

Chairman, APPGs on: Tajikistan; corruption; pensions. Cllr, Amber Valley BC, 2004-11; Heanor & Loscoe TC, 2007-11. Ed: Loughborough GS; Newcastle University (BA classics).

CHALLENGERS
Adam Thompson (Lab) Engineering researcher, University of Nottingham. Worked at Rolls Royce. Vice-chairman for policy, Scientists for Labour. Sings in a band. **Kate Smith** (LD) Gift shop assistant in the National Tramway Museum. Cllr, Crich PC, 2003-08. **Lian Pizzey** (Green) Community worker, Derby University.

CONSTITUENCY PROFILE
A bellwether since its creation in 1983, this rural, west Derbyshire constituency was won by the Conservatives by only 536 votes in 2010, though Nigel Mills has increased his majority at every election since and it now exceeds Labour's 1997 record. The constituency contains former mining towns, such as Alfreton, Heanor, Ripley and Oakerthorpe. House prices and median weekly pay are lower than the national average.

EU REFERENDUM RESULT
65.3% Leave   Remain 34.7%

Angus

DAVE DOOGAN
BORN Mar 4, 1973
MP 2019-

Spent 18 years with the Ministry of Defence, first as a helicopter engineer and later as a commercial programme manager. Left the civil service to study international relations and drove taxis part-time to support his studies. Also a self-employed landscape gardener. Born in Perth to Irish parents. Cllr, Perth & Kinross, 2012-20; SNP group leader, 2017-20. Contested Mid-Scotland & Fife in Scottish parliament elections, 2016. Voted Remain in 2016. Served on NHS Tayside board. Ed: University of Dundee (MA politics and international relations).

	Electorate	Share %	Change from 2017 %
	63,952		
D Doogan SNP	21,216	49.15	+10.57
*K Hair C	17,421	40.35	-4.80
B Lawrie LD	2,482	5.75	+2.49
M Miller Lab	2,051	4.75	-8.27

CHALLENGERS
Kirstene Hair (C) MP for this seat, 2017-19. PPS to David Mundell, Scotland secretary, 2019. Worked as an events manager and executive personal assistant. Did not vote in the 2016 Brexit referendum, but supported Theresa May's withdrawal agreement. Born and brought up in Angus. **Ben Lawrie** (LD) Recent graduate and mental health campaigner. **Monique Miller** (Lab) Student and agency worker who campaigned on homelessness. Failed to secure 5 per cent of the vote and thus lost her deposit.

CONSTITUENCY PROFILE
Angus and its predecessor seats were mostly represented by Conservatives in the postwar era, until the SNP claimed it in 1987, with two different SNP MPs holding it for 30 years. During this period the party often won with slim majorities over the Tories. This rural seat relies on the agricultural sector. It contains Arbroath, where the 1320 declaration of Scottish independence was signed, although 56 per cent of constituents voted against independence in 2014.

EU REFERENDUM RESULT
48.2% Leave   Remain 51.8%

Antrim East

SAMMY WILSON
BORN Apr 4, 1953
MP 2005-

DUP's Commons chief whip, 2019-. MLA, Belfast East, 1998-2003; East Antrim, 2003-15. Dismissed environmental campaigns as "green guff" and called Irish "the leprechaun language". Brexiteer. Voted against plain cigarette packaging and increasing alcohol duty. Voted against LGBT-inclusive sex education in English schools. Stormont minister of finance, 2009-13. Previously DUP Westminster spokesman for Brexit, Treasury, work and pensions. Former member, Northern Ireland policing board. Cllr, Belfast CC, 1981-

		Electorate	Share %	Change from 2017 %
		64,830		
*S Wilson	DUP	16,871	45.28	-12.07
D Donnelly	Alliance	10,165	27.28	+11.68
S Aiken	UUP	5,475	14.69	+2.83
O McMullan	SF	2,120	5.69	-3.63
A Rankin	C	1,043	2.80	+0.27
A Mulholland	SDLP	902	2.42	-0.93
P Randle	Green	685	1.84	

2010. Former teacher. Ed: Queen's University, Belfast (BA economics and politics); Stranmillis Teaching Coll (DipEd).

CHALLENGERS
Danny Donnelly (Alliance) Cllr, Mid & East Antrim BC. Car attacked with acid in January 2019. **Steve Aiken** (UUP) MLA, South Antrim, 2016-. Ulster Unionist Party chief whip. **Oliver**

McMullan (SF) Publican. MLA, East Antrim, 2011-17; lost his seat to a DUP candidate. **Aaron Rankin** (C) Geologist.

CONSTITUENCY PROFILE
This seat and its predecessor have been held by unionists since the 19th century, although 2019 was the best ever result for the non-aligned Alliance Party. Located in the northeast of Northern Ireland, the seat's most populated towns, Carrickfergus and Larne, are largely Protestant. There is a large Catholic population in the north of the seat. Home to the University of Ulster campus at Jordanstown.

EU REFERENDUM RESULT
55.2% Leave   Remain 44.8%

Antrim North

IAN PAISLEY JR
BORN Dec 12, 1966
MP 2010-

Career politician nicknamed Baby Doc after his father, Papa Doc, the late founder of the DUP, the Rev Ian Paisley. Campaigned for Brexit. Has consistently put in among the highest expenses claims of all MPs, claiming more than £1 million between 2010 and 2015. Suspended from parliament for 30 days in 2018 for failing to declare two holidays paid for by the Sri Lankan government; a recall petition against him did not garner enough signatures to trigger a by-election. DUP spokesman in Westminster for local government, 2015-; culture,

		Electorate	Share %	Change from 2010 %
		77,134		
*I Paisley	DUP	20,860	47.35	-11.50
R Swann	UUP	8,139	18.48	+11.29
P O'Lynn	Alliance	6,231	14.14	+8.53
C McShane	SF	5,632	12.79	-3.47
M McKillop	SDLP	2,943	6.68	+1.37
S Palmer	Ind	246	0.56	

2015-; energy, 2015-17; agriculture and work and pensions, 2010-15. Select cttees include: panel of chairs, 2016-; Northern Ireland, 2010-. MLA, Antrim North, 1998-2010. Ed: Methodist Coll Belfast GS; Queen's University Belfast (BA history; MSc Irish politics).

CHALLENGERS
Robin Swann (UUP) Party leader, 2017-19; chief whip, 2012-17. Board member, Volunteer

Development Agency. President and County Antrim Chairman, Young Farmers' Clubs of Ulster. **Patricia O'Lynn** (Alliance) PhD student, Queen's University Belfast. **Cara McShane** (SF) Cllr, Causeway Coast & Glens BC, 2014-; has condemned the DUP for its anti-LGBT stances.

CONSTITUENCY PROFILE
This solidly unionist seat in the northeast contains a mix of rural villages and manufacturing towns. Held by the late Rev Ian Paisley from 1970 until his retirement in 2010. A relatively prosperous area, containing a quarter of Northern Irish manufacturing.

EU REFERENDUM RESULT
62.2% Leave   Remain 37.8%

Antrim South

MAJORITY 2,689 (6.26%)   DUP HOLD   TURNOUT 59.93%

PAUL GIRVAN
BORN Jul 6, 1963
MP 2017-

Electorate	Share %	Change from 2017 %
71,711		
*P Girvan DUP	15,149 35.25	-2.99
D Kinahan UUP	12,460 28.99	-1.81
J Blair Alliance	8,190 19.06	+11.64
D Kearney SF	4,887 11.37	-6.69
R Lynch SDLP	2,288 5.32	-0.15

DUP spokesman for transport and education since 2017. Criticised for saying during a radio interview in 2013 that he had "no problem about burning a tricolour on top of a bonfire". Subsequently issued a statement saying he wanted to see a reduction in flag burning, but suggested that perceived attacks on "Eleventh Night" bonfires, an annual Ulster Protestant celebration, could provoke "an increase of incidents where flags and other emblems are burnt". Voted against LGBT-inclusive sex education in English schools. MLA, Antrim South, 2010-17,

2003-07. Transport select cttee, 2017-19. Cllr, Newtownabbey BC, 1997-2013; mayor, 2002-04. Worked as an electronics engineer and parliamentary assistant.

CHALLENGERS
Danny Kinahan (UUP) MP, this seat, 2015-17. Helped to thwart a Sinn Fein campaign to abolish grammar schools in Northern Ireland. **John Blair** (Alliance) MLA, 2018-. **Declan Kearney** (SF) MLA, 2016-. Party's national

chairman; apologised for "lives lost during the Troubles", 2015. **Roisin Lynch** (SDLP) Vice-chairwoman, party central executive.

CONSTITUENCY PROFILE
This commuter seat to the east of Belfast has been held by five different unionist MPs since 1997, having switched multiple times between the DUP and the UUP. It has been held by its sitting MP only twice since then, in 2015 and 2019, both times by the DUP. The nationalist parties won more than 10,000 votes combined for the first time in 2017. The constituency is about two-thirds Protestant.

EU REFERENDUM RESULT
50.6% Leave   Remain 49.4%

Arfon

MAJORITY 2,781 (9.57%)   PLAID CYMRU HOLD   TURNOUT 68.87%

HYWEL WILLIAMS
BORN May 14, 1953
MP 2001-

Electorate	Share %	Change from 2017 %
42,215		
*H Williams PC	13,134 45.17	+4.34
S Williams Roberts Lab	10,353 35.61	-4.90
G Daniels C	4,428 15.23	-1.13
G Gribben Brexit	1,159 3.99	

Plaid Cymru leader in Westminster, 2015-17. Career as a mental health lecturer, social worker and consultant. Has never rebelled against the Plaid Cymru whip. Party spokesman: Brexit, Cabinet Office, trade, 2017-; work and pensions, 2001-. MP for Caenarfon, 2001-2010, before boundary changes. Advocate of "radical alliance" with SNP and Green Party in 2017. Chairman, Catalonia APPG. Campaigned to Remain in the EU and voted in favour of a second referendum. Ed: Glan y Mor Sch; University of Wales, Cardiff (BSc psychology).

CHALLENGERS
Steffie Williams Roberts (Lab) Best-selling erotic author, with work featuring in Amazon Top 10 Erotica list; books described as "steamier than *Fifty Shades of Grey*". Grew up on a Bangor estate. Joined Labour in 2015. Welsh speaker. Previously a beauty pageant contestant. Law graduate. **Gonul Daniels** (C) Trustee, Ashmole Academy Board; chairman, Ashmole Primary School. Worked at the Bank of England and in the Houses of Parliament.

CONSTITUENCY PROFILE
This northwest Wales seat and its predecessor, Caernarfon, have been held by Plaid Cymru since 1974, when the party defeated the Labour Party candidate, Goronwy Robert, who was a minister under Harold Wilson and later a member of the House of Lords. Labour came within 92 votes of winning it back in 2017, and within 1,455 votes in 2010, but it has otherwise been held with decent majorities by Plaid Cymru. The Lib Dems did not put up a candidate here as part of the pro-European Union "Unite to Remain" coalition. There is a large student population in the seat.

EU REFERENDUM RESULT
35.8% Leave   Remain 64.2%

Argyll & Bute

MAJORITY 4,110 (8.55%)   **SNP HOLD**   **TURNOUT 72.23%**

BRENDAN O'HARA
BORN Apr 27, 1963
MP 2015-

SNP spokesman for inclusive society, 2018-; culture, 2017-18. Stepped down from culture role "for personal reasons". SNP Westminster group leader, defence, 2015-17. One of the beneficiaries of the Liberal Democrat wipeout in 2015. Supported Remain in the referendum; voted against the triggering of Article 50. Independent television producer prior to politics. Contested: Glasgow Central, 1992; Springburn, 1987. Ed: St Andrew's, Carntyne; University of Strathclyde (MA economic and modern history).

	Electorate	Share %	Change from 2017 %
	66,525		
*B O'Hara SNP	21,040	43.79	+7.79
G Mulvaney C	16,930	35.23	+2.00
A Reid LD	6,832	14.22	-3.97
R Barnes Lab	3,248	6.76	-5.81

CHALLENGERS
Gary Mulvaney (C) Chartered accountant and business manager of a theatre company. Cllr, Argyll & Bute C, 2003-; council deputy leader and policy lead for financial services. **Alan Reid** (LD) MP for this seat from 2001 until 2015, when he lost to Brendan O'Hara by 8,000 votes. Former whip. Criticised during 2009 expenses scandal for claiming £1,500 for B&B stays in his own constituency, which he said were necessary because of the size of his constituency.

CONSTITUENCY PROFILE
A seat in west Scotland that was held by the Liberal Democrats for 18 years before being taken in the SNP's 2015 landslide. The predecessor seats of Argyll and Argyllshire were held mostly by Unionist and Conservative MPs between 1924 and 1987. The constituency covers a swathe of sparsely populated countryside and 26 islands, including Mull, Tiree and Iona. Its main towns are Oban, a ferry port, and Helensburgh, which is within commuting distance of Glasgow. It also contains HM Naval Base Clyde, which is home to the submarines that carry Britain's Trident nuclear missiles.

EU REFERENDUM RESULT
39.4% Leave   Remain 60.6%

Arundel & South Downs

MAJORITY 22,521 (36.67%)   **CONSERVATIVE HOLD**   **TURNOUT 75.14%**

ANDREW GRIFFITH
BORN Feb 23, 1971
MP 2019-

Hired as a business adviser to Boris Johnson in the previous parliament after the prime minister was forced to deny saying "f*** business". Parachuted into this Conservative safe seat, which had been held by the retiring Nick Herbert since 2005. Allowed Mr Johnson to stay in his £9.5 million Westminster townhouse during his leadership bid. Chief operating officer, Sky, 2016-19; finance chief, 2008-16; executive, 1999-2008. Non-executive director, Just Eat, 2014-19. Youngest ever FTSE 100 finance director. Worked

	Electorate	Share %	Change from 2017 %
	81,726		
A Griffith C	35,566	57.92	-4.44
A Bennett LD	13,045	21.24	+13.31
B Sankey Lab	9,722	15.83	-6.89
I Thurston Green	2,519	4.10	-0.12
R Wheal Ind	556	0.91	

for PwC and Rothschild. Ed: St Mary's & St Joseph's Sch, Sidcup; University of Nottingham (BA law).

CHALLENGERS
Alison Bennett (LD) Joined party after the 2015 wipeout. Previously worked for British Airways, Powergen and Legal & General. Cllr, Mid Sussex DC, 2019-; Lib Dem group leader. **Bella Sankey** (Lab) Director, Detention Action, an immigration charity.

Policy director, Liberty. **Isabel Thurston** (Green) Secretary, West Sussex Green Party. **Robert Wheal** (Ind) Former Conservative councillor initially standing for the Brexit Party.

CONSTITUENCY PROFILE
This rural West Sussex seat has been safely held by the Conservatives since its creation in 1997. Only in 2005 has the Tory vote share dipped below 50 per cent. The seat's predecessors also returned Conservative MPs at every postwar election. Three quarters of households are owner occupied, and the seat's residents are generally middle class.

EU REFERENDUM RESULT
49.7% Leave   Remain 50.3%

Ashfield

LEE ANDERSON
BORN Jan 6, 1967
MP 2019-

Went from Labour campaigner to Conservative MP in less than two years. Worked as a coalminer and joined the strikes in the 1980s. Caseworker for Gloria De Piero, the Labour MP for Ashfield since 2010, who resigned from the shadow cabinet and voted for Boris Johnson's Brexit deal. Cllr, Mansfield DC, 2015-19; deselected by Labour in January 2018 and joined the Tories a few months later, condemning the opposition's handling of Brexit and the rise of Momentum. Received national media attention during the campaign

	Electorate	Share %	Change from 2017 %
	78,204		
L Anderson C	19,231	39.26	-2.43
J Zadrozny Ash	13,498	27.56	
N Fleet Lab	11,971	24.44	-18.14
M Daubney Brexit	2,501	5.11	
R Wain LD	1,105	2.26	+0.32
R Woods Green	674	1.38	+0.58

for saying that "nuisance" council tenants should have to live in tents and pick vegetables for 12 hours a day. Caught by the journalist Michael Crick using a friend as a canvassing stooge.

CHALLENGERS
Jason Zadrozny (Ash) Leader, Ashfield DC, 2018-, 2007-09. Leader of the Ashfield Independents. Brexiteer. Contested this seat as a Lib Dem in 2010, losing by 192 votes.

Stood again in 2015, but was deselected after being charged with child sex offences; the charges were later dropped. **Natalie Fleet** (Lab) Trade unionist. **Martin Daubney** (Brexit) MEP, 2019-20. Former editor, *Loaded*, a men's magazine.

CONSTITUENCY PROFILE
A west Nottinghamshire seat that had elected Labour MPs at every general election since its creation in 1955, although a Tory won a by-election in 1977. Held by the Labour cabinet minister Geoff Hoon from 1992 until 2010. It became marginal: Gloria De Piero's majorities in 2010 and 2017 were both less than 500.

EU REFERENDUM RESULT
70.5% Leave   Remain 29.5%

Ashford

DAMIAN GREEN
BORN Jan 17, 1956
MP 1997-

First secretary of state and Theresa May's de facto deputy, 2017; he resigned after lying following the discovery of pornography on his work computer. Backed Boris Johnson for leader, 2019. Chairman, Parliamentary Mainstream. Vice-president, Tory Reform Group. Chairman, One Nation Conservative caucus, 2019-. First appointed to the front bench in 1998. Work and pensions secretary, 2016-17. Home Office minister, 2010-12. Select cttees: national security strategy, 2015-16; European scrutiny, 2015-16. Shadow secretary:

	Electorate	Share %	Change from 2017 %
	89,550		
*D Green C	37,270	62.06	+3.07
D Farrell Lab	13,241	22.05	-7.75
A Gee-Turner LD	6,048	10.07	+4.89
M Rossi Green	2,638	4.39	+2.05
S De Sanvil Ind	862	1.44	

transport, 2003-04; education, 2001-03. Shadow home affairs minister, 2005-10. Voted Remain. Financial journalist at the BBC, Channel 4 and *The Times*. Contested Brent East, 1992. Ed: Balliol Coll, Oxford (BA PPE; president, Oxford Union).

CHALLENGERS
Dara Farrell (Lab) Sales executive and former nightclub DJ. Cllr, Ashford BC, 2017-. **Adrian Gee-Turner** (LD) Medical business consultant.

Executive member, Association Lib Dem Trade Unionists. **Mandi Rossi** (Green) Qualified in forensic psychology.

CONSTITUENCY PROFILE
The Conservative majority in Ashford has grown from a low of just over 5,000 in 1997 at most successive elections. Held by the Conservatives since 1931, including by the former cabinet minister and *Daily Telegraph* editor, Bill Deedes, between 1950 and 1975. This Kent seat contains large rural areas, while the town of Ashford itself is a commuter hotspot, with an international station on the Eurostar route and a high-speed link to London.

EU REFERENDUM RESULT
59.9% Leave   Remain 40.1%

Ashton-under-Lyne

MAJORITY 4,263 (11.05%)   LABOUR HOLD   TURNOUT 56.29%

ANGELA RAYNER
BORN Mar 28, 1980
MP 2015-

Favourite to become deputy leader of the Labour Party after the 2019 election, having struck a deal with her flatmate, the leadership contender Rebecca Long Bailey (Salford & Eccles), to endorse each other for the respective roles. A rare breed: loyal to Jeremy Corbyn but also criticised by the far left after she praised Tony Blair and defended New Labour's legacy. Shadow education secretary, 2016-; shadow work and pensions minister, 2016. Opposition whip, 2015-16. Remainer. Former regional convener, Unison. Worked as a care assistant.

	Electorate	Share %	Change from 2017 %
	68,497		
*A Rayner Lab	18,544	48.09	-12.26
D Costello C	14,281	37.04	+5.08
D Brocklehurst Brexit	3,131	8.12	
G Rice LD	1,395	3.62	+1.99
L Huntbach Green	1,208	3.13	+1.79

Nominated Andy Burnham for the leadership in 2015 and Mr Corbyn in 2016. Has spoken of how becoming a mother at 16 helped to give her life purpose. Became a grandmother at 37. Ed: Avondale HS. Advocate of lifelong education after leaving with no GCSEs above a grade D. Ed: Stockport Coll.

CHALLENGERS
Dan Costello (C) Hurst resident, born in Tameside. **Derek Brocklehurst** (Brexit) Vehicle

fleet manager for a Manchester taxi firm. **George Rice** (LD) Final year student, University of Manchester. Youth mentor with the National Citizen Service.

CONSTITUENCY PROFILE
This seat has returned a Labour MP since 1935, though the party's majority in 2019 was its smallest since 1970. The town of Ashton, in the east of the constituency, is the biggest population centre. Droylsden and Failsworth, in the west, are more affluent and closer to Manchester city centre. The seat has a sizeable south Asian and Asian British population of about 10,000 residents.

EU REFERENDUM RESULT
61.8% Leave   Remain 38.2%

Aylesbury

MAJORITY 17,373 (28.68%)   CONSERVATIVE HOLD   TURNOUT 69.90%

ROB BUTLER
BORN Jun 19, 1967
MP 2019-

Replaced Sir David Lidington, who had held the seat since 1992 and was at one time Theresa May's deputy in all but name; he resigned from government before Boris Johnson became prime minister and stood down before the election. Owner of Butler Corporate Communications and Media Ltd, a reputation management agency providing advice and media training to protect the standing of companies, NGOs and prominent individuals. Worked as an ITV news anchor and presenter on Channel 5's *News at Noon* for seven years.

	Electorate	Share %	Change from 2017 %
	86,665		
R Butler C	32,737	54.04	-0.96
L Hind Lab	15,364	25.36	-4.63
S Lambert LD	10,081	16.64	+7.01
C Simpson Green	2,394	3.95	+1.85

Non-executive director, HM Prison & Probation Service, 2019. Magistrate: chairman, adult court; winger, youth court. Opposed HS2. Voted Leave. Ed: Bicester Sch, Oxford; University of Sheffield (BA French and economics).

CHALLENGERS
Liz Hind (Lab) Publican with a PhD. Formerly of the British Science Association. **Steven Lambert** (LD) Cllr, Buckinghamshire CC, 2013-. Post Office project manager.

Contested this seat in the previous three general elections.

CONSTITUENCY PROFILE
This affluent Buckinghamshire seat has returned a Conservative MP at every election since 1924, the party's majority not having fallen below 8,000 in more than 50 years. It is a middle-class area that contains large rural areas as well as semi-rural commuter towns and villages in the south. There is a relatively large Asian population for a rural seat. HS2, which would pass through the constituency, is a controversial local issue: a petition calling for a vote to scrap the project garnered 1,500 signatures.

EU REFERENDUM RESULT
51.8% Leave   Remain 48.2%

Ayr, Carrick & Cumnock

MAJORITY 2,329 (5.00%) SNP GAIN FROM CONSERVATIVE TURNOUT 64.74%

ALLAN DORANS
BORN July 30, 1955
MP 2019-

A former policeman, like his Conservative opponent. Joined the Metropolitan Police as a cadet, before becoming a detective inspector aged 28. Later worked as a personnel and training executive at Butlins in Ayr. Vocal supporter of Waspi women. Cllr, South Ayrshire C, 2012-17; SNP group leader, 2014-17. Ed: Carrick Academy; University of the West of Scotland (Dip public service leadership).

CHALLENGERS
Martin Dowey (C) Stood in place of Bill Grant, a Tory

	Electorate	Share %	Change from 2017 %
	71,970		
A Dorans SNP	20,272	43.51	+9.38
M Dowey C	17,943	38.51	-1.62
D Townson Lab	6,219	13.35	-10.50
H Bongard LD	2,158	4.63	+2.75

moderate who did not stand again after winning the seat from the SNP in 2017, having always maintained he wished to serve only one term. Cllr, South Ayrshire C, 2017-; leader, Conservative group. Voted Remain. Left school at 16 to work as a fisherman, before becoming a policeman for 25 years. **Duncan Townson** (Lab) Critical of Jeremy Corbyn, saying that the party leader was on a "one-man crusade to destroy Labour". Classics graduate. **Helena Bongard** (LD)

Parliamentary researcher and recent history graduate of the University of Edinburgh.

CONSTITUENCY PROFILE
Until the SNP landslide in 2015, this Ayrshire seat in southwest Scotland had been held by Labour in all but one election since 1918, if its predecessors before boundary changes are included. The Conservatives won it for one term in 2017. The constituency consists of the coastal town of Ayr, the more rural and prosperous Carrick, and Cumnock, which has higher levels of deprivation. It also encompasses several former mining villages.

EU REFERENDUM RESULT
44.1% Leave Remain 55.9%

Ayrshire Central

MAJORITY 5,304 (11.40%) SNP HOLD TURNOUT 66.72%

PHILIPPA
WHITFORD
BORN Dec 24, 1958
MP 2015-

Consultant breast surgeon until the 2015 election. Helped to develop Scottish breast cancer care guidelines. Spent a 2016 parliamentary recess in the West Bank and Gaza, operating on Palestinian women with breast cancer. Medical volunteer at a UN hospital in Gaza, 1991-92. Left Labour in protest at Iraq War and joined the SNP in 2011. Active in Women for Independence campaign. Voted against triggering Article 50. SNP Westminster spokeswoman, health, 2010-. Select cttees: European scrutiny, 2017-; health, 2019-, 2015-17. Feminist blogger.

	Electorate	Share %	Change from 2017 %
	69,742		
*P Whitford SNP	21,486	46.17	+8.98
D Stillie C	16,182	34.77	+0.39
L McPhater Lab	6,583	14.15	-11.94
E Farthing LD	2,283	4.91	+2.58

Born in Belfast and moved to Scotland aged ten. Ed: University of Glasgow (MBChB).

CHALLENGERS
Derek Stillie (C) Former goalkeeper for Scottish and English clubs, including Aberdeen, Wigan Athletic and Dundee United. Signed by Aberdeen aged 18. After retiring from the game, he qualified in English law with the Open University and was a legal consultant for the BBC Scotland drama *Guilt*. **Louise McPhater**

(Lab) Cllr, North Ayrshire C, 2016-. Beat Robin Sturgeon, the father of Nicola, the first minister of Scotland since 2014, in a council by-election.

CONSTITUENCY PROFILE
A coastal seat held by Labour until being taken by the Scottish National Party in its 2015 landslide. The constituency was split from 1983 to 2005 between Cunninghame South, which returned Labour Party MPs each time, and Ayr, which swung between Labour and the Conservatives. The biggest towns include Irvine and Troon. Nicola Sturgeon was born and raised in the area.

EU REFERENDUM RESULT
41.6% Leave Remain 58.4%

Ayrshire North & Arran

MAJORITY 8,521 (17.70%)   **SNP HOLD**   **TURNOUT 65.49%**

PATRICIA GIBSON
BORN May 12, 1968
MP 2015-

	Electorate	Share %	Change from 2017 %
	73,534		
*P Gibson SNP	23,376	48.54	+9.65
D Rocks C	14,855	30.85	-0.39
C Gilmore Lab	6,702	13.92	-13.57
L Young LD	2,107	4.38	+2.01
D Nairn Green	1,114	2.31	

Former teacher. Campaigns against medical negligence after the stillbirth of her son in 2009. Voted against triggering Article 50, and conducted SNP MPs' rendition of *Ode to Joy* in the Commons chamber during that vote. SNP spokeswoman, consumer affairs, 2017-; education, 2007-11. Cllr, Glasgow CC, 2007-12. Contested this seat in the 2010 election. Successfully lobbied for a change in the law to tackle nuisance telephone callers. Married to the SNP MSP Kenneth Gibson. Ed: St Gerald's Secondary Sch; University of Glasgow (BA English and politics); Open University (modules included child development and approaches to literature).

CHALLENGERS
David Rocks (C) Secondary school music teacher for 13 years. Contested this seat in 2017, the first election at which his party pushed Labour into third place here. **Cameron Gilmore** (Lab) Critical of zero-hours contracts, having previously worked in the gig economy. **Louise Young** (LD)

Corporate planning manager. Cllr, Edinburgh CC, 2017-, 2007-12. Humanist. **David Nairn** (Green) Works for the Fairlie Coastal Trust.

CONSTITUENCY PROFILE
The seat was created in 2005 and held for ten years by Labour's Katy Clark, who worked in Jeremy Corbyn's office after losing to the SNP in 2015. The seat's predecessor had been held by Labour since 1987, the Conservatives having won it in 1983. The constituency includes former mining areas, with tourism and nuclear energy among the most important parts of the economy.

EU REFERENDUM RESULT

42.4% Leave	Remain 57.6%

Banbury

MAJORITY 16,813 (26.72%)   **CONSERVATIVE HOLD**   **TURNOUT 69.82%**

VICTORIA PRENTIS
BORN Mar 24, 1971
MP 2015-

	Electorate	Share %	Change from 2017 %
	90,113		
*V Prentis C	34,148	54.27	+0.04
S Watson Lab	17,335	27.55	-6.54
T Bearder LD	8,831	14.04	+8.43
I Middleton Green	2,607	4.14	+2.15

Barrister who spent 17 years in the civil service and defended the government in cases such as the inquiry into the 7/7 terrorist attacks. Moderate; voted Remain in 2016 and backed Rory Stewart in the 2019 Conservative leadership election. Parly under-sec, Defra, 2020-. PPS to Andrea Leadsom (Northamptonshire South), 2017-19. Former director of the anti-HS2 group Transport Sense. Campaigned for bereaved mothers after losing three babies; vice-chairwoman, APPG on baby loss, 2016-. Founder and former chairwoman, benefactors' board of the Oxford Hospital Trust. Organised the Singing for Syria and Great British Spring Clean campaigns. Select cttees: justice, 2015-; statutory instruments, 2015-17. Daughter of Tim Boswell, the Conservative MP for Daventry, 1987-2010. Ed: Royal Holloway, University of London (BA English literature); Downing Coll, Cambridge (LLB).

CHALLENGERS
Suzette Watson (Lab) Self-employed arts and culture consultant, having studied dance. Made redundant as a council worker after 20 years. **Tim Bearder** (LD) Worked as a BBC journalist; runs an independent production company. Cllr, Oxfordshire CC, 2018-.

CONSTITUENCY PROFILE
Banbury is a safe Conservative seat in north Oxfordshire. It has returned Conservative MPs consistently since 1922, the party's majority last falling below 5,000 in 1997. It is dominated by the market towns of Banbury and Bicester and there are high levels of employment. The M40 and rail links mean that it is home to many commuters who work in both London and Birmingham.

EU REFERENDUM RESULT

50.3% Leave	Remain 49.7%

Banff & Buchan

MAJORITY 4,118 (9.74%) CONSERVATIVE HOLD TURNOUT 63.40%

DAVID DUGUID
BORN Oct 8, 1970
MP 2017-

Electorate	Share %	Change from 2017 %
66,655		
*D Duguid C	21,182 50.12	+2.15
P Robertson SNP	17,064 40.38	+1.28
A Smith LD	2,280 5.40	+1.92
B Balcombe Lab	1,734 4.10	-5.35

Parliamentary private secretary to the departments of health and social care, and business, energy and industrial strategy, 2019. Backed Michael Gove for leader, 2019. Scottish affairs select committee, 2017-. Career in oil and gas industry; first as a production chemist, later moved into planning and management. Spent most of his career at BP before going freelance in 2016. Has worked in Azerbaijan, the North Sea, Asia and the Americas. Project manager, Hitachi Consulting. Director of a consultancy firm. Grew up on a farm on the banks of the River Deveron. Ed: Banff Academy; Robert Gordon University (MSc chemistry).

CHALLENGERS
Paul Robertson (SNP) Communications and public affairs consultant. Head of research and policy for the SNP, 2015-17. Local organiser for the Yes campaign in the 2014 referendum. Worked for Eilidh Whiteford MP, 2014-15; 2011-12. **Alison Smith** (LD) Academic specialising in European and Russian politics at University of Oxford. Cllr, Aberdeen City C, 2003-07. Worked for Sir Malcolm Bruce MP, 2001-06.

CONSTITUENCY PROFILE
A large, sparsely populated seat in northern Aberdeenshire that has swung between the Conservatives and the SNP since 1935. Held by the Conservatives without interruption until 1974, the seat was then represented by Alex Salmond, the former SNP leader and first minister, from 1987 to 2010. His successor lost the seat in 2015. Mostly rural; the biggests towns are all on the coast and include Fraserburgh and Peterhead.

EU REFERENDUM RESULT
61.4% Leave Remain 38.6%

Barking

MAJORITY 15,427 (34.67%) LABOUR HOLD TURNOUT 57.09%

DAME MARGARET HODGE
BORN Sep 8, 1944
MP 1994-

Electorate	Share %	Change from 2017 %
77,946		
*M Hodge Lab	27,219 61.17	-6.62
T Shaikh C	11,792 26.50	+4.03
K Batley Brexit	3,186 7.16	
A Haigh LD	1,482 3.33	+2.07
S Butterfield Green	820 1.84	+0.32

Vocal critic of Jeremy Corbyn: subject of a party investigation, later dropped, for calling Mr Corbyn an antisemite, 2018, and refused to say whether she would prefer him over Boris Johnson as prime minister a month before election. Lost trigger ballot in 2019, but chosen again after full selection process. Supported Jess Phillips for leader, 2020. Remainer; supported a second referendum. Minister: culture, 2009-10, 2007-08; trade and investment, 2006-07; work and pensions, 2005-06; education, 1998-2005. Select cttee chairwoman: public accounts, 2010-15; liaison, 2010-15. Consultant, Price Waterhouse, 1992-94. Became a dame in 2015. Vice-president, Fabian Society. Ed: Bromley HS; LSE (BSc government studies).

CHALLENGERS
Tamkeen Shaikh (C) Journalist in India. Domestic violence researcher. Welfare sector worker, department of work and pensions, 2005-12. **Karen Batley** (Brexit) NHS medical secretary. Has worked in banking.

CONSTITUENCY PROFILE
Held by Labour since 1945, this riverside east London seat is ethnically diverse: it has significant Indian, Pakistani and Bangladeshi communities, and more than a fifth of residents are black. The far-right British National Party came third here in 2005 and 2010, playing on fears over housing in a constituency where about a third of residents rent from the local authority. The party's leader Nick Griffin was its candidate in the latter election. The seat has relatively high levels of unemployment; the transport and construction sectors provide some local jobs.

EU REFERENDUM RESULT
60.0% Leave Remain 40.0%

Barnsley Central

MAJORITY 3,571 (9.68%) | **LABOUR HOLD** | **TURNOUT 56.53%**

DAN JARVIS
BORN Nov 30, 1972
MP 2011-

	Electorate	Share %	from 2017 %	Change %
	65,277			
*D Jarvis Lab	14,804	40.12	-23.79	
V Felton Brexit	11,233	30.44		
I Ahmed C	7,892	21.39	-2.75	
W Sapwell LD	1,176	3.19	+1.78	
T Heyes Green	900	2.44	+0.98	
R Williams Yorkshire	710	1.92		
D Wood Ind	188	0.51		

Elected mayor of the Sheffield City region in 2018, vowing to stay in parliament to fight for greater power for the role. Was tipped to run for party leader in 2015, but ruled himself out to prioritise his family. Rebelled to vote for airstrikes against Isis, 2015. Remainer, but one of 19 Labour MPs to vote for Boris Johnson's withdrawal agreement. Shadow minister: foreign affairs, 2015; justice, 2013-15; culture, 2011-13. Former army officer; deployed in Kosovo, Northern Ireland, Afghanistan and Iraq. First person to resign military commission to contest parliamentary by-election since the Second World War. Ed: Rushcliffe CS; Aberystwyth University (BA international politics and strategic studies); RMA Sandhurst.

CHALLENGERS
Victoria Felton (Brexit) Cllr, Barnsley MBC, 2019-. **Iftikhar Ahmed** (C) Management consultant. Former president, Bradford Conservative Association. Contested Bradford East, 2015. **Will Sapwell** (LD) NHS doctor. Held national roles in the BMA.

CONSTITUENCY PROFILE
This South Yorkshire seat and its predecessor have been won by Labour at all but one election since 1922, the exception being 1931, when the Liberal National Party took the seat. The 2019 result is Labour's lowest tally since men and women's suffrage was equalised in 1928. The Brexit Party secured its highest share of the vote in the election here. This is a somewhat deprived area: in the 1980s a fifth of workers were in coalmining.

EU REFERENDUM RESULT
68.2% Leave | **Remain 31.8%**

Barnsley East

MAJORITY 3,217 (8.45%) | **LABOUR HOLD** | **TURNOUT 54.77%**

STEPHANIE PEACOCK
BORN Dec 19, 1986
MP 2017-

	Electorate	Share %	from 2017 %	Change %
	69,504			
*S Peacock Lab	14,329	37.64	-21.91	
J Ferguson Brexit	11,112	29.19		
A Gregg C	10,377	27.26	+0.29	
S Thornton LD	1,330	3.49	+1.65	
R Trotman Green	922	2.42		

Opposition whip, 2018-19; resigned to rebel against Labour's second referendum policy. Voted for Boris Johnson's Brexit withdrawal agreement. Backed Lisa Nandy for the leadership in the 2020 contest. Select cttees: women and equalities, 2019-; international trade, 2017-18. Parliamentary assistant to John Cryer (Leyton & Wanstead), 2010; Sylvia Heal MP, 2005-10. Secondary school teacher. Regional political officer, GMB, 2013-17. Former partner of Tom Watson, who stood down as an MP and Labour deputy leader in 2019. Ed: Queen Mary, UoL (BA modern and contemporary history); Canterbury Christ Church University (PGCE); UCL Institute of Education (MA educational leadership).

CHALLENGERS
Jim Ferguson (Brexit) Former business owner. Member, Scotland Crimestoppers advisory board. **Adam Gregg** (C) Works in event management. **Sophie Thornton** (LD) Bid writer for HealthBid. Chairwoman, University of Birmingham Liberal Democrats Society, 2018-19. Contested EU parliament, 2019. **Richard Trotman** (Green) IT consultant. Contested Barnsley Central, 2017.

CONSTITUENCY PROFILE
This seat, which mostly consists of towns to the south and east of Barnsley, has been a safe one for Labour since its creation in 1983. The 2019 result is by far the party's smallest majority in that time, however, the Labour vote having never fallen below 15,000 in the postwar period. The area is an ex-mining community; construction and manufacturing account for more than a fifth of local employment.

EU REFERENDUM RESULT
71.0% Leave | **Remain 29.0%**

Barrow & Furness

MAJORITY 5,789 (12.57%)   CONSERVATIVE GAIN FROM LABOUR   TURNOUT 65.63%

SIMON FELL
BORN Feb 9, 1981
MP 2019-

Chairman, Barrow and District
Credit Union. Director of a not-
for-profit company that prevents
fraud and other financial crimes.
Previously worked in telecoms.
Helped run two charities.
Ran his own communications
business. Member, British
Council TN2020 network
of future leaders. Patron,
Fair Votes for All campaign.
Brexiteer. Supported the decision
to revoke the franchise of
Northern Rail "after years of
poor performance". Contested
this constituency, 2017, 2015.
Ed: University of Warwick (BA
English literature).

	Electorate	Share %	Change from 2017 %
	70,158		
S Fell C	23,876	51.85	+4.82
C Altree Lab	18,087	39.28	-8.19
L Birchall LD	2,025	4.40	+1.71
G McGrath Brexit	1,355	2.94	
C Loynes Green	703	1.53	+0.74

CHALLENGERS
Chris Altree (Lab) Engineer,
Network Rail. Former Royal
Marines commando. Board
member, Bluebirds Trust.
Loraine Birchall (LD) Partner,
Artemis Media. Consultant, West
Cumbria Development Agency.
Chair of trustees, Friends of
X112. Contested: this seat in 2017;
Carlisle, 2015. Gerald McGrath
(Brexit) Cllr, Copeland BC, 2017-;
mayor of Copeland BC, 2019.
Resigned from the Conservative
Party in 2019. School governor.

Chris Loynes (Green) Teacher
and social worker.

CONSTITUENCY PROFILE
Until 2019, the Conservatives
had only won Barrow & Furness
twice in the postwar period, in
1983 and 1987, although Labour
held it by only 209 votes in 2017.
Previous MPs include John
Woodcock, who resigned from
the Labour Party in opposition
to Corbyn's leadership, and
the one-time Labour defence
secretary John Hutton. BAE
Systems is a significant local
employer, providing 5,000 jobs
in ship-building. The world's
largest offshore wind farm lies
nine miles off the coast.

EU REFERENDUM RESULT
57.3% Leave   Remain 42.7%

Basildon & Billericay

MAJORITY 20,412 (46.26%)   CONSERVATIVE HOLD   TURNOUT 63.12%

JOHN BARON
BORN Jun 21, 1959
MP 2001-

Quiet backbencher after serving
as an opposition whip from
2007 to 2010 and shadow health
minister, 2003-07 and 2002-03.
Captain, Fusiliers; served in
Northern Ireland, Cyprus and
Germany. Has opposed military
interventions since being elected,
except for the first deployment
in Afghanistan. Resigned from
the shadow cabinet to vote
against the Iraq War. Ardent
Eurosceptic; supported a no-deal
Brexit and voted against Theresa
May's deal three times. Backed
Dominic Raab for leader, 2019.
Foreign affairs select cttee,
2010-17. Former investment

	Electorate	Share %	Change from 2017 %
	69,906		
*J Baron C	29,590	67.05	+6.10
A Gordon Lab	9,178	20.80	-10.33
E Sainsbury LD	3,741	8.48	+5.03
S Goshawk Green	1,395	3.16	
S Breedon Soc Dem	224	0.51	

fund manager. Ed: Queen's Coll,
Taunton; Jesus Coll, Cambridge
(BA history and politics); RMA
Sandhurst.

CHALLENGERS
Andrew Gordon (Lab) Social
worker. Cllr, Basildon BC, 2011-;
vice-chairman, housing. First
elected as a councillor at the age
of 18. Mental health campaigner.
Edward Sainsbury (LD)
Secondary school teacher. Scout
leader, 3rd Billericay Scouts.
Contested Basildon BC, 2019.

CONSTITUENCY PROFILE
The seats of Basildon and
Billericay were combined in
the boundary changes of 2010.
Basildon had been a bellwether
seat, held by Labour from 1997,
while Billericay had been held
by the Conservatives from its
creation in 1983. The seat is
now safely Conservative, and
the party has garnered half of
the vote in every election since
2010. Ukip had its strongest
performance here in 2015,
coming third with 20 per cent
of the vote. The construction
and financial services industries
each make up about a tenth of
employment in this southern
Essex constituency.

EU REFERENDUM RESULT
67.1% Leave   Remain 32.9%

Basildon South & Thurrock East

MAJORITY 19,922 (43.98%)   CONSERVATIVE HOLD   TURNOUT 60.85%

STEPHEN METCALFE
BORN Jan 9, 1966
MP 2010-

Backbench Brexiteer who rejected Theresa May's deal in the first meaningul vote before supporting it thereafter. Backed Dominic Raab, and then Michael Gove, in the 2019 leadership contest. Chairman, select cttees: science and technology, 2016-17, 2010-15; liason, 2016-17. Chairman, APPGs: artifical intelligence; print; scientific. Cllr, Epping Forest DC, 2002-05; Worked in family's printing business. Government envoy for the Year of Engineering, 2018. Contested Ilford South, 2005. Ed: Davenant Foundation Sch; Buckhurst Hill County HS.

	Electorate	Share %	from 2017 %	Change
	74,441			
*S Metcalfe C	29,973	66.17	+9.27	
J Ferguson Lab	10,051	22.19	-10.33	
K Smith Ind	3,316	7.32		
M Bukola LD	1,957	4.32	+2.77	

CHALLENGERS
Jack Ferguson (Lab) Cllr, Basildon BC, 2018-. Community worker, Arsenal Football Club. Contested Essex CC, 2017. **Kerry Smith** (Ind) Cllr, Basildon BC, 2013-; deputy council leader. Resigned from Ukip after using racist and homophobic slurs. Contested this seat in the 2015 and 2010 general elections. **Michael Bukola** (LD) NHS nurse. Worked as a tax consultant. Cllr, Southwark LBC, 2010-14; Lib Dem spokesman for housing management and

community safety. Lost deposit. Contested Camberwell & Peckham, 2017.

CONSTITUENCY PROFILE
The Conservatives have increased their majority in this seat at every successive election since its creation in 2010. The area has been split between Thurrock, Basildon and Billericay seats in various boundary changes, and both Basildon and Billericay have historically been dominated by the Conservatives, with occasional Labour victories. The Thameside seat is a commuter area just beyond Greater London's eastern border.

EU REFERENDUM RESULT
73.0% Leave   Remain 27.0%

Basingstoke

MAJORITY 14,198 (25.95%)   CONSERVATIVE HOLD   TURNOUT 65.98%

MARIA MILLER
BORN Mar 26, 1964
MP 2005-

Culture secretary and minister for women and equalities, 2012-14. Work and pensions minister, 2010-12. Forced to resign from cabinet after she over-claimed expenses. Early believer in the Cameron project. Voted Remain but backed Dominic Raab for leader in 2019. Campaigns on women, LGBT, family and equality issues. Has accused government of "mishandling" trans issues. Led calls for a law aginst revenge pornography and for compulsory sex and relationship education in schools. Chairwoman, women and equalities select cttee, 2015-

	Electorate	Share %	from 2017 %	Change
	82,926			
*M Miller C	29,593	54.09	+1.35	
K Marchant Lab	15,395	28.14	-7.68	
S Mylvaganam LD	6,841	12.50	+6.42	
J Jenkin Green	2,138	3.91	+1.93	
A Stone ND	746	1.36		

20. Vice-chairwoman, APPG on domestic violence. Background in advertising and PR before parliament. Ed: Brynteg CS; LSE (BSc economics).

CHALLENGERS
Kerena Marchant (Lab) TV producer and journalist. Disability rights campaigner. Founding member, the Special Educational Needs and Disability Discrimination Tribunal. **Sashi Mylvaganam** (LD) Cllr, Surrey Heath BC,

2019-. Vice-chairman, South East Lib Dems, 2018-. Chartered accountant and finance director.

CONSTITUENCY PROFILE
This seat has elected Conservative MPs at every election since 1924, although Maria Miller's predecessor, Andrew Hunter, was briefly an Independent Conservative and a Democratic Unionist, 2002-05. Labour came within 1,000 votes of winning the seat in 2001, but the Conservatives now have their largest majority in Basingstoke since 1992. This commuter town is demographically young, relatively affluent and residents are highly likely to be in work.

EU REFERENDUM RESULT
53.6% Leave   Remain 46.4%

Bassetlaw

MAJORITY 14,013 (27.56%)   CONSERVATIVE GAIN FROM LABOUR   TURNOUT 63.52%

BRENDAN CLARKE-SMITH
BORN Aug 17, 1980
MP 2019-

Teacher. Cllr, Newark and Sherwood BC, 2019-. Vote Leave campaigner. Attended ERG meeting. In 2019, he claimed food banks in the UK were a "political weapon" and denied that people couldn't afford to buy food on a regular basis. Named by *The Guardian* as one of the seven "most controversial" new Conservative MPs. Contested European parliament, 2019, 2014. Ed: Nottingham Trent University (BA politics; PGCE).

CHALLENGERS
Keir Morrison (Lab) Cllr, Ashfield DC, 2011-19. Works

	Electorate	Share %	Change from 2017 %
	80,035		
B Clarke-Smith C	28,078	55.23	+11.94
K Morrison Lab	14,065	27.66	-24.90
D Soloman Brexit	5,366	10.55	
H Tamblyn-Saville LD	3,332	6.55	+4.35

for the Advisory, Conciliation and Arbitration Service (Acas). Chosen to replace the journalist and campaigner Sally Gimson, who had been nominated by the local party but removed by the national executive committee. Lord Mann, the MP for this seat, 2001-19, and an independent antisemitism adviser to the government since 2019, described the selection as a "Momentum stitch-up". **Debbie Soloman** (Brexit) GIS consultant. **Helen Tamblyn-Saville** (LD) Cllr, Bassetlaw

DC, 2019-. Children's bookshop owner. Worked in comms for a national sports governing body.

CONSTITUENCY PROFILE
A Red Wall seat in Nottinghamshire which had, until this election, been held by Labour since 1935. Labour's smallest postwar majority was 3,800 in the 1983 Conservative landslide under Margaret Thatcher; the Conservatives did not secure more than 40 per cent of the vote in this former mining area between the 1970s and 2017. The seat had the biggest decrease in Labour's vote share from 2017 of any seat that the party contested in 2019.

EU REFERENDUM RESULT
68.3% Leave   Remain 31.7%

Bath

MAJORITY 12,322 (23.63%)   LIBERAL DEMOCRAT HOLD   TURNOUT 76.98%

WERA HOBHOUSE
BORN Feb 8, 1960
MP 2017-

Liberal Democrat spokeswoman for transport, the environment and climate change, and justice, 2019-; housing, communities and local government, 2017-19. First to throw hat in the ring for the leadership, 2020. Presented private member's bill on "upskirting"; it failed but a government bill was passed as the Voyeurism (Offences) Act 2019. Apologised during campaign for a 2014 tweet comparing Gaza to a "Nazi ghetto". Cllr, Rochdale BC, 2004-14; leader, Lib Dem group, 2011-14; had first been elected as a Conservative but defected in

	Electorate	Share %	Change from 2017 %
	67,725		
*W Hobhouse LD	28,419	54.51	+7.24
A Tall C	16,097	30.87	-4.91
M Davies Lab	6,639	12.73	-1.95
J Ogunnusi Brexit	642	1.23	
B Blockhead Ind	341	0.65	

2005. Former radio journalist, professional artist and teacher of modern languages. Born in Hanover; came to Britain in 1990 and was naturalised in 2007. Ed: Munster University (BA history).

CHALLENGERS
Annabel Tall (C) Chartered engineer. Cllr, North Somerset DC, 2011-15. Trainee, Avon & Somerset Search and Rescue Team. **Mike Davies** (Lab) Cllr, Bristol CC, 2016-. **Jimi Ogunnusi** (Brexit) Management consultant.

Lecturer in leadership and management, University of the West of England. **Bill Blockhead** (Ind) Political satirist and artist.

CONSTITUENCY PROFILE
Although it was a Conservative seat for most of the last century, Bath has flipped between the Liberal Democrats and the Conservatives in recent times. This Somerset seat comprises the ancient Roman town of Bath and, with the universities of Bath and Bath Spa in the constituency, it is home to more than 15,000 students. The Greens stood aside for the Lib Dems here as part of the "Unite to Remain" alliance.

EU REFERENDUM RESULT
31.7% Leave   Remain 68.3%

Batley & Spen

MAJORITY 3,525 (6.66%)   **LABOUR CO-OP HOLD**   **TURNOUT 66.53%**

TRACY BRABIN
BORN May 9, 1961
MP 2016-

Appointed shadow secretary of state for digital, culture, media and sport, 2020. Shadow minister for early years, 2017-20. Backed Sir Keir Starmer for leader in 2020. Career as an actress, including in the soap operas *Coronation Street*, *EastEnders* and *Emmerdale*. Combined a 30-year acting and writing career with role as a Labour and trade union activist. Women and equalities select cttee, 2016-17. Co-chairwoman, art APPG. Ed: Heckmondwike GS; Loughborough University (BA drama); London Coll of Printing (MA screenwriting).

	Electorate	Share %	Change from 2017 %
	79,558		
*T Brabin Lab Co-op	22,594	42.69	-12.80
M Brooks C	19,069	36.03	-2.80
P Halloran Woollen	6,432	12.15	
J Lawson LD	2,462	4.65	+2.38
C Minihan Brexit	1,678	3.17	
T Akram Green	692	1.31	+0.02

CHALLENGERS
Mark Brooks (C) Chairman, Bexleyheath & Crayford Conservative Association. Awarded OBE in 2019 for services to male victims of domestic abuse. **Paul Halloran** (Woollen) Business manager. Former professional rugby league player for Batley Bulldogs. **John Lawson** (LD) Cllr, Kirklees MBC, 2010-; Liberal Democrat group leader. Contested this seat, 2017, 2015. **Clive**

Minihan (Brexit) Managing director, Centaur management consulting.

CONSTITUENCY PROFILE
This seat was previously held by the Labour MP Jo Cox, who was elected in 2015 but murdered outside a constituency surgery by a far-right terrorist one week before the 2016 EU referendum. The seat had been represented by the Conservatives between 1983 and 1997, and by Labour MPs ever since. It is located between Bradford, Leeds, Huddersfield and Wakefield. About a fifth of the seat's population have Indian or Pakistani heritage.

EU REFERENDUM RESULT
59.6% Leave   Remain 40.4%

Battersea

MAJORITY 5,668 (9.45%)   **LABOUR HOLD**   **TURNOUT 75.62%**

MARSHA DE CORDOVA
BORN Jan 23, 1976
MP 2017-

Shadow minister for disabled people, 2017-. Work and pensions select committee, 2017. Sir Keir Starmer supporter, 2020. Registered blind from birth; disability rights campaigner. Engagement and advocacy director, Thomas Pocklington Trust, 2016-17. Worked as policy manager, Action for Blind People. Campaigns to make parliament accessible. Criticised for putting a £17 Remembrance Day wreath on expenses; said it was an administrative error. Cllr, Lambeth BC, 2014-18. Ed: London South Bank University (LLB law).

	Electorate	Share %	Change from 2017 %
	79,309		
*M De Cordova Lab	27,290	45.50	-0.44
K Caddy C	21,622	36.05	-5.50
M Gitsham LD	9,150	15.26	+7.26
L Davis Green	1,529	2.55	+0.98
J Thomas Brexit	386	0.64	

CHALLENGERS
Kim Caddy (C) Cllr, Wandsworth LBC, 2014-; cabinet member for housing. Qualified chartered accountant. School and hospital governor. Actively campaigned for Boris Johnson during the 2019 Conservative leadership election. Contested Streatham, 2017, 2015. **Mark Gitsham** (LD) Events manager. Worked on the organising committee of the 2012 Olympic and Paralympic Games. **Lois Davis** (Green) Teaches English

as a foreign language. Contested this seat in 2017.

CONSTITUENCY PROFILE
This west London marginal seat had mostly tracked winners of general elections until it was won by Labour in 2017. The seat was held until 1987 by the Labour MP Alf Dubs, the refugee rights campaigner who now sits in the House of Lords. The preceding seat of Battersea North was one of very few to have elected a Communist MP, doing so in 1922 and 1924. It has a high proportion of university-educated residents and residents in employment. The average house price is £720,000.

EU REFERENDUM RESULT
22.0% Leave   Remain 78.0%

Beaconsfield

MAJORITY 15,712 (27.15%)   **CONSERVATIVE HOLD**   **TURNOUT 74.46%**

JOY MORRISSEY
BORN Jan 30, 1981
MP 2019-

	Electorate	Share %	Change from 2017 %
	77,720		
J Morrissey C	32,477	56.12	-9.13
*D Grieve Ind	16,765	28.97	
A Collins Lab	5,756	9.95	-11.50
Z Hatch Green	2,033	3.51	+1.02
A Cleary Ind	837	1.45	

Ohio-born Brexiteer who has worked for the Centre for Social Justice. Has undertaken humanitarian work in Albania, Kosovo, China and India. Former Hollywood actress and producer under the stage name Joy Boden. Self-described One Nation "compassionate conservative". Cllr, Ealing LBC, 2014-19. Unsuccessfully sought nomination to be the Conservative candidate for the 2020 London mayoral election. Former parliamentary staffer. Member, ERG. Contested: Ealing Central & Acton, 2017; EU parliament, 2019; London assembly, 2016. Ed: LSE (MSc European social policy).

CHALLENGERS
Dominic Grieve (Ind) MP for this constituency, 1997-2019. Attorney general, 2010-14. Chairman, intelligence and security select committee, 2015-19. Stood as an independent after his expulsion from the Conservative Party for voting against a no-deal Brexit. Supported a second referendum. Lost vote of confidence among local Conservative association members, 2019. **Alexa Collins** (Lab) Secretary of the Beaconsfield Labour Party. **Zoe Hatch** (Green) Runs a mindful singing business.

CONSTITUENCY PROFILE
This south Buckinghamshire seat and its predecessor have returned Conservative MPs since 1950. The Liberal Democrats stood aside here to help Dominic Grieve's campaign, which was dominated by his stance on Brexit. The town of Beaconsfield itself is one of the richest towns in the UK, with high average earnings among residents and high property prices.

EU REFERENDUM RESULT
49.0% Leave   Remain 51.0%

Beckenham

MAJORITY 14,258 (28.20%)   **CONSERVATIVE HOLD**   **TURNOUT 73.62%**

BOB STEWART
BORN Jul 7, 1949
MP 2010-

	Electorate	Share %	Change from 2017 %
	68,671		
*B Stewart C	27,282	53.96	-5.36
M Ahmad Lab	13,024	25.76	-4.35
C Ross LD	8,194	16.21	+8.32
R Fabricant Green	2,055	4.06	+1.39

Decorated colonel; completed seven tours in Northern Ireland. Admitted in 2017 to having been "kind of a torturer", carrying out interrogation techniques now considered illegal during the Troubles. Critical about cuts to military spending. Brexiteer; rebelled twice on Theresa May's Brexit deal. Backed Boris Johnson in the 2019 leadership election. Select cttees: Northern Irish affairs, 2017-, 2016-17; defence, 2010-17; arms export controls, 2010-14. Ed: RMA Sandhurst; Wales (international politics), Army Staff Coll; Joint Services Staff Coll.

CHALLENGERS
Marina Ahmad (Lab) Qualified barrister. Worked at the Crown Prosecution Service. Helps set up grassroots projects in housing estates. Contested this seat in the previous two elections, and stood for the London Assembly in 2016. **Chloe-Jane Ross** (LD) Works in finance and corporate planning. Road safety campaigner. Runs the largest residents association in Beckenham. **Ruth Fabricant** (Green) Retired teacher. Member, Bromley TUC.

CONSTITUENCY PROFILE
This suburban southeast London seat has been held by the Conservatives since 1950. Labour managed to reduce the Conservative majority to just under 5,000 in 1997 and 2001, and to 1,200 in a 1997 by-election prompted by the resignation of Piers Merchant, the Conservative MP for the previous five years who had been caught out in a tabloid sex scandal. It is an affluent area, with high incomes, and high levels of home ownership and self-employment. Many residents work in finance and insurance and an above-average proportion work in managerial roles.

EU REFERENDUM RESULT
48.4% Leave   Remain 51.6%

Bedford

MAJORITY 145 (0.31%)   LABOUR HOLD   TURNOUT 66.08%

MOHAMMAD YASIN
BORN Oct 15, 1971
MP 2017-

Backbencher who worked as a taxi driver in Milton Keynes before his election in 2017. One of several Muslim MPs to receive a package in 2018 with an Islamophobic letter and sticky liquid, which was later found to be harmless. Backed Sir Keir Starmer for the leadership, 2020. Remainer; voted for a second Brexit referendum. Housing, communities and local government select committee, 2019-. Cllr, Bedford BC, 2006-19. Born in Pakistan; moved to the UK at the age of 21. Ed: Mirpur Degree Coll, Kashmir (BA commerce).

	Electorate	Share %	Change from 2017 %
	71,579		
*M Yasin Lab	20,491	43.32	-3.53
R Henson C	20,346	43.01	-2.21
H Vann LD	4,608	9.74	+3.89
A Spurrell Green	960	2.03	-0.05
C Bunker Brexit	896	1.89	

CHALLENGERS
Ryan Henson (C) Cllr, East Herts CC, 2015-19. Works in international development. Former civil servant. Criticised for comparing Scottish Labour MPs to a marauding tribe of pillagers from the Dark Ages, 2014. **Henry Vann** (LD) Teacher. Cllr, Bedford BC, 2011-19; portfolio holder for education. Contested this seat in the 2017 and 2010 elections. **Adrian Spurrell** (Green) Consultant. Sits on board of local credit union.

CONSTITUENCY PROFILE
Mohammad Yasin had the third smallest majority in the Commons after the 2019 election. Something of a bellwether since the Second World War, this Midlands seat had been won by the Labour Party only in elections in which the party won a comfortable governing majority. That remained true until 2017, the first time Labour won here while losing nationally, partly because boundary changes had removed rural areas. The constituency has a significant south Asian community. It is close to Milton Keynes and has a fast railway link to London.

EU REFERENDUM RESULT
51.9% Leave   Remain 48.1%

Bedfordshire Mid

MAJORITY 24,664 (38.11%)   CONSERVATIVE HOLD   TURNOUT 73.71%

NADINE DORRIES
BORN May 21, 1957
MP 2005-

Outspoken former nurse, social conservative and Brexiteer who was given her first frontbench job by Boris Johnson after she had backed him for leader in 2019. Parliamentary under-secretary, housing, 2019-. Had whip withdrawn in 2012 for appearing on *I'm a Celebrity ... Get Me Out of Here!* without the whips' permission; reinstated in 2013. Christian who has attempted to lower the time limit for abortions. Sobbed in press conference in which Mr Johnson announced he would not stand in 2016 leadership contest. Spad to Sir Oliver Letwin, 2002-05.

	Electorate	Share %	Change from 2017 %
	87,795		
*N Dorries C	38,692	59.79	-1.87
R Meades Lab	14,028	21.68	-6.75
R McGann LD	8,171	12.63	+6.61
G Ellis Green	2,478	3.83	+0.99
A Victor Ind	812	1.25	
A Kelly Loony	536	0.83	-0.23

Sold childcare company to Bupa in 1998, then served as Bupa director. Worked in Zambia, 1983-84. Ed: Halewood Grange; Warrington General Hospital.

CHALLENGERS
Rhiannon Meades (Lab) Actor and musician. Co-founder of the Bedfordshire Rail Access Network. Contested this seat in 2017. **Rachel McGann** (LD) Software engineer. Retrained as a primary school teacher. Cllr,

Arlesey TC, 2016-19. **Gareth Ellis** (Green) Energy and environment manager, Cranfield University.

CONSTITUENCY PROFILE
This constituency has been held continuously by the Conservatives since their 1931 landslide victory, and the party hasn't received less than 45 per cent of the vote in the seat since 1950. It is mostly sparse and rural, and its largest towns, Ampthill and Flitwick, are home to about 12,000 people each. It is an affluent seat: incomes are high and residents are more likely to be in managerial-level jobs.

EU REFERENDUM RESULT
52.9% Leave   Remain 47.1%

Bedfordshire North East

MAJORITY 24,283 (37.35%)   **CONSERVATIVE HOLD**   **TURNOUT 71.70%**

RICHARD FULLER
BORN May 30, 1962
MP 2019-; 2010-17

Electorate	Share %	from 2017 % Change
90,679		
R Fuller C	38,443	59.13 -1.82
J Vaughan Lab	14,160	21.78 -6.68
D Norton LD	7,999	12.30 +6.55
A Zerny Ind	2,525	3.88
P Fleming Green	1,891	2.91 +1.02

Brexiteer and small business ambassador. Patron, Tory Reform Group. MP for Bedford from 2010 until he lost his seat to Labour by 789 votes in 2017. International business career before returning to politics. Executive chairman, Impero Software. Former partner: Investcorp, venture capital firm; LEK Consulting. Select cttees: business, energy and industrial strategy, 2016-17; regulatory reform, 2015-17; business, innovation and skills, 2015-16; regulatory reform, 2012-15. National chairman, Young Conservatives, 1985-87. Theatre enthusiast. Ed: Bedford Mod Sch; University Coll, Oxford (BA PPE; chairman, Conservative Association; provided a platform for Nelson Mandela's ANC party, which was then a proscribed terrorist organisation in South Africa); Harvard Business Sch (MBA).

CHALLENGERS
Julian Vaughan (Lab) London Underground train driver. Aslef union rep, 2007-. **Daniel Norton** (LD) Hedging strategy manager, British Gas. Contested Bedfordshire South West, 2017. **Philippa Fleming** (Green) Qualified nurse.

CONSTITUENCY PROFILE
This constituency has returned Conservative MPs since its creation in 1997, as did its predecessor, Bedfordshire North, which was established in 1983. The smallest Conservative majority was 5,800 in 1997. A mostly rural seat, its biggest towns are Biggleswade and Sandy, which are home to about 17,000 and 11,000 residents respectively. Incomes and levels of home ownership are well above average.

EU REFERENDUM RESULT
53.4% Leave   Remain 46.6%

Bedfordshire South West

MAJORITY 18,583 (34.86%)   **CONSERVATIVE HOLD**   **TURNOUT 66.70%**

ANDREW SELOUS
BORN Apr 27, 1962
MP 2001-

Electorate	Share %	from 2017 % Change
79,926		
*A Selous C	32,212	60.43 +1.18
C Anderson Lab	13,629	25.57 -8.21
E Matanle LD	5,435	10.20 +5.47
A Waters Green	2,031	3.81 +2.10

Territorial Army officer with the Honourable Artillery Company. Served with the Royal Regiment of Fusiliers, 1981-94. Campaigned to Remain in 2016; backed Sajid Javid for leader, 2019. Frontbench roles: assistant whip, 2014-16; justice minister, 2014-16; PPS to Iain Duncan Smith (Chingford & Woodford Green), 2010-14; shadow work and pensions minister, 2006-10; opposition whip, 2004-06. Select cttees: health and social care, 2016-; European statutory instruments, 2018-; work and pensions, 2001-05. Contested Sunderland North, 1997.

CHALLENGERS
Callum Anderson (Lab) Senior business and policy adviser for City of London Corporation. Campaign organiser, Britain Stronger in Europe. **Emma Matanle** (LD) Worked as a journalist and press officer, Chatham House, UN and BBC. Cllr, St Albans CDC, 2019-. Vice-chairwoman, St Albans Lib Dems, 2017-. **Andrew Waters** (Green) Contested Central Bedfordshire C, 2019.

CONSTITUENCY PROFILE
A safe Conservative seat, which the party has held since its creation in 1983. Labour came within 132 votes of winning the seat in 1997. When the constituency's predecessor included parts of Luton, Labour MPs were elected with slim majorities in 1950 and 1966. Just to the west of Luton, the constituency contains the towns of Leighton Buzzard and Dunstable, and is generally less affluent than its similarly rural, Conservative-held neighbours.

EU REFERENDUM RESULT
58.1% Leave   Remain 41.9%

Belfast East

GAVIN ROBINSON
BORN Nov 22, 1984
MP 2015-

Barrister and DUP spokesman on defence, 2017-; home affairs, 2015-; justice and human rights, 2015-17. Brexiteer. Called on government to save Bombardier jobs in Belfast, 2017. Select cttees: defence, 2016-; ecclesiastical, 2015-; Northern Irish affairs, 2015-16. Secretary, armed forces covenant APPG. Other APPGs: aerospace; air passenger duty reform; armed forces; fintech; funerals and bereavement; Queen's University Belfast; strengthening the Union; war heritage. Special adviser to Peter Robinson, Northern Ireland first minister, 2011-15. Cllr, Belfast

	Electorate	Share % from 2017	Change %
	66,245		
*G Robinson DUP	20,874	49.18	-6.58
N Long Alliance	19,055	44.89	+8.89
C McClean UUP	2,516	5.93	+2.64

City C, 2010-15; lord mayor of Belfast, 2012-13. Ed: Queen's University Belfast (LLB; MA Irish politics).

CHALLENGERS
Naomi Long (Alliance) Party leader since 2016; held the seat 2010-15. MEP, Northern Ireland, 2019-20. MLA, Belfast East, 2016-19, 2003-10. Lord mayor of Belfast, 2009-10. Former engineering consultant. Member, Bloomfield Presbyterian Church; expressed "great concern" and considered leaving over its decision to exclude those in

same-sex relationships from being members. Contested this seat, 2017, 2015. **Carl McClean** (UUP) Cllr, Ards & North Down BC, 2019. Manager, Airinc, an HR consultancy firm. Former manager, PwC. Contested Northern Ireland assembly, 2016.

CONSTITUENCY PROFILE
The seat has historically been unionist. It was held for one parliament by the Alliance Party, from 2010 to 2015, after Naomi Long took it from the sitting first minister, Peter Robinson, who had been the MP since 1979. It became the party's first ever seat in Westminster. It contains majority Protestant areas.

EU REFERENDUM RESULT
51.4% Leave   Remain 48.6%

Belfast North

JOHN FINUCANE
BORN March, 1980
MP 2019-

Solicitor who unseated the DUP heavyweight Nigel Dodds. Cllr, Belfast City C, 2019-; lord mayor of Belfast, 2019-. Youngest son of Pat Finucane, who was shot dead in front of his wife and children by loyalist paramilitaries in 1989. Has spent his life campaigning for "truth and justice". His father was a Roman Catholic from west Belfast but his mother came from a Protestant family in the east. Was spoken to by the police in 2019 after he was caught urinating in the streets of Belfast. Goalkeeper and captain of Lamh Dhearg Gaelic games club. Contested this seat, 2017.

	Electorate	Share % from 2017	Change %
	72,225		
J Finucane SF	23,078	47.06	+5.35
*N Dodds DUP	21,135	43.10	-3.14
N McAllister Alliance	4,824	9.84	+4.45

CHALLENGERS
Nigel Dodds (DUP) MP for this seat, 2001-19. Democratic Unionist Party leader at Westminster, 2010-19; deputy leader, 2008-10. Negotiated confidence and supply arrangement with Theresa May, 2017. DUP's spokesman: Brexit, 2017-19; foreign affairs and constitutional issues, 2015-19. Trained barrister, later worked at European parliament secretariat. **Nuala McAllister** (Alliance) Lord mayor of Belfast, 2017-18. Cllr, Belfast City C, 2014-. Alliance whip's assistant in the

Northern Ireland assembly. Criticised by constituents after her mayoral portrait cost £10,850.

CONSTITUENCY PROFILE
This seat had elected only unionist MPs for 125 years until 2019. This may be explained by the Roman Catholic population of Belfast North having overtaken the Protestant population for the first time in the 2011 census. The seat is home to a higher than average proportion of workless and single-parent families. The moderate nationalist SDLP stood aside for Sinn Fein in 2019 and the Ulster Unionist Party also decided not to stand.

EU REFERENDUM RESULT
49.6% Leave   Remain 50.4%

Belfast South

SDLP GAIN FROM DUP

TURNOUT 67.66%

CLAIRE HANNA
BORN Jun 19, 1980
MP 2019-

Won seat back for the SDLP after she had resigned the party whip and stood down as Brexit spokeswoman less than a year before because the SDLP agreed an electoral alliance with Fianna Fail. Remained a party member and was selected as the SDLP candidate over the former party leader Alasdair McDonnell, who held this seat from 2005 to 2017. Previously an aid worker. MLA, Belfast South, 2015-19. Cllr, Belfast City C, 2011-14. Contested: Strangford, 2010; Northern Ireland assembly, 2017, 2016. Ed: Rathmore GS; the Open University (BA

	Electorate	Share %	Change from 2017 %
	69,984		
C Hanna SDLP	27,079	57.19	+31.32
*E Little Pengelly DUP	11,678	24.66	-5.77
P Bradshaw Alliance	6,786	14.33	-3.85
M Henderson UUP	1,259	2.66	-0.84
C McHugh Aontu	550	1.16	

international relations); Queen's University Belfast (law).

CHALLENGERS
Emma Little Pengelly (DUP) MP for this seat, 2017-19. DUP spokeswoman on equality, justice and trade, 2017-19. MLA, Belfast South, 2015-17. Junior minister at Stormont, 2015-17; spad to Ian Paisley and Peter Robinson, 2007-15. **Paula Bradshaw** (Alliance) MLA, Belfast South, 2016-. Defected from the UUP, denouncing it as "sexist,

homophobic and sectarian". Cllr, Belfast City C, 2014-16. Contested this seat, 2017, 2015, 2010. **Michael Henderson** (UUP) Contested: this seat, 2017; Northern Ireland assembly, 2017.

CONSTITUENCY PROFILE
Elected unionists at every election from 1985 until 2005, when the DUP stood against the incumbent UUP candidate and split the vote. It then elected SDLP MPs until 2017, when the DUP won. Contains Queen's University Belfast and most of its student population. Sinn Fein stood aside for the SDLP in this seat, the reverse of the parties' actions in Belfast North.

EU REFERENDUM RESULT
30.5% Leave   Remain 69.5%

Belfast West

MAJORITY 14,672 (37.83%)

SINN FEIN HOLD

TURNOUT 59.08%

PAUL MASKEY
BORN Jun 10, 1967
MP 2011-

Development co-ordinator of the Welcome to Belfast tourism organisation. Lifelong republican activist. Cllr, Belfast City C, 2001-09; Sinn Fein council group leader, 2005-07. MLA, Belfast West, 2007-12. Two of his brothers jailed for dissident republican activities during the Troubles; one, Alex Maskey, represents Belfast West at Stormont. Ed: Edmund Rice Coll.

CHALLENGERS
Gerry Carroll (PBP) Long-time activist who was previously banned from Belfast city centre for taking part in student

	Electorate	Share %	Change from 2017 %
	65,644		
*P Maskey SF	20,866	53.80	-12.91
G Carroll PBP	6,194	15.97	+5.80
F McCoubrey DUP	5,220	13.46	+0.03
P Doherty SDLP	2,985	7.70	+0.66
D Higgins Alliance	1,882	4.85	+3.05
M Digney Aontu	1,635	4.22	

protests. MLA, Belfast West, 2016-. Cllr, Belfast City C, 2014-16. Contested this seat, 2017, 2015. Atheist and revolutionary socialist. **Frank McCoubrey** (DUP) Researcher. Cllr, Belfast City C, 1997-; deputy mayor, 2000-01. **Paul Doherty** (SDLP) Community activist. Organiser, Foodstock festival, which supports local food banks. Contested Belfast City C, 2019. **Donnamarie Higgins** (Alliance) Member of the Belfast Feminist

Network. Contested Belfast City C, 2019.

CONSTITUENCY PROFILE
Belfast West is the only seat in Northern Ireland's capital with a long history of electing nationalists. It was held by Gerry Adams, then the leader of Sinn Fein, from 1983 until 1992 and again between 1997 and 2011. Although the seat was mainly held by the Ulster Unionists between 1922 and 1966, it has since flipped between Sinn Fein and the SDLP, the former having held it since 1997. The seat has approximately five times as many Roman Catholic residents as Protestants.

EU REFERENDUM RESULT
25.9% Leave   Remain 74.1%

---

98 | THE NEW PARLIAMENT

Bermondsey & Old Southwark

MAJORITY 16,126 (27.51%) **LABOUR HOLD** **TURNOUT 62.82%**

NEIL COYLE
BORN Dec 30, 1978
MP 2015-

Outspoken moderate and disability rights campaigner. Threatened to sue Jeremy Corbyn after appearing on a leaked list of MPs accused of abusive behaviour towards Mr Corbyn, an allegation he denied. Voted Remain and rebelled to vote against Article 50 in 2017. Nominated Mr Corbyn for leadership in 2015 but expressed regret for doing so and backed Owen Smith in 2016 and Jess Phillips in 2020. Work and pensions select cttee, 2016-. PPS to Chris Bryant (Rhondda), 2015-16. APPG chairman: counter-extremism, foodbanks,

	Electorate	Share %	Change from 2017 %
	93,313		
*N Coyle Lab	31,723	54.12	+0.87
H Ali LD	15,597	26.61	-4.47
A Baker C	9,678	16.51	+3.56
A Matthews Brexit	1,617	2.76	

homelessness, wine and spirits. Previously director of policy and campaigns, Disability Rights UK; head of policy, National Centre for Independent Living. Cllr, Southwark BC, 2010-16; deputy mayor, 2014-15. Ed: Bedford Sch; University of Hull (BA British politics and legislative studies).

CHALLENGERS
Humaira Ali (LD) Department for the Environment, Food and Rural Affairs programme director. Cllr, Southwark LBC, 2018-. **Andrew Baker** (C)

Corporate solicitor. Treasurer, Tory Reform Group.

CONSTITUENCY PROFILE
A central London Labour stronghold until the 1983 Bermondsey by-election, in which the gay rights campaigner and Labour candidate Peter Tatchell was defeated with a huge swing to the Liberal candidate Simon Hughes, after a notoriously homophobic and abusive campaign. Mr Hughes held the seat until 2015. The constituency contains a high proportion of students and EU migrants and many of its residents work in financial services.

EU REFERENDUM RESULT
26.1% Leave   Remain 73.9%

Berwick-upon-Tweed

MAJORITY 14,835 (35.23%) **CONSERVATIVE HOLD** **TURNOUT 70.25%**

ANNE-MARIE TREVELYAN
BORN Apr 6, 1969
MP 2015-

International development secretary since February 2020. Junior defence minister, 2019-20. ERG member who sat on the board of Vote Leave; rejected Theresa May's Brexit deal twice, resigning as PPS to Gavin Williamson in 2018 over Mrs May's so-called Chequers plan. Backed Boris Johnson for leader, 2019. Campaigned for improvements to transport and broadband infrastructure. Public accounts select committee, 2018-19, 2015-17. Vice-chairwoman of APPGs on armed forces, forestry (founder), women's health. Member, Conservatives for

	Electorate	Share %	Change from 2017 %
	59,939		
*A Trevelyan C	23,947	56.87	+4.41
T Williams Lab	9,112	21.64	-2.91
T Hancock LD	7,656	18.18	-2.94
T Stewart Green	1,394	3.31	+1.45

Britain. Chartered accountant, worked at PWC. First contested this seat in 2010. Ed: St Paul's Girls' Sch; Oxford Polytechnic (BA mathematics).

CHALLENGERS
Trish Williams (Lab) IT consultant, mainly employed in public sector. **Tom Hancock** (LD) "Yes" campaigner in AV referendum. Musician. Contested Easington, 2017; Wansbeck, 2015. **Thomas Stewart** (Green) Contested this constituency in the 2017 general election.

CONSTITUENCY PROFILE
The northernmost English constituency, this huge, sparse Northumberland seat has swung between the Conservatives and the Liberals for more than a century. The seat was once held by William Beveridge, father of the welfare state. Alan Beith, now Lord Beith, a Liberal, won the seat at a by-election in 1973 and held it until his retirement in 2015. Since then the Conservatives have increased their majority at every election. Labour came second in the seat in 2017 for the first time since 1997. About one fifth of residents are retired, a higher proportion than the national average.

EU REFERENDUM RESULT
55.3% Leave   Remain 44.7%

Berwickshire, Roxburgh & Selkirk

MAJORITY 5,148 (9.69%)   CONSERVATIVE HOLD   TURNOUT 71.32%

JOHN LAMONT
BORN Apr 15, 1976
MP 2017-

	Electorate	Share %	Change from 2017 %
	74,518		
*J Lamont C	25,747	48.45	-5.43
C Kerr SNP	20,599	38.76	+6.00
J Marr LD	4,287	8.07	+3.33
I Davidson Lab	2,513	4.73	-3.90

Solicitor. Backed Jeremy Hunt in the 2019 Conservative leadership contest. Voted against the Brexit withdrawal agreement in the first meaningful vote. Member, 1922 exec cttee, 2017-. Select cttees: Scottish affairs, 2017-; statutory instruments, 2017-. Also contested this seat in 2015, 2010 and 2005. MSP for Ettrick, Roxburgh & Berwickshire, 2007-17: Conservative chief whip, 2011-16; parliamentary business manager, 2011-16; Conservative justice spokesman, 2010-11, and community safety spokesman, 2007-10. Marathon runner and first UK politician to complete an Ironman triathlon. Ed: University of Glasgow (MA law).

CHALLENGERS
Calum Kerr (SNP) MP for this seat, 2015-17. Spokesman: digital, 2016-17; environment and rural affairs, 2015-17. **Jenny Marr** (LD) Customs and logistics co-ordinator, National Oilwell Varco. Secretary, Robert Smith MP, 2013-15. **Ian Davidson** (Lab) MP for Glasgow South West, 2005-15; and Glasgow Pollok, which was previously constituted as Glasgow Govan, 1992-2005.

CONSTITUENCY PROFILE
Created in 2005, the seat was held by the Liberal Democrat and coalition-era Scotland secretary Michael Moore from 2005 to 2015. Like all but three Scottish seats, it fell to the SNP in 2015. The two seats from which this one was created both tended to return Liberal and Liberal Democrat MPs, including the Liberal leader David Steel. It is a large and mostly rural seat; the combined population of its two largest towns, Galashiels and Hawick, is about 30,000. The seat has a high proportion of agricultural workers compared with the rest of Britain.

EU REFERENDUM RESULT
43.3% Leave   Remain 56.7%

Bethnal Green & Bow

MAJORITY 37,524 (61.96%)   LABOUR HOLD   TURNOUT 68.69%

RUSHANARA ALI
BORN Mar 14, 1975
MP 2010-

	Electorate	Share %	Change from 2017 %
	88,169		
*R Ali Lab	44,052	72.74	+0.91
N Stovold C	6,528	10.78	-1.88
J Babarinde LD	5,892	9.73	+4.74
S Ali Green	2,570	4.24	+1.71
D Axe Brexit	1,081	1.78	
V Hudson AWP	439	0.72	

First MP of Bangladeshi origin and trade envoy to Bangladesh since 2016. Remainer who rebelled to vote against Article 50. Briefly stood for deputy leadership in 2015; backed Jeremy Corbyn for leader in that year but Owen Smith in 2016 and Sir Keir Starmer in 2020. Backbencher since 2014, having resigned from front bench to abstain on airstrikes against Isis in Iraq. Shadow minister: education, 2013-14; international development, 2010-13. Select cttees: Treasury, 2017-, 2014-15; housing, 2016-17; energy and climate change, 2015-16. Vocal supporter of Palestine. Co-founder: Uprising, an employability charity; One Million Mentors. Ed: Mulberry Sch; Tower Hamlets Coll; St John's Coll, Oxford (BA PPE).

CHALLENGERS
Nicholas Stovold (C) Shipbroker. Contested Wiltshire C, 2017. **Josh Babarinde** (LD) Founder, Cracked It, a social enterprise supporting young ex-offenders. **Shahrar Ali** (Green)

Party's home affairs spokesman. Former deputy leader. **David Axe** (Brexit) Director, Invoke Democracy Now.

CONSTITUENCY PROFILE
This seat and its predecessors have elected Labour MPs consistently in the postwar era, with one exception: when the former Labour MP George Galloway, of the newly created Respect Party, narrowly defeated the Labour MP Oona King in 2005. Rushanara Ali's majority has grown at every election since 2010. This seat, in the East End of London, is one of the most ethnically diverse, with a large Bangladeshi community.

EU REFERENDUM RESULT
30.9% Leave   Remain 69.1%

Beverley & Holderness

MAJORITY 20,448 (38.19%)   CONSERVATIVE HOLD   TURNOUT 67.19%

GRAHAM STUART
BORN Mar 12, 1962
MP 2005-

	Electorate	Share %	Change from 2017 %
	79,683		
*G Stuart C	33,250	62.10	+3.73
C Hopkins Lab	12,802	23.91	-9.24
D Healy LD	4,671	8.72	+3.68
A Shead Yorkshire	1,441	2.69	+0.61
I Pires Green	1,378	2.57	+1.22

Junior minister for international trade, 2018-. Remainer in 2016, but voted for no-deal and for Boris Johnson in the 2019 leadership election. Campaigned against the "caravan tax" in 2012, because many were manufactured in East Yorkshire. Assistant government whip, 2016-18. Chairman, education select committee, 2010; member, 2007-15; criticised Michael Gove for "rushed" education reforms. Conservative Party Board, 2006-10. Cllr, Cambridge CC, 1998-2004. Entrepreneur: Go Enterprises; director, Marine Publishing Company. Founder, Community Hospitals Acting Nationally Together, 2005. Contested Cambridge, 2001. Ed: Glenalmond Coll; Selwyn Coll, Cambridge (read BA law and philosophy, but did not graduate; chairman, Conservative Association, 1985).

CHALLENGERS
Chloe Hopkins (Lab) Cllr, Beverley TC, 2019-. Customer experience manager, William Hill. Member, Unite. **Denis Healy** (LD) Business development manager, Institute of Mechanical Engineers. Cllr, East Riding C, 2016-; deputy leader, Liberal Democrat group. Contested: this seat, 2017, 2015; Hull North, 2010.

CONSTITUENCY PROFILE
Although Labour came within a thousand votes of winning this East Riding seat in 1997 and 2001, the Conservative majority has grown steadily in the elections since. Mostly rural, it sits to the north and east of Hull. The biggest town is Beverley, home to about 30,000 people. The seat has high rates of home ownership and a large number of retired residents.

EU REFERENDUM RESULT
58.7% Leave   Remain 41.3%

Bexhill & Battle

MAJORITY 26,059 (44.10%)   CONSERVATIVE HOLD   TURNOUT 72.09%

HUW MERRIMAN
BORN Jul 13, 1973
MP 2015-

	Electorate	Share %	Change from 2017 %
	81,968		
*H Merriman C	37,590	63.61	+1.64
C Bayliss Lab	11,531	19.51	-5.19
M Saunders LD	7,280	12.32	+4.78
J Kent Green	2,692	4.56	+2.14

Chairman, transport select cttee, 2020-. One of a handful of Conservative MPs who showed sympathy for a second EU referendum. Claimed Brexit stress caused his waist size to fall from 34 to 30. PPS to: Philip Hammond, 2018-19; work and pensions, 2017-18, publicly inviting Theresa May to sack him rather than resigning as a PPS. The only MP to vote both for a second referendum and for no-deal in indicative votes, March 2019. Backed Jeremy Hunt in 2019 leadership race. Cttee member: transport, 2015-; procedure, 2016-17. Cllr, Wealden DC, 2007-15. Barrister, moved from criminal to commercial law early in his career. Led team of lawyers unwinding Lehman Brothers insolvency. Contested Derbyshire North East, 2010. Ed: Buckingham Co Sec Mod; Aylesbury Coll; Durham University (LLB law).

CHALLENGERS
Christine Bayliss (Lab) Cllr, Rother DC, 2019. Education consultant. Former civil servant at the Treasury and Department for Education, after spending nine years as a police officer. **Martin Saunders** (LD) Solicitor. Trustee: RSPB; Citizens' Advice Bureau. **Jonathan Kent** (Green) Contested this seat, 2017, 2015.

CONSTITUENCY PROFILE
A safe Conservative seat since its creation in 1983, Tory candidates rarely receive fewer than half of the votes cast and the party has never failed to achieve a five-figure majority. Between Hastings and Eastbourne, it serves as a retirement hotspot with a high rate of home ownership and self-employment. The town in the second half of the seat's name was the site of the Battle of Hastings in 1066.

EU REFERENDUM RESULT
57.7% Leave   Remain 42.3%

Bexleyheath & Crayford

MAJORITY 13,103 (30.30%)　　　　CONSERVATIVE HOLD　　　　TURNOUT 66.06%

SIR DAVID EVENNETT
BORN Jun 3, 1949
MP 2005-; 1983-97

	Electorate	Share %	from 2017 %	Change
	65,466			
*D Evennett C	25,856	59.79	+4.21	
A Day Lab	12,753	29.49	-6.01	
D McBride LD	2,819	6.52	+3.86	
T Ball Green	1,298	3.00	+1.67	
G Moore Eng Dem	520	1.20		

Vice-chairman of the Conservative Party, 2019-. Most recently on front bench as a government whip, 2012-18, and a junior minister at the culture department for six months in 2016, providing maternity cover for Tracey Crouch (Chatham & Aylesford). Shadow business minister, 2009-10. Opposition whip, 2005-09. Initially supported Mark Harper in 2019 leadership race but then backed Boris Johnson. MP for Erith & Crayford, 1983-97. PPS: Michael Gove, 2010-12; Gillian Shepherd, 1996-97; John Redwood, 1993-95. Select cttees include: European statutory instruments, 2018-; procedure, 2018-; selection, 2013-18. Contested: this seat, 2001; Hackney South & Shoreditch, 1979. Knighted in 2018. Cllr, Redbridge BC, 1974-78. Former insurance broker. Ed: Buckhurst Hill County HS; LSE (BSc, analytical and descriptive economics; MSc government).

CHALLENGERS
Anna Day (Lab) Caseworker and housing officer. Contested Bexley BC, 2018. **David McBride** (LD) Teacher. Former cllr, mayor of Bromley, 2011. **Tony Ball** (Green) Retired youth worker.

CONSTITUENCY PROFILE
This seat, created in 1997, narrowly elected a Labour MP in that year and again in 2001 but has been solidly Conservative since 2005. A predecessor constituency, Bexley, was held by Edward Heath, the prime minister 1970-74, from 1950 until boundary changes in 1974. This is a middle-class commuter area in the far east of London on the border with Kent. It has high levels of home ownership.

EU REFERENDUM RESULT
65.3% Leave　　　　Remain 34.7%

Birkenhead

MAJORITY 17,705 (41.83%)　　　　LABOUR HOLD　　　　TURNOUT 66.39%

MICK WHITLEY
BORN Nov 17, 1951
MP 2019-

	Electorate	Share %	from 2017 %	Change
	63,762			
M Whitley Lab	24,990	59.04	-17.82	
*F Field BSJP	7,285	17.21		
C Rowles C	5,540	13.09	-5.33	
S Kelly LD	1,620	3.83	+1.27	
D Lythgoe Brexit	1,489	3.52		
P Cleary Green	1,405	3.32	+1.16	

Leftwinger and former car factory worker who had served in the merchant navy. Trade union organiser: Transport and General Workers Union shop steward then Vauxhall plant convenor for 27 years. Unite regional secretary for the North West, 2013-17. Supported Rebecca Long Bailey for leadership, 2020. Voted Remain but later embraced Brexit. Selection campaign run jointly by Unite and Momentum.

CHALLENGERS
Frank Field (BSJP) Birkenhead MP, 1979-2019. Critical of Jeremy Corbyn. Resigned Labour whip in 2018, saying that the party was becoming "a force for antisemitism" and had a culture of "nastiness and intimidation". Voted for the Brexit withdrawal agreement. Chairman, work and pensions select committee, 2015-19. Welfare reform minister, 1997-98. **Claire Rowles** (C) Former solicitor. Cllr, West Berkshire Council, 2019-. Chairwoman, West Berkshire Conservative Association. **Stuart Kelly** (LD) Electrical apprenticeship assessor. Cllr, Wirral MBC, 1998-; 1991-95. Contested this seat, 2010.

CONSTITUENCY PROFILE
This Merseyside seat and its predecessors have elected Labour MPs at every election since the Second World War. The former MP Frank Field had won more than 60 per cent of the vote since 1987 and the Conservatives have failed to win more than 10,000 votes since 1992. Shipbuilding was once a strong industry in the area, which has high levels of unemployment and relative poverty.

EU REFERENDUM RESULT
51.7% Leave　　　　Remain 48.3%

Birmingham Edgbaston

MAJORITY 5,614 (13.26%)   LABOUR CO-OP HOLD   TURNOUT 61.50%

PREET KAUR GILL
BORN Nov 21, 1972
MP 2017-

First female Sikh MP. Shadow minister for international development, 2018-. Successfully amended offensive weapons bill to give Sikhs an exemption for carrying kirpan knives. Backed Sir Keir Starmer for leader, 2020. Voted Remain. Home affairs select cttee, 2017-18. APPG chairwoman: mentoring; Sikhs. Career in social care and children's services. Researched street children in India with Unicef. Spent time on a kibbutz after graduation. Daughter of a bus driver who moved from India to Birmingham in the 1950s. Cllr, Sandwell BC, 2012-18.

	Electorate	Share %	from 2017 %	Change
	68,828			
*P Gill Lab Co-op	21,217	50.13	-5.19	
A Yip C	15,603	36.86	-2.59	
C Green LD	3,349	7.91	+4.33	
P Simpson Green	1,112	2.63	+1.34	
D Wilks Brexit	1,047	2.47		

Ed: Lordswood Girls' Sch; University of East London (BA sociology and social work).

CHALLENGERS
Alex Yip (C) Self-employed businessman. Magistrate, 2009-. Cllr, Birmingham City C, 2015-. Governor, Wilson Stuart Sch. **Colin Green** (LD) Software engineer. Contested: this constituency, 2017; Birmingham Selly Oak, 2015. **Phil Simpson** (Green) Works for Birmingham city council.

CONSTITUENCY PROFILE
Held by the Conservatives for most of the 20th century. Gisela Stuart, who went on to become a prominent Brexiteer, won the seat in 1997 for Labour and held it until she stepped down in 2017. The Conservatives had come within 1,300 votes of regaining it in 2010. The seat has been represented by women at every election since 1953 and, therefore, for longer than any other constituency. Neville Chamberlain, the Conservative prime minister, 1937-40, was its MP from 1929 until 1940. The seat, in the west of the city, contains the University of Birmingham.

EU REFERENDUM RESULT
47.3% Leave   Remain 52.7%

Birmingham Erdington

MAJORITY 3,601 (10.22%)   LABOUR HOLD   TURNOUT 53.26%

JACK DROMEY
BORN Sep 21, 1948
MP 2010-

Opposition frontbencher who put his name to a bill ruling out a no-deal Brexit. Shadow minister: pensions, 2018-; labour, 2016-18; home affairs, 2013-16; housing, 2010-13. Resigned as shadow minister in 2016 in opposition to Jeremy Corbyn's leadership. Backed Lisa Nandy for leader, 2020. Labour treasurer during "cash for honours" allegations of the Tony Blair years. Trade unionist who worked his way up the TGWU and was elected deputy general secretary in 2003. Founder member, Greater London Enterprise Board. Married to

	Electorate	Share %	from 2017 %	Change
	66,148			
*J Dromey Lab	17,720	50.30	-7.66	
R Alden C	14,119	40.08	+1.69	
W Garcarz Brexit	1,441	4.09		
A Holtom LD	1,301	3.69	+1.68	
R Grant Green	648	1.84	+0.20	

Harriet Harman (Camberwell & Peckham). Ed: Cardinal Vaughan Sch, London.

CHALLENGERS
Robert Alden (C) Cllr, Birmingham City C, 2006-; leader, Conservative group, 2014-. Deputy chairman, Local Government Association. Contested this seat, 2017, 2015, 2010. **Wendy Garcarz** (Brexit) Management consultant. Non-executive director, Agewell UK. Fellow, Institute of Leadership

and Management. **Ann Holtom** (LD) Cllr, Birmingham City C, 2002-12. Contested this seat, 2017, 2015, 2010. **Rob Grant** (Green) Lecturer, South & City College Birmingham.

CONSTITUENCY PROFILE
The Birmingham seat that voted Leave by the largest margin, Erdington has had a Labour MP since 1974, although with slim, three-figure majorities in 1979 and 1983. In the northeast of the city there are significant areas of deprivation and unemployment. About three in ten residents live in social housing, well above the national average, and there are high levels of poor health.

EU REFERENDUM RESULT
63.0% Leave   Remain 37.0%

Birmingham Hall Green

MAJORITY 28,508 (53.88%)   LABOUR HOLD   TURNOUT 65.91%

TAHIR ALI
BORN Oct 15, 1971
MP 2019-

Trade union official and Royal Mail employee. Served as the Midlands political officer for the CWU. Supported Rebecca Long Bailey for leader, 2020. Cllr, Birmingham City C, 2004-; 1999-2003. Parliamentary campaign was marred by intimidation from supporters of the former MP Roger Godsiff; this resulted in three investigations, one arrest for malicious communications and police patrols outside polling stations.

CHALLENGERS
Penny-Anne O'Donnell (C) Speech therapist. Co-founder,

	Electorate	Share %	Change from 2017 %
	80,283		
T Ali Lab	35,889	67.83	-9.77
P O'Donnell C	7,381	13.95	-1.15
*R Godsiff Ind	4,273	8.08	
I Knowles LD	3,673	6.94	+1.17
R Cuckston Brexit	877	1.66	
P Cox Green	818	1.55	+0.02

Voice Camps Warwickshire, which provides vocal coaching. Cllr, Stratford DC, 2017-. **Roger Godsiff** (Ind) Labour MP for this seat, 2010-19, and its predecessor, 1992-2010. Deselected by constituency party, mainly over support for local campaign against LGBT-inclusive education. Former bank clerk and GMB political officer. Backed Leave in 2016, but later supported Remain options in line with his constituents' views.

Cllr, Lewisham LBC, 1971-90; mayor, 1977-90. **Izzy Knowles** (LD) Outreach worker. Worked in a children's home. Retired police sergeant. **Rosie Cuckston** (Brexit) School governor.

CONSTITUENCY PROFILE
Conservative from 1950, but held by Labour since 1997. The strongest challenge to Labour since it gained the seat came from Salma Yaqoob for the Respect Party, who came within 3,800 votes of winning in 2010. A densely populated and young constituency to the south of the city centre. About half of its residents are Asian or of Asian descent.

EU REFERENDUM RESULT
33.6% Leave   Remain 66.4%

Birmingham Hodge Hill

MAJORITY 28,655 (63.67%)   LABOUR HOLD   TURNOUT 57.48%

LIAM BYRNE
BORN Oct 2, 1970
MP 2004-

Left infamous "I'm afraid there is no money" note to his successor as chief secretary to the Treasury after the 2010 election. Nominated Jess Phillips for leader, 2020. Selected as the Labour candidate for the West Midlands mayoral election, 2020. Shadow front bench: digital minister, 2017-; business minister, 2013-15; work and pensions secretary, 2011-13; Cabinet Office, 2010-11. Home Office minister, 2006-08; created UK Border Agency and drafted immigration reforms. Select cttees: trade, 2016-17; European scrutiny, 2005. APPG chairman: children of

	Electorate	Share %	Change from 2017 %
	78,295		
*L Byrne Lab	35,397	78.65	-2.40
A Sidhu C	6,742	14.98	+0.80
J Dagnan Brexit	1,519	3.38	
W Rafiq LD	760	1.69	-0.05
J McKears Green	328	0.73	-0.11
H Johani CPA	257	0.57	

alcoholics. Author of books on entrepreneurship and counter-extremism. Ed: University of Manchester (BA politics and history); Harvard Business School (MBA; Fulbright scholar).

CHALLENGERS
Akaal Singh Sidhu (C) Criminal law barrister. Contested Birmingham City C, 2018, 2016. Fluent in Punjabi, Hindi, and Urdu. **Jill Dagnan** (Brexit) Salon owner. Former teacher

and school governor. **Waheed Rafiq** (LD) Suspended by party for historic social media posts described as "clearly antisemitic".

CONSTITUENCY PROFILE
Represented by Labour since its creation in 1983, although the Lib Dems came within 500 votes of winning in the 2004 by-election won by Liam Byrne. In the east of the city; it has a large Asian community and one of the highest proportions of Muslim residents of any constituency. As of May 2019 it had the second highest number of people claiming jobseekers' allowance or universal credit and nearly half of children lived in poverty.

EU REFERENDUM RESULT
51.5% Leave   Remain 48.5%

Birmingham Ladywood

MAJORITY 28,582 (67.86%)   **LABOUR HOLD**   TURNOUT 56.22%

SHABANA MAHMOOD
BORN Sep 17, 1980
MP 2010-

	Electorate	Share %	Change from 2017 %
	74,912		
*S Mahmood Lab	33,355	79.19	-3.52
M Noone C	4,773	11.33	-1.87
L Dargue LD	2,228	5.29	+2.49
A Nettle Green	931	2.21	+0.92
A Garcarz Brexit	831	1.97	

One of the first female Muslim MPs. Briefly served as shadow chief secretary to the Treasury in 2015 before stepping down over disagreements with Jeremy Corbyn. Defended constituents protesting against LGBT-inclusive education, but later said that she did not share their views. Criticised for role in protest that caused temporary closure of supermarket because it stocked Israeli goods. Former barrister specialising in professional indemnity litigation. Shadow minister: Treasury, 2013-15; business, 2011-13; home affairs, 2010-11. Select cttees:

public accounts, 2017-; trade, 2016-17; work and pensions, 2010. Ed: Lincoln Coll, Oxford (BA jurisprudence); Inns of Court School of Law.

CHALLENGERS
Mary Noone (C) Cllr, Warwick DC, 2016-. **Lee Dargue** (LD) Teacher and mental health campaigner. Contested: this seat, 2017; Birmingham Edgbaston, 2015. **Alex Nettle** (Green) Third-year politics student. **Andrew Garcarz** (Brexit) Criticised for

controversial views on race posted on social media.

CONSTITUENCY PROFILE
Labour's seventh safest seat at the 2019 general election. The party has won every general election here since 1945, although the Liberals held the seat for a year after a 1969 by-election and the former MP Clare Short was an independent for four years from 2006 after resigning from Labour. More than 40 per cent of the population are of Asian descent. As of May 2019, more constituents claimed jobseekers' allowance or universal credit than in any other seat.

EU REFERENDUM RESULT
35.6% Leave   Remain 64.4%

Birmingham Northfield

MAJORITY 1,640 (3.81%)   **CONSERVATIVE GAIN FROM LABOUR**   TURNOUT 58.48%

GARY SAMBROOK
BORN Jun 25, 1989
MP 2019-

	Electorate	Share %	Change from 2017 %
	73,694		
G Sambrook C	19,957	46.31	+3.62
*R Burden Lab	18,317	42.50	-10.71
J Scott LD	1,961	4.55	+2.39
K Rowe Brexit	1,655	3.84	
E Masters Green	954	2.21	+0.27
K Lowry Ukip	254	0.59	

Parliamentary assistant to James Morris (Halesowen & Rowley Regis), 2015-19. Ousted Labour incumbent of 27 years. Cllr, Birmingham City C, 2014-. Campaign manager, Conservative Party, 2013-15. Trustee: Kingstanding Regeneration Trust; Birmingham YMCA. Freemason. Ed: Birmingham City University (BA human resource management and PR; Dip international human resource management).

CHALLENGERS
Richard Burden (Lab) Lost the seat he had held since 1992.

Two stints as shadow transport minister: 2013-16, when he resigned in opposition to Jeremy Corbyn's leadership, and 2016-17. PPS to Jeff Rooker, 1997-2001. Chairman, Labour Campaign for Electoral Reform, 1996-98. Select cttees: international development, 2017-19, 2005-13; trade and industry, 2001-05. Former amateur racing driver. **Jamie Scott** (LD) Criminal barrister. Former housing and homelessness caseworker

in Brixton, south London. Contested Halesowen & Rowley Regis, 2017.

CONSTITUENCY PROFILE
First Birmingham seat to elect a Conservative since 1992. Dominated by Labour since its creation in 1950 but went Conservative under Margaret Thatcher. Held by John Spellar (Warley) between a 1982 by-election and the 1983 general election. In the southwest of the city and one of the less ethnically diverse seats in Birmingham, with a higher-than-average rate of residents who lack education qualifications.

EU REFERENDUM RESULT
61.8% Leave   Remain 38.2%

Birmingham Perry Barr

MAJORITY 15,317 (36.34%)   LABOUR HOLD   TURNOUT 58.53%

KHALID
MAHMOOD
BORN Jul 13, 1961
MP 2001-

Shadow Europe minister under
Jeremy Corbyn from 2016. Left
the Vote Leave campaign to
back Remain, citing the group's
emphasis on immigration.
Briefly entered competition to be
Labour deputy leader, 2020, but
pulled out citing lack of support.
Nominated Rebecca Long Bailey,
2020; had backed Owen Smith
in 2016, and Yvette Cooper
in 2015. Select cttees: home
affairs, 2009-10; broadcasting,
2001-05. Chairman, business
improvement districts APPG.
Claimed £1,350 in expenses
for stays in a five-star London
hotel. Had lifesaving kidney

	Electorate	Share %	Change from 2017 %
	72,006		
*K Mahmood Lab	26,594	63.10	-5.03
R Shamji C	11,277	26.76	+0.23
G Jerome LD	1,901	4.51	+2.07
A Willcox Brexit	1,382	3.28	
K Dennis Green	845	2.00	+0.67
T Braich Yeshua	148	0.35	

transplant in 2014; previously
on dialysis for kidney failure in
2008. Born in Pakistan. Worked
as a mechanical engineer. Cllr,
Birmingham City C, 1990-93. Ed:
University of Central England
(engineering).

CHALLENGERS
Raaj Shamji (C) Events host and
toastmaster. Senior development
manager, Birmingham City
University. Gerry Jerome (LD)
Contested Birmingham City C,

2018. Annette Willcox (Brexit)
NHS accountant, commissioner
and consultant. Kefentse
Dennis (Green) Pizza maker
at Dominos. Contested
Birmingham Ladywood, 2017.

CONSTITUENCY PROFILE
Represented by Labour MPs
since 1970, this seat has elected
a Conservative only twice since
its creation in 1950. Labour's
vote share has not fallen below
50 per cent since 2005. North of
the city centre with a young and
ethnically diverse population.
Alexander Stadium, in the seat,
is undergoing a £70 million
expansion in preparation for the
2022 Commonwealth Games.

EU REFERENDUM RESULT
51.2% Leave   Remain 48.8%

Birmingham Selly Oak

MAJORITY 12,414 (25.10%)   LABOUR HOLD   TURNOUT 59.84%

STEVE MCCABE
BORN Aug 4, 1955
MP 1997-

Glaswegian who represented
Birmingham Hall Green from
1997 to 2010, before switching
seat after boundary changes.
Shadow education minister,
2013-15. Opposition whip, 2010;
government whip, 2007-10;
assistant government whip,
2006-07. PPS to Charles Clarke,
2004-05. Select cttees: work and
pensions, 2015-; panel of chairs,
2015-; home affairs, 2010-13,
2005-06; Northern Ireland, 1998-
2003; deregulation, 1997-99. Cllr,
Birmingham City C, 1990-98. Ed:
University of Edinburgh (social
work); Bradford University (MA
social work).

	Electorate	Share %	Change from 2017 %
	82,665		
*S McCabe Lab	27,714	56.03	-6.92
H Campbell C	15,300	30.93	-0.98
D Radcliffe LD	3,169	6.41	+3.05
J Peacock Green	1,848	3.74	+1.95
J Tawonezvi Brexit	1,436	2.90	

CHALLENGERS
Hannah Campbell (C) Account
director, QA Ltd, corporate
training provider. Cllr, Malvern
Hills DC, 2011-19. Deputy mayor,
Malvern TC, 2016-17. Contested
Malvern Hills DC, 2019.
David Radcliffe (LD) Head of
resource planning, University of
Birmingham. Cllr, Birmingham
City C, 2004-14. Contested this
constituency in 2017 and 2010.
Joe Peacock (Green) Heritage
project co-ordinator at Casba, an
education charity.

CONSTITUENCY PROFILE
A Conservative seat for much
of its early history from 1950,
Selly Oak first elected a Labour
MP at the October 1974 general
election but the seat returned to
the Conservatives in Margaret
Thatcher's 1979 landslide victory.
Labour regained the seat in
1992 and has held it since.
Steve McCabe's majority has
fallen below 8,000 only once,
in 2010. The seat, which is in
the south of Birmingham, is
one of the city's less ethnically
diverse constituencies and has a
significant student population.
The seat contains a Cadbury
factory and the Cadbury World
tourist attraction.

EU REFERENDUM RESULT
46.9% Leave   Remain 53.1%

Birmingham Yardley

MAJORITY 10,659 (24.98%) LABOUR HOLD TURNOUT 57.13%

JESS PHILLIPS
BORN Oct 9, 1981
MP 2015-

Outspoken backbencher who has taken a strong stance on online abuse and the safety of MPs. Stood in 2020 leadership election, drawing support from party moderates, but withdrew saying she was unable to unite the party and subsequently backed Lisa Nandy. Women's rights advocate; clashed with Jeremy Corbyn over the number of women in the shadow cabinet. Said she would rather lose her seat by voting against Brexit than endanger her constituents' jobs. Select cttees: women and equalities, 2015-; backbench business, 2015-. APPG

	Electorate	Share %	Change from 2017 %
	74,704		
*J Phillips Lab	23,379	54.78	-2.29
V Garrington C	12,720	29.80	+9.98
R Harmer LD	3,754	8.80	-9.14
M McKenna Brexit	2,246	5.26	
C Garghan Green	579	1.36	+0.73

chairwoman/co-chairwoman: domestic violence; sex equality; women and work. Author of two books. Ed: University of Leeds (BA history and social policy); University of Birmingham (PG Dip public sector management).

CHALLENGERS
Vincent Garrington (C) General manager, Cairn Hotel Group. Vice-chairman, Birmingham Southside Business District. **Roger Harmer** (LD) Business consultant. Cllr, Birmingham

City C, 2014-, 1995-2001, 2008-12. Contested Birmingham Northfield, 2017; Birmingham Edgbaston, 2010.

CONSTITUENCY PROFILE
Formerly a bellwether, Yardley changed hands between Labour and the Conservatives nine times from 1918 until 2005, when it was gained by the Liberal Democrat John Hemming, who held the seat for ten years and came third in 2017. Contains Stechford, which as a constituency was represented by Roy Jenkins, a Labour moderniser and later a founder of the SDP, in 1950-77. Home to a large Irish community.

EU REFERENDUM RESULT
60.1% Leave Remain 39.9%

Bishop Auckland

MAJORITY 7,962 (17.77%) CONSERVATIVE GAIN FROM LABOUR TURNOUT 65.73%

DEHENNA DAVISON
BORN Jul 27, 1993
MP 2019-

First Conservative to represent Bishop Auckland since the seat's creation in 1885. Former analyst at the tax advisory firm Lumo. Also worked as a parliamentary assistant to Jacob Rees-Mogg (Somerset North East). Father died after being attacked in a pub when she was 13; represented her family at the criminal injuries compensation tribunal at 16. Married John Fareham, a Conservative councillor 35 years her senior, in 2018; their wedding featured on the Channel 4 series *Bride and Prejudice*. They separated before the 2019 election. Contested: Sedgefield,

	Electorate	Share %	Change from 2017 %
	68,170		
D Davison C	24,067	53.71	+6.80
*H Goodman Lab	16,105	35.94	-12.13
N Brown Brexit	2,500	5.58	
R Georgeson LD	2,133	4.76	+2.04

2017; Kingston-upon-Hull North, 2015. Ed: University of Hull (BA politics and legislative studies).

CHALLENGERS
Helen Goodman (Lab) MP for this seat since 2005; had clung on by 502 votes in 2017. Shadow minister: Foreign Office, 2017-19; work and pensions, 2014-15; culture, 2011-14; justice, 2010-11. Shadow secretary of state for work and pensions, 2010. In government: junior minister, work and pensions, 2009-10; assistant whip, 2008-09;

deputy leader of the Commons, 2007-08. Senior civil servant before election. **Nicholas Brown** (Brexit) Software consultant. **Ray Georgeson** (LD) Recycling and resource management specialist. Cllr, Otley TC, 2014-; council leader, 2015-19.

CONSTITUENCY PROFILE
One of seven Conservative gains in the North East. Until 2019, this seat had elected a Labour MP at every election since 1931. It was twice represented by Hugh Dalton, chancellor under Clement Attlee. Predominantly rural, Bishop Auckland itself is a former mining town with a population of about 16,000.

EU REFERENDUM RESULT
60.9% Leave Remain 39.1%

Blackburn

MAJORITY 18,304 (40.92%)   LABOUR HOLD   TURNOUT 62.81%

KATE HOLLERN
BORN Apr 12, 1955
MP 2015-

Served as PPS to Jeremy Corbyn from 2017, despite having backed Owen Smith for the Labour leadership in 2016. Shadow minister: housing, 2017-18; armed forces, 2016. Accused the Ministry of Defence of cost-cutting after an incident in which six Gurkhas were allowed to wander into the line of fire at a training range in Kent in 2016. Waspi campaigner. Select cttees: education, 2015-16; armed forces bill, 2015; education, skills and economy sub, 2015-16. Cllr, Blackburn & Darwen BC, 1995-2015; council leader 2010-15, 2004-07. Former manager,

	Electorate	Share %	from 2017 % Change
	71,229		
*K Hollern Lab	29,040	64.91	-4.85
C Gill C	10,736	24.00	-2.90
R Moore Brexit	2,770	6.19	
B Waller-Slack LD	1,130	2.53	+1.03
R Hossain Green	741	1.66	
R Shah Ind	319	0.71	-1.13

Newman's Footwear. Contracts manager, Blackburn College.

CHALLENGERS
Claire Gill (C) Served in the army before becoming a nurse. Worked in Sierra Leone during the Ebola crisis. Contested Hambleton DC, 2019. **Rick Moore** (Brexit) Local businessman. **Beth Waller-Slack** (LD) Contested Salford City C, 2018; Manchester City C, 2018. **Reza Hossain** (Green)

GP. Contested: Chelmsford, 2017; Brentwood & Ongar, 2015; Saffron Walden, 2010.

CONSTITUENCY PROFILE
Solidly Labour since its re-creation in 1955. Two of Blackburn's previous MPs were the Wilson-era cabinet minister Barbara Castle and the New Labour stalwart Jack Straw. The Labour majority has not fallen below 5,000 since 1983. Blackburn itself is an old industrial town once home to a thriving textiles industry. Manufacturing remains one of the largest employment sectors. About a third of its population is of south Asian descent.

EU REFERENDUM RESULT
53.7% Leave   Remain 46.3%

Blackley & Broughton

MAJORITY 14,402 (37.29%)   LABOUR HOLD   TURNOUT 52.63%

GRAHAM STRINGER
BORN Feb 17, 1950
MP 1997-

Backbencher since 2002, having served as a government whip from 2001 to 2002 and a minister in the Cabinet Office, 1999-2001. One of the first MPs to call for Gordon Brown to resign and a vocal critic of Ed Miliband as leader. Called for Margaret Thatcher's funeral to be privatised. Prominent Labour Brexiteer involved with Leave Means Leave pressure group; his views aligned with the ERG "Spartans". Backed Lisa Nandy for leader, 2020. Trustee of Global Warming Policy Foundation, a group for climate change sceptics. Select cttees:

	Electorate	Share %	from 2017 % Change
	73,372		
*G Stringer Lab	23,887	61.85	-8.59
A Elias C	9,485	24.56	+2.98
J Buckley Brexit	2,736	7.08	
I Donaldson LD	1,590	4.12	+2.28
D Jones Green	920	2.38	+1.23

panel of chairs, 2017-; transport, 2011-; science and technology, 2009-. Cllr, Manchester City C, 1979-96; council leader, 1984-96. Ed: Moston Brook HS; University of Sheffield (BSc chemistry).

CHALLENGERS
Alexander Elias (C) President, Oxford Conservative Association 2009-10. **James Buckley** (Brexit) Criticised for attending meetings of the far-right group Britain First. **Iain Donaldson**

(LD) Research administrator, Manchester University. Former school governor. **David Jones** (Green) Environmental scientist and academic.

CONSTITUENCY PROFILE
Blackley & Broughton and the seat it was formed mostly from, Manchester Blackley, have elected Labour MPs since 1964. Salford, which the seat also contains part of, has returned only Labour MPs since the Second World War. This seat had the sixth lowest turnout of any constituency in 2019. It is home to a large number of Muslim and Jewish residents. The child poverty rate is 45 per cent.

EU REFERENDUM RESULT
50.0% Leave   Remain 50.0%

Blackpool North & Cleveleys

MAJORITY 8,596 (22.15%)   CONSERVATIVE HOLD   TURNOUT 60.93%

PAUL MAYNARD
BORN Dec 16, 1975
MP 2010-

Strong advocate for people with disabilities. Has cerebral palsy and epilepsy and said he was mocked in parliament for his disability, leading to some Labour MPs being disciplined. Initially backed Kit Malthouse (Hampshire North West) for the Tory leadership before supporting Boris Johnson. Parly under-sec: transport, 2019-20, 2016-18; justice, 2019. Government whip, 2018-19. PPS to Sir Oliver Letwin, 2012-15. Select cttees: work and pensions, 2014-15; transport, 2010-12. Special adviser to Liam Fox (Somerset North), 1999-2007.

Electorate	Share %	from 2017 %	Change
63,691			
*P Maynard C	22,364	57.63	+8.24
C Webb Lab	13,768	35.48	-8.98
S Close LD	1,494	3.85	+2.03
D Royle Green	735	1.89	+0.97
N Holden Ind	443	1.14	

Speechwriter for William Hague. Contested Twickenham, 2005. Ed: Stambrose Coll; University Coll, Oxford (BA modern history).

CHALLENGERS
Chris Webb (Lab) Head of communications and trustee, CWU Humanitarian Aid charity. Head of office, Wajid Khan MEP. Cllr, Manchester City C, 2015-18. Deputy police and crime commissioner, Lancashire, 2018-. Contested this constituency, 2017,

2015. **Sue Close** (LD) Contested this seat in the previous two general elections.

CONSTITUENCY PROFILE
A bellwether that has been through several different incarnations owing to boundary changes, this coastal west Lancashire seat has been Conservative-held since 2010. Labour held the seat, then called Blackpool North & Fleetwood, from the landslide general election of 1997; its predecessor Blackpool North was held by the Conservatives in every election from 1945 to 1992. About 20,000 of its residents are aged 65 or over.

EU REFERENDUM RESULT
66.9% Leave   Remain 33.1%

Blackpool South

MAJORITY 3,690 (11.27%)   CONSERVATIVE GAIN FROM LABOUR   TURNOUT 56.77%

SCOTT BENTON
BORN Jul 1, 1987
MP 2019-

Parliamentary assistant to Craig Whittaker (Calder Valley), 2013-19. Former primary school teacher. Cllr, Calderdale MBC, 2011-19; leader, Conservative group, 2015-19; deputy council leader, 2014-15. Brexiteer. Urged council to make every school fly the Union Jack and sing the national anthem. Thatcherite with strong unionist links in Northern Ireland. Trustee, Bridgehouse War Memorial. Contested: Huddersfield, 2017; Northern Ireland assembly, 2017. Ed: Rastrick Comprehensive Sch; University of Nottingham (BA theology; MA theology).

Electorate	Share %	from 2017 %	Change
57,688			
S Benton C	16,247	49.61	+6.53
*G Marsden Lab	12,557	38.34	-11.96
D Brown Brexit	2,009	6.13	
B Greene LD	1,008	3.08	+1.26
B Daniels Green	563	1.72	+0.74
G Coleman Ind	368	1.12	

CHALLENGERS
Gordon Marsden (Lab) MP for this seat since 1997. Shadow minister: education, 2015-19; business 2015-16, 2010-13; transport, 2013-15. PPS to: John Denham, 2009-10; Tessa Jowell, 2003-05; Lord Irvine of Lairg, 2001-03. Chairman, Fabian Society, 2000-01. Editor: *History Today; New Socialist.* Contested this seat, 1992. Kennedy scholar. **David Brown** (Brexit) Online retailer and former hotelier.

Bill Greene (LD) Retired IT professional. Contested: this seat, 2017, 2015; Blackpool North & Cleveleys, 2010.

CONSTITUENCY PROFILE
More marginal than its neighbour to the north, Labour had slim majorities here in the previous three elections, despite having lost nationally. Conservative for 52 years after the 1945 general election and first won by Labour in 1997, the party held onto it until this election. The seat, which contains the coastal resort's three piers and Blackpool Pleasure Beach, is highly reliant on tourism.

EU REFERENDUM RESULT
67.8% Leave   Remain 32.2%

Blaenau Gwent

MAJORITY 8,647 (28.61%)   LABOUR HOLD   TURNOUT 59.56%

NICK SMITH
BORN Jan 14, 1960
MP 2010-

Served as an opposition whip under Jeremy Corbyn from 2016, despite having resigned as shadow food and farming minister earlier that year citing fears for Labour's future. Supported Sir Keir Starmer for leader, 2020; in previous years he backed Owen Smith and Liz Kendall. Select cttees: procedure, 2017-; standing orders, 2017-; public accounts, 2010-15. Cllr, Camden LBC, 1998-2005. Ran the 2018 London marathon, raising money for Hospice of the Valleys. Married to the former Darlington MP Jenny Chapman. Ed: Tredegar Comp

	Electorate	Share %	Change from 2017 %
	50,736		
*N Smith Lab	14,862	49.18	-8.83
R Taylor Brexit	6,215	20.57	
L Jones C	5,749	19.02	+4.25
P Owen Griffiths PC	1,722	5.70	-15.55
C Annett LD	1,285	4.25	+3.34
S Priestnall Green	386	1.28	

Sch; Coventry University (BA history, politics and international relations); Birkbeck, University of London (MSc economic and social change).

CHALLENGERS
Richard Taylor (Brexit) Businessman. Former Labour voter. **Laura Jones** (C) Member, Welsh assembly, 2003-07. Cllr, Monmouth TC, 2017-. **Peredur Owen Griffiths** (PC) Manager at Christian Aid.

CONSTITUENCY PROFILE
Solidly Labour except during the 2005 parliament, when Peter Law, a Welsh assembly member, quit Labour in protest at all-women shortlists and held the seat as an independent until he died of a brain tumour in 2006. His campaign manager, Dai Davies, won the resulting by-election, which was contested for Labour by Owen Smith, a future MP for Pontypridd and party leadership contender in 2016. Its predecessor, Ebbw Vale, was represented by Aneurin Bevan and Michael Foot. Contains several former mining and steel towns; the biggest sector today is manufacturing.

EU REFERENDUM RESULT
62.0% Leave   Remain 38.0%

Blaydon

MAJORITY 5,531 (12.11%)   LABOUR HOLD   TURNOUT 67.32%

LIZ TWIST
BORN Jul 10, 1956
MP 2017-

Backbencher who worked as a caseworker for her predecessor Dave Anderson. Former trade union official: head of health for northern region, Unison, 2000-12. Cllr, Gateshead BC, 2012-18. Widowed in 2000 when her husband took his own life. Samaritans listener and chairwoman of the APPG on suicide and self-harm prevention. Select cttees: European statutory instruments, 2018-; petitions, 2017-; housing, communities and local government, 2017-19. Ed: University College of Wales, Aberystwyth (BA history; PG Dip archive administration).

	Electorate	Share %	Change from 2017 %
	67,853		
*L Twist Lab	19,794	43.33	-12.78
A Pepper C	14,263	31.22	+3.14
M Robinson Brexit	5,833	12.77	
V Anderson LD	3,703	8.11	-0.97
D Cadman Green	1,279	2.80	+1.59
K King Lib	615	1.35	
L Marschild Space	118	0.26	+0.09
L Garrett ND	76	0.17	

CHALLENGERS
Adrian Pepper (C) PR executive. Director of the opinion research company SRU. Speechwriter and policy adviser, Syed Kamall MEP, 2008-13. Contested: Burton, 2005; Wolverhampton South East, 2001; European parliament, 2019, 2014. **Michael Robinson** (Brexit) Small business owner. Former maths teacher. Worked for the National Coal Board. **Vicky Anderson** (LD) Online events co-ordinator. Cllr, Gateshead MBC, 2019-.

CONSTITUENCY PROFILE
Labour has won here at every election since 1935. In 2019, the party had its lowest vote share in Blaydon since 1918. An old coalmining seat southwest of Newcastle, consisting of a small area of western Gateshead, several towns, including Whickham and Ryton, and the surrounding rural area. The town of Blaydon has a population of about 16,000. Slightly higher employment and earnings than the average in the North East.

EU REFERENDUM RESULT
56.1% Leave   Remain 43.9%

Blyth Valley

MAJORITY 712 (1.74%) CONSERVATIVE GAIN FROM LABOUR TURNOUT 63.42%

IAN LEVY
BORN Feb 14, 1966
MP 2019-

Knocked the first brick out of the Labour Red Wall with surprise victory. Won Newcomer of the Year at the *Spectator* magazine's Parliamentarian of the Year awards, 2020. Left school to become a gravedigger. NHS mental health nursing assistant for 28 years; *Nursing Times* alleged that he had "deceived voters" by claiming in his campaign literature that he was a nurse. Member of Unison. Volunteer for the Royal British Legion. Contested: this constituency, 2017; Northumberland CC, 2017. Ed: Blyth Ridley HS.

	Electorate	Share %	from 2017 %	Change
	64,429			
I Levy C	17,440	42.68	+5.37	
S Dungworth Lab Co-op	16,728	40.94	-15.00	
M Peart Brexit	3,394	8.31		
T Chapman LD	2,151	5.26	+0.68	
D Furness Green	1,146	2.80	+0.64	

CHALLENGERS
Susan Dungworth (Lab Co-op) Former social worker. Cllr, Northumberland CC, 2017-. Associate, Local Government Association. Member: Unison; GMB; Co-operative Party. **Mark Peart** (Brexit) Lifelong local resident whose campaign website promised to "Make Blyth Valley Great Again". **Thom Chapman** (LD) Postgraduate international relations student at the University of Newcastle. Labour member for six years but left citing antisemitism in the party and its Brexit policy.

CONSTITUENCY PROFILE
The first Conservative gain on election night. Returned Labour MPs at every election since its creation in 1950, with the exception of February 1974, when the incumbent Labour MP, Eddie Milne, who had been deselected by his local party, stood and won as an independent. Consists of the south Northumberland towns of Blyth and Cramlington. Blyth was once home to coalmining and shipbuilding industries; Cramlington is a postwar new town.

EU REFERENDUM RESULT
60.5% Leave Remain 39.5%

Bognor Regis & Littlehampton

MAJORITY 22,503 (43.93%) CONSERVATIVE HOLD TURNOUT 66.10%

NICK GIBB
BORN Sep 3, 1960
MP 1997-

Longstanding schools minister, 2014-, 2010-12, having been shadow schools minister, 2005-10. Supported Michael Gove's leadership bid, 2019. Parly under-sec, equalities, 2017-18. Spokesman: trade and industry, 1999-2001, 1997-98; Treasury, 1998-99. Select cttees: draft voting eligibility (prisoners) bill, 2013; education and skills, 2003-05; public accounts, 2001-03; Treasury, 1998; social security, 1997-98. KPMG corporate tax accountant, 1984-97. Worked on a kibbutz in 1983. Brother of the former No 10 communications director Robbie Gibb. Contested:

	Electorate	Share %	from 2017 %	Change
	77,488			
*N Gibb C	32,521	63.49	+4.53	
A Butcher Lab	10,018	19.56	-5.33	
F Oppler LD	5,645	11.02	+4.49	
C Birch Green	1,826	3.56	+1.63	
D Kurten UKIP	846	1.65	-1.97	
A Elston Ind	367	0.72	-3.35	

Rotherham by-election, 1994; Stoke Central, 1992. Ed: Maidstone GS, Kent; Roundhay School, Leeds; Thornes House Sch, Wakefield; Durham University (BA law).

CHALLENGERS
Alan Butcher (Lab) Works for an air ambulance company. Contested this constituency, 2017. **Francis Oppler** (LD) Runs an office equipment firm. Cllr: Arun DC, 1989-; chairman, Arun DC, 2019-; West Sussex CC, 2005-. Twice mayor of Bognor Regis. Contested this seat, 2017, 2015. **Carol Birch** (Green) Cllr, Aldwick PC, 2019-. Contested Arun DC, 2019, 2017.

CONSTITUENCY PROFILE
A safe seat on the West Sussex coast in which the Conservative majority has increased at every election since 2001. The seat's predecessors, Arundel and Arundel & Shoreham, have also consistently elected Conservative MPs at every election since 1950. The constituency has a large retired population, with a quarter of residents over 65, and high levels of home ownership.

EU REFERENDUM RESULT
64.8 Leave Remain 35.2%

Bolsover

MAJORITY 5,299 (11.54%)   **CONSERVATIVE GAIN FROM LABOUR**   **TURNOUT 61.12%**

MARK FLETCHER
BORN Sep 29, 1985
MP 2019-

Praised Dennis Skinner as a "wonderful constituency MP" after he unseated him to become the first Conservative to win the seat since its creation in 1950. Director of communications, Synergix Health. Former chief of staff to Lord Popat, trade envoy to Uganda and Rwanda. Grandson of a miner. First in his family to go to university. Passionate campaigner for Brexit. Contested: Stockton North, 2017; Doncaster North, 2015. Ed: Ridgewood Sch; Danum Sixth Form; Jesus Coll, Cambridge (BA land economy; students' union president).

	Electorate	Share %	Change from 2017 %
	75,157		
M Fletcher C	21,791	47.44	+6.88
*D Skinner Lab	16,492	35.90	-16.02
K Harper Brexit	4,151	9.04	
D Hancock LD	1,759	3.83	+0.88
D Kesteven Green	758	1.65	
R Walker Ind	517	1.13	
N Hoy Ind	470	1.02	

CHALLENGERS
Dennis Skinner (Lab) MP for this seat, 1970-2019, known as the Beast of Bolsover. Heckled Black Rod at state openings of parliament and was suspended from the Commons several times for "unparliamentary language". A coalminer for 21 years who joined Labour in 1956 and rose through the National Union of Mineworkers. Became the party's longest continuously serving MP

in 2017. **Kevin Harper** (Brexit) Former Derbyshire policeman. Used to vote Labour.

CONSTITUENCY PROFILE
Bolsover, in east Derbyshire, had elected a Labour MP at every election since 1950, and Labour never received fewer than 20,000 votes in the seat until 2019. Its predecessor, Clay Cross, had also elected Labour MPs since 1922, and was represented by Arthur Henderson, the Labour leader and foreign secretary from 1933-35. A classic Red Wall seat, it was one of only 17 constituencies to vote Leave by a margin of more than 40 per cent.

EU REFERENDUM RESULT
70.4% Leave   Remain 29.6%

Bolton North East

MAJORITY 378 (0.87%)   **CONSERVATIVE GAIN FROM LABOUR**   **TURNOUT 64.47%**

MARK LOGAN
BORN Jan 28, 1984
MP 2019-

Former diplomat and longtime Brexiteer who unseated the veteran backbencher Sir David Crausby. Head of global communications for Sanpower Group. Head of communications, British Consulate in Shanghai, 2012-16. Speaks Mandarin. Voted for Boris Johnson in the 2019 leadership contest. Founder, Oxford PR, a strategic communications agency. Volunteers at a Tourette's care facility. Contested: Antrim East, 2017. Ed: Queen's University Belfast (LLB); LSE (MSc politics); Oxford University (MSc contemporary Chinese studies).

	Electorate	Share %	Change from 2017 %
	67,564		
M Logan C	19,759	45.36	+3.15
*D Crausby Lab	19,381	44.50	-6.12
T Jones Brexit	1,880	4.32	
W Fox LD	1,847	4.24	+1.33
L Spencer Green	689	1.58	+0.79

CHALLENGERS
Sir David Crausby (Lab) MP for this seat, 1997-2019. Delegate: Council of Europe parliamentary assembly, 2013-17; Nato parliamentary assembly, 2005-15. Voted against same-sex marriage in 2013. Supported challenge to Jeremy Corbyn's leadership in 2016. Knighted in 2017. Was a works convenor at the Amalgamated Engineering Union. **Trevor Jones** (Brexit) Owner and director, Britannia Building Services. Contested

Bolton MBC, 2019. **Warren Fox** (LD) Marketing manager. Contested this seat, 2017.

CONSTITUENCY PROFILE
One of the ten most marginal seats in the 2019 parliament, this Greater Manchester constituency elected Tories from its creation in 1983 until Labour gained the seat in 1997. The Labour majority was stable at about 4,000 from 2005 to 2017. A young and diverse constituency with nearly 20,000 residents aged under 16 and more than 16,000 ethnic minority residents. On average, the seat has higher pay and lower unemployment than Bolton South East.

EU REFERENDUM RESULT
58.1% Leave   Remain 41.9%

Bolton South East

MAJORITY 7,598 (18.71%)   LABOUR HOLD   TURNOUT 58.71%

YASMIN QURESHI
BORN Jul 5, 1963
MP 2010-

Electorate	Share %	from 2017 %	Change
69,163			
*Y Qureshi Lab	21,516	52.99	-7.68
J Lee C	13,918	34.28	+4.62
M Cunningham Brexit	2,968	7.31	
K Walsh LD	1,411	3.48	+1.63
D Figgins Green	791	1.95	+0.68

Barrister and former policy adviser for the Crown Prosecution Service. Appointed shadow justice minister in 2016. APPGs: communities engagement (chairwoman); British Muslims; religion in the media; Sudan. Headed criminal legal section of the UN mission in Kosovo. Human rights adviser to Ken Livingstone during his second term as London mayor. Volunteer legal adviser, South Law Centre, 1993-2000. Largely supportive of Jeremy Corbyn. Nominated Emily Thornberry in 2020 leadership race. Apologised following criticism for appearing to draw a parallel between the Israeli treatment of Palestinians and the Holocaust, 2014. Born in Pakistan; moved to Britain aged nine. Ed: Westfield Comp; London South Bank University (BA law); Council of Legal Education; UCL (LLM).

CHALLENGERS
Johno Lee (C) Cllr, Newark & Sherwood DC, 2015-. Lost a leg while serving in Afghanistan. Mark Cunningham (Brexit) Cllr, Bolton MBC, 2016-. Defected from Ukip in August 2019. Kev Walsh (LD) Contested Bolton MBC, 2019, 2018, 2016. David Figgins (Green) Football coach and referee. Has contested Bolton MBC three times in the past four years.

CONSTITUENCY PROFILE
Has elected a Labour MP at every election since it was created in 1983, mostly with large majorities. The result in 2019 was Labour's worst ever in the seat. A diverse community; about a fifth of residents are of Asian descent. It is a relatively poor constituency, with low levels of home ownership and a child poverty rate of 37 per cent.

EU REFERENDUM RESULT
63.0% Leave   Remain 37.0%

Bolton West

MAJORITY 8,855 (17.96%)   CONSERVATIVE HOLD   TURNOUT 67.36%

CHRIS GREEN
BORN Aug 12, 1973
MP 2015-

Electorate	Share %	from 2017 %	Change
73,191			
*C Green C	27,255	55.29	+7.38
J Hilling Lab	18,400	37.32	-8.75
R Forrest LD	2,704	5.49	+2.58
P Hayes Green	939	1.90	

Appointed parliamentary private secretary to the Department for Education in 2019. Served as PPS to the Department for Transport in 2018, but resigned over concerns that the government was failing to deliver Brexit. Voted for no-deal during indicative votes; supported Dominic Raab, then Boris Johnson, in the 2019 leadership election. Opposed fracking in his own constituency. Supporter of regional devolution. Select cttees: home affairs, 2018-; work and pensions, 2017-18; science and technology, 2015-17. APPGs: medical research (chairman); British parliamentary awards. Has worked in the pharmaceutical and manufacturing industries. Former member, Territorial Army. Contested Manchester Withington, 2010.

CHALLENGERS
Julie Hilling (Lab) MP for this seat, 2010-15. Opposition whip, 2013-15. Former senior regional organiser, TSSA; North West learning organiser, NASUWT. Chairwoman, Socialist Education Association. Rebecca Forrest (LD) Office manager, Jane Brophy MEP and Chris Davies MEP. Former science teacher. Contested this seat, 2017.

CONSTITUENCY PROFILE
Recently a very marginal seat, Bolton West stayed Labour in 2010, but was gained by the Conservatives in 2015. Until 2019, no MP had enjoyed a majority of more than 1,000 since the New Labour cabinet minister Ruth Kelly in 2005. In 2019 Chris Green won the largest majority that any MP for the seat has had since its creation in 1950. It is the largest and most rural of the three Bolton constituencies.

EU REFERENDUM RESULT
55.6% Leave   Remain 44.4%

Bootle

PETER DOWD
BORN Jun 20, 1957
MP 2015-

Electorate	Share %	Change from 2017 %
74,832		
*P Dowd Lab	39,066	79.44	-4.59
T Onuluk C	4,510	9.17	-2.88
K Knight Brexit	2,610	5.31	
R Hanson LD	1,822	3.71	+2.04
M Carter Green	1,166	2.37	+0.96

Appointed shadow chief secretary to the Treasury in 2017. Shadow Treasury minister, 2016-17. Nominated Rebecca Long Bailey in the 2020 Labour leadership election and was supportive of Jeremy Corbyn, despite backing Andy Burnham in 2015. Campaigned to remain in the EU. APPGs: beauty, aesthetics and wellbeing; health. Qualified social worker who worked for 35 years in Merseyside. Long career in local government before entering parliament. Cllr, Sefton MBC, 1991-2015; leader, 2011-15. Cllr, Merseyside CC, 1981-86.

Ed: Hugh Baird Coll; University of Liverpool; Lancaster University.

CHALLENGERS
Tarsilo Onuluk (C) Parlimentary assistant, Crispin Blunt MP (Reigate). **Kim Knight** (Brexit) Small business owner. Contested Blackpool BC, 2015. **Rebecca Hanson** (LD) Education consultant. Former maths lecturer, Manchester Metropolitan University. Cllr: Cumbria CC, 2017-;

Cockermouth TC, 2016-. **Mike Carter** (Green) Contested Sefton Central, 2017.

CONSTITUENCY PROFILE
In only two constituencies, both also in Merseyside, did the Labour candidate receive a higher percentage of the vote than in Bootle, an old docking town to the north of Liverpool. The constituency was one of only 12 where Labour won more than three quarters of the vote. It has elected Labour MPs since the Second World War. Two by-elections were held in 1990, the second after Michael Carr, who had been the MP for only 57 days, died from a heart attack.

EU REFERENDUM RESULT
54.8% Leave   Remain 45.2%

Boston & Skegness

MATT WARMAN
BORN Sep 1, 1981
MP 2015-

Electorate	Share %	Change from 2017 %
68,895		
*M Warman C	31,963	76.66	+13.06
B Cook Lab	6,342	15.21	-9.74
H Jones LD	1,963	4.71	+2.91
P Watson Ind	1,428	3.42	

Appointed a junior minister for digital and broadband when Boris Johnson, whom Mr Warman backed in the 2019 Conservative leadership race, became prime minister. Remainer in 2016, but embraced Brexit and voted for no-deal in the indicative votes. Assistant whip, 2019. PPS to Karen Bradley (Staffordshire Moorlands), 2017-19. Led parliamentary debate on bereavement counselling. Science and tech select cttee, 2015-17. APPGs: broadband; rural crime; women in parliament. Technology editor, *The Daily*

Telegraph, 1999-2015. Called the newspaper a "Fleet Street tragedy" after its "Brexit mutineers" headline targeting Tory colleagues in 2017. Ed: Haberdashers' Aske's Boys' Sch; Durham University (BA English).

CHALLENGERS
Ben Cook (Lab) GMB trade union representative, Asda. Contested Linconshire CC, 2017. **Hilary Jones** (LD) Director, design engineering company. Cllr, Derby City C, 2000-16; leader, 2008-12. Contested

Derbyshire Mid, 2017. **Peter Watson** (Ind) Driving instructor. Cllr, Boston CC, 2019-.

CONSTITUENCY PROFILE
Britain's most pro-Brexit constituency and the only seat where more than 75 per cent of voters backed Leave in 2016. The seat has elected Conservatives since it was created in 1997. In 2019 it had one of the largest increases in the Conservative's vote share. Ukip reduced the Tory majority to less than 5,000 in 2015, though in 2017 Paul Nuttall, the Ukip leader, won less than 8 per cent of the vote. The coastal town of Skegness relies on tourism.

EU REFERENDUM RESULT
75.6% Leave   Remain 24.4%

Bosworth

MAJORITY 26,278 (46.57%)   **CONSERVATIVE HOLD**   **TURNOUT 69.21%**

LUKE EVANS
BORN Jan 10, 1983
MP 2019-

GP. Taught anatomy at the University of Birmingham after his junior doctor training. Member of the Birmingham and Edgbaston Debating Society; British public speaking champion, 2017. His debating experience spurred him to enter politics. Played for Harborne rugby club and sang in a barbershop chorus. Based in Oxford and criticised by the leader of Hinckley & Bosworth council for standing for this seat despite living in Abingdon. Wife, father and two brothers are all doctors and his mother was a nurse. Contested Birmingham

	Electorate	Share %	Change from 2017 %
	81,537		
L Evans C	36,056	63.89	+7.16
R Middleton Lab	9,778	17.33	-6.73
M Mullaney LD	9,096	16.12	-1.23
M Gregg Green	1,502	2.66	+0.80

Edgbaston, 2015. Ed: University of Birmingham (medicine).

CHALLENGERS
Rick Middleton (Lab) Runs a web consultancy business. Contested: Hinckley & Bosworth BC, 2019; Leicestershire CC, 2017. **Michael Mullaney** (LD) Carer for elderly and disabled people. Cllr, Hinckley & Bosworth BC, 2011-. Contested this seat, 2017, 2015, 2010. **Mick Gregg** (Green) Social worker. Worked in mental health and child protection. Contested this seat, 2017.

CONSTITUENCY PROFILE
A safe Tory seat in rural west Leicestershire. Labour held it for the first 25 years after the Second World War, but it has been Conservative since 1970, although Labour came within about 1,000 votes of winning it in 1997. The constituency encompasses the area around the town of Market Bosworth and the constituency is affluent with high levels of home ownership. Woodrow Wyatt, known for his *News of the World* column and closeness to the Queen Mother, represented the seat for Labour from 1959-70, before becoming a Thatcherite and being made a life peer.

EU REFERENDUM RESULT
60.8% Leave   **Remain 39.2%**

Bournemouth East

MAJORITY 8,806 (17.87%)   **CONSERVATIVE HOLD**   **TURNOUT 66.47%**

TOBIAS ELLWOOD
BORN Aug 12, 1966
MP 2005-

Former army officer; chairman of the defence select cttee since 2020. Junior defence minister, 2017-19. Backed Matt Hancock and then Rory Stewart in the Conservative leadership race, 2019. Mostly voted in favour of overseas military operations. Called a hero by colleagues and the press after he was pictured with blood on his face giving mouth-to-mouth resuscitation to Keith Palmer, the PC who was fatally stabbed during the 2017 Westminster terrorist attack. Apologised in 2015 after saying he would have to "watch the pennies" if MPs did not

	Electorate	Share %	Change from 2017 %
	74,127		
*T Ellwood C	24,926	50.59	-1.29
C Drew Lab	16,120	32.72	-2.84
P Dunn LD	5,418	11.00	+4.48
A Keddie Green	2,049	4.16	+1.62
B Aston ND	447	0.91	
E Johnson Ind	314	0.64	+0.01

get a £7,000 pay rise, despite earning almost £90,000. Junior Foreign Office minister, 2014-17. PPS to: Jeremy Hunt, 2013-14; David Lidington, 2011-13; Liam Fox, 2010-11. Shadow culture minister, 2007-10. Opposition whip, 2005-07. Ed: Vienna Int Sch; Loughborough University (design and technology); City, University of London (MBA).

CHALLENGERS
Corrie Drew (Lab) Social media

co-ordinator. Climate change and human rights campaigner. **Philip Dunn** (LD) Humanities teacher. Former insurance investigator. **Alasdair Keddie** (Green) IT engineer. Contested this seat, 2017, 2015.

CONSTITUENCY PROFILE
Neither Bournemouth seat has failed to elect a Conservative at any election since 1922, although Tobias Ellwood's predecessor had his majority reduced to less than 5,000 by the Liberal Democrats in 1997 and 2001. This half of the Dorset town stretches further along Poole Bay and contains more of the town's beaches, with tourism an important industry.

EU REFERENDUM RESULT
53.7% Leave   **Remain 46.3%**

Bournemouth West

MAJORITY 10,150 (22.08%)   CONSERVATIVE HOLD   TURNOUT 61.95%

CONOR BURNS
BORN Sep 24, 1972
MP 2010-

Appointed minister for international trade in 2019 after serving as Boris Johnson's PPS, 2017-18, and backing him for leader, 2019. Thatcherite Eurosceptic who voted against Theresa May's withdrawal agreement twice and for a no-deal Brexit. Expressed reservations about same-sex marriage, despite being a gay man, but ultimately voted for it. He said that doing so left him feeling unable to take Holy Communion at his local Roman Catholic church. PPS to: Owen Paterson (Shropshire North), 2012; Hugo Swire, 2010-12. Select

	Electorate	Share %	Change from 2017 %
	74,211		
*C Burns C	24,550	53.40	-0.11
D Stokes Lab	14,400	31.32	-4.86
J Nicholas LD	4,931	10.72	+4.14
S Bull Green	2,096	4.56	+1.76

cttees: administration, 2014-15; culture, 2012-15. Career in lobbying and finance: Associate director, PLMR; head of business development, Dehavilland; Zurich Insurance. Chairman, Conservative Way Forward. Ed: St Colomba's Coll, St Albans; University of Southampton (BA modern history and politics).

CHALLENGERS
David Stokes (Lab) Construction worker. Contested this seat, 2017, 2015. **Jon Nicholas** (LD) Conflict management consultant who

has worked in Yugoslavia and Indonesia. Contested this seat, 2017, 2015. **Simon Bull** (Green) Cllr, Bournemouth CC, 2015-.

CONSTITUENCY PROFILE
Bournemouth West has been represented by Tory MPs since it was created in 1950. The party's majority fell below 5,000 in 2001 and 2005. The constituency contains the University of Bournemouth, so there is a sizable student population and residents are generally younger than average. The seat is better off than its neighbour, with higher average earnings and lower unemployment.

EU REFERENDUM RESULT
57.7% Leave   Remain 42.3%

Bracknell

MAJORITY 19,829 (36.48%)   CONSERVATIVE HOLD   TURNOUT 68.62%

JAMES SUNDERLAND
BORN Jun 6, 1970
MP 2019-

Bracknell-born veteran who entered politics after a 27-year career in the Army. Selected in November 2019 to replace Phillip Lee, who stood in neighbouring Wokingham after defecting to the Liberal Democrats in September 2019. Claimed to possess no lofty ambitions in parliament, instead focusing on being a good constituency MP. Keen to support extra funding for social care and people with special educational needs and disabilities. Army diversity champion. Commanded 27 Regiment Royal Logistic Corps, 2014-16. Wrote for Conservative

	Electorate	Share %	Change from 2017 %
	79,206		
J Sunderland C	31,894	58.68	-0.15
P Bidwell Lab	12,065	22.20	-7.98
K Beheshtizadeh LD	7,749	14.26	+6.77
D Florey Green	2,089	3.84	
O Barreto Ind	553	1.02	+0.24

Home in support of the Armed Forces Covenant. Volunteer for Samaritans, Help for Heroes and British Legion.

CHALLENGERS
Paul Bidwell (Lab) Project manager for a security firm. Cllr, Bracknell Forest C, 2015-. Trustee, elderly day centre and a local community centre. Contested this seat, 2017. **Kaweh Beheshtizadeh** (LD) Asylum and immigration solicitor. Shortlisted for Human Rights Lawyer of

the Year by the Law Society in 2017. Refugee. Contested Merton LBC, 2018.

CONSTITUENCY PROFILE
A safe Conservative seat. The party's majority was more than 10,000 even in 1997, although it fell below 7,000 in 2001. A compact and affluent Berkshire seat, in which a large proportion of residents are in managerial jobs. Andrew MacKay, the MP, 1997-2010, quit after he and his wife, Julie Kirkbride, were among the most criticised MPs in the expenses scandal; he was reportedly heckled and called a "thieving toad" as he tried to explain himself to constituents.

EU REFERENDUM RESULT
53.2% Leave   Remain 46.8%

Bradford East

LABOUR HOLD

IMRAN HUSSAIN
BORN Jun 7, 1978
MP 2015-

Barrister who was appointed shadow justice minister in 2017. On the far left of the party. Nominated Rebecca Long Bailey in 2020 Labour leadership race, having backed Jeremy Corbyn in 2015 and 2016. Rejected Tony Blair's donation to his 2015 general election campaign, citing his opposition to the Iraq War. One of 48 Labour MPs to vote against the welfare bill in 2015, defying Labour's position to abstain. Shadow minister for international development, 2016-17. Regulatory reform select cttee, 2015-17. APPGs: Kashmir; Pakistan; race and community;

	Electorate	Share %	Change from 2017 %
	73,206		
*I Hussain Lab	27,825	62.98	-2.41
L Kemkaran C	9,681	21.91	+1.55
J Sunderland LD	3,316	7.50	+5.66
J Barras Brexit	2,700	6.11	
A Stanford Green	662	1.50	+0.86

Rohingya. Cllr, Bradford DC, 2002-18; deputy leader, 2010-15. Contested: Bradford West by-election, 2012, losing to George Galloway. Ed: University of Huddersfield; Honourable Society of Lincoln's Inn (BPTC).

CHALLENGERS
Linden Kemkaran (C) Former BBC broadcast journalist. Retweeted claims that there were "no-go areas in Bradford and that Muslims had a "nasty culture". Denied she agreed with

the tweets. An investigation was launched after Naz Shah (Bradford West) complained to the Conservative Party. **Jeanette Sunderland** (LD) Cllr, Bradford MDC, 2019-.

CONSTITUENCY PROFILE
Bradford East's predecessor, Bradford North, was Labour from 1987 and 2010, but after boundary changes for the 2010 election the seat fell for one term to the Liberal Democrats' David Ward. One of the most densely populated constituencies in West Yorkshire. About two fifths of residents are of Asian descent, mostly Pakistani. More than 30,000 residents under 16.

EU REFERENDUM RESULT
55.2% Leave   Remain 44.8%

Bradford South

LABOUR HOLD

JUDITH CUMMINS
BORN Jun 26, 1967
MP 2015-

Appointed shadow minister for international trade in 2018. Opposition whip, 2015-18. Backed Owen Smith in his 2016 attempt to oust Jeremy Corbyn and supported Sir Keir Starmer in the 2020 Labour leadership race. Standing orders select cttee, 2017-. APPGs: beauty, aesthetics and wellbeing (co-chairwoman); dementia; dentistry and oral health; policing and security; rugby league (chairwoman). Cllr: Leeds City C, 2012-16; Bradford MDC, 2004-07. Former benefits adviser. Worked across FE colleges in Yorkshire and the Humber. Ed: University of Leeds

	Electorate	Share %	Change from 2017 %
	69,046		
*J Cummins Lab	18,390	46.27	-8.21
N Sekhon C	16,044	40.37	+2.21
K Manik Brexit	2,819	7.09	
A Griffiths LD	1,505	3.79	+2.53
M Edwards Green	983	2.47	+1.57

(BA politics and parliamentary studies); Ruskin Coll, Oxford.

CHALLENGERS
Narinder Sekhon (C) Barrister specialising in crime and serious injury, Park Square Barristers. **Kulvinder Manik** (Brexit) Barrister and GP. Residential doctor at a local winter homeless shelter. Voted Remain in 2016, but defected from Labour after feeling aggrieved at MPs trying to obstruct Brexit. **Alun Griffiths** (LD) GP. Cllr. Bradford MDC,

2016-. Stood in the neighbouring seat of Bradford West, 2017.

CONSTITUENCY PROFILE
Bradford South has been held by Labour since 1945, but the Conservatives came within 400 votes of gaining it in 1983 and 1987. In 2019 the Labour majority was the lowest it had been since then; the Brexit Party vote was bigger than the MP's majority. Of the three seats in the city, Bradford South is the least ethnically diverse, with a population that is about three quarters white. It also has the lowest unemployment and the highest proportion of managerial jobs.

EU REFERENDUM RESULT
63.6% Leave   Remain 36.4%

Bradford West

NAZ SHAH
BORN Nov 13, 1973
MP 2015-

	Electorate	Share %	Change from 2017 %
	70,694		
*N Shah Lab	33,736	76.22	+11.55
M Afzal C	6,717	15.18	-1.39
D Hodgson Brexit	1,556	3.52	
M Christie LD	1,349	3.05	+1.48
D Parkinson Green	813	1.84	+0.78
A Bukhari ND	90	0.20	-13.73

Appointed shadow minister for women and equalities in 2018. Briefly suspended by Labour in 2016 and investigated over antisemitic posts on social media before her election; she apologised in the Commons and admitted mistakes. Nominated Emily Thornberry in 2020 leadership election. PPS to John McDonnell (Hayes & Harlington), 2016. Home affairs select cttee, 2015-18. Endured a turbulent childhood: had an arranged marriage in Pakistan at 15 and her mother was imprisoned for murder. Spent 12 years campaigning with the Southall Black Sisters, an anti-domestic abuse group, for her mother's release. Worked as a carer for children with disabilities. Former chairwoman, Sharing Voices, a mental health charity. Once worked in a crisp-packing factory.

CHALLENGERS
Mohammed Afzal (C) Criminal lawyer. Director, Conservative Friends of Pakistan. Contested: Birmingham Yardley, 2017;

Manchester Gorton, 2015. **Derrick Hodgson** (Brexit) Contested this seat in 2017 for Ukip.

CONSTITUENCY PROFILE
Although it has elected Labour MPs at every general election for more than 40 years, Bradford West was won by George Galloway for the Respect Party at a 2012 by-election. About 50,000 residents are under the age of 25 and a similar number are of Pakistani descent. The constituency has one of the largest Muslim populations in the country. It was the only seat to have a child poverty rate of more than 50 per cent in 2018.

EU REFERENDUM RESULT
46.7% Leave   Remain 53.3%

Braintree

JAMES CLEVERLY
BORN Sep 4, 1969
MP 2015-

	Electorate	Share %	Change from 2017 %
	75,208		
*J Cleverly C	34,112	67.55	+4.73
J Garfield Lab	9,439	18.69	-8.93
D Graham LD	4,779	9.46	+5.16
J Beavis Ind	1,488	2.95	
D Mansell Ind	420	0.83	
A Dorkins Ind	261	0.52	

Minister in the Foreign Office and Department for International Development, 2020-. Stood for the Tory leadership in 2019 but withdrew before the first ballot and endorsed Boris Johnson. Brexiteer. Conservative Party co-chairman and minister without portfolio, 2019-20. Briefly a junior Brexit minister at the end of Theresa May's premiership, 2019. Conservative deputy chairman, 2018-19. Trade select cttee, 2016-18. GLA member for Bexley & Bromley, 2008-16. Appointed youth ambassador for Mr Johnson as London mayor in 2009. Territorial Army officer from 1991; called up during the Iraq War in 2004. Awarded the Territorial Decoration, 2003. Worked in magazine publishing. Contested Lewisham East, 2005. Ed: Colfe's Sch; Thames Valley University (BA hospitality management).

CHALLENGERS
Joshua Garfield (Lab) Cllr, Newham LBC, 2018-. Former public health worker for

Hackney LBC. Campaigns officer, LGBT Labour. Appeared in *Panorama* episode about Labour's antisemitism crisis. **Dominic Graham** (LD) Cllr, Colchester BC, 2014-17.

CONSTITUENCY PROFILE
Created in 1974, this Essex seat has been held mostly by Conservatives, although Labour won it narrowly in 1997 and 2001. The Conservatives have increased their vote share at every election since winning the seat back in 2005. Large skilled working-class population. The area is sparsely populated, with most of its residents based in the towns of Braintree and Halstead.

EU REFERENDUM RESULT
61.5% Leave   Remain 38.5%

Brecon & Radnorshire

MAJORITY 7,131 (17.26%)   **CONSERVATIVE GAIN FROM LIB DEM**   **TURNOUT 74.46%**

FAY JONES
BORN Jan 18, 1985
MP 2019-

Lobbyist who ran Boris Johnson's 2019 leadership campaign in Wales. Was one of the first three female Conservative MPs elected to a Welsh seat, all of them in 2019. Head of Wales for Grayling, a communications agency. Communications adviser to the National Farmers' Union, 2013-17. Researcher, HRH The Prince of Wales, 2009-13. Worked for David Jones (Clwyd West) and the MEP Jonathan Evan. Chairwoman, Public Affairs Cymru. Stood for the EU parliament, 2019. Ed: King's College London (BA French).

	Electorate	Share %	from 2017 %	Change %
	55,490			
F Jones C	21,958	53.14	+4.56	
*J Dodds LD	14,827	35.88	+6.75	
T Davies Lab	3,944	9.55	-8.20	
L The Pink Loony	345	0.83		
J Green Christian	245	0.59		

CHALLENGERS
Jane Dodds (LD) MP for this seat since August 2019. Leader of the Welsh Liberal Democrats who won a by-election and served for 97 days, becoming the shortest-serving female MP in history. Worked for the Salvation Army in child protective services for 27 years. Former Labour member, but left after the Iraq War. Cllr, Richmond-upon-Thames LBC, 2006-10. Contested Montgomeryshire, 2017, 2015. **Tomos Davies** (Lab)

Barrister. Cllr, Brecon TC, 2019-.

CONSTITUENCY PROFILE
A Conservative-Liberal Democrat swing seat, although it elected Labour MPs between 1939 and 1979. It held a by-election in August 2019 when its Conservative MP, Chris Davies, was unseated by a recall petition after being convicted of making a false expenses claim. It is the largest constituecy in Wales by area and its most-populated towns, Brecon and Ystradgynlais, have about 8,000 residents. More than half of the residents are 45 or older, 98 per cent are white, and almost 70 per cent own their home.

EU REFERENDUM RESULT
51.9% Leave   Remain 48.1%

Brent Central

MAJORITY 20,870 (42.48%)   **LABOUR HOLD**   **TURNOUT 58.35%**

DAWN BUTLER
BORN Nov 3, 1969
MP 2015-; 2005-10

Candidate in the 2020 contest for deputy Labour leader. Nominated Emily Thornberry for leader; backed Jeremy Corbyn in 2015. Shadow secretary of state for women and equalities from 2017, having been shadow minister for diverse communities, 2016-17. Briefly quit to vote against triggering Article 50, but was reappointed a few months later. Chairwoman of the women's parliamentary Labour party, 2015-16; ousted by Jess Phillips (Birmingham Yardley) in 2016 after a vote. Represented Brent South from 2005, then lost when contesting

	Electorate	Share %	from 2017 %	Change %
	84,204			
*D Butler Lab	31,779	64.68	-8.38	
D Brescia C	10,909	22.20	+2.68	
D Unger LD	4,844	9.86	+5.04	
W Relton Green	1,600	3.26	+1.72	

Brent Central in 2010 after being criticised during the 2009 expenses scandal. Minister for young citizens, 2009-10; first black woman to speak from the dispatch box. Whip, 2008-09. Education select cttee, 2007-09. Third Afro-Caribbean woman elected to Commons. Ed: Waltham Forest Coll of FE (Dip).

CHALLENGERS
David Brescia (C) Works in organic chemical research. Contested Camden LBC, 2018. **Deborah Unger** (LD) Editor,

Strategy+Business magazine.

CONSTITUENCY PROFILE
A safe Labour seat, Brent Central was created in 2010 after boundary changes. Its predecessor, Brent East, was Ken Livingstone's constituency from 1974 to 2001. The Liberal Democrats won it in a 2003 by-election, holding Brent East and then Brent Central until 2015. The constituency has one of the largest black populations in the country, with more than 40,000 residents of mixed race or Afro-Caribbean descent. It also has one of the largest Irish populations and a significant Hindu community.

EU REFERENDUM RESULT
42.9% Leave   Remain 57.1%

Brent North

MAJORITY 8,079 (15.57%) LABOUR HOLD TURNOUT 61.93%

BARRY GARDINER
BORN Mar 10, 1957
MP 1997-

New Labour junior minister turned passionate defender of Jeremy Corbyn. Shadow trade secretary, 2016-. Considered running for leader in 2020, but failed to receive sufficient support. PM's special envoy for forestry, 2007-08, but removed after criticising Gordon Brown. Shadow energy secretary, 2016. Shadow minister, the Department for Environment, Food and Rural Affairs, 2013-16. Parliamentary under-secretary: biodiversity, 2006-07; delivery, 2005-06; Northern Ireland, 2004-05. Cllr, Cambridge City C, 1988-94; mayor, 1992-93. Son

	Electorate	Share %	from 2017 %	Change
	83,772			
*B Gardiner Lab	26,911	51.87	-11.01	
A Patel C	18,832	36.30	+3.64	
P Lorber LD	4,065	7.84	+4.98	
S O'Brien Brexit	951	1.83		
S Rebbitt Green	850	1.64	+0.47	
N Coonan Ind	169	0.33		
E Jeffers Ind	101	0.19		

of a Scottish footballer, John Gardiner. Ed: University of St Andrews (MA philosophy); Harvard (philosophy, Kennedy scholar); Corpus Christi, Cambridge (PhD philosophy).

CHALLENGERS
Anjana Patel (C) Deleted Twitter account after being accused of sending an Islamaphobic tweet. Cllr, Harrow LBC, 2002-10. **Paul Lorber** (LD)

Refugee who came to Britain from Czechoslovakia in 1968. Cllr, Brent LBC, 1982-2014; leader, 2006-10.

CONSTITUENCY PROFILE
Held by Labour since 1997, with the party's majority not falling below 5,000. It was previously held by Sir Rhodes Boyson, a right-wing junior minister under Margaret Thatcher recognisable for his mutton-chop sideburns. The seat is diverse, with a large Asian community of about 70,000, most of whom are of Indian descent. In 2011, this constituency had the highest proportion of residents born outside the EU.

EU REFERENDUM RESULT
42.6% Leave Remain 57.4%

Brentford & Isleworth

MAJORITY 10,514 (18.03%) LABOUR HOLD TURNOUT 68.00%

RUTH CADBURY
BORN May 14, 1959
MP 2015-

Descendent of the chocolatier and Quaker philanthropist John Cadbury. Appointed shadow minister for housing in 2016, but sacked in 2017 after defying the whip to back a closer relationship with the EU after Brexit. Opposed to expansion of Heathrow. Backed Jess Phillips for leader, 2020. Select cttees: transport, 2018-; justice, 2017-18; women and equalities, 2015-17. Former local government officer. Cllr, Hounslow LBC, 1998-2015. Ed: The Mount Sch, York; Bournville FE Coll; University of Salford (BSc social science, geography and statistics).

	Electorate	Share %	from 2017 %	Change
	85,770			
*R Cadbury Lab	29,266	50.18	-7.21	
S Shah C	18,752	32.15	-5.47	
H Cross LD	7,314	12.54	+7.54	
D Goldsmith Green	1,829	3.14		
L O'Sullivan Brexit	1,165	2.00		

CHALLENGERS
Seena Shah (C) Worked on marketing campaigns for brands and technology companies. Founded her own consultancy, Splash Creative London. President, Conservative Young Women. **Helen Cross** (LD) Career in technology and the digital economy, specialising in robotics and AI. **Daniel Goldsmith** (Green) IT consultant. **Lucy O'Sullivan** (Brexit) Worked at the European parliament and commission.

CONSTITUENCY PROFILE
Brentford & Isleworth was a bellwether seat between 1997 and 2015, but was one of four London seats that Labour won from the Tories in 2015. Ruth Cadbury's majority in 2015 was only 465; in 2017, the Greens did not field a candidate to help her maintain her control of the seat. Ms Cadbury's margin of victory has shot up since then. The west London constituency stretches from Chiswick to Hounslow, and has some of the largest Buddhist, Hindu and Sikh communities in the UK. A significant proportion of residents commute further into London and many have managerial jobs.

EU REFERENDUM RESULT
43.3% Leave Remain 56.7%

Brentwood & Ongar

MAJORITY 29,065 (54.89%)   **CONSERVATIVE HOLD**   **TURNOUT 70.35%**

ALEX BURGHART
BORN Sep 7, 1977
MP 2017-

Appointed PPS to Boris Johnson in 2019. Previously PPS to the attorney-generals Geoffrey Cox and Jeremy Wright, and to Karen Bradley while she was Northern Ireland secretary. Initially backed Kit Malthouse in Conservative leadership contest before switching to Mr Johnson. Special adviser to Theresa May on social policy, 2016-17. Director of policy, Centre for Social Justice. Director of strategy and advocacy, Children's Commissioner for England. Author of book on social policy and vulnerable children. Taught history at Warwick School.

	Electorate	Share %	Change from 2017 %
	75,253		
*A Burghart C	36,308	68.58	+2.79
O Durose Lab	7,243	13.68	-6.75
D Kendall LD	7,187	13.58	+5.21
P Jeater Green	1,671	3.16	+1.43
R Tilbrook Eng Dem	532	1.00	

Contested Islington North against Jeremy Corbyn in 2015. Ed: Millfield Sch, Somerset; Christ Church, Oxford (BA history); King's Coll London (PhD history).

CHALLENGERS
Oliver Durose (Lab) Researcher, specialising in criminal justice reform. **David Kendall** (LD) Business owner, carpet and upholstery cleaning specialist. Cllr, Brentwood BC, 1991-. **Paul Jeater** (Green) Former politics and history teacher. Contested: this seat, 2017; Braintree, 2015. **Robin Tilbrook** (Eng Dem) Solicitor. Party founder.

CONSTITUENCY PROFILE
Brentwood & Ongar has elected Conservatives since its creation in 1974 and was held between 1992 and 2017 by Eric Pickles, a chairman of the Conservative Party and communities secretary. The independent MP Martin Bell stood in 2001, cutting Mr Pickles's majority to less than 3,000. The Essex seat, on Greater London's northeast border, has high levels of home ownership and self-employment.

EU REFERENDUM RESULT
61.2% Leave   Remain 38.8%

Bridgend

MAJORITY 1,157 (2.74%)   **CONSERVATIVE GAIN FROM LABOUR**   **TURNOUT 66.72%**

JAMIE WALLIS
BORN Jun 2, 1984
MP 2019-

Managing director of Fields Associates, a data recovery company. He has been a shareholder in numerous other companies, including Quickie Divorve, a legal services firm. Removed from Pencoed town council in 2018 after he failed to attend for six months. The council said it did not receive any advanced notice of his absence, but Mr Wallis told Wales Online: "I sent my resignation letter by post. I assumed they had got it." Contested Ogmore, 2017. Ed: Christ Church, Oxford (MChem chemistry); University of Cardiff

	Electorate	Share %	Change from 2017 %
	63,303		
J Wallis C	18,193	43.07	+3.28
*M Moon Lab	17,036	40.34	-10.32
J Pratt LD	2,368	5.61	+3.48
L Lewis PC	2,013	4.77	+0.64
R Morgan Brexit	1,811	4.29	
A Harris Green	815	1.93	

(MA maths; PhD planetary astronomy and science).

CHALLENGERS
Madeleine Moon (Lab) MP for this seat, 2005-19. President of the Nato parliamentary assembly, 2018-19, having been a member of the delegation since 2010. Cllr, Bridgend BC, 1991-2004; mayor of Porthcawl, 1995-96. **Jonathan Pratt** (LD) Former Royal Fleet Auxiliary member. Works for family business, selling Welsh and Celtic giftware. Contested this seat, 2017. **Leanne Lewis** (PC) Nurse. Cllr, Pencoed TC, 2019-.

CONSTITUENCY PROFILE
Bridgend had been represented by Labour MPs for 32 years and its Welsh assembly member is the former first minister of Wales Carwyn Jones. A small part of south Wales that stretches east from the town of Bridgend, which has a population of about 50,000. Many residents are employed in manufacturing, retail, health and social care. A Ford plant was expected to close in September 2020, with the loss of 1,700 jobs.

EU REFERENDUM RESULT
50.3% Leave   Remain 49.7%

Bridgwater & Somerset West

MAJORITY 24,439 (42.39%)   **CONSERVATIVE HOLD**   **TURNOUT 67.57%**

IAN LIDDELL-GRAINGER
BORN Feb 23, 1959
MP 2001-

Electorate	Share %	Change from 2017 %
85,327		
*I Liddell-Grainger C	35,827	62.14 +7.03
O Thornton Lab	11,388	19.75 -8.84
B Revans LD	7,805	13.54 +2.67
M Ritchie Green	1,877	3.26 +1.44
F Moussa Lib	755	1.31

Aristocratic social conservative, descended from Queen Victoria on his mother's side. Compared the town of Taunton, in a neighbouring seat, to the war-torn Syrian city of Aleppo in 2019. Backed Boris Johnson for leader, 2019. Accused of trivialising mental health issues after allegedly shouting "suicide" in parliament when another MP asked during a heated Brexit debate what options were available. Locally, councillors backed calls for him to be deselected in 2015. In 2014 he admitted that a fellow Tory had been erased from a photograph on his website. He told the BBC: "I was narked and my researcher did it as a bit of a joke. These things happen." A member of the right-wing Cornerstone Group of Tory MPs. Former managing director of a building and property company. Contested Torridge & West Devon, 1997. Ed: Millfield Sch, Somerset; South of Scotland Agricultural Coll.

CHALLENGERS
Oliver Thornton (Lab) Works in financial crime prevention. **Bill Revans** (LD) History teacher. Cllr, Somerset CC, 2017-.

CONSTITUENCY PROFILE
The seat's predecessor, Bridgwater, returned Conservative MPs at every election since 1950. Tom King, the defence secretary under John Major during the Gulf War, represented it from 1970 to 2001. The Liberal Democrats came within 2,000 votes of winning in 1997. A large area stretching from Exmoor National Park to the Somerset Levels. Lucrative tourist industry, especially on Exmoor, the Quantocks and in the coastal town of Minehead.

EU REFERENDUM RESULT
62.1% Leave   Remain 37.9%

Brigg & Goole

MAJORITY 21,941 (50.55%)   **CONSERVATIVE HOLD**   **TURNOUT 65.82%**

ANDREW PERCY
BORN Sep 18, 1977
MP 2010-

Electorate	Share %	Change from 2017 %
65,939		
*A Percy C	30,941	71.29 +10.88
M Khan Lab	9,000	20.74 -12.24
D Dobbie LD	2,180	5.02 +3.17
J Baker Green	1,281	2.95 +1.73

Served as Theresa May's trade envoy to Canada, 2017-19, but resigned in July 2019 in protest at Liam Fox's plans for a no-deal Brexit. Rebellious Eurosceptic. Minister for the northern powerhouse, 2016-17. Secondary school history teacher who once taught in the US and Canada. Supporter: Countryside Alliance; National Trust; Campaign Against Political Correctness. Converted to Judaism in 2017. Cllr, Hull City C, 2000-10. Contested Normanton, 2005. Ed: Wyke Sixth Form Coll; University of York (BA politics); Leeds University (PgDip law).

CHALLENGERS
Majid Khan (Lab) Businessman. Was managing director of Electrical Aid. First ethnic minority vice-chairman of Doncaster metropolitan borough council and deputy civic mayor of Doncaster. Cllr, Doncaster MBC, 2015-. **David Dobbie** (LD) Security officer. Cllr, Gainsborough TC, 2005-; leader, 2017-. Cllr, West Lindsey DC, 2011-15, 2019-. **Jo Baker** (Green) Occupational therapist working in Scunthorpe and studying canine behaviour.

CONSTITUENCY PROFILE
Created in 1997, Brigg & Goole was represented by the Labour MP Ian Cawsey, a former government whip under Tony Blair and Gordon Brown. Its MP has been Conservative since 2010, making it a bellwether. The Conservative majority has increased at every election since the party gained the seat. A large and sparse constituency to the south of the Humber, with residents older than the national average. It also has higher than average levels of home ownership and median income. The small market town of Brigg and industrial port of Goole are either side of Scunthorpe.

EU REFERENDUM RESULT
66.2% Leave   Remain 33.8%

Brighton Kemptown

MAJORITY 8,061 (16.61%) **LABOUR CO-OP HOLD** **TURNOUT 69.50%**

LLOYD RUSSELL-MOYLE
BORN Sep 14, 1986
MP 2017-

Left-wing Remainer who voted to revoke Article 50. Nominated Rebecca Long Bailey in the 2020 leadership contest. Said he would fight the Conservatives "in the streets" in fiery acceptance speech, 2019. Ejected from the chamber for picking up the mace during a debate in 2018. Became the second sitting MP to live openly with HIV, revealing his diagnosis on World Aids Day in 2018. Cllr, Brighton and Hove City C, 2016-17. Worked for National Youth Agency. Contested Lewes in 2015. Ed: Priory Sch, Lewes; Sussex Downs Coll; University

	Electorate	Share %	Change from 2017 %
	69,833		
*L Russell-Moyle Lab Co-op	25,033	51.58	-6.75
J Miller C	16,972	34.97	-3.31
B Thomas LD	2,964	6.11	+3.15
A Phillips Green	2,237	4.61	
G Cushway Brexit	1,327	2.73	

of Bradford (BA peace studies); University of Sussex (LLM international law).

CHALLENGERS
Joe Miller (C) Trainee barrister. Cllr, Brighton & Hove City C, 2015-. **Ben Thomas** (LD) Pub manager. **Alexandra Phillips** (Green) Former policy lead, Terrence Higgins Trust. MEP for South East England, 2019-20. Mayor of Brighton and Hove, 2019-. **Graham Cushway** (Brexit) Former soldier. Bassist in Stuka

Squadron, a heavy-metal band that dresses in Nazi clothing.

CONSTITUENCY PROFILE
A bellwether between 1979 and 2017. Labour came close to winning Brighton Kemptown in 2015, before doing so in 2017 with a big increase in its share of the vote. It was the first time that Labour had won the seat without winning a majority. Before 1997, the seat had only elected a Labour MP twice, in the 1964 and 1966 elections. Kemptown stretches beyond the east of Brighton into rural Sussex, and the seat contains the heart of Brighton's large LGBT community.

EU REFERENDUM RESULT
43.6% Leave   Remain 56.4%

Brighton Pavilion

MAJORITY 19,940 (34.38%) **GREEN HOLD** **TURNOUT 73.36%**

CAROLINE LUCAS
BORN Dec 9, 1960
MP 2010-

Sole Green Party MP. Co-leader of the party, 2016-18; leader, 2008-12; principal speaker, 2007-08 and 2003-06. Arrested during an anti-fracking protest in 2013, but later cleared of obstructing a public highway. Environmental audit select cttee, 2010-. Endorsed Jeremy Corbyn's campaign to be Labour leader in 2015. Critical of free trade and GM crops. Vice-president, RSPCA. Parliamentary champion for Unicef. MEP for South East England, 1999-2010. Worked for charities including Oxfam before entering politics. Cllr, Oxfordshire CC, 1993-97.

	Electorate	Share %	Change from 2017 %
	79,057		
*C Lucas Green	33,151	57.16	+4.90
A Imanpour Lab	13,211	22.78	-4.01
E Hogan C	10,176	17.55	-1.67
R Milton Brexit	770	1.33	
C Skwith Loony	301	0.52	
B Dobbs Ind	212	0.37	-0.29
N Furness UKIP	177	0.31	-0.79

Contested Oxford East, 1992. Ed: Malvern Girls' Coll; University of Exeter (BA English literature; PhD English); University of Kansas (Dip journalism).

CHALLENGERS
Adam Imanpour (Lab) Business manager at Brighton MOT centre. **Emma Hogan** (C) Psychiatrist who has advised MPs on mental health issues. **Richard Milton** (Brexit) Writer

and journalist whose latest book is a "feminist thriller".

CONSTITUENCY PROFILE
Elected Conservative MPs from 1950 to 1997, a Labour MP during the New Labour years, and the Greens' Caroline Lucas since 2010. The University of Sussex is in the north of the seat, and more of Brighton's students live in Pavilion than in Kemptown or Hove, which Pavilion sits between. The seat also has the highest average income of Brighton's three constituencies. A viral petition to "revoke Article 50 and remain in the EU" garnered 30,000 signatures in the seat.

EU REFERENDUM RESULT
25.9% Leave   Remain 74.1%

Bristol East

LABOUR HOLD

TURNOUT 70.61%

KERRY MCCARTHY
BORN Mar 26, 1965
MP 2005-

Electorate	Share %	Change from 2017 %
73,867		
*K McCarthy Lab	27,717 53.14	-7.58
S Codling C	16,923 32.45	-1.91
N Coombes LD	3,527 6.76	+4.03
C Connolly Green	2,106 4.04	+1.85
T Page Brexit	1,881 3.61	

Claims to have been the first vegan MP and is a campaigner on environmental issues, reducing food waste and food poverty. Patron of Food Cycle, a charity that provides community meals. Founder of the APPG on food waste. Nominated Sir Keir Starmer for leader, 2020. Appointed shadow environment secretary in 2015 but resigned a year later over Jeremy Corbyn's leadership. Shadow minister: Foreign Office, 2011-15; Treasury, 2010-11; pensions, 2010. Assistant whip, 2010. PPS to: Douglas Alexander, 2007-09; Rosie Winterton, 2007. Worked

as a solicitor and director of Luton Airport. Cllr, Luton BC, 1999-2003. Ed: Denbigh HS; University of Liverpool (BA Russian and politics); City of London Polytechnic (LLB law).

CHALLENGERS
Sarah Codling (C) Charity worker. Worked in local government. Cllr, North Somerset C, 2015-. **Nicholas Coombes** (LD) Chartered town planner. **Conan Connolly** (Green) Military career in

Ireland. **Tim Page** (Brexit) Corporate lawyer and former partner at Clifford Chance.

CONSTITUENCY PROFILE
This seat was first contested with these boundaries in 1983, when it elected a Conservative MP. Tony Benn, who had been the Labour MP for Bristol South East, contested this seat that year and lost. Labour then won the seat back in 1992, and has held it since, the party's majority falling to about 4,000 in 2010 and 2015. Stafford Cripps, one of Clement Attlee's chancellors, once held the seat. Highest rate of home ownership of the Bristol seats, but lower average income.

EU REFERENDUM RESULT

46.8% Leave	Remain 53.2%

Bristol North West

LABOUR HOLD

TURNOUT 73.27%

DARREN JONES
BORN Nov 13, 1986
MP 2017-

Electorate	Share %	Change from 2017 %
76,273		
*D Jones Lab	27,330 48.90	-1.75
M Weston C	21,638 38.72	-3.13
C Coleman LD	4,940 8.84	+3.64
H Mack Green	1,977 3.54	+1.24

Voted Remain in 2016 and said softening or stopping Brexit was his "number one obligation". Nominated Jess Phillips in 2020 leadership race. Director of the technology think tank Labour Digital. Select cttees: European scrutiny, 2017-; science and tech, 2017-. Worked as a consumer rights lawyer at Bond Dickinson. Claimed in his maiden speech to be the first Darren elected to the House of Commons. Contested: this seat, 2015; Torridge & Devon West, 2010. Ed: Plymouth University (BSc human bioscience); UWE (PgDip law); University of Law (LPC).

CHALLENGERS
Mark Weston (C) Works for a facilities management company. Has run nightclubs and worked for BT and Bristol & West Mortgages. Cllr, Bristol City C, 2006-; leader, Conservative group. **Chris Coleman** (LD) Solicitor advocate for a regional law firm specialising in legal aid work. Cllr, Cheltenham BC, 2012-, 2002-08. Contested: Devizes, 2017; Forest of Dean, 2015. **Heather Mack** (Green) Worked for the Green MEP Molly Scott Cato.

CONSTITUENCY PROFILE
Changed hands from Labour to the Conservatives ten times since 1950, mostly corresponding with whichever party was in government. The 2017 election was the first time since 1955 that Labour had won the seat despite having lost nationally, Darren Jones having defeated Charlotte Leslie MP, who had backed Leave in the 2016 Brexit referendum. The constituency stretches from the northwest suburbs of Bristol up to the port of Avonmouth. Bristol North West is the second most affluent of the Bristol constituencies and the most marginal seat in the city.

EU REFERENDUM RESULT

38.9% Leave	Remain 61.1%

124 | THE NEW PARLIAMENT

Bristol South

KARIN SMYTH
BORN Sep 8, 1964
MP 2015-

Appointed shadow Northern
Ireland minister in 2018. Voted
Remain in 2016; supported
holding a second Brexit
referendum and revoking Article
50. Corbynsceptic. In the 2020
leadership race she supported Sir
Keir Starmer, to whom she was
a PPS, 2016-17. Public accounts
select cttee, 2015-17. Former
manager, NHS Bristol clinical
commissioning group. Non-
executive director, Bristol North
PCT, 2002-06. Political assistant
to Valerie Davey MP, 1997-2001.
Ed: Uxbridge Technical Coll;
UEA (BA economic and social
studies); Bath University (MBA).

	Electorate	Share %	Change from 2017 %
	84,079		
*K Smyth Lab	27,895	50.54	-9.53
R Morgan C	18,036	32.68	+2.01
A Brown LD	4,227	7.66	+4.31
T Dyer Green	2,713	4.92	+2.29
R de Vito Boutin Brexit	2,325	4.21	

CHALLENGERS
Richard Morgan (C)
Business director of a training
consultancy. Cllr, Cotswold DC,
2017-; leader of the Conservative
group. **Andrew Brown** (LD)
Works in financial services.
Member of LGBT+ Lib Dems.
Tony Dyer (Green) IT trainer
and former construction worker.
Stood for Bristol mayor, 2016.
Contested this constituency, 2017.
Robert de Vito Boutin (Brexit)
Counsellor. Previously a head
teacher and freelance writer.

CONSTITUENCY PROFILE
Bristol South has elected Labour
MPs since 1935. The Liberal
Democrats reduced Labour's
majority to less than 5,000 in
2010, and the Conservatives
came within 1,500 votes in
1987, after the deselection of
the former Labour chief whip
Michael Cocks. Mr Cocks had
beaten Terry Dicks, a right-wing
Tory who later became known
for his insistence that Nelson
Mandela was a terrorist, in
1979. Dawn Primarolo, a former
deputy speaker, held the seat
from 1987 to 2015. John Bercow,
the Speaker 2009-19, stood here
in 1992. It is Bristol's least diverse
and most working class seat.

EU REFERENDUM RESULT
48.0% Leave   Remain 52.0%

Bristol West

**THANGAM
DEBBONAIRE**
BORN Aug 3, 1966
MP 2015-

Shadow Brexit minister, 2020-.
Nominated Sir Keir Starmer for
leader, 2020. Appointed shadow
culture minister early in 2016
without her knowledge, part way
through treatment for breast
cancer; later told the role was
not hers, before being reinstated.
Resigned in opposition to Jeremy
Corbyn's leadership in June
2016 but rejoined front bench
as a whip in October 2016.
Campaigner against domestic
violence; has written academic
papers and journals on the topic.
Women's Aid's first ever national
children's officer. Director and
lead independent practitioner,

	Electorate	Share %	Change from 2017 %
	99,253		
*T Debbonaire Lab	47,028	62.27	-3.67
C Denyer Green	18,809	24.90	+12.03
S Aujla C	8,822	11.68	-2.11
N Hipkiss Brexit	869	1.15	

Domestic Violence Responses.
Professional cellist. Ed: Bradford
Girls' GS; Chetham's School of
Music; University of Bristol (MSc
management).

CHALLENGERS
Carla Denyer (Green) Worked
in the wind energy sector.
Cllr, Bristol City C, 2015-; led
successful efforts to get the
council to become the first in
the UK to declare a climate
emergency. **Suria Aujla** (C)
Legal executive; worked at the
Financial Ombudsman Service.

CONSTITUENCY PROFILE
Labour's biggest majority in
Bristol and the only seat where
any candidate won more than
45,000 votes. This was the
Green Party's second best result
after Brighton Pavillion, the
Liberal Democrats having stood
aside as part of the parties'
"Unite to Remain" pact. It was
Conservative for more than 100
years before turning to Labour
in 1997. The Lib Dem Stephen
Williams won it in 2005 and
2010. The densest, most diverse
and most affluent Bristol seat, it
contains the biggest portion of
the city's student population and
had the second highest Remain
vote in the country.

EU REFERENDUM RESULT
20.7% Leave   Remain 79.3%

Broadland

CONSERVATIVE HOLD

JEROME MAYHEW
BORN Apr 11, 1970
MP 2019-

Managing director of Go Ape. Former barrister. Replaced the BBC Norfolk presenter Nick Conrad as the Conservative candidate after controversy about Mr Conrad's past on-air comments during a debate about rape and sexual assault. Son of Patrick Mayhew, who served in the cabinets of Margaret Thatcher and John Major, including five years as attorney general. Director of an agricultural company. Ed: Edinburgh University (BA politics); Inns of Court (LLB); Cranfield University (BGP business growth).

	Electorate	Share %	Change from 2017 %
	78,151		
J Mayhew C	33,934	59.56	+1.66
J Barnard Lab	12,073	21.19	-8.45
B Goodwin LD	9,195	16.14	+8.19
A Boswell Green	1,412	2.48	+0.81
S Rous Universal	363	0.64	

CHALLENGERS
Jess Barnard (Lab) Senior youth worker at a Norfolk-based youth charity. GMB union activist. Cllr, Norfolk CC, 2017-. **Ben Goodwin** (LD) Served in the armed forces in Iraq, Syria and Afghanistan. Worked as a military assistant in London and at Nato in Brussels. **Andrew Boswell** (Green) Computing researcher. Contested this constituency, 2017, 2015. **Simon Rous** (Universal) Founder of the Universal Good Party, which had two members

and advocated the abolition of income tax.

CONSTITUENCY PROFILE
Home to part of the Norfolk Broads, Broadland has been a Conservative safe seat since its creation in 2010, with the number of Conservative votes rising at every election since. A large and sparsely populated seat in rural Norfolk, the biggest town is Fakenham, which has a population of about 8,000. More than half of the seat's residents are aged 45 or over and it has high rates of home ownership and self-employment. The area has one of the lowest levels of violent crime in the country.

EU REFERENDUM RESULT
54.1% Leave   Remain 45.9%

Bromley & Chislehurst

CONSERVATIVE HOLD

BOB NEILL
BORN Jun 24, 1952
MP 2006-

Justice select committee chairman since 2015, having had the same role in 2012-13 and 2007-10. Became the MP in a closely fought by-election after the death of the libertarian Tory Eric Forth in 2006. Remainer in 2016, but voted for Theresa May and Boris Johnson's withdrawal agreements. Backed Michael Gove for leader, 2019. Planning minister, 2010-12. Vice-chairman, Conservative Party, 2012-15. Select cttees: national security strategy, 2015-; liaison, 2015-; political and constitutional reform, 2013-15; constitutional affairs, 2006-07. Contested

	Electorate	Share %	Change from 2017 %
	66,711		
*B Neill C	23,958	52.58	-1.37
A Wilkins Lab	13,067	28.68	-4.72
J Ireland LD	6,621	14.53	+7.31
M Ion Green	1,546	3.39	+0.93
Z Amodu CPA	255	0.56	
J Dialani Renew	119	0.26	

Dagenham, 1987, 1983. Ed: Abbs Cross GS, Hornchurch; LSE (law).

CHALLENGERS
Angela Wilkins (Lab) Described herself as "chief heifer" at Drunken Dairy, an alcoholic ice cream company. Previously a consultant at the National Democratic Institute. Cllr, Bromley BC, 2014-. **Julie Ireland** (LD) IT consultant for small and medium-sized local businesses.

Mary Ion (Green) Teacher and environmental campaigner. **Zion Amodu** (CPA) Founded City Revival Church. **Jyoti Dialani** (Renew) Lawyer.

CONSTITUENCY PROFILE
A Conservative safe seat; the party's majority has fallen below 10,000 at general elections only in 2001 and 2017. The Liberal Democrats came within 634 votes of winning it at a 2006 by-election, which was the last time a by-election was triggered by the death of a Conservative MP. A suburban, affluent seat in the southeast of London, about a sixth of residents are non-white. Self-employment is common.

EU REFERENDUM RESULT
49.8% Leave   Remain 50.2%

Bromsgrove

MAJORITY 23,106 (42.57%) CONSERVATIVE HOLD TURNOUT 72.29%

SAJID JAVID
BORN Dec 5, 1969
MP 2010-

	Electorate	Share %	Change from 2017 %
	75,079		
*S Javid C	34,408	63.40	+1.42
R Shannon Lab	11,302	20.82	-10.49
D Nicholl LD	6,779	12.49	+7.89
K White Green	1,783	3.29	+1.18

First chancellor not to deliver a budget since Iain Macleod died suddenly in 1970. Quit in February 2020 after six months in post, when Boris Johnson insisted that he sack advisers as No 10 sought more control over the Treasury. Came fourth in the 2019 leadership contest. Became first British Asian to hold one of the great offices of state when appointed home secretary in 2018. Secretary of state: housing, 2016-18; business, 2015-16; culture, 2014-15. Minister: equality, 2014; financial secretary to Treasury, 2013-14; economic secretary, 2012-13. Eurosceptic,

but supported the Remain campaign in 2016. Seen as a free-market Thatcherite. Strong supporter of Israel. Career in business and finance. Vice-president, Chase Manhattan Bank. Was earning £3 million a year working for Deutsche Bank when he quit to pursue politics. Born in Rochdale to Pakistani immigrants; raised in Bristol. Ed: University of Exeter (BA economics and politics).

CHALLENGERS
Rory Shannon (Lab) Unison

member. Cllr, Bromsgrove DC. **David Nicholl** (LD) Consultant neurologist. **Kevin White** (Green) Organiser of vegan festivals across the Midlands.

CONSTITUENCY PROFILE
Bromsgrove has returned a Conservative MP at every general election since 1950, although Labour won the 1971 by-election. Labour came within 4,000 votes of winning in 1997, but the Conservative majority has increased at every subsequent election. This affluent, mostly rural Worcestershire seat has high levels of home ownership. Half of residents are aged over 45.

EU REFERENDUM RESULT
55.4% Leave   Remain 44.6%

Broxbourne

MAJORITY 19,807 (42.41%) CONSERVATIVE HOLD TURNOUT 63.82%

SIR CHARLES WALKER
BORN Sep 11, 1967
MP 2005-

	Electorate	Share %	Change from 2017 %
	73,182		
*C Walker C	30,631	65.58	+3.43
S Waters Lab	10,824	23.17	-5.72
J Bird LD	3,970	8.50	+5.38
N Cox Green	1,281	2.74	+0.96

Procedure select committee chairman, 2012-19. Made headlines in 2012 for speaking in the Commons about his mental health issues. Brexit supporter who voted for both Theresa May's and Boris Johnson's Brexit deals. Appointed OBE in 2015 and knighted in Mrs May's resignation honours. Other select cttees: liaison, 2012; Speaker's committee for Ipsa, 2010-; panel of chairs, 2010-. Cllr, Wandsworth LBC, 2002-06. Former board director, Blue Arrow. Worked in communication and marketing in the IT sector. Stepson of the

Conservative MP Christopher Chataway. Contested Ealing North, 2001. Ed: University of Oregon (BSc political science).

CHALLENGERS
Sean Waters (Lab) Chairman of Broxbourne Young Labour, having joined the party in 2016. **Julia Bird** (LD) Economist who worked in transport and green energy investments. Lived in France for six years. **Nicholas Cox** (Green) Leading authority on sustainable refrigeration and air conditioning.

CONSTITUENCY PROFILE
No Conservative candidate in Broxbourne has received less than half the vote since 1997. It was represented by the right-wing Eurosceptic Dame Marion Roe from 1983 to 2005. The Hertfordshire seat consists mainly of the towns of Cheshunt, Hoddeson and Broxbourne. It has a higher than average median income and high levels of home ownership. Workers are twice as likely to commute by train compared with the UK average. A significant proportion of residents work in construction. Several newspapers, including *The Times*, are printed in Broxbourne.

EU REFERENDUM RESULT
65.5% Leave   Remain 34.5%

Broxtowe

DARREN HENRY
BORN Aug 4, 1968
MP 2019-

Former RAF squadron leader. General manager of a wholesale food distributor 2014-15. NHS Great Western Hospital programme manager with Carillion. Cllr, Wiltshire C, 2017-. Suggested during a campaign hustings that people who used foodbanks struggled with managing their budget. Contested Wolverhampton North East, 2015. Mentored veterans for Help for Heroes. Ed: University of Lincoln (BSc logistics management).

CHALLENGERS
Greg Marshall (Lab) Water

	Electorate	Share %	Change from 2017 %
	73,895		
D Henry C	26,602	48.13	+1.32
G Marshall Lab	21,271	38.48	-6.77
*A Soubry Change	4,668	8.45	
K Boettge Green	1,806	3.27	+2.04
A Dalla Mura Eng Dem	432	0.78	
T Khong Ind	321	0.58	
D Bishop Elvis	172	0.31	

resource adviser, Environment Agency. Cllr, Broxtowe BC, 2011-. Contested Broxtowe, 2017. **Anna Soubry** (Change) Broxtowe MP, 2010-19. One of the three Conservative MPs to defect to the Independent Group, which later became Change UK, in February 2019. Party leader, Jun-Dec 2019. Staunch Remainer; voted against all withdrawal agreements. Minister: business, 2015-16; defence, 2013-15;

health, 2012-13. Journalist and barrister. **Kat Boettge** (Green) Psychotherapist. Cllr, Kimberley TC. Appeared on a Brexit special of *Wife Swap*.

CONSTITUENCY PROFILE
A bellwether, Broxtowe has been won by whichever party went on to form the government at every election since its creation in 1983. Darren Henry won the largest majority of any Broxtowe MP since 2001. The Tories held on by 389 votes in 2010 and 863 in 2017. This west Nottinghamshire seat has high levels of home ownership and many residents work in education.

EU REFERENDUM RESULT

52.5% Leave	Remain 47.5%

Buckingham

GREG SMITH
BORN Mar 3, 1979
MP 2019-

Marketing and design consultant for clients in manufacturing, medical technology and charity. Cllr, Hammersmith & Fulham LBC, 2006-18; deputy leader, 2012-14; cabinet member 2006-14; Conservative group leader 2014-18. Co-founded the Young Britons' Foundation, the "madrassa" for Tory activists. Campaigned to Leave. "Back Boris" regional coordinator for the South East. Contested Hayes & Harlington, 2017. Board member, Riverside Studios, 2008-19. Ed: Bromsgrove Sch; University of Birmingham (BA political science).

	Electorate	Share %	Change from 2017 %
	83,146		
G Smith C	37,035	58.36	-6.75
S Dorrell LD	16,624	26.20	
D Morgan Lab	7,638	12.04	
A Bell Brexit	1,286	2.03	
N Thompson Ind	681	1.07	-9.63
A Vitiello Eng Dem	194	0.31	

CHALLENGERS
Stephen Dorrell (LD) Tory MP, Loughborough, 1979-97; Charnwood, 1997-2015. Secretary of state for: health, 1995-97; national heritage, 1994-95. Financial secretary to the Treasury, 1992-94. Government whip, 1988-90. Defected to Change UK before joining the Liberal Democrats in August 2019. **David Morgan** (Lab) Local radio presenter in Milton Keynes. Law lecturer. Contested

Blaby, 2005, 2001. **Andrew Bell** (Brexit) Former banker. Son of the former Tory MP Ronald Bell.

CONSTITUENCY PROFILE
From 1997 Buckingham was held by John Bercow, the Commons Speaker from 2009-19. It has elected Conservative MPs for most of the past century but was won by Labour in 1966, 1964 and 1945. Robert Maxwell represented the seat for two terms before he went on to buy Mirror Group Newspapers. It is a large, rural constituency in which almost half the population is aged over 45. Wages are about a fifth higher than the national average.

EU REFERENDUM RESULT

48.9% Leave	Remain 51.1%

Burnley

MAJORITY 1,352 (3.47%) | **CONSERVATIVE GAIN FROM LABOUR** | **TURNOUT 60.59%**

ANTONY HIGGINBOTHAM
BORN Dec 16, 1989
MP 2019-

First Conservative to hold Burnley since 1910. Former banker; before the election he worked for Nat West on Brexit preparations. Former NHS worker. Volunteer at the young offender charity Trailblazers. Pupil referral unit school governor. Former army cadet. First in his family to attend university. Mother was a trade union representative. Ed: University of Hull (BSc politics). Contested Greenwich LBC, 2018.

CHALLENGERS
Julie Cooper (Lab) Burnley MP, 2015-19. Shadow community

	Electorate	Share %	Change from 2017 %
	64,343		
A Higginbotham C	15,720	40.32	+9.35
*J Cooper Lab	14,368	36.86	-9.88
G Birtwistle LD	3,501	8.98	-6.03
S Scott Brexit	3,362	8.62	
C Briggs Burnley	1,162	2.98	
L Fisk Green	739	1.90	+0.75
K Helsby Entwistle Ind	132	0.34	

health minister, 2016-19. PPS to Seema Malhotra, 2015-16. Health and social care cttee, 2015-16. APPG treasurer, adverse childhood experiences. Cllr, Burnley BC, 2005-16; council leader, 2012-14. Contested Burnley, 2010. **Gordon Birtwistle** (LD) Burnley MP, 2010-15. Career in engineering and textile manufacture. Cllr, Burnley BC. Contested Burnley 2017, 2015, 1997, 1992; 1982 for SDP. **Stewart**

Scott (Brexit) Marketing consultant. Contested Hyndburn DC for Ukip, 2016.

CONSTITUENCY PROFILE
Labour had held Burnley in all but two elections in the past century, losing it to the National Liberals in 1931 and the Liberal Democrats in 2010. This east Lancashire constituency, containing the former cotton town of Burnley, has an Asian community of about 10,000. A large proportion of constituents work in manufacturing, with more than 20,000 residents in routine and manual jobs. It suffers from higher than average unemployment.

EU REFERENDUM RESULT
66.6% Leave   Remain 33.4%

Burton

MAJORITY 14,496 (29.74%) | **CONSERVATIVE HOLD** | **TURNOUT 64.96%**

KATE GRIFFITHS
BORN 1971
MP 2019-

Hospitality coordinator at Burton Albion football club. Estranged wife of the former Burton MP Andrew Griffiths, who had the Conservative whip temporarily removed in 2018 after sending more than 2,000 sexually explicit texts to two constituents. Mrs Griffiths rejected support from her estranged husband after he stood aside for her in the constituency's nomination contest. Campaigned on improving high streets. APPG on domestic violence and abuse. Called on Burton's breweries to make a "Brexit beer" to celebrate

	Electorate	Share %	Change from 2017 %
	75,030		
K Griffiths C	29,560	60.65	+2.68
L Walker Lab	15,064	30.91	-6.94
A Wain LD	2,681	5.50	+2.97
K Copeland Green	1,433	2.94	+1.29

Britain leaving the EU. Ed: Derby High Sch; University of Exeter (BA classics).

CHALLENGERS
Louise Walker (Lab) Retired Macmillan chemotherapy specialist nurse. Fought for creation of oncology and chemotherapy unit at Queen's Hospital, Burton. Volunteer with homelessness and domestic abuse charities. **Adam Wain** (LD) IT professional. Contested Derbyshire Mid, 2017. **Kate Copeland** (Green) Worked for

the Globe Foundation's Eco Centre, a community garden.

CONSTITUENCY PROFILE
Burton has mostly elected Conservative MPs for the past century, the exceptions being Labour victories in the 1945 general election and the three elections that the party fought under Tony Blair. The Conservatives' vote share has grown at every election since 2001. The north Staffordshire seat has Burton-upon-Trent in its south and stretches west to Uttoxeter, but is mostly rural. The manufacturing and retail sectors are important sources of employment.

EU REFERENDUM RESULT
64.8% Leave   Remain 35.3%

Bury North

JAMES DALY
BORN Mar 19, 1980
MP 2019-

Legal aid solicitor. Cllr, Bury MBC, 2012-; leader of the Conservative group, 2017-. Tabled a failed emergency motion calling on Bury council to buy Bury Football Club to prevent its expulsion from the EFL in 2019 and pledged to raise the team's troubles in parliament. Board member, Bury Citizens Advice. Law society member. Campaigned to protect the green belt. Contested: Bolton North East, 2017, 2015; Oldham West & Royton by-election, 2015. Ed: Edge Hill University (BA history); University of Leeds (LLM law).

	Electorate	Share %	from 2017 %	Change %
	68,802			
J Daly C		21,660	46.24	+1.76
*J Frith Lab		21,555	46.02	-7.60
G Lloyd-Johnson LD		1,584	3.38	+1.48
A McCarthy Brexit		1,240	2.65	
C Allen Green		802	1.71	

CHALLENGERS
James Frith (Lab) MP, 2017-19. PPS in Labour's shadow housing team, 2018-19. Education select cttee, 2017-19. Founder and director, All Together, a youth unemployment social enterprise. Cllr, Bury MBC, 2011-15. **Gareth Lloyd-Johnson** (LD) Researcher and organiser for MPs, most recently Layla Moran (Oxford West). **Alan McCarthy** (Brexit) Lorry driver. Cllr, Rochdale BC, 2000-. Defected to the Brexit Party in 2019.

CONSTITUENCY PROFILE
The second smallest majority in parliament. Created in 1983, Bury North had been a bellwether seat until James Frith's 2017 victory. The constituency was won by Labour under Tony Blair and by the Tories under Margaret Thatcher, John Major and David Cameron. This Greater Manchester seat covers most of the old mill town of Bury, as well as the market town of Ramsbottom. Unemployment is higher than average, but so are average earnings. A greater than average proportion of residents in this constituency own their own home.

EU REFERENDUM RESULT
53.7% Leave   Remain 46.3%

Bury South

CHRISTIAN WAKEFORD
BORN Nov 9, 1984
MP 2019-

Insurance broker. Cllr, Pendle BC, 2015-; leader of Conservative group, 2019-. Cllr, Lancashire CC, 2013-. Caseworker for Andrew Stephenson (Pendle). "Back Boris" North West coordinator during 2019 leadership campaign. Backed by Ivan Lewis, the former MP and a fellow candidate, during campaign. Ed: Open University (BSc chemistry); University of Lancaster (BA politics).

CHALLENGERS
Lucy Burke (Lab) English lecturer, Manchester Metropolitan University.

	Electorate	Share %	from 2017 %	Change %
	75,152			
C Wakeford C		22,034	43.83	+2.25
L Burke Lab		21,632	43.03	-10.25
R Kilpatrick LD		2,315	4.60	+2.52
A Livesey Brexit		1,672	3.33	
*I Lewis Ind		1,366	2.72	
G Heath Green		848	1.69	
M Boyle Ind		277	0.55	
G Evans Women		130	0.26	

Co-chairwoman of disabled staff forum. **Richard Kilpatrick** (LD) Communications manager. Cllr, Manchester CC, 2018-. Contested: Leigh, 2017; Middlesbrough, 2015. **Andrea Livesey** (Brexit) Retired NHS manager. **Ivan Lewis** (Ind) MP, 1997-2019. Various ministerial roles, 2001-10. Shadow cabinet roles under Ed Miliband. Suspended by Labour

in 2017 over claims of sexual harassment, which he denied. Resigned from party in 2018, citing antisemitism crisis and his continued suspension.

CONSTITUENCY PROFILE
Created in 1983, it initially elected Tories but was held by Labour 1997-2019. As in Bury North, has one of the smallest majorities. Bury South covers a little of the town's southern edge but consists mainly of the former mill towns Radcliffe, Whitefield and Prestwich. The seat has a Jewish population of about 10,000, one of the largest of any constituency. Earnings are lower than the national average.

EU REFERENDUM RESULT
54.5% Leave   Remain 45.5%

Bury St Edmunds

MAJORITY 24,988 (40.33%)   CONSERVATIVE HOLD   TURNOUT 69.11%

JO CHURCHILL
BORN Mar 18, 1964
MP 2015-

Junior health minister, 2019-. Remainer. As assistant whip, 2018-19, it was reported that she had forgotten to vote against an amendment put forward by Dominic Grieve and this helped to frustrate the possibility of a no-deal Brexit. PPS to: Jeremy Hunt, 2017-18; Mike Penning, 2016-17. Select cttees: environmental audit, 2015-16; women and equalities, 2015-17. Exec cttee of Commonwealth Parliamentary Association, 2016-. Survived thyroid and breast cancer. Campaigner for the charity Breast Cancer Now. Cllr, Lincolnshire CC,

	Electorate	Share %	Change from 2017 %
	89,644		
*J Churchill C	37,770	60.96	+1.77
C Waterman Lab	12,782	20.63	-8.89
H Geake Green	9,711	15.67	+11.50
P Hopfensperger Ind	1,694	2.73	+1.36

2013-15. Ed: Dame Alice Harpur Sch; University of Lincoln (BSc business); University of Nottingham (MSc occupational psychology).

CHALLENGERS
Cliff Waterman (Lab) Bikeability instructor and retired teacher. Cllr, W Suffolk DC, 2019-. **Helen Geake** (Green) Archaeologist. Cllr, Mid Suffolk DC, 2019-. Contested this seat, 2017, 2015. **Paul Hopfensperger** (Ind) Deputy mayor, Bury St Edmunds. Cllr: West Suffolk

DC, 2019-; St Edmundsbury BC, 2011-19; Bury St Edmunds TC, 2016-.

CONSTITUENCY PROFILE
Has elected Tory MPs since it became a single-member constituency in 1885, although Labour came within 400 votes in 1997. The Green Party almost tripled its support in 2019, after the Liberal Democrats stood aside. With Bury St Edmunds in the west and the smaller town of Stowmarket in the southeast the constituency also consists of rural Suffolk villages. A higher than average number of residents work in higher managerial jobs.

EU REFERENDUM RESULT
54.0% Leave   Remain 46.0%

Caerphilly

MAJORITY 6,833 (17.03%)   LABOUR HOLD   TURNOUT 63.51%

WAYNE DAVID
BORN Jul 1, 1957
MP 2001-

Remainer who had to apologise in 2016 for saying in a radio interview that the only people in his area who had "coloured skin" ran takeaways. Backed Sir Keir Starmer for leader. Shadow minister: defence, 2016-; cabinet office, 2015-16; Scotland, 2015-16; justice, 2015-16. PPS to: Ed Miliband, 2013-15; constitutional reform, 2011-13; foreign affairs, 2010-11; Wales, 2010. Junior minister for Wales, 2008-10; assistant whip, 2007-08. Select cttees: European scrutiny, 2001-07; Welsh affairs, 2007. Ranked number one in Change.org's 2019 People-Power Index.

	Electorate	Share %	Change from 2017 %
	63,166		
*W David Lab	18,018	44.91	-9.55
J Pratt C	11,185	27.88	+2.67
L Whittle PC	6,424	16.01	+1.58
N Gill Brexit	4,490	11.19	

APPG chairman: role of the House of Lords, Vietnam. MEP, 1989-99. Ed: Cardiff University (BA history and Welsh history, PGCE); Swansea University (economic history).

CHALLENGERS
Jane Pratt (C) Cllr and cabinet member for infrastructure, Monmouthshire CC, 2017-. **Lindsay Whittle** (PC) Former housing manager. Cllr, Caerphilly BC 1976-; leader, 2008-11, 1999-2004. Welsh assembly member, 2011-16.

Contested this seat eight times since 1983. **Nathan Gill** (Brexit) MEP, Wales, 2014-20. Leader, Welsh Ukip, 2014-16.

CONSTITUENCY PROFILE
Has returned Labour MPs for a century but briefly represented by the SDP when the Labour MP defected in 1981. The 2019 and 2017 elections are the only ones since 1931 in which the Conservatives have won more than a quarter of the vote. In 2019 Labour's majority fell to its lowest since 1924. A former industrial area north of Cardiff with a fairly elderly population. About a fifth of residents live in social housing.

EU REFERENDUM RESULT
55.1% Leave   Remain 44.9%

Caithness, Sutherland & Easter Ross

MAJORITY 204 (0.65%) **LIB DEM HOLD** **TURNOUT 67.03%**

JAMIE STONE
BORN Jun 16, 1954
MP 2017-

The Liberal Democrats'
Scotland spokesman in
Westminster, 2019-, 2017.
Defence spokesman, 2017-19.
Said he believed himself to have
been a victim of identity theft in
2018, with details allegedly stolen
by a drug dealer in Manchester.
Three-decade career in local and
Scottish politics: MSP, Caithness,
Sutherland & Ross, 1999-2011;
Holyrood housing spokesman.
Cllr, Highland C, 2012-17, 1995-
99. Cllr, Ross & Cromarty DC,
1986-95. Select cttees: Scottish
affairs, 2019-. Former teacher,
fish gutter and director of
Highland Fine Cheeses. Ed: Tain

	Electorate	Share %	Change from 2017 %
	46,930		
*J Stone LD	11,705	37.21	+1.41
K Rosie SNP	11,501	36.56	+7.38
A Sinclair C	5,176	16.45	-6.17
C McDonald Lab	1,936	6.15	-6.25
S Skinner Brexit	1,139	3.62	

Royal Academy; University of
St Andrews (MA history and
geology).

CHALLENGERS
Karl Rosie (SNP) Worked
in nuclear and oil industries.
Constituency manager for Paul
Monaghan, MP, 2015-17. Cllr,
Highland C, 2017-. Campaigned
for better access to banking
in the Highlands. **Andrew
Sinclair** (C) Cllr, Highland C,
2017-. **Cheryl McDonald** (Lab)
Resettlement officer and former

nurse. Regional police liaison
cttee member.

CONSTITUENCY PROFILE
Created in 1997, this seat
has been won by the Liberal
Democrats at every election
except the SNP's 2015 landslide.
Its predecessor, Caithness &
Sutherland, had been Labour
from 1966 until the defection to
the SDP of its MP, after which
it voted for the SDP and the Lib
Dems. The seat has the sixth
smallest majority in parliament.
It includes the northernmost tip
of mainland Scotland. Much of
the electorate is concentrated in
Easter Ross in the south, where
there is a strong oil industry.

EU REFERENDUM RESULT
51.3% Leave Remain 48.7%

Calder Valley

MAJORITY 5,774 (9.99%) **CONSERVATIVE HOLD** **TURNOUT 72.89%**

CRAIG WHITTAKER
BORN Aug 30, 1962
MP 2010-

Eurosceptic who rebelled to
support the holding of an EU
referendum before it became
Conservative policy. Supported
Remain, but voted for no-deal
in unwhipped indicative votes.
Criticised in 2015 for sharing an
article entitled *Trust Labour?
I'd rather trust Jimmy Savile to
babysit*, partly given his role
at the time on the APPG for
children in care. Founder of the
charity Together for Looked-
after Children. Held three
different roles in government
whips' office during 2017-19
parliament. PPS to: James
Brokenshire, 2015-16; Karen

	Electorate	Share %	Change from 2017 %
	79,287		
*C Whittaker C	29,981	51.88	+5.73
J Fenton-Glynn Lab	24,207	41.89	-3.21
J Bashir LD	2,884	4.99	+1.63
R Phillips Lib	721	1.25	

Bradley, 2016-17. Select cttees:
selection, 2018-19; education,
2010-15. Cllr, Calderdale, MCB,
2003-11; cabinet member 2007-
10. Heptonstall PC, 1998-2003.
Retail manager, 1998-2009. Ed:
Belmont HS.

CHALLENGERS
Josh Fenton-Glynn (Lab)
Oxfam, 2008-09; Child Poverty
Action Group, 2009-10; End
Hunger UK, 2017-. North West
field director, Britain Stronger
In Europe. Cllr, Calderdale
BC, 2016-. **Javed Bashir** (LD)

Innovation adviser, University
of York. Director, Techno Peers,
management consultancy.

CONSTITUENCY PROFILE
A bellwether since its creation
in 1983, Labour was 609 votes
from gaining this seat in 2017.
The Conservative vote has
grown at every election since
2010, although Craig Whittaker's
majority shrank in 2015 and
2017. Calder Valley is a relatively
affluent West Yorkshire seat,
where incomes are higher than
the Yorkshire and Humber
average. More people are
employed in managerial-level
jobs than average and home
ownership is relatively high.

EU REFERENDUM RESULT
53.2% Leave Remain 46.8%

Camberwell & Peckham

MAJORITY 33,780 (59.80%)   LABOUR HOLD   TURNOUT 63.44%

HARRIET HARMAN
BORN Jul 30, 1950
MP 1982-

Prominent feminist and longest continuously serving woman MP. Accused Gordon Brown of sexism after he declined to make her deputy prime minister when she was elected deputy Labour leader, a role she held from 2007-15. Leader of the House of Commons and minister for equality, 2007-10, during which time she was an architect of the Equality Act. Leader of the opposition during leadership elections in 2010 and 2015. Shadow culture secretary, 2011-15; shadow international development secretary, 2010-11. Stood to succeed John Bercow as

	Electorate	Share %	Change from 2017 %
	89,042		
*H Harman Lab	40,258	71.26	-6.53
P Quentin C	6,478	11.47	-1.33
J Ogiehor LD	5,087	9.00	+3.06
C Sheppard Green	3,501	6.20	+3.36
C Cass-Horne Brexit	1,041	1.84	
J Ogunleye WRP	127	0.22	-0.00

Speaker, coming fourth. Recent cttees: liaison, 2015-; human rights, 2015-. Qualified solicitor. Married to Jack Dromey (Birmingham Erdington). Ed: University of York (BA politics).

CHALLENGERS
Peter Quentin (C) Adviser to Lord Hague of Richmond. Associate fellow, RUSI. Army reservist and Fusiliers veteran. **Julia Ogiehor** (LD) Cllr, Haringey BC, 2018-. Spoke out

about suffering racist abuse on public transport.

CONSTITUENCY PROFILE
A very safe Labour seat in south London. Since its creation in 1997 Labour has won at every election, the party's share of the vote falling to a low of 59 per cent in 2010. Its predecessor seat, Peckham, had elected Labour MPs since the Second World War. A densely populated area, fewer than one in twelve residents are 65 or above, less than half the UK average, and more than 30 per cent are under 25. Highest black, African and Caribbean demographic of any seat in the country.

EU REFERENDUM RESULT
31.5% Leave   Remain 68.5%

Camborne & Redruth

MAJORITY 8,700 (17.27%)   CONSERVATIVE HOLD   TURNOUT 71.70%

GEORGE EUSTICE
BORN Sep 28, 1971
MP 2010-

Environment secretary, 2020-, having been the minister for agriculture, fisheries and food since 2015, barring the five months between his resignation in February 2019 over delays to Brexit and his reappointment by Boris Johnson. Junior minister, Defra, 2013-15. Backed Michael Gove for leader in 2019. Environment, food and rural affairs select cttee, 2010-13. Secretary of the APPG for the South West. Portland Communications, 2008-10. Press secretary to David Cameron, 2005-07; Tory head of press, 2003-05. Campaign director,

	Electorate	Share %	Change from 2017 %
	70,250		
*G Eustice C	26,764	53.14	+5.67
P Farmer Lab	18,064	35.86	-8.35
F MacDonald LD	3,504	6.96	+0.81
K La Borde Green	1,359	2.70	+0.53
P Holmes Lib	676	1.34	

No campaign against the euro, 1999-2003. Ukip MEP candidate, 1999. Farming background, having worked in the family fruit business. Ed: Truro Cathedral Sch; Truro Sch; Cornwall Coll.

CHALLENGERS
Paul Farmer (Lab) Film and TV lecturer. Writer and director. Co-founder, A39 Theatre Group. **Florence MacDonald** (LD) Primary school teacher and musician. **Karen La Borde** (Green) Farm owner.

CONSTITUENCY PROFILE
This west Cornwall seat has been won by the Tories since 2010, although George Eustice only narrowly beat the Liberal Democrats in 2010 and Labour in 2017. Camborne & Falmouth, the seat's predecessor, flipped between Labour and the Conservatives during its postwar history. It was represented by Sebastian Coe, the Olympic gold medallist, for the Tories from 1992-97. Labour then took the seat before losing it to the Lib Dems in 2005. Once a prosperous copper and tin mining area, the decline of the industry means that incomes are below average.

EU REFERENDUM RESULT
58.4% Leave   Remain 41.6%

Cambridge

MAJORITY 9,639 (17.94%)   **LABOUR HOLD**   **TURNOUT 67.20%**

DANIEL ZEICHNER
BORN Nov 9, 1956
MP 2015-

Soft-left Remainer who rebelled to vote against triggering Article 50 despite being shadow transport minister, 2015-17. Resigned after the 2017 general election to vote for a pro-single market amendment. Nominated Sir Keir Starmer for leader in 2020. Electoral and Lords reform advocate. Select cttees: transport, 2017-; petitions, 2018-; science and tech, 2015. APPG chairman: bullying; data analytics; east of England; innovation corridor; life sciences. Contested this seat, 2010; Norfolk Mid, 2005, 2001, 1997. National officer, Unison, 2002-15. Ed: Trinity Sch; King's

	Electorate	Share %	from 2017 %	Change
	79,951			
*D Zeichner Lab	25,776	47.97	-3.93	
R Cantrill LD	16,137	30.03	+0.77	
R Perrin C	8,342	15.53	-0.80	
J Caddick Green	2,164	4.03	+1.77	
P Dawe Brexit	1,041	1.94		
M Hurley Ind	111	0.21		
J Robins Soc Dem	91	0.17		
K Garrett Rebooting	67	0.12	-0.11	

Coll, Cambridge (BA history).

CHALLENGERS
Rod Cantrill (LD) Financial consultant. Cllr, Newham LBC, 2004-. Trustee, Wintercomfort for the Homeless. **Russell Perrin** (C) Assistant head teacher. Cllr, Harlow DC, 2008-. **Jeremy Caddick** (Green) Dean, Emmanuel Coll, Cambridge. **Peter Dawe** (Brexit) Trustee,

Dawe Charitable Trust.

CONSTITUENCY PROFILE
Narrowly elected a Labour MP in 2015, having backed the Liberal Democrats in 2010 and 2005. The seat last elected a Tory in 1987. A strongly Remain seat, about 30,000 constituents signed the "revoke Article 50 and remain in the EU" petition. Home to Cambridge University and Anglia Ruskin, the seat also contains high-tech industry. More than one in six adults is in full-time education and Cambridge has among the highest proportions in the country of residents in professional occupations.

EU REFERENDUM RESULT
26.2% Leave   Remain 73.8%

Cambridgeshire North East

MAJORITY 29,993 (56.63%)   **CONSERVATIVE HOLD**   **TURNOUT 63.28%**

STEVE BARCLAY
BORN May 3, 1972
MP 2010-

Chief secretary to the Treasury, 2020-. Brexiteer; became Brexit secretary in 2018 after Dominic Raab resigned over Theresa May's Brexit strategy. Kept in the role after backing Boris Johnson for leader. Health minister, 2018; economic secretary to the Treasury, 2017-18; government whip, 2016-17; assistant whip, 2015-16. Public accounts cttee, 2010-14. Adviser to Liam Fox as Conservative party chairman, 2005. Contested: Lancaster & Wyre, 2001, losing by only 481 votes; Manchester Blackley, 1997. Solicitor. Previous career included positions at Barclays

	Electorate	Share %	from 2017 %	Change
	83,699			
*S Barclay C	38,423	72.55	+8.10	
D Boyd Lab	8,430	15.92	-8.61	
R Moss-Eccardt LD	4,298	8.11	+3.64	
R Johnson Green	1,813	3.42	+1.50	

Bank, the Financial Services Authority, Guardian Royal Exchange and AXA insurance. Served in the army briefly, sponsored through university. Ed: Peterhouse, Cambridge (BA history); Coll of Law, Chester.

CHALLENGERS
Diane Boyd (Lab) Criminal barrister. Involved in shelter and food provisions for the homeless. **Rupert Moss-Eccardt** (LD) Security consultant. Cllr, Cambridgeshire CC, 2005-10. Contested: Norfolk North West,

2017; Norfolk South West, 2015. **Ruth Johnson** (Green) Career in financial services. Contested this seat, 2017.

CONSTITUENCY PROFILE
Has elected Conservative MPs since 1987, having initially been held by the broadcaster and Liberal MP Clement Freud, who was posthumously accused of child sex abuse. Labour reduced the Tory majority to 5,101 in 1997 but the Conservatives have increased their majority at every election since. This is a rural and agricultural area. The seat includes small Indian and Chinese communities. Home ownership levels are fairly high.

EU REFERENDUM RESULT
69.4% Leave   Remain 30.6%

Cambridgeshire North West

MAJORITY 25,983 (40.26%)   **CONSERVATIVE HOLD**   **TURNOUT 67.99%**

SHAILESH VARA
BORN Sep 4, 1960
MP 2005-

Electorate	Share %	from 2017 %	Change
94,909			
*S Vara C	40,307	62.46	+3.81
C Cordiner-Achenbach Lab	14,324	22.20	-8.31
B Smith LD	6,881	10.66	+5.71
N Day Green	3,021	4.68	+2.72

First minister to resign over Theresa May's EU withdrawal agreement in 2018. Voted Remain, against the withdrawal agreement twice and for no-deal in the indicative votes. Junior minister: Northern Ireland, 2018; work and pensions, 2015-16; justice, 2013-16. Assistant whip, 2010-12; shadow deputy leader of the House of Commons, 2006-10. Select cttees: finance and services, 2011-13; administration, 2010-11; environment, food and rural affairs, 2005-06. Party vice-chairman, 2001-05. Stood to succeed John Bercow as Speaker but withdrew before the first

round of voting, endorsing the eventual winner Sir Lindsay Hoyle. Initially backed Dominic Raab for the leadership before supporting Boris Johnson. Contested: Northampton South, 2001; Birmingham Ladywood, 1997. Solicitor and legal adviser. Born in Uganda to Indian parents and moved to Britain aged 4. Ed: Aylesbury GS; Brunel University (LLB law).

CHALLENGERS
Cathy Cordiner-Achenbach (Lab) Teacher. Cllr, Great Yarmouth BC, 2018-. Said she was punched while campaigning in the 2019 European elections. **Bridget Smith** (LD) Former teacher. Author. Cllr, S Cambridgeshire DC, 2008-. Contested this seat, 2017.

CONSTITUENCY PROFILE
This seat has elected Tory MPs since its creation in 1997, with the party's majority rising at every election except 2017. It contains suburban areas to the south of Peterborough, mostly residential developments, and there are pockets of deprivation. Employment levels are high and the constituency includes many affluent rural villages.

EU REFERENDUM RESULT
56.9% Leave   Remain 43.1%

Cambridgeshire South

MAJORITY 2,904 (4.34%)   **CONSERVATIVE HOLD**   **TURNOUT 76.68%**

ANTHONY
BROWNE
BORN Jan 19, 1967
MP 2019-

Electorate	Share %	from 2017 %	Change
87,288			
A Browne C	31,015	46.34	-5.46
I Sollom LD	28,111	42.00	+23.36
D Greef Lab	7,803	11.66	-15.57

Former journalist: chief political correspondent, *The Times*, 2002-07. Covered 9/11 attacks for *The Guardian*. Also worked for the BBC and *The Observer*. Founding columnist, Conservative Home. Wrote columns arguing against holding an EU referendum. Has sought to distance himself from previous comments claiming that immigrants brought "too many germs" and were the "main cause of HIV" in Britain. Later apologised, saying the comments were made when in a "phase of being deliberately contrary". Director, Policy Exchange, 2007-08. Policy director for economic

development under Boris Johnson while he was mayor of London. Chairman, Regulatory Policy Committee. Head of British Bankers' Association, 2012-17, responsible for reforms after the Libor scandal. Board member, Blockchain (cryptocurrency company), 2018-. Ed: Cambridge University (BA mathematics).

CHALLENGERS
Ian Sollom (LD) Cllr, South Cambridgeshire DC. Board member, Greater Cambridgeshire Partnership. **Dan Greef** (Lab) Former teacher. Contested this seat, 2017, 2015.

CONSTITUENCY PROFILE
Won by the Conservatives at every election since its creation in 1997, although the Tory majority is at a record low. The seat's previous MP, Heidi Allen, a rising star in the Tory party who resigned in February 2019 and served as leader of Change UK before joining the Liberal Democrats, announced she would not stand after suffering online abuse. Mostly rural with much of the electorate scattered across small, prosperous villages, the seat also contains one area in the south of Cambridge.

EU REFERENDUM RESULT
38.5% Leave   Remain 61.5%

Cambridgeshire South East

MAJORITY 11,490 (17.85%) CONSERVATIVE HOLD TURNOUT 74.20%

LUCY FRAZER
BORN May 17, 1972
MP 2015-

	Electorate	Share %	Change from 2017 %
	86,769		
*L Frazer C	32,187	49.99	-3.34
P Heylings LD	20,697	32.15	+13.17
J Bull Lab	10,492	16.30	-11.39
E Fordham Ind	1,009	1.57	

Prisons and probation minister since Boris Johnson's first reshuffle in July 2019. Barrister; appointed Queen's Counsel in 2013. Introduced a bill to make "upskirting" an offence in England and Wales, which was passed in 2019. Solicitor-general, 2019. Justice minister, 2018-19. PPS to Ben Gummer (Ipswich), 2016-17. Education select cttee, 2015-17. Campaigned for Remain in the referendum and voted against no-deal in indicative votes. Supported Boris Johnson in the 2019 leadership race. Forced to apologise after jokingly referring in her maiden speech to Oliver Cromwell's sale of Scots into colonial slavery. Ed: Leeds Girls' HS; Newnham Coll, Cambridge (BA law; president of Cambridge Union).

CHALLENGERS
Pippa Heylings (LD) Founder, sustainability company. Cllr, South Cambridgeshire DC, 2018-. Worked in Africa and South America as an expert on governance of natural resources. **James Bull** (Lab) Lifelong trade unionist; regional and local organiser, Unison,

2011-. **Edmund Fordham** (Ind) Physicist and engineer.

CONSTITUENCY PROFILE
A safe Conservative seat since its creation in 1983, with the Liberal Democrats typically coming a distant second. The Conservatives have never received less than 40 per cent of the vote. The constituency covers rural areas between Cambridge and Newmarket. Residents are more likely than average to be economically active, with about two thirds of constituents in employment. A high proportion work in professional jobs and in scientific or technical industries.

EU REFERENDUM RESULT
45.3% Leave Remain 54.7%

Cannock Chase

MAJORITY 19,879 (42.92%) CONSERVATIVE HOLD TURNOUT 61.91%

AMANDA MILLING
BORN Mar 12, 1975
MP 2015-

	Electorate	Share %	Change from 2017 %
	74,813		
*A Milling C	31,636	68.31	+13.33
A Hobbs Lab	11,757	25.39	-12.06
P Woodhead Green	2,920	6.30	+4.60

Chairwoman of the Conservative Party and minister without portfolio since the reshuffle in February 2020. Deputy chief whip, 2019-20; assistant whip, 2018-19. PPS to: Foreign Office, 2017-18; Baroness Anelay of St Johns, 2016-17. Opposed Brexit in 2016 but did not join campaign to Remain; voted for withdrawal agreements every time and for no-deal. Backed Boris Johnson in the 2019 leadership contest. Select cttees: selection, 2019-; arms export controls, 2016; business, 2015-17. Subject to police investigation into 2015 election expenses, but she was cleared and the case dropped. Background in market research, specialising in financial services, including as director and head of clients at Optimisa and director of Quaestor. Cllr, Rossendale BC, 2009-14; deputy group leader. Ed: Moreton Hall Sch; UCL (BSc economics and statistics).

CHALLENGERS
Anne Hobbs (Lab) Retired cardiac nurse. Cllr, Stafford BC, 2019-. **Paul Woodhead** (Green) Environmental consultant and tutor, De Montfort University. Cllr, Cannock Chase DC, 2011-;

group leader. Presenter on a local radio station.

CONSTITUENCY PROFILE
Staffordshire seat held by Labour from its creation in 1997 until the Conservatives won it in one of the biggest swings of the 2010 election. The party's majority has increased at every election since. In 2019 the Liberal Democrats stood aside for the Green Party. The constituency's predecessor, Cannock Chase & Burntwood, elected Conservatives from 1983 before being gained by Labour in 1992. Not an affluent constituency and the main sources of jobs include construction and manufacturing.

EU REFERENDUM RESULT
68.9% Leave Remain 31.1%

Canterbury

MAJORITY 1,836 (3.05%)   **LABOUR HOLD**   **TURNOUT 74.95%**

ROSIE DUFFIELD
BORN Jul 1, 1971
MP 2017-

Held on to the seat, which she gained in one of the most unexpected results of the 2017 election. Remainer and second referendum campaigner. Backed Jess Phillips for leader, 2020. Spoke in parliament during debate on a domestic abuse bill about her experience of an abusive partner. Chairwoman, Women's Parliamentary Labour Party, 2019-. PPS to Dawn Butler (Brent Central), 2017-18. Select cttees: work and pensions, 2018-; women and equalities, 2017-18. APPGs: civic societies; homelessness; net zero; single-parent families. Co-founder,

	Electorate	Share %	from 2017 %	Change %
	80,203			
*R Duffield Lab	29,018	48.27	+3.25	
A Firth C	27,182	45.22	+0.53	
C Malcomson LD	3,408	5.67	-2.36	
M Gould Ind	505	0.84		

Canterbury Action Network. Former teaching assistant; turned to writing political satire full-time in 2016. Animal rights campaigner. Ed: Guy's Hospital (YTS).

CHALLENGERS
Anna Firth (C) Career in financial services before retraining as barrister; Hailsham Chambers, 2005-. Cllr, Sevenoaks DC, 2019-, 2011-15. Contested Erith & Thamesmead, 2015. **Claire Malcomson** (LD) Actor and singer; started a

Leatherhead theatre company in 2002. Cllr: Mole Valley DC, 2019-; Surrey CC, 2017-.

CONSTITUENCY PROFILE
Historically a safe Conservative seat. The party had claimed it continuously from 1874 until Labour's surprise victory in 2017. Before that the postwar low points for the Conservatives had been in 1997 and 2001, when their majority fell below 10,000. The seat contains the relatively economically active cathedral town and the largest campus of the University of Kent. Surrounding villages and towns include the seaside resort of Whitstable.

EU REFERENDUM RESULT
45.3% Leave   Remain 54.7%

Cardiff Central

MAJORITY 17,179 (41.08%)   **LABOUR HOLD**   **TURNOUT 65.31%**

JO STEVENS
BORN Sep 6, 1966
MP 2015-

Human rights lawyer; former director, Thompsons Solicitors. Resigned from the shadow cabinet to vote against triggering Article 50 in 2017. Introduced a bill to register voters automatically. Nominated Sir Keir Starmer for the leadership, 2020. Shadow Welsh secretary, 2016-17. Shadow solicitor-general for England and Wales, 2016. Shadow justice minister, 2016. Chairwoman, GMB parliamentary group. Select cttees: culture, 2017-; justice, 2017; business, 2015-16; standards, 2015-16; privileges, 2015-16. Chairwoman,

	Electorate	Share %	from 2017 %	Change %
	64,037			
*J Stevens Lab	25,605	61.22	-1.19	
M Jenkins C	8,426	20.15	+0.34	
B Molik LD	6,298	15.06	+1.64	
G Pearce Brexit	1,006	2.41		
S Caiach Gwlad	280	0.67		
A Kata Ind	119	0.28		
B Johnson SPGB	88	0.21		

occupational health and safety APPG. Ed: Elfred HS; University of Manchester (LLB law); Manchester Poly (solicitors' professional examination).

CHALLENGERS
Meirion Jenkins (C) International trade adviser, UK Trade & Investment, 2008-. Cllr, Birmingham City C, 2012-. Contested: Bridgend, 2015; Birmingham Yardley,

2010. **Bablin Molik** (LD) Chief executive, Sight Cymru, a sight support charity. Cllr, Cardiff City C, 2017-. **Gareth Pearce** (Brexit) Architect.

CONSTITUENCY PROFILE
Created in 1983 and initially held by the Conservatives before Labour won in 1992. Held by the Liberal Democrats from 2005 to 2015. The smallest and most densely populated seat in Cardiff. Home to about 24,000 full-time students, who make up more than a quarter of the population. One of the more diverse Welsh seats: about 10 per cent of residents are Asian or of Asian descent.

EU REFERENDUM RESULT
32.0% Leave   Remain 68.0%

Cardiff North

ANNA MCMORRIN
BORN Sep 23, 1971
MP 2017-

Climate change and sustainability campaigner. Voted for a second Brexit referendum and to revoke Article 50. PPS to Barry Gardiner (Brent North), 2017-18, but resigned to rebel in a vote on membership of the single market. Nominated Sir Keir Starmer for leader, 2020. Select cttees: Welsh affairs, 2017-; environmental audit, 2017-. APPGs: climate change; future generations; net zero. Adviser to Welsh government on environment and sustainability, 2008-14. Campaigns and communications officer, Friends of the Earth; climate

Electorate	Share %	from 2017 %	Change
68,438			
*A McMorrin Lab	26,064	49.49	-0.65
M Ali C	19,082	36.23	-5.88
R Taylor LD	3,580	6.80	+3.50
S Webb PC	1,606	3.05	-0.29
C Butler Brexit	1,311	2.49	
M Cope Green	820	1.56	
R Jones Ind	203	0.39	

change negotiator, the UN. Ed: University of Southampton (BA French and politics); Cardiff University (PG Dip journalism).

CHALLENGERS
Mo Ali (C) Child refugee from Somaliland, raised by a single mother on a Cardiff estate. Senior account manager, M&C Saatchi. Volunteer adviser on counterterrorism, Metropolitan Police. **Rhys Taylor** (LD) Cllr,

Cardiff City C, 2017-. **Steffan Webb** (PC) Teacher. **Chris Butler** (Brexit) Conservative MP for Warrington South, 1987-92; former special adviser to Margaret Thatcher. Lobbyist.

CONSTITUENCY PROFILE
Until recently a bellwether seat, with the party of government holding it from 1979 to 2015, when it was regained by Labour. The Conservatives had won it with small majorities at the previous two elections. Cardiff North contains the largest hospital in Wales and about 8,000 students, meaning that health and education are big sources of employment.

EU REFERENDUM RESULT
39.1% Leave   Remain 60.9%

Cardiff South & Penarth

STEPHEN DOUGHTY
BORN Apr 15, 1980
MP 2012-

Jeremy Corbyn critic who resigned from the shadow cabinet on live television in 2016. Supported a second Brexit referendum and revoking Article 50. Called on tech companies to tackle online abuse. Supported leadership bids of: Sir Keir Starmer, 2020; Owen Smith, 2016; Liz Kendall, 2015. Shadow minister, Foreign Office, 2015-16; quit in protest at the sacking of Pat McFadden (Wolverhampton South East). Shadow business minister, 2015; opposition whip, 2013-15. Select cttees: home affairs, 2017-; international development,

Electorate	Share %	from 2017 %	Change
78,837			
*S Doughty Lab Co-op	27,382	54.14	-5.35
P Broom C	14,645	28.95	-1.24
D Schmeising LD	2,985	5.90	+3.08
N Adam PC	2,386	4.72	+0.46
T Price Brexit	1,999	3.95	
K Barker Green	1,182	2.34	+1.29

2016-17; arms export controls, 2016-17. Co-chairman, LGBT+ group of Labour MPs. Chairman, HIV/Aids APPG. Adviser to Douglas Alexander, international development secretary, 2009-10. Former head of Oxfam Cymru. Ed: Llantwit Major Comp Sch; Corpus Christi Coll, Oxford (BA PPE); St Andrews University.

CHALLENGERS
Philippa Broom (C) Consultant. Director, Conservative Party

international office, 2001-15. Cllr, Spelthorne BC, 2007-15. Head of appeals, NSPCC Wales, 1992-2001. **Dan Schmeising** (LD) Cardiff University graduate. **Nasir Adam** (PC) PhD in geography and planning.

CONSTITUENCY PROFILE
A safe Labour seat for seven decades. Represented for many years by James Callaghan, the Labour prime minister from 1976 to 1979. This coastal area is the least affluent Cardiff seat by income. Home ownership is well below average, with more than a fifth of households privately rented, and there is relatively high unemployment.

EU REFERENDUM RESULT
42.8% Leave   Remain 57.2%

Cardiff West

MAJORITY 10,986 (23.79%)   **LABOUR HOLD**   **TURNOUT 67.40%**

KEVIN BRENNAN
BORN Oct 16, 1959
MP 2001-

	Electorate	Share %	from 2017 %	Change %
	68,508			
*K Brennan Lab	23,908	51.77	-4.90	
C Webster C	12,922	27.98	-1.77	
B Clack PC	3,864	8.37	-1.11	
C Littlemore LD	2,731	5.91	+3.31	
N Mullins Brexit	1,619	3.51		
D Griffin Green	1,133	2.45		

Shadow culture minister, 2016-. Researcher for his predecessor Rhodri Morgan, 1995-2001. Ran the "Yes for Wales" devolution campaign. Nominated Lisa Nandy for leader, 2020. Critical of Jeremy Corbyn and backed Owen Smith in 2016. Shadow minister: business, 2015-16, 2010; education, 2010-15. Minister: education, 2009-10; business, 2010. Whip, 2006-07; assistant whip, 2005-06. Select cttees: public administration, 2010-11, 2001-05. APPG chairman: folk arts (chairman); music (co-chairman). Guitarist in the cross-party parliamentary rock band MP4. Cllr, Cardiff City C, 1991-2001. Economics teacher, 1985-1994. Ed: St Alban's RC Comp Sch, Pontypool; Pembroke Coll, Oxford (BA PPE; president, Oxford Union); Cardiff University (PGCE); University of Glamorgan (MSc education and management).

CHALLENGERS
Caroline Webster (C) Career in event logistics and construction. Cllr, Bridgend BC, 2017-. **Boyd**

Clack (PC) Canadian-born writer and actor; appeared in films including *Twin Town*. **Callum Littlemore** (LD) Parliamentary assistant, Jane Dodds MP.

CONSTITUENCY PROFILE
Has returned a Labour MP since its creation in 1950, with two exceptions: the first in 1979, when it returned the sitting Speaker, and the second in 1983, when the Conservatives narrowly won it. The constituency has the smallest population of full-time students of any Cardiff seat. Home ownership is slightly below the Welsh average.

EU REFERENDUM RESULT
43.8% Leave   Remain 56.2%

Carlisle

MAJORITY 8,319 (19.40%)   **CONSERVATIVE HOLD**   **TURNOUT 65.85%**

JOHN STEVENSON
BORN Jul 4, 1963
MP 2010-

	Electorate	Share %	from 2017 %	Change %
	65,105			
*J Stevenson C	23,659	55.18	+5.31	
R Alcroft Lab	15,340	35.78	-8.05	
J Aglionby LD	2,829	6.60	+3.68	
F Mills UKIP	1,045	2.44	-0.94	

Qualified solicitor and partner, Bendles and Tiffen Estate Agents. Backed Theresa May's withdrawal agreement every time; supported soft Brexit options in indicative votes. Remainer in 2016. Backed Michael Gove for the leadership in 2019. Member, 1922 exec cttee, 2017-. Select cttees: privileges, 2017-; standards, 2017-; Scottish affairs, 2015-16; housing, 2012-15. APPG chairman: family business; food and drink manufacturing; inheritance and intergenerational fairness; West Coast mainline. Cllr, Carlisle City C, 1999-2010. Ed: Aberdeen GS;

Dundee University (MA history and politics); Chester Coll of Law (LLB).

CHALLENGERS
Ruth Alcroft (Lab) Supply teacher. Cllr, Carlisle City C, 2016-; previously a councillor on Rossendale BC. **Julia Aglionby** (LD) Chartered surveyor; professor, University of Cumbria. Former board member, Natural England. **Fiona Mills** (Ukip) NHS accountant. Chairwoman, Ukip Cumbria. Party spokeswoman, health. Contested:

this seat, 2017, 2015; European parliament, 2019.

CONSTITUENCY PROFILE
First won by Labour in 1922 before flipping between the two main parties until 1964. Labour then held the seat until 2010, when the Conservatives gained it by a narrow margin. The party has increased its vote share at every election since. Only a few miles from the Scottish border, Carlisle itself contains the main campus of the University of Cumbria. Part-time, routine and semi-routine work is more common in this constituency than nationally and there are high levels of poor health.

EU REFERENDUM RESULT
60.6% Leave   Remain 39.4%

Carmarthen East & Dinefwr

MAJORITY 1,809 (4.41%)   **PLAID CYMRU HOLD**   **TURNOUT 71.42%**

JONATHAN EDWARDS
BORN Apr 26, 1976
MP 2010-

	Electorate	Share %	from 2017 % Change
	57,407		
*J Edwards PC	15,939	38.87	-0.43
H Hughes C	14,130	34.46	+8.19
M Carroll Lab	8,622	21.03	-8.75
P Prosser Brexit	2,311	5.64	

Dubbed "the member for Wales" for his strong criticism of Westminster and for being one of the party's main strategic thinkers. Was chief of staff to Adam Price, this seat's MP 2001-10 who joined the Welsh assembly in 2016 and became the party's leader, 2018-. Supported Conservative plans to relax the foxhunting ban in 2017, saying that he was reflecting the views of his agricultural constituents. Plaid Cymru Westminster spokesman: transport, 2010-; Treasury, 2010-; business, 2010-; foreign intervention, 2015-. Spokesman for culture, Wales and housing, 2010-15. Ed: Ysgol Gymraeg Rhydaman; Ysgol Gyfun Maes yr Yrfa; University of Wales, Aberystwyth (BA history and politics; MA international history).

CHALLENGERS
Harvard Hughes (C) Chief executive, the lobbying firm Barndoor Strategy. Previously: associate, financial conduct authority; campaign director, Electoral Reform Society. Chairman, Northwest London Conservatives, 2014-17.

Contested this seat in 2017. **Maria Carroll** (Lab) Contested Carmarthenshire CC, 2017. **Peter Prosser** (Brexit) Firefighter. Narrowly won back deposit by achieving 5 per cent of the vote.

CONSTITUENCY PROFILE
Created in 1997, this seat was initially held by Labour before being gained by Plaid Cymru in 2001. The predecessor seat of Carmarthen elected only Labour MPs from 1979 and Labour last finished in third place in 1923. The Liberal Democrats stood aside for Plaid in 2019. More than a fifth of residents are aged 65 or over and three quarters of households are owner-occupied.

EU REFERENDUM RESULT
53.2% Leave   Remain 46.8%

Carmarthen West & Pembrokeshire South

MAJORITY 7,745 (18.39%)   **CONSERVATIVE HOLD**   **TURNOUT 71.83%**

SIMON HART
BORN Aug 15, 1963
MP 2010-

	Electorate	Share %	from 2017 % Change
	58,629		
*S Hart C	22,183	52.67	+5.85
M Tierney Lab	14,438	34.28	-5.17
R Thomas PC	3,633	8.63	-0.69
A Cameron LD	1,860	4.42	+2.15

Appointed Welsh secretary in February 2020 reshuffle. Cabinet Office minister, 2019-20. Remainer in the referendum, but voted for Theresa May's withdrawal agreements as a backbencher. Backed Boris Johnson for leader, 2019. Vocal against abuse faced by politicians. Supports foxhunting. Chairman, Countryside Alliance, 2015-19; chief executive, 2003-10. Was criticised for continuing to work with the campaign group while serving on the environment committee, 2015-17. Other select cttees: standards, 2017; privileges, 2017; culture, 2017; Welsh affairs, 2012-15. Worked as a chartered surveyor in Carmarthen. Served with the TA for seven years. Ed: Radley College; Royal Agricultural College, Cirencester.

CHALLENGERS
Marc Tierney (Lab) Manager at Radio Pembrokeshire and involved with the community media project Cleddau Radio. Previous charity work providing respite for those affected by the Chernobyl nuclear disaster. **Rhys Thomas** (PC) Consultant anaesthetist. Retired army medical officer. World Iron Man representative for Wales. **Alistair Cameron** (LD) English teacher. Contested: this seat, 2017; Tewkesbury, 2015, 2010, 2005.

CONSTITUENCY PROFILE
A coastal seat created in 1997 from parts of the marginal seats of Pembroke and Carmarthen, and a bellwether since then. Held by Labour from 1997-2010 but by the Conservatives ever since. This constituency has a higher than average proportion of retirees, and residents are more likely to be self-employed than the national average. There are high levels of poor health.

EU REFERENDUM RESULT
55.2% Leave   Remain 44.8%

Carshalton & Wallington

MAJORITY 629 (1.28%)   **CONSERVATIVE GAIN FROM LIB DEM**   **TURNOUT 67.33%**

ELLIOT COLBURN
BORN Aug 6, 1992
MP 2019-

Brought to an end more than 20 years of Liberal Democrat dominance in this seat. Public affairs officer, South West London Health and Care Partnership, 2018-19. Parliamentary assistant, 2015-18. Voted Leave. LGBT rights campaigner who faced homophobic abuse during the campaign. Supported reforming the Gender Recognition Act in favour of trans rights. Cllr, Sutton BC, 2018-. Ed: Carshalton Boys Sports College; Aberystwyth University (law with politics; MA postcolonial politics).

	Electorate	Share %	from 2017 %	Change
	72,926			
E Colburn C	20,822	42.41	+4.09	
*T Brake LD	20,193	41.13	+0.11	
A Wattoo Lab	6,081	12.39	-6.06	
J Woudhuysen Brexit	1,043	2.12		
T Hague Green	759	1.55	+0.56	
A Dickenson CPA	200	0.41	+0.03	

CHALLENGERS
Tom Brake (LD) MP for this seat, 1997-2019. Party spokesman, Brexit and trade, 2017-19. Chief whip, shadow Commons leader and foreign affairs spokesman, 2015-17. Treasury whip, 2014-15. Deputy leader of the Commons, 2012-15. First contested the seat in 1992. Former computer software consultant, Hoskyns. Cllr: Sutton BC, 1994-97; Hackney LBC, 1988-90. Schooled in France before

a degree in physics at Imperial College, London. **Ahmad Wattoo** (Lab) Criminal duty solicitor. **James Woudhuysen** (Brexit) Technology consultant and visiting professor, London South Bank University.

CONSTITUENCY PROFILE
Created in 1983, this south London constituency bordering Surrey was the only seat in all of London and the southeast to elect a Liberal Democrat MP in 2015. It had elected Conservative MPs before it was won by Tom Brake in 1997. Consistently marginal, the largest majority came when the Lib Dems won by 5,260 votes in 2010.

EU REFERENDUM RESULT
56.3% Leave   Remain 43.7%

Castle Point

MAJORITY 26,634 (60.15%)   **CONSERVATIVE HOLD**   **TURNOUT 63.58%**

REBECCA HARRIS
BORN Dec 22, 1967
MP 2010-

Government whip, 2018-; assistant whip, 2017-18. Voted to leave the EU; backed Theresa May's withdrawal agreements and supported no-deal in the indicative votes. Championed a daylight-saving bill in 2012 that would have moved Britain to Central European Time. PPS to: Theresa Villiers (Chipping Barnet), 2016-17; Sajid Javid (Bromsgrove), 2016-17. Select cttees: selection, 2018; regulatory reform, 2012-17; business, 2010-15. Marketing executive at Phillimore & Co, publishers of British local history, 1997-2007. In 2001 she took a sabbatical

	Electorate	Share %	from 2017 %	Change
	69,643			
*R Harris C	33,971	76.72	+9.45	
K Curtis Lab	7,337	16.57	-8.49	
J Howson LD	2,969	6.71	+4.36	

to work in the Conservative research department, focusing on the foot and mouth epidemic. Campaigned against green belt development. Cllr, Chichester DC, 1999-2003. Former House of Commons caseworker. Ed: Bedales Sch; London School of Economics (BSc government).

CHALLENGERS
Katie Curtis (Lab) Events manager, Progress, the New Labour campaigning group. Contested Epping Forest, 2010. **John Howson** (LD) Founding trustee, charity for children

with parents in prison. Cllr, Oxfordshire CC, 2013-. Twice stood for police and crime commissioner. Contested Banbury, 2015.

CONSTITUENCY PROFILE
Labour has held this coastal Essex seat, between Basildon and Southend-on-Sea, for only one term, winning it in 1997 before narrowly losing it to the Conservatives in 2001. Bob Spink, MP in 1992-97 and 2001-10, was the first to represent Ukip in parliament after his defection in 2008. Rebecca Harris's majority has grown at every election since 2010. Very high levels of home ownership.

EU REFERENDUM RESULT
72.7% Leave   Remain 27.3%

Ceredigion

MAJORITY 6,329 (15.78%)   PLAID CYMRU HOLD   TURNOUT 71.30%

BEN LAKE
BORN Jan 22, 1993
MP 2017-

Plaid Cymru's youngest ever MP when first elected aged 24. He has been a party spokesman for: environment, education, skills, health, communities, local goverment, culture and constitutional affairs. Welsh affairs select cttee, 2017-. APPG chairman, Western Sahara; vice-chairman: hill farming, university, youth employment. Has been vocal about concerns over the potential impact of Brexit on rural areas. Former press officer to the Welsh assembly member Elin Jones. Ed: Lampeter Comprehensive Sch; Trinity Coll, Oxford (BA history).

	Electorate	Share %	from 2017 % Change
	56,250		
*B Lake PC	15,208	37.92	+8.69
A Jenner C	8,879	22.14	+3.76
M Williams LD	6,975	17.39	-11.57
D Mulholland Lab	6,317	15.75	4.41
G James Brexit	2,063	5.14	
C Simpson Green	663	1.65	+0.29

CHALLENGERS
Amanda Jenner (C) Solicitor turned teacher. Cllr, Powys CC, 2017-; health and care scrutiny cttee. **Mark Williams** (LD) MP for this seat, 2005-17. Former teacher. Leader of the Welsh Liberal Democrats and the party's Wales spokesman, 2016-17, and innovation, universities and skills spokesman, 2007-10. Was the first non-Welsh speaker to hold the seat since 1867. Majority grew from 219 in

2005 to 8,000 in 2010. **Dinah Mulholland** (Lab) Worked in learning support at University of Wales, Trinity St David. Contested this seat, 2017. **Gethin James** (Brexit) Contested this seat for Ukip, 2017.

CONSTITUENCY PROFILE
Plaid Cymru is establishing dominance in this western seat after the Liberal Democrats won it in the three elections before 2017. The Conservatives have historically done poorly here; the last time they came second was in 1979. The coastal town of Aberystwyth contains a university and about 3,000 students live in the constituency.

EU REFERENDUM RESULT
45.4% Leave   Remain 54.6%

Charnwood

MAJORITY 22,397 (40.45%)   CONSERVATIVE HOLD   TURNOUT 69.59%

EDWARD ARGAR
BORN Dec 9, 1977
MP 2015-

Party loyalist. Appointed health minister by Boris Johnson in 2019 despite having backed Sajid Javid in the Conservative leadership election. Voted to remain in the EU but toed government line on Brexit in parliament. Appointment as justice minister, 2018-19, caused controversy because of his past job as a lobbyist for Serco, an outsourcing company that runs prisons. PPS to: Sajid Javid (Bromsgrove), 2019; Nick Gibb (Bognor Regis & Littlehampton), 2015-19. Cllr, Westminster City C, 2006-15; tried and failed to become leader, 2012. Contested

	Electorate	Share %	from 2017 % Change
	79,556		
*E Argar C	35,121	63.44	+3.05
G Godden Lab	12,724	22.98	-7.79
K Tipton LD	4,856	8.77	+5.05
L Needham Green	2,664	4.81	+2.93

Oxford East, 2010. Ed: Harvey GS; Oriel Coll, Oxford (BA history; MSt historical research).

CHALLENGERS
Gary Godden (Lab) Apprenticeships co-ordinator and former policy officer, GMB. Former police officer. Contested European parliament, 2019. **Kate Tipton** (LD) Deputy head and maths teacher, Scarborough Coll. Former housemistress at Framlingham Coll. **Laurie Needham** (Green) Cllr, Charnwood BC, 2019-.

CONSTITUENCY PROFILE
A safe Conservative seat in which the party's majority has dipped below 6,000 only in 1997, the year it was created, amid Tony Blair's national landslide victory. Held until 2015 by Stephen Dorrell, a Conservative health secretary under John Major. The constituency is made up mainly of satellite towns located between Leicester and Loughborough. It has a greater proportion of those aged 65 or over than the national average. There is also a significant population of Asians, who are mostly of Indian descent and comprise about one in ten residents.

EU REFERENDUM RESULT
57.9% Leave   Remain 42.1%

Chatham & Aylesford

MAJORITY 18,540 (42.78%)   CONSERVATIVE HOLD   TURNOUT 60.50%

TRACEY CROUCH
BORN Jul 24, 1975
MP 2010-

	Electorate	Share %	from 2017 %	Change
	71,642			
*T Crouch C	28,856	66.58	+9.58	
V Maple Lab	10,316	23.80	-9.90	
D Naghi LD	2,866	6.61	+4.13	
G Wilkinson Green	1,090	2.51	+1.24	
J Gibson CPA	212	0.49	-0.09	

Moderniser and self-described One Nation Conservative. Culture minister, 2015-18, but resigned over delays to measures to curb the use of fixed-odds betting terminals. Did not declare her vote in the EU referendum; voted against Theresa May's withdrawal agreement in first meaningful vote. Backed Boris Johnson for leader, 2019. One of two Tories to abstain in tuition fees vote. Opposed press regulations. Anti-foxhunting and called badger-culling barbaric. Select cttees: culture, 2012-15; political and constitutional reform, 2013-15.

Would-be lawyer who shunned being a solicitor for a political career. Lobbyist, Aviva, 2005-10. Football enthusiast: FA-qualified coach. First Tory minister to take maternity leave, 2016. Ed: University of Hull (LLB law and politics).

CHALLENGERS
Vince Maple (Lab) Cllr, Medway C, 2011-; leader of Labour and Co-operative group. Former regional organiser, GMB. **David Naghi** (LD) Self-employed

builder. Cllr, Maidstone BC, 2002-. **Geoff Wilkinson** (Green) Managing director, construction consultancy.

CONSTITUENCY PROFILE
A compact seat in Kent held by Labour after its creation in 1997 before being taken by the Conservatives in 2010. The Conservative vote share has not fallen below 50 per cent since. The constituency contains most of Chatham and further to the south are smaller towns and villages including Snodland, Ditton and Aylesford. About a third of residents are under 25 and the seat has a below-average proportion of over-65s.

EU REFERENDUM RESULT
63.9% Leave   Remain 36.1%

Cheadle

MAJORITY 2,336 (4.18%)   CONSERVATIVE HOLD   TURNOUT 74.90%

MARY ROBINSON
BORN Aug 23, 1955
MP 2015-

	Electorate	Share %	from 2017 %	Change
	74,639			
*M Robinson C	25,694	45.96	+1.38	
T Morrison LD	23,358	41.78	+5.46	
Z Chauhan Lab	6,851	12.26	-6.83	

Owned an accountancy practice with her husband until it went into administration. Supported Remain and voted with Theresa May's government on every meaningful vote on Brexit. Backed Sajid Javid for leader, 2019. Select cttees: European statutory instruments, 2018-; administration, 2017-; housing, 2017-. APPG vice-chairwoman: Rohingya; sales; women in parliament. Investigated over alleged overspending in the 2015 election, but cleared and no charges were brought. Founded a fashion design business with her daughter in 2012, although

the company has since become dormant. Cllr, South Ribble BC, 2007-13. Ed: Leyton Hill Convent Sch; Preston Polytechnic (accountancy foundation); Lancashire Polytechnic (LLB law).

CHALLENGERS
Tom Morrison (LD) Former community engagement adviser, Liberal Democrats. Cllr: Stockport MBC, 2019-; Liverpool City C, 2010-14. Contested St Helens North, 2017. **Zahid Chauhan** (Lab) Doctor. Cllr, Oldham MBC, 2013-; cabinet

member, health and social care, 2018-.

CONSTITUENCY PROFILE
Has for the most part elected Conservative MPs since its creation in 1950. It was won by the Liberals in 1966 and by the Liberal Democrats from 2001 until the party's collapse in 2015. Cheadle is on the southern edge of Greater Manchester, bordering the Cheshire seats of Macclesfield and Tatton. More than a fifth of residents are aged 65 or above and the seat has an Asian population of about 7,000. About five in six households are owner-occupied, one of the highest proportions of any seat.

EU REFERENDUM RESULT
42.7% Leave   Remain 57.3%

Chelmsford

MAJORITY 17,621 (30.85%)   CONSERVATIVE HOLD   TURNOUT 70.98%

VICKY FORD
BORN Sep 21, 1967
MP 2017-

	Electorate	Share %	from 2017 % Change
	80,481		
*V Ford C	31,934	55.90	+2.22
M Goldman LD	14,313	25.06	+12.89
P Richards Lab	10,295	18.02	-11.79
M Lawrence Loony	580	1.02	

Appointed a junior education minister in the February 2020 reshuffle. Vice-president, loan syndication at JP Morgan. MEP, 2009-17; chairwoman, internal market and consumer affairs cttee, 2014-17. Bureau of the European Conservative and Reformist Group; lead negotiator, inter-group political discussions. Supported Jeremy Hunt in 2019 leadership race. Select cttees: European statutory instruments, 2018-; women and equalities, 2018-; science and technology, 2017-. Chairwoman, women in parliament APPG. Member: bees; plastic waste;

climate change APPGs. Cllr, South Cambridgeshire DC, 2006-09. Contested Birmingham Northfield, 2005. Born and raised in Northern Ireland. Ed: Trinity Coll, Cambridge (BSc maths and economics).

CHALLENGERS
Marie Goldman (LD) Cllr, Chelmsford City C, 2019-; deputy leader. Co-founded Piktical, a digital ticket-selling services provider. Director, Red Glazing Systems and the IT consultancy Making Solutions.

Contested European parliament, 2019. **Penny Richards** (Lab) Immigration compliance officer, Cats colleges. Contested Chelmsford City C, 2019.

CONSTITUENCY PROFILE
This Essex constituency has not elected anyone other than a Conservative since 1924. Having been split between two Conservative-held seats from 1997, Chelmsford was re-created in 2010 and the party's vote share has grown at every election since. Its MP for more than two decades was Norman St John-Stevas, a minister in Margaret Thatcher's government.

EU REFERENDUM RESULT
50.7% Leave   Remain 49.3%

Chelsea & Fulham

MAJORITY 11,241 (24.00%)   CONSERVATIVE HOLD   TURNOUT 69.77%

GREG HANDS
BORN Nov 14, 1965
MP 2005-

	Electorate	Share %	from 2017 % Change
	67,110		
*G Hands C	23,345	49.86	-2.79
N Horlick LD	12,104	25.85	+14.87
M Uberoi Lab	10,872	23.22	-9.99
S Morland AWP	500	1.07	

Minister in the Department for International Trade, 2020-. Former City banker who speaks five languages. Has British and American dual nationality. Trade and investment minister, 2016-18. Backed Jeremy Hunt for leader, 2019. Supported Remain but voted for Theresa May's deal on second and third attempts. Co-chairman of the Alternative Arrangements Commission, which sought to replace the Irish backstop with a technological solution. Chief secretary to the Treasury, 2015-16; deputy chief whip, 2013-15; assistant whip, 2011-13; PPS to George Osborne,

2010-11. Member: Conservative Way Forward; Conservative Friends of Israel. Former president, Conservative Friends of Poland. Ed: Dr Challoner's GS; Robinson Coll, Cambridge (BA history).

CHALLENGERS
Nicola Horlick (LD) Chief executive, Money and Co; Bramdean Asset Management. Advisory board member, Red Badger consultancy. **Matt Uberoi** (Lab) Imprisoned aged 21 after being found guilty of

insider dealing while interning at a bank; discovered to have been sending tips to his father. Cllr, Hammersmith & Fulham LBC, 2018-; vice-chairman, planning development and control cttee.

CONSTITUENCY PROFILE
No party other than the Conservatives has represented any incarnation of this seat since 1910. Situated on the north bank of the Thames in west London, it has one of the highest average incomes in the country, rivalled only by the neighbouring constituencies of Cities of London & Westminster and Kensington. The average property price is £950,000.

EU REFERENDUM RESULT
29.1% Leave   Remain 70.9%

Cheltenham

MAJORITY 981 (1.65%)   CONSERVATIVE HOLD   TURNOUT 73.24%

ALEX CHALK
BORN Aug 8, 1976
MP 2015-

	Electorate	Share %	Change from 2017 %
	81,043		
*A Chalk C	28,486	47.99	+1.31
M Wilkinson LD	27,505	46.34	+4.16
G Penny Lab	2,921	4.92	-4.56
G Ridgeon Loony	445	0.75	

Junior minister in the Ministry of Justice and asssistant whip, 2020-. Barrister who represented journalists during the phone-hacking scandal and prosecuted terrorism offences. Supported Matt Hancock for leader in 2019. Advocate for legal aid. Campaigned to change minimum sentence for stalking from five to ten years. Tried to enshrine in law that the UK should be carbon-neutral by 2050. Remainer who supported Theresa May's Brexit deal. Member: Criminal Bar Association; Serious Fraud Office Panel of Counsel. APPG chairman: cyber security; pro bono. Justice select cttee, 2015-. Cllr, Hammersmith & Fulham LBC, 2006-14. Ed: Magdalen Coll, Oxford (BA modern history); City, University of London (GDL); Inns of Court.

CHALLENGERS
Max Wilkinson (LD) Cllr, Cheltenham BC, 2014-; chairman of the standards committee. Senior account manager, Camargue, a communications agency. Clean air activist. Led campaigns to declare

Cheltenham a "Remain town" and to name it one of the country's cities of sanctuary for refugees. Former journalist. Contested Stroud, 2017. **George Penny** (Lab) Twenty-two-year-old law graduate.

CONSTITUENCY PROFILE
Relatively affluent seat in the Cotswolds held by the Conservatives for most of the 20th century. The Liberal Democrats gained the seat in 1992 and held on to it until 2015; the party has cut Alex Chalk's majority at every general election since. This seat is home to Gloucestershire University and its 9,000 students.

EU REFERENDUM RESULT
42.9% Leave   Remain 57.1%

Chesham & Amersham

MAJORITY 16,223 (29.13%)   CONSERVATIVE HOLD   TURNOUT 76.76%

DAME CHERYL GILLAN
BORN Apr 21, 1952
MP 1992-

	Electorate	Share %	Change from 2017 %
	72,542		
*C Gillan C	30,850	55.40	-5.26
D Gallagher LD	14,627	26.27	+13.27
M Turmaine Lab	7,166	12.87	-7.72
A Booth Green	3,042	5.46	+2.46

Longest-serving female Conservative MP. Chairwoman, 1922 committee, 2019-. Brexiteer. Opposed HS2, which would cross her constituency. Welsh secretary, 2010-12. Shadow minister, home affairs, 2003-05; foreign and commonwealth affairs, 1998-2001; trade and industry, 1997-98. Opposition whip, 2001-03. Embroiled in the 2009 expenses scandal for putting dog food on her expenses and for having made excess mortgage claims, which she later repaid. Former marketing consultant, Ernst & Young. Marketing director, Kidsons Impey 1991-93. Made a dame in 2018. Ed: Cheltenham Ladies Coll; Coll of Law.

CHALLENGERS
Dan Gallagher (LD) Company manager responsible for an extensive housebuilding programme. **Matt Turmaine** (Lab) Project manager, Hertfordshire council integrated care programme. Cllr, Watford BC, 2012-. Contested Watford, 2015. **Alan Booth** (Green) Editorial designer. Cllr, Chartridge PC. Contested this

seat, as well as Buckinghamshire CC, in 2017.

CONSTITUENCY PROFILE
The Conservatives have never won fewer than half of the votes cast in this constituency, which was created in 1974. The Liberals or Liberal Democrats historically came in second place, but three different parties have come second in the past three elections, with Ukip and Labour achieving that feat in 2015 and 2017 respectively. This mainly rural south Buckinghamshire seat on the outskirts of Greater London is characterised by high incomes and high levels of self-employment.

EU REFERENDUM RESULT
45.0% Leave   Remain 55.0%

Chester, City of

CHRIS MATHESON
BORN Jan 2, 1968
MP 2015-

	Electorate	Share %	Change from 2017 %
	76,057		
*C Matheson Lab	27,082	49.64	-7.12
S George C	20,918	38.34	-2.15
B Thompson LD	3,734	6.84	+4.09
N Brown Green	1,438	2.64	
A Argyle Brexit	1,388	2.54	

First won this seat with the third smallest majority of the 2015 election. Shadow Cabinet Office secretary, 2018-. Remain campaigner. Resigned as a PPS for justice in 2016, backed Owen Smith for leader in the same year, then re-joined the shadow cabinet when he lost. Supported Sir Keir Starmer in 2020. PPS to John Healey, 2016-17. Culture select cttee, 2017-18, 2015-17. APPGs: aerospace; Argentina; BBC; Peru. Formerly a manager in the electricity industry. HR manager and officer, Unite. Ed: Manchester GS; LSE (BSc economics and politics).

CHALLENGERS
Samantha George (C) Chartered accountant and director of business support and outsourcing at the tax and audit management outsourcer BDO UK. First female Conservative candidate for the constituency. Cllr, Merton LBC, 2006-14, deputy council leader, 2006-10, made honorary alderman, 2014. Fellow, RSA. **Bob Thompson** (LD) Former HR director at the chemical company Ineos. Cllr, Cheshire West & Chester BC,

2008-15. Contested this seat, 2015; Eddisbury, 2010. **Nicholas Brown** (Green) Teacher.

CONSTITUENCY PROFILE
This relatively affluent seat returned Conservative MPs to parliament for almost the entire 20th century but Labour won the seat for the first time in 1997. Although the Conservatives gained the constituency in 2010, Labour won it back by only 93 votes in 2015, increasing that majority to more than 9,000 in 2017. Chester is the second largest settlement and the only city in Cheshire, on the Welsh border. The seat contains 8,000 students.

EU REFERENDUM RESULT
42.3% Leave   Remain 57.7%

Chesterfield

TOBY PERKINS
BORN Aug 12, 1970
MP 2010-

	Electorate	Share %	Change from 2017 %
	71,030		
*T Perkins Lab	18,171	40.21	-14.59
L Higgins C	16,720	37.00	+2.24
J Scotting Brexit	4,771	10.56	
E Coy LD	3,985	8.82	+3.37
N Jackson Green	1,148	2.54	+0.92
J Daramy Ind	391	0.87	

Moderate who was critical of Jeremy Corbyn's leadership. Voted Remain. Ran Liz Kendall's 2015 leadership campaign and backed Sir Keir Starmer in 2020. Shadow armed forces minister between 2015 and his resignation in 2016. Shadow minister: small businesses, 2011-15; children and families, 2010-11. Select cttees: home affairs, 2019-; international trade, 2016-17. Former Sheffield Tigers rugby union player. Founder, Club Rugby, a rugby clothing company. Cllr, Chesterfield BC, 2003-10. Ed: Trinity Sch, Leamington; Silverdale Sch, Sheffield.

CHALLENGERS
Leigh Higgins (C) Director, Open Solutions Ltd, a telecoms company. Cllr, Melton BC, 2015-. Regional chairman, East Midlands Conservatives. Former project manager, Lloyds Banking Group. **John Scotting** (Brexit) Property developer. Contested: Chesterfield BC, 2019; Derbyshire CC, 2017; Sheffield City C, 2016, all as a Conservative. **Emily Coy** (LD) Cllr, Chesterfield BC, 2019-.

Owner, Business Doctors Sheffield, a mentoring coaching service for companies.

CONSTITUENCY PROFILE
The Labour Party's historic domination of Chesterfield was challenged by the Liberals in the 1980s and 1990s, when the seat was represented by the leftwinger Tony Benn. The Lib Dems eventually won in 2001, the year that Mr Benn retired, but it swung back to Labour in 2010, with Toby Perkins's first majority standing at below 600. A compact seat in northern Derbyshire, but closer to Sheffield than Derby. Incomes are relatively low.

EU REFERENDUM RESULT
59.3% Leave   Remain 40.7%

Chichester

MAJORITY 21,490 (35.09%)   CONSERVATIVE HOLD   TURNOUT 71.63%

GILLIAN KEEGAN
BORN May 13, 1968
MP 2017-

	Electorate	Share %	from 2017 % Change
	85,499		
*G Keegan C	35,402	57.81	-2.33
K O'Kelly LD	13,912	22.72	+11.45
J Morton Lab	9,069	14.81	-7.57
H Barrie Green	2,527	4.13	+0.80
A Brown Libertarian	224	0.37	
A Emerson Patria	109	0.18	+0.04

Junior minister in the Department for Education since 2020. Apprentice at Delco Electronics in Merseyside aged 16; became parliament's apprenticeship ambassador in 2019. Worked abroad in manufacturing, banking and IT for 25 years. PPS to: Gavin Williamson (Staffordshire South), 2019; the Treasury, 2018-19. Voted Remain; supported Theresa May's Brexit deals. Endorsed Rory Stewart for leader, 2019. Select cttees: standing orders, 2017-; public accounts, 2017-18. Chairwoman, APPG on UN global goals

for sustainable development. Director, Women 2 Win, 2015-17. Cllr, Chichester DC, 2014-18. Godmother to two children of the former Speaker John Bercow. Contested St Helens South & Whiston, 2015. Ed: John Moores University (BA business studies); London Business School (Sloan Fellowship, MSc leadership and strategy).

CHALLENGERS
Kate O'Kelly (LD) Psychiatrist.

Cllr: West Sussex CC, 2017-; Chichester DC, 2018-. **Jay Morton** (Lab) Associate, Bell Phillips Architects. Campaigner, Generation Rent.

CONSTITUENCY PROFILE
The election of 1923, when the seat returned a Liberal MP, was the only time the Conservatives have lost Chichester since the Great Reform Act of 1867. The constituency, located between Portsmouth and Bognor Regis, has an ageing population, of which about a quarter are aged 65 or over. There are high levels of self-employment, and home ownership is slightly above the national average.

EU REFERENDUM RESULT
50.7% Leave   Remain 49.3%

Chingford & Woodford Green

MAJORITY 1,262 (2.61%)   CONSERVATIVE HOLD   TURNOUT 74.08%

SIR IAIN DUNCAN SMITH
BORN Apr 9, 1954
MP 1992-

	Electorate	Share %	from 2017 % Change
	65,393		
*I Duncan Smith C	23,481	48.47	-0.67
F Shaheen Lab	22,219	45.87	+1.92
G Seeff LD	2,744	5.66	+1.31

Conservative leader between 2001 and 2003; the "quiet man" who was ousted by his own MPs. Hardliner whose seat was specifically targeted by opposition activists. Work and pensions secretary, 2010-16, and architect of universal credit reforms; resigned from position in protest at proposed disability cuts, 2016. Founder, Centre for Social Justice. Eurosceptic; ultimately supported Theresa May's withdrawal agreement. Former Scots Guard lieutenant; active service in Northern Ireland and Rhodesia. Knighted in 2020; 200,000 people signed

a petition demanding that the honour be rescinded. Supported Boris Johnson for leader, 2019. Contested Bradford West, 1987. Ed: HMS Conway Cadet Sch; RMA Sandhurst.

CHALLENGERS
Faiza Shaheen (Lab) One of Labour's rising stars since her selection in 2018; led prolonged charge to unseat Mr Duncan Smith. Director, Centre for Labour and Social Studies. Former head of inequality and development, Save the Children. **Geoff Seeff** (LD) Chartered

accountant. Refused to stand aside for Ms Shaheen, saying that Labour was in the hands of "union paymasters" who would "prevent Remain". Contested Harlow, 2017, 2015; this seat, 2010; Romford, 2005.

CONSTITUENCY PROFILE
The Conservative majority in this seat has fallen at three successive elections and it was a key Labour target in 2019. Created in 1997, it is on the northern edge of London and has always elected Conservatives; its predecessor seat, Chingford, was held for 18 years by the Thatcherite cabinet minister Norman Tebbit.

EU REFERENDUM RESULT
49.9% Leave   Remain 50.1%

Chippenham

MICHELLE DONELAN
BORN Apr 8, 1984
MP 2015-

	Electorate	Share %	Change from 2017 %
	77,225		
*M Donelan C	30,994	54.28	-0.44
H Belcher LD	19,706	34.51	+8.90
M Anachury Lab	6,399	11.21	-8.46

Minister of state in the Department of Education, 2020-; parly under-sec, education, 2019-20; whip, 2019-20; assistant whip, 2018-19. Made her first speech at a Conservative Party conference aged 15. Eurosceptic, but voted Remain; supported Theresa May's withdrawal agreement. Select cttees: petitions, 2017-; education, 2015-18. APPG vice-chairwoman: Australia and New Zealand; family business. Had Lyme disease diagnosed by a constituent during a surgery in 2016. Worked in marketing at AETN UK, the broadcasting company. Contested Wentworth & Dearne, 2010. Ed: County HS, Leftwich; University of York (BA history and politics).

CHALLENGERS
Helen Belcher (LD) Campaigner, Trans Media Watch, a charity influencing media coverage of trans issues. Gave evidence to the Leveson Inquiry on the misrepresentation of trans people. Chairwoman, Consortium of LGBT Voluntary and Community Organisations. Former managing director, Aurum Solutions, a software provider. Contested this constituency, 2017. **Martha Anachury** (Lab) Education convener, GMB. Activist, Operation Black Vote.

CONSTITUENCY PROFILE
This western Wiltshire seat was created in 2010 from two Conservative seats. It was first won by the Lib Dem Duncan Hames, husband of the former Lib Dem leader Jo Swinson and PPS to her predecessor Nick Clegg. It had previously returned Conservative MPs in all but three 20th-century elections: 1905, 1922 and 1923. Home ownership and incomes are slightly above the regional average.

EU REFERENDUM RESULT
51.6% Leave   Remain 48.4%

Chipping Barnet

THERESA VILLIERS
BORN Mar 5, 1968
MP 2005-

	Electorate	Share %	Change from 2017 %
	79,960		
*T Villiers C	25,745	44.72	-1.61
E Whysall Lab	24,533	42.61	-3.08
I Parasram LD	5,932	10.30	+4.87
G Bailey Green	1,288	2.24	-0.30
J Sheffield Advance	71	0.12	

Sacked as environment secretary after six months in post in the February 2020 reshuffle. Brexit "Spartan" who voted consistently against Theresa May's deal but backed that of Boris Johnson, whose leadership campaign she supported in 2019. Northern Ireland secretary, 2012-16; left the front bench after refusing a demotion in Mrs May's first reshuffle, 2016. Transport minister, 2010-12; shadow transport secretary, 2007-10; shadow chief secretary to the Treasury, 2005-07. MEP, 1999-2005. National security strategy select cttee, 2016-19. Barrister, Lincoln's Inn. Former law lecturer, King's College London. Member of the aristocratic Villiers family. Ed: Francis Holland Sch; University of Bristol (LLB law); Jesus Coll, Oxford (BCL).

CHALLENGERS
Emma Whysall (Lab) Trade union lawyer, Thomson's Solicitors. Reselection as the candidate was endorsed by Unison and the Jewish Labour Movement. Contested this seat in 2017. **Isabelle Parasram** (LD) Vice-president, Liberal Democrats. Head of legal practice, Greycoat Law. Former senior prosecution lawyer, Department for Business, Innovation and Skills. Contested Walsall North, 2017.

CONSTITUENCY PROFILE
This constituency to the north of London has elected Conservative MPs at every election since its creation in 1974. Labour came within four hundred votes of winning it in 2017, having come within about a thousand votes in 1997. It was previously held by the Conservative cabinet minister Reginald Maudling.

EU REFERENDUM RESULT
41.1% Leave   Remain 58.9%

Chorley

MAJORITY 17,392 (43.62%)   **SPEAKER WIN**   **TURNOUT 51.00%**

SIR LINDSAY HOYLE
BORN Jun 10, 1957
MP 1997-

	Electorate	Share %	Change from 2017 %
	78,177		
*L Hoyle Speaker	26,831	67.30	+12.03
M Brexit-Smith Ind	9,439	23.67	
J Melling Green	3,600	9.03	+8.08

Speaker of the Commons since November 2019 after being first elected for Labour. Known for his menagerie of politically named pets, including Boris the parrot and Maggie the tortoise. Deputy speaker, 2010-19. Reprimanded SNP MPs for singing *Ode to Joy* during the vote to trigger Article 50 in 2017. Called on social media companies to crack down on offensive posts, arguing that they deterred minority groups from entering politics. Son of the former Labour MP and peer Lord Hoyle. Cllr, Chorley BC, 1980-98; mayor, 1997-98. Former textile-printing business owner. Knighted in 2018 for public and political service. Ed: Lord's Coll, Bolton; Horwich FE Coll.

CHALLENGERS
Mark Brexit-Smith (Ind) Was to stand for the Brexit Party but it did not field a candidate after the election of Sir Lindsay as Speaker. Changed his name so that "Brexit" could appear on the ballot paper. Contested South Ribble, 2017, and this seat, 2015, both for Ukip. **James Melling** (Green) Teacher. Campaigns officer, Cheshire Wildlife Trust.

CONSTITUENCY PROFILE
With other Labour seats in Lancashire, such as Burnley and Hyndburn, falling to the Conservatives, Sir Lindsay Hoyle might well be relieved that he was elevated to the Speaker's chair before the 2019 general election took place. Chorley was first won by Labour in 1945 and had been held by the party for most of its postwar history, although the Conservatives did win it in 1970 and subsequently held it from 1979 to 1997. Situated between Preston and Wigan, the town of Chorley itself is home to about 35,000 people and the seat has high levels of home ownership.

EU REFERENDUM RESULT
56.7% Leave   Remain 43.3%

Christchurch

MAJORITY 24,617 (47.39%)   **CONSERVATIVE HOLD**   **TURNOUT 72.64%**

SIR CHRISTOPHER CHOPE
BORN May 19, 1947
MP 1997-; 1983-92

	Electorate	Share %	Change from 2017 %
	71,521		
*C Chope C	33,894	65.24	-4.34
M Cox LD	9,277	17.86	+9.92
A Dunne Lab	6,568	12.64	-7.22
C Rigby Green	2,212	4.26	+1.64

Controversial carrier of the Thatcherite flame who has received opprobrium for objecting to private member's bills being passed without extensive debate; bills he has blocked include one attempting to make "upskirting" a specific offence and another introducing measures to protect girls at risk of genital mutilation. Honorary vice-president and former chairman, Conservative Way Forward. Climate-change sceptic. Brexit "Spartan"; consistently voted against Theresa May's withdrawal agreement but approved Boris Johnson's. MP for Southampton Itchen, 1983-92; parly under-sec, environment, 1986-90, and transport, 1990-92. Former barrister and consultant, Ernst & Young. Knighted in 2018 for political service. Ed: Marlborough Coll; University of St Andrews (LLB law).

CHALLENGERS
Mike Cox (LD) Chartered accountant. Non-executive director, Curtin and Co, a communications consultancy. Cllr, Bournemouth, Christchurch & Poole BC, 2019-. Contested: this seat, 2017; Uxbridge & South Ruislip, 2015, 2010. **Andrew Dunne** (Lab) Former police officer, Hampshire Constabulary.

CONSTITUENCY PROFILE
Christchurch and its various predecessors have been won by the Conservatives at every general election since 1910, although the Lib Dems won at a 1993 by-election before losing narrowly to the Conservatives at the next general election. This Dorset constituency stretches north and east along the coast from Bournemouth. More than a third of residents are aged 65 or above, giving it one of the oldest populations of any seat.

EU REFERENDUM RESULT
60.0% Leave   Remain 40.0%

Cities of London & Westminster

MAJORITY 3,953 (9.25%) CONSERVATIVE HOLD **TURNOUT 67.07%**

NICKIE AIKEN
BORN Feb 4, 1969
MP 2019-

	Electorate	Share %	Change from 2017 %
	63,700		
N Aiken C	17,049	39.91	-6.67
C Umunna LD	13,096	30.65	+19.61
G Nardell Lab	11,624	27.21	-11.23
Z Polanski Green	728	1.70	-0.42
J McLachlan CPA	125	0.29	
D van Heck Lib	101	0.24	

Head of PR for Bradford &
Bingley. Previously William
Hague's press secretary,
a consultant and a crisis
management trainer. Began her
career working in the Welsh
Conservatives' press office. Cllr,
Westminster LBC, 2014-; council
leader. Shadow lead for crime
and policing; education and
children services lead, London
Councils. Voted Remain in 2016.
Her husband, Alex Aiken, is
executive director of government
communications. Board member,
Children and Family Court
Advisory and Support Service,
2014-17. Ed: University of Exeter.

CHALLENGERS
Chuka Umunna (LD) A former
rising star of the Labour Party
and MP for Streatham, 2010-19.
Left the party in protest at the
leadership and co-founded The
Independent Group; he later
left that too and joined the Lib
Dems. Remainer. Employment
law solicitor, 2002-11. Tipped
for the Labour leadership in
2015 but withdrew, citing press
intrusion. **Gordon Nardell**
(Lab) QC. Became Labour's first

in-house general counsel, 2018;
established its legal operation
before returning to the Bar.

CONSTITUENCY PROFILE
The Conservatives' vote share
fell to a historic low in 2019.
Mark Field, MP 2001-19, was
sacked as a Foreign Office
minister after he was accused
of assaulting, on camera, a
protester at the Mansion House.
Mr Field denied the allegations.
No charges were brought and
he referred himself to the
Cabinet Office for investigation.
The seat contains the Houses
of Parliament and the Bank
of England and the average
property price is £1.1 million.

EU REFERENDUM RESULT
28.1% Leave Remain 71.9%

Clacton

MAJORITY 24,702 (56.78%) CONSERVATIVE HOLD **TURNOUT 61.34%**

GILES WATLING
BORN Feb 18, 1953
MP 2017-

	Electorate	Share %	Change from 2017 %
	70,930		
*G Watling C	31,438	72.26	+11.03
K Bonavia Lab	6,736	15.48	-9.89
C Robertson LD	2,541	5.84	+3.83
C Southall Green	1,225	2.82	+1.19
A Morgan ND	1,099	2.53	
C Bennett Ind	243	0.56	-0.46
J Sexton Loony	224	0.51	

Actor and director best known
for playing Vicar Oswald in the
sitcom *Bread*; has also appeared
in *'Allo 'Allo!*, *Grange Hill* and
Upstairs, Downstairs. Stood
against Douglas Carswell in the
2014 by-election prompted by
Mr Carswell's defection from
the Conservatives to Ukip, and
also in the 2015 general election.
Cllr, Tendring DC, 2007-;
cabinet member for planning
and regeneration. Eurosceptic
but supported Remain in the
referendum; voted for the
withdrawal agreements. Culture
select cttee, 2017-19. APPG
chairman, theatre. Ed: Forest HS.

CHALLENGERS
Kevin Bonavia (Lab) Cllr,
Lewisham LBC, 2018-; cabinet
member for democracy, refugees
and accountability. Solicitor.
Contested Rochford & Southend
East, 2010. **Callum Robertson**
(LD) Law clinic director and
legal adviser. Former civil
servant. **Chris Southall** (Green)
Contested this seat in 2017, 2015
and 2010.

CONSTITUENCY PROFILE
Created in 2010, Clacton's
predecessor seat, Harwich, had
been held by Labour from 1997
until Douglas Carswell won it
as a Conservative in 2005. In
2014 Mr Carswell defected from
the Conservatives and fought
a by-election to become Ukip's
first elected MP. Although he
held the seat for Ukip in 2015,
he left the party to sit as an
independent a few months
before the 2017 election, in
which he did not stand. About a
third of residents in this coastal
Essex seat are aged 65 or over,
and the constituency has one
of the lowest proportions of
graduates of any in the country.

EU REFERENDUM RESULT
73.0% Leave Remain 27.0%

Cleethorpes

MARTIN VICKERS
BORN Sep 13, 1950
MP 2010-

Eurosceptic backbencher who voted for an EU referendum in 2011 and supported Leave in 2016. Supported Theresa May's withdrawal agreement on second and third attempt. Backed Boris Johnson for leader, 2019. Voted against same-sex marriage in 2013, also in Northern Ireland in 2019; voted against LGBT sex education in schools. Select cttees: ecclesiastical, 2019; health and social care, 2018-19; transport, 2013-2018. Contested this seat in 2005. Cllr: North East Lincolnshire BC, 1999-2011; Great Grimsby BC, 1980-94. Member, Conservative Christian

	Electorate	Share %	from 2017 %	Change
	73,689			
*M Vickers C	31,969	68.99	+11.89	
R James Lab	10,551	22.77	-12.60	
R Horobin LD	2,535	5.47	+3.15	
J Shanahan Green	1,284	2.77	+1.79	

Fellowship. Background in printing industry and retail. Ed: Havelock Comp, Grimsby; Grimsby College; University of Lincoln (BA politics, which he studied part-time, 2004-10).

CHALLENGERS
Ros James (Lab) Member, Unite. Brexiteer because of her "unease with the democratic deficit within the EU". Cllr, North East Lincolnshire BC, 2008-. **Roy Horobin** (LD) Teacher. Campaigned to give Grimsby's historic dock conservation

status. Contested this seat, 2017, 2015. **Jodi Shanahan** (Green) Freelance social media coach.

CONSTITUENCY PROFILE
Cleethorpes had a Labour MP from its creation in 1997, but since the Conservatives gained it in 2010 they have consistently increased their majority. More than 40,000 people live in the north Lincolnshire town of Cleethorpes itself, which, like neighbouring Grimsby, is an old fishing town. The seat, which contains several caravan parks, also stretches north along a more rural area on the southern side of the Humber estuary. It has an ageing population.

EU REFERENDUM RESULT

69.5% Leave	Remain 30.5%

Clwyd South

SIMON BAYNES
BORN Apr 21, 1960
MP 2019-

Ran a second-hand bookshop after a career in finance for JPMorgan Cazenove, 1982-2006. Brexiteer. Backed Boris Johnson in 2019 leadership contest. Cllr, Llanfyllin TC, 2008-13; mayor, 2018-19. Cllr, Powys CC, 2008-12; joint leader of the Conservative group. Former chairman, Welsh Historic Gardens Trust. Founder, Concertina, a charity providing live music for the elderly. Contested this seat, 2017, 2015. Ed: Shrewsbury Sch, Magdalene Coll, Cambridge (BA history; chairman of both the Cambridge Union and the Conservative Association, 1982).

	Electorate	Share %	from 2017 %	Change
	53,919			
S Baynes C	16,222	44.68	+5.60	
*S Jones Lab	14,983	41.27	-9.44	
C Allen PC	2,137	5.89	-0.23	
C Davies LD	1,496	4.12	+2.17	
J Adams Brexit	1,468	4.04		

CHALLENGERS
Susan Elan Jones (Lab) MP for this seat, 2010-19. Critical of Jeremy Corbyn. Shadow Wales minister, 2015-16; opposition whip, 2011-15. PPS to Harriet Harman (Camberwell & Peckham), 2010-11. Select cttees: standards, 2016-17; privileges, 2016-17; Welsh affairs, 2010-12. Former fundraiser. Contested Surrey Heath, 1997. **Chris Allen** (PC) Contested this seat, 2017. **Calum Davies** (LD) Twenty-three-year-old retail worker.

CONSTITUENCY PROFILE
Had been held by Labour since its creation in 1997, but became one of the seats to fall as part of the party's collapse in north Wales in 2019. The predecessor seat, Clwyd South West, also elected Labour MPs continuously from 1987. Clwyd South is a rural seat to the south and west of Wrexham, containing some of Wrexham's suburbs. Much of it lies along Wales's border with Shropshire. Manufacturing is a common source of jobs and residents' incomes are below the Welsh average. The proportion of households in the social-rented sector is above average.

EU REFERENDUM RESULT

59.9% Leave	Remain 40.1%

Clwyd West

MAJORITY 6,747 (16.78%)　　　　CONSERVATIVE HOLD　　　　**TURNOUT 69.66%**

DAVID JONES
BORN Mar 22, 1952
MP 2005-

Did not plan to contest the seat again but reconsidered when the snap election was called. Brexit minister, 2016-17; appointed after his successful leadership of the Vote Leave campaign in Wales. Supported Boris Johnson for the party leadership, 2019. Wales secretary, 2012-14; parly under-sec for Wales, 2010-12; shadow Wales minister, 2006-10. Member, Welsh assembly, 2002-03. Voted against same-sex marriage and the legalisation of abortion in Northern Ireland. Qualified solicitor who set up law practice, David Jones & Co, where he was a senior partner.

	Electorate	Share %	from 2017 %	Change
	57,714			
*D Jones C	20,403	50.75	+2.68	
J Thomas Lab	13,656	33.97	-5.64	
E Williams PC	3,907	9.72	+0.08	
D Wilkins LD	2,237	5.56	+2.88	

Honorary life fellow, Cancer Research UK. Fluent in Welsh. Contested: City of Chester, 2001; Conwy, 1997. Ed: Ruabon GS; UCL (LLB Law); Coll of Law, Chester.

CHALLENGERS
Jo Thomas (Lab) Former PA and shopkeeper. Contested Welsh assembly, 2016. Married to Gareth Thomas, the MP for this seat between 1997 and 2005. **Elfed Williams** (PC) Services director for a local mental health charity. **David Wilkins** (LD)

Physics teacher who helped to reform the Welsh curriculum. Environmentalist.

CONSTITUENCY PROFILE
This constituency elected Labour MPs with modest majorities in 1997 and 2001. The Conservatives narrowly won it in 2005, and have increased their share of the vote at every general election since. The residents of this large, rural north Wales seat are disproportionately older than the UK average. The biggest town, Colwyn Bay, on the north Welsh coast, is home to about 31,000 people and has a significant tourism industry.

EU REFERENDUM RESULT
53.0% Leave　　　　Remain 47.0%

Coatbridge, Chryston & Bellshill

MAJORITY 5,624 (11.66%)　　　　SNP GAIN FROM LABOUR　　　　**TURNOUT 66.11%**

STEVEN BONNAR
BORN Aug 27, 1981
MP 2019-

First caught media attention when he crossed his fingers during his pledge of allegiance to the Queen as he was being sworn in as an MP. Cllr, North Lanarkshire C, 2015-19. Internal auditor at John Lewis Partnership, 2011-15. Loss prevention manager at BHS, 2000-03; Debenhams, 2003-11. Policy priorities include ensuring an independence vote and protecting the environment, workers' rights and rights of disabled people. Volunteer, Caledonian Crushers, a Glasgow wheelchair rugby club. Ed: Cardinal Newman HS.

	Electorate	Share %	from 2017 %	Change
	72,943			
S Bonnar SNP	22,680	47.03	+7.94	
*H Gaffney Lab	17,056	35.37	-7.24	
N Wilson C	6,113	12.68	-3.57	
D Stevens LD	1,564	3.24	+1.20	
P McAleer Green	808	1.68		

CHALLENGERS
Hugh Gaffney (Lab) MP for this seat, 2017-19. Royal Mail postman; political officer, Communication Workers Union and regional secretary, TUC. Founding member, Keir Hardie Society. **Nathan Wilson** (C) Cllr, North Lanarkshire C, 2017-; shadow cabinet secretary for European and external relations, culture and tourism. Parliamentary researcher. **David Stevens** (LD) Former teacher. Contested Inverclyde,

2017. **Patrick McAleer** (Green) Scientist.

CONSTITUENCY PROFILE
This North Lanarkshire constituency and its predecessors had been held by Labour since 1935 until the SNP landslide of 2015. The seat was then one of the six SNP seats to return to Labour two years later; it swung back to the SNP again in 2019. The seat contains the old industrial towns of Coatbridge and Bellshill, along with a rural area to their north. Coatbridge has suffered long-term industrial decline due to the exhaustion of local iron deposits; the last ironworks closed in 1967.

EU REFERENDUM RESULT
38.8% Leave　　　　Remain 61.2%

Colchester

MAJORITY 9,423 (17.65%)   CONSERVATIVE HOLD   TURNOUT 64.60%

WILL QUINCE
BORN Dec 27, 1982
MP 2015-

Parliamentary under-secretary, work and pensions, 2019-. PPS to Gavin Williamson, 2018; resigned in opposition to Theresa May's withdrawal agreement. Select cttees: home affairs, 2017-18; transport, 2015-17. Supported greater funding for the upkeep of war graves and has campaigned against cuts to maternity services. Supported Jeremy Hunt in 2019 leadership contest. Cllr: Colchester BC, 2011-16; East Herts DC, 2007-09. Auditioned for *Britain's Got Talent* in 2016 as part of a charity bet with a constituent. Solicitor at Thompson Smith and Puxton,

	Electorate	Share %	Change from 2017 %
	82,625		
*W Quince C	26,917	50.43	+4.55
T McKay Lab	17,494	32.78	-2.50
M Goss LD	7,432	13.92	-3.05
M Goacher Green	1,530	2.87	+1.32

2013-15; customer development manager, Britvic, 2007-10. Contested this seat in 2010. Ed: The Windsor Boys' Sch; Aberystwyth University (LLB); UWE (PG Dip legal practice).

CHALLENGERS
Tina McKay (Lab) Community activist, experience working with disadvantaged children and veterans. Member, Unite. Contested this seat in 2017. **Martin Goss** (LD) Cllr, Colchester BC, 2008-19. Project manager in finance.

CONSTITUENCY PROFILE
Created in 1997, this seat was held by the Liberal Democrats from 1997 to 2015, but has been Conservative for its more recent history, with the Lib Dems falling to third in 2017 and the Conservative vote share rising at the past three elections. The constituency has elected a Labour MP just once, at the 1945 general election. Colchester is the second largest town in Essex after Southend-on-Sea. Although the campus of the University of Essex is located in another constituency, many of its students live in Colchester. Income is significantly below average for the east of England.

EU REFERENDUM RESULT
51.5% Leave   Remain 48.5%

Colne Valley

MAJORITY 5,103 (8.38%)   CONSERVATIVE GAIN FROM LABOUR   TURNOUT 72.36%

JASON MCCARTNEY
BORN Jan 29, 1968
MP 2019-; 2010-17

Former journalist and RAF officer who reclaimed the seat he unexpectedly lost in 2017. Head of public affairs at Huddersfield University, 2017-19. Director, Fairandfunky, 2018-. Senior lecturer at Leeds Beckett University after a career as a broadcast and radio journalist with BBC Leeds and ITV. Member, 1922 exec cttee, 2013-17. Brexiteer. HS2 advocate. Transport select cttee, 2013-15. UK delegate for Nato parliamentary assembly, 2010. Director, Yorkshire Chamber of Commerce, 2018-. RAF officer, 1988-97. Served in Turkey and

	Electorate	Share %	Change from 2017 %
	84,174		
J McCartney C	29,482	48.40	+2.22
*T Walker Lab	24,379	40.02	-7.67
C Burke LD	3,815	6.26	+2.14
S Harrison Brexit	1,286	2.11	
D Gould Green	1,068	1.75	+0.28
O Aspinall Yorkshire	548	0.90	
M Roberts UKIP	230	0.38	
C Peel Ind	102	0.17	-0.35

Iraq; reached flight lieutenant. Ed: Lancaster Royal GS; Leeds Trinity & All Saints Coll (PG Dip broadcast journalism).

CHALLENGERS
Thelma Walker (Lab) MP for this seat, 2017-19. Signed the No Border Guards pledge not to report constituents in breach of immigration law. Education

consultant. **Cahal Burke** (LD) Contested this seat in 2017.

CONSTITUENCY PROFILE
The seat alternated between the Liberals and Labour for years, before being won from Labour by the Conservatives in 1987. It has swung between the two since, with Labour holding it from 1997 until 2010, winning it again in 2017. It was held by Labour's first chancellor of the exchequer, Philip Snowden, in the 1920s. Contains some of Huddersfield's western suburbs and a large chunk of the eastern Pennines. The BBC sitcom *The Last of the Summer Wine* was filmed here.

EU REFERENDUM RESULT
50.1% Leave   Remain 49.9%

Congleton

MAJORITY 18,561 (32.43%)   CONSERVATIVE HOLD   TURNOUT 70.72%

FIONA BRUCE
BORN Mar 26, 1957
MP 2010-

Brexiteer with a strong interest in human rights. Has introduced several early day motions on the rights of Hong Kong protestors. Chairwoman, Conservative Party human rights inquiry into prostitution, 2019. Select cttees: human rights, 2015-; ecclesiastical, 2016-; international development, 2012-17; draft modern slavery bill, 2014. Chairwoman, pro-life APPG; has said her priority in Westminster is fighting for the sanctity of human life. Supported the Conservative leadership campaign of Sajid Javid in the 2019 contest. Contested

	Electorate	Share %	from 2017 %	Change
	80,930			
*F Bruce C	33,747	58.96	+2.36	
J Dale Lab	15,186	26.53	-7.63	
P Duffy LD	6,026	10.53	+5.37	
R McCarthy Green	1,616	2.82	+1.05	
J Smith AWP	658	1.15		

Warrington South, 2005. Cllr, Warrington BC, 2004-10. Solicitor; Fiona Bruce & Co. Co-author, *There is Such a Thing as Society.* Ed: Burnley HS; Howell's Sch; University of Manchester (LLB law).

CHALLENGERS
Jo Dale (Lab) Cllr, Alsager TC, 2019-. Market stall owner. **Paul Duffy** (LD) Supply chain manager in healthcare industry. **Richard McCarthy** (Green) Former teacher.

CONSTITUENCY PROFILE
This safe seat in Cheshire has elected Conservative MPs since it was created in 1983. Labour's best performance was in 1997, when it was about 6,000 votes away from the winning candidate. The Conservatives' vote share has increased at successive elections since 2005. Demographically, it is older than average, and has high levels of home ownership and retirement among its residents. A high proportion of residents work in managerial jobs. The biggest town in the constituency is Congleton, but the region also contains smaller towns such as Sandbach and Middlewich.

EU REFERENDUM RESULT
52.6% Leave   Remain 47.4%

Copeland

MAJORITY 5,842 (13.74%)   CONSERVATIVE HOLD   TURNOUT 68.93%

TRUDY HARRISON
BORN Apr 19, 1976
MP 2017-

Brexiteer who snatched the seat from Labour in a by-election in February 2017, less than six months after joining the Conservative Party. Appointed PPS to Boris Johnson after the 2019 election; formerly PPS to Gavin Williamson (Staffordshire South). Education select cttee, 2017-. Supported Michael Gove in the 2019 leadership election. Supporter of nuclear energy; former technical clerk at the Sellafield nuclear site. Project manager at Bootle2020, a local campaign to promote a sustainable rural community. Stopped holding

	Electorate	Share %	from 2017 %	Change
	61,693			
*T Harrison C	22,856	53.75	+4.69	
T Lywood Lab	17,014	40.01	-5.10	
J Studholme LD	1,888	4.44	+1.17	
J Lenox Green	765	1.80		

public constituency surgeries in 2017, citing safety concerns after the murder of Jo Cox. Cllr, Bootle PC, 2004-07. Ed: Salford University (FdSc sustainable communities).

CHALLENGERS
Tony Lywood (Lab) Cllr, Allerdale BC, 2015-; Keswick TC, 2017-. Community housing champion. **John Studholme** (LD) Retired chartered surveyor. Former chairman of South Lakeland district council. **Jack Lenox** (Green) Design engineer.

CONSTITUENCY PROFILE
Copeland and its predecessor, Whitehaven, had elected Labour MPs since 1931, but the party lost it at a by-election in early 2017, triggered when Jamie Reed, the MP for Copeland since 2005, took a job at Sellafield, the nuclear processing plant in the constituency that employs 10,000 people. The Conservative majority increased significantly in 2019. This large Cumbrian constituency consists of land contained within the Lake District national park, including England's highest peak, Scafell Pike. Its largest town, Whitehaven, is home to about 23,000 people.

EU REFERENDUM RESULT
59.2% Leave   Remain 40.8%

Corby

TOM PURSGLOVE
BORN Nov 5, 1988
MP 2015-

Ardent campaigner for Leave who said that he would choose Brexit over a Conservative majority in 2016. Assistant whip, 2019-. PPS to: Robert Goodwill (Scarborough & Whitby), 2016-17; Liam Fox, 2017-18; Sajid Javid, 2018-19. Supported Dominic Raab, then Boris Johnson, for leader in 2019. Co-founder and chief executive of the pro-Leave campaign Grassroots Out!. Director, anti-wind farm group Together Against Wind; has advocated abolishing the Department of Energy and Climate Change. Party vice-chairman for youth, 2018-19.

	Electorate	Share %	from 2017 %	Change %
	86,151			
*T Pursglove C	33,410	55.24	+6.01	
B Miller Lab	23,142	38.26	-6.48	
C Stanbra LD	3,932	6.50	+3.93	

Worked as parliamentary assistant to Chris Heaton-Harris (Daventry) and Peter Bone (Wellingborough). Cllr, Wellingborough BC, 2007-15. Ed: Sir Christopher Hatton Sch, Northants; QMUL (BA politics).

CHALLENGERS
Beth Miller (Lab) Started out as a kitchen porter and hairdresser before becoming an adviser to Lord Blunkett, a former home secretary. Contested this seat in 2017. **Chris Stanbra** (LD) Bookkeeper. Cllr, Northamptonshire CC, 2009-.

CONSTITUENCY PROFILE
Corby is a bellwether and has been since its creation in 1983. Tom Pursglove's majority in 2019 was the largest of any MP for Corby since 1997. Labour won it in a 2012 by-election after the resignation of Louise Mensch, the MP since 2010. This east Northamptonshire seat consists of the former iron and steelworks town from which it takes its name, and several smaller towns. Sometimes described as the most Scottish place in England, after migration from Scotland during the decline of the Clyde shipyards. More than 8,000 residents were born north of the border.

EU REFERENDUM RESULT
60.1% Leave　　　Remain 39.9%

Cornwall North

SCOTT MANN
BORN Jun 24, 1977
MP 2015-

Royal Mail postman who took his parliamentary oath in the Cornish language. Voted Leave. Champion of British fishing and farming. Typically toes the party line but voted for the Assisted Dying Bill, 2015. PPS to: Department for Transport, 2017-18; Treasury, 2018; resigned the latter in opposition to Chequers plan. Select cttees: human rights, 2019; environmental audit, 2016-17. Initially backed Mark Harper in the 2019 Conservative leadership race before switching to Boris Johnson. Cllr, North Cornwall DC, 2009-16. Almost drowned in 2016 when he was

	Electorate	Share %	from 2017 %	Change %
	69,935			
*S Mann C	30,671	59.35	+8.64	
D Chambers LD	15,919	30.80	-5.78	
J Bassett Lab	4,516	8.74	-3.34	
E Liepins Lib	572	1.11		

embarrassed to admit he could not swim; was saved by fellow MP Johnny Mercer (Plymouth Moor View). Honorary vice-president, Wadebridge Cricket Club. Ed: Wadebridge Sch.

CHALLENGERS
Danny Chambers (LD) Veterinary surgeon. Member, Royal College of Veterinary Surgeons, 2017-. *New Scientist* contributor. **Joy Bassett** (Lab) Contested this seat in 2017. **Elmars Liepins** (Lib) Retired building sub-contractor.

CONSTITUENCY PROFILE
The largest constituency in Cornwall. The seat was held by Liberal Democrat MPs from 1992 to 2015, when it was won by Scott Mann. The seat, which was created in 1918, had flipped between the two parties for most of its postwar history, only briefly held by Labour when a Liberal MP defected in 1947. Cornwall North contains the towns of Bude, Bodmin, Launceston and Wadebridge, and is mainly rural, containing much of Bodmin Moor. About a quarter of the population is aged 65 or above and its working residents are more likely than average to be self-employed.

EU REFERENDUM RESULT
60.2% Leave　　　Remain 39.8%

Cornwall South East

MAJORITY 20,971 (39.08%)   CONSERVATIVE HOLD   TURNOUT 74.70%

SHERYLL MURRAY
BORN Feb 4, 1956
MP 2010-

Passionate fishing industry campaigner; wife of a trawler skipper who died in an accident at sea in 2011. Voted Leave. Submitted letter of no confidence in Theresa May, December 2018. 1922 exec cttee, 2017-. Supported Boris Johnson for leader, 2019. Spokeswoman, Save Britain's Fish; director, the Fishermen's Association; Looe Fisherman's Protection Association. Select cttees: high speed rail bill, 2018-; environment, 2017-, 2012-15; environmental audit, 2010-12. Worked as a part-time doctor's receptionist for 20 years. Called

	Electorate	Share %	Change from 2017 %
	71,825		
*S Murray C	31,807	59.28	+3.86
G Derrick Lab	10,836	20.20	-2.45
C Martin LD	8,650	16.12	-3.30
M Green Green	1,493	2.78	+0.27
J Latham Lib	869	1.62	

for greater regulation of social media after receiving online abuse during the 2017 election campaign. Cllr, Caradon DC, 2003-09, Conservative group leader, 2003-07. Cllr, Cornwall CC, 2001-05. Ed: Torpoint CS.

CHALLENGERS
Gareth Derrick (Lab) Royal Navy commodore. Served in Iraq in 1991 and 2003; awarded US Bronze Star. **Colin Martin** (LD) Teacher. Cllr, Cornwall C, 2017-. Vice-chairman, Cornwall LDs.

CONSTITUENCY PROFILE
Since its creation in 1983, this seat has returned Conservative MPs whenever the party has been the largest in parliament; the Liberal Democrats won control of the constituency during the New Labour years. Ukip pushed Labour into fourth place in 2015. A large rural constituency encompassing the Tamar towns of Saltash and Torpoint in its east, with Liskeard further west and Looe to its south. More than half of residents in work are aged over 45 and are among the most likely to be self-employed of anywhere in the UK. Home ownership is well above average.

EU REFERENDUM RESULT
55.1% Leave   Remain 44.9%

Cotswolds, The

MAJORITY 20,214 (33.04%)   CONSERVATIVE HOLD   TURNOUT 74.66%

SIR GEOFFREY CLIFTON-BROWN
BORN Mar 23, 1953
MP 1992-

Veteran MP knighted in 2018 for political and public service. Ranked last in an index of MPs based on openness and responsiveness to constituents by the campaign group change.org, 2019. Instrumental in schools funding rebellion, 2017, voicing concerns about underfunding. Thrown out of 2019 Tory party conference after an altercation with security staff caused a temporary lockdown. Shadow international development secretary, 2007-10; opposition whip, 2004-05; asst chief whip, 2005. Shadow foreign minister, 2005-07. Chairman, Conservative

	Electorate	Share %	Change from 2017 %
	81,939		
*G Clifton-Brown C	35,484	58.00	-2.63
L Webster LD	15,270	24.96	+8.63
A MacKenzie Lab	7,110	11.62	-6.30
S Poole Green	3,312	5.41	+2.49

Friends of the Chinese. Treasurer, 1922 committee. Ed: Eton Coll; Royal Agricultural College.

CHALLENGERS
Liz Webster (LD) Self-employed recruitment agent. Anti-Brexit campaigner and founding member of Farmers for a People's Vote. Contested Swindon North, 2017. **Alan MacKenzie** (Lab) Trade unionist and former officer, British Transport Police. Contested Cirencester TC, 2019.

CONSTITUENCY PROFILE
This seat and its predecessor have elected only Conservative MPs at every election since 1918, with the exception of the 1955 general election, when its MP William Morrison was the Speaker of the House of Commons. A safe seat, the Conservatives have not won less than 50 per cent of the vote in the seat since 2005. The largest town in this sparse Gloucestershire constituency is Cirencester, with a population of about 19,000. More than half of residents are aged 45 or above, but unlike most older seats it contains a significant proportion of graduates.

EU REFERENDUM RESULT
47.9% Leave   Remain 52.1%

Coventry North East

MAJORITY 7,692 (17.31%)　　　　　　LABOUR HOLD　　　　　　TURNOUT 58.48%

COLEEN FLETCHER
BORN Nov 23, 1954
MP 2015-

First woman to represent Coventry North East; stood for the seat while supporting her husband through cancer. Stepped down from her role as PPS to Kerry McCarthy in 2016 in protest at Jeremy Corbyn's leadership. Backed Jess Phillips in 2020, Owen Smith in 2016 and Yvette Cooper in 2015. Opposition whip, 2017-. Administration cttee, 2017-19. Remain campaigner. Cllr, Coventry CC at various points in 1992-2011. Previously customer services officer in the housing sector. Ed: Hall CS; Henly Coll, Coventry University.

	Electorate	Share %	Change from 2017 %
	76,002		
*C Fletcher Lab	23,412	52.68	-10.75
S Richards C	15,720	35.37	+5.44
I Sufyan Brexit	2,110	4.75	
N Proctor LD	2,061	4.64	+2.15
M Handley Green	1,141	2.57	+1.49

CHALLENGERS
Sophie Richards (C) Deputy chairwoman, Conservative Young Women. Contested Hammersmith & Fulham LBC, 2018. **Iddrisu Sufyan** (Brexit) British-Ghanaian law student with background in logistical supply services. **Nukey Proctor** (LD) Senior programme management consultant. Executive member of the Liberal Democrat Health and Care Association. Vice-chairwoman, Coventry Liberal Democrats.

CONSTITUENCY PROFILE
Coventry North East has been Labour since its creation in 1974, although the party's majority was much reduced in 2019. Only in 1983 and 2010 has Labour's vote share dipped below half of the votes cast. It is the biggest of the three Coventry seats and also the most diverse, with an Asian population exceeding 22,000 and more than 11,000 black and mixed race residents. Islam and Sikhism are prominent religions among residents, with 11,000 Muslims and 7,000 Sikhs living in the seat. It is a relatively deprived constituency and unemployment is higher than average.

EU REFERENDUM RESULT
57.8% Leave　　　　Remain 42.2%

Coventry North West

MAJORITY 208 (0.44%)　　　　　　LABOUR HOLD　　　　　　TURNOUT 63.46%

TAIWO OWATEMI
BORN Jul 22, 1992
MP 2019-

A rising star replacing Geoffrey Robinson, who had held the seat since 1976. A former senior oncology pharmacist, specialising in cancer and palliative care. Interned at the House of Commons through the Social Mobility Foundation, in the office of the former Conservative minister Sir Oliver Letwin. Served in a number of roles in the Young Fabian Health Network. Supported Lisa Nandy for the party leadership in 2020. Voted Remain in the 2016 referendum. Member, GMB. Her father died when she was six due to a shortage of organ donors.

	Electorate	Share %	Change from 2017 %
	75,240		
T Owatemi Lab	20,918	43.81	-10.14
C Golby C	20,710	43.38	+6.64
G Judge LD	2,717	5.69	+3.11
J Richardson Brexit	1,956	4.10	
S Gray Green	1,443	3.02	+1.69

Originally from Greenwich. Ed: The Business Academy Bexley. University of Kent (Mst pharmacy).

CHALLENGERS
Clare Golby (C) IT systems administrator. Cllr: Arbury, Warwickshire CC, 2017-; Nuneaton and Bedworth BC, 2016-. **Greg Judge (LD)** Policy manager at bone marrow charity Anthony Nolan. Contested Coventry South, 2017.

CONSTITUENCY PROFILE
This seat has been Labour since its creation in 1974, the party never having received less than two fifths of the vote. Geoffrey Robinson, the former owner of the *New Statesman* magazine and a New Labour cabinet minister, stood down in 2019 after serving as MP for 43 years. In terms of demographics and economics, it lies somewhere between its neighbours to the west and south. About a third of its residents are aged under 25. It has a roughly equal population of Muslims and Sikhs. The seat has lower than average levels of home ownership and high levels of private renting.

EU REFERENDUM RESULT
58.4% Leave　　　　Remain 41.7%

Coventry South

MAJORITY 401 (0.89%)   LABOUR HOLD   TURNOUT 63.47%

ZARAH SULTANA
BORN Oct 31, 1993
MP 2019-

Replaced Jim Cunningham, the MP for this seat since 1992. Labour Party community organiser, 2018-19. Backed Rebecca Long Bailey early on in the 2020 leadership contest. PPS to Dan Carden (Liverpool Walton), 2020-. Called for an end to "40 years of Thatcherism" in her maiden speech. Member: Unite; Momentum. NUS national executive council, 2014-15; cttee member, NUS black students' campaign, 2015-16, 2013-14. Marketing and engagement officer. Contested EU elections, 2019. Apologised for posting on social media in

	Electorate	Share %	from 2017 %	Change
	70,970			
Z Sultana Lab	19,544	43.39	-11.65	
M Heaven C	19,143	42.50	+4.36	
S Richmond LD	3,398	7.54	+4.69	
J Crocker Brexit	1,432	3.18		
B Finlayson Green	1,092	2.42	+1.14	
E Manning Ind	435	0.97	+0.49	

2015 that she would celebrate when "the likes of Blair, Netanyahu and Bush die". Ed: University of Birmingham (BA international relations and economics).

CHALLENGERS
Mattie Heaven (C) Associate, Fine & Country, 2014-19, selling residential properties. Cllr, Coventry City C, 2019-. **Stephen Richmond** (LD) Chairman, Coventry Lib Dems.

CONSTITUENCY PROFILE
This constituency has elected a Conservative only in 1959. A Coventry South West seat with different boundaries elected a Conservative MP during the Labour "wilderness years" from 1979 until 1997. Contains the city centre and cathedral as well as Coventry University and most of its student halls of residence, hence the high proportion of 16 to 24-year-olds. Petition to "bring the date for the post-study work visa closer to help current students" is popular in the constituency. It is the most affluent of the three Coventry seats, with its residents earning more than the regional average.

EU REFERENDUM RESULT
50.4% Leave   Remain 49.6%

Crawley

MAJORITY 8,360 (16.75%)   CONSERVATIVE HOLD   TURNOUT 67.24%

HENRY SMITH
BORN May 14, 1969
MP 2010-

Advocate for English votes for English laws; co-authored *Direct Democracy* arguing for devolution of powers. Ardent Brexiteer and one of the first Tory MPs to send a letter of no confidence in Theresa May; backed Boris Johnson to replace her in 2019. Select cttees: arms export controls, 2017-19; international development, 2017-19; European scrutiny, 2010-15. Chairman, animal welfare APPG. Heavily involved in campaigns for the rights of expelled Chagos Islanders. PPS to Greg Clark (Tunbridge Wells), 2015-16. Cllr, West Sussex

	Electorate	Share %	from 2017 %	Change
	74,207			
*H Smith C	27,040	54.19	+3.61	
P Lamb Lab	18,680	37.44	-8.25	
K Yousuf LD	2,728	5.47	+1.73	
I Dickson Green	1,451	2.91		

CC, 1997-2010; leader, 2003-10. Contested this seat in 2005 and 2001. Ed: Frensham Heights Sch, Farnham; UCL (BA philosophy).

CHALLENGERS
Peter Lamb (Lab) Social scientist. Cllr, Crawley BC, 2010-; leader, 2014-. Joined council while still in sixth form. **Khalil Yousuf** (LD) Corporate solicitor for a global aviation company based near Crawley; pro bono work for a number of refugee charities. Negotiator at UN on refugee rights.

CONSTITUENCY PROFILE
Henry Smith's majority in 2019 was the largest since the 1987 election, when the seat was held by Sir Nicholas Soames. It is a Labour and Conservative marginal, and a bellwether since its creation in 1983, although Labour held onto it by only 37 votes in 2005. Contains Gatwick Airport, the source of more than 20,000 local jobs. The town of Crawley itself contains 13,000 people who are of Asian descent and there are significant Muslim and Hindu communities. The constituency is more affluent than the national average, but slightly less than the regional average for the southeast.

EU REFERENDUM RESULT
58.4% Leave   Remain 41.6%

Crewe & Nantwich

MAJORITY 8,508 (15.75%)   CONSERVATIVE GAIN FROM LABOUR   TURNOUT 67.27%

KIERAN MULLAN
BORN Jun 6, 1984
MP 2019-

Accident and emergency doctor since 2010. Head of engagement and strategy, the Patients Association, 2009-10; director of policy and public affairs, 2010-13. Independent adviser to 2013 inquiry into NHS hospital complaints procedures in England. Volunteer special constable, 2014-18. Founder and trustee of a volunteer scheme, 2013-. Intern, World Food Programme. Brexiteer. One of 20 Conservative LGBT candidates. Contested: Wolverhampton South East, 2017; Birmingham Hodge Hill, 2015. Ed: Imperial Coll Healthcare NHS Trust.

	Electorate	Share %	Change from 2017 %
	80,321		
K Mullan C	28,704	53.12	+6.09
*L Smith Lab	20,196	37.38	-9.74
M Theobald LD	2,618	4.85	+2.42
M Wood Brexit	1,390	2.57	
T Browne Green	975	1.80	
A Kinsman Libertarian	149	0.28	

CHALLENGERS
Laura Smith (Lab) MP for this seat, 2017-19. Shadow Cabinet Office minister, 2018, resigned to vote against joining the European Economic Area. One of 19 rebel Labour MPs to vote for Boris Johnson's Brexit bill in October 2019. Former teacher. **Matthew Theobald** (LD) Legal director of a global aviation group. Cllr, Stapeley & District PC, 2013-. Contested Chesire East C, 2019. School governor.

CONSTITUENCY PROFILE
This Cheshire seat was an unexpected narrow victory for Labour in 2017, with the party winning by 48 votes. The Conservatives had gained it in a 2008 by-election after the death of the long-serving MP Gwyneth Dunwoody. It had been held by Labour since 1983, with the predecessor Crewe seat electing Labour MPs continuously since 1945. The constituency consists primarily of the railway town of Crewe and the much smaller Roman town of Nantwich. It has high levels of home ownership and residents are relatively likely to work in retail or manufacturing.

EU REFERENDUM RESULT
60.3% Leave   Remain 39.7%

Croydon Central

MAJORITY 5,949 (11.01%)   LABOUR HOLD   TURNOUT 66.39%

SARAH JONES
BORN Dec 20, 1972
MP 2017-

Croydon's first female MP. Shadow housing minister, 2018-; PPS to John Healey, 2018. Home affairs select cttee, 2017-18. Backed Sir Keir Starmer for leadership, 2020; supported Owen Smith in 2016. Made maiden speech during debate on Grenfell Tower. Former head of campaigns, Shelter; deputy communications director, London Olympics and Paralympics, 2008-11. Founded APPG on knife crime, 2017. Contested this seat, 2015. Former parliamentary assistant to Mo Mowlam and Geraint Davies. Ed: Durham University (BA history).

	Electorate	Share %	Change from 2017 %
	81,410		
*S Jones Lab	27,124	50.19	-2.14
M Creatura C	21,175	39.18	-3.24
S Sprague LD	3,532	6.54	+4.64
E Sutton Green	1,215	2.25	+1.15
P Sonnex Brexit	999	1.85	

CHALLENGERS
Mario Creatura (C) Spad to Theresa May, the prime minister, 2017-19. Head of digital communications, Virgin Money UK, 2019-. Parliamentary adviser to Gavin Barwell MP, 2012-15. Cllr, Croydon LBC, 2014-. Has Italian heritage. **Simon Sprague** (LD) Research scientist for six years in pharmaceutical manufacturing industries. Diversity and community outreach officer, Croydon Lib Dems, 2019-.

CONSTITUENCY PROFILE
The only Croydon constituency to have changed hands in the last twenty years, it has mainly elected Conservative MPs with Labour only previously winning the seat in 1997, 2001 and 2017. Its former MP, Gavin Barwell, went on to serve as Theresa May's chief of staff after losing the seat in 2017. More than 60 per cent of residents in this south London constituency are aged under 45. There is a significant community of people with Caribbean heritage, of about 21,000. This seat contains the New Addington estate, at one time a place of significant British National Party activity.

EU REFERENDUM RESULT
50.3% Leave   Remain 49.7%

Croydon North

STEVE REED
BORN Nov 12, 1963
MP 2012-

Won 2012 by-election after the death of Malcolm Wicks, the MP since 1992. Shadow minister: culture, 2016-19; communities, 2015-16; home affairs, 2013-15. Wanted to make Lambeth Britain's first co-op council, with residents running services. Resigned as shadow communities minister in protest at Jeremy Corbyn's leadership in 2016. Supported Sir Keir Starmer, 2020, Owen Smith, 2016 and Liz Kendall, 2015. Passed a bill to make hospitals reveal physical force used against patients. Chairman: Central London Forward,

	Electorate	Share %	from 2017 %	Change
	88,466			
*S Reed Lab Co-op	36,495	65.63	-8.53	
D Ekekhomen C	11,822	21.26	+1.39	
C Bonham LD	4,476	8.05	+5.27	
R Chance Green	1,629	2.93	+1.28	
C Ngwaba Brexit	839	1.51		
C Mitchell CPA	348	0.63		

2010-11; Vauxhall Nine Elms regeneration strategy board. Former educational publisher. Awarded OBE, 2013. Cllr, Lambeth LBC, 1998-2012; leader, 2006-12. Ed: University of Sheffield (BA English).

CHALLENGERS
Donald Ekekhomen (C) Pharmacist. Advocate for tougher sentencing. **Claire Bonham** (LD) Strategic lead, the Salvation Army.

Previously head of operations for Prison Fellowship England and Wales. **Rachel Chance** (Green) Extinction Rebellion campaigner.

CONSTITUENCY PROFILE
Labour candidates have consistently been elected with five-figure majorities since this seat was re-created in 1997. The party's majority exceeded 32,000 at the previous general election. This constituency has one of the largest black and mixed race populations of any seat in the UK, and it contains significant Hindu and Muslim populations. More than a third of residents are above the age of 45.

EU REFERENDUM RESULT
41.2% Leave   Remain 58.9%

Croydon South

CHRIS PHILP
BORN Jul 6, 1976
MP 2015-

Entrepreneur and self-made millionaire who founded multiple financial and travel businesses. Parly under-sec, Home Office, 2020-. Parly under-sec, justice, and minister for London, 2019-20. PPS to: Sajid Javid, 2018-19; the Treasury, 2017-18. Author, *Work for the Dole: A Proposal to Fix Welfare Dependency*. Backed Sajid Javid, 2019. Founder of Next Big Thing, a mentoring charity for entrepreneurs. Cllr, Camden LBC, 2006-10. Ed: St Olave's GS, Orpington; University Coll, Oxford (BA physics; MA theoretical quantum mechanics).

	Electorate	Share %	from 2017 %	Change
	83,977			
*C Philp C	30,985	52.20	-2.22	
O Fitzroy Lab	18,646	31.41	-4.38	
A Jones LD	7,503	12.64	+6.86	
P Underwood Green	1,782	3.00	+1.17	
K Garner Ukip	442	0.74	-1.08	

CHALLENGERS
Olga Fitzroy (Lab) Music recording engineer; helped produce albums by Coldplay, Foo Fighters and Muse. Executive, UK Music Producers Guild. **Anna Jones** (LD) Former HR director for a travel company. Contested this seat in the 2017 general election. **Peter Underwood** (Green) Chairman, Croydon Friends of the Earth. Opted against standing aside for "Unite to Remain" alliance in constituency.

CONSTITUENCY PROFILE
A safe Conservative seat, held by the party since the constituency was created in 1974. Sir William Clark represented it between 1974 and 1992, followed by Sir Richard Ottaway until 2005. The Conservative majority has only once fallen below 10,000, in 2001. Consists of affluent, leafy, middle-class suburbs, with the north of the seat incorporating Waddon, which contains a large tower-block council estate and sometimes returns Labour councillors. Large Hindu, Muslim and Buddhist communities. Employment rates are high in the financial and scientific sectors.

EU REFERENDUM RESULT
45.8% Leave   Remain 54.2%

Cumbernauld, Kilsyth & Kirkintilloch East

MAJORITY 12,976 (28.40%)   SNP HOLD   TURNOUT 69.14%

STUART C MCDONALD
BORN May 2, 1978
MP 2015-

SNP parliamentary spokesman on immigration, asylum and border control, 2015-; criticised Theresa May's immigration policies for splitting families. Select cttees: home affairs, 2015-; draft investigatory powers bill, 2015-16. Campaigned for the Yes vote in the referendum on same-sex marriage in Northern Ireland. Human rights solicitor for the Immigration Advisory Service, 2005-09. Began political career as a researcher for Shirley-Anne Somerville MSP and Jim Eadie MSP. Head of information, Yes Scotland. Former parliamentary and

	Electorate	Share %	from 2017 % Change
	66,079		
*S McDonald SNP	24,158	52.88	+9.25
J McPhilemy Lab	11,182	24.48	-9.42
R McCall C	7,380	16.15	-2.12
S Murray LD	2,966	6.49	+3.67

public affairs officer, Coalition for Racial Equality and Rights. Ed: Craighead Primary; Kilsyth Academy; University of Edinburgh (LLB).

CHALLENGERS
James McPhilemy (Lab) Lives locally, in Condorrat. Supporter of a green industrial revolution.
Roz McCall (C) Cllr, Perth & Kinross C, 2017-; business ambassador for the council.
Susan Murray (LD) Career in medical marketing. Cllr, East Dunbartonshire C, 2017-.

CONSTITUENCY PROFILE
Cumbernauld, Kilsyth & Kirkintilloch East had been Labour since its creation in 2005, and both of its predecessor seats had elected Labour MPs since the 1980s. The SNP won it with a majority of nearly 15,000 in 2015, holding it in 2017 with a majority of about 4,000. The seat encompasses towns in North Lanarkshire and East Dunbartonshire. Cumbernauld is home to more than 50,000 people, with higher levels of home ownership and lower levels of unemployment than the Scottish average. The seat has the longest name of any parliamentary constituency.

EU REFERENDUM RESULT
37.0% Leave   Remain 63.0%

Cynon Valley

MAJORITY 8,822 (29.18%)   LABOUR HOLD   TURNOUT 59.13%

BETH WINTER
BORN Oct 4, 1974
MP 2019-

Welsh academic who inherited this safe Labour seat from Ann Clwyd, who had held it for the 35 years since 1984 and spent most of her time in parliament as a backbencher. Supported Rebecca Long Bailey for the leadership, 2020. Research associate in housing and social policy at Swansea University. Specialises in disadvantages faced by older people living in rural communities. Policy and communicatoins officer for University and College Union Wales. First time running for an elected office. Welsh speaker. Ed: University of Bristol (BSc social

	Electorate	Share %	from 2017 % Change
	51,134		
B Winter Lab	15,533	51.37	-9.64
P Church C	6,711	22.20	+2.81
R Rees-Evans Brexit	3,045	10.07	
G Benney PC	2,562	8.47	-5.29
A Chainey Cynon	1,322	4.37	
S Bray LD	949	3.14	+1.30
I Mclean Soc Dem	114	0.38	

policy; MA housing studies); Swansea University (PhD).

CHALLENGERS
Pauline Church (C) Shopkeeper. Cllr, Wiltshire CC, 2017-.
Rebecca Rees-Evans (Brexit) Born-again Christian. Contested this seat in 2015 for Ukip.
Geraint Benney (PC) Spiritual life coach. **Andrew Chainey** (Cynon) Video production company owner; co-founder of

the Cynon Valley Party. **Steve Bray** (LD) Known for shouting "Stop Brexit" outside parliament and heckling pro-Leave MPs during broadcast interviews.

CONSTITUENCY PROFILE
Cynon Valley has elected Labour MPs since it was created in 1983, as did its predecessor seat, Aberdare, from 1922. Beth Winter's majority was the smallest her party had ever received here. The south Wales seat consists of former coalmining and ironworks towns, the largest of which, Aberdare, is home to about 14,000 people. Levels of economic inactivity are well above average.

EU REFERENDUM RESULT
56.7% Leave   Remain 43.3%

Dagenham & Rainham

MAJORITY 293 (0.67%)   LABOUR HOLD   TURNOUT 61.56%

JON CRUDDAS
BORN Apr 7, 1962
MP 2001-

Deputy political secretary
to Tony Blair, 1997-2001.
Supported Lisa Nandy in 2020
Labour leadership election,
having backed Jeremy Corbyn
in 2015 and Owen Smith in
2016. Labour policy review
co-ordinator, 2010-15. Contested
Labour deputy leadership
election, 2007. Rebelled on
tuition fees vote, 2004. Visiting
professor at Oxford and the
University of Leicester; also
University of Wisconsin, 1987-
89. Ed: Oaklands RC Comp,
Portsmouth; Warwick University
(BSc economics; MA industrial
relations; PhD philosophy).

	Electorate	Share %	from 2017 %	Change %
	71,043			
*J Cruddas Lab	19,468	44.51	-5.57	
D White C	19,175	43.84	+3.91	
T Bewick Brexit	2,887	6.60		
S Fisk LD	1,182	2.70	+1.69	
A Minott Green	602	1.38	+0.19	
R Emin Ind	212	0.48		
T London Ind	209	0.48		

CHALLENGERS
Damian White (C) Cllr,
Havering BC, 2010-; leader,
cabinet chairman. **Tom
Bewick** (Brexit) International
development adviser. Former
Labour Party member for 27
years; Cllr, Brighton & Hove
City C. Chairman, local Vote
Leave campaign. **Sam Fisk**
(LD) Public relations associate
at Room to Read; previously
communications for Hitachi Rail.

CONSTITUENCY PROFILE
Including its predecessor
seat of Dagenham, this east
London constituency has been
represented by Labour since
its creation in 1945, though
Labour's majority has never
been lower and in 2019 was one
of the ten smallest in parliament.
Average earnings in the seat
are in line with the UK average
but below that of London. The
British National Party held
council seats here in the 2000s
and won 11 per cent of the vote
at the 2010 general election. The
old Ford plant in Dagenham was
the scene of a 1968 strike that
became a catalyst for equal pay
for women.

EU REFERENDUM RESULT
70.3% Leave   Remain 29.7%

Darlington

MAJORITY 3,294 (7.57%)   CONSERVATIVE GAIN FROM LABOUR   TURNOUT 65.51%

PETER GIBSON
BORN May 22, 1975
MP 2019-

First Conservative to represent
Darlington in parliament since
1992. Solicitor specialising
in personal injury litigation.
Managing director of Coles
Solicitors, his own legal practice
with nine offices across the
region, taken over by the
national firm Kingly Solicitors in
2019. Voted Remain in the 2016
referendum. Previously worked
in the insurance industry. Board
member, Herriot Hospice.
Newcastle University student
union, 2012-18. Contested
Redcar, 2017. Ed: University of
Newcastle (BA law); University
of Law (LPC).

	Electorate	Share %	from 2017 %	Change %
	66,395			
P Gibson C	20,901	48.05	+4.76	
*J Chapman Lab	17,607	40.48	-10.13	
A Curry LD	2,097	4.82	+2.52	
D Mawson Brexit	1,544	3.55		
M Snedker Green	1,057	2.43	+1.26	
M Brack Ind	292	0.67		

CHALLENGERS
Jenny Chapman (Lab) MP
for this seat, 2010-19. Shadow
minister: Brexit, 2016-19;
childcare and early years,
2016; prisons, 2011-16. Former
vice-chairwoman, Progress.
Resigned from shadow cabinet
over Jeremy Corbyn's leadership
in 2016. Cllr, Darlington BC,
2003-10. Married to Nick Smith,
the Labour MP for Blaenau
Gwent. **Anne-Marie Curry**
(LD) Member of a domestic

abuse charity, Family Help. Cllr,
Darlington BC, 2008-.

CONSTITUENCY PROFILE
A Conservative gain in the
north of England, but not
necessarily a Red Wall seat, since
a Conservative MP represented
from 1983-92. Mostly held by
Labour since 1945, but was also
held by the Conservatives while
the party was in government
from 1951 until 1964. Darlington
itself is the biggest town in
County Durham. Average
earnings are below both the
UK and regional average, and
residents are more likely than
average to be in part-time work
or have an apprenticeship.

EU REFERENDUM RESULT
58.1% Leave   Remain 41.9%

Dartford

MAJORITY 19,160 (35.47%)   CONSERVATIVE HOLD   TURNOUT 65.71%

GARETH JOHNSON
BORN Oct 12, 1969
MP 2010-

Low-key Brexiteer, who did not actively campaign during the 2016 referendum. Assistant whip, 2018-19; resigned in opposition to Theresa May's withdrawal agreement, which he eventually ended up supporting. PPS to: Matt Hancock, 2015-; David Gauke, 2014-15. Supported Boris Johnson for leader, 2019. Select cttees: human rights, 2014-15; justice, 2013-14. Defence solicitor and son of a milkman. Cllr, Bexley LBC, 1998-2002. Contested: this seat, 2005; Lewisham West, 2001. Ed: Dartford GS; Coll of Law (LPC); UWE (PG Dip law).

	Electorate	Share %	Change from 2017 %
	82,209		
*G Johnson C	34,006	62.95	+5.39
S Gosine Lab	14,846	27.48	-5.76
K Marsh LD	3,735	6.91	+4.28
M Lindop Green	1,435	2.66	+1.17

CHALLENGERS
Sacha Gosine (Lab) Cllr, Dartford BC, 2019-; Labour group leader. **Kyle Marsh** (LD) Special educational needs teacher. Joint leader, North Kent District NEU. Canadian; moved to the UK in 2009. **Mark Lindop** (Green) Local government officer in housing. Contested: Sittingbourne & Sheppey, 2017; Gravesham, 2015.

CONSTITUENCY PROFILE
Dartford was a safe Labour seat in the aftermath of the

Second World War, but has been a bellwether since 1970. Labour's majority in 2005 was a slim 706, and the Conservative majority has grown at every successive election since the party reclaimed it in 2010. Ukip received nearly 20 per cent of the vote in this seat in the 2015 general election. Margaret Thatcher stood for the constituency under her premarital name Margaret Roberts in 1950 and 1951. Overrepresented industries in this constituency include construction and transport. Dartford enjoys low levels of unemployment and higher than average earnings.

EU REFERENDUM RESULT

64.0% Leave   Remain 36.0%

Daventry

MAJORITY 26,080 (45.43%)   CONSERVATIVE HOLD   TURNOUT 74.08%

CHRIS HEATON-HARRIS
BORN Nov 28, 1967
MP 2010-

Fierce Eurosceptic and advocate of small government. Criticised for "McCarthyite" tactics in 2017 after writing to all UK universities to request the names of any academics lecturing on Brexit, along with copies of their course materials. Transport minister, 2019-; parly under-sec, Brexit, 2018-19; assistant whip, 2017-18; government whip, 2016-17. Supported Andrea Leadsom then Boris Johnson in the 2019 leadership race. Assistant whip, 2016-17. ERG chairman, 2010-16. MEP, East Midlands, 1999-2009. Select cttees: selection, 2018; European

	Electorate	Share %	Change from 2017 %
	77,493		
*C Heaton-Harris C	37,055	64.55	+0.84
P Joyce Lab	10,975	19.12	-5.55
A Simpson LD	7,032	12.25	+5.04
C Slater Green	2,341	4.08	+2.36

scrutiny, 2010-15; public accounts, 2010-15. Ran family's wholesale fruit and vegetables company. Contested Leicester South, 2004 by-election, 1997. Ed: Tiffin GS.

CHALLENGERS
Paul Joyce (Lab) Health and safety rep, Communication Workers Union. Cllr, Northampton BC, 2017-. **Andrew Simpson** (LD) Cllr, Northampton BC, 1995-2011; deputy leader of Lib Dem group, 1999-2004. **Clare Slater** (Green)

Pharmacist. Manages a local sustainable living forum.

CONSTITUENCY PROFILE
Daventry is a safe seat that has elected a Conservative MP at every election since 1945. From 1979 to 1987 it was represented by the Labour defector Reg Prentice, a minister in both Labour and Conservative governments. Daventry was also the seat of Edward Fitzroy, the Commons Speaker from 1928 until his death in 1943. Half of the residents in the east Northamptonshire seat are aged over 45. The area has high levels of home ownership and low levels of unemployment.

EU REFERENDUM RESULT

58.6% Leave   Remain 41.4%

Delyn

CONSERVATIVE GAIN FROM LABOUR

ROB ROBERTS
BORN Oct 15, 1979
MP 2019-

	Electorate	Share %	from 2017 %	Change %
	54,552			
R Roberts C	16,756	43.67	+2.23	
*D Hanson Lab	15,891	41.42	-10.78	
A Parkhurst LD	2,346	6.11	+3.50	
N Williams Brexit	1,971	5.14		
P Rowlinson PC	1,406	3.66	-0.09	

Ended 27 years of Labour reign in this constituency. Worked as an independent financial planner and adviser with a number of local firms. Previously a mortgage adviser. Long-term local resident. Speaks English, French and Welsh. Campaigned on improving infrastructure for north Wales. Former school governor. Ed: Ysgol Maes Garmon; Liverpool John Moores University.

CHALLENGERS
David Hanson (Lab) MP for this seat, 1992-2019. Spent 17 years on Labour's front bench in

relatively junior positions. Quit in 2015 to chair debates. Shadow minister: Foreign Office, 2015; immigration, 2013-15; policing, 2011-13; Treasury, 2010-11. Supported Remain. PPS to: Tony Blair, 2001-05; Alistair Darling, 1997-98. Minister: crime, 2009-10; justice, 2007-09; Northern Ireland, 2005-07. Parly under-sec for Wales, 1999-2001. Assistant whip, Treasury, 1998-99. **Andrew Parkhurst** (LD) Chartered insurance risk manager. **Nigel Williams** (Brexit) Contested

this seat in 2015 for Ukip. **Paul Rowlinson** (PC) Contested this seat, 2017, 2015.

CONSTITUENCY PROFILE
Delyn is one of several north Wales seats which, despite Labour's dominance in recent elections, fell to the Conservatives in 2019. The constituency was created in 1983 from parts of a safe Labour seat and a safe Conservative one. While it initially elected a Conservative MP in the 1983 and 1987 general elections, Labour claimed control in 1992 and went on to hold it for the next 27 years. The seat has a significant population of over-65s.

EU REFERENDUM RESULT
54.4% Leave   Remain 45.6%

Denton & Reddish

LABOUR HOLD

ANDREW GWYNNE
BORN Jun 4, 1974
MP 2005-

	Electorate	Share %	from 2017 %	Change %
	66,579			
*A Gwynne Lab	19,317	50.06	-13.48	
I Bott C	13,142	34.06	+6.07	
M Power Brexit	3,039	7.88		
D Hardwick LD	1,642	4.26	+2.10	
G Lawson Green	1,124	2.91	+1.69	
F Dave Loony	324	0.84	+0.29	

Became England's youngest ever councillor in 1996, and was subsequently the youngest Labour MP in the 2005 parliament. Party general election campaign chief, 2017. Supported Sir Keir Starmer for leader, 2020, having previously backed Jeremy Corbyn, 2016, Andy Burnham, 2015, and Ed Balls, 2010. Shadow communities minister, 2018-. PPS to: Ed Balls, 2009-10; Jacqui Smith, 2007-09; Baroness Scotland, 2005-07. Shadow minister: without portfolio, 2016-17; health, 2011-16; public health, 2015-16; transport, 2010-11. Select cttees:

Crossrail bill, 2007; procedure, 2005-10. Previously European co-ordinator for Arlene McCarthy MEP. Cllr, Tameside MBC, 1996-2008. Ed: Tameside Coll; North East Wales Institute (HND business & finance); University of Salford (BA politics and history).

CHALLENGERS
Iain Bott (C) Dentist. Cllr, City of Westminster LBC, 2013-. **Martin Power** (Brexit)

Former Ukip member. **Dominic Hardwick** (LD) Works for a family clothing company.

CONSTITUENCY PROFILE
A safe seat in which Labour has not won less than half of the votes cast at any election since the 1980s. However, the party's majority is now at its lowest level since 1983. Situated in the south-east outskirts of Manchester, the seat crosses into Stockport to its south. Local industry used to consist of cotton spinning and engineering; the seat still retains many manual and skilled workers, but residents earn less than the UK average. It is part of the M60 investment corridor.

EU REFERENDUM RESULT
61.0% Leave   Remain 39.0%

Derby North

MAJORITY 2,540 (5.4%)   CONSERVATIVE GAIN FROM LABOUR   TURNOUT 64.22%

AMANDA SOLLOWAY
BORN June 4, 1961
MP 2019-; 2015-17

Reclaimed the seat that she had lost to Chris Williamson in 2017. Parly under-sec, business, 2020-. PPS to Rory Stewart, then an international development minister, 2016-17. Voted Remain. Appointed as parliamentary ambassador for HS2. Select cttees: business, energy and industrial strategy, 2015-17; human rights, 2015-17; consolidation bills, 2015-17. Was a retail manager with Sainsbury's. Worked in HR with charities including Save the Children and Help the Aged. Patron: Friends of the Baby Unit, Royal Derby Hospital. Ed: Bramcote Hills GS.

	Electorate	Share %	from 2017 %	Change
	73,212			
A Solloway C	21,259	45.22	+0.82	
T Tinley Lab	18,719	39.81	-8.72	
G Webb LD	3,450	7.34	+2.69	
A Graves Brexit	1,908	4.06		
H Hitchcock Green	1,046	2.22		
*C Williamson Ind	635	1.35		

CHALLENGERS
Tony Tinley (Lab) Unite regional officer for 22 years; former chairman, Rolls-Royce works cttee. **Gregory Webb** (LD) Software engineer. **Alan Graves** (Brexit) Cllr, Derby City C, 2014-. **Helen Hitchcock** (Green) Teacher and classical musician. **Chris Williamson** (Ind) Labour MP for this seat, 2017-19, 2010-15. Shadow fire and emergency services minister, 2017-18. Staunch Jeremy Corbyn supporter, but investigated for his views on the handling of antisemitism within Labour. He was barred from standing for the party and lost his deposit as an independent.

CONSTITUENCY PROFILE
A yo-yo marginal that has changed hands at the past three general elections. Labour, having gained the seat in 1997, held on to it by 613 votes in 2010 before losing by 41 votes in 2015. The seat contains the University of Derby. Nearly one in five of the voting-age population is aged under 25, largely due to the 10,000-strong student population.

EU REFERENDUM RESULT
54.3% Leave   Remain 45.7%

Derby South

MAJORITY 6,019 (14.18%)   LABOUR HOLD   TURNOUT 58.10%

DAME MARGARET BECKETT
BORN Jan 15, 1943
MP 1983-; 1974-9

The longest-serving female MP in history. Deputy leader of the Labour Party, 1992-94; became acting leader between John Smith's death and Tony Blair's victory in the 1994 leadership election, in which she herself came third. Called herself a "moron" for nominating Jeremy Corbyn for leader in 2015; described his supporters as "members of a fan club", not of Labour. Backed Sir Keir Starmer to replace him in 2020. Communities and local government minister, 2008-09; foreign secretary, 2006-07; environment secretary, 2001-06.

	Electorate	Share %	from 2017 %	Change
	73,079			
*M Beckett Lab	21,690	51.08	-7.26	
E Barker C	15,671	36.91	+3.40	
J Naitta LD	2,621	6.17	+3.46	
T Prosser Brexit	2,480	5.84		

MP for Lincoln, 1974-79. Author of report into Labour's election loss in 2015. Ed: Notre Dame HS, Norwich; UMIST.

CHALLENGERS
Ed Barker (C) Music tutor and saxophonist for George Michael and Wham!. Performed on *Strictly Come Dancing* and *The X Factor*. **Joe Naitta** (LD) Head coach with local sports group. Cllr, Derby City C, 2013-; chairman, communities scrutiny cttee. **Timothy Prosser** (Brexit) Local businessman.

CONSTITUENCY PROFILE
Unlike its neighbour to the north, Derby South is something of a safe seat, won by Labour at every election since its creation in 1950, although the Conservatives came close in 1983 and 1987. Labour's majority in 2019 was its lowest in the seat since 2005, the only time since the 1980s that it had dipped below 6,000. The constituency contains the city centre as well as Derby's southern suburbs. It has a significant south Asian population, with more than one in ten residents of Pakistani heritage. About 15 per cent of residents were born outside the European Union.

EU REFERENDUM RESULT
61.4% Leave   Remain 38.6%

Derbyshire Dales

MAJORITY 17,381 (34.75%)   CONSERVATIVE HOLD   TURNOUT 76.88%

SARAH DINES
BORN May 27, 1965
MP 2019-

Inherited seat from Sir Patrick McLoughlin, who first won it in 1986 and later became transport secretary, 2012-16, and chairman of the Conservative Party, 2016-18. Family law barrister. Member, Lincoln's Inn; called to the Bar in 1988. Voted Leave. Described by this constituency's former MP Matthew Parris as the "sensible choice" candidate for her proactive attitude to flooding in the region in 2019. Passionate about the green belt; has a farming background. Originally from Essex. Ed: Brunel University; Inns of Court School of Law.

Electorate	Share %	Change from 2017 %
65,060		
S Dines C	29,356	58.69	-1.31
C Raw Lab	11,975	23.94	-7.16
R Court LD	6,627	13.25	+6.94
M Buckler Green	2,058	4.11	+2.09

CHALLENGERS
Claire Raw (Lab) Service and commissioning manager at Derbyshire county council for 13 years. Local NHS assistant general manager. Experience as social worker with adults in independent living and as a mental health team manager in Doncaster and South Humber. Cllr, Derbyshire Dales DC, 2019-. **Robert Court** (LD) Physics teacher and headmaster. Village cricketer. **Matt Buckler** (Green) Conservationist for the Peak District National Park Authority.

CONSTITUENCY PROFILE
A safe seat since its creation in 2010; the preceding seat, West Derbyshire, elected Conservative MPs from 1950, having returned a Labour MP only in the 1945 general election. Matthew Parris, a columnist for *The Times* and *The Spectator*, was MP for this seat between 1979 and 1986 before resigning to begin his career in journalism. The constituency is large and sparsely populated. It is located to the northwest of Derby itself, and stretches up to the Peak District. More than half of its residents are over 45, and home ownership is well above the national average.

EU REFERENDUM RESULT
51.2% Leave   Remain 48.8%

Derbyshire Mid

MAJORITY 15,385 (31.17%)   CONSERVATIVE HOLD   TURNOUT 73.19%

PAULINE LATHAM
BORN Feb 4, 1948
MP 2010-

Brexiteer with a long history in local government. ERG member; voted against Theresa May's Brexit deal on first two occasions but supported it on the third. Nominated Esther McVey for leader in 2019. Advocates greater support for children with diabetes. Lobbied the East Midlands Drugs Fund to alter its funding for various types of cancer. Select cttees: international development, 2010-; arms exports, 2017-; administration, 2017-. Director, Michael St Development. Proprietor, Humble Plc. Led social action projects in Uganda.

Electorate	Share %	Change from 2017 %
67,437		
*P Latham C	29,027	58.81	+0.22
E Monkman Lab	13,642	27.64	-7.89
F Dodds LD	4,756	9.64	+6.08
S MacFarlane Green	1,931	3.91	+1.59

Contested Broxstowe, 2001. Ed: Bramcote Hill Technical GS.

CHALLENGERS
Emma Monkman (Lab) Former cabin crew co-ordinator with Thomas Cook. Cllr: Belper TC, 2019-; Amber Valley BC 2019-. Trustee, Rural Action Derbyshire, British Red Cross. **Felix Dodds** (LD) Sustainable development adviser. Senior affiliate with University of North Carolina Water Institute. **Sue MacFarlane** (Green) Contested this seat in the 2017 election.

CONSTITUENCY PROFILE
This seat was created in 2010, and has been held by the Conservatives since. The party's vote share has risen at each successive election. Its predecessor seats, Amber Valley and Erewash, were both held by Labour during the New Labour period. The seat's largest town is Belper, home to more than 20,000 people. Mostly covering the east and north of Derby, this seat also contains some suburban areas in the north of the city. More than a fifth of the seat's residents are aged 65 or above, and it has high levels of home ownership. The University of Derby falls within its borders.

EU REFERENDUM RESULT
52.5% Leave   Remain 47.5%

Derbyshire North East

MAJORITY 12,876 (26.16%)   CONSERVATIVE HOLD   TURNOUT 68.02%

LEE ROWLEY
BORN Sep 11, 1980
MP 2017-

Electorate	Share %	from 2017 % Change
72,360		
*L Rowley C	28,897	58.71 +9.52
C Peace Lab	16,021	32.55 -10.96
R Shipman LD	3,021	6.14 +3.38
F Adlington-Stringer Green	1,278	2.60 +1.17

Elected in 2017 as the constituency's first non-Labour MP since 1935. Son of a milkman who spent his early years in the family business before pursuing a career in finance: former senior manager of corporate change, Santander; also KPMG, Barclays, Co-op. Eurosceptic. Publicly opposed Theresa May's Chequers proposal, and supported her withdrawal agreement only in the third vote. Backed Boris Johnson for leader, 2019. Select cttes: public accounts, 2018-; statutory instruments, 2017-18. Contested this seat, 2015, and Bolsover, 2010. Worked for the Centre for Social Justice. Cllr, Westminster City C, 2006-14. Ed: St Mary's High Sch; Lincoln Coll, Oxford (BA history); University of Manchester (MA history).

CHALLENGERS
Chris Peace (Lab) Trade unionist, Unite. Campaigner, Orgreave Truth and Justice. **Ross Shipman** (LD) Cllr, North East Derbyshire DC, 2019-. **Frank Adlington-Stringer** (Green) Politics student aged 21.

CONSTITUENCY PROFILE
Something of a precursor to the raft of Red Wall seats that the Conservatives gained from Labour in 2019, Derbyshire North East was one of just six seats, all in the north of England or the Midlands, which the Conservatives won from Labour two years earlier. Labour had, until that loss, continuously held the seat from 1935. It is a rural constituency spread around the town of Chesterfield. Its biggest town is Dronfield, with a population of more than 21,000. More than half of residents are aged 45 or over and incomes are above the UK and East Midlands average.

EU REFERENDUM RESULT
62.1% Leave   Remain 37.9%

Derbyshire South

MAJORITY 19,335 (36.22%)   CONSERVATIVE HOLD   TURNOUT 67.26%

HEATHER WHEELER
BORN May 14, 1959
MP 2010-

Electorate	Share %	from 2017 % Change
79,365		
*H Wheeler C	33,502	62.76 +4.04
R Pearson Lab	14,167	26.54 -9.44
L Johnson LD	3,924	7.35 +3.80
A Baker Green	1,788	3.35 +1.61

Former Lloyd's broker and associate at the Chartered Institute. Parly under-sec: Asia and the Pacific, 2019-20; housing, 2018-19. Leave campaigner. Backed Andrea Leadsom, and then Boris Johnson, for leader in 2019. PPS to: John Whittingdale (Maldon), 2015-16; Jeremy Wright (Kenilworth & Southam), 2014-15. Assistant whip, 2016-17. Select cttees: communities, 2011-15; standards and privileges, 2010-13. Director, Brety Inns. Manager, Rics Insurance. Insurance broker, Lloyds. Criticised for sharing an image on Twitter suggesting that the British Empire won the 2016 Olympics. Cllr, South Derbyshire DC, 1995-2010; leader, 2007-10. Contested Coventry South, 2005, 2001. Ed: Grey Coat Hospital.

CHALLENGERS
Robert Pearson (Lab) Assistant registrar, Loughborough University. Cllr, South Derbyshire DC, 2011-. **Lorraine Johnson** (LD) Retired; worked for BT for 30 years in IT and project management. Barnardo's trustee and volunteer. **Amanda Baker** (Green) Charity manager.

CONSTITUENCY PROFILE
Effectively a bellwether seat, Derbyshire South was initially held by the Conservatives' Edwina Currie from its creation in 1983 until Labour gained the seat in 1997. Since winning it in 2010, the Conservatives have increased their majority at every successive election. A large and mostly rural seat to the south and west of Derby, the largest town, Swandlincote, is home to about 32,000 people. It is relatively young for such a rural seat. A high proportion of residents, about three quarters, own their own homes, and earnings are slightly higher than the East Midlands average.

EU REFERENDUM RESULT
60.4% Leave   Remain 39.6%

Devizes

CONSERVATIVE HOLD

TURNOUT 69.44%

DANNY KRUGER
BORN 23 Oct, 1974
MP 2019-

	Electorate	Share %	Change from 2017 %
	73,379		
D Kruger C	32,150	63.10	+0.35
J Waltham LD	8,157	16.01	+6.71
R Schneider Lab	7,838	15.38	-5.58
E Dawnay Green	2,809	5.51	+2.34

Former speechwriter for David Cameron and a leader writer at the *Telegraph*. Political secretary to Boris Johnson for the first four months of his premiership; resigned to stand for office. Advisor to culture department, 2018-19. Director of research, Centre for Policy Studies, 2001-03. Founder, trustee and chairman, Only Connect, a criminal justice charity, 2006-. Awarded an MBE in 2017 for charity work. Author, *On Fraternity: Politics Beyond Liberty and Equality*. Selected to contest Tony Blair's Sedgefield seat, 2005, but stood down after being

quoted as calling for "a period of creative destruction in the public services". Son of the TV chef Prue Leith and the author Rayne Kruger. Ed: Eton Coll; University of Edinburgh (BA history); University of Oxford (DPhil history).

CHALLENGERS
Jo Waltham (LD) Web designer. **Rachael Schneider** (Lab) Director of a business specialising in leadership. **Emma Dawnay** (Green) Contested this seat, 2017, 2015.

CONSTITUENCY PROFILE
Devizes has elected Conservative MPs since 1924, and has never returned a Labour MP to parliament. The second-placed party has changed at every election this decade, with Ukip and Labour the main challenger to the former MP Claire Perry in 2015 and 2017 respectively. It is a rural Wiltshire seat encompassing the town of Devizes, home to about 12,000 people, in its west. Unemployment and earnings are lower than the UK averages. This seat contains Larkhill artillery range and part of Salisbury Plain. Employment in the defence sector is high.

EU REFERENDUM RESULT

53.5% Leave   Remain 46.5%

Devon Central

CONSERVATIVE HOLD

TURNOUT 77.51%

MEL STRIDE
BORN Sept 30, 1961
MP 2010-

	Electorate	Share %	Change from 2017 %
	74,926		
*M Stride C	32,095	55.27	+1.19
L Robillard Webb Lab	14,374	24.75	-2.21
A Eden LD	8,770	15.10	+3.40
A Williamson Green	2,833	4.88	+2.23

Chairman, Treasury select cttee, 2019-. Opposed Brexit in 2016, but voted for all withdrawal agreements. Backed Michael Gove for leader, 2019. Leader of the House of Commons, 2019; dismissed by Boris Johnson after two months in the role. Paymaster general and financial secretary to the Treasury, 2017-19; various positions in the whips' office, 2014-17. PPS to John Hayes (South Holland & The Deepings), 2012-14. Northern Ireland affairs select cttee, 2010-11. Set up his own business in 1987 specialising in trade exhibitions, conferences

and publishing. Ed: Portsmouth Grammar Sch; St Edmund Hall, Oxford (BA PPE; Oxford Union president).

CHALLENGERS
Lisa Robillard Webb (Lab) Runs a small business. Chairwoman, Central Devon Labour Party, 2013-. Contested this seat, 2017. **Alison Eden** (LD) Healthcare communications specialist. Contested this seat, 2017. **Andy Williamson** (Green) Musician and music teacher. Contested this seat, 2015, 2017.

CONSTITUENCY PROFILE
This constituency was created from other Devon seats in 2010, and the Conservatives have increased their vote share in every election since. Initially a Conservative-Liberal Democrat contest, Ukip came second here in 2015 and Labour have since cemented their place as the second biggest party in the seat. It is a relatively large, rural constituency containing a chunk of Dartmoor National Park, and it has Devon's capital, Exeter, to its east. More than half of its residents are aged 45 or older, and the seat has one of the highest rates of self-employment in the country.

EU REFERENDUM RESULT

50.9% Leave   Remain 49.1%

Devon East

MAJORITY 6,708 (10.47%)   CONSERVATIVE HOLD   **TURNOUT 73.78%**

SIMON JUPP
BORN Sep 8, 1985
MP 2019-

Plymouth-born former BBC and ITV radio journalist who saw off a challenge from a popular independent candidate to maintain East Devon's record 184-year streak of being held by a single party. Presented shows on various local radio stations, including Radio Exe and Radio Plymouth, which he helped to establish in 2010. Station manager, BBC Radio Solent. Special adviser to Dominic Raab in the Foreign Office before the election. Voted Remain. Campaigned on improving broadband provision for local homes and businesses.

	Electorate	Share %	Change from 2017 %
	86,841		
S Jupp C	32,577	50.84	+2.31
C Wright Ind	25,869	40.37	
D Wilson Lab	2,870	4.48	-6.88
E Rylance LD	1,771	2.76	+0.33
H Gent Green	711	1.11	
P Faithfull Ind	275	0.43	

CHALLENGERS
Claire Wright (Ind) Columnist for the *Express & Echo*. Remainer. Contested this seat, 2015, 2017, winning more than 13,000 and 21,000 votes respectively. Increased her vote share again in 2019. Cllr, Devon CC, 2013-. **Dan Wilson** (Lab) Property manager. Ran 26 marathons in one year to raise money for Parkinson's UK. **Eleanor Rylance** (LD) Cllr, East Devon DC, 2017-; deputy leader,

Lib Dem group. Translator and languages teacher.

CONSTITUENCY PROFILE
Relatively safe seat for the Conservative Party. The independent local councillor Claire Wright has displaced the Lib Dems as the perennial second-placed candidate. The constituency is mostly rural; the largest town is Exmouth, on the south coast. It also contains two of the more Conservative areas in the southeast of Exeter. More than a quarter of constituents are aged 65 or older and a much greater than average proportion of residents are employed in the tourism sector.

EU REFERENDUM RESULT
50.4% Leave   Remain 49.6%

Devon North

MAJORITY 14,813 (26.65%)   CONSERVATIVE HOLD   **TURNOUT 73.27%**

SELAINE SAXBY
BORN Nov 25, 1970
MP 2019-

Business support consultant, who was training as a maths teacher before being selected. Director, LessBounce.com, a sports bra retailer, 2012-16. Founded and led breast cancer charity Pink Aerobics, 2003-13. Served as chief of staff for Ben Howlett MP, 2015-17. Cllr, North Devon DC, 2019-. Contested Llanelli, 2015, where she caused controversy by claiming that the Welsh language would not offer "value for money" if it were a business. Former member, teachers' union. Helped to arrange local beach cleans at Instow. Nordic

	Electorate	Share %	Change from 2017 %
	75,853		
S Saxby C	31,479	56.64	+10.83
A White LD	16,666	29.99	-8.05
F ONeill Lab	5,097	9.17	-3.51
R Mack Green	1,759	3.16	+1.81
S Cotten Ind	580	1.04	

walker. Ed: Cambridge (BSc mathematics and management studies); Bideford Coll (PGCE secondary maths; NQT, did not complete).

CHALLENGERS
Alex White (LD) County court advocate and trainee solicitor. Former Unicef adviser; previously worked on anti-AIDS campaign in Jamaica. Contested this seat, aged 22, in 2015. **Finola ONeill** (Lab) GP. Supporter of Extinction Rebellion.

CONSTITUENCY PROFILE
For much of its postwar history, Devon North had been a swing seat, alternating between the Conservatives and the Liberals or Liberal Democrats. It was represented by the Liberal leader Jeremy Thorpe between 1959 and 1979. The Conservatives won it and held it under Margaret Thatcher, but the Lib Dems won it back in 1992 and held it for the next 23 years. The biggest towns are Barnstaple and Ilfracombe, both on the coast, with populations of 24,000 and 11,000 respectively. The constituency has a significant tourist industry, low unemployment and an older than average population.

EU REFERENDUM RESULT
57.0% Leave   Remain 43.0%

Devon South West

MAJORITY 21,430 (40.16%)   CONSERVATIVE HOLD   TURNOUT 73.57%

SIR GARY STREETER
BORN Oct 2, 1955
MP 1992-

Electorate	Share %	from 2017 % Change
72,535		
*G Streeter C	33,286	62.37 +2.52
A Beverley Lab	11,856	22.22 -7.71
S Davarian LD	6,207	11.63 +6.46
I Poyser Green	2,018	3.78 +1.64

Elected temporary deputy speaker after the election. Solicitor for 14 years. Knighted in 2019. MP for Plymouth Sutton, 1992-97. Cllr, Plymouth CC, 1986-92. Evangelical Christian. Among MPs who signed a letter to the Advertising Standards Authority in 2012 trying to overturn a ban on adverts that claimed God could heal people. Interested in human rights and the developing world. Voted Remain; consistently supported the government's Brexit deals. Select cttees: privileges, 2017-; standards, 2017-; ecclesiastical, 2015-17; panel of chairs, 2009-. Speaker's cttee on the electoral commission, 2006-17. Vice-chairman, Conservative Party, 2001-02. Ed: King's College London (BA law).

CHALLENGERS
Alex Beverley (Lab) Mental health clinician and parliamentary assistant. Co-chairman, LGBT+ Labour South West. Former domestic abuse and youth support worker. Sima Davarian (LD) English teacher. Campaigner for Bowel Cancer UK after having the disease diagnosed while pregnant with her first child. Ian Poyser (Green) Local government environmental worker.

CONSTITUENCY PROFILE
Has been Conservative since its creation in 1997. It is a safe seat for the party, although Labour had a strong performance in the 2017 election. Dartmoor is in its north, and south Devon's coastline runs along its southern edge. Like other mostly rural Devon seats, it is demographically older than the national average and, like much of the southwest, its levels of home ownership are higher than average.

EU REFERENDUM RESULT
55.1% Leave   Remain 44.9%

Devon West & Torridge

MAJORITY 24,992 (41.84%)   CONSERVATIVE HOLD   TURNOUT 74.82%

GEOFFREY COX
BORN Apr 30, 1960
MP 2005-

Electorate	Share %	from 2017 % Change
79,831		
*G Cox C	35,904	60.11 +3.60
D Chalmers LD	10,912	18.27 +0.57
S Strode Lab	10,290	17.23 -4.50
C Jordan Green	2,077	3.48 +0.75
B Wootton Ind	547	0.92 -0.42

Attorney-general from July 2018 to February 2020. His legal advice on Brexit and the Irish backstop was hugely influential over political proceedings. Known for distinctive deep voice and rousing speech introducing Theresa May at the 2018 party conference. Supported Boris Johnson for the leadership in the 2019 contest. QC; co-founded Thomas More Chambers. Formerly: standing counsel to Mauritius; defence attorney in Operation Elveden trial involving allegations of payments by journalists to public officials. President, Tavistock FC. One of the wealthiest MPs; apologised to MPs for failing to declare £400,000 of outside earnings from legal work, 2015. Brexiteer. Contested this seat, 2001. Ed: King's Coll, Taunton; Downing Coll, Cambridge (BA English and law).

CHALLENGERS
David Chalmers (LD) Former advertising and sales manager, The Economist. Compared stopping Brexit to resisting Nazi sympathisers in the 1930s. Cllr, Fremington PC, 2015-. Contested this seat, 2017. Siobhan Strode (Lab) Copywriter and supply teacher. Cllr, Great Torrington TC, 2017-.

CONSTITUENCY PROFILE
Held by the Lib Dems for ten years after the Conservative MP Emma Nicholson defected in 1995. The 2017 election was the first time that the Lib Dems had been beaten to second place by Labour since the seat was created in 1983. This sparse, rural constituency north of Plymouth has a long border with Cornwall. It has a large retired population and nearly three quarters of residents are homeowners.

EU REFERENDUM RESULT
57.2% Leave   Remain 42.8%

Dewsbury

MAJORITY 1,561 (2.77%)   **CONSERVATIVE GAIN FROM LABOUR**   **TURNOUT 69.40%**

MARK EASTWOOD
BORN Mar 14, 1971
MP 2019-

Businessman. Left school at 17 to work as an insurance clerk. Most recently worked supplying furniture and equipment to the NHS. Self-described social liberal. Deputy chairman, Dewsbury County Conservative Association. Member: Prospect Union; Conservatives for Liberty; Blue Collar Conservatives. Stood for Kirklees district council multiple times, including in 2012, when he called for the council's abolition. Campaigned to protect local green spaces. Yorkshire and the Humber representative, Conservative Workers & Trade Unionists.

	Electorate	Share %	Change from 2017 %
	81,253		
M Eastwood C	26,179	46.43	+1.34
*P Sherriff Lab	24,618	43.66	-7.30
J Rossington LD	2,406	4.27	+2.12
P James Brexit	1,874	3.32	
S Cope Green	1,060	1.88	+0.07
S Stanton Loony	252	0.45	

CHALLENGERS
Paula Sherriff (Lab) MP for this seat, 2015-19. Sucessfully lobbied to abolish the tampon tax, 2016. Shadow minister: social care and mental health, 2018-19; women and equalities, 2016-18. Accused Boris Johnson of inflammatory rhetoric and warned of abuse and threats to female MPs, prompting Mr Johnson to call her complaints "humbug". Member, Unison. **John Rossington** (LD) Retired

manager of a drug and alcohol treatment service. **Philip James** (Brexit) Works in construction industry. **Simon Cope** (Green) Co-ordinator, Kirklees Greens. Former chairman, Scarborough Athletic FC.

CONSTITUENCY PROFILE
Until 2019 Dewsbury had mostly elected only Labour MPs since 1935, with the exceptions of 1983 and 2010. Sayeeda Warsi contested it for the Conservatives in 2005. The West Yorkshire seat consists of the old mill town of Dewsbury, home to 63,000 people, the smaller town of Mirfield and a large rural area south of the two towns.

EU REFERENDUM RESULT
57.1% Leave   Remain 42.9%

Don Valley

MAJORITY 3,630 (7.99%)   **CONSERVATIVE GAIN FROM LABOUR**   **TURNOUT 60.30%**

NICK FLETCHER
BORN Jul 15, 1972
MP 2019-

Lifelong Doncaster resident who ousted the incumbent of more than two decades to become the first Conservative MP elected in Don Valley since the seat's creation in 1918. Established an electrical contracting business, Analogue Electrics, with his wife in 1994. Sat on board of Doncaster Chamber of Commerce in 2019. Described his victory as a miracle. Ed: Doncaster Coll (electrical engineering).

CHALLENGERS
Caroline Flint (Lab) MP for this seat, 1997-2019. Blamed her

	Electorate	Share %	Change from 2017 %
	75,356		
N Fletcher C	19,609	43.16	+1.45
*C Flint Lab	15,979	35.17	-17.78
P Whitehurst Brexit	6,247	13.75	
M Alcock LD	1,907	4.20	+2.34
K Needham Green	872	1.92	
C Holmes Yorkshire	823	1.81	-1.67

defeat on "Corbynistas and uber-Remainers". One of the strongest anti-Jeremy Corbyn voices in the parliamentary party. Contested deputy leadership, 2015. Shadow secretary: energy, 2011-15; communities and local government, 2010-11. Europe minister, 2008-09. Joined a growing ministerial rebellion in 2009 and resigned from government, accusing Gordon Brown of treating her like "female window dressing" at

cabinet meetings. Voted Remain, but supported Brexit deals owing to her Leave-voting constituency. Vice-chairwoman, children of alcoholics APPG; her mother died from alcoholism.

CONSTITUENCY PROFILE
A Red Wall constituency in South Yorkshire that had elected only Labour MPs since 1922. The party's majority had previously fallen below 4,000 only once in its postwar history, in 2010. This seat encompasses Doncaster's southern outskirts and several smaller towns in the area, such as Hatfield and Conisbrough. It has a large population aged 65 or over, numbering about 12,000.

EU REFERENDUM RESULT
68.5% Leave   Remain 31.5%

Doncaster Central

MAJORITY 2,278 (5.48%)	LABOUR HOLD	TURNOUT 58.25%

DAME ROSIE WINTERTON
BORN Aug 10, 1958
MP 1997-

	Electorate	Share %	Change from 2017 %
	71,389		
*R Winterton Lab	16,638	40.01	-17.90
R Weeden-Sanz C	14,360	34.54	+0.17
S Duhre Brexit	6,842	16.45	
P Horton LD	1,748	4.20	+1.94
L French Yorkshire	1,012	2.43	-0.69
F Sheridan Green	981	2.36	

Deputy speaker, 2017-19; stood to replace John Bercow as Speaker but came fifth. Appointed chief whip by Ed Miliband in 2010; sacked by Jeremy Corbyn after his 2016 leadership victory. Made a dame in 2016. Began political career as a constituency assistant to John Prescott, 1980-86, and managed his office, 1994-97. Parliamentary officer: Southwark Council, 1986-88; Royal Coll of Nursing, 1988-90. Managing director, Connect Public Affairs consultancy firm. Lobbied for Channel Tunnel rail link to north of England. Minister: regional affairs, 2008-

10; transport, 2007-08; health, 2003-07. Ed: Doncaster GS; Hull University (BA history).

CHALLENGERS
Roberto Weeden-Sanz (C) Former charity worker and volunteer special constable. Cllr, Barnet LBC 2018-. Council policing lead. Candidate, GLA elections, 2020. Ambassador, White Ribbon UK. **Surjit Duhre** (Brexit) Party colleagues claimed that his campaign trailer was run

off the road in a political attack; police later said it was more likely to have been knocked over by the wind. **Paul Horton** (LD) Business consultant.

CONSTITUENCY PROFILE
Has elected Labour MPs since its creation in 1983, as the old seat of Doncaster had done since 1964. Labour's majority in 2019 was smaller than in 1983, the only other time that the party's winning margin had fallen below 3,000. The seat covers most of the town of Doncaster. It is the most diverse of the Doncaster seats, although about 90 per cent of its residents are white.

EU REFERENDUM RESULT

66.7% Leave	Remain 33.3%

Doncaster North

MAJORITY 2,370 (5.82%)	LABOUR HOLD	TURNOUT 56.24%

ED MILIBAND
BORN Dec 24, 1969
MP 2005-

	Electorate	Share %	Change from 2017 %
	72,362		
*E Miliband Lab	15,740	38.68	-22.09
K Sale C	13,370	32.85	+5.23
A Stewart Brexit	8,294	20.38	
J Otten LD	1,476	3.63	+1.96
S Manion Yorkshire	959	2.36	+0.61
F Calladine Eng Dem	309	0.76	-0.10
E Todd ND	220	0.54	
W Bailey Ind	188	0.46	
N Wood Ind	142	0.35	

Leader of the opposition, 2010-15. Brownite and youngest ever Labour leader who managed to unite the party despite persistent concerns about his leadership and ridicule within the media for his presentational style. Energy secretary, 2008-10; Cabinet Office minister, 2007-08. Special adviser to Gordon Brown, including in the Treasury, 1997-2002. Researcher and speechwriter for Harriet Harman (Camberwell & Peckham), 1993-94. Son of the Marxist academic, Ralph, and brother of David, the former foreign secretary whom he beat in the 2010 leadership

contest. Supported Sir Keir Starmer, 2020. Ed: Corpus Christi Coll, Oxford (BA PPE); LSE (MSc economics).

CHALLENGERS
Katrina Sale (C) Former brand manager, Ford. **Andy Stewart** (Brexit) Said that Brexit Party members were victims of "racism of opinion".

CONSTITUENCY PROFILE
Labour MPs have held this seat since its creation in 1983, but in 2019 the party's majority was not only the lowest it had been in any election since it was created, it was the first time that the winning margin had been less than 10,000 votes. An area to the north of Doncaster rather than an area in the north of Doncaster, it is even sparser than its mirror seat to the south, Don Valley. Of the three Doncaster seats, its residents are least likely to have high qualification levels, although unemployment is not as high as in the neighbouring seat of Doncaster Central.

EU REFERENDUM RESULT

71.7% Leave	Remain 28.3%

Dorset Mid & Poole North

MAJORITY 14,898 (13.45%)   CONSERVATIVE HOLD   TURNOUT 74.79%

MICHAEL TOMLINSON
BORN Oct 1, 1977
MP 2015-

	Electorate	Share %	from 2017 % Change
	65,426		
*M Tomlinson C	29,548	60.39	+1.15
V Slade LD	14,650	29.94	+2.49
J Oldale Lab	3,402	6.95	-6.36
N Carswell Green	1,330	2.72	

Government whip since 2020. Qualified barrister. Campaign manager for Nick King, the Conservative candidate in this seat in 2010. ERG member; co-deputy chairman, 2016-18. Backed Boris Johnson for leader, 2019. Voted for his Brexit deal, having supported Theresa May's only on the third occasion. Served as Dominic Raab's PPS in November 2018 for less than 48 hours, as it coincided with Mr Raab's resignation in protest at Mrs May's Brexit strategy. European scrutiny cttee, 2016-. Ed: King's Coll London (BA classics; PG Dip law).

CHALLENGERS
Vikki Slade (LD) Regional financial services manager. Contested this constituency in the previous two general elections. Cllr, Poole BC, 2011-16. **Joanne Oldale** (Lab) Teacher. Granddaughter of a coalminer, and attended workers' rallies as a child with her mother. Former roadie for the Austrian folk band Graymalkin. **Natalie Carswell** (Green) Sustainability consultant; former business and finance lecturer. Contested Dorset CC, 2019.

CONSTITUENCY PROFILE
Dorset Mid & Poole North was represented by a Liberal Democrat between 2001 and 2015, but the Conservatives have held it safely since their former coalition partner's collapse in 2015, each time with five-figure majorities. The seat is mainly rural with the exception of the northern suburban areas of Poole in its east. The constituency has older residents than the UK average, with a fifth at retirement age or above. It is characterised by high levels of home ownership and part-time employment, and is a relatively affluent constituency with high levels of economic activity.

EU REFERENDUM RESULT
57.1% Leave   Remain 42.9%

Dorset North

MAJORITY 24,301 (43.31%)   CONSERVATIVE HOLD   TURNOUT 73.87%

SIMON HOARE
BORN Jun 28, 1969
MP 2015-

	Electorate	Share %	from 2017 % Change
	75,956		
*S Hoare C	35,705	63.64	-1.27
D Chadwick LD	11,404	20.33	+6.77
P Osborne Lab	6,737	12.01	-6.64
K Huggins Green	2,261	4.03	+1.15

Previous careers in PR and public affairs, including at Charles Barker, Ketchum and Four Communications. Chairman, Northern Ireland affairs select cttee, 2019-. Supported the leadership campaign of Sajid Javid in the 2019 contest. Voted Remain and has supported both versions of the government's withdrawal agreement; also voted for soft Brexit options and against no-deal during indicative votes. Select cttees: liaison, 2019-; Welsh affairs, 2017-18; Speaker's cttee on works of art, 2015-18; regulatory reform, 2015-. APPG

chairman: multiple sclerosis; thalidomide. Member, Tory Reform Group. Contested: Cardiff South & Penarth, 2010; Cardiff West, 1997. Ed: University of Oxford (BA modern history).

CHALLENGERS
David Chadwick (LD) London-based data privacy consultant. Author of Centre for Policy Studies article *How Capitalism Can Kill Class*. **Pat Osborne** (Lab) Transformation manager for an insurance company. Cllr, Blandford Forum TC, 2016-.

Ken Huggins (Green) Cllr, Hazelbury Bryan PC, 2013-.

CONSTITUENCY PROFILE
Has elected a Conservative MP at every election since 1950, although by small majorities between 1997 and 2010, when the Liberal Democrats performed strongly. Only three places in Dorset North, the towns of Verwood, Gillingham and Blandford Forum, have a population of more than 10,000. It is a large constituency that borders Somerset, Wiltshire and Hampshire. One in four residents is aged 65 or above. Average earnings are slightly lower than the national average.

EU REFERENDUM RESULT
56.6% Leave   Remain 43.4%

Dorset South

RICHARD DRAX
BORN Jan 29, 1958
MP 2010-

Electorate	Share %	Change from 2017 %
72,924		
*R Drax C	30,024	58.80	+2.67
C Parkes Lab	12,871	25.21	-8.39
N Ireland LD	5,432	10.64	+4.76
J Orrell Green	2,246	4.40	+0.01
J Green Ind	485	0.95	

Career in the army before becoming a reporter in 1991, including for *The Daily Telegraph*, the *Daily Express* and the BBC. Brexiteer; backed Boris Johnson for leader, 2019. Cleared by a tribunal after being accused of sexual harassment by a former employee at an unfair dismissal case in 2013. The case was thrown out. Cttees: European scrutiny, 2015-; environment, 2010-15. Ed: Harrow; Royal Agricultural College; PG Dip (journalism).

CHALLENGERS
Carralyn Parkes (Lab) Artist and art historian. Former lecturer, Weymouth College. Trade union activist. Taught at Weymouth Women's Refuge, and Portland Outlook Family Centre. **Nick Ireland** (LD) IT worker. Completed a solo channel swim. Cllr: Dorset CC, 2017-19; Dorset UA, 2019-; LD council leader. Proposed successful resolution declaring a climate emergency in Dorset in 2019. **Jon Orrell** (Green) GP. Cllr, Weymouth C, 2016-. Contested this seat, 2017. Stood in the Melcombe Regis by-election, 2013.

CONSTITUENCY PROFILE
One of only two seats that Labour gained in 2001, Tony Blair's second landslide. The party held it until the Conservatives won it in 2010. Aside from 2001 and 2005, and a 1962 by-election, the Conservatives have held the seat for a century, increasing their majority in the last three elections. Weymouth dominates the constituency and has a population of more than 52,000. Nearly a quarter of the seat's residents are over 65 and a greater than average proportion of residents work part-time. Home ownership is lower than

EU REFERENDUM RESULT
59.4% Leave　　　Remain 40.6%

Dorset West

CHRIS LODER
BORN Sept 5, 1981
MP 2019-

Electorate	Share %	Change from 2017 %
80,963		
C Loder C	33,589	55.13	-0.38
E Morello LD	19,483	31.98	+8.50
C Sorin Lab	5,729	9.40	-8.88
K Clayton Green	2,124	3.49	+0.75

Started work as a train guard aged 18; head of new trains at South Western Railway before standing for parliament. Volunteered as a guard to break an RMT strike during the election campaign; accused by the TSSA of hampering negotiations to further his political career. Former head of service planning for SWR, responsible for Waterloo station upgrade. Voted Leave. Interested in rural services, transport, farming and agriculture. Organist and church bell-ringer. Former chairman, Institute of Railway Operators; Freeman of the City of London. Cllr, West Dorset DC, 2013-15. Fourth generation of Dorset-based farmers.

CHALLENGERS
Edward Morello (LD) Renewable energy assets manager, Zestec, 2018-. Previous roles in geopolitics and security risk. **Claudia Sorin** (Lab) Health and safety representative, Unison. Former chairwoman, West Dorset Labour Party. **Kelvin Clayton** (Green) Philosopher and ethics lecturer.

CONSTITUENCY PROFILE
Sir Oliver Letwin, who led rebellions against the government's Brexit programme, stood down from this seat in 2019. The seat has only ever elected Tory MPs, although Sir Oliver, having won the seat in 1997, never had a majority over the Lib Dems of more than 4,000 until 2015. It is a large, sparse seat. The largest town, Dorchester, is home to about 19,000 people. More than 30 per cent of the population are aged 65 or above and a greater proportion than average are homeowners. Self-employment and part-time employment are both common.

EU REFERENDUM RESULT
51.0% Leave　　　Remain 49.0%

Dover

MAJORITY 12,278 (24.22%)   **CONSERVATIVE WIN**   **TURNOUT 66.40%**

NATALIE ELPHICKE
BORN Nov 5, 1970
MP 2019-

Housing finance policy expert and former barrister. Replaced her husband, Charlie Elphicke, MP for Dover since 2010, who was facing trial on sexual assault charges, which he denies. Co-authored the Elphicke-House report, which led to the creation of the Housing and Finance Institute in 2015, of which she became CEO. Awarded an OBE for services to housing in 2015. Has been vocal in her opposition to migrants crossing the Channel to Britain. Volunteered at Dover Winter Night Shelter, 2017-19. Former non-executive director, Student Loans Company. Former

Electorate	Share %	from 2017 % Change
76,355		
N Elphicke C	28,830	56.86 +4.50
C Cornell Lab	16,552	32.65 -7.33
S Dodd LD	2,895	5.71 +3.14
B Sawbridge Green	1,371	2.70 +0.93
N Sutton Ind	916	1.81
E Morais Women	137	0.27

director, Dover People's Port Trust. Established Conservative Policy Forum, 2010. Ed: University of Kent (LLB law).

CHALLENGERS
Charlotte Cornell (Lab) Chief of staff for Rosie Duffield (Canterbury). Former English teacher studying for a PhD at the University of Kent. **Simon Dodd** (LD) Solicitor specialising in EU and competition law. Contested: this seat, 2017; Scunthorpe,

2015. **Beccy Sawbridge** (Green) Community representative, Unite. Contested this seat, 2017.

CONSTITUENCY PROFILE
Elected Conservatives from its reconstitution in 1983, before returning a Labour MP 1997-2010. Since 2010 the Tories have increased their majority at every election, with Natalie Elphicke almost doubling her husband's majority from 2017 at this election. This east Kent seat is best known for its port town's connections to Calais. Dover and Deal have about 30,000 residents, and the remaining inland area is rural. One in five residents is 65 or above.

EU REFERENDUM RESULT

63.0% Leave   **Remain 37.0%**

Down North

MAJORITY 2,968 (7.30%)   **ALLIANCE GAIN FROM INDEPENDENT**   **TURNOUT 60.57%**

STEPHEN FARRY
BORN Apr 22, 1971
MP 2019-

Won shock victory in what was widely expected to be a DUP gain. Deputy leader, Alliance Party. MLA, Down North, 2007-19. Minister, employment and learning, Northern Ireland executive, 2011-16. Mayor of Down North, 2013-14. Cllr, Down North BC, 1993-2011. UN international peace scholar. Constituency office was set on fire in 2012 after Alliance's decision to limit the number of days that the Union flag would fly over Belfast City Hall. Sat on Stormont economy and business committee until the assembly's collapse in 2017. Alliance

Electorate	Share %	from 2017 % Change
67,099		
S Farry Alliance	18,358	45.17 +35.88
A Easton DUP	15,390	37.87 -0.26
A Chambers UUP	4,936	12.14
M Robinson C	1,959	4.82 +2.42

Brexit spokesman. Ed: Queen's University, Belfast (BSc politics; PhD international relations).

CHALLENGERS
Alex Easton (DUP) Orangeman. Previously worked in healthcare. MLA, Down North, 2003-. Cllr, Ards and North Down BC, 2001-14. Contested this seat in past two elections. **Alan Chambers** (UUP) MLA, 2016-. Cllr, Ards and North Down BC, 1991-2014. Mayor, Down North, 2000-01. Contested 1995 Down North by-election. Independent until 2015.

CONSTITUENCY PROFILE
Lady Sylvia Hermon, who had represented the seat for the UUP, 2001-10, and as an independent since, stood down in 2019. Alliance, who won under 10 per cent in 2017, quintupled their vote tally to gain the seat, their only representation in the Commons. This was the only parliamentary seat in Northern Ireland not held by the DUP or Sinn Fein after the 2017 election; after 2019 it was one of three. Centred on the town of Bangor. 67,000 residents are Protestant and about 11,000 Catholic. The UUP won 97 per cent and 98 per cent of the vote here in 1955 and 1959.

EU REFERENDUM RESULT

47.6% Leave   **Remain 52.4%**

Down South

MAJORITY 1,620 (3.25%)   SINN FEIN HOLD   TURNOUT 62.85%

CHRIS HAZZARD
BORN Aug 20, 1984
MP 2017-

	Electorate	Share %	from 2017 %	Change
	79,175			
*C Hazzard SF	16,137	32.43	-7.51	
M Savage SDLP	14,517	29.17	-5.96	
G Hanna DUP	7,619	15.31	-2.11	
P Brown Alliance	6,916	13.90	+10.33	
J Macauley UUP	3,307	6.65	+2.71	
P Brady Aontu	1,266	2.54		

Member of the Northern Ireland assembly for Down South, 2012-17, and the youngest MLA at the time of his election. Campaigned for local infrastructure projects and served as minister for infrastructure in the Northern Ireland executive, 2016-17. Community activist focused on rural areas. Ed: Our Lady & St Patrick's Coll, Knock; Queen's University Belfast (PhD international studies and political philosophy).

CHALLENGERS
Michael Savage (SDLP) Business consultant and journalist. Chief executive, SDLP, 2009-12. Cllr, Newry, Mourne & Down DC, 2017-. Co-founded the *Down Democrat*, and *Newry Democrat* newspapers. **Glyn Hanna** (DUP) Cllr, Newry, Mourne & Down DC. **Patrick Brown** (Alliance) Cllr, Newry, Mourne & Down DC, 2014-; suspended from the council for six months in 2018 after a drink-driving conviction in 2017. Was director of a water charity in east Africa. **Jill Macauley**

(UUP) Communications officer, Northern Ireland assembly, 2007-17.

CONSTITUENCY PROFILE
This was Enoch Powell's constituency while he was an MP for the Ulster Unionist Party from 1974 to 1987. The UUP had held the seat for its entire postwar history until the SDLP won it in 1987 and held it for the next 30 years. Sinn Fein gained the seat for the first time in 2017. A large, sparse coastal seat in the southeast, containing the alleged burial site of St Patrick. There are about 79,000 Catholics and 29,000 Protestants living in the constituency.

EU REFERENDUM RESULT
32.8% Leave   Remain 67.2%

Dudley North

MAJORITY 11,533 (31.44%)   CONSERVATIVE GAIN FROM LABOUR   TURNOUT 59.23%

MARCO LONGHI
BORN Apr 22, 1967
MP 2019-

	Electorate	Share %	from 2017 %	Change
	61,936			
M Longhi C	23,134	63.06	+16.63	
M Dudley Lab	11,601	31.62	-14.87	
I Flynn LD	1,210	3.30	+2.35	
M Harrison Green	739	2.01	+1.40	

Trained as a pilot, but "lost interest" in flying and worked in oil and gas. Born in Walsall but his Italian father worked for an airline and he spent much of his childhood in Rome. Brexiteer. Has campaigned to protect the green belt. Voted for himself to serve a second year as mayor of Walsall in 2018, making him the first person for 70 years to serve in the position for two consecutive terms. Cllr, Walsall BC, 1999-2019. His grandfather, Wilfred Clarke, was a Conservative councillor in Walsall and the mayor in 1978. Contested this seat in 2005. Ed:

Manchester University (BEng civil engineering).

CHALLENGERS
Melanie Dudley (Lab) Replaced the longtime Labour incumbent Ian Austin, who did not stand. Assistant chief executive, Sandwell MBC. Trained as a teacher. Told a local newspaper in the campaign: "I've been saddled with this name all my life, it's about time it got me some benefit." **Ian Flynn** (LD) Worked in teaching, marketing and business development.

CONSTITUENCY PROFILE
Since its creation in 1997, Dudley North had been held by Labour MPs. Ian Austin held the seat by 649 votes in 2010 and by 22 in 2017. He resigned from Labour in February 2019 to sit as an independent. A vocal critic of Jeremy Corbyn's leadership and of the handling of antisemitism within the party, Mr Austin urged his constituents to vote Conservative at the 2019 election. The town of Dudley sits just to the south of Wolverhampton and to the west of Birmingham. There are high levels of unemployment and poor health. About one in four people live in social housing.

EU REFERENDUM RESULT
71.4% Leave   Remain 28.6%

Dudley South

MAJORITY 15,565 (42.56%)   CONSERVATIVE HOLD   TURNOUT 60.23%

MIKE WOOD
BORN Mar 17, 1976
MP 2015-

Nearly died from sepsis in 2017 and later urged Theresa May to improve treatment for the condition. Brexiteer who voted for the withdrawal agreement every time, but supported no-deal in indicative votes. Backed Sajid Javid for the leadership, 2019. His private member's bill became the Riot Compensation Act 2016. Parliamentary assistant, House of Commons, 2011-14. Caseworker to Andrew Griffiths, 2010-11. Senior researcher, JDS Associates, a business consultancy, 2006-08. Cllr, Dudley MBC, 2014-16. European scrutiny select cttee,

	Electorate	Share %	Change from 2017 %
	60,731		
*M Wood C	24,835	67.90	+11.45
L Caldicott Lab	9,270	25.34	-10.89
J Bramall LD	1,608	4.40	+2.76
C Mohr Green	863	2.36	+1.36

2016-17. Former policy adviser to the European parliament on matters including internal market legislation and environmental regulation. Ed: University of Aberystwyth (BSc economics and law); University of Cardiff (PG Dip Bar vocational course).

CHALLENGERS
Lucy Caldicott (Lab) Career in charities and fundraising. Cllr, Lambeth LBC, 2018-. **Jonathan Bramall** (LD) Fourth time contesting this constituency.

CONSTITUENCY PROFILE
Dudley South initially elected Labour MPs after it was created in 1997, but the constituency has been Conservative since 2010. The party's vote share has grown at each election, from just over two fifths in 2010 to more than two thirds in 2019. Labour's vote had not fallen below five figures until the 2019 election. The seat contains much of the residential area outside the town of Dudley, in the West Midlands, but also includes areas still in the metropolitan district, such as Kingswinford. Residents here earn slightly more, on average, than in Dudley North, and unemployment is also lower.

EU REFERENDUM RESULT
70.4% Leave   Remain 29.6%

Dulwich & West Norwood

MAJORITY 27,310 (48.96%)   LABOUR HOLD   TURNOUT 65.88%

HELEN HAYES
BORN Aug 8, 1974
MP 2015-

Background in planning and architectural practice. Director, Allies and Morrison: Urban Practitioners, 2011-15, created from the merger of A&M with Urban Practitioners, of which she was a director, 1998-2012. Co-sponsor of the homelessness reduction bill, 2017. Co-founder of the APPG on Southern Rail. Campaigned to remain in the EU; voted against Theresa May's Brexit deal every time and campaigned for a second referendum. Voted for soft Brexit options and revoke in the indicative votes. Housing select cttee, 2015-. Cllr, Southwark

	Electorate	Share %	Change from 2017 %
	84,663		
*H Hayes Lab	36,521	65.48	-4.16
J Bartley Green	9,211	16.51	+14.01
J Lyons C	9,160	16.42	-3.06
J Stephenson Brexit	571	1.02	
A Hodgson CPA	242	0.43	
J Plume UKIP	73	0.13	

LBC, 2010-16. Ed: Ormskirk GS; Balliol Coll, Oxford (BA PPE); LSE (MA social policy and administration).

CHALLENGERS
Jonathan Bartley (Green) Co-leader of the Green Party, 2016-; Unite to Remain candidate for this seat and endorsed by the Liberal Democrats. Founder of Ekklesia, a Christian think tank, 2002-. Arrested in October 2019 during an Extinction Rebellion

protest. Cllr, Lambeth LBC, 2018-; leader of the opposition. Contested Streatham, 2015. **Jane Lyons** (C) PR professional.

CONSTITUENCY PROFILE
This south London constituency has been Labour since its creation in 1997, although its predecessor seats, Dulwich and Norwood, were sometimes Conservative. It was represented from 1992 by Tessa Jowell, the Labour minister who brought the Olympics to London. It was one of the highest Remain-voting seats and in March 2019 more than 25,000 constituents signed a petition that called for Brexit to be cancelled.

EU REFERENDUM RESULT
22.9% Leave   Remain 77.1%

Dumfries & Galloway

MAJORITY 1,805 (3.51%)   CONSERVATIVE HOLD   TURNOUT 68.96%

ALISTER JACK
BORN Jul 15, 1963
MP 2017-

	Electorate	Share %	Change from 2017 %
	74,580		
*A Jack C	22,678	44.10	+0.79
R Arkless SNP	20,873	40.59	+8.22
T Thompson Lab	4,745	9.23	-11.66
M Laurie LD	3,133	6.09	+3.69

Appointed secretary of state for Scotland in July 2019. PPS to the leader of the Lords, 2018-19. Assistant whip, then whip, 2019. Treasury select cttee, 2017-18. Voted for Theresa May's Brexit deal each time, and against no-deal in the indicative votes. Former entrepreneur specialising in self-storage marketing, with an estimated £20 million fortune; he sold two self-storage businesses for a total of £54 million in 2017. Co-founder of a tent-hire firm Field & Lawn. Farmer of 1,200 acres near Lockerbie. Contested Tweeddale, Ettrick & Lauderdale, 1997.

Former vice-chairman, Scottish Conservatives. Scottish Conservative spokesman for industry, 1998. Ed: Glenalmond Sch; Heriot-Watt University.

CHALLENGERS
Richard Arkless (SNP) MP for this seat, 2015-17. Previously worked as a solicitor in consumer litigation before running an online business. **Ted Thompson** (Lab) Lecturer. Served in the merchant navy before working as a mechanical engineer. **McNabb Lawrie** (LD)

CONSTITUENCY PROFILE
Created in 2005 from parts of Galloway, a longstanding Conservative seat, and Dumfries, which had been Labour since 1997. This seat was held by Labour until 2015, then won by the SNP in the party's 2015 landslide, before the Conservatives gained it with a large swing in 2017. The southernmost constituency in Scotland, it is a large, sparse seat where more than half the population is aged over 45. Has a significant fishing industry.

Farming background. Leader, Galloway Glens Landscape Partnership.

EU REFERENDUM RESULT
45.1% Leave   Remain 54.9%

Dumfriesshire, Clydesdale & Tweeddale

MAJORITY 3,781 (7.69%)   CONSERVATIVE HOLD   TURNOUT 71.93%

DAVID MUNDELL
BORN May 27, 1962
MP 2005-

	Electorate	Share %	Change from 2017 %
	68,330		
*D Mundell C	22,611	46.00	-3.38
A Burgauer SNP	18,830	38.31	+8.21
N Chisholm Lab	4,172	8.49	-8.06
J Ferry LD	3,540	7.20	+3.22

Scotland secretary, 2015-19; shadow Scotland secretary, 2005-10. Became the first openly gay Conservative cabinet minister in 2016. Campaigned for Remain, but voted for the withdrawal agreement each time. Supported Michael Gove for the leadership, 2019. MSP, South of Scotland, 1999-2005. The only Scottish Conservative MP between the 2015 and 2017 elections. Scottish affairs select cttee, 2005-10. Social Democratic Party cllr: Dumfries & Galloway, 1986-87; Annandale and Eskdale, 1984-86. His son Oliver is MSP for Dumfriesshire, 2016-. Former

solicitor and legal adviser to BT. Ed: Lockerbie Academy; University of Edinburgh (MA law, Dip LP); Strathclyde Business School (MBA).

CHALLENGERS
Amanda Burgauer (SNP) Director, Arena Peak, IT company, 2011-; founder, Sharedbase, software company, 1999-2007. **Nick Chisholm** (Lab) Environmentalist. **John Ferry** (LD) Founder, media consultancy; financial journalist. Contested this seat, 2017.

CONSTITUENCY PROFILE
Held by the Conservatives since its creation in 2005, this was one of the three Scottish seats that was not won by the SNP in the party's 2015 landslide. Mostly farther inland than its neighbouring seat of Dumfries & Galloway, this is a large, sparse constituency, with a relatively old population. Many residents are employed in agriculture and fishing. It is more affluent than Dumfries & Galloway, with a higher average income and likelihood of home ownership. The seat contains Lockerbie, the site of the deadliest terror attack in UK history in 1988, in which 270 people were killed.

EU REFERENDUM RESULT
44.6% Leave   Remain 55.4%

Dunbartonshire East

MAJORITY 149 (0.28%)   SNP GAIN FROM LIB DEM   TURNOUT 80.26%

AMY CALLAGHAN
BORN May 21, 1992
MP 2019-

A 27-year-old administrator who narrowly unseated Jo Swinson, the leader of the Liberal Democrats. Aspired to become a teacher but switched to pursuing a career in politics after being diagnosed with melanoma at the age of 19. Cancer-free since 2014, but cites her experience with the disease as motivation to safeguard the NHS. Worked as an office manager to Rona Mackay, MSP for Strathkelvin & Bearsden, between 2018 and 2019; also had various jobs in the Scottish parliament, 2015-18. Ed: University of Strathclyde (BA politics).

	Electorate	Share %	Change from 2017 %
	66,075		
A Callaghan SNP	19,672	37.10	+6.82
*J Swinson LD	19,523	36.81	-3.77
P Gosal C	7,455	14.06	-0.54
C McNally Lab	4,839	9.12	-5.41
C Scrimgeour Green	916	1.73	
R Dickson Ind	221	0.42	
D MacKay UKIP	208	0.39	
L McKechnie Scot Family	197	0.37	

CHALLENGERS
Jo Swinson (LD) Leader of the Liberal Democrats, 2019; MP for Dunbartonshire East, 2017-19, 2005-15. Party's youngest and first female leader. Pledged to revoke Article 50 and cancel Brexit; began campaign claiming she could be the next prime minister. Deputy leader, 2017-19. Minister: employment, 2012-15; women and equalities, 2012-15.

Former marketing manager, Viking FM. **Pam Gosal** (C) Head of economy and culture, Milton Keynes council. **Callum McNally** (Lab) Aged 21. Contested this seat in the 2017 election.

CONSTITUENCY PROFILE
Had the highest turnout of any constituency in 2019, and Amy Callaghan has the fourth smallest majority in this parliament. The seat lies north of Glasgow; its main population centre, Bearsden, is effectively a Glasgow suburb. It is one of the more affluent seats in Scotland, with average incomes higher than in the wider city.

EU REFERENDUM RESULT
26.9% Leave   Remain 73.1%

Dunbartonshire West

MAJORITY 9,553 (21.16%)   SNP HOLD   TURNOUT 67.86%

MARTIN DOCHERTY-HUGHES
BORN Jan 21, 1971
MP 2015-

Left school with no qualifications and worked in a sweet factory. Later went to university and spent a decade in the voluntary sector, including at West Dunbartonshire Community and Volunteering Services, and Volunteer Scotland. Was Scotland's youngest councillor when elected to Clydebank DC, 1992-96. Cllr, Glasgow City C, 2012-15. Read out the names of all 520 victims of the Blitz in Clydebank during a Commons debate. Voted against the Brexit deals every time. Defence select cttee, 2017-. Party spokesman

	Electorate	Share %	Change from 2017 %
	66,517		
*M Docherty-Hughes SNP	22,396	49.61	+6.76
J Mitchell Lab	12,843	28.45	-9.21
A Mathieson C	6,436	14.26	-2.94
J Lang LD	1,890	4.19	+1.90
P Connolly Green	867	1.92	
A Muir Ind	708	1.57	

for the voluntary sector, 2016-. Ed: Glasgow Coll of Food Technology (HND business administration); University of Essex (BA politics); Glasgow Sch of Art (MPhil).

CHALLENGERS
Jean-Anne Mitchell (Labour) Managing director for a charity development consultancy. Formerly Scottish head of sales, Mirror Group. **Alix Mathieson** (C) Voted Leave. **Jennifer Lang**

(LD) Head of communications, People's Energy.

CONSTITUENCY PROFILE
Had voted Labour since its reconfiguration in 2005 and its main predecessor elected Labour MPs from 1936, but the seat was won by the SNP in the party's 2015 landslide. In 2017 the SNP's majority fell to just over 2,000 votes, from more than 14,000 in 2015. It is less affluent and suffers from much higher unemployment than its neighbour to the east. Clydebank, the largest town in the seat, was once the main home of Upper Clyde Shipbuilders.

EU REFERENDUM RESULT
38.0% Leave   Remain 62.0%

Dundee East

STEWART HOSIE
BORN Jan 3, 1963
MP 2005-

Veteran party activist who spent 20 years in IT. SNP deputy leader, 2014-16. Long-time ally of Alex Salmond, the party's former leader. Advocates tax cuts and fiscal probity. Resigned as SNP deputy leader after an extramarital affair came to light. In 2005 he and his wife, Shona Robison, became the first married couple to represent the same seat at Westminster and Holyrood. Voted against the Brexit deal every time; backed a second referendum and revoking Article 50 in the indicative votes. SNP Westminster economy spokesman, 2015-; organisation

	Electorate	Share %	Change from 2017 %
	66,210		
*S Hosie SNP	24,361	53.80	+10.96
P Scott C	10,986	24.26	-3.10
R Garton Lab	6,045	13.35	-12.68
M Crichton LD	3,573	7.89	+4.13
G Morton Ind	312	0.69	

convenor, 2003-05; national secretary, 1999-03; first youth convener, 1986-89. Contested: this seat, 2001; Kirkcaldy in 1997, 1992. Ed: Carnoustie HS; Dundee Institute of Technology (HD computer studies).

CHALLENGERS
Philip Scott (C) Cllr, Dundee City C. **Rosalind Garton** (Lab) Tutor, St Andrews University and trade union activist. **Michael Crichton** (LD) Politics student at the University of Glasgow.

CONSTITUENCY PROFILE
This has been a Labour seat for most of its history, but it was gained narrowly by the SNP in 2005 and has been held by the party ever since. The SNP also held the seat from 1974 to 1987. Dundee was the authority in which a greater proportion of voters backed Scottish independence than in any other. The seat stretches slightly beyond the city of Dundee itself, and contains the towns of Monifieth and Carnoustie. Its residents are older on average than those living in Dundee West and home ownership is much higher. Unemployment is high.

EU REFERENDUM RESULT
38.4% Leave   Remain 61.6%

Dundee West

CHRIS LAW
BORN Oct 21, 1969
MP 2015-

Ponytailed financial adviser. Once nearly drowned in Mozambique. Spent ten years leading motorcycle expeditions in the Himalayas. Trained as a chef, specialising in French food. Led flamboyant Spirit of Independence fire engine tour during the Scottish referendum campaign. Questioned by police but later cleared of all wrongdoing over financial arrangements connected with the tour in 2016. Voted against Theresa May's Brexit deals and for both a second referendum and revoke in the indicative votes. At the start of the 2015

	Electorate	Share %	Change from 2017 %
	64,431		
*C Law SNP	22,355	53.77	+7.11
J Malone Lab	10,096	24.28	-8.77
T White C	5,149	12.38	-3.79
D Coleman LD	2,468	5.94	+2.86
S Waiton Brexit	1,271	3.06	
Q Arrey CPA	240	0.58	

parliament he attempted, unsuccessfully, to take over the front bench seat that had been traditionally occupied by Dennis Skinner. International development select cttee, 2017-. Ed: Madras College; University of St Andrews (MA cultural and social anthropology).

CHALLENGERS
Jim Malone (Lab) Painter and decorator; former firefighter.
Tess White (C) First time

contesting a general election.
Daniel Coleman (LD) Contested this seat, 2015. **Stuart Waiton** (Brexit) Sociology lecturer, Abertay University.

CONSTITUENCY PROFILE
Elected only Labour MPs from 1950 to 2015. The old constituency of Dundee was represented by Winston Churchill, as a Liberal MP, 1908-22. Dundee West contains the University of Dundee and has a much higher student population than Dundee East. It is a slightly more affluent seat than its neighbour, but also has higher unemployment. There are high levels of poor health.

EU REFERENDUM RESULT
40.7% Leave   Remain 59.3%

Dunfermline & West Fife

MAJORITY 10,699 (20.00%) **SNP HOLD** **TURNOUT 69.77%**

DOUGLAS
CHAPMAN
BORN Jan 5, 1955
MP 2015-

Career in finance and business development. Spent 12 years in retail banking, then ran the youth training scheme at TSB. Has led vocal campaigns against defence cuts and in favour of better road safety. Censured for taking a selfie on a Commons bench in 2015. Rejected Theresa May's Brexit deal and voted for a second referendum in the indicative votes. Select cttees: public accounts, 2018-; European scrutiny, 2017-18; defence, 2015-17. Cllr, Fife C, 2007-15, 1997-98. Contested: Kirkcaldy & Cowdenbeath, 2010; this seat in a 2006 by-election and in 2005.

	Electorate	Share %	Change from 2017 %
	76,652		
*D Chapman SNP	23,727	44.36	+8.84
C Hilton Lab Co-op	13,028	24.36	-9.51
M Benny C	11,207	20.95	-3.73
R Bell LD	4,262	7.97	+2.05
M Hall Green	1,258	2.35	

Ed: West Calder HS; Edinburgh Napier University (BA personnel management).

CHALLENGERS
Cara Hilton (Lab Co-op) MSP for Dunfermline, 2013-16. Backed by Momentum. **Moira Benny** (C) Campaign manager for Luke Graham, the MP for Ochil & South Perthshire, 2017-19. Financial controller, Murray & Currie. **Rebecca Bell** (LD) Broadcast journalist for BBC Politics and Sky News.

CONSTITUENCY PROFILE
Created in 2005, this seat elected Labour MPs at that election and in 2010, although it was held by the Liberal Democrats for four years after a by-election in 2006 called after the death of the sitting MP, Rachel Squire. The various predecessor seats that contained Dunfermline elected Labour MPs in almost every election since 1935. The constituency consists of the town of Dunfermline, the smaller coastal towns to its south of Rosyth and Inverkeithing, and the rural areas surrounding them. Incomes are above the national average.

EU REFERENDUM RESULT
39.4 Leave Remain 60.6%

Durham, City of

MAJORITY 5,025 (10.28%) **LABOUR HOLD** **TURNOUT 68.55%**

MARY FOY
BORN Feb 27, 1968
MP 2019-

A party member of 30 years and a staunch trade unionist. Describes herself as the working-class daughter of Irish migrants and was raised on a council estate in Jarrow. Replaced Roberta Blackman-Woods, who retired after holding the seat for Labour since 2005. Backed Rebecca Long Bailey for leader, 2020. Candidacy was endorsed by Len McCluskey, the general secretary of Unite; she won selection by one vote at the second count. Cites experience as mother of a disabled daughter as motivation for prioritising the NHS. Was parliamentary

	Electorate	Share %	Change from 2017 %
	71,271		
M Foy Lab	20,531	42.02	-13.38
W Morgan C	15,506	31.74	+1.92
A Hopgood LD	7,935	16.24	+6.33
L Wright Brexit	3,252	6.66	
J Elmer Green	1,635	3.35	+1.70

assistant to Stephen Hepburn, the Labour MP for Jarrow from 1997 to 2019 who was barred from standing after being suspended from the party during the investigation of an accusation of sexual harassment, which he denied. Member, Labour's national policy forum, 2015-. Cllr, Gateshead BC, 2006-. Ed: YTS; gained social sciences degree as a mature student.

CHALLENGERS
William Morgan (C) Mental health nurse, University Hospital of North Durham, 2012-. **Amanda Hopgood** (LD) Cllr, Durham CC, 2008-; group leader, 2013-. Contested this seat, 2017.

CONSTITUENCY PROFILE
Labour has not failed to win this seat since 1931, but the party's majority in 2019 was its lowest since 1983, when the Social Democratic Party reduced it to about 2,000. The seat consists of the city of Durham and the rural area around it, including former collieries. Contains the medieval city centre, Durham University's many colleges and most of its 18,000 students.

EU REFERENDUM RESULT
43.3% Leave Remain 56.7%

Durham North

MAJORITY 4,742 (11.24%)   LABOUR HOLD   TURNOUT 63.17%

KEVAN JONES
BORN Apr 25, 1964
MP 2001-

Senior national organiser, GMB, 1999; previously officer and regional organiser, and led the union's campaign for compensation for the industrial victims of asbestos. Son of a coalminer. Shadow defence minister, 2010-16. Parly under-sec, veterans, 2008-10. His private member's bill, the Christmas Day Trading Act 2004, was passed by parliament. Voted against Theresa May's deal every time; voted against a second referendum in indicative votes. Corbyn critic; has backed Andy Burnham, Yvette Cooper, Owen Smith and Sir Keir

	Electorate	Share %	Change from 2017 %
	66,796		
*K Jones Lab	18,639	44.17	-15.70
E Parson C	13,897	32.94	+2.95
P Telford Brexit	4,693	11.12	
C Martin LD	2,879	6.82	+2.25
D Morse Green	1,126	2.67	
K Rollings Ind	961	2.28	

Starmer for the leadership. Spoke in parliament about his struggles with depression, 2012. Cllr, Newcastle City C, 1990-2001. Ed: Newcastle Polytechnic, University of Southern Maine (BA government and public policy).

CHALLENGERS
Edward Parson (C) Management consultant, PwC. Contested Durham North West, 2010. **Peter Telford** (Brexit)

Opposed the Brexit deal. **Craig Martin** (LD) Teacher. Contested this seat, 2017.

CONSTITUENCY PROFILE
Has elected only Labour MPs since its creation in 1983, as did its predecessor, Chester-le-Street, from 1906. Labour's majority in 2019 was its lowest at a general election in either seat since 1931. Slightly smaller and denser than the City of Durham, the biggest towns here are Stanley, once a mining town, and Chester-le-Street, with populations of 32,000 and 24,000 respectively. It has above-average unemployment and below-average pay.

EU REFERENDUM RESULT
60.3% Leave   Remain 39.7%

Durham North West

MAJORITY 1,144 (2.40%)   CONSERVATIVE GAIN FROM LABOUR   TURNOUT 66.05%

RICHARD HOLDEN
BORN Mar 11, 1985
MP 2019-

Party apparatchik who stood only after the previous candidate withdrew. First Conservative to win the seat in its history. Spad to: Gavin Williamson (Staffordshire South), 2019; Chris Grayling (Epsom & Ewell), 2018-19; Sir Michael Fallon, 2016-17; Baroness Stowell of Beeston, leader of the Lords, 2015-16. Conservative deputy head of press, 2012-15, after several junior jobs in the party press office. Senior manager, Vodafone, 2017-18. Resigned from political roles in 2017 for 15 months after an allegation of sexual assault, which he denied;

	Electorate	Share %	Change from 2017 %
	72,166		
R Holden C	19,990	41.94	+7.46
*L Pidcock Lab	18,846	39.54	-13.29
J Wolstenholme Brexit	3,193	6.70	
M Peacock LD	2,831	5.94	-1.15
W Stelling Ind	1,216	2.55	
D Sewell Green	1,173	2.46	+1.35
D Lindsay Ind	414	0.87	

later cleared of all charges and said the case was a "cruel public shaming". Contested Preston, 2015. Ed: LSE (BSc government and history).

CHALLENGERS
Laura Pidcock (Lab) MP for this seat since 2017. Shadow minister and Jeremy Corbyn ally once touted as a future Labour leader. Maiden speech decrying the "archaic" systems of the

Commons drew media interest, as did her assertion that she had no intention of being friends with any Conservative MPs. Shadow minister: employment rights, 2019; labour, 2018-19. **John Wolstenholme** (Brexit) Microbiologist. **Michael Peacock** (LD) Business owner.

CONSTITUENCY PROFILE
Had elected Labour MPs at every election since its creation in 1950 and the party had never previously won less than 40 per cent of the vote. Theresa May and Tim Farron both stood in this seat in 1992, before going on to become Tory and Liberal Democrat leaders respectively.

EU REFERENDUM RESULT
55.0% Leave   Remain 45.0%

Dwyfor Meirionnydd

MAJORITY 4,740 (15.84%)   **PLAID CYMRU HOLD**   **TURNOUT 67.46%**

LIZ SAVILLE ROBERTS
BORN Dec 16, 1964
MP 2015-

	Electorate	Share %	from 2017 %	Change
	44,362			
*L Saville Roberts PC	14,447	48.27	+3.17	
T Davies C	9,707	32.43	+3.32	
G Hogg Lab	3,998	13.36	-7.31	
L Hughes Brexit	1,776	5.93		

Former reporter in London and north Wales, and further education lecturer. Plaid Cymru's first female MP. Elected as the party's leader in the House of Commons, 2017. Rejected Brexit deals and voted for a second referendum, revoke and UK membership of the Efta and EEA in the indicative votes. Her 2017 private member's bill to prevent the cross-examination of rape victims in court prompted an emergency government review. She became the first person to speak Irish in the Commons since 1901 when asking the Northern Ireland secretary to introduce an Irish Language Act. Plaid Cymru spokeswoman, 2015-: energy and natural resources; local government; women and equalities; environment, food and rural affairs; health; education; home affairs. Ed: Aberystwyth University (BA languages).

CHALLENGERS
Tomos Davies (C) Associate director, Fleishman Hillard Fishburn, lobbying company. Special adviser, Welsh secretary, 2015-16. **Graham Hogg** (Lab)

Worked in hospitality. **Louise Hughes** (Brexit) Contested this seat as an independent in 2017, 2015 and 2010.

CONSTITUENCY PROFILE
This seat in northwest Wales and its main predecessor, Meirionnydd Nant Conwy, have elected Plaid Cymru MPs since 1983. The seat covers the Snowdonia national park, making it a mountainous, isolated and rural area. Its largest towns, Porthmadog and Pwllheli, are home to fewer than 5,000 people each. One in four residents is 65 or above. David Lloyd George, the last Liberal prime minister, grew up here.

EU REFERENDUM RESULT
47.4% Leave   Remain 52.6%

Ealing Central & Acton

MAJORITY 13,300 (24.27%)   **LABOUR HOLD**   **TURNOUT 72.58%**

RUPA HUQ
BORN Apr 2, 1972
MP 2015-

	Electorate	Share %	from 2017 %	Change
	75,510			
*R Huq Lab	28,132	51.33	-8.37	
J Gallant C	14,832	27.06	-7.69	
S Badiani LD	9,444	17.23	+11.68	
K Crossland Green	1,735	3.17		
S Alsoodani Brexit	664	1.21		

Former researcher and lecturer in sociology at Kingston University. Voted for soft-Brexit options, a second referendum and revoke in the indicative votes. Backed Sir Keir Starmer in the 2020 leadership election and supported Owen Smith in 2016. Nominated Jeremy Corbyn in 2015, but later backed Yvette Cooper. Shadow crime prevention minister, 2016-17. Select cttees: public administration, 2017-19; regulatory reform, 2015-17; justice, 2015-16. APPG chairwoman, London planning and built environment. Deputy mayor, Ealing LBC, 2010-11. DJ. Sister of the broadcaster Konnie Huq. Contested Chesham & Amersham, 2005. Ed: Montpelier Primary Sch; Ealing & Notting Hill High Sch; Newnham Coll, Cambridge (BA political and social sciences and law); University of East London (PhD cultural studies).

CHALLENGERS
Julian Gallant (C) Professional conductor and composer. **Sonul Badiani** (LD) Adviser, World Animal Protection; previously campaign director, Peta. **Kate Crossland** (Green) Palliative care doctor.

CONSTITUENCY PROFILE
The seat was gained by the Conservatives upon its creation in 2010 before Labour won it back in 2015 with a majority of 274. Before 2015, the seat's various predecessors had been bellwethers as far back as 1979, with Acton switching between Labour and the Conservatives for most of the 20th century. About 15 per cent of residents were born in the EU-27 nations. It is also the most affluent Ealing constituency.

EU REFERENDUM RESULT
29.2% Leave   Remain 70.8%

Ealing North

JAMES MURRAY
BORN Jul 13, 1983
MP 2019-

Local politician who has ascended to parliament by replacing the retiring Labour grandee Steve Pound, MP for this seat, 1997-2019. London deputy mayor for housing, 2016-19. Executive member for housing and development at Islington council for six years; oversaw initiative to build 10,000 new homes. Worked closely with Jeremy Corbyn and Emily Thornberry, local MPs. Campaigner for shared property ownership and high-density accommodation. Backed by Unite but considered to be soft left by much of the party. Won

	Electorate	Share %	Change from 2017 %
	74,473		
J Murray Lab Co-op	28,036	56.49	-9.46
A Pickles C	15,767	31.77	+3.32
H Bewley LD	4,370	8.80	+6.38
J Parker Green	1,458	2.94	+1.52

party selection in first round of voting. Born in Ealing. Ed: Wadham Coll, Oxford (PPE).

CHALLENGERS
Anthony Pickles (C) Head of tourism affairs at VisitBritain, 2017-. Trustee, Institute of Welsh Affairs, 2018-. Chief of staff, Welsh Conservatives, 2012-15. **Henrietta Bewley** (LD) Computer programmer and business analyst, British Airways. Opera singer and tango dancer. **Jeremy Parker** (Green) Critical of local development projects.

CONSTITUENCY PROFILE
For much of its postwar history this was a swing seat, won by the Conservatives under Anthony Eden and Margaret Thatcher but by Labour under Harold Wilson and Tony Blair; in more recent times it has become a relatively safe Labour seat. The Labour majority in Ealing North in 2019, although reduced, was still almost twice the size it was in 2005 and larger than it was in 2010 as well. More than a quarter of residents are of Asian descent and another sixth are black or mixed race. Constituents are far less likely than average to own their homes and more likely to rent.

EU REFERENDUM RESULT
46.3% Leave   Remain 53.7%

Ealing Southall

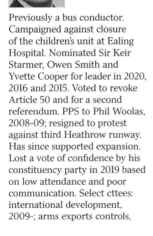

VIRENDRA SHARMA
BORN Apr 5, 1947
MP 2008-

Previously a bus conductor. Campaigned against closure of the children's unit at Ealing Hospital. Nominated Sir Keir Starmer, Owen Smith and Yvette Cooper for leader in 2020, 2016 and 2015. Voted to revoke Article 50 and for a second referendum. PPS to Phil Woolas, 2008-09; resigned to protest against third Heathrow runway. Has since supported expansion. Lost a vote of confidence by his constituency party in 2019 based on low attendance and poor communication. Select cttees: international development, 2009-; arms exports controls,

	Electorate	Share %	Change from 2017 %
	64,580		
*V Sharma Lab	25,678	60.82	-9.44
T Bennett C	9,594	22.73	+1.39
T Mahmood LD	3,933	9.32	+5.13
D Moore Green	1,688	4.00	+1.70
R Beattie Brexit	867	2.05	
S Fernandes CPA	287	0.68	
H Zulkifal WRP	170	0.40	-0.40

2016-17; human rights, 2007-15. APPG chairman: India; Nepal; honour-based abuse; Indian traditional sciences. Cllr, Ealing BC, 1982-2010. Ed: London School of Economics (MA).

CHALLENGERS
Tom Bennett (C) Management consultant; now owns a technology firm. Cllr, Kensington and Chelsea LBC, 2018-. Educated in America.

Tariq Mahmood (LD) NHS consultant. **Darren Moore** (Green) Earth scientist.

CONSTITUENCY PROFILE
This seat and its predecessor have elected Labour MPs at every election since 1945. As in Ealing North, Labour's 2019 majority was larger than its majorities in 2005 and 2010. Ealing Southall is one of the few seats in the country where more than half the residents are of Asian descent; about two thirds are Indian or of Indian descent, and it has the largest proportion of Sikh residents in Britain. Its socio-economic profile is similar to Ealing North.

EU REFERENDUM RESULT
41.8% Leave   Remain 58.2%

Easington

MAJORITY 6,581 (19.03%)   **LABOUR HOLD**   **TURNOUT 56.52%**

GRAHAME MORRIS
BORN Mar 13, 1961
MP 2010-

Medical lab scientific officer and caseworker for his predecessor John Cummings, MP for Easington 1987-2010. Shadow housing secretary, 2016. Select cttees: transport, 2018-; health, 2010-15. Pioneered recognition of Palestinian statehood as party policy; chairman, Labour Friends of Palestine & the Middle East. Chairman, the Unite Group in Parliament. APPG vice-chairman: Cuba; bees & pollution; housing in the North; radiotherapy. Received treatment for lymphatic cancer, 2016. Backed Rebecca Long Bailey for leadership, 2020, and

	Electorate	Share %	Change from 2017 %
	61,182		
*G Morris Lab	15,723	45.46	-18.20
C Ambrosino C	9,142	26.43	+3.72
J Maughan Brexit	6,744	19.50	
D Haney LD	1,526	4.41	+3.15
S McDonnell NE Party	1,448	4.19	-2.29

Jeremy Corbyn in 2015 and 2016. Cllr, Easington DC, 1987-2002. Ed: Newcastle Polytechnic (BTec medical laboratory sciences).

CHALLENGERS
Clare Ambrosino (C) Senior account manager, Newington, 2019-. Executive officer and president, Parliament Street think tank. Founder, Women 4 Westminster. Friend of Carrie Symonds, Boris Johnson's partner. **Julie Maughan** (Brexit) Self-described as northern and

working-class; climate sceptic. **Dominic Haney** (LD) Former civil servant.

CONSTITUENCY PROFILE
This constituency has elected Labour MPs at every election since 1950; never in that time had the Labour candidate received less than half the vote. A coastal seat between Sunderland and Hartlepool. Once a thriving area for coal-mining, Easington provided the backdrop to the film *Billy Elliot*. The largest towns are Seaham and Peterlee. Constituents have relatively low earnings and the average property price is £85,000.

EU REFERENDUM RESULT
66.0% Leave   **Remain 34.0%**

East Ham

MAJORITY 33,176 (60.73%)   **LABOUR HOLD**   **TURNOUT 55.78%**

STEPHEN TIMMS
BORN July 29, 1955
MP 1997-

Chairman of the work and pensions select committee since 2020. Manager of Logica, 1978-86; Ovum, 1986-94. Survived a stabbing in his constituency in 2010. Evangelical Christian; threatened to resign from shadow front bench if the party did not grant free vote on same-sex marraige in 2013. Supported Sir Keir Starmer for leader, 2020; backed Owen Smith, 2016, and Liz Kendall, 2015. Financial secretary to the Treasury, 2008-10; 2006-07. Shadow work and pensions secretary, 2015; shadow minister, 2010-15. Select cttees: Brexit, 2016-; education, 2016.

	Electorate	Share %	Change from 2017 %
	97,942		
*S Timms Lab	41,703	76.34	-6.87
S Pattenden C	8,527	15.61	+2.82
M Fox LD	2,158	3.95	+2.79
A Sehgal Cuthbert Brexit	1,107	2.03	
M Spracklin Green	883	1.62	+0.78
K Malik Communities	250	0.46	

APPG chairman: Egypt; faith and society. Ed: Emmanuel Coll, Cambridge (MA mathematics, MPhil operational research).

CHALLENGERS
Scott Pattenden (C) Telecomms programme manager: Cyient, 2017-; BT, 2016-17. RAF cadet and Royal British Legion fundraiser. **Michael Fox** (LD) Construction project manager. Former NHS administrator and Royal Navy commissioned

officer; served in the Middle East. **Alka Sehgal Cuthbert** (Brexit) English teacher and former research assistant. **Mike Spracklin** (Green) IT consultant.

CONSTITUENCY PROFILE
One of Labour's safest seats; the party won its fifth biggest vote total at the 2019 election here, and it is one of three seats in which more than 47,000 people voted Labour in 2017. Young and ethnically diverse; about a quarter of residents are aged over 45 and more than half are of Asian descent, including significant Indian, Pakistani and Bengali populations. Also contains London City Airport.

EU REFERENDUM RESULT
46.3% Leave   **Remain 53.7%**

East Kilbride, Strathaven & Lesmahagow

MAJORITY 13,322 (23.65%)   SNP HOLD   TURNOUT 69.36%

LISA CAMERON
BORN Apr 8, 1972
MP 2015-

Former NHS consultant psychologist. Accredited risk assessor in historical abuse cases, Scottish court service. Shadow SNP spokeswoman, climate justice, 2015-17. Select cttees: health, 2017-; international development, 2015-17. APPG chairwoman: disabilities; health; psychology; dog welfare. Spoke about receiving death threats after the murder of Jo Cox, 2016. Criticism from party for voting against extending abortion rights to Northern Ireland. Ed: Strathclyde University (BA psychology); Stirling University

	Electorate	Share %	Change from 2017 %
	81,224		
*L Cameron SNP	26,113	46.35	+7.49
M McAdams Lab	12,791	22.70	-9.01
G MacGregor C	11,961	21.23	-4.10
E McRobert LD	3,760	6.67	+3.74
E Bradley-Young Green	1,153	2.05	
D Mackay Ukip	559	0.99	-0.17

(MSc psychology and health); Glasgow University (PhD clinical psychology).

CHALLENGERS
Monique McAdams (Lab) Former marketing manager. Cllr, South Lanarkshire C, 2017-. Chief executive, East Kilbride Community Trust, 2009-. **Gail MacGregor** (C) Caseworker for David Mundell (Dumfriesshire, Clydesdale & Tweeddale). Cllr, Dumfries & Galloway C,

2002-. Secretary of the regional Conservative group, 2007-18. **Ewan McRobert** (LD) Web developer. Contested Airdrie & Shotts, 2017.

CONSTITUENCY PROFILE
Created in 2005, this seat initially elected Labour MPs until it was gained by the SNP in its 2015 landslide. Its predecessor seats had also elected Labour MPs since 1959. Located in South Lanarkshire, just south of Glasgow. The town of East Kilbride, in the north, is home to 74,000 people, about three quarters of the seat's population. The seat has fairly high levels of home ownership.

EU REFERENDUM RESULT
36.9% Leave   Remain 63.1%

East Lothian

MAJORITY 3,886 (6.64%)   SNP GAIN FROM LABOUR   TURNOUT 71.71%

KENNY MACASKILL
BORN Apr 28, 1958
MP 2019-

Former solicitor operating with his own practice. Member of the Scottish parliament, 1999-2016; Scottish justice secretary, 2007-14. Shadow minister: justice, 2004-07; transport, 2003-04; enterprise, 2001-03. Organised release of Lockerbie bomber on compassionate grounds, 2009. Lifted ban on sale of alcohol at rugby union matches at Murrayfield rugby stadium. Led "Can't Pay, Won't Pay" campaign to oppose poll tax during the 1980s. Favours a more gradualist approach to pursuing Scottish independence. Ed: University of Edinburgh (law).

	Electorate	Share %	Change from 2017 %
	81,600		
K MacAskill SNP	21,156	36.16	+5.60
*M Whitfield Lab	17,270	29.51	-6.56
C Hoy C	15,523	26.53	-3.07
R O'Riordan LD	4,071	6.96	+3.85
D Sisson UKIP	493	0.84	

CHALLENGERS
Martin Whitfield (Lab) MP for this seat, 2017-19. Personal injury lawyer; retrained as a primary school teacher. Stood in 2017 only so that an outsider was not parachuted into constituency. Voted Remain. Trans and non-binary advocate. Led Commons debate on World Menopause Day. Chairman, Prestonpans community council, 2016-17. **Craig Hoy** (C) Former lobby correspondent and publisher; established *Holyrood* magazine.

Cllr, East Lothian DC, 2019-. **Robert O'Riordan** (LD) Former investment professional.

CONSTITUENCY PROFILE
A yo-yo seat between Labour and the SNP for the past few elections, East Lothian was solely a Labour seat from its creation in 1983 until the SNP landslide in 2015. The predecessor seat was gained by the Conservatives in 1974 but was otherwise won at every election by Labour since 1966. Just to Edinburgh's east, East Lothian is a large coastal seat made up of relatively small towns, the largest of which are Musselburgh and Tranent.

EU REFERENDUM RESULT
35.4% Leave   Remain 64.6%

Eastbourne

MAJORITY 4,331 (7.86%)   **CONSERVATIVE GAIN FROM LIB DEM**   **TURNOUT 69.52%**

CAROLINE ANSELL
BORN Jan 12, 1971
MP 2019; 2015-17

Former French teacher and MP for this seat, 2015-17; was the constituency's first female MP. Voted with the government whip on every vote while she was in parliament the first time. Championed victims of revenge porn and constituents facing deportation. Lost seat in 2017 by fewer than 1,500 votes, having won it by just over 700 in 2015. Select cttees: ecclesiastical, 2015-17; environment audit, 2015-17. Voted Leave. Christian; attends both Evangelical and Roman Catholic churches. Cllr, Eastbourne BC, 2012-15. One of her three children survived

	Electorate	Share %	Change from 2017 %
	79,307		
C Ansell C	26,951	48.88	+4.80
*S Lloyd LD	22,620	41.03	-5.86
J Lambert Lab	3,848	6.98	-1.16
S Gander Brexit	1,530	2.78	
K Pollock Ind	185	0.34	

diagnosis of a brain tumour. Ed: Beresford House School; Royal Holloway (BA French); University of Brighton (MA education).

CHALLENGERS
Stephen Lloyd (LD) MP for this seat, 2017-19; 2010-15. Voted against increasing tuition fees. Former commodities broker and business development consultant. Contested: this seat, 2005; Beaconsfield, 2001. **Jake Lambert** (Lab) Secondary school

teacher. Chairman, Eastbourne Labour Party, 2012-. **Stephen Gander** (Brexit) Retail manager.

CONSTITUENCY PROFILE
Eastbourne has flipped between the Conservatives and the Lib Dems since 2010. It elected Conservative MPs at almost every election in the 20th century, although it was gained by the Lib Dems at a 1990 by-election after the assassination of Ian Gow by the IRA. The Victorian seaside town in Sussex is sometimes stereotyped for its ageing population; about a quarter of residents are 65 or over, compared to about a sixth in the UK overall.

EU REFERENDUM RESULT
57.5% Leave   **Remain 42.5%**

Eastleigh

MAJORITY 15,607 (26.47%)   **CONSERVATIVE HOLD**   **TURNOUT 70.30%**

PAUL HOLMES
BORN Aug 25, 1988
MP 2019-

Head of public affairs, Clarion Housing Group, the UK's largest housing association, 2018-19. Replaced Mims Davies, who became the MP for Sussex Mid in the 2019 election. Spad to: Damian Hinds (Hampshire East) 2018; Damian Green (Ashford), 2017. Previously an adviser to Stephen Hammond, 2011-15. Local to Southampton. Brexiteer. Cllr, Southampton CC, 2008-12. Contested: Southampton Test, 2017; Mitcham & Morden, 2015. Ed: Kelsey Park Sports Coll; Southampton University (BSc politics and international relations).

	Electorate	Share %	Change from 2017 %
	83,880		
P Holmes C	32,690	55.43	+5.00
L Murphy LD	17,083	28.97	+3.29
S Jordan Lab	7,559	12.82	-7.18
R Meldrum Green	1,639	2.78	+1.47

CHALLENGERS
Lynda Murphy (LD) Climate change activist; maths graduate with additional degree in wildlife management. Born in Scotland. Cllr, Winchester CC, 2018-; cabinet member for transport and the environment, 2019-. **Sam Jordan** (Lab) Market expansion manager and consultant in telecommunications. Local to the area in Eastleigh. Decried a dearth of local infrastructure. **Ron Meldrum** (Green) Counsellor and mental health campaigner.

CONSTITUENCY PROFILE
This Hampshire constituency was held by the Liberal Democrats from 1994 until 2015, including by Chris Huhne, the coalition energy secretary from 2010 to 2012, until he stood down from the seat in 2013 after pleading guilty to perverting the course of justice. This prompted a by-election, won by Mike Thornton for the Lib Dems. The Conservatives claimed the seat in 2015, however, and have increased their majority at every election since. The constituency consists of several towns to the north and east of Southampton and is younger and more affluent than the UK average.

EU REFERENDUM RESULT
54.3% Leave   **Remain 45.7%**

Eddisbury

CONSERVATIVE HOLD

EDWARD TIMPSON
BORN Dec 26, 1973
MP 2019; 2008-17

Family law barrister. MP for Crewe & Nantwich, 2008-17; lost his seat to the Lib Dems. Minister for children and families, 2015-17; parly under-sec, children and families, 2012-15. PPS to Theresa May, home secretary, 2010-12. Published independent inquiry into school exclusions, 2017-19. Chairman: National Child Safeguarding Panel; Children and Family Court Advisory and Support Service. Brought up in Cheshire alongside 80 children fostered by his parents. Marathon runner; had completed six to date. Ed: Durham University (BA law).

Electorate	Share %	Change from 2017 %
73,700		
E Timpson C	30,095	56.81	-0.07
T Savage Lab	11,652	22.00	-11.62
*A Sandbach LD	9,582	18.09	+12.63
L Jewkes Green	1,191	2.25	+0.72
A Allen Ukip	451	0.85	-1.31

CHALLENGERS
Terry Savage (Lab) NHS employee. Lifelong trade unionist; national officer, shop workers' union. **Antoinette Sandbach** (LD) MP for this seat, 2015-19. One of the 21 Conservative MPs who had the whip removed for rebelling over Brexit. Initially sat as an independent before joining the Lib Dems in October 2019. Former barrister; left the Bar to run family farm in Elwy Valley, north Wales. Former researcher

for David Jones (Clwyd West). Member of the Welsh assembly, 2011-15. **Louise Jewkes** (Green) Counsellor and mature student. **Andrea Allen** (Ukip) Contested Shropshire North, 2015.

CONSTITUENCY PROFILE
The seat has elected only Conservative MPs since it was reconstituted in 1983, although Labour came within 1,200 votes of victory in 1997. Eddisbury is the largest, sparsest constituency in Cheshire and about half its residents are aged 45 or above. Earnings are about 20 per cent higher than the regional average and about three quarters of residents own their homes.

EU REFERENDUM RESULT

52.2% Leave	Remain 47.8%

Edinburgh East

SNP HOLD

TOMMY SHEPPARD
BORN Mar 6, 1959
MP 2015-

Founder and former manager of Edinburgh stand-up comedy club. Member, SNP national executive committee. Vice-president of the National Union of Students for two terms. Member, Scottish Comedy Agency. Edinburgh South "Yes" campaign organiser in 2012; joined SNP, 2014. Cllr, Hackney BC, 1986-92; deputy council leader, 1990-92. Honorary associate, National Secular Society. Anti-royalist: remarked "off with their heads" during the royal wedding of Prince William and Kate Middleton. Contested Bury St Edmunds, 1992. Ed:

Electorate	Share %	Change from 2017 %
69,424		
*T Sheppard SNP	23,165	48.45	+5.92
S Gilmore Lab	12,748	26.66	-8.00
E Price C	6,549	13.70	-4.87
J Reilly LD	3,289	6.88	+2.63
C Miller Green	2,064	4.32	

University of Aberdeen (BA politics & sociology).

CHALLENGERS
Sheila Gilmore (Lab) MP for this seat, 2010-15. Family lawyer. Born in Aberdeen, later moved to Edinburgh. Marxist in her youth before joining the Socialist Labour Party in the 1970s. Family lawyer. Cllr, Edinburgh CC, 1991-2007. **Eleanor Price** (C) Asset manager. Contested Dundee East, 2017. **Jill Reilly** (LD) Senior project manager,

Standard Life Assurance. **Claire Miller** (Green) Cllr, Edinburgh CC, 2017-.

CONSTITUENCY PROFILE
Held by the Labour Party from its creation in 1974 until the Scottish National Party's landslide in 2015. Gavin Strang was the constituency's Labour MP for almost 40 years, until 2010. Unlike most SNP-held seats, the party's majority here was larger in 2019 than it was in 2015. Compact and urban, it contains the Palace of Holyroodhouse and the Scottish parliament building, as well as some of the city's other biggest tourist attractions.

EU REFERENDUM RESULT

27.6% Leave	Remain 72.4%

Edinburgh North & Leith

MAJORITY 12,808 (21.58%)   SNP HOLD   TURNOUT 72.96%

DEIDRE BROCK
BORN Dec 8, 1961
MP 2015-

Popular local figure; former deputy lord provost of Edinburgh city council. Shadow environment spokeswoman, 2015-. Raised in Perth, Australia, before moving to Scotland in 1996. Former office manager for Rob Gibson MSP. Board member: Edinburgh International Festival Council; the Centre for the Moving Image; Creative Edinburgh. Select cttees: Scottish affairs, 2016-; public accounts, 2015-16. APPG vice-chairwoman: Syria; Commonwealth; BBC. Cllr, Edinburgh City C, 2007-15. Ed: John Curtin University

	Electorate	Share %	Change from 2017 %
	81,336		
*D Brock SNP	25,925	43.69	+9.66
G Munro Lab Co-op	13,117	22.10	-9.05
I McGill C	11,000	18.54	-8.67
B Wilson LD	6,635	11.18	+6.62
S Burgess Green	1,971	3.32	+0.27
R Speirs Brexit	558	0.94	
H Astbury Renew	138	0.23	

(BA English); West Australian Academy of Performing Arts.

CHALLENGERS
Gordon Munro (Lab Co-op) Cllr, Edinburgh City C, 2003-. Co-founder, Edinburgh Sculpture Workshop. **Iain McGill** (C) Oversaw aid and development projects in Africa, South America and eastern Europe. Contested this seat, 2017, 2015. **Bruce Wilson** (LD) Former

Royal Marines commando. **Steve Burgess** (Green) Cllr, Edinburgh City C, 2007-.

CONSTITUENCY PROFILE
Elected Labour MPs from 1950, as did the predecessor seat of Edinburgh Leith, but was gained by the SNP in 2015. Labour came within 2,000 votes of winning it back in 2017. It is the Edinburgh seat with the highest level of unemployment and the largest proportion of EU citizens. Dense and urban, it contains the Port of Leith and was the economically depressed setting for Irvine Welsh's novel *Trainspotting*, and the film by Danny Boyle based on it.

EU REFERENDUM RESULT
21.8% Leave   Remain 78.2%

Edinburgh South

MAJORITY 11,095 (22.31%)   LABOUR HOLD   TURNOUT 75.14%

IAN MURRAY
BORN Aug 10, 1976
MP 2010-

Labour's only MP in Scotland. Second candidate after Angela Rayner to secure enough nominations to stand for deputy leader, 2020; nominated Jess Phillips for leader. Shadow Scotland secretary, 2015-16; resigned on live television after EU referendum result. Corbyn critic. Member, Progress. Shadow trade minister, 2011-15. PPS to Ivan Lewis, 2010-15. Select cttees: foreign affairs, 2016-; Scottish affairs, 2016-17; public accounts, 2015-17. APPG chairman, ITV. Cllr, Edinburgh City C, 2003-10. Born and raised in Edinburgh. Ed: Wester Hailes Ed Centre;

	Electorate	Share %	Change from 2017 %
	66,188		
*I Murray Lab	23,745	47.75	-7.16
C MacDonald SNP	12,650	25.44	+2.96
N Cook C	8,161	16.41	-3.30
A Beal LD	3,819	7.68	+4.78
K Nevens Green	1,357	2.73	

University of Edinburgh (social policy and law).

CHALLENGERS
Catriona MacDonald (SNP) Joined SNP aged 16, when independence referendum was announced. Café owner. Schooled in China; youth ambassador, Scotland-China Education Network. **Nick Cook** (C) Cllr, Edinburgh City C, 2017-. Contested Scottish parliament, 2016. **Alan Beal** (LD) Energy consultant. **Kate Nevens** (Green)

Co-convenor of the Edinburgh Greens.

CONSTITUENCY PROFILE
This seat was also Labour's only one in Scotland in 2015. It has elected Labour MPs ever since it was won from the Conservatives in 1987, having previously elected Conservative and Unionist MPs since the end of the First World War. The Lib Dems came within a few hundred votes of claiming it in both 2005 and 2010. It has the lowest unemployment of the Edinburgh constituencies, the highest average income and the second highest student population.

EU REFERENDUM RESULT
22.2% Leave   Remain 77.8%

Edinburgh South West

MAJORITY 11,982 (22.98%)   SNP HOLD   TURNOUT 70.93%

JOANNA CHERRY
BORN Mar 18, 1966
MP 2005-

Barrister in constitutional and family law. Nicola Sturgeon loyalist. SNP group leader, justice and home affairs, 2015-. Member, Brexit select committee, 2016-. Co-founder and leader, Lawyers for Yes independence group. Credited alongside the businesswoman Gina Miller with successfully overturning the suspension of parliament, September 2019. Previously junior counsel to the Scottish government, 2003-08. Took silk in 2009. Former tutor, University of Edinburgh. Member, Scottish Women's Rights Centre Advisory Group.

	Electorate	Share %	Change from 2017 %
	73,501		
*J Cherry SNP	24,830	47.63	+12.05
C Laidlaw C	12,848	24.65	-8.72
S Cooke Lab	7,478	14.34	-12.41
T Inglis LD	4,971	9.54	+5.24
B Parker Green	1,265	2.43	
D Ballantine Brexit	625	1.20	
M Brown Soc Dem	114	0.22	

LGBT; opposes reform to the Gender Recognition Act. Ed: University of Edinburgh (LLB law; LLM, Vans Dunlop Scholar; Dip).

CHALLENGERS
Callum Laidlaw (C) Corporate communications consultant. Cllr, Edinburgh City C, 2017-. Contested Falkirk, 2017. **Sophie Cooke** (Lab) Former SNP member; joined Labour in

2017 because she thought the SNP was failing on health and education. **Tom Inglis** (LD) Technology specialist.

CONSTITUENCY PROFILE
Initially voted Labour from its creation in 2005, having been the seat of Alistair Darling, the chancellor of the exchequer under Gordon Brown and chairman of the Better Together campaign during the 2014 independence referendum. The Scottish National Party has held it since Mr Darling's retirement in 2015. Contains a large rural area beyond Edinburgh. Significant student population; high level of private renting.

EU REFERENDUM RESULT
27.9% Leave   Remain 72.1%

Edinburgh West

MAJORITY 3,769 (6.91%)   LIB DEM HOLD   TURNOUT 75.21%

CHRISTINE
JARDINE
BORN Nov 24, 1960
MP 2017-

Lib Dem spokeswoman: home affairs, 2019-; women and equalities, 2019-. Deputy chief whip, 2019-. No 10 media adviser during coalition government. Unsuccessfully stood to be party president in 2019. Background in journalism and broadcasting: BBC, *Deeside Piper*, *The Scotsman*, and Scotland editor of the Press Association. Lecturer, University of the West of Scotland and Scottish Centre for Journalism Studies. Select cttee: Scottish affairs, 2017-. APPG vice-chairwoman, immigration detention. Widowed; her husband, Calum Macdonald,

	Electorate	Share %	Change from 2017 %
	72,507		
*C Jardine LD	21,766	39.91	+5.61
S Masson SNP	17,997	33.00	+4.36
G Hutchison C	9,283	17.02	-4.87
C Bolton Lab	4,460	8.18	-6.74
E Gunn Green	1,027	1.88	

died of a heart attack during the 2017 election. Ed: Braidfield HS; University of Glasgow (modern history & politics).

CHALLENGERS
Sarah Masson (SNP) Office manager and communications officer, Scottish parliament. SNP equalities officer, 2016. Background in theatre and the performing arts. **Graham Hutchison** (C) Accountant and valuations manager. Cllr, Edinburgh City C, 2017-. Elder,

Church of Scotland. **Craig Bolton** (Lab) Criticised SNP education policy. **Elaine Gunn** (Green) Project manager.

CONSTITUENCY PROFILE
Has elected Liberal Democrats at every election from 1997, other than in 2015 when it was gained by the SNP. Before 1997 the seat had been held continuously by Conservative and Unionist MPs from 1931. Dissimilar to the other Edinburgh seats in that it contains the oldest population and is the least ethnically diverse. The constituency also contains Edinburgh Airport and the coastal town of Queensferry.

EU REFERENDUM RESULT
28.8% Leave   Remain 71.2%

Edmonton

MAJORITY 16,015 (39.70%)   LABOUR CO-OP HOLD   TURNOUT 61.53%

KATE OSAMOR
BORN Aug 15, 1968
MP 2015-

	Electorate	Share %	Change from 2017 %
	65,568		
*K Osamor Lab Co-op	26,217	64.99	-6.49
J Hockney C	10,202	25.29	+2.15
D Schmitz LD	2,145	5.32	+3.35
B Maydon Green	862	2.14	+0.69
S Sehgal Brexit	840	2.08	
S Warsame Ind	75	0.19	

Worked for *The Big Issue* and spent 15 years in the NHS. Advocated abolishing the monarchy when prorogation was approved, 2019. Accused of misleading the public in 2018 by claiming she did not know about her son's arrest on drugs charges while he was employed as her communications officer; threatened to assault a *Times* reporter when questioned about it. Nominated Jeremy Corbyn for leader, 2015. NEC, 2014-. Unite member. Shadow international development secretary, 2016-18; shadow women and equalities minister, 2016. Active in campaigns: Women for Refugee Women; Set Her Free, to end the detention of women asylum seekers in the UK. Chairwoman, Nigeria APPG, 2015-. Ed: University of East London (Third World studies).

CHALLENGERS
James Hockney (C) Cllr: Enfield LBC, 2018-; South Cambridgeshire DC, 2004-16. **David Schmitz** (LD) Barrister. Contested this seat in 2017 and 2015, and Tottenham in 2010. **Benjamin Maydon** (Green) Contested Enfield LBC, 2018.

CONSTITUENCY PROFILE
Now a Labour safe seat in north London; Kate Osamor's majority in 2019 is second only to her majority in 2017 as the largest in the history of the constituency. It was Labour in 1935-83, Conservative in 1983-97 and has been held by Labour since then. More than a quarter of its population are aged under 16. About a third of residents are black or mixed race; it also has a large European population, especially from the post-2000 EU accession states.

EU REFERENDUM RESULT
45.5% Leave   Remain 54.5%

Ellesmere Port & Neston

MAJORITY 8,764 (17.98%)   LABOUR HOLD   TURNOUT 69.31%

JUSTIN MADDERS
BORN Nov 22, 1972
MP 2015-

	Electorate	Share %	Change from 2017 %
	70,327		
*J Madders Lab	26,001	53.34	-5.82
A Rodwell C	17,237	35.36	-1.44
E Gough LD	2,406	4.94	+3.18
C Stevens Brexit	2,138	4.39	
C Copeman Green	964	1.98	+1.31

Employment solicitor, 1998-2015; legally represented the rugby league players Ian Sibbit and Andrew Henderson. Shadow minister: health, 2015-19; business, 2018-19. Petitions select cttee, 2015. Defied Labour whip in a vote on a second referendum; resigned from the shadow cabinet in March 2019. Supported Lisa Nandy and Owen Smith for leader in 2020 and 2016 respectively. APPG chairman: social mobility; vice-chairman: football, foodbanks, leasehold reform. Cllr, Cheshire West & Chester BC, 2008-15; Ellesmere Port and Neston BC, 1998-2009; leader, 2007-09. First in family to attend university. Contested Tatton, 2005. Ed: University of Sheffield (LLB law).

CHALLENGERS
Alison Rodwell (C) Scientific researcher and management accountant. Worked in sustainable development for Shell, 1996-2014. Environmentalist. **Ed Gough** (LD) Software engineer, including project management with NHS systems. **Christopher Stevens** (Brexit) Career in car manufacturing, technical research and development. **Chris Copeman** (Green) Veterinary surgeon.

CONSTITUENCY PROFILE
Held by the Conservatives from its creation in 1983 until 1992 but has been a Labour seat since. Just north of Chester, Ellesmere Port lies on the southern banks of the River Mersey, below the Wirral peninsula. Its residents enjoy higher than average home ownership but lower than average median pay. The Stanlow oil refinery and the Vauxhall car plant are significant employers.

EU REFERENDUM RESULT
58.3% Leave   Remain 41.7%

Elmet & Rothwell

MAJORITY 17,353 (29.80%) CONSERVATIVE HOLD TURNOUT 71.92%

ALEC SHELBROOKE
BORN Jan 1, 1976
MP 2010-

Privy councillor and the UK representative to the Nato parliamentary assembly since 2015. Member, 1922 exec cttee. Vice-chairman, Conservative Party, 2015-. Voted for Jeremy Hunt in the 2019 leadership contest. Member: Blue Collar Conservatism; Trade Union Reform Group. Introduced private member's bill to ban unpaid internships. PPS to: Hugo Swire, 2014-15; Mike Penning (Hemel Hempstead), 2012-14; Theresa Villiers (Chipping Barnet), 2010-12. Select cttees: European scrutiny, 2015-16; housing, 2014-15; backbench

	Electorate	Share %	Change from 2017 %
	80,957		
*A Shelbrooke C	33,726	57.92	+3.59
D Nagle Lab	16,373	28.12	-9.75
S Golton LD	5,155	8.85	+4.48
P Stables Green	1,775	3.05	+1.38
M Clover Yorkshire	1,196	2.05	+0.30

business, 2013-14. Former kitchen and bathroom fitter. Later project manager, University of Leeds; became researcher and assistant to pro-vice-chancellor. Ed: Brunel University (BEng mechanical engineering).

CHALLENGERS
David Nagle (Lab) Cllr, Leeds City C, 2012-. Manager, ISS cleaning and security services company. Contested this seat, 2017. **Stewart Golton** (LD) Cllr, Leeds City C, 1998-; group

leader, 2010-. **Penny Stables** (Green) Nutritional therapist. Former marketing manager.

CONSTITUENCY PROFILE
This West Yorkshire seat has elected Conservatives since its creation in 2010, with the party's majority rising at every successive election. Its two predecessor seats were both represented by Labour from 1997. A relatively large seat encompassing several towns to the east of Leeds. Nearly half of its residents are aged 45 or above and it has high levels of home ownership. Income is also well above average for Yorkshire and the Humber.

EU REFERENDUM RESULT
56.8% Leave   Remain 43.2%

Eltham

MAJORITY 3,197 (7.32%) LABOUR HOLD TURNOUT 68.17%

CLIVE EFFORD
BORN Jul 10, 1958
MP 1997-

Nominated Jeremy Corbyn in the 2015 leadership contest but resigned from his position as a shadow culture minister, 2011-16, amid mass resignations from the shadow cabinet. Supported Sir Keir Starmer's leadership bid in 2020 and Owen Smith's in 2016. Voted Remain; supported a second referendum. Made a formal complaint to the police complaints authority after Stephen Lawrence was murdered in this constituency in 1993. PPS to John Healey (Wentworth & Deane), 2009-19; Dame Margaret Beckett (Derby South), 2008-09. Select cttees:

	Electorate	Share %	Change from 2017 %
	64,084		
*C Efford Lab	20,550	47.04	-7.41
L French C	17,353	39.72	-1.08
C Hasted LD	2,941	6.73	+3.57
S Kelleher Brexit	1,523	3.49	
M Stratford Green	1,322	3.03	

culture, 2018-19; public accounts commission, 2017-19; transport, 2016-17. Former taxi driver. Previously a youth worker who set up a job club for young people. Contested this seat, 1992. Ed: Southwark College.

CHALLENGERS
Louie French (C) Cllr, Bexley LBC, 2014-. Career in environmental research and investment. School governor. Local campaigner. **Charley Hasted** (LD) NHS emergency

services worker. Contested: Swansea East, 2017; Lambeth LBC, 2018.

CONSTITUENCY PROFILE
Won by the Conservatives when it was created in 1983, but then gained by Labour in 1997 and held by the party ever since, although often with slim majorities. One of the less ethnically diverse London seats; about two thirds of its residents are white British. Home ownership is low, albeit higher than the London average, and levels of social renting are high, with more than a quarter of households in the social rented sector, mostly from the council.

EU REFERENDUM RESULT
51.8% Leave   Remain 48.2%

The 2019 House of Commons

Seats by party

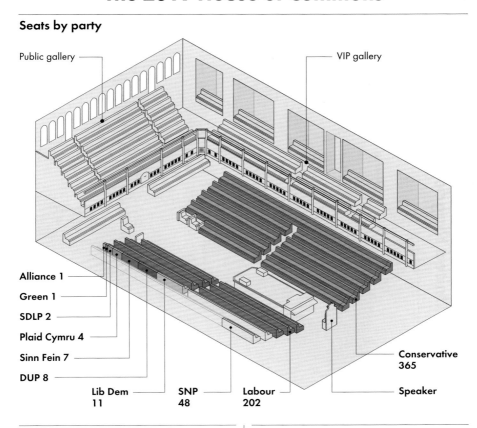

Public gallery

VIP gallery

Alliance 1
Green 1
SDLP 2
Plaid Cymru 4
Sinn Fein 7
DUP 8
Lib Dem 11
SNP 48
Labour 202
Speaker
Conservative 365

Vote share, %

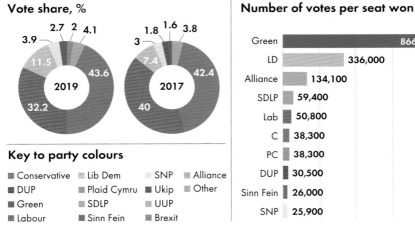

2019
2.7 2 4.1
3.9
11.5
43.6
32.2

2017
1.8 1.6 3.8
3
7.4
42.4
40

Key to party colours

- Conservative
- DUP
- Green
- Labour
- Lib Dem
- Plaid Cymru
- SDLP
- Sinn Fein
- SNP
- Ukip
- UUP
- Brexit
- Alliance
- Other

Number of votes per seat won

Party	Votes
Green	866,400
LD	336,000
Alliance	134,100
SDLP	59,400
Lab	50,800
C	38,300
PC	38,300
DUP	30,500
Sinn Fein	26,000
SNP	25,900

The political map of the United Kingdom 2019

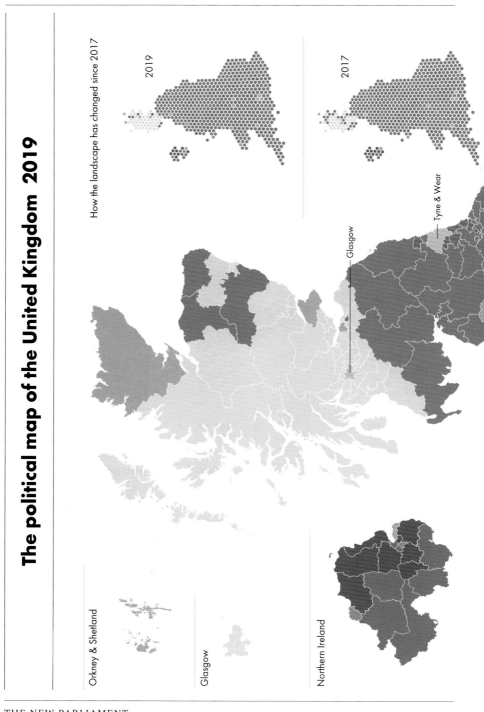

How the landscape has changed since 2017

2019

2017

Glasgow

Tyne & Wear

Orkney & Shetland

Glasgow

Northern Ireland

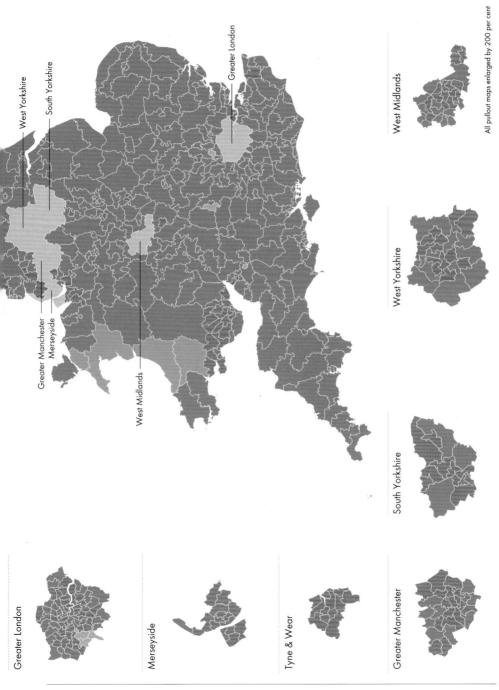

West Yorkshire

South Yorkshire

Greater London

Greater Manchester
Merseyside

West Midlands

West Midlands

West Yorkshire

South Yorkshire

All pullout maps enlarged by 200 per cent

Greater London

Merseyside

Tyne & Wear

Greater Manchester

Anatomy of the election

Voters

Gender

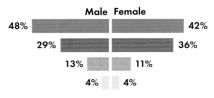

	Male	Female
48%		42%
29%		36%
13%		11%
4%		4%

How the Remain vote split

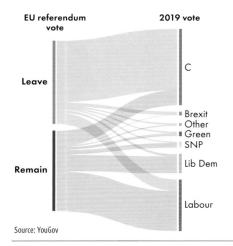

EU referendum vote — 2019 vote

Leave

Remain

C
Brexit
Other
Green
SNP
Lib Dem
Labour

Source: YouGov

Social class

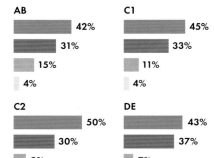

AB

| 42% |
| 31% |
| 15% |
| 4% |

C1

| 45% |
| 33% |
| 11% |
| 4% |

C2

| 50% |
| 30% |
| 9% |
| 4% |

DE

| 43% |
| 37% |
| 7% |
| 4% |

AB Professionals and managers; C1 Supervisory or clerical and junior managerial, administrative or professional; C2 Skilled manual workers; DE Semi-skilled and unskilled manual workers

Age

%				
18-24	19	57	12	4
25-34	23	55	11	5
35-44	30	45	13	5
45-54	43	35	11	4
55-64	49	27	13	4
65+	62	18	12	3

MPs

Women

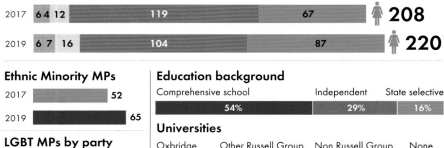

| 2017 | 6 | 4 | 12 | 119 | 67 | 208 |
| 2019 | 6 | 7 | 16 | 104 | 87 | 220 |

Ethnic Minority MPs

| 2017 | 52 |
| 2019 | 65 |

LGBT MPs by party

| 23 | 16 | 10 | 1 |

50 out of 650

Education background

Comprehensive school	Independent	State selective
54%	29%	16%

Universities

Oxbridge	Other Russell Group	Non Russell Group	None
21%	33%	32%	14%

THE NEW PARLIAMENT

Enfield North

MAJORITY 6,492 (14.41%) LABOUR HOLD TURNOUT 66.19%

FERYAL CLARK
BORN Jan 6, 1979
MP 2019-

Worked in diagnostic biochemistry and virology for four years at the University College Hospital and Barts. Labour's first Kurdish MP. Cllr, Hackney LBC, 2006-; deputy mayor, 2018-19; also a cabinet member for health and social care. Member, Unison. Voted for Lisa Nandy in the 2020 leadership contest, having supported Yvette Cooper in 2015. Interested in community safety, the environment and health. Born in Turkey to Alevi parents. Ed: University of Kingston (BSc biomedical science); University of Exeter (MSc bioinformatics).

	Electorate	Share %	from 2017 % Change
	68,066		
F Clark Lab	23,340	51.81	-6.21
J Laban C	16,848	37.40	+0.48
G Russo LD	2,950	6.55	+4.42
I Whittaker Green	1,115	2.48	+1.29
I Ijeh Brexit	797	1.77	

CHALLENGERS
Joanne Laban (C) Cllr, Enfield LBC, 2010-; opposition leader, 2017-. First woman to lead a political group on Enfield council. Works in public relations. Director of the Nightingale Cancer Support Centre. Contested London assembly, 2016. **Guy Russo** (LD) Bartender. Helped lead StrongerIn Enfield campaign during the EU referendum, aged 18. **Isobel Whittaker** (Green) Former legal aid lawyer.

CONSTITUENCY PROFILE
Joan Ryan, Enfield North's Labour MP in 1997-2010 and 2015-19, joined The Independent Group in 2019 before choosing not to stand for election again. Ms Ryan and the Conservative Nick de Bois had stood against each other in this constituency at every election since 2001, with Mr de Bois victorious just once, in 2010. It is the northernmost seat in Greater London, and the M25 runs along its northern border. A young and diverse seat, where about a quarter of residents are too young to vote and nearly two thirds are aged under 45. About a fifth are black or mixed race.

EU REFERENDUM RESULT
49.2% Leave Remain 50.8%

Enfield Southgate

MAJORITY 4,450 (9.41%) LABOUR HOLD TURNOUT 72.67%

BAMBOS CHARALAMBOUS
BORN Dec 2, 1967
MP 2017-

Opposition whip and parliamentary private secretary to Rebecca Long Bailey since 2018, although he nominated Sir Keir Starmer for leader over her in 2020. Remainer who voted for a second referendum and to revoke Article 50. First MP of full Cypriot descent. Select cttees: finance, 2019; procedure, 2017-19; justice, 2017-19. APPG: future generations; legal and constitutional affairs; sex equality. Qualified solicitor. Housing lawyer for Hackney LBC. Cllr, Enfield BC, 2014-18. Member, Unison and GMB. Founder and chairman, Enfield

	Electorate	Share %	from 2017 % Change
	65,055		
*B Charalambous Lab	22,923	48.49	-3.22
D Burrowes C	18,473	39.07	-3.62
R Wilson LD	4,344	9.19	+5.21
L Balnave Green	1,042	2.20	+0.59
P Shah Brexit	494	1.04	

Law Centre. Formerly director of the London Arts Board. Ed: Liverpool Polytechnic (LLB Law); University of North London (LPC).

CHALLENGERS
David Burrowes (C) MP for this seat, 2005-17. Solicitor and consultant. Brexit campaigner. Contested: this seat, 2017; Edmonton, 2001. **Rob Wilson** (LD) Project manager. Contested Enfield LBC, 2018. **Luke Balnave** (Green) Teacher. Volunteer, local

climate action group. Contested Chatham & Aylesford in 2015 and Enfield LBC in 2018.

CONSTITUENCY PROFILE
Conservative from its creation in 1950 until it became the site of the "Portillo moment" in the 1997 election, in which the incumbent defence secretary Michael Portillo unexpectedly lost his seat. Labour went onto lose the seat in 2005 before regaining it in 2017. A diverse north London constituency with more than 10,000 Muslims, 4,000 Hindus and 3,000 Jews. It is semi-rural and includes Middlesex University. One of the poorer seats in London.

EU REFERENDUM RESULT
37.9% Leave Remain 62.1%

Epping Forest

MAJORITY 22,173 (44.11%)   CONSERVATIVE HOLD   TURNOUT 67.65%

DAME ELEANOR LAING
BORN Feb 1, 1958
MP 1997-

	Electorate	Share %	Change from 2017 %
	74,305		
*E Laing C	32,364	64.38	+2.42
V Ashworth Te Velde Lab	10,191	20.27	-5.76
J Whitehouse LD	5,387	10.72	+5.04
S Neville Green	1,975	3.93	+1.50
T Hall Young	181	0.36	+0.14
J Newham Soc Dem	170	0.34	

Deputy speaker from 2013; stood for the speakership in 2019 but was eliminated in the third round of voting. Advocate of constitutional reform. Brexiteer; abstained on the vote to trigger Article 50. Made a dame in 2018. Shadow minister: justice, 2007-10; women and equalities, 2006-07. Select cttees: standing orders, 2017-; Scottish affairs, 2013-14. Former solicitor. Special adviser to John MacGregor, 1989-94. Contested Paisley North, 1987. Ed: St Columba's Sch; University of Edinburgh (LLB law; first female president, students' union).

CHALLENGERS
Vicky Ashworth Te Velde (Lab) Cllr, Waltham Forest LBC, 2018-. Director, Smart Squash. Former director, Commonwealth Policy Studies, University of London. Vice-chairwoman, North East London Fabians. Jon Whitehouse (LD) Cllr, Epping Forest DC, 1999-. Contested this seat in the past two general election campaigns. Steven Neville (Green) Cllr, Epping Forest DC, 2014-.

CONSTITUENCY PROFILE
Has been held by the Conservatives since its creation in 1974. The party's majority has dipped below five figures only twice in the last 40 years, in the Labour landslides of 1997 and 2001. The Liberal Democrats replaced Labour as the second-placed party in 2010 before Ukip had a strong performance and finished second here in 2015. The west Essex constituency borders northeast London. The seat has higher than average levels of home ownership and income. It also has a relatively large Jewish population, at about 4,000 residents.

EU REFERENDUM RESULT
61.0% Leave   Remain 39.0%

Epsom & Ewell

MAJORITY 17,873 (30.06%)   CONSERVATIVE HOLD   TURNOUT 73.27%

CHRIS GRAYLING
BORN Apr 1, 1962
MP 2001-

	Electorate	Share %	Change from 2017 %
	81,138		
*C Grayling C	31,819	53.52	-6.06
S Gee LD	13,946	23.46	+10.97
E Mayne Lab	10,226	17.20	-7.84
J Baker Green	2,047	3.44	+0.55
C Woodbridge Ind	1,413	2.38	

The transport secretary between 2016 and 2019 whose controversial spell included awarding a no-deal Brexit ferrying contract to a company that had never run a ferry service, the cancellation of which cost the taxpayer £1 mill ion. Brexiteer; one of six ministers to support the Leave campaign. Voted for Boris Johnson in the 2019 leadership contest. Campaign manager for Theresa May's leadership bid in 2016. Leader of the Commons, 2015-16; justice secretary, 2012-15; work and pensions minister, 2010-12. Criticised while justice secretary

for introducing tribunal fees, cutting legal aid, banning books for prisoners and making a deal with Saudia Arabia to sell prison training. Worked in television production and as a marketing director. Cllr, Merton BC, 1998-2002. Ed: Royal GS; Sidney Sussex Coll, Cambridge (BA history).

CHALLENGERS
Steve Gee (LD) Surveyor. Contested this seat in the 2017 and 2015 elections. Ed Mayne (Lab) Train driver. Contested this seat, 2017.

CONSTITUENCY PROFILE
Conservative MPs have been elected here consistently since the seat's creation in 1974. The predecessor seat, Epsom, elected Conservatives from 1885. This northern Surrey seat is best-known for the Epsom Derby. It is an affluent constituency in which many residents commute to work by train and work in professional jobs. Incomes are well above average. High levels of home ownership and one of the smallest proportions of residents renting from their local council in the country.

EU REFERENDUM RESULT
47.8% Leave   Remain 52.2%

Erewash

MAJORITY 10,606 (21.73%) CONSERVATIVE HOLD **TURNOUT 67.31%**

MAGGIE THROUP
BORN Jan 27, 1957
MP 2015-

Government whip since 2019; also a parliamentary private secretary since 2018 to Matt Hancock, whom she backed for the leadership. Voted Remain but has embraced Brexit, voting to allow no-deal. Marketing consultant with her own business, Maggie Throup Marketing, and previously for a pharmaceutical company. Former medical scientist and an advocate for the wider use of diagnostic testing. Contested: Solihull 2010, losing narrowly; Colne Valley, 2005. Ed: Bradford Girls' GS; University of Manchester (BSc biology).

	Electorate	Share %	from 2017 %	Change
	72,519			
*M Throup C	27,560	56.46	+4.35	
C Atkinson Lab	16,954	34.73	-8.27	
J Archer LD	2,487	5.09	+2.60	
B Poland Green	1,115	2.28	+0.93	
D Ball Ind	388	0.79		
R Shaw Ind	188	0.39		
R Dunn Ind	122	0.25		

CHALLENGERS
Catherine Atkinson (Lab) Barrister specialising in personal injury and employment law. Awarded the Lincoln's Inn Gluckstein prize. Cllr, Kensington & Chelsea LBC, 2006-10. Contested: this seat, 2017, 2015; Kensington & Chelsea, 2005. **James Archer** (LD) Engineering group leader, Rolls-Royce. Member, Unite. Contested Erewash BC, 2019.

Brent Poland (Green) Member, Stop HS2 Erewash. Contested Derbyshire CC, 2017.

CONSTITUENCY PROFILE
Has been a bellwether since its creation in 1983. Held by the Conservatives under Margaret Thatcher and John Major before being won by Labour in the 1997 landslide and reclaimed by David Cameron in 2010. The Conservative majority has steadily grown since. Located between Derby and Nottingham. The average income in the seat is slightly higher than the east Midlands average, but lower than average compared to the country as a whole.

EU REFERENDUM RESULT
63.2% Leave Remain 36.8%

Erith & Thamesmead

MAJORITY 3,758 (9.08%) LABOUR HOLD **TURNOUT 63.28%**

ABENA OPPONG-ASARE
BORN Feb 8, 1983
MP 2019-

One of two candidates elected in 2019 to become the first female Ghanaian-British MPs, alongside Bell Ribeiro-Addy (Streatham). PPS to Luke Pollard (Plymouth Sutton & Davenport), 2019-. Chairwoman, Labour Women's Network. Cllr, Bexley LBC, 2014-18. Parliamentary assistant and constituency liaison officer. Advised the shadow minister on preventing violence against women and girls. Researcher and equalities lead at City Hall. Seconded in 2017 to be Grenfell community liaison manager. Ed: University of Kent (BA politics with international relations;

	Electorate	Share %	from 2017 %	Change
	65,399			
A Oppong-Asare Lab	19,882	48.04	-9.50	
J Robertson C	16,124	38.96	+3.94	
T Bright Brexit	2,246	5.43		
S Webber LD	1,984	4.79	+3.11	
C Letsae Green	876	2.12	+0.98	
R Mitchell CPA	272	0.66	+0.11	

MA international law with international relations).

CHALLENGERS
Joe Robertson (C) Business development, Dementia UK. Former family lawyer. Vice-president of the Hampshire Law Society. Member of the Society of Conservative Lawyers. **Tom Bright** (Brexit) Primary school teacher. **Sam Webber** (LD) External relations manager for Vuelio. Former communications

consultant for PoliticsHome. Contested Bromley & Chislehurst, 2017.

CONSTITUENCY PROFILE
This east London seat has been a Labour one since its creation in 1997, although the party's majority had not fallen below 5,000 until the 2019 election. One of its predecessor seats, Woolwich, was mostly Labour, while the other, Erith & Crayford, had been held by the Conservatives since its 1983 landslide. About a third of the constituency's residents are black, Afro-Caribbean or mixed race. About a quarter are under the age of 15.

EU REFERENDUM RESULT
54.6% Leave Remain 45.4%

Esher & Walton

MAJORITY 2,743 (4.35%)   CONSERVATIVE HOLD   TURNOUT 77.70%

DOMINIC RAAB
BORN Feb 25, 1974
MP 2010-

Ardent Brexiteer on the free-market right of the party who was appointed foreign secretary in 2019. Brexit secretary, 2018; resigned in opposition to Theresa May's withdrawal agreement. Minister: housing, communities and local government, 2018; justice, 2017-18. Parly under-sec, justice, 2015-16. Stood in the 2019 leadership election, finishing in sixth place and subsequently backing Boris Johnson. International lawyer at Linklaters who was seconded to the human rights NGO Liberty. Has written books on human rights and the coalition. Joined

	Electorate	Share %	Change from 2017 %
	81,184		
*D Raab C	31,132	49.35	-9.26
M Harding LD	28,389	45.00	+27.67
P Ashurst Lab	2,838	4.50	-15.17
K Keens Ind	347	0.55	+0.22
B Badger Loony	326	0.52	-0.01
K Taylor Advance	52	0.08	

the Foreign Office in 2000; led team in The Hague to bring war criminals to justice. Black belt in karate. Ed: Dr Challoners GS, Amersham; Lady Margaret Hall, Oxford (LLB law); Jesus Coll, Cambridge (LLM law).

CHALLENGERS
Monica Harding (LD) Associate consultant. Former chief executive: Industry and Parliament Trust; Refugees International Japan. Lifelong

Conservative voter. **Peter Ashurst** (Lab) Communications consultant. Former researcher.

CONSTITUENCY PROFILE
Seen as the possible site of a "Portillo moment" as the Lib Dems surged in seats such as this during the campaign; the Greens' decision to stand aside allowed Dominic Raab's majority to be cut by more than 20,000 votes. This Surrey seat borders southwest London and many of its residents commute into the capital. It is one of the most affluent seats in the country, with finance, property and communications among the most over-represented sectors.

EU REFERENDUM RESULT
41.6% Leave   Remain 58.4%

Exeter

MAJORITY 10,403 (18.51%)   LABOUR HOLD   TURNOUT 68.49%

BEN BRADSHAW
BORN Aug 30, 1960
MP 1997-

Junior minister in the New Labour years before serving as culture secretary in 2009-10; has returned to the backbenches since. Jeremy Corbyn critic; supported Sir Keir Starmer for the leadership, 2020. Remainer who supported a second referendum. Shadow culture secretary, 2010. Minister: the South West, 2007-09; health, 2007-09; environment, 2006-07. Parly under-sec: environment, 2003-06; Foreign Office, 2001-02. Deputy leader of the Commons, 2002-03. Select cttees: health and social care 2015-19; culture, media and

	Electorate	Share %	Change from 2017 %
	82,043		
*B Bradshaw Lab	29,882	53.18	-8.77
J Gray C	19,479	34.67	+1.79
J Levy Green	4,838	8.61	+6.76
L Willis Brexit	1,428	2.54	
D Page Ind	306	0.54	+0.16
D Odgers UKIP	259	0.46	

sport, 2012-15. Former journalist for BBC Radio 4; won the Sony News Reporter Award in 1993 and reported on the fall of the Berlin Wall. Ed: Thorpe St Andrew Sch, Norwich; University of Sussex (BA German).

CHALLENGERS
John Gray (C) Consultant for a start-up. **Joe Levy** (Green) Postgraduate administrator, University of Exeter. Member,

Unison. Community campaigner. Runs a free food initiative to support the homeless. Contested this seat, 2017.

CONSTITUENCY PROFILE
Before 1997, Exeter had been held by the Labour Party only once, at the 1966 election, and had otherwise been held by the Conservatives since 1911. The Liberal Democrats stood aside for the Green Party in this seat. The three largest employers in the city are its university, the Met Office's weather forecasting headquarters and the county council offices. One in five residents is a student. There is also a large Chinese community.

EU REFERENDUM RESULT
44.8% Leave   Remain 55.2%

Falkirk

MAJORITY 14,948 (26.75%)   SNP HOLD   TURNOUT 66.14%

JOHNNY MCNALLY
BORN Feb 2, 1951
MP 2015-

Shadow Scottish National Party environment spokesman, 2017-. Won the largest SNP majority in 2015 and received the highest number of votes for any SNP candidate in election history. Voted to remain in the EU in 2016 and against triggering Article 50. Environmental audit select cttee, 2015-19. Chairman, APPG on the hair industry; vice-chairman of the one on air pollution. Barber; owns a barbershop in his constituency. Cllr, Falkirk C, 2005-15. Contested this seat in the 2010 general election. Ed: St Patrick's PS; St Modans Sch.

	Electorate	Share %	Change from 2017 %
	84,472		
*J McNally SNP	29,351	52.53	+13.59
L Munro C	14,403	25.78	-0.40
S Ali Lab	6,243	11.17	-18.61
A Reid LD	3,990	7.14	+5.06
T McLaughlin Green	1,885	3.37	+1.69

CHALLENGERS
Lynn Munro (C) Cllr, Falkirk C, 2017-. Director of a nuclear engineering consultancy. **Safia Ali** (Lab) Deselected after allegedly antisemitic posts on her Facebook account were revealed. Contested Falkirk C, 2017. **Austin Reid** (LD) Educational consultant who has worked in Zambia and Bhutan. International observer, Turkish elections, 2015. Contested this seat, 2017. **Tom McLaughlin** (Green) IT consultant.

CONSTITUENCY PROFILE
Falkirk and its predecessor seats elected only Labour MPs from 1935, but it was won by the SNP in 2015. Eric Joyce, the MP in 2000-15, announced in 2013 he would not stand at the next election after admitting to an assault in Westminster; the selection process for his successor was dogged by scandal and led to strained relations between Labour and Unite. On the southern bank of the River Forth, Falkirk once had significant iron and steel industries, but these have been in decline in recent years. Earnings in the seat are lower than the Scottish average.

EU REFERENDUM RESULT
42.1% Leave   Remain 57.9%

Fareham

MAJORITY 26,086 (45.57%)   CONSERVATIVE HOLD   TURNOUT 73.08%

SUELLA
BRAVERMAN
BORN Apr 3, 1980
MP 2015-

Attorney-general since the February 2020 reshuffle. Chairwoman of the ERG, 2017-18, who resigned as parliamentary under-secretary to the Treasury in 2018 in protest at Theresa May's draft Brexit deal. Backed Boris Johnson for leader, 2019. Criticised by the Board of Deputies of British Jews for using the phrase "cultural Marxism", which is linked to antisemitic conspiracy theories. Barrister specialising in planning and public law. Defended Home Office in immigration cases and MoD in Guantanamo Bay inquiry. Researcher for Dominic

	Electorate	Share %	Change from 2017 %
	78,337		
*S Braverman C	36,459	63.68	+0.69
M Randall Lab	10,373	18.12	-7.07
M Winnington LD	8,006	13.98	+7.15
N Lyle Green	2,412	4.21	+1.93

Grieve MP. Co-founder, Africa Justice Foundation. Daughter of Kenyan and Mauritian immigrants. Ed: Queen's Coll, Cambridge (MA law; president, Conservative association); Université de Paris Panthéon-Sorbonne (LLM); New York Bar.

CHALLENGERS
Matthew Randall (Lab) Senior mentor, NCS. Duty Manager, Southern Co-op. Contested: this seat, 2017; Fareham BC, 2018, 2017. **Matthew Winnington** (LD) Cllr, Portsmouth CC,

2012-. Support worker at a local children and families charity. Contested this seat, 2017, 2015.

CONSTITUENCY PROFILE
Since its creation in 1885, Fareham has been a safe Conservative seat. The party's majority fell to a contemporary low of 7,000 in 2001. About four in five homes are owner occupied, a figure well above the national average. It is a relatively affluent constituency between Southampton and Portsmouth, where jobs are skewed towards managerial and professional occupations. Incomes, however, are lower than the southeast average.

EU REFERENDUM RESULT
55.5% Leave   Remain 44.5%

Faversham & Kent Mid

MAJORITY 21,976 (43.61%)   CONSERVATIVE HOLD   TURNOUT 68.65%

HELEN WHATELY
BORN Jun 23, 1976
MP 2015-

	Electorate	Share %	Change from 2017 %
	73,404		
*H Whately C	31,864	63.23	+2.14
J Reeves Lab	9,888	19.62	-6.46
H Perkin LD	6,170	12.24	+5.71
H Temple Green	2,103	4.17	+1.30
G Butler Ind	369	0.73	

Junior health minister since the reshuffle in February 2020. Deputy chairwoman of the Conservative party, 2019-. Parly under-sec, the arts and tourism, 2019-20. Remain campaigner who later supported Brexit. Voted for Jeremy Hunt in the 2019 leadership election. Conservative parliamentary representative at President Trump's inauguration, 2016; faced a backlash after tweeting about it enthusiastically. Criticised for accepting several thousand pounds' worth of hospitality from the Saudi Arabian government before defending the country's record in a parliamentary debate. Select cttees: draft domestic abuse bill, 2019; health, 2015-17. Worked at PWC, AOL and NHS as a healthcare consultant. President, Mencap Maidstone. Ed: Westminster Sch; Lady Margaret Hall, Oxford (BA PPE).

CHALLENGERS
Jenny Reeves (Lab) Unpaid carer for her disabled husband. Environmental and animal rights campaigner. Contested Swale BC, 2019. **Hannah Perkin** (LD) Cllr, Faversham TC, 2019-. Owns a catering business. **Hannah Temple** (Green) Volunteers with a charity that supports victims of human trafficking.

CONSTITUENCY PROFILE
This seat has been held by the Conservatives since its creation in 1997. Faversham, its predecessor seat, was won by Labour in 1945 and held until 1970. The seat contains Faversham in its east and some suburbs of Maidstone in its west. It is fairly affluent with relatively high levels of home ownership. The population is predominantly white and born in this country.

EU REFERENDUM RESULT
58.7% Leave   Remain 41.3%

Feltham & Heston

MAJORITY 7,859 (16.44%)   LABOUR CO-OP HOLD   TURNOUT 59.08%

SEEMA MALHOTRA
BORN Aug 7, 1972
MP 2011-

	Electorate	Share %	Change from 2017 %
	80,932		
*S Malhotra Lab Co-op	24,876	52.03	-9.19
J Keep C	17,017	35.59	+3.80
H Malik LD	3,127	6.54	+3.92
M Nelson Brexit	1,658	3.47	
T Firkins Green	1,133	2.37	+0.84

Shadow chief secretary to the Treasury, 2015-16; resigned in protest at Jeremy Corbyn's leadership. Voted Remain and for a second referendum. Backed Sir Keir Starmer for the leadership in 2020, having nominated Yvette Cooper in 2015. Shadow Home Office minister, 2014-15. Brexit select cttee, 2017-. One of 18 London MPs to vote for a third runway at Heathrow. Founder and director, Fabian Women's Network. Former freelance business and public service advisor in the video game and film industries. Ed: University of Warwick (BA politics and philosophy); Aston University (MSc business IT).

CHALLENGERS
Jane Keep (C) Has worked in the NHS for 40 years. Visiting associate professor in health innovation. Contested Richmond-upon-Thames LBC, 2018. Unpaid carer of an elderly relative. **Hina Malik** (LD) Chief executive, Voice of Women Society. Named a Community Champion by Save the Children UK. Contested this seat, 2017.

CONSTITUENCY PROFILE
The constituency has voted to put a Labour candidate in parliament in all but two elections since its creation in 1974 — the two Margaret Thatcher landslides of 1983 and 1987. Though the party won big majorities in 2015 and 2017, its winning margin in 2019 was still larger than that of 2010. Feltham & Heston lies just east of Heathrow Airport in west London. The seat is characterised by high levels of social and private renting and incomes are substantially lower than the London average. About two fifths of residents are Asian, mostly of Indian descent.

EU REFERENDUM RESULT
55.9% Leave   Remain 44.1%

Fermanagh & South Tyrone

MAJORITY 57 (0.11%)   SINN FEIN HOLD   TURNOUT 69.68%

MICHELLE GILDERNEW
BORN Mar 28, 1970
MP 2017-

Sinn Fein spokeswoman for heath. MP for this constituency, 2001-15; held the seat by four votes in 2010 before losing it to the UUP in 2015. MLA for Fermanagh & South Tyrone, 2016-, 1998-2012; dealt with the spread of bluetongue disease during her time as agriculture and rural development minister, 2007-11. Vice-chairwoman, committee for social development, 2007-11. Anti-Brexit. Women's rights campaigner. Part of the first Sinn Fein delegation to visit Downing Street. Ed: St Catherine's Coll, Aramagh; University of Ulster.

	Electorate	Share %	Change from 2017 %
	72,848		
*M Gildernew SF	21,986	43.31	-3.86
T Elliott UUP	21,929	43.20	-2.34
A Gannon SDLP	3,446	6.79	+1.95
M Beaumont Alliance	2,650	5.22	+3.56
C Wheeler Ind	751	1.48	

CHALLENGERS
Tom Elliott (UUP) MP for this constituency, 2015-17. Leader of the UUP, 2010-12; resigned after facing hostility from party colleagues. MLA for Fermanagh & South Tyrone, 2003-15. Previously County Grand Master of the Orange Order within Fermanagh; assistant secretary to the Grand Lodge of Ireland. Spent 18 years as a part-time member of the Ulster Defence Regiment and the Royal Irish Regiment. **Adam Gannon**

(SDLP) Science and maths teacher. Cllr, Fermanagh & Omagh DC, 2019-.

CONSTITUENCY PROFILE
Michelle Gildernew won the smallest majority of the 2019 election. Since the creation of the seat in 1950, representation has swapped between unionists and nationalists. It was briefly represented by Bobby Sands, a republican who died on hunger strike in 1981. The sparse and largely rural seat shares a long border with the Republic of Ireland. Its residents are about 58 per cent Catholic and 32 per cent Protestant. It has relatively high unemployment.

EU REFERENDUM RESULT
41.4% Leave   Remain 58.6%

Fife North East

MAJORITY 1,316 (2.87%)   LIB DEM GAIN FROM SNP   TURNOUT 75.33%

WENDY CHAMBERLAIN
BORN Dec 20, 1976
MP 2019-

Worked for a global drinks manufacturer. Police officer, Lothian and Borders Police, 1999-2011. Former lecturer in communications, Fife College. Worked for MoD in Rosyth, supporting service personnel leaving the forces. Passionate about mental health. Chair of Camanachd Association. Voted and campaigned for Remain in 2016. Contested: Stirling, 2017; Fife C, 2017. Ed: Edinburgh University (English).

CHALLENGERS
Stephen Gethins (SNP) MP for this seat, 2015-17; had won

	Electorate	Share %	Change from 2017 %
	60,905		
W Chamberlain LD	19,763	43.08	+10.22
*S Gethins SNP	18,447	40.21	+7.35
T Miklinski C	5,961	12.99	-11.13
W Haynes Lab	1,707	3.72	-5.91

it by just two votes in 2015. SNP shadow spokesman: international affairs and Europe, 2018-19; Europe, 2015-18. Former consultant on international development in the Balkans and South Caucasus and on democratisation in Africa. Former special adviser to the first minister of Scotland, Alex Salmond. **Tom Miklinski** (C) Cllr, Fife C, 2017-. Former teacher and Royal Navy commando; Falklands veteran. Former defence director of training and education, MoD.

Appointed CBE in 2006. Contested this seat, 2017.

CONSTITUENCY PROFILE
Represented by the onetime Liberal Democrat leader Sir Menzies Campbell from 1987 until 2015, when it was won by the SNP in their landslide victory. In 2017, it became the most marginal seat of any in parliament. It is large and rural, containing the coastal university town of St Andrews, which is also famous as the home of the Royal and Ancient golf club. Education and tourism are significant industries for the local economy and as such provide a sizeable share of employment.

EU REFERENDUM RESULT
36.3% Leave   Remain 63.7%

Filton & Bradley Stoke

MAJORITY 5,646 (10.50%)   **CONSERVATIVE HOLD**   **TURNOUT 72.62%**

JACK LOPRESTI
BORN Aug 23, 1969
MP 2010-

Brexiteer who lent his support to all withdrawal agreements. PPS to: Stephen Barclay (Cambridgeshire North East), 2018-; Sir Desmond Swayne (New Forest West), 2014-15. Backed Boris Johnson for leader, 2019. Select cttees: Welsh affairs, 2018-; defence, 2016-17; Northern Ireland affairs, 2010-18. Cllr, Bristol CC, 1999-2007. TA reservist; served a five-month tour in Afghanistan, 2008-09. Survivor of bowel cancer, later sharing his experience in parliament, 2015. Consultant in financial services. Married to fellow MP Andrea Jenkyns

	Electorate	Share %	from 2017 % Change
	74,016		
*J Lopresti C	26,293	48.92	-1.05
M Threlfall Lab	20,647	38.41	-3.31
L Harris LD	4,992	9.29	+3.27
J Vernon Green	1,563	2.91	+0.62
E Hardwick Citizens	257	0.48	

(Morley & Outwood). Contested: Bristol East, 2001; European parliament, 2004. Ed: Brislington Comp Sch.

CHALLENGERS
Mhairi Threlfall (Lab) Development manager, University of the West of England. Cllr, Bristol City C, 2013-. Contested Kingswood, 2017. Member and UWE officer, Unison. **Louise Harris** (LD) Cllr: South Gloucestershire C, 2018-; Eastleigh BC, 2002-17.

CONSTITUENCY PROFILE
This south Gloucestershire seat has been represented by Jack Lopresti for the Conservatives since its creation in 2010. Just north of Bristol, it maintains some Labour-leaning areas, particularly the towns of Filton and Patchway. This is a mostly suburban seat characterised by low unemployment and a slight skew towards professional and managerial-level jobs, with finance and insurance among the most over-represented industries. The last Concorde plane to fly was built in this constituency and remains within it, at the Aerospace Bristol museum.

EU REFERENDUM RESULT
48.8% Leave   Remain 51.2%

Finchley & Golders Green

MAJORITY 6,562 (11.91%)   **CONSERVATIVE HOLD**   **TURNOUT 71.04%**

MIKE FREER
BORN Jun 29, 1960
MP 2010-

Whip, 2019-; assistant whip, 2017-19. PPS to: Eric Pickles, 2013-14; Nick Boles, 2014, resigning to vote against recognition of Palestinian state. Forced to hide when 12 men attacked his surgery in 2011, incited by a group called Muslims Against Crusades. Barnet LBC leader, 2006-09, and pioneer of streamlined "easyCouncil" model; cllr, 2002-10, 1990-94. Supported Jeremy Hunt for leader, 2019. Career in financial services. Contested Harrow West, 2005. Ed: University of Stirling (accountancy & business law — did not graduate).

	Electorate	Share %	from 2017 % Change
	77,573		
*M Freer C	24,162	43.84	-3.11
L Berger LD	17,600	31.94	+25.33
R Houston Lab	13,347	24.22	-19.58

CHALLENGERS
Luciana Berger (LD) Liberal Democrat health and social care spokeswoman, 2019, having joined the party that year. Had previously defected from Labour to The Independent Group over antisemitism and Jeremy Corbyn's leadership. Labour MP for Liverpool Wavertree, 2010-19. Shadow minister: mental health, 2015-2016; public health, 2013-15; energy and climate change, 2010-13. **Ross Houston** (Lab) Cllr, Barnet LBC, 2006-. Operations manager of a housing association.

CONSTITUENCY PROFILE
Although Margaret Thatcher held Finchley, the predecessor seat, from 1959 to 1992, Labour gained the newly created Finchley & Golders Green in 1997. The party then lost the seat in 2010 and recorded its worst vote share in 2019, partly because of a strong performance by the Lib Dems, who benefited from the Greens standing down as part of the "Unite to Remain" pact. This northwest London seat has the largest Jewish population of any parliamentary seat in the country, at more than a fifth of residents. It also has a significant Muslim population, roughly one in ten.

EU REFERENDUM RESULT
31.1% Leave   Remain 68.9%

Folkestone & Hythe

DAMIAN COLLINS
BORN Feb 4, 1974
MP 2010-

Chairman of the culture select committee, 2016-20, with a focus on fake news, big tech, and attempted Russian influence in British politics. Chief of staff to Michael Howard, the Conservative leader, 2003-05, and MP for this seat, 1983-2010. Voted Remain in 2016; supported withdrawal agreements in third and fourth bills. Backed Boris Johnson for leader, 2019. Select cttees: culture, 2010-20; liaison, 2016-19. M&C Saatchi advertising agency, 1999-2008. Author of a 2016 biography of the politician and art collector Philip Sassoon, a former MP for

	Electorate	Share %	Change from 2017 %
	88,273		
*D Collins C	35,483	60.14	+5.45
L Davison Lab	14,146	23.97	-4.54
S Bishop LD	5,755	9.75	+2.58
G Treloar Green	2,706	4.59	+0.34
H Bolton Ind	576	0.98	+0.14
C Menniss Soc Dem	190	0.32	
R Kapur Young	80	0.14	
A Thomas SPGB	69	0.12	

Hythe. Contested Northampton North, 2005. Ed: St Benet's Hall, University of Oxford (BA modern history).

CHALLENGERS
Laura Davison (Lab) Radio journalist; national organiser, NUJ. Cllr, Folkestone & Hythe DC, 2019. Contested this seat, 2017. **Simon Bishop** (LD) Deputy chief executive, Plan

International UK. Adviser to Justine Greening, international development secretary, 2015-17. **Georgina Treloar** (Green) Freelance copywriter.

CONSTITUENCY PROFILE
Held by the Conservatives since its creation in 1950. Damian Collins has increased his majority at every election since his first victory in 2010. A southeast Kent seat bordering the English Channel. Residents are older than average, with nearly a quarter aged 65 or over. It is also characterised by higher than average levels of private sector renting and lower than average wages.

EU REFERENDUM RESULT

61.6% Leave	Remain 38.4%

Forest of Dean

MARK HARPER
BORN Feb 26, 1970
MP 2005-

Stood in the 2019 Conservative leadership election but was eliminated in the first round, receiving ten votes. Chief whip, 2015-16. Supported Remain; backed no-deal in indicative votes. Minister: disabled people, 2014-15; immigration, 2012-14; Cabinet Office, 2010-12. Resigned as immigration minister in 2014 after his cleaner was found to be an illegal immigrant. Shadow minister: work and pensions, 2007-10; defence, 2005-07. Contested this seat, 2001. Chartered accountant, KPMG and Intel. Ed: Brasenose Coll, Oxford (BA PPE).

	Electorate	Share %	Change from 2017 %
	71,438		
*M Harper C	30,680	59.60	+5.33
D Martin Lab Co-op	14,811	28.77	-7.15
C McFarling Green	4,681	9.09	+6.70
J Burrett Ind	1,303	2.53	+1.43

CHALLENGERS
Di Martin (Lab Co-op) Cllr, Forest of Dean, 1989-. Independent domestic violence adviser working for Greensquare Housing Association. Contested Gloucestershire CC, 2017. **Chris McFarling** (Green) Part-time handyman. Deputy leader, Forest of Dean DC; proposed motion to declare climate emergency, 2017.

CONSTITUENCY PROFILE
Labour held this seat from its creation in 1997 until 2005. Its

predecessor, before boundary changes, was also held by Labour from 1918 until 1979. The Liberal Democrats did not field a candidate here, endorsing the Greens as part of the "Unite to Remain" alliance. Situated in rural west Gloucestershire with Gloucester and Stroud to its east, Forest of Dean consists of towns with populations of no more than 10,000. More than half of its residents are over the age of 45, and fewer than 2 per cent are non-white. About 75 per cent of households are owner-occupied, which is significantly above the national average. The area has historically been associated with mining and industry.

EU REFERENDUM RESULT

57.9% Leave	Remain 42.1%

Foyle

MAJORITY 17,110 (46.89%) **SDLP GAIN FROM SINN FEIN** **TURNOUT 63.41%**

COLUM EASTWOOD
BORN Apr 30, 1983
MP 2019-

Leader of the SDLP, 2015-. MLA for Foyle, 2011-19. Confirmed allegiance to the Queen "under protest" as he was sworn into parliament. Cllr, Derry City C, 2005-11. Mayor of Londonderry, 2011-12; at the age of 27, he was the youngest mayor of the city to date. In 2012 he was criticised by unionists for carrying the coffin at the funeral of a former paramilitary in the Irish National Liberation Army. Contested European parliament elections, 2019. Ed: St Columb's College; University of Liverpool (BA Latin American studies — did not finish).

	Electorate	Share %	Change from 2017 %
	74,346		
C Eastwood SDLP	26,881	57.02	+17.67
*E McCallion SF	9,771	20.73	-18.99
G Middleton DUP	4,773	10.12	-5.97
A McCloskey Aontu	2,032	4.31	
S Harkin PBP	1,332	2.83	-0.17
R Ferguson Alliance	1,267	2.69	+0.84
D Guy UUP	1,088	2.31	

CHALLENGERS
Elisha McCallion (SF) MP for this seat, 2017-19. Cllr, Derry City C 2005-17; mayor, 2015. **Gary Middleton** (DUP) MLA, Foyle, 2015-; deputy chairman, health committee. Derry councillor, 2011-15. Contested this seat in the past two elections. **Anne McCloskey** (Aontu) Cllr, Derry City & Strabane DC, 2019-. **Shaun Harkin** (PBP) Cllr, Derry City & Strabane DC, 2019-.

Rachael Ferguson (Alliance) O2 sales adviser. Cllr, Derry City & Strabane DC, 2019-.

CONSTITUENCY PROFILE
Although the old seat of Londonderry elected unionists until 1983, it was split that year, with East Londonderry held by unionists and Foyle by nationalists since. It was won by Sinn Fein with a majority of 179 in 2017. Containing Northern Ireland's second largest city, Londonderry, Foyle has high levels of unemployment, and below average levels of income. This seat had the strongest Remain vote in Northern Ireland in the 2016 referendum.

EU REFERENDUM RESULT

21.7% Leave   Remain 78.3%

Fylde

MAJORITY 16,611 (35.60%) **CONSERVATIVE HOLD** **TURNOUT 69.80%**

MARK MENZIES
BORN May 18, 1971
MP 2010-

Trade envoy to Argentina, Colombia, Chile and Peru. Has campaigned against fracking and for the liberalisation of Sunday trading laws. Voted Remain. Backed Michael Gove for the Conservative Party leadership, 2019. PPS to: Sir Alan Duncan, 2013-14; Mark Prisk, 2012-13; Charles Hendry, 2010-12. Allegations that he had paid a male escort for sex and drugs forced him to resign as PPS to Sir Alan; he denied the claims. Select cttees: international development, 2018-; regulatory reform, 2017; finance, 2016-; transport, 2015-17. Marketing

	Electorate	Share %	Change from 2017 %
	66,847		
*M Menzies C	28,432	60.94	+2.11
M Mitchell Lab	11,821	25.33	-8.08
M Jewell LD	3,748	8.03	+2.99
G Dowding Green	1,731	3.71	+0.99
A Higgins Ind	927	1.99	

career at Asda, Morrisons and M&S. Member of the Armed Forces Parliamentary Scheme. Contested: Selby, 2005; Glasgow Govan, 2001. Ed: University of Glasgow (MA economics and social history; president, Conservative Association).

CHALLENGERS
Martin Mitchell (Lab) Cllr, Blackpool C, 2011-. Royal Mail employee. Contested: Bradford East, 2017; Denton & Reddish 2015; Preston, 2010. **Mark Jewell** (LD) Works for BAE systems. Cllr, Preston CC, 2019-, 2006-10.

CONSTITUENCY PROFILE
A safe Conservative seat, which the party has held since 1918. The Conservative majority fell into four figures in 1997 and 2001, the only times it has done so since the introduction of universal suffrage. Situated in Lancashire, Fylde lies between Preston and Blackpool, on the north bank of the River Ribble. More than a quarter of its residents are aged 65 or over, which is well above the national average; a similar number of constituents are aged under 25. Unemployment is relatively low.

EU REFERENDUM RESULT

56.7% Leave   Remain 43.3%

Gainsborough

MAJORITY 22,967 (44.99%)   CONSERVATIVE HOLD   TURNOUT 66.86%

SIR EDWARD LEIGH
BORN Jul 20, 1950
MP 1983-

	Electorate	Share %	Change from 2017 %
	76,343		
*E Leigh C	33,893	66.40	+4.58
P Smith Lab	10,926	21.40	-7.31
L Rollings LD	5,157	10.10	+3.04
M Cavill Ind	1,070	2.10	

Backbench Brexiteer who stood to succeed John Bercow as Speaker, promising to "not put himself in the limelight"; came second to last with 12 votes. Select cttees: procedure, 2018-, 2015-17; international trade, 2016-17; liaison, 2001-10. Supported Michael Gove for leader, 2019. Trade and industry minister, 1990-93; sacked for opposing the Maastricht Treaty. Private secretary to Margaret Thatcher, 1974-81. Barrister, Goldsmiths Chambers. Fellow, Chartered Institute of Arbitrators. Knighted in 2013. Suffers from rosacea, a condition that reddens skin on the face. Contested Middlesbrough, 1974. Ed: Lycée Français, London; Durham University (BA modern history).

CHALLENGERS
Perry Smith (Lab) Chairman, Gainsborough CLP. Retired lecturer. Contested West Lindsey DC, 2019. **Lesley Rollings** (LD) Teacher, Gainsborough Academy. Mayor of Gainsborough, 2012-14. Cllr, West Lindsey DC, 2006-. Contested this seat, 2017, 2015.

CONSTITUENCY PROFILE
The Conservative Party has held Gainsborough since 1924, during which time the seat has been represented by only three MPs. Sir Edward Leigh's majority has grown at every election since 2005, and the closest challenge to the party was during the 1970s and 1980s, when the Liberals repeatedly reduced the Conservative majority without ever managing to gain the constituency. A town in the West Lindsey district of Lincolnshire gives its name to this agricultural seat. About one in five residents are pensioners. The area has above-average home ownership and is known for pig farming.

EU REFERENDUM RESULT
62.0% Leave   Remain 38.0%

Garston & Halewood

MAJORITY 31,624 (59.30%)   LABOUR HOLD   TURNOUT 70.06%

MARIA EAGLE
BORN Feb 17, 1961
MP 1997-

	Electorate	Share %	Change from 2017 %
	76,116		
*M Eagle Lab	38,578	72.34	-5.38
N Novaky C	6,954	13.04	-4.62
K Brown LD	3,324	6.23	+3.01
J Fraser Brexit	2,943	5.52	
J Roberts Green	1,183	2.22	+0.82
H Williams Lib	344	0.65	

Charity worker and lawyer. Hillsborough justice campaigner. Resigned from front bench in June 2016, expressing no confidence in Jeremy Corbyn. Campaigned to Remain and voted for a second referendum. Backed Sir Keir Starmer for leader, 2020. Shadow secretary: culture, 2016; defence, 2015-16; environment, 2013-15; transport, 2010-13. Five different junior ministerial jobs in New Labour governments before serving as a minister in the Ministry of Justice and equalities office, 2009-10. PPS to John Hutton, 1999-2001. Public accounts cttee, 1997-99. Contested Crosby, 1992. Twin sister of Angela Eagle (Wallasey). Ed: St Peter's CofE Sch; Formby HS; Pembroke, Oxford (PPE); College of Law, London.

CHALLENGERS
Neva Novaky (C) EU policy expert and commentator on European affairs. Contested EU parliament, 2019. **Kris Brown** (LD) Mental health care worker. Cllr, Liverpool City C, 2018-.

CONSTITUENCY PROFILE
The predecessor seat, Liverpool Garston, was created in 1950 and held by the Conservatives until Labour won it in 1974. Though the Tories won it back in 1979, it was one of few Labour gains in the 1983 landslide election; it has since become one of Labour's twenty safest seats. There are some areas of deprivation in this south Merseyside seat, although the Woolton suburb in its north is one of Liverpool's most affluent. Levels of social renting are high, and the number of residents paid less than the Living Wage is above the regional average. John Lennon Airport is in the seat's south.

EU REFERENDUM RESULT
48.0% Leave   Remain 52.0%

Gateshead

MAJORITY 7,200 (18.88%)   **LABOUR HOLD**   **TURNOUT 59.19%**

IAN MEARNS
BORN Apr 21, 1957
MP 2010-

Left-winger who criticised his party colleagues for attempting to remove Jeremy Corbyn as leader in 2016. One of 16 Labour MPs who wrote to Ed Miliband in 2015 demanding stronger opposition to austerity. Resigned as PPS to rebel against workfare policy in 2013, on which Labour was whipping to abstain. Backed Rebecca Long Bailey for leader in 2020. Cllr, Gateshead C, 1983-2010. Member: Unison; Unite. Select cttees: liaison, 2015-; backbench business, 2010-, chairman since 2015; education, 2010-. Anti-HS2. APPG chairman: football supporters;

	Electorate	Share %	Change from 2017 %
	64,449		
*I Mearns Lab	20,450	53.61	-11.53
J MacBean C	13,250	34.74	+10.80
P Maughan LD	2,792	7.32	+3.26
R Cabral Green	1,653	4.33	+2.88

foster care work; housing in the North; rail in the North. Ed: St Mary's RC Technical College.

CHALLENGERS
Jane MacBean (C) Chartered accountant. Cllr, Chiltern DC, 2015-; Member of the National Trust. **Peter Maughan** (LD) Solicitor. Cllr, Gateshead C, 2012-. Chairman of the Newcastle and North Northumberland RSPCA for more than 30 years. Contested: Jarrow, 2017; Durham North, 2015; Blaydon, 2005, 2001,

1997. **Rachel Cabral** (Green) Contested Gateshead C, 2019, 2018.

CONSTITUENCY PROFILE
Gateshead has elected Labour MPs at every general election since the Second World War, although it was split in two for much of that time. The constituency was re-created in 2010, and Labour's majority had been growing at successive elections until 2019, when it fell to below its 2010 level and into four figures for the first time. The town lies along the southern bank of the River Tyne, opposite Newcastle. The seat has a significant Jewish population.

EU REFERENDUM RESULT
56.2% Leave   Remain 43.8%

Gedling

MAJORITY 679 (1.36%)   **CONSERVATIVE GAIN FROM LABOUR**   **TURNOUT 69.92%**

TOM RANDALL
BORN Jul 4, 1981
MP 2019-

First Conservative MP to represent Gedling since Andrew Mitchell (Sutton Coalfield) did in 1987-97. Policy officer, Royal College of Pathologists. Flag protocol manager, London Olympic and Paralympic Games, 2012. Previously worked as a solicitor specialising in construction issues. Editor, *Flagmaster*, a magazine published by the Flag Institute, a charity that promotes the use of flags, 2015-19. Campaigned for Vote Leave. Voted for Boris Johnson in the leadership contest, 2019. Passionate about protecting the green belt.

	Electorate	Share %	Change from 2017 %
	71,438		
T Randall C	22,718	45.48	+2.64
*V Coaker Lab	22,039	44.12	-7.80
A Prabhakar LD	2,279	4.56	+2.53
G Hunt Brexit	1,820	3.64	
J Norris Green	1,097	2.20	+1.20

Contested EU parliament, 2019. Ed: Redhill Comprehensive Sch; Christchurch Coll, Oxford University (LLB Law); Nottingham Law School (LPC).

CHALLENGERS
Vernon Coaker (Lab) MP for this seat, 1997-2019. Jeremy Corbyn critic. Shadow secretary: Northern Ireland, 2015-16, 2011-13; defence, 2013-15. Shadow minister: education 2010; home affairs, 2010-11. **Anita Prabhakar** (LD) Solicitor specialising in

constitutional and corporate law. **Graham Hunt** (Brexit) Retired manager for a local energy utility.

CONSTITUENCY PROFILE
Although Labour had held Gedling for 22 years, Vernon Coaker's majorities were often fairly narrow, peaking at about 5,000 in 2001. Historically, Gedling and its predecessor, Carlton, were regarded as safe Conservative seats, but by 2019 it had become a marginal. Tom Randall has one of the ten smallest majorities among his Conservative colleagues. Mostly comprised of an urban area northeast of Nottingham.

EU REFERENDUM RESULT
56.3% Leave   Remain 43.7%

Gillingham & Rainham

MAJORITY 15,119 (32.90%)　　　CONSERVATIVE HOLD　　　TURNOUT 62.49%

REHMAN CHISHTI
BORN Oct 4, 1978
MP 2010-

The prime minister's special envoy for freedom of religion or belief, 2019-. Conservative Party vice-chairman for communities, 2018, and PM's trade envoy to Pakistan, 2017-18, resigning over the Asia Bibi asylum case. Political adviser to Benazir Bhutto, the two-time prime minister of Pakistan, 1999–2007. Brexiteer; eventually supported Theresa May's deal. Backed Boris Johnson, 2019. PPS to: Jeremy Wright (Kenilworth & Southam), 2015-16; Nick Gibb (Bognor Regis & Littlehampton), 2014-15. Select cttees: home affairs, 2017-; petitions, 2017-18; backbench

	Electorate	Share %	Change from 2017 %
	73,549		
*R Chishti C	28,173	61.30	+5.86
A Stamp Lab	13,054	28.40	-7.74
A Bullion LD	2,503	5.45	+2.64
G Salomon Green	1,043	2.27	+1.21
R McCulloch Martin Ukip	837	1.82	-2.47
P Cook Ind	229	0.50	
R Peacock CPA	119	0.26	-0.00

business, 2017. Adviser to Francis Maude, 2006-07, having stood against him in Horsham in 2005 for Labour. Cllr, Medway C, 2003-07, defecting from Labour to the Conservatives in 2006. Barrister, Goldsmith Chambers. Ed: Aberystwyth University (LLB); Inns of Court Sch of Law.

CHALLENGERS
Andy Stamp (Lab) Environment Agency employee. Cllr, Medway

C, 2007-. **Alan Bullion** (LD) Associate lecturer, the Open University, 1992-2014.

CONSTITUENCY PROFILE
This Kent constituency was created in 2010 to replace Gillingham. Since then, the Conservative vote share has increased at every election. The old seat had been consistently Conservative, other than in the Labour landslide of 1945 and during New Labour's national dominance, 1997-2010. Local retail and business parks, and convenient access to the City of London, provide constituents with a high level of employment and home ownership.

EU REFERENDUM RESULT
63.6% Leave　　　Remain 36.4%

Glasgow Central

MAJORITY 6,474 (16.14%)　　　SNP HOLD　　　TURNOUT 57.93%

ALISON THEWLISS
BORN Sep 13, 1982
MP 2015-

Campaigned against so-called rape clause in the child tax credit policy of the 2015 budget, which required women to prove exceptional circumstances, such as rape, to claim tax credits for a third child. Shadow SNP spokeswoman for the Treasury, 2017-; housing, 2018-20; cities, 2015-18. Select cttees: Treasury, 2019-; procedure, 2017-; communities, 2015-17. Cllr, Glasgow City C, 2007-15. Worked as a researcher for Bruce McFee MSP. Member of Scottish CND. APPG chairwoman: immigration detention; infant feeding and inequalities; working at height.

	Electorate	Share %	Change from 2017 %
	69,230		
*A Thewliss SNP	19,750	49.25	+4.51
F Hameed Lab	13,276	33.10	-5.33
F Scarabello C	3,698	9.22	-4.71
E Hoyle LD	1,952	4.87	+1.96
E Gallagher Green	1,429	3.56	

Ed: Carluke HS; University of Aberdeen (BA politics and international relations).

CHALLENGERS
Faten Hameed (Lab) Project manager, Glasgow city council. Born in Iraq and led drive to help Iraqi refugees. Founder, Scottish Iraqi Association. Contested this seat in 2017. **Flora Scarabello** (C) Suspended from the party for alleged "anti-Muslim language". **Ewan Hoyle** (LD) Founder, Liberal

Democrats for Drug Policy Reform, 2009-.

CONSTITUENCY PROFILE
First gained by Labour in the 1950s, this was a safe seat for the party until the 2015 SNP landslide. Before that, it had mostly elected Conservative MPs, including the short-lived prime minister Andrew Bonar Law. Its residents are the most educated and affluent of any in the Glasgow seats, but there are still fairly high levels of poverty. The Calton area in particular suffers severe deprivation, and high levels of unemployment and crime. A quarter of the seat's residents are students.

EU REFERENDUM RESULT
28.8% Leave　　　Remain 71.2%

Glasgow East

DAVID LINDEN
BORN May 14, 1990
MP 2017-

SNP whip who has supported campaigns against fixed-odds betting terminals and for equalising the minimum wage for young people. Career in financial sector as an underwriter at Access Loans & Mortgages and Glasgow Credit Union. Caseworker for Alison Thewliss (Glasgow Central), 2015-17, and John Mason while he was MP for this seat, 2008-10. Has been a campaigner and researcher for the SNP in the Scottish, European and UK parliaments. Cttees: procedure, 2017-; standing orders, 2017-. Ed: Bannerman HS, Baillieston.

	Electorate	Share %	from 2017 % Change
	67,381		
*D Linden SNP	18,357	47.70	+8.93
K Watson Lab	12,791	33.24	-5.32
T Kerr C	5,709	14.84	-4.01
J Harrison LD	1,626	4.23	+2.63

CHALLENGERS
Kate Watson (Lab) Former director of operations, the Better Together campaign. Contested this seat in 2017. **Thomas Kerr** (C) Twenty-two-year-old PR and advertising student. Cllr, Glasgow City C, 2017-. Better Together campaigner. Member of the Tory Reform Group. Contested this seat in 2017. **James Harrison** (LD) Lead policy officer, QAA. Member, Scottish Liberal Democrats NEC, 2016-17. Contested Glasgow North West, 2015.

CONSTITUENCY PROFILE
Like most of the Glasgow seats, this had been safely held in general elections by Labour for generations, in this case since the 1930s. A by-election in 2008 following the death of David Marshall was won by the SNP on a swing of 22 per cent. Although Labour regained the seat in 2010, the SNP won it back again in their 2015 landslide. The winning MP, Natalie McGarry, resigned the party whip in 2015 after an investigation into fraud, which she denied but for which she was later charged. The SNP majority in 2017 was just 75. Home to Celtic Park, Celtic FC's stadium.

EU REFERENDUM RESULT
43.8% Leave　　　　　Remain 56.2%

Glasgow North

PATRICK GRADY
BORN Feb 5, 1980
MP 2015-

SNP's Westminster chief whip, 2017-. Party spokesman for international development, 2015-17. Select committees include: European statutory instruments, 2018-; selection, 2017-; administration, 2017-18; procedure, 2015-17. Chairman, Malawi APPG, having previously lived there. Before parliament: Scottish Catholic International Aid Fund, 2011-15. SNP national secretary, 2012-16. Contested this seat in 2010. Joined the SNP in 1997. Born in Edinburgh and raised in Inverness. Ed: Inverness Royal Academy; University of Strathclyde.

	Electorate	Share %	from 2017 % Change
	57,130		
*P Grady SNP	16,982	46.92	+9.29
P Duncan-Glancy Lab	11,381	31.45	-3.02
T Curtis C	3,806	10.52	-4.23
A Chamberlain LD	2,394	6.61	+3.17
C Macgregor Green	1,308	3.61	-6.10
D Cocozza Brexit	320	0.88	

CHALLENGERS
Pam Duncan-Glancy (Lab) Senior communications and engagement officer, NHS Scotland, 2015-; policy officer, Independent Living in Scotland, 2009-. Contested this seat in 2017. **Tony Curtis** (C) Cllr, Glasgow City C, 2017-. Affiliate owner of a crossfit gym. Researcher in Scottish parliament, 2016-18. **Andrew Chamberlain** (LD) Contested Ayrshire Central, 2010.

CONSTITUENCY PROFILE
Even in the days of Scottish Labour's hegemony, this seat was less overwhelmingly likely to return Labour MPs than the others in Glasgow. Its predecessor, Glasgow Hillhead, was won by the Conservatives from 1918 until Roy Jenkins, once a Labour cabinet minister but by then the leader of the Social Democratic Party, won it in a by-election in 1982. As Glasgow Hillhead & Glasgow Kelvin it was represented by Labour from 1987 until the SNP took control in 2015. The seat's outskirts include large council estates but the centre is more middle class.

EU REFERENDUM RESULT
21.6% Leave　　　　　Remain 78.4%

Glasgow North East

MAJORITY 2,548 (7.51%)   SNP GAIN FROM LABOUR CO-OP   TURNOUT 55.55%

ANNA
MCLAUGHLIN
BORN Mar 8, 1966
MP 2019-; 2015-17

Regained seat she won with a record-breaking 39 per cent swing from Labour in 2015. Shadow SNP civil liberties spokeswoman, 2015-17. Worked in consultancy during brief political hiatus, 2017-19. Former fundraiser and adviser in the charity sector, including African Caribbean Network. Glasgow MSP, 2009-11. Campaigned to remain in the EU; voted against Article 50 being triggered. Contested this seat in 2017. Ed: Port Glasgow HS; Royal Scottish Academy of Music and Drama; University of Glasgow (BA dramatic studies).

	Electorate	Share %	from 2017 % Change
	61,075		
A McLaughlin SNP	15,911	46.90	+4.74
*P Sweeney Lab Co-op	13,363	39.39	-3.53
L Bennie C	3,558	10.49	-2.43
N Moohan LD	1,093	3.22	+1.22

CHALLENGERS
Paul Sweeney (Lab Co-op) MP for this seat, 2017-19; shadow Scotland minister, 2017-19. Named the "Best Scot at Westminster" in the *Herald*'s Scottish Politician of the Year awards, 2018. Territorial Army reservist, 2006-18. **Lauren Bennie** (C) Owns a small crafts business. Cllr, Dennistoun Community C. Community volunteer. Secretary, Scottish Conservative Women. **Nicholas Moohan** (LD) Sales director, family tyre business.

CONSTITUENCY PROFILE
Like most of Glasgow, the seat was Labour but fell to the SNP in 2015. However, this was also the only seat to return to Labour in 2017. Including its predecessor, Glasgow Springburn, the constituency was represented between 1979 and 2009 by Michael Martin, the Speaker of the Commons from 2000. After he stood down in 2009, it was won by Labour. Almost half of all residents in this area live in social housing, and crime and unemployment are higher than average. This constituency ranks highly in Scotland for the proportion of residents with no qualifications.

EU REFERENDUM RESULT
40.7% Leave   Remain 59.3%

Glasgow North West

MAJORITY 8,359 (21.04%)   SNP HOLD   TURNOUT 62.67%

CAROL
MONAGHAN
BORN Aug 2, 1972
MP 2015-

Shadow SNP spokeswoman for education; armed forces and veterans, 2017-. Group leader, public services and education, 2015-2017. Science and technology select cttee, 2015-. Chairwoman, photonics APPG. Has led multiple debates in parliament on myalgic encephalomyelitis (ME), and spoken about the challenges of balancing motherhood with life as an MP in Westminster. Physics teacher and university lecturer who joined the SNP after the 2014 independence referendum. Ed: University of Strathclyde (BSc laser physics

	Electorate	Share %	from 2017 % Change
	63,402		
*C Monaghan SNP	19,678	49.52	+7.02
P Ferguson Lab	11,319	28.49	-7.42
A Aibinu C	6,022	15.16	-2.87
J Speirs LD	2,716	6.84	+3.26

and optoelectronics); St Andrews College, Bearsden (PGCE).

CHALLENGERS
Patricia Ferguson (Lab) MSP, 1999-2016. Worked as a health service administrator. **Ade Aibinu** (C) Cllr, Glasgow City C, 2017-. Graduate teaching assistant, Glasgow Caledonian University. Trained pharmacologist. **James Speirs** (LD) Mental health and learning disabilities charity worker. Contested this seat in the 2017 general election.

CONSTITUENCY PROFILE
A Labour seat from its creation in 2005 until 2015. Its predecessors, Glasgow Anniesland and Glasgow Garscadden, were represented by Donald Dewar, the first minister of the first Scottish parliament, from 1978 until his death in 2000. The seat lies on the north bank of the Clyde and covers areas to the city's northwest, encompassing the deprived Drumchapel housing estate as well as the more affluent areas of Scotstoun and Jordanhill. Less than half of households are owner-occupied. Unemployment is lower than in other parts of Glasgow.

EU REFERENDUM RESULT
31.5% Leave   Remain 68.5%

Glasgow South

MAJORITY 9,005 (18.98%)   **SNP HOLD**   **TURNOUT 66.92%**

STEWART MALCOLM MCDONALD
BORN Aug 24, 1986
MP 2015-

Worked as a retail manager and holiday rep in Tenerife before becoming a caseworker for two MSPs. SNP campaign manager, Glasgow & Cathcart, 2011. Defence spokesman, 2017-; condemned Theresa May for "gesture bombing" Syria and not getting the military action approved by parliament. Supported PrEP pill for HIV prevention; said that opposition to treatment was rooted in homophobia. Private members bill against unpaid trial shifts. Select cttees: standards, 2019; transport, 2015-17. Ed: Govan HS.

	Electorate	Share %	Change from 2017 %
	70,891		
*S McDonald SNP	22,829	48.12	+7.01
J Lamont Lab Co-op	13,824	29.14	-7.42
K Thornton C	6,237	13.15	-5.95
C Ford LD	2,786	5.87	+2.62
D Hutchison Green	1,251	2.64	
D Raja Brexit	516	1.09	

CHALLENGERS
Johann Lamont (Lab Co-op) Leader, Scottish Labour, 2011-14; deputy leader, 2008-11. Resigned the leadership saying that party in Westminster had prevented her attempts at reform. MSP, Glasgow, 2016-; Glasgow Pollok, 1999-2016. **Kyle Thornton** (C) Operations manager. Cllr, Glasgow City C, 2017-. Voted Remain. **Carole Ford** (LD) Former head teacher. **Dan Hutchison** (Green) Co-convenor,

Glasow & West of Scotland Young Greens.

CONSTITUENCY PROFILE
A safe Labour seat before it was gained by the SNP in 2015. Labour had held it and its predecessor, Glasgow Cathcart, from 1979, before which it was Conservative for nearly 60 years. Primarily consists of leafy, residential areas as well as sprawling housing estates built for families displaced by Glasgow's slum clearances. Has a significant Pakistani community and, in common with other Glasgow seats, a relatively high proportion of residents living in social housing.

EU REFERENDUM RESULT
28.2% Leave   Remain 71.8%

Glasgow South West

MAJORITY 4,900 (13.30%)   **SNP HOLD**   **TURNOUT 57.06%**

CHRIS STEPHENS
BORN Mar 20, 1973
MP 2015-

Former local government officer for Glasgow City C. Trade unionist: senior Unison activist; secretary, SNP trade union group; spokesman, trade unions and workers' rights, 2017-18. Criticised by party members for poor handling of constituency office redundancies in 2018. Contested: this seat, 2010; European parliament, 2014; Scottish parliament, 2011, 2007. Campaigned to Remain; voted for second referendum and to revoke Article 50 in indicative votes. Select cttees: work and pensions, 2017-19; European scrutiny, 2017. APPG

	Electorate	Share %	Change from 2017 %
	64,575		
*C Stephens SNP	17,643	47.88	+7.22
M Kerr Lab Co-op	12,743	34.58	-5.91
T Haddow C	4,224	11.46	-4.15
B Denton-Cardew LD	1,435	3.89	+2.03
P Brown Brexit	802	2.18	

vice-chairman: Botswana; South Africa; shipbuilding. Member, SNP national executive cttee. Ed: Trinity HS, Renfrew.

CHALLENGERS
Matt Kerr (Lab Co-op) Cllr, Glasgow City C, 2007-, Former postman. **Thomas Haddow** (C) Manager, Tesco 2006-. Contested Glasgow City C, 2017, 2016. **Ben Denton-Cardew** (LD) Railway consultant and music tutor. **Peter Brown** (Brexit) First time contesting an election.

CONSTITUENCY PROFILE
The 60 votes separating the Scottish National Party from Labour at the 2017 election had made this seat one of the most marginal in parliament. Historically a Labour stronghold, it was gained in 2015 by the SNP with a significant swing. Its predecessor constituency, Glasgow Pollok, had elected Labour MPs at every general election since 1964. The area suffers from poor health and relatively high rates of crime and deprivation. Residents tend to have few qualifications and unemployment is high. The seat is home to Rangers FC's Ibrox Stadium.

EU REFERENDUM RESULT
40.9% Leave   Remain 59.1%

Glenrothes

MAJORITY 11,757 (28.30%)   **SNP HOLD**   **TURNOUT 63.18%**

PETER GRANT
BORN Oct 12, 1960
MP 2015-

Accountant in the NHS; former physics teacher. Recovered more than £93,000 for constituents who had been wrongly assessed by the Department for Work and Pensions. SNP shadow to chief secretary to the Treasury, 2020-; Europe spokesman, 2017-20. Cllr, Fife C, 1992-2015; leader, 2007-12. Contested by-election in this seat, 2008. Select cttees: Brexit, 2016-19; consolidation, 2015-17; European scrutiny, 2015-16. Member of SNP's international affairs team. Brought up in Lanarkshire in a working-class Labour household. Ed: Glasgow University (BSc).

	Electorate	Share %	from 2017 % Change
	65,762		
*P Grant SNP	21,234	51.11	+8.31
P Egan Lab	9,477	22.81	-11.90
A Thomson C	6,920	16.66	-2.84
J Liston LD	2,639	6.35	+3.36
V Farrell Brexit	1,276	3.07	

CHALLENGERS
Pat Egan (Lab) Trade unionist; learning organiser, Unite, 2007-. Former coalminer. Assistant training manager, Scottish Coal. Lung cancer survivor. **Amy Thomson** (C) Senior HR consultant; previously with Epam systems and Deloitte. Contested Paisley & Renfrewshire South, 2017. **Jane Ann Liston** (LD) Former IT specialist, RBS. Cllr, Fife C, 1995-2007; 2017-. **Victor Farrell** (Brexit) Evangelical pastor.

CONSTITUENCY PROFILE
This, along with its predecessor constituency of Fife Central, was a safe Labour seat before 2015, having been held continuously by the party from its creation in 1974. The town of Glenrothes itself is the administrative centre of the historic county of Fife, on the east coast. It was once a mining town but has since become a centre for technology and industry: Bosch Rexroth, a German engineering firm, is one of the biggest employers. The proportion of households in the social rented sector is above average and the unemployment rate is also relatively high.

EU REFERENDUM RESULT
47.6% Leave   Remain 52.4%

Gloucester

MAJORITY 10,277 (19.12%)   **CONSERVATIVE HOLD**   **TURNOUT 66.10%**

RICHARD GRAHAM
BORN Apr 4, 1958
MP 2010-

Former investment banker, diplomat and airline manager. Previously general manager, Cathay Pacific in France and the Philippines; first secretary, British embassy in Beijing; British trade commissioner, China; consul for Macau. Speaks eight languages. Supported Remaining in the EU but voted for Theresa May's deal, 2019. Supported Jeremy Hunt's leadership bid, 2019. Successfully campaigned to extend the maximum penalty for stalking and to abolish visa fees for Commonwealth service people bringing their families to Britain.

	Electorate	Share %	from 2017 % Change
	81,332		
*R Graham C	29,159	54.24	+3.92
F Boait Lab Co-op	18,882	35.12	-4.99
R Trimnell LD	4,338	8.07	+3.05
M Byfield Green	1,385	2.58	+1.18

PPS to: Hugo Swire, 2012-14; Lord Howell of Guildford, 2010-12. Cllr, Cotswold DC, 2003-07. Ed: Eton Coll; Christ Church, Oxford (BA history).

CHALLENGERS
Fran Boait (Lab Co-op) Executive director, the financial reform group Positive Money. Senior fellow, Finance Innovation Lab; adviser, Avon Mutual Bank. **Rebecca Trimnell** (LD) Political researcher, Gloucestershire Liberal Democrats, 2011-18.

CONSTITUENCY PROFILE
This city and district in southwest England has been a bellwether between Labour and the Conservatives since 1979. Labour gained the seat in 1945 and held it until 1970, after which it spent nearly three decades returning Conservative MPs. Famous for its cathedral, which featured in the Harry Potter films, the city is home to about 150,000 people, although parts of its northern and eastern suburbs sit outside the constituency. The seat is relatively affluent: unemployment is below the national average and the level of home ownership is above it.

EU REFERENDUM RESULT
58.9% Leave   Remain 41.1%

Gordon

RICHARD THOMSON
BORN June 16, 1976
MP 2019-

Previously worked in financial services for firms including Scottish Widows. Columnist, *Scots Independent*. Former SNP head of research and campaigns. Cllr, Aberdeenshire C, 2012-; leader, SNP group, 2015-17. Among *The Spectator's* "ones to watch" of the 2019 intake. Campaign backed by Scottish Whisky Association and leading figures in Scottish fishing industry. Contested: Tweeddale, Ettrick & Lauderdale, 2001; this seat, 2010. Ed: University of Stirling (history and politics), Edinburgh Business School (MBA).

	Electorate	Share %	Change from 2017 %
	79,629		
R Thomson SNP	23,885	42.72	+6.85
*C Clark C	23,066	41.25	+0.53
J Oates LD	5,913	10.57	-1.03
H Herbert Lab	3,052	5.46	-6.35

CHALLENGERS
Colin Clark (C) At the centre of one of the biggest upsets of 2017 when he unseated Alex Salmond, the first minister of Scotland, in 2007-14. MP for Gordon, 2015-17 and for Banff & Buchan, 1987-2010. Parly under-sec, Scotland, 2019. Contested this seat, 2015. **James Oates** (LD) Human rights campaigner in central and eastern Europe. Nephew of this seat's former MP, Sir Malcolm Bruce. **Heather Herbert** (Lab) Works at University of Aberdeen; she also previously

worked for Aberdeenshire council.

CONSTITUENCY PROFILE
Alex Salmond gained this Aberdeenshire constituency with a large majority during the SNP's 2015 landslide in Scotland, but lost it to the Conservatives in the 2017 election. The seat had been represented by Sir Malcolm Bruce, a Liberal then Lib Dem MP, from 1983 until 2015. Mostly rural and sparse, covering much of central Aberdeenshire and a northern part of the city of Aberdeen. Earnings are significantly higher than average, and three quarters of residents are homeowners.

EU REFERENDUM RESULT
38.8% Leave   Remain 61.2%

Gosport

CAROLINE DINENAGE
BORN Oct 28, 1971
MP 2010-

Minister of state for digital and culture, 2020-. Former director of Dinenages, a small business supplying corporate identity products. Campaigned to Remain but approved Theresa May's deal and voted for no-deal. Supported leadership bids of Matt Hancock then Jeremy Hunt, 2019. Social care minister, 2018-20. Parly under-sec: work and pensions, 2017-18; education, 2016-17; justice, 2015-16. Equalities minister, 2015-16; previously had a mixed record on same-sex marriage. PPS to Nicky Morgan, 2014-15. Select cttees: science and technology,

	Electorate	Share %	Change from 2017 %
	73,482		
*C Dinenage C	32,226	66.51	+4.57
T Chatwin Lab	8,948	18.47	-8.69
M Pepper LD	5,473	11.30	+6.59
Z Aspinall Green	1,806	3.73	+1.66

2012-13; business, 2012-15. Contested Portsmouth South, 2005. Cllr, Winchester City C, 1998-2003. Ed: Oaklands RC Comp, Waterlooville; University of Wales, Swansea (BA politics and English).

CHALLENGERS
Tom Chatwin (Lab) Head of English at a special educational needs school. **Martin Pepper** (LD) Former army officer. Board member, police and crime commissioner. Cllr, Gosport BC, 2018-.

CONSTITUENCY PROFILE
A Conservative safe seat with consistent five-figure majorities. Labour came closest to winning it in 2001, when the Conservative majority was reduced to less than 3,000. The MP between 1974 and 2010, Sir Peter Viggers, was forced to retire after it was revealed during the expenses scandal that he had claimed £1,600 for a floating duck house. The seat contains the south coast naval town of Gosport and a few small villages to its west. Many of the working residents hold managerial and professional occupations; public administration and defence are significant sources of local jobs.

EU REFERENDUM RESULT
61.8% Leave   Remain 38.2%

Gower

MAJORITY 1,837 (4.13%)   LABOUR HOLD   TURNOUT 72.02%

TONIA ANTONIAZZI
BORN Oct 5, 1971
MP 2017-

Spent more than 20 years as a language teacher; head of languages, Bryngwyn School, Llanelli. Stint as a tighthead prop for the Welsh national rugby team; won nine caps in three years. Remainer; voted in favour of a second referendum. Daughter of Italian immigrants who made ice cream and ran a chain of cafés. Accused of spreading pseudoscience by claiming that 5G was carcinogenic, 2019. Supports the legalisation of medical cannabis. Select cttees: women and equalities, 2017-19; Welsh affairs, 2017-19. Ed: St John Lloyd

	Electorate	Share %	Change from 2017 %
	61,762		
*T Antoniazzi Lab	20,208	45.43	-4.44
F O'Brien C	18,371	41.30	-1.39
J Davies PC	2,288	5.14	+1.48
S Bennett LD	2,236	5.03	+2.98
R Ross Brexit	1,379	3.10	

RC Sch, Llanelli; Gower Coll, Swansea; University of Exeter (BA French and Italian); Cardiff University (PGCE).

CHALLENGERS
Francesca O'Brien (C) Former RAF commanding officer. Faced calls to stand down during campaign for having said that people on the Channel 4 programme *Benefits Street* needed "putting down". **John Davies** (PC) Self-employed financier. Organises annual

St David's Day parade. **Sam Bennett** (LD) Works in Swansea University recruitment.

CONSTITUENCY PROFILE
Labour lost this west Glamorgan seat in 2015 by 27 votes, having previously won control of the constituency at every election for 105 years. The party regained the seat in 2017 with a majority of more than 3,000. It consists of the Gower peninsula, including the popular coastal resort of The Mumbles and the former mining towns of Gorseinon and Pontarddulais. The area is predominantly middle class: wages are high and constituents are generally highly educated.

EU REFERENDUM RESULT
49.3% Leave   Remain 50.7%

Grantham & Stamford

MAJORITY 26,003 (46.43%)   CONSERVATIVE HOLD   TURNOUT 68.71%

GARETH DAVIES
BORN Mar 31, 1984
MP 2019-

Chosen to take over from Nick Boles, MP for this seat, 2010-19. Director-general of the Department for Transport, 2019-; Department for Business, Energy and Industrial Strategy, 2015-19. Previously executive director, Cabinet Office; No 10 private secretary, 2003-07, and deputy director, PM's strategy unit. One of his first acts in parliament was to ask the government to confirm its commitment to improving transport infrastructure. State educated, originally from Yorkshire. Contested: Leeds Central & Doncaster, 2017;

	Electorate	Share %	Change from 2017 %
	81,502		
G Davies C	36,794	65.70	+3.70
K Salt Lab	10,791	19.27	-7.23
H Bisnauthsing LD	6,153	10.99	+5.47
A Gayfer Green	2,265	4.04	+2.66

Doncaster Central, 2010. Ed: University of Oxford (MA PPE), LSE (MSc economics).

CHALLENGERS
Kathryn Salt (Lab) History and business studies teacher. Fiction and poetry author; received MBE for charity work, offering publishing copyright to charities. **Harrish Bisnauthsing** (LD) Counsellor and managing director of a computer firm. Former RAF electronics engineer. **Anne Gayfer** (Green) Secretary, local Green Party.

CONSTITUENCY PROFILE
Historically Conservative, although representation has changed twice in recent years. Quentin Davies, MP 1987-2010, defected to Labour in 2007, while in 2019 Nick Boles left his party over Brexit and sat as an independent for his last few months in parliament. Mr Boles, who was skills minister, 2014-16, and a cancer survivor, did not to contest the 2019 election. The seat has never elected a Labour MP and has elected Conservatives since 1950. It is associated with the Conservative prime minister Margaret Thatcher, who grew up in the town of Grantham.

EU REFERENDUM RESULT
61.0% Leave   Remain 39.0%

Gravesham

| MAJORITY 15,581 (32.76%) | CONSERVATIVE HOLD | TURNOUT 64.94% |

ADAM HOLLOWAY
BORN July 29, 1965
MP 2005-

Former ITN journalist: foreign affairs correspondent in Sarajevo and undercover investigative reporter. Grenadier Guards, 1991-97. Campaigned to Leave the EU; voted against Theresa May's withdrawal agreement on all three meaningful votes. Supported Boris Johnson's leadership bid, 2019. Faced criticism for claiming that rough sleeping was more comfortable than military exercises, 2018. Prepared to rebel: voted against military action in Syria, 2014. PPS to David Lidington, 2010-11. Select cttees: science and technology, 2017-18;

	Electorate	Share %	Change from 2017 %
	73,234		
*A Holloway C	29,580	62.20	+6.61
L Sullivan Lab	13,999	29.43	-7.08
U Obasi LD	2,584	5.43	+2.96
M Gilligan Green	1,397	2.94	+1.46

foreign affairs, 2015-17; public administration, 2016, 2014-15; defence, 2012-14, 2006-10. Chairman, drones APPG. Ed: Magdalene Coll, Cambridge (BA theology; MA social and political science); Imperial Coll, London (MBA); RMA Sandhurst.

CHALLENGERS
Lauren Sullivan (Lab) Cllr, Kent CC, 2017-. Member, Francis Crick Institute. **Ukonu Obasi** (LD) Public health specialist. **Marna Gilligan** (Green) Contested this seat, 2017.

CONSTITUENCY PROFILE
Gravesham, and its predecessor seat of Gravesend, has mostly been a bellwether since the Second World War, with only a few exceptions. Labour won it in 1951 despite the Conservatives forming a government and the Conservatives gained the seat in 2005 despite Labour winning a third term under Tony Blair. Its largest town, Gravesend, has a population of about 75,000. On the south bank of the Thames, this constituency is poorer, more ethnically diverse and has a higher proportion of council housing than other Kent seats. Dominant industries include construction and retail.

EU REFERENDUM RESULT
65.4% Leave   Remain 34.6%

Great Grimsby

| MAJORITY 7,331 (22.16%) | CONSERVATIVE GAIN FROM LABOUR | TURNOUT 53.88% |

LIA NICI
BORN Aug 1, 1969
MP 2019-

The first Conservative MP to be elected in this constituency since 1935. Media studies lecturer, Grimsby Institute. Executive producer, Estuary TV, 2013-18; faced controversy after it received £300,000 in BBC local funding, despite some programmes having fewer than 200 viewers. Contested Hull North, 2017. Cllr, North East Lincolnshire C, 2018-; chairwoman, economic scrutiny panel. Ed: Huddersfield University (BA education).

CHALLENGERS
Melanie Onn (Lab) MP for this

	Electorate	Share %	Change from 2017 %
	61,409		
L Nici C	18,150	54.86	+12.68
*M Onn Lab	10,819	32.70	-16.69
C Barker Brexit	2,378	7.19	
I Barfield LD	1,070	3.23	+0.55
L Emmerson Green	514	1.55	
N Winn Ind	156	0.47	-0.64

seat, 2015-19. Worked in Labour Party head office for ten years. Former regional organiser, Unison. Shadow housing minister, 2017-19; shadow deputy Commons leader, 2015-16. Proposed making wolf-whistling a hate crime. Corbyn sceptic. Remainer; voted against Theresa May's deal but approved Boris Johnson's. **Christopher Barker** (Brexit) Campaigned on British fishing rights. **Ian Barfield** (LD) Cllr, North Lincolnshire C, 2016-.

CONSTITUENCY PROFILE
Great Grimsby had consistently been won by the Labour Party since 1945, although it was not always a safe seat in that time. The Conservatives came within about 800 votes of gaining it in 1983 and 2010 and Labour's majority tipped into five figures only in 1997 and 2001. The seat's MP from 1959 until 1977 was Anthony Crosland, a Labour moderniser and foreign secretary under Jim Callaghan. Located in northeast Lincolnshire, the market town and port of Grimsby was once a thriving industrial centre for fishing and remains an important centre for fish processing.

EU REFERENDUM RESULT
71.4% Leave   Remain 28.6%

Great Yarmouth

MAJORITY 17,663 (40.64%) CONSERVATIVE HOLD TURNOUT 60.40%

BRANDON LEWIS
BORN Jun 20, 1971
MP 2010-

Secretary of state for Northern Ireland since the February 2020 reshuffle. Minister for security and deputy to the home secretary for no-deal preparation, 2019-20. Chairman of the Conservative Party, 2018-19, in which role he allowed an investigation into Boris Johnson's comment about women in Muslim dress looking like "letterboxes". Voted Remain but for Theresa May's withdrawal agreement. Minister: without portfolio, 2018-19; immigration, 2017-18; policing and fire service, 2016-17; housing, 2014-16. Parly under-sec, local government,

	Electorate	Share %	Change from 2017 %
	71,957		
*B Lewis C	28,593	65.79	+11.65
M Smith-Clare Lab Co-op	10,930	25.15	-10.93
J Joyce LD	1,661	3.82	+1.59
A Killett Green	1,064	2.45	+1.17
D Harding VPP	631	1.45	
A Myers Ind	429	0.99	
M McMahon-Morris Ind	154	0.35	

2012-14. Cllr, Brentwood BC, 1998-2009; leader, 2004-09. Contested Sherwood, 2001. Member of the Carlton Club. CBE. Barrister; called to the Bar in 1995. Ed: Forest Sch; Walthamstow; University of Buckingham (BSc economics; LLB law); King's College London (LLM commercial law).

CHALLENGERS
Mike Smith-Clare (Lab Co-op)

Cllr, Great Yarmouth BC, 2017-. MBE for community work. Contested this seat, 2017. **James Joyce** (LD) Postmaster, Broadlands DC, 2004-11. Contested this seat in the previous two elections.

CONSTITUENCY PROFILE
Looks like a safe Conservative seat from recent results but it has been a bellwether since 1979, electing Labour MPs in 1997, 2001 and 2005. Labour also won in 1945, 1950 and 1966, breaking spells of Conservative dominance. Known for its oil industry and offshore gas rigs. Contains two of the most deprived wards in the country.

EU REFERENDUM RESULT
71.5% Leave Remain 28.5%

Greenwich & Woolwich

MAJORITY 18,464 (34.76%) LABOUR HOLD TURNOUT 66.40%

MATTHEW PENNYCOOK
BORN Oct 29, 1982
MP 2015-

Shadow minister for Brexit, 2016-19; resigned to campaign for a second referendum. Background with various charities, such as Child Poverty Action Group and Fair Pay Network. Researcher, Resolution Foundation; Institute for Public Policy Research. PPS to John Healey, 2015-16. Select cttee: energy and climate change, 2016-19. Nominated Yvette Cooper, Owen Smith and Sir Keir Starmer for the leadership in 2015, 2016 and 2020. Remainer; backed options including revoking Article 50 in indicative votes. Signed early day

	Electorate	Share %	Change from 2017 %
	79,997		
*M Pennycook Lab	30,185	56.82	-7.60
T Turrell C	11,721	22.07	-3.36
R O'Connor LD	7,253	13.65	+6.53
V Rance Green	2,363	4.45	+1.43
K Trivedi Brexit	1,228	2.31	
E Odesanmi CPA	245	0.46	
S Gaikwad Ind	125	0.24	

motion to deny President Trump an invitation to Westminster. Cllr, Greenwich BC, 2010-15. Raised by a single mother; first person in family to go to university. Ed: LSE (BSc history and international relations); Balliol Coll, Oxford (MPhil international relations).

CHALLENGERS
Thomas Turrell (C) Deputy area chairman, London South East

Conservatives. **Rhian O'Connor** (LD) Economist. **Victoria Rance** (Green) Party campaigns officer for Greenwich and Bexley.

CONSTITUENCY PROFILE
A safe Labour seat: the party has not won with less than a five-figure majority since the seat was created in 1997. Its two predecessors, Greenwich and Woolwich, were held during the 1980s by the Social Democratic Party but both returned to Labour in 1992. This southeast London constituency is mostly working class, with a quarter of people in council properties. The unemployment rate is above the national average.

EU REFERENDUM RESULT
35.7% Leave Remain 64.3%

Guildford

MAJORITY 3,337 (5.69%) CONSERVATIVE HOLD TURNOUT 75.46%

ANGELA RICHARDSON
BORN Oct 21, 1974
MP 2019-

Former PFI administrator, Axa Investment Managers, 2001-02; Schroders, 1999-2000. Grew up in New Zealand and attended school with Simon Bridges, the leader of that country's conservative National Party. Vice-chairwoman, Cranleigh PC, 2017-. Chairwoman, 1867 Patrons Club; former deputy chairwoman, Guildford Conservative Association. National officer, Conservative Women's Association, 2017-18. Voted Leave; originally supported Dominic Raab in leadership election but sided with Boris Johnson in final vote.

	Electorate	Share %	Change from 2017 %
	77,729		
A Richardson C	26,317	44.87	-9.71
Z Franklin LD	22,980	39.18	+15.30
A Rouse Lab	4,515	7.70	-11.30
*A Milton Ind	4,356	7.43	
J Morris Peace	483	0.82	+0.45

CHALLENGERS
Zöe Franklin (LD) Career in publishing. Contested this seat, 2017. **Anne Rouse** (Lab) Director, Surrey Nurturing Links, 2009-. **Anne Milton** (Ind) Conservative MP for this seat, 2005-19; had whip removed over Brexit. Former NHS nurse. Deputy chief whip, 2012-17. Parly under-sec, health, 2010-12.

CONSTITUENCY PROFILE
The Liberal Democrats had hoped to win this seat, the Greens having stood aside for them, but Anne Milton's decision to stand as an independent may have reduced their chances. This Surrey seat has historically been a Conservative stronghold, held by the party in every election since 1910 with the sole exception of 2001, when it was captured for one parliamentary term by the Lib Dems. A large constituency dominated by the town that gives its name, which has a population of about 77,000. An affluent seat, which also contains the University of Surrey, residents are more likely than average to work in professional occupations.

EU REFERENDUM RESULT
41.2% Leave Remain 58.8%

Hackney North & Stoke Newington

MAJORITY 33,188 (58.36%) LABOUR HOLD TURNOUT 61.51%

DIANE ABBOTT
BORN Sep 27, 1953
MP 1987-

Britain's first black female MP who in 2019 also became the first black MP to appear at the dispatch box during PMQs. Shadow home secretary, 2016-. Absent during the 2019 campaign after blunders in 2017. Firebrand leftwinger with interests in police reform and anti-racism. Receives almost half of all online abuse directed at female MPs, according to Amnesty UK. Rebel during New Labour years; also defied Jeremy Corbyn to vote against replacing Trident, 2016. Remainer; abstained on revoke motion during indicative votes. Stood for

	Electorate	Share %	Change from 2017 %
	92,451		
*D Abbott Lab	39,972	70.29	-4.78
B Obese-Jecty C	6,784	11.93	-0.73
A Armitage Green	4,989	8.77	+4.14
B Mathis LD	4,283	7.53	+0.75
R Ings Brexit	609	1.07	
H Ur-Rehman Renew	151	0.27	
L Lixenberg ND	76	0.13	

leader in 2010; backed Rebecca Long Bailey in 2020. Shadow international development secretary, 2015-16. Race relations officer, National Council for Civil Liberties (now Liberty). Cllr, Westminster City C, 1982-86. Ed: Harrow County GS; Newnham Coll, Cambridge (BA history).

CHALLENGERS
Benjamin Obese-Jecty (C) Army veteran; served in Iraq and Afghanistan. Former project manager, JP Morgan. **Alex Armitage** (Green) Hospital doctor. **Ben Mathis** (LD) Dropped by the party over controversial tweets.

CONSTITUENCY PROFILE
Labour's sixth safest seat by numerical majority. One of the smallest and most compact seats in parliament. Young and diverse; less than a quarter of residents are aged over 45. Two fifths are from an ethnic minority, most of them black or mixed race. About one in ten residents was born in the EU-27 nations and another quarter were born outside the EU.

EU REFERENDUM RESULT
20.5% Leave Remain 79.5%

Hackney South & Shoreditch

MAJORITY 33,985 (62.43%)   LABOUR CO-OP HOLD   TURNOUT 60.91%

MEG HILLIER
BORN Feb 14, 1969
MP 2005-

	Electorate	Share %	Change from 2017 %
	89,380		
*M Hillier Lab Co-op	39,884	73.26	-6.18
M Beckett C	5,899	10.84	-0.08
D Raval LD	4,853	8.91	+3.19
T Scott Green	2,948	5.42	+2.67
R Lloyd Brexit	744	1.37	
J Leff WRP	111	0.20	+0.05

Former journalist. Remainer; voted against triggering Article 50. Corbyn sceptic; nominated Emily Thornberry for leader, 2020. Short-lived attempt to become Speaker in 2019. Campaigner against parliamentary bullying. Chairwoman, public accounts cttee, 2015-. Other cttees: parliamentary buildings, 2018-19, public accounts, 2011-, Commons liaison, 2015-19. Parly under-sec, Home Office, 2009-10; 2007-08. Shadow minister, Home Office, 2010; energy and climate change, 2010-11. PPS to Ruth Kelly, 2006-07. Cllr, Islington LBC, 1994-98;

mayor, 1998-99. Greater London Assembly, 2000-04. Member, Fabian Society. Ed: Portsmouth HS; St Hilda's Coll, Oxford (BA PPE); City, University of London (Dip newspaper journalism).

CHALLENGERS
Mark Beckett (C) Executive director, The Enterprise Forum. Former PR manager, National Pharmacy Association. **Dave Raval** (LD) Chief executive, Loftzone. Contested Leicester

East, 2015; this seat in 2010. **Tyrone Scott** (Green) Campaigns officer, Young Greens. **Robert Lloyd** (Brexit) Former lawyer.

CONSTITUENCY PROFILE
This northeast London seat, including its predecessor of Shoreditch & Finsbury, has returned Labour MPs at every election since 1950 and the party has received less than half the vote only twice in that time, in 1983 and 1987. The seat stretches from Old Street in its west to Stratford's Olympic Park in the East End. Half of its households are socially rented. Two fifths of residents were born overseas.

EU REFERENDUM RESULT
22.8% Leave   Remain 77.2%

Halesowen & Rowley Regis

MAJORITY 12,074 (28.51%)   CONSERVATIVE HOLD   TURNOUT 62.00%

JAMES MORRIS
BORN Feb 4, 1967
MP 2010-

	Electorate	Share %	Change from 2017 %
	68,300		
*J Morris C	25,607	60.47	+8.62
I Cooper Lab	13,533	31.96	-8.06
R Priest LD	1,738	4.10	+2.17
J Windridge Green	934	2.21	+1.21
J Cross Ind	232	0.55	
I Fleming Ind	190	0.45	
T Weller Ind	111	0.26	

Entrepreneur who started a string of software companies. Founding director, London Policy Institute. Staunch advocate of localism: former chief executive, Localis think tank. Resigned as a PPS to vote for law change to require planning permission to demolish local pubs. Campaigned to Remain in the EU but voted for Theresa May's withdrawal agreement. Supported Jeremy Hunt's leadership bid, 2019. Government whip, 2020-; assistant whip, 2019-20. PPS to Esther McVey, employment minister, 2014-15. APPG

chairman, mental health, 2010-17. Ed: University of Birmingham (BA English literature); Wadham Coll, Oxford (postgraduate research); Cranfield School of Management (MBA).

CHALLENGERS
Ian Cooper (Lab) English and drama teacher. Cllr, Dudley MBC, 2014-18; cabinet member. Branch president, GMB. **Ryan Priest** (LD) Twenty-two years

old; joined the party in 2016. **James Windridge** (Green) Scientific researcher.

CONSTITUENCY PROFILE
This West Midlands seat was held by Labour between 1997 and 2010 but the Conservatives won it in 2010 and since then James Morris's majority has grown at every election. The predecessor seats covering Halesowen were held by Labour from 1950-70, then by the Conservatives from 1970-97. It is a metropolitan area between the urban centres of Birmingham and Dudley. The population is less ethnically diverse and older than in most nearby seats.

EU REFERENDUM RESULT
66.6% Leave   Remain 33.4%

Halifax

HOLLY LYNCH
BORN Oct 8, 1986
MP 2015-

Halifax born and bred former fast-food worker. Shadow environment minister, 2017-19. Opposition whip, 2015-16; resigned when Rosie Winterton, a chief whip, was sacked. Long-time champion of Protect the Protectors, a campaign for tougher punishments on people who assault police officers. Oversaw constituency office of Batley & Spen after the murder of its MP, Jo Cox. Nominated Jess Phillips in the 2020 Labour leadership contest. Wrote open letter of support to Meghan Markle signed by 72 female MPs. Select cttees: women and

	Electorate	Share %	Change from 2017 %
	71,904		
*H Lynch Lab	21,496	46.27	-6.57
K Ali C	18,927	40.74	-0.96
S Wood Brexit	2,813	6.05	
J Baker LD	2,276	4.90	+2.68
B Jessop Green	946	2.04	

equalities, 2017; procedure, 2016-17; environmental audit, 2015. Ed: Brighouse HS; Lancaster University (BA politics and history).

CHALLENGERS
Kashif Ali (C) Practising barrister and law tutor, Manchester University and ICC. Trained mediator. Contested Oldham East & Saddleworth, 2010. **Sarah Wood** (Brexit) Former RAF pilot, qualified teacher and chartered

accountant. **James Baker** (LD) Cllr: Calderdale BC, 2012-; Hebden Royd PC, 2010-12.

CONSTITUENCY PROFILE
A Labour seat since 1945, with three exceptions during the Conservatives' 1983 landslide, and their victories in 1955 and 1959, when Harold Macmillan's son, Maurice, represented the seat. The Conservatives came within 500 votes of gaining it in 1992 and 2015. In West Yorkshire, the seat contains both Halifax itself and the nearby town of Sowerby Bridge. More than a fifth of residents are aged under 16. About one in eight residents is of Pakistani heritage.

EU REFERENDUM RESULT
58.8% Leave   Remain 41.2%

Haltemprice & Howden

DAVID DAVIS
BORN Dec 23, 1948
MP 1987-

Eurosceptic catapulted onto front line as Brexit secretary, 2016-18, and chief Brexit negotiator, 2016-17. Resigned in opposition to Theresa May's Chequers plan. Initially supported Dominic Raab in the 2019 Tory leadership election, then Boris Johnson. Contested party leadership himself in 2005 and 2001. Declined to be a part of the coalition cabinet and was a frequent critic of its stance on tuition fees, civil liberties and airstrikes against Isis. Resigned his seat to force a by-election in 2008 in the hope of provoking a debate on the erosion of civil

	Electorate	Share %	Change from 2017 %
	71,062		
*D Davis C	31,045	62.37	+1.41
G Ayre Lab	10,716	21.53	-9.48
L Johnson LD	5,215	10.48	+5.65
A Stone Green	1,764	3.54	+2.16
R Honnoraty Yorkshire	1,039	2.09	+0.26

liberties. Shadow home secretary, 2003-08. Europe minister, 1994-97. Former senior executive, Tate & Lyle. Territorial SAS. Ed: Tooting Bec GS; University of Warwick (BSc molecular and computer sciences); London Business Sch (MSc business); Harvard University (advanced management programme).

CHALLENGERS
George Ayre (Lab) Cllr, Wakefield DC, 2014-; resigned from council front bench after

leading a failed coup against the council leader in 2018. **Linda Johnson** (LD) Safeguarding trainer and local preacher.

CONSTITUENCY PROFILE
A large and rural area north of the Humber estuary and west of Kingston-upon-Hull, which has been held in various forms by the Conservatives for more than a century. Despite being boycotted by Labour and the Lib Dems, the by-election that David Davis prompted in 2008 set the record for the most candidates in a by-election, at 26. One of the highest levels of home ownership in the country, with four fifths of households owner-occupied.

EU REFERENDUM RESULT
55.2% Leave   Remain 44.8%

Halton

MAJORITY 18,975 (41.07%) LABOUR HOLD TURNOUT 64.23%

DEREK TWIGG
BORN Jul 9, 1959
MP 1997-

Civil servant in the departments for education and employment, 1975-94. Became CPSA union branch secretary aged 18. Voted against same-sex marriage in 2013, and was absent for 2019 votes on abortion and same-sex marriage in Northern Ireland. Supported Lisa Nandy for leader, 2020; backed Andy Burnham in both 2015 and 2010. PPS to: Helen Liddell, 1998-2001; Stephen Byers, 2001-02. Defence minister, 2006-08; parly under-sec, transport, 2004-06; government whip, 2002-04. Select cttees: liaison, 2015-17; statutory instruments, 2015-17.

	Electorate	Share %	Change from 2017 %
	71,930		
*D Twigg Lab	29,333	63.49	-9.45
C Rowley C	10,358	22.42	+0.79
J Balfe Brexit	3,730	8.07	
S Gribbon LD	1,800	3.90	+2.09
D O'Keefe Green	982	2.13	

Cllr, Cheshire CC, 1980-85. Member, Labour Friends of Israel. Interested in military history. Widower; his wife died during the election campaign. Ed: Bankfield HS, Widnes; Halton Coll of FE.

CHALLENGERS
Charles Rowley (C) Cllr, East Herts DC, 2019-. **Janet Balfe** (Brexit) Business owner. **Stephen Gribbon** (LD) Watch commander for local fire service. Cllr, Stockport MBC, 2018-.

CONSTITUENCY PROFILE
The north Cheshire seat of Halton, created in 1983, has only ever elected Labour MPs. It was created from the seats of Widnes and Runcorn, which had been represented by Labour and the Conservatives respectively since the Second World War. To the southeast of Liverpool, consisting of Widnes and most of the railway town of Runcorn, residents earn well below the Cheshire average, but only slightly less than the North West average. The seat contains Spike Island, formerly an important centre for the chemical industry and the site of a famous concert by *The Stone Roses* in 1990.

EU REFERENDUM RESULT
57.7% Leave Remain 42.3%

Hammersmith

MAJORITY 17,847 (34.34%) LABOUR HOLD TURNOUT 69.51%

ANDREW SLAUGHTER
BORN Sep 29, 1960
MP 2005-

Trained barrister who worked as a researcher for the BBC and for Michael Meacher MP. Campaigned for constituents to take in refugees from Syria and Calais. Shadow housing minister, 2016-17; sacked for defying Labour whip to vote for a pro-single market amendment to Queen's Speech. Shadow justice minister, 2010-16; resigned in protest against Jeremy Corbyn's leadership. Supported Sir Keir Starmer's leadership campaign, 2020. Select cttees: justice, 2019; human rights, 2010. MP for Ealing, Acton & Shepherd's Bush, 2005-10. Cllr, Hammersmith

	Electorate	Share %	Change from 2017 %
	74,759		
*A Slaughter Lab	30,074	57.87	-6.00
X Wang C	12,227	23.53	-4.65
J Venegas LD	6,947	13.37	+8.01
A Horn Green	1,744	3.36	+1.82
J Keyse Brexit	974	1.87	

& Fulham LBC, 1986-2005; leader, 1996-2005. Contested Uxbridge, 1997. Ed: Latymer Upper Sch; University of Exeter (BA English).

CHALLENGERS
Xingang Wang (C) Financial consultant; named in *Top 100 People in Finance Magazine*. Contested Manchester Central, 2017, 2015. **Jessie Venegas** (LD) Law teacher and EU parliamentary caseworker. Contested Hammersmith and

Fulham LBC, 2019, 2018. **Alex Horn** (Green) NHS worker, St Mary's Hospital, London.

CONSTITUENCY PROFILE
After this west London seat's reconstitution in 2010, Andy Slaughter increased his majority from 3,500 to more than 18,000 in 2017. Represented, in different forms, by Labour since 1950, except for 2005-10, when, as Hammersmith & Fulham, it was held by the Conservative Greg Hands (Chelsea & Fulham). House prices have soared: on average a terraced house costs at least £1 million. Just under half the residents were born outside the country.

EU REFERENDUM RESULT
31.3% Leave Remain 68.7%

Hampshire East

MAJORITY 19,696 (34.62%)   CONSERVATIVE HOLD   TURNOUT 74.39%

DAMIAN HINDS
BORN Nov 27, 1969
MP 2010-

	Electorate	Share %	Change from 2017 %
	76,478		
*D Hinds C	33,446	58.79	-4.86
D Buxton LD	13,750	24.17	+9.00
G Austin Lab	6,287	11.05	-5.93
Z Parker Green	2,600	4.57	+1.39
J Makin Ukip	616	1.08	
E Trotter JACP	196	0.34	-0.69

Education secretary, 2018-19; left the role upon Boris Johnson's ascension to the premiership, having supported Michael Gove in the leadership contest. Criticised unconditional university offers as unethical. Employment minister, 2016-18; Treasury secretary, 2015-16; assistant whip, 2014-15. Career in pubs, breweries and hotels as a strategist and marketer: Greene King; Intercontinental Hotels; Holiday Inn. Contested Stretford & Urmston, 2005. Ed: St Ambrose GS, Altrincham; Trinity Coll, Oxford (BA PPE; president, students' union).

CHALLENGERS
David Buxton (LD) Chief executive of a charity. Disability adviser to Paddy Ashdown; founder, Lib Dem Disability Association. Born deaf, first councillor to use a sign language interpreter. Cllr: Epsom & Ewell BC, 2007-11; Southwark BC, 1990-94. **Gaynor Austin** (Lab) Teacher, previously NHS auditor. Cllr, Rushmoor BC, 2019-. **Zoe Parker** (Green) Cllr, Petersfield TC, 2019-.

Education researcher, College of Occupational Therapists and Kingston University.

CONSTITUENCY PROFILE
Conservative since its creation in 1983; its predecessor, Petersfield, was held by the party from 1892. The second-placed party has alternated recently, with Ukip and Labour runners-up in 2015 and 2017 respectively. A largely rural area north of Portsmouth and east of Winchester, much of it is in the South Downs. Home ownership levels and average incomes are above the national and regional averages. About a fifth of residents are of pensionable age.

EU REFERENDUM RESULT
49.3% Leave   Remain 50.7%

Hampshire North East

MAJORITY 20,211 (34.10%)   CONSERVATIVE HOLD   TURNOUT 75.07%

RANIL
JAYAWARDENA
BORN Sep 3, 1986
MP 2015-

	Electorate	Share %	Change from 2017 %
	78,954		
*R Jayawardena C	35,280	59.52	-5.99
G Cockarill LD	15,069	25.42	+13.30
B Jones Lab	5,760	9.72	-7.60
C Walsh Green	1,754	2.96	+0.40
T Durrant Ind	831	1.40	+0.77
H L Hope Loony	576	0.97	

Conservative Party vice-chairman, 2019-. Resigned as PPS to the Ministry of Justice in protest at Theresa May's Brexit deal. Backed Boris Johnson's leadership bid, 2019. Worked as a Brussels lobbyist and government relations manager at Lloyds Banking. Voted against LGBT-inclusive sex education in schools. PPS to work and pensions, 2019. Select cttees: arms export controls, 2017-19; procedure, 2017-19; international trade, 2016-19; home affairs, 2015-17. Director, Conservative Christian Fellowship. Ed: Alton Coll; LSE (BSc government).

CHALLENGERS
Graham Cockarill (LD) Insurance broker, Willis Group Holdings. Former telemarketing executive. Cllr, Hart DC, 2002-. **Barry Jones** (Lab) Graduate student in railway studies, University of York. Systems architect. Cllr, Rushmoor BC, 2012-19. Contested this seat, 2017. **Culann Walsh** (Green) Contested Haringey BC, 2018. Party staffer since 2017. **Tony Durrant** (Ind) Retired software

company director. Chairman, Bramley parish council.

CONSTITUENCY PROFILE
The safest Conservative seat in the country in 2015, partly because opposition votes were so evenly split between the other parties. The Conservatives have never won less than half of the votes cast in the constituency. Ukip's candidate in 2015 was suspended after threatening to "put a bullet in" Ranil Jayawardena. Sprawled around the town of Basingstoke, about three quarters of households are owner-occupied, and it is one of the most affluent areas in the country.

EU REFERENDUM RESULT
46.2% Leave   Remain 53.8%

Hampshire North West

MAJORITY 26,308 (44.65%)   **CONSERVATIVE HOLD**   **TURNOUT 70.91%**

KIT MALTHOUSE
BORN Oct 27, 1966
MP 2015-

	Electorate	Share %	from 2017 % Change
	83,083		
*K Malthouse C	36,591	62.10	+0.05
L Gregori LD	10,283	17.45	+7.74
L Bell Lab	9,327	15.83	-7.64
L Mitchell Green	2,717	4.61	+2.34

Minister for crime, policing and the fire service since 2019 and a justice minister, 2020-. Voted Leave, fearing the EU would cause the "elimination of the nation state". Gave name to the Malthouse Compromise, a Brexit proposal for redrafting the Irish backstop, 2019. Minister: housing, 2018-19; family support, 2018. Announced he would stand in the 2019 party leadership contest, but dropped out before the first ballot and backed Boris Johnson. Qualified chartered accountant. Asked by Andover MS society to step down as patron after voting for disability benefit cuts, 2016. Deputy mayor of London, 2008-15; London assembly member, 2008-16. Contested Liverpool Wavertree, 1997. Ed: Liverpool Coll; Newcastle University (BA economics and politics).

CHALLENGERS
Luigi Gregori (LD) Former army officer and civil servant. Cllr, Andover TC, 2015-19. Chairman, Andover and District Lib Dems. **Liz Bell** (Lab) Scientist. Associate director, ALP Synergy Ltd, a sustainability consultancy firm.

Former head of policy, Ucas. **Lance Mitchell** (Green) Former military surveyor. Attended naval cadet school.

CONSTITUENCY PROFILE
Since the seat's creation in 1983, the Conservative vote share has fallen below 50 per cent only once, in 1997. Previous MPs include the one-time chief whip Sir George Young and the novelist David Mitchell. The biggest town in this sparse, mostly rural seat is Andover, home to about 40,000 people. Home ownership and average earnings are slightly lower than in Hampshire North East, but the seats are otherwise similar.

EU REFERENDUM RESULT
54.8% Leave   Remain 45.2%

Hampstead & Kilburn

MAJORITY 14,188 (24.72%)   **LABOUR HOLD**   **TURNOUT 69.61%**

TULIP SIDDIQ
BORN Sep 16, 1982
MP 2015-

	Electorate	Share %	from 2017 % Change
	82,432		
*T Siddiq Lab	28,080	48.93	-10.07
J Luk C	13,892	24.21	-8.16
M Sanders LD	13,121	22.86	+15.85
D Stansell Green	1,608	2.80	+1.53
J Pointon Brexit	684	1.19	

Delayed planned caesarean to vote against Theresa May's Brexit deal, and subsequently became the first MP to vote by proxy. Shadow education minister, 2016-17; resigned to vote against triggering Article 50. Former policy adviser to Tessa Jowell. Select cttees: women and equalities, 2015-19; public administration, 2018-19. Niece of Sheikh Hasina, the prime minister of Bangladesh; criticised for not challenging her aunt about human rights abuses. Vocal supporter of Nazanin Zaghari-Ratcliffe, a British-Iranian constituent imprisoned in Iran since 2016. Worked for Amnesty International and Save the Children. Cllr, Camden LBC, 2010-14. Ed: UCL (BA English); King's Coll, London (MA politics, policy and government).

CHALLENGERS
Johnny Luk (C) Head of policy and strategy, The Adecco Group. Senior policy adviser, Brexit department, 2017-19. Head of policy and projects, culture department, 2016-17. **Matt Sanders** (LD) Director for London Union, operator of Street Feast events. Special adviser to Nick Clegg, 2011-15.

CONSTITUENCY PROFILE
A north London seat held by the Oscar-winning actress turned Labour MP Glenda Jackson from 1992 to 2015, before which Labour had previously won Hampstead only once, in 1966. In the 2010 general election Ms Jackson held the seat by just 42 votes. Both John McDonnell and Sir Oliver Letwin have unsuccessfully contested this seat. Home to Muslim and Jewish populations of about 14,000 and 8,000 respectively. Social renting is common.

EU REFERENDUM RESULT
23.7% Leave   Remain 76.3%

Harborough

NEIL O'BRIEN
BORN Nov 6, 1978
MP 2017-

Think tank guru and special adviser to George Osborne, 2012-16. Director: Policy Exchange, 2008-12; Open Europe, 2005-08. Longtime Eurosceptic. Directed Vote 2004 campaign for an EU referendum. Author, *Reforming the EU for the 21st Century*. PPS to: the justice secretary Robert Buckland (Swindon South), 2019-; department of business, 2018-19. Select cttees: science and technology, 2017-19; standing orders, 2017-19. Lead adviser, industrial strategy and the northern powerhouse in David Cameron's policy unit. Ed: Christ

	Electorate	Share %	Change from 2017 %
	79,366		
*N O'Brien C	31,698	55.30	+2.98
C Hibbert Lab	14,420	25.16	-5.58
Z Haq LD	9,103	15.88	+3.23
D Woodiwiss Green	1,709	2.98	+1.05
R Lambert Ind	389	0.68	

Church Coll, Oxford University (BA PPE).

CHALLENGERS
Celia Hibbert (Lab) Sports educator. Disabilities activist. Campaigner, Street Pastoring. Trained FA referee. Part-time model. Cllr, Wolverhampton CC, 2018-. **Zuffar Haq** (LD) Health campaigner involved in various Leicestershire patient groups. Founder, International Medical Aid Appeal. Awarded MBE in 2019. **Darren Woodiwiss**

(Green) Co-founder, Transition Market Harborough.

CONSTITUENCY PROFILE
Safe Conservative seat which has elected a Labour MP only once, in 1945. Represented by Conservatives for 70 years since, although the Liberal Democrats reduced the party's majority to less than 4,000 in 2005. This south Leicestershire seat countains Market Harborough to its south, and Oadby and Wigston, two small towns just south of Leicester, to its north. About one in seven of residents is Asian or of Asian descent. Home ownership levels are well above the national average.

EU REFERENDUM RESULT

52.4% Leave	Remain 47.6%

Harlow

ROBERT HALFON
BORN Mar 22, 1969
MP 2010-

Career politician who extols blue-collar conservatism and published a pamphlet urging more Tories to join trade unions. Named by *The Spectator* as Campaigning MP of the Year, 2013. As a backbencher, petitioned to make St George's Day a public holiday, and successfully lobbied government to lower fuel duty and cut petrol and diesel costs. Minister: education, 2016-17; without portfolio, Cabinet Office, 2015-16. PPS to George Osborne, 2014-15. Chairman, education select cttee, 2017-. Former chief of staff to Sir Oliver Letwin. Backed

	Electorate	Share %	Change from 2017 %
	68,078		
*R Halfon C	27,510	63.45	+9.43
L McAlpine Lab	13,447	31.02	-7.33
C Cane LD	2,397	5.53	+3.37

Sajid Javid's leadership bid, 2019. Member, Conservative Way Forward. Contested this seat, 2005, 2001. Ed: University of Exeter (BA politics; MA Russian and eastern European politics).

CHALLENGERS
Laura Ann McAlpine (Lab) Contested Harborough DC, 2018. Criticised during campaign for defending campaign manager, who in 2018 wrote a blog calling for a "Jewish final solution to the Palestine problem". **Charlotte Cane** (LD) Chartered accountant and trained

archaeologist. Financial director, environmental charity. Treasurer of local solar farm.

CONSTITUENCY PROFILE
Held by Labour from its creation in 1974 until 1983, it has since been a bellwether, although Labour's majority at the 2005 election was just 97. In 2019, Robert Halfon had the largest majority that any Harlow MP has commanded since its creation. Comprises the Essex town of Harlow and some of the rural area around it. Incomes are slightly below the national average, and residents are less likely than average to have been educated to degree level.

EU REFERENDUM RESULT

67.7% Leave	Remain 32.3%

Harrogate & Knaresborough

MAJORITY 9,675 (16.99%) CONSERVATIVE HOLD TURNOUT 73.08%

ANDREW JONES
BORN Nov 28, 1963
MP 2010-

Campaigns on environmental
issues; champion of renewable
energy and recycling.
Campaigned for Remain but
voted for no-deal. Backed Jeremy
Hunt's leadership bid, 2019.
Socially liberal; consistently
voted in favour of LGBT
legislation. Parly under-sec,
transport, 2018-19, 2015-17;
Treasury minister 2017-18. Vice-
chairman, business engagement,
CCHQ, 2018. Select cttees: public
accounts, 2017-19; regulatory
reform, 2010-15. Previously in
sales and marketing, including
for M&C Saatchi. Contested
this constituency, 2001. Long-

	Electorate	Share %	from 2017 %	Change
	77,914			
*A Jones C	29,962	52.62	-2.85	
J Rogerson LD	20,287	35.63	+12.17	
M Sewards Lab	5,480	9.62	-10.46	
K George Yorkshire	1,208	2.12		

standing member, Yorkshire
County Cricket Club. Ed:
Bradford GS; University of Leeds
(BA English).

CHALLENGERS
Judith Rogerson (LD) Barrister
in healthcare law. Previously
taught in northern France.
Called to the Bar in 2003. "Unite
to Remain" candidate. Mark
Sewards (Lab) Maths teacher,
Cockburn School; background
in finance. Executive council
of the NUS, 2012-13. Kieron
George (Yorkshire) Advocated

implementing Brexit and
scrapping all taxes except the
land value tax.

CONSTITUENCY PROFILE
Harrogate had continuously
elected Conservative MPs since
1950 before boundary changes
in 1997. Those changes split the
Kingston-upon-Thames seat
held by the former chancellor
Norman Lamont, leading him
to stand instead in the new
Harrogate & Knaresborough. He
lost to the Liberal Democrats,
who held it from 1997 to 2010.
Home ownership in this north
Yorkshire area is relatively high,
with incomes slightly above the
regional average.

EU REFERENDUM RESULT
47.2% Leave Remain 52.8%

Harrow East

MAJORITY 8,170 (16.51%) CONSERVATIVE HOLD TURNOUT 68.62%

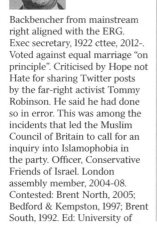

BOB BLACKMAN
BORN Apr 26, 1956
MP 2010-

Backbencher from mainstream
right aligned with the ERG.
Exec secretary, 1922 cttee, 2012-.
Voted against equal marriage "on
principle". Criticised by Hope not
Hate for sharing Twitter posts
by the far-right activist Tommy
Robinson. He said he had done
so in error. This was among the
incidents that led the Muslim
Council of Britain to call for an
inquiry into Islamophobia in
the party. Officer, Conservative
Friends of Israel. London
assembly member, 2004-08.
Contested: Brent North, 2005;
Bedford & Kempston, 1997; Brent
South, 1992. Ed: University of

	Electorate	Share %	from 2017 %	Change
	72,120			
*B Blackman C	26,935	54.42	+5.00	
P Fitzpatrick Lab	18,765	37.92	-8.05	
A Bernard LD	3,791	7.66	+4.57	

Liverpool (BSc physics & maths).

CHALLENGERS
Pamela Fitzpatrick (Lab)
Activist and lecturer on social
security rights. Director, Harrow
Law Centre, 2011-. Trustee of the
Women's Budget Group. Cllr,
Harrow LBC, Headstone South,
2014-. Welfare rights adviser,
Child Poverty Action Group.
Adam Bernard (LD) Freelance
software engineer. Previously
worked as a computer scientist
at Queen Mary, University of
London. Gardening volunteer in
Canons Park.

CONSTITUENCY PROFILE
Held by Labour only when
the party won comfortable
governing majorities nationally:
1945, 1966 and Tony Blair's
three election victories. This
northwest London seat has
one of the country's largest
proportions of Indian residents:
more than three in ten residents
have Indian heritage. Almost
two fifths of residents were born
outside the UK. Home to large
Hindu and Muslim communities,
as well as more than a thousand
Buddhists. Home ownership
is higher here than both the
London and UK averages. The
area has low unemployment and
a significant student population.

EU REFERENDUM RESULT
47.5% Leave Remain 52.5%

Harrow West

MAJORITY 8,692 (18.14%)   LABOUR CO-OP HOLD   TURNOUT 66.12%

GARETH THOMAS
BORN Jul 15, 1967
MP 1997-

	Electorate	Share %	from 2017 %	Change
	72,477			
*G Thomas Lab Co-op	25,132	52.44	-8.40	
A Ali C	16,440	34.31	-0.10	
L Bornemann LD	4,310	8.99	+6.48	
R Langley Green	1,109	2.31	+1.02	
R Jones Brexit	931	1.94		

Chairman of the Co-operative Party, 2000-. Former parliamentary under-secretary for trade and international development; promoted by Gordon Brown to minister: business, 2008-09; international development, 2008-10. Shadow minister: communities, 2016-; Africa and the Middle East, 2014-15; Europe, 2013-14; civil society, 2011-13; higher education and science, 2010-11. Select cttees: international trade, 2019; environmental audit, 1997-99. Unsuccessfully sought Labour candidacy for 2016 London mayoral election. Nominated Emily Thornberry in 2020 leadership contest. PPS to Charles Clarke, 1999-2003. Ed: Hatch End HS; Aberystwyth University (BSc economics and politics); King's Coll, London (MA imperial and commonwealth studies); Thames Polytechnic (PGCE).

CHALLENGERS
Anwara Ali (C) GP. Mayoral candidate for Tower Hamlets, 2018. Cllr, Tower Hamlets LBC, 2006-10. MBE for services to community healthcare. Former PR director for Lycamobile. **Lisa-Maria Bornemann** (LD) Online retailer, and international healthcare relations manager.

CONSTITUENCY PROFILE
Returned Conservative MPs from 1945 until 1997, when Gareth Thomas was first elected. A Labour marginal for many years, the party increased its majority by more than 10,000 in 2017. Demographically a slightly younger seat than the neighbouring Harrow East, with two thirds of residents aged 45 or under. About a quarter of residents are of Indian heritage.

EU REFERENDUM RESULT
45.1% Leave   Remain 54.9%

Hartlepool

MAJORITY 3,595 (8.76%)   LABOUR HOLD   TURNOUT 57.92%

MIKE HILL
BORN May 12, 1963
MP 2017-

	Electorate	Share %	from 2017 %	Change
	70,855			
*M Hill Lab	15,464	37.68	-14.83	
S Houghton C	11,869	28.92	-5.30	
R Tice Brexit	10,603	25.84		
A Hagon LD	1,696	4.13	+2.35	
J Bousfield Ind	911	2.22		
K Cranney Soc Lab	494	1.20		

Won re-election despite being a Remainer in a heavily pro-Leave constituency, partly thanks to a split Leave vote. Supported Sir Keir Starmer for leader, 2020. Campaigner on health issues, including protecting local assisted fertility units and GP practices. Suspended by the Labour Party over a sexual harassment accusation in September 2019; subsequently reinstated. An employment tribunal will consider the allegations in 2020. He has "completely rejected" the claims. Former librarian and Unison activist. Contested Richmond (Yorks), 2015. Ed: Lancaster University (BA drama and English literature).

CHALLENGERS
Stefan Houghton (C) Cllr, Stockton-on-Tees BC, 2015-. Taxation assistant. **Richard Tice** (Brexit) Chairman of the Brexit Party. Founder of Leave Means Leave and Leave.EU. MEP for the East of England, 2019-. Chief executive, Quidnip Capital LLP. Contested this seat after Nigel Farage stood down candidates in Conservative seats. **Andy Hagon** (LD) Assistant head teacher.

CONSTITUENCY PROFILE
Hartlepool, including its predecessor seat The Hartlepools, has elected a Conservative MP just once in its postwar history, in 1959. Represented by Peter Mandelson from 1992 until his appointment to the European Commission in 2004. A coastal town just north of the River Tees, Hartlepool had the highest Leave vote in the North East region. Although incomes are in line with the rest of the region, unemployment is well above average.

EU REFERENDUM RESULT
69.6% Leave   Remain 30.4%

Harwich & Essex North

MAJORITY 20,182 (38.84%) CONSERVATIVE HOLD TURNOUT 70.08%

SIR BERNARD JENKIN
BORN Apr 9, 1959
MP 1992-

Electorate	Share %	Change from 2017 %
74,153		
*B Jenkin C	31,830	61.26 +2.75
S Rice Lab	11,648	22.42 -8.02
M Beckett LD	5,866	11.29 +5.84
P Banks Green	1,945	3.74 +1.71
R Browning-Smith Ind	411	0.79
T Francis Ind	263	0.51

Eurosceptic right-winger who was among the first ten ERG members. Called John Bercow "an irretrievably politicised and radicalised" Speaker. Knighted in 2018 for political service. Member, 1922 exec cttee, 2015-. MP for: Essex North, 1997-2010; Colchester North, 1992-97. Policy adviser to Leon Brittan, 1986-88. Chairman, public administration and constitutional affairs select cttee, 2015-19. Shadow minister: regions, 2003-05; defence, 2001-03. Long-time friend of the screenwriter Richard Curtis, who regularly names characters Bernard. Contested Glasgow Central, 1987. Ed: William Ellis Sch; Corpus Christi Coll, Cambridge (BA English).

CHALLENGERS
Stephen Rice (Lab) Essex County Fire and Rescue Service. RNLI volunteer. Trade union background. Volunteer, Festival Friends, an adult learning disability charity. **Mike Beckett** (LD) Cllr, Brightlingsea TC, 2019-. Manager at Colchester food bank. Contested Scarborough & Whitby, 2015.

CONSTITUENCY PROFILE
A safe Conservative seat in which the party's majority has never fallen below five figures. Created in 2010 from Harwich, which was Labour from 1997 until 2005, and Essex North, which Sir Bernard Jenkin held in 1997 by 5,000 votes. The constituency contains the University of Essex's Colchester campus, although most students in the area live in Colchester itself. More than a fifth of residents are aged 65 or over. About three quarters of households are owner-occupied. Self-employment is common.

EU REFERENDUM RESULT
59.0% Leave Remain 41.0%

Hastings & Rye

MAJORITY 4,043 (7.45%) CONSERVATIVE HOLD TURNOUT 67.40%

SALLY-ANN HART
BORN Mar 6, 1968
MP 2019-

Electorate	Share %	Change from 2017 %
80,524		
S Hart C	26,896	49.56 +2.69
P Chowney Lab	22,853	42.11 -4.13
N Perry LD	3,960	7.30 +3.85
P Crosland Ind	565	1.04 +0.29

Subject of two internal party investigations during the election for engaging with Islamophobic content on social media, and also shared a video that claimed that the Jewish billionaire George Soros owned the EU. Wrote an article appearing to suggest that people with disabilities should not be guarenteed a minimum wage because "they don't understand money". Brexiteer, sympathetic to the ERG. Corporate finance lawyer, 1992-96. Cllr: Udimore PC, 2019-; Rother DC, 2015-. Magistrate. Contested Durham North West, 2017. Ed: Kings' Coll London (BA geography).

CHALLENGERS
Peter Chowney (Lab) Food and pharmaceutical researcher. Cllr, Hastings BC, 2015-; leader, 2015-. Trade unionist backed by Momentum. Nearly unseated Amber Rudd in this seat in 2017, losing by 346 votes after a full recount. **Nick Perry** (LD) Mental health social worker. Contested this seat in the previous three general election campaigns.

CONSTITUENCY PROFILE
A bellwether since its creation in 1983, although the old individual seats of Hastings and Rye consistently returned Conservative MPs in the postwar period. Represented since 2010 by Amber Rudd, the home secretary, 2016-18, and work and pensions secretary, 2018-19. She stood down in 2019, having resigned the Tory whip over Brexit in September. Hastings and Rye are coastal Sussex towns; Hastings is about ten times the size in terms of population, with over 90,000 residents. The area has relatively high levels of self-employment and lower than average wages.

EU REFERENDUM RESULT
55.9% Leave Remain 44.1%

Havant

CONSERVATIVE HOLD

ALAN MAK
BORN Nov 15, 1983
MP 2015-

Parliamentary private secretary since 2017 in departments including housing, business and justice. Backed Jeremy Hunt for the leadership, 2019. Voted consistently for Brexit deals, after angering local party members by campaigning for Remain in 2016. Former corporate lawyer at Clifford Chance. Born in Leeds to Chinese parents; the first ethnically Chinese MP. Family ran a shop in York. Has campaigned for the Tories since sixth form. Non-executive director and investor in a range of businesses. Former president, Magic Breakfast, a charity

	Electorate	Share %	Change from 2017 %
	72,130		
*A Mak C	30,051	65.39	+5.63
R Knight Lab	8,259	17.97	-7.34
P Gray LD	5,708	12.42	+6.37
J Colman Green	1,597	3.47	+1.05
A Black Soc Dem	344	0.75	

for disadvantaged children. Member, Conservative Christian Fellowship. Ed: St Peter's Sch, York (assisted-place scholarship; Peterhouse, Cambridge (BA law); Oxford Institute of Legal Practice (PG Dip law and business).

CHALLENGERS
Rosamund Knight (Lab) Teenage mother from local area who went on to study fine art. **Paul Gray** (LD) Worked in financial services.

CONSTITUENCY PROFILE
Held by the Conservatives since 1950, and the party has increased its majority at every election since 1997, when the margin of victory dipped below 4,000 for the only time in its postwar history. The MP before Alan Mak was David Willetts, a Conservative minister under John Major and David Cameron nicknamed "two brains". More than a fifth of this Hampshire constituency's residents are aged 65 or above. While home ownership is average for the southeast, there is a high proportion of households in the social rented sector. Unemployment is low.

EU REFERENDUM RESULT
62.6% Leave   Remain 37.4%

Hayes & Harlington

LABOUR HOLD

JOHN MCDONNELL
BORN Sep 8, 1951
MP 1997-

Shadow chancellor under Jeremy Corbyn after managing his leadership campaign in 2015; stepped down after the 2019 election, calling for "a new generation" to lead the party. Stood for the leadership himself in 2007 and 2010 but struggled to gain sufficient nominations. Rebecca Long Bailey, whom he nominated for leader in 2020, was considered to be his protégé. History of rebelling, for example on Iraq, tuition fees, and identity cards. Chief executive, association of London Authorities, 1987-95. Chairman of Socialist Campaign

	Electorate	Share %	Change from 2017 %
	72,356		
*J McDonnell Lab	24,545	55.79	-10.72
W Bridges C	15,284	34.74	+6.12
A Cunliffe LD	1,947	4.43	+3.17
H Boparai Brexit	1,292	2.94	
C West Green	739	1.68	+0.49
C Amadi CPA	187	0.43	

Group during New Labour era. Campaigned to Remain; less Eurosceptic than Mr Corbyn. Ed: Brunel University London (BSc government and politics); Birkbeck, London (MSc politics and sociology).

CHALLENGERS
Wayne Bridges (C) Director, signage and stationery printing company. Cllr, Hillingdon BC, 2010-. **Alexander Cunliffe** (LD) Barrister.

CONSTITUENCY PROFILE
Held by Labour from its creation in 1950 until 1981, when its Labour MP defected to the Social Democratic Party and the Conservatives took advantage of the split in 1983. The Tories then narrowly held off John McDonnell in his first attempt to become the seat's MP in 1992, winning by 53 votes. This west London seat contains Heathrow airport, a significant source of jobs. About a quarter of residents are aged under 16, more than a third are of Asian descent, and there are large Muslim and Sikh communities. Incomes and house prices are below the London average.

EU REFERENDUM RESULT
58.2% Leave   Remain 41.8%

Hazel Grove

MAJORITY 4,423 (9.99%)   CONSERVATIVE HOLD   TURNOUT 67.63%

WILLIAM WRAGG
BORN Dec 11, 1987
MP 2015-

	Electorate	Share %	from 2017 % Change
	65,457		
*W Wragg C	21,592	48.77	+3.35
L Smart LD	17,169	38.78	+5.85
T Wilson Lab	5,508	12.44	-8.03

Brexiteer who voted to leave the EU without a deal in indicative votes. Member: ERG, 1992 exec cttee. Chairman of the public administration and constitutional affairs cttee. Former primary school teacher who mentored children with special educational needs. Teach First graduate. Caseworker for David Nuttall, MP. Cllr, Stockport MBC, 2011-15. Moved in with his parents so he could save for a deposit for a house in 2016. Rebelled to vote against liberalising Sunday trading law. Ed: Poynton HS; University of Manchester (BA history).

CHALLENGERS
Lisa Smart (LD) Deputy leader of the Liberal Democrat group on Stockport council. School governor for 16 years. Former director, Stockport Credit Union. Active member of the Women's Institute. Contested this seat, 2017, 2015. **Tony Wilson** (Lab) IT worker at Transport for Greater Manchester and a senior Unison activist.

CONSTITUENCY PROFILE
William Wragg overturned a Liberal Democrat majority of more than 6,000 in 2010 to win the seat by about 6,000 votes in 2015. Before that, Hazel Grove had elected a Lib Dem MP from 1997 and had otherwise elected Conservative MPs from its creation in 1974. It was created from parts of the Cheadle constituency, which had elected Conservatives since 1950, with the exception of a Liberal MP in 1966. On the outskirts of Greater Manchester, just east of Stockport, the seat is partly rural and partly metropolitan. About three quarters of homes are owner-occupied and one in five residents is over 65, both well above the UK average. Median pay is slightly above the North West average.

EU REFERENDUM RESULT
52.2% Leave   Remain 47.8%

Hemel Hempstead

MAJORITY 14,563 (28.40%)   CONSERVATIVE HOLD   TURNOUT 69.25%

SIR MIKE PENNING
BORN Sep 29, 1957
MP 2005-

	Electorate	Share %	from 2017 % Change
	74,033		
*M Penning C	28,968	56.50	+1.54
N Ahmed Lab	14,405	28.10	-8.80
S Barry LD	6,317	12.32	+6.14
S Hassan Green	1,581	3.08	+1.13

Former soldier, firefighter and journalist. Political reporter, the *Express*. Long-standing Brexiteer and right-winger, though he did not actively campaign in 2016. Minister: armed forces, 2016-17; justice, 2014-16; disabled people, 2013-14; Northern Ireland, 2012-13. Privy councillor, 2014-. Head of media, CCHQ, 2000-04. Chief adviser to William Hague as leader of the opposition. Grenadier Guards, 1974-80; served in Kenya, Germany and Northern Ireland. Knighted in 2017. Contested Thurrock, 2001. Ed: Appleton CS; King Edmund Sch, Essex.

CHALLENGERS
Nabila Ahmed (Lab) Master's student at the University of Manchester and former Labour Party staff member. Has worked in schools as a teacher trainer for Unite. Speaks fluent Mandarin after living in Taiwan for two years. **Sammy Barry** (LD) Youth worker. Cllr, Dacorum BC, 2019-. Animal rights campaigner. **Sherief Hassan** (Green) Community radio presenter. Previously worked for the Ministry of Defence and the NHS.

CONSTITUENCY PROFILE
Hemel Hempstead was held by Labour from 1997 to 2005, and the party won it in the October election of 1974, but otherwise it has elected only Conservative MPs at every election since 1924, and the Conservatives have not won less than half of the vote for the last four elections. The seat, just north of Watford, consists of the town of Hemel Hempstead itself, with its population of about 95,000, and some of the more rural areas to its north. A significantly greater than average proportion of households are in the social rented sector — about one in four, compared with one in six nationally.

EU REFERENDUM RESULT
55.5% Leave   Remain 44.5%

Hemsworth

JON TRICKETT
BORN Jul 2, 1950
MP 1996-

Former plumber and builder. Loyal to Jeremy Corbyn but removed as his campaign co-ordinator before two by-elections in 2017 after allegations of a spat with his chief of staff Karie Murphy. Supported Rebecca Long Bailey in the 2020 leadership contest. Eurosceptic; sought permission from leadership to vote Leave. Shadow lord president of the council and Cabinet Office minister, 2017-. Among the first to call for Tony Blair's resignation. PPS to: Gordon Brown, 2008-10; Peter Mandelson, 1997-98. Cllr, Leeds CC, 1984-96. Ed: Roundhay GS,

	Electorate	Share %	Change from 2017 %
	73,726		
*J Trickett Lab	16,460	37.49	-18.54
L Calland C	15,280	34.80	+0.92
W Ali Brexit	5,930	13.51	
I Womersley Ind	2,458	5.60	
J Monaghan LD	1,734	3.95	+1.96
M Roberts Yorkshire	964	2.20	-0.27
L Morton Green	916	2.09	
P Wilks Ind	165	0.38	

Leeds; University of Hull (BA politics); University of Leeds (MA political sociology).

CHALLENGERS
Louise Calland (C) Senior lobbyist for the Swiss pharmaceutical company Novartis. Cllr, Wandsworth BC, 2018-. Cllr, Lambeth BC, 2014-18. **Wajid Ali** (Brexit) Pledged to donate his salary to local causes.

CONSTITUENCY PROFILE
Hemsworth has been held by the Labour Party for more than a hundred years, the seat having elected a Labour MP in 1918, the year it was created. However, the party's majority in 2019 was the smallest it had ever been, smaller even than before the introduction of universal suffrage in 1928. This West Yorkshire seat is made up of former coalmining towns and villages. Many of its residents commute to work in nearby Wakefield or Leeds. More than a fifth of the workforce are employed in the wholesale and retail sector and there is a reliance of routine-level jobs.

EU REFERENDUM RESULT
68.1% Leave   Remain 31.9%

Hendon

MATTHEW OFFORD
BORN Sep 3, 1969
MP 2010-

Former political analyst at the BBC. Brexiteer who initially rejected Theresa May's deal but later backed it. Voted against same-sex marriage. Investigated by police in 2016 for swearing at a Labour candidate and a former fire officer from his office window. Environmental audit select committee, 2016-17, 2012-15. Helped to establish Holocaust Memorial Day. Former deputy leader of Barnet council. Fellow, Royal Geographical Society. Contested Barnsley East & Mexborough, 2001. Ed: Amery Hill Sch, Alton; Nottingham Trent University; Lancaster

	Electorate	Share %	Change from 2017 %
	82,661		
*M Offord C	26,878	48.80	+0.77
D Pinto-Duschinsky Lab	22,648	41.12	-4.85
C Enderby LD	4,628	8.40	+4.60
P Vincent-Kirby Green	921	1.67	+0.57

University (MA environment, culture and society); King's College London (PhD rural governance).

CHALLENGERS
David Pinto-Duschinsky (Lab) Management consultant. Member, GMB. Contested Tatton against George Osborne, 2015. Jewish; his father was a Holocaust survivor who came to Britain as an unaccompanied child refugee. **Clareine Enderby** (LD) Business communications trainer; former actress.

CONSTITUENCY PROFILE
This northwest London seat was re-created in 1997 and held by Labour until 2010. Before 1997, the seat had been split between Hendon North and Hendon South, which were almost exclusively won by the Conservatives. It is an ethnically diverse seat, with a little more than half of its residents born in the UK. The seat has one of the biggest Jewish populations, at more than 20,000, second only to the neighbouring Finchley & Golders Green. It is also home to 17,000 Muslim and 10,000 Hindu residents. The area contains Middlesex University and has a large student population.

EU REFERENDUM RESULT
41.6% Leave   Remain 58.4%

Henley

MAJORITY 14,053 (23.92%) CONSERVATIVE HOLD TURNOUT 76.65%

JOHN HOWELL
BORN Jul 27, 1955
MP 2008-

Electorate	Share %	from 2017 %	Change
76,660			
*J Howell C	32,189	54.78	-4.32
L Coyle LD	18,136	30.87	+16.00
Z Marham Lab	5,698	9.70	-10.36
J Robb Green	2,736	4.66	+1.39

Former partner, Ernst & Young. Led attempts to establish UK trading links with eastern Europe; awarded OBE for his efforts in 2000. Business reporter, BBC World Service, 1994-95. Has published books on archaeology and international affairs. Backed Jeremy Hunt over Boris Johnson in the 2019 leadership election. Campaigned to Remain in the EU in 2016 and voted for all withdrawal agreements. PPS to: Andrew Lansley, 2012-14; Sir George Young, 2010-12; Greg Clark, 2010-11. Select cttees: justice, 2014-17; work and pensions, 2008-10. Member, Council of Europe. Ed: University of Edinburgh (MA archaeology); St John's Coll, Oxford (DPhil archaeology).

CHALLENGERS
Laura Coyle (LD) Housing solicitor, Turpin & Miller. Cllr, Haringey BC, 2004-10. **Zaid Marham** (Lab) Loyal to Jeremy Corbyn. Private tutor.

CONSTITUENCY PROFILE
A large, affluent and rural Oxfordshire seat that has been held continuously by the Conservatives since 1910. The two previous MPs have been the prime minister, Boris Johnson, who held the seat from 2001 until he became mayor of London in 2008, and Michael Heseltine, who served as a cabinet minister under Margaret Thatcher and John Major. Henley itself is famous for its annual royal regatta, and the seat stretches from north of Oxford towards Reading. Income in the constituency is far above the national average and the workforce is disproportionately skewed towards professional occupations. The level of home ownership is high.

EU REFERENDUM RESULT
43.1% Leave   Remain 56.9%

Hereford & Herefordshire South

MAJORITY 19,686 (39.65%) CONSERVATIVE HOLD TURNOUT 68.87%

JESSE NORMAN
BORN Jun 23, 1962
MP 2010-

Electorate	Share %	from 2017 %	Change
72,085			
*J Norman C	30,390	61.21	+7.72
A Coda Lab	10,704	21.56	-2.19
L Hurds LD	6,181	12.45	+5.41
D Toynbee Green	2,371	4.78	+2.36

Financial secretary to the Treasury, 2019-. Considered standing for the Conservative leadership in 2019. Refused to make public his vote in the Brexit referendum but supported all withdrawal agreements. Former philosophy researcher and teacher, UCL. Worked at Barclays, 1991-97. Sacked as a government adviser by David Cameron for abstaining from Syrian intervention vote. Parly under-sec, transport, 2017-19; business, 2016-17. Friend and Eton contemporary of Boris Johnson, to whom he was a policy adviser during his mayoral campaign. Also advised George Osborne while he was shadow chancellor. Director, Hay Festival of Literature and the Arts. Ed: Eton Coll; Merton Coll, Oxford (MA classics); UCL (MPhil; PhD philosophy).

CHALLENGERS
Anna-Maria Coda (Lab) Retired chemistry teacher; lives on small family farm. Former volunteer, Oxfam. Former trade union representative. **Lucy Hurds** (LD) Business consultant and former charity worker.

CONSTITUENCY PROFILE
Jesse Norman won a narrow victory when this seat was created in 2010, winning just under 2,500 more votes than his Liberal Democrat rival. The Tory vote share has risen at every election since. Before Mr Norman won the seat back for the Conservatives, the predecessor seat of Hereford was held by the Lib Dems from 1997, and before this it had been in Conservative hands since 1931. A mostly rural seat, except for the towns of Hereford and Ross-on-Wye on the Welsh border. One in five residents are aged 65 or over, while about one in fifteen was born across the border.

EU REFERENDUM RESULT
60.4% Leave   Remain 39.6%

Herefordshire North

MAJORITY 24,856 (48.71%)   CONSERVATIVE HOLD   TURNOUT 72.64%

BILL WIGGIN
BORN Jun 4, 1966
MP 2001-

Former financier and TA officer. Particular interest in agriculture; named Countryside Alliance's first Westminster champion and owns a farm stocked with Hereford cattle. Chairman, 92 Group of right-wing Tories. Chief whip for the Leave campaign during the Brexit referendum. Voted for no-deal in indicative votes. Initially rejected Theresa May's deal but later backed it. Voted against same-sex marriage. Apologised for mistakenly claiming £11,000 for a phantom mortgage. Treasury whip, 2010-12. Member, 1992 exec cttee, 2015-. Son of

	Electorate	Share %	from 2017 %	Change
	70,252			
*B Wiggin C		32,158	63.01	+1.04
P Howells LD		7,302	14.31	+2.60
J Wood Lab		6,804	13.33	-5.59
E Chowns Green		4,769	9.34	+3.82

the former Tory MP Sir Jerry Wiggin. Contemporary of David Cameron at Eton. Contested Burnley, 1997. Ed: University Coll of North Wales (BA economics).

CHALLENGERS
Phillip Howells (LD) IT worker and former lieutenant. **Joe Wood** (Lab) Sustainability consultant and climate change activist. Member: Unite; Sera. **Ellie Chowns** (Green) First Green MEP for the West Midlands, elected in 2019. Cllr, Herefordshire CC, 2017.

CONSTITUENCY PROFILE
Herefordshire North has been Conservative since its creation in 2010, while its predecessor, Leominster, elected only Conservative MPs at every election from 1910. The seat's former MP, Peter Temple-Morris, defected to the Labour Party in 1998. A large and sparse seat along the English border with Wales. Nearly a quarter of Herefordshire North's residents are aged 65 or above. The seat has relatively high levels of home ownership, and incomes are above average. Residents in work are also about twice as likely as average to be self-employed.

EU REFERENDUM RESULT
58.0% Leave   Remain 42.0%

Hertford & Stortford

MAJORITY 19,620 (32.65%)   CONSERVATIVE HOLD   TURNOUT 72.92%

JULIE MARSON
BORN Mar 23, 1965
MP 2019-

Former corporate banker at Natwest who describes herself as a "working-class grammar school girl". Lifelong Eurosceptic and ardent Brexiteer. Experience as a magistrate shaped her attitudes to crime; she thought many of the young people she saw should have been helped to avoid the criminal justice system after suffering neglect, abuse and a lack of opportunities. Cllr, Thanet DC, 2011-15. Has a "blonde and lively" cockapoo called Boris. Unsuccessfully sought selection in Grantham & Stamford before beating the former MP Nick de Bois to

	Electorate	Share %	from 2017 %	Change
	82,407			
J Marson C		33,712	56.10	-4.22
C Vince Lab		14,092	23.45	-5.14
C Lucas LD		8,596	14.30	+6.23
L Downes Green		2,705	4.50	+1.48
A Lindsay UKIP		681	1.13	
B Percival Ind		308	0.51	

become the candidate for this seat. Contested: EU parliament, 2014; Dagenham & Rainham, 2017, 2015. Ed: Downing Coll, Cambridge (BA History).

CHALLENGERS
Chris Vince (Lab) Maths teacher and former community radio presenter. Cllr, Harlow DC, 2018-. Stood for the EU parliament, 2019. Contested Chelmsford, 2017, 2015. **Chris Lucas** (LD) Business and law

teacher. Cllr, Three Rivers DC, 2010-14.

CONSTITUENCY PROFILE
A safe Conservative seat, which the party has held at every election since it was created in 1983. Only in 1997 and 2001 did the Tories win less than half of the votes cast, with the majority falling below 6,000 only in 2001. The seat runs along Hertfordshire's border with Essex, with Hertford in its southwest and Bishop's Stortford in the northeast. A high proportion of residents are economically active, and are more likely to be in managerial and professional occupations.

EU REFERENDUM RESULT
49.2% Leave   Remain 50.8%

Hertfordshire North East

MAJORITY 18,189 (32.88%)   **CONSERVATIVE HOLD**   **TURNOUT 72.68%**

SIR OLIVER HEALD
BORN Dec 15, 1954
MP 1992-

Former barrister and QC. Solicitor general, 2012-14; led attempts to digitally modernise the criminal justice system. Soft Tory; campaigned for Remain in 2016. Supported Jeremy Hunt in the 2019 leadership contest. Argued for tightening of female genital mutilation laws. Backed a campaign to scrap the convention that parliament must approve military action. Justice minister, 2016-17. Vociferously opposed reforms to the House of Lords. Shadow minister: justice, 2004-07; work and pensions, 2002-03; leader of the Commons, 2003-05. Select cttees: Commons

	Electorate	Share %	from 2017 % Change
	76,123		
*O Heald C	31,293	56.56	-2.07
K Green Lab	13,104	23.68	-4.66
A Finch LD	8,563	15.48	+7.78
T Lee Green	2,367	4.28	-1.06

governance, 2014; standards and privileges, 2010-12; work and pensions, 2007-12. Received knighthood in 2014. Contested Southwark & Bermondsey, 1987. Ed: Reading Sch; Pembroke Coll, Cambridge (BA law); City Law School.

CHALLENGERS
Kelley Green (Lab) Farm shop owner and sloe gin producer. Member, GMB. **Amy Finch** (LD) Party member for less than two years. **Tim Lee** (Green) Data protection officer.

CONSTITUENCY PROFILE
The seat has voted Conservative since its creation in 1997, and its predecessor seat, Hertfordshire North, elected Conservatives from its creation in 1983. Sir Oliver's majorities in 1997 and 2001 were less than 4,000 votes, but have grown as the Conservatives have recovered nationally. Many London commuters reside in the south of the seat and it is close to Stansted airport. The seat contains a larger than average Sikh community, with well over a thousand living in the seat. The workforce in this seat is more likely than average to work in professional jobs.

EU REFERENDUM RESULT
51.4% Leave   Remain 48.6%

Hertfordshire South West

MAJORITY 14,408 (23.55%)   **CONSERVATIVE HOLD**   **TURNOUT 76.06%**

GAGAN
MOHINDRA
BORN Apr 7, 1978
MP 2019-

Selected after the incumbent David Gauke had the Conservative whip removed for rebelling against no-deal and stood as an independent. Founder of the Chromex Group, a property investment company, 2003-15. Cllr, Essex CC, 2017-; cabinet member for finance, property and housing. Board member, West Essex Clinical Commissioning Group. Chairman, Essex Conservatives, 2018-; Epping Forest Conservative Association, 2015-18. Contested North Tyneside, 2010. Ed: King's Coll, London (BSc mathematics).

	Electorate	Share %	from 2017 % Change
	80,449		
G Mohindra C	30,327	49.56	-8.36
*D Gauke Ind	15,919	26.02	
A Aklakul Lab	7,228	11.81	-13.87
S Symington LD	6,251	10.22	-1.45
T Pashby Green	1,466	2.40	-0.20

CHALLENGERS
David Gauke (Ind) Conservative MP for this seat, 2005-19. Justice secretary and lord chancellor, 2018-19; work and pensions secretary, 2017-18; various positions in the Treasury, 2010-17. Leader of the so-called "Gaukward squad" which made Boris Johnson's life difficult on the issue of no-deal. Voted Remain, but backed Theresa May's deal in all four votes. **Ali Aklakul** (Lab) Catering and hospitality employee. Contested

Reigate, 2015. **Sally Symington** (LD) Former financial manager. Contested Hemel Hempstead in the 2017 election.

CONSTITUENCY PROFILE
Has elected only Conservative MPs since 1950, and the party's candidate has never received less than 40 per cent of the vote. Stretches north from its border with Ruislip in northwest London and lies along the border with Buckinghamshire. It has a small Asian community, mostly Indian, making up about one in sixteen residents, and a Jewish community of almost 2,000. Many residents commute into London.

EU REFERENDUM RESULT
46.2% Leave   Remain 53.8%

Hertsmere

MAJORITY 21,313 (40.83%) **CONSERVATIVE HOLD** **TURNOUT 70.57%**

OLIVER DOWDEN
BORN Aug 1, 1978
MP 2015-

Culture secretary since 2020. Worked for the Conservative research department and later for a PR company. Returned to the Conservative Party to work as an adviser and then deputy chief of staff to David Cameron as PM; he was rewarded with a CBE and this safe seat in 2015. Opposed Brexit before the referendum; voted with the government on withdrawal agreements and indicative votes. Backed Boris Johnson for the leadership in 2019. Paymaster general, 2019-20. Parliamentary secretary for the Cabinet Office, 2018-19. Select cttees: petitions,

	Electorate	Share %	Change from 2017 %
	73,971		
*O Dowden C	32,651	62.55	+1.44
H Kal-Weiss Lab	11,338	21.72	-6.94
S Barrett LD	6,561	12.57	+7.22
J Humphries Green	1,653	3.17	+1.27

2015-17; public administration and constitutional affairs, 2015-16. Ed: Parmiters' Sch, Watford; Trinity Hall, Cambridge (BA law).

CHALLENGERS
Holly Kal-Weiss (Lab) Specialist teacher for children with dyslexia. Former member, Jewish Labour Movement. **Stephen Barrett** (LD) School business manager. Cllr, St Albans DC, 2019-. **John Humphries** (Green) Management training business manager.

CONSTITUENCY PROFILE
Hertsmere has elected Conservative MPs since its creation in 1983 and was once the seat of Cecil Parkinson, a former chairman of the party. The biggest towns in this seat on Greater London's northern border are Borehamwood, home of Elstree Studios, and Potters Bar. The seat has about 14,000 Jewish residents and there is also a significant Asian and Asian-British population, mostly of Indian descent. The constituency has high levels of self-employment and good levels of health and education, while incomes are well above the national average.

EU REFERENDUM RESULT
50.8% Leave   Remain 49.2%

Hexham

MAJORITY 10,549 (22.86%) **CONSERVATIVE HOLD** **TURNOUT 75.26%**

GUY OPPERMAN
BORN May 18, 1965
MP 2010-

Parliamentary under-secretary for pensions and financial inclusion, 2017-. A vocal party moderate. Backed Michael Gove for the leadership in 2019. Former barrister; won 2007 Bar Pro Bono Award for Free Representation Unit work, a judicial review challenge and a campaign against local hospital closures. Entered politics after leading a campaign against the closure of a hospital that he credited with saving his mother's life. Voted Remain but toed the government line on withdrawal agreement and indicative votes. Whip, 2016-17; assistant whip,

	Electorate	Share %	Change from 2017 %
	61,324		
*G Opperman C	25,152	54.50	+0.42
P Grennan Lab	14,603	31.64	-2.45
S Howse LD	4,672	10.12	+3.02
N Morphet Green	1,723	3.73	+1.02

2015-16. One of the first MPs to take on an apprentice. Amateur jockey. Contested: Caernarfon, 2005; Swindon North, 1997. Ed: University of Buckingham (LLB law); University of Lille, France (diploma).

CHALLENGERS
Penny Grennan (Lab) Supply teacher. Member, National Education Union and Unite. Lead singer and ukulele player for the Cherry Pickers Band. **Stephen Howse** (LD) Research manager, Wise Campaign.

CONSTITUENCY PROFILE
A huge and sparsely populated Northumberland seat on the Scottish border, Hexham has elected only Tory MPs since 1951, although Labour was about 200 votes away from winning it in 1997. The town of Hexham itself is the only settlement in this rural constituency with a population of more than 10,000. Its residents are older than average, with more than half of them aged over 45, and more than one fifth over the age of 65. The seat is characterised by higher than average self-employment and is one of the richest seats in the context of typical incomes in the region.

EU REFERENDUM RESULT
45.3% Leave   Remain 54.7%

Heywood & Middleton

MAJORITY 663 (1.40%)   CONSERVATIVE GAIN FROM LABOUR   TURNOUT 59.24%

CHRIS CLARKSON
BORN Dec 12, 1982
MP 2019-

	Electorate	Share %	Change from 2017 %
	80,162		
C Clarkson C	20,453	43.07	+5.05
*L McInnes Lab	19,790	41.67	-11.63
C Lambert Brexit	3,952	8.32	
A Smith LD	2,073	4.37	+2.19
N Ainsworth-Barnes Green	1,220	2.57	

Corporate development manager and consultant with Iris Legal and Virgin who initially trained as a lawyer. Leave campaigner. Cllr, Salford CC, 2011-. Describes himself as a liberal Tory and wine enthusiast. Member: Tory Reform Group, LGBT+ Conservatives, Conservative Friends of Israel, Countryside Alliance, Mensa. Friend of the Lowry Theatre. Speaks French and German. Interested in electoral reform. Regular marathon runner. Contested this seat, 2017; Wallasey, 2015. Ed: Dundee University (LLB).

CHALLENGERS
Liz McInnes (Lab) MP for this seat, 2014-19. Supported Jeremy Corbyn in the vote of confidence against him, but resigned as shadow communities minister, 2015-16, because she believed Mr Corbyn should have stood down in response to vote. Rejoined the front bench later that year as shadow foreign minister, 2016-19. **Colin Lambert** (Brexit) Teacher, pupil referral unit. Labour leader, Rochdale BC, 2010-14, but later defected from the party.

CONSTITUENCY PROFILE
Had elected only Labour MPs since its creation in 1983, although it nearly fell to Ukip in the 2014 by-election that Labour won by 617 votes. Its two predecessor seats were initially held by Conservatives after 1945, but by 1974 both were held by Labour. The Conservatives more than doubled their vote share in 2017 – though they still lagged behind Labour by 8,000 votes – before gaining it this time. The constituency comprises the Greater Manchester towns of Heywood and Middleton and some of the rural area to their north. Many residents work in routine occupations.

EU REFERENDUM RESULT
62.4% Leave   Remain 37.6%

High Peak

MAJORITY 590 (1.09%)   CONSERVATIVE GAIN FROM LABOUR   TURNOUT 72.87%

ROBERT LARGAN
BORN May 29, 1987
MP 2019-

	Electorate	Share %	Change from 2017 %
	74,343		
R Largan C	24,844	45.86	+0.49
*R George Lab	24,254	44.77	-4.91
D Lomax LD	2,750	5.08	+0.12
A Graves Brexit	1,177	2.17	
R Hodgetts-Haley Green	1,148	2.12	

Moderate Remainer who believed it was necessary to honour the outcome of the referendum. His father was a postman and trade unionist, which helped shape his politics. Strong interest in infrastructure projects and defence. First job was as a fishmonger to support his studies. Former parliamentary researcher for Greg Hands (Chelsea & Fulham). Also worked as a chartered accountant for M&W and in equity capital markets at Deloitte. Cllr, Hammersmith & Fulham BC, 2014-17. Contested Bury South, the constituency where he grew up, in 2017. Ed: University of Manchester (BA economics and politics).

CHALLENGERS
Ruth George (Lab) MP for this seat, 2017-19. Voted Remain. Introduced and passed bill to ban sky lanterns after they were found to cause fires. Apologised in February 2019 after criticism for invoking an antisemitic conspiracy theory in relation to Luciana Berger, then an MP for The Independent Group.

CONSTITUENCY PROFILE
A Midlands seat gained by the Conservatives from Labour, but not a Red Wall seat. Though Labour held it between 1997 and 2010, the Conservatives represented it for seven years from 2010, and held it from 1970 until 1997. 2017 was the first time Labour had held High Peak despite being in opposition. This large north Derbyshire seat contains the towns of Glossop, Buxton and New Mills, and stretches across a large rural and largely uninhabited area of the Peak District. Typical incomes are slightly higher than the East Midlands average and unemployment is below average.

EU REFERENDUM RESULT
50.5% Leave   Remain 49.5%

Hitchin & Harpenden

MAJORITY 6,895 (11.71%)   CONSERVATIVE HOLD   TURNOUT 77.14%

BIM AFOLAMI
BORN Feb 11, 1986
MP 2017-

Moderate who has served
as a parliamentary private
secretary to several ministers:
Thérèse Coffey (Suffolk Coastal),
2020-; Alok Sharma (Reading
West), 2019-20; Chris Grayling
(Epsom & Ewell), 2018-19. Was
a senior executive at HSBC.
Also worked in corporate law:
Freshfields Bruckhaus Deringer;
Simpson Thacher and Bartlett.
Voted Remain but backed the
Brexit withdrawal agreement
four times. Voted against no-
deal in the indicative votes.
Supported Boris Johnson in
the 2019 leadership election.
Former treasurer, Bow Group.

	Electorate	Share %	Change from 2017 %
	76,321		
*B Afolami C	27,719	47.08	-5.97
S Collins LD	20,824	35.37	+24.76
K Tart Lab	9,959	16.92	-15.67
S Cordle CPA	268	0.46	+0.04
P Marshall Advance	101	0.17	

Was once a political adviser to
George Osborne. Select cttees:
regulatory reform, 2017-; public
accounts, 2017-. Father came to
Britain from Nigeria in the 1980s
and is an NHS doctor. Contested
Lewisham Deptford, 2015. Ed:
Eton Coll; University Coll,
Oxford (BA modern history;
vice-president, Oxford Union);
BPP Law Sch, London (PG Dip
law).

CHALLENGERS
Sam Collins (LD) Technology

consultant and author of books
about motor racing. Cllr, North
Hertfordshire DC, 2018-. **Kay
Tart** (Lab) Project manager. Cllr,
North Hertfordshire DC, 2019-.

CONSTITUENCY PROFILE
Has elected only Conservatives
since the seat was created in
1997. The previous MP was
Peter Lilley, a cabinet minister
under Margaret Thatcher and
John Major. Labour was 6,671
votes short of winning even in
1997, and the Liberal Democrats
have been the main challenger
in three of the elections since.
A large Hertfordshire seat that
sprawls around Luton and has a
long border with Bedfordshire.

EU REFERENDUM RESULT
39.8% Leave   Remain 60.2%

Holborn & St Pancras

MAJORITY 27,763 (48.89%)   LABOUR HOLD   TURNOUT 65.09%

SIR KEIR STARMER
BORN Sep 2, 1962
MP 2015-

Favourite to become Labour
leader in 2020. Mild-mannered,
distinguished human rights
lawyer and shadow Brexit
secretary, 2016-. Director of
public prosecutions, 2008-13.
Drafted a victims' law with
Doreen Lawrence, mother of
the murdered teenager Stephen,
which was included in Labour's
2015 manifesto. Mentioned as
a possible candidate for 2015
Labour leadership election, but
did not stand, supporting Andy
Burnham. Nominated Owen
Smith in 2016. Voted Remain;
called for a second referendum.
Voted against the withdrawal

	Electorate	Share %	Change from 2017 %
	87,236		
*K Starmer Lab	36,641	64.52	-5.55
A Hayward C	8,878	15.63	-2.73
M Kirk LD	7,314	12.88	+6.07
K De Keyser Green	2,746	4.84	+1.48
H Birchwood Brexit	1,032	1.82	
M Bhatti Ukip	138	0.24	-0.99
T Scripps Soc Eq	37	0.07	

agreement. Shadow Home Office
minister, 2015-16. Co-founder,
Doughty Street Chambers.
Appointed Queen's Counsel,
2002. Ed: Reigate GS; University
of Leeds (LLB law); St Edmund
Hall, Oxford (BCL).

CHALLENGERS
Alexandra Hayward (C) Former
nurse and financial director;
used medical knowledge to save
man having a seizure during the

campaign. Cllr, Three Rivers
DC, 2018-. **Matthew Kirk** (LD)
Barrister. **Kirsten De Keyser**
(Green) Danish TV producer.
Hector Birchwood (Brexit)
Immigrant from El Salvador.

CONSTITUENCY PROFILE
A Labour seat since its creation
in 1983, the party's majority fell
below 5,000 only in 2005 after a
Liberal Democrat surge. Frank
Dobson, the health secretary
from 1997 to 1999, represented
the seat until 2015. A central
London seat in which incomes
and house prices are well above
the average for the capital.
About a third of residents are
from ethnic minorities.

EU REFERENDUM RESULT
26.7% Leave   Remain 73.3%

Hornchurch & Upminster

MAJORITY 23,308 (43.18%)   **CONSERVATIVE HOLD**   **TURNOUT 66.83%**

JULIA LOPEZ
BORN Jun 4, 1984
MP 2017-

Parliamentary secretary to the Cabinet Office since February 2020 reshuffle. Photographed entering Downing Street with "have cake and eat it" Brexit strategy notes on display in November 2016, while an aide to Mark Field MP. Voted Leave and against Theresa May's Brexit withdrawal agreement three times, but backed Boris Johnson's deal. Supported no-deal in indicative votes. Select cttees: European statutory instruments, 2018-; international trade, 2017-. Researching and writing a book, *London in the Noughties*, having contributed to *The Best of*

	Electorate	Share %	Change from 2017 %
	80,765		
*J Lopez C	35,495	65.76	+5.61
T Lawal Lab	12,187	22.58	-5.99
T Clarke LD	3,862	7.16	+4.71
P Caton Green	1,920	3.56	+1.64
D Furness BNP	510	0.94	+0.27

Times and *Between the Crashes* by Mr Field. Former trustee, Inspire Malawi. Cllr, Tower Hamlets LBC, 2014-18, where she encountered corruption. Ed: Herts & Essex HS; Queens' Coll, Cambridge (BA social and political sciences).

CHALLENGERS
Tele Lawal (Lab) Caseworker for Meg Hillier, 2019-. Cllr, Havering BC, 2018-. **Thomas Clarke** (LD) Senior content editor, *Golf Monthly* magazine. **Peter**

Caton (Green) Ran company manufacturing adhesives. Author of six travel books.

CONSTITUENCY PROFILE
Created in 2010, this is a safe Conservative seat, although Ukip won more than a quarter of the vote in 2015. Labour won the predecessor seat of Upminster in 1997. London's easternmost constituency, it is demographically more similar to Essex, which it borders, than to much of London, being both older and less ethnically diverse. About one in ten residents is from an ethnic minority, compared to four in ten in London as a whole.

EU REFERENDUM RESULT
53.7% Leave   Remain 46.3%

Hornsey & Wood Green

MAJORITY 19,242 (31.49%)   **LABOUR HOLD**   **TURNOUT 74.69%**

CATHERINE WEST
BORN Sep 14, 1966
MP 2015-

Formerly worked helping migrants to secure welfare and housing. Taught English in Nanjing. Caseworker for David Lammy (Tottenham). Nominated Emily Thornberry for leader in 2020 after supporting Jeremy Corbyn in 2015 and 2016. Anti-Trident renewal. Shadow foreign minister, 2015-17; sacked after voting to remain in the single market. Voted against the Brexit withdrawal agreement four times, and for a second referendum. Select cttees: foreign affairs, 2019-; international trade 2017-19. Introduced a

	Electorate	Share %	Change from 2017 %
	81,814		
*C West Lab	35,126	57.48	-7.91
D Barnes LD	15,884	25.99	+9.94
E McGuinness C	6,829	11.18	-3.67
J Francis Green	2,192	3.59	+1.69
D Corrigan Brexit	763	1.25	
H Spiby-Vann CPA	211	0.35	+0.20
S Wakie Ind	100	0.16	

private member's bill to grant asylum seekers the right to work. Founded UK-EU relations APPG, 2016. Cllr, Islington LBC, 2002-14; leader, 2010-13. Ed: Ravenswood Sch for Girls, Sydney; Soas (BA social science and languages; MA Chinese studies).

CHALLENGERS
Dawn Barnes (LD) Marketing manager, King's College London.

Contested: this seat, 2017; Witney, 2010. Cllr, Haringey LBC, 2018-. **Ed McGuinness** (C) Financial analyst. **Jarelle Francis** (Green) Contested Tottenham, 2017.

CONSTITUENCY PROFILE
Initially won by the Conservatives after its creation in 1983, then gained by Labour in 1992 before it was held by the Liberal Democrats from 2005 to 2015. Compact north London seat between Finchley & Golders Green and Tottenham. Includes Alexandra Palace. About one in three residents is from an ethnic minority and one in eight was born in the EU-27.

EU REFERENDUM RESULT
25.0% Leave   Remain 75.0%

Horsham

MAJORITY 21,127 (33.41%)   CONSERVATIVE HOLD   TURNOUT 72.92%

JEREMY QUIN
BORN Sep 24, 1968
MP 2015-

Defence procurement minister, 2020-. PPS to: the Cabinet Office, 2019-20; the Brexit department, 2016-18. Whip, 2018-19; assistant whip, 2018. Was company adviser at Natwest Securities, now Deutsche Bank; seconded to the Treasury, 2008-09, advising on the response to the financial crisis. A Remainer who embraced Brexit; voted for the withdrawal agreement four times. Volunteer: City UK; Debate Mate; Countryside Alliance Foundation; Aylesbury Homeless Shelter. Involved in establishing a free school for children with autism. Supporter

	Electorate	Share %	from 2017 %	Change
	86,730			
*J Quin C	35,900	56.77	-2.77	
L Potter LD	14,773	23.36	+11.03	
M Jones Lab	9,424	14.90	-6.75	
C Ross Green	2,668	4.22	+1.24	
J Duggan Peace	477	0.75	+0.33	

of expanding Heathrow airport rather than Gatwick; the latter is in his constituency. Select cttees: regulatory reform, 2015-18; work and pensions, 2015-16. Contested Meirionnydd Nant Conwy, 1997. Ed: St Albans Sch; Hertford Coll, Oxford (BA history; president, Oxford Union).

CHALLENGERS
Louise Potter (LD) History and politics teacher. Cllr, Horsham DC, 2019-. **Michael Jones** (Lab) Qualified solicitor.

Former parliamentary assistant. **Catherine Ross** (Green) Contested this seat, 2017.

CONSTITUENCY PROFILE
Horsham and its predecessors have elected only Conservative MPs since 1880, making it one of the country's safest seats. The Conservatives have won more than half the votes cast at every election since 1974. The majority of residents live in the town of Horsham itself, with just under half living in the rural areas of Sussex around the town. There is low unemployment and relatively high home ownership. Many constituents work at Gatwick airport.

EU REFERENDUM RESULT
49.5% Leave   Remain 50.5%

Houghton & Sunderland South

MAJORITY 3,115 (7.82%)   LABOUR HOLD   TURNOUT 57.84%

BRIDGET PHILLIPSON
BORN Dec 19, 1983
MP 2010-

Managed a women's refuge and worked on regeneration projects in Sunderland. First elected aged 26. Remainer who voted against the Brexit withdrawal agreement four times and for a second referendum. Nominated Sir Keir Starmer for leader in 2020, having backed Owen Smith in 2016, Yvette Cooper in 2015 and David Miliband in 2010. Select cttees: Electoral Commission, 2010-19; public accounts, 2015-; home affairs, 2010-13; procedure, 2010-11. PPS to Jim Murphy, 2010-13. Whip, 2013-15. GMB member. Ed: St Robert of Newminister RC Sch,

	Electorate	Share %	from 2017 %	Change
	68,835			
*B Phillipson Lab	16,210	40.72	-18.75	
C Howarth C	13,095	32.89	+3.18	
K Yuill Brexit	6,165	15.49		
P Edgeworth LD	2,319	5.83	+3.64	
R Bradley Green	1,125	2.83	+1.08	
R Elvin Ukip	897	2.25	-3.48	

Washington; Hertford Coll, Oxford (BA modern history; chairwoman, Labour club).

CHALLENGERS
Christopher Howarth (C) Senior researcher, ERG, 2015-. Former tax adviser. Qualified solicitor. Researcher to Mark Francois (Rayleigh & Wickford), 2006-10. **Kevin Yuill** (Brexit) Associate professor of history, University of Sunderland. **Paul Edgeworth** (LD) Parliamentary assistant:

Layla Moran (Oxford West & Abingdon), 2017-19; Sarah Olney (Richmond Park), 2016-17. Contested this seat, 2017.

CONSTITUENCY PROFILE
Including its predecessors, Houghton & Sunderland South has elected only Labour MPs since 1935. This election was the first time that Labour had not won more than half of the vote since the constituency was created in 2010. Includes the towns of Houghton-le-Spring, Hetton-le-Hole and Sunderland's southern suburbs. The workforce is skewed towards routine and semi-routine jobs, and there are relatively few young people.

EU REFERENDUM RESULT
62.4% Leave   Remain 37.6%

Hove

MAJORITY 17,044 (30.22%)   **LABOUR HOLD**   **TURNOUT 75.88%**

PETER KYLE
BORN Sep 9, 1970
MP 2015-

Aid worker in Eastern Europe and the Balkans for almost a decade. Overcame difficulties with dyslexia to return to school aged 25, before becoming a mature student and completing a PhD. Nominated Jess Phillips for leader in 2020. Remainer who voted against the Brexit withdrawal agreement four times. Co-authored the "Kyle-Wilson amendment", which sought to break the Brexit stalemate by passing a deal with the proviso that this would be put to a public vote. Co-founder of Fat Sand Films, a Brighton-based production company.

	Electorate	Share %	Change from 2017 %
	74,313		
*P Kyle Lab	32,876	58.30	-5.84
R Nemeth C	15,832	28.08	-3.50
B Bass LD	3,731	6.62	+4.34
O Sykes Green	2,496	4.43	+2.74
A Hancock Brexit	1,111	1.97	
D Dixon Loony	195	0.35	
C Sabel Ind	150	0.27	-0.06

Chief executive, Working for Youth, an unemployment charity, 2013-15. Former trustee, Brighton Pride. Business select cttee, 2015-. APPGs: fourth industrial revolution; LGBT rights. Ed: University of Sussex (BA human geography and international development; PhD community economic development).

CHALLENGERS
Robert Nemeth (C) Commercial bee farmer. Cllr, Brighton & Hove CC, 2015-. **Beatrice Bass** (LD) Trainee solicitor. **Ollie Sykes** (Green) Senior project manager, Environment Agency. Cllr, Brighton & Hove CC, 2011-19.

CONSTITUENCY PROFILE
Labour had never won Hove until 1997, but the Conservatives have only held the seat for one term since, from 2010-15. More than a third of residents in this West Sussex seat, which fringes Brighton, are aged between 24 and 45, well above the national average. Levels of private renting are almost double the national average.

EU REFERENDUM RESULT

32.9% Leave   Remain 67.1%

Huddersfield

MAJORITY 4,937 (11.79%)   **LABOUR CO-OP HOLD**   **TURNOUT 63.92%**

BARRY SHEERMAN
BORN Aug 17, 1940
MP 1979-

Unlikely leader of an attempt to overthrow Gordon Brown in 2009. Nominated Sir Keir Starmer for leader in 2020 and backed Owen Smith in his 2016 challenge to Jeremy Corbyn. Supported Remain; voted against the withdrawal agreement four times and supported a second referendum. Shadow spokesman: disability rights, 1992-94; home affairs, 1988-92; education and employment, 1983-88. Select cttees: education, 2001-10; liaison, 1999-2010; public accounts, 1981-83. APPGs: learning disability; miscarriages of justice; skills

	Electorate	Share %	Change from 2017 %
	65,525		
*B Sheerman Lab Co-op	20,509	48.97	-11.42
K Davy C	15,572	37.18	+4.18
J Wilkinson LD	2,367	5.65	+3.02
A Cooper Green	1,768	4.22	+1.04
S Hale Brexit	1,666	3.98	

and employment. Chairman, The Skills Commission. Former lecturer. Contested Taunton in 1974. Ed: Hampton GS; Kingston Tech Coll; LSE (BSc economics); University of London (MSc political sociology).

CHALLENGERS
Ken Davy (C) Said he had voted for the Brexit Party in the 2019 EU elections. **James Wilkinson** (LD) Accountant for a large retailer. **Andrew Cooper** (Green) Cllr, Kirklees C, 1999-.

CONSTITUENCY PROFILE
Held by Labour since its 1983 creation, although 2019 marked the party's smallest majority in that time. Before that, the seat was split between Huddersfield East, which returned Labour MPs from 1950, and Huddersfield West, which was held variously by the Liberals, Labour and the Conservatives. This West Yorkshire seat contains most of the large former wool-making town of Huddersfield, home to more than 160,000 people. One in ten constituents is of Pakistani origin. The seat also contains Huddersfield University and most of its 20,000 students.

EU REFERENDUM RESULT

51.9% Leave   Remain 48.1%

Hull East

MAJORITY 1,239 (3.82%)   LABOUR HOLD   TURNOUT 49.35%

KARL TURNER
BORN April 15, 1971
MP 2010-

	Electorate	Share %	Change from 2017 %
	65,745		
*K Turner Lab	12,713	39.19	-19.10
R Storer C	11,474	35.37	+5.46
M Hall Brexit	5,764	17.77	
B Morgan LD	1,707	5.26	+1.83
J Brown Green	784	2.42	+1.07

Born to a seafaring family. Sold antiques before returning to education and becoming a barrister. Remainer who vowed not to block Brexit after Hull voted to Leave, but voted against the withdrawal agreement four times. Voted for a second referendum. Brought his baby daughter to the Article 50 vote in 2017. Nominated Sir Keir Starmer in 2020. Jeremy Corbyn critic who backed Owen Smith in his 2016 leadership challenge. Tends not to rebel. Shadow minister: transport, 2017-; attorney-general, 2016; justice, 2015-16; solicitor-general

2014-16. Opposition whip, 2017. Select cttees: regulatory reform, 2017-19. First Hull-born MP to represent the constituency since 1784. Confronted Dominic Cummings in Westminster, claiming he had received death threats for his Brexit stance. Ed: University of Hull (LLB law).

CHALLENGERS
Rachel Storer (C) Constituency manager, Victoria Atkins (Louth & Horncastle). **Marten Hall** (Brexit) Ecological consultant.

Former army commando and police constable. **Bob Morgan** (LD) Community worker. Served in the RAF. Former policeman.

CONSTITUENCY PROFILE
Hull East has returned a Labour MP since 1935, though in 2019 the party's majority was at its lowest since it first won the seat. For the 40 years between 1970 and 2010, it was held by John Prescott, the Labour stalwart and deputy prime minister under Tony Blair. The seat contains several middle-class suburbs of Hull as well as deprived areas such as Marfleet. It is the least affluent of the Hull seats by income.

EU REFERENDUM RESULT
72.8% Leave   Remain 27.2%

Hull North

MAJORITY 7,593 (22.20%)   LABOUR HOLD   TURNOUT 52.21%

DIANA JOHNSON
BORN Jul 25, 1966
MP 2005-

	Electorate	Share %	Change from 2017 %
	65,515		
*D Johnson Lab	17,033	49.80	-13.88
H Whitbread C	9,440	27.60	+2.36
D Abram Brexit	4,771	13.95	
M Ross LD	2,084	6.09	+1.06
R Howarth Green	875	2.56	+0.82

Resigned from the front bench in 2016 in protest at Jeremy Corbyn's leadership during the EU referendum. Voted against the withdrawal agreement four times, and for a second referendum. Behind bill to remove criminal sanctions facing women and doctors under abortion rules. In September 2019, she became the first Labour MP to face reselection process, but was overwhelmingly reselected. Shadow minister: Foreign Office, 2015-16; Home Office, 2010-15; health 2010. Junior minister, education, 2009-10. Asstistant whip, 2007-09. PPS

to Stephen Timms (East Ham), 2005-07. Select cttee: health and social care, 2017-. Contested Brentwood & Ongar, 2001. Cllr, Tower Hamlets LBC, 1994-2002. Former barrister. Ed: Northwich County GS; Brunel University (law).

CHALLENGERS
Holly Whitbread (C) Self-employed communications consultant. Previously worked as a parliamentary researcher. Cllr, Epping Forest DC, 2016-.

Derek Abram (Brexit) HR consultant. **Mike Ross** (LD) Cllr, Hull City C, 2002-; group leader. Contested: Hull North, 2017, 2015; Hull West & Hessle, 2010.

CONSTITUENCY PROFILE
Including its predecessors, Hull North has been represented by Labour MPs since 1964, having been held by the Conservatives from 1950. It includes the University of Hull campus. The seat is characterised by slightly higher average pay than the other two Hull seats, although median income in all three seats is below the regional average. Lowest level of home ownership in Hull.

EU REFERENDUM RESULT
59.8% Leave   Remain 40.2%

Hull West & Hessle

MAJORITY 2,856 (9.11%)　　　LABOUR HOLD　　　TURNOUT 51.91%

EMMA HARDY
BORN Jul 17, 1979
MP 2017-

Electorate	Share %	from 2017 %	Change
60,409			
*E Hardy Lab	13,384	42.68	-10.38
S Bell C	10,528	33.58	+3.73
M Dewberry Brexit	5,638	17.98	
D Nolan LD	1,756	5.60	-0.79
M Lammiman Green	50	0.16	-0.80

PPS to Sir Keir Starmer since 2017 and backed him for leader, 2020. Former primary school teacher and deputy general secretary, Socialist Education Association. Replaced the retiring former home secretary Alan Johnson, MP for this seat from 1997 to 2017, after beating Jeremy Corbyn's speechwriter David Prescott, son of John, to be selected as candidate. Voted against the Brexit withdrawal agreement four times, and for a second referendum. Education select cttee, 2017-. Worked closely with the women's health charity Endometriosis UK to successfully push for "menstrual wellbeing" to be part of sex education in schools. Member, Unite. Cllr, Hessle TC, 2015-19. Ed: University of Liverpool (BA politics); University of Leeds (PGCE).

CHALLENGERS
Scott Bell (C) Brexit project manager, management consultancy. Raised in Hull. Voted to Remain but has since campaigned for Leave. **Michelle Dewberry** (Brexit) Businesswoman; set up own consultancy. Winner of the second series of *The Apprentice*. Co-presenter, *The Pledge* on Sky News. Contested this seat as an independent, 2017. **David Nolan** (LD) Ran market research firm.

CONSTITUENCY PROFILE
This seat has voted Labour since its creation in 1997, as did its predecessor Hull West from 1955. It has the highest unemployment rate of the three Hull seats, although it has a relatively high number of manufacturing jobs. Home ownership levels are low and about a quarter of homes are socially rented.

EU REFERENDUM RESULT
68.0% Leave　　　Remain 32.0%

Huntingdon

MAJORITY 19,383 (32.77%)　　　CONSERVATIVE HOLD　　　TURNOUT 69.87%

JONATHAN DJANOGLY
BORN Jun 3, 1965
MP 2001-

Electorate	Share %	from 2017 %	Change
84,657			
*J Djanogly C	32,386	54.76	-0.36
S Sweek Lab	13,003	21.98	-8.89
M Argent LD	9,432	15.95	+7.42
D Laycock Green	2,233	3.78	+1.94
P Bullen Ind	1,789	3.02	
T Varghese Ind	304	0.51	

Solicitor and former partner at the commercial law firm SJ Berwin LLP. Ran mail-order retail business with his wife. Wealthy son of the multimillionaire textile magnate and philanthropist Sir Harry Djanogly. Justice minister, 2010-12. Voted to Remain in the EU; backed the withdrawal agreement four times. In the shadow cabinet until 2010. Select cttee: Brexit, 2017-. Supported Matt Hancock, then Jeremy Hunt, for the Conservative leadership in 2019. He was ranked as 645th out of 650 MPs for "openness and responsiveness" by the petitions platform Change.org in the same year. Cllr, Westminster CC, 1994-2001. Contested Oxford East, 1997. Ed: University Coll Sch; Oxford Polytechnic (BA law and politics); Coll of Law, Guildford.

CHALLENGERS
Samuel Sweek (Lab) Parliamentary assistant. **Mark Argent** (LD) Background in publishing, web design and consultancy. **Daniel Laycock** (Green) Contested Peterborough CC, 2018. **Paul Bullen** (Ind) Owned a company in private marine sector. Former RAF officer.

CONSTITUENCY PROFILE
Safe Conservative seat, held by John Major from its creation in 1983 until 2001. The predecessor seat, Huntingdonshire, had been held by Conservative MPs since 1964 and was never won by Labour. This west Cambridgeshire constituency is demographically balanced but has very low levels of unemployment. It includes the towns of St Neots and Huntingdon.

EU REFERENDUM RESULT
53.5% Leave　　　Remain 46.5%

Hyndburn

MAJORITY 2,951 (6.96%)   CONSERVATIVE GAIN FROM LABOUR   TURNOUT 59.80%

SARA BRITCLIFFE
BORN Feb 21, 1995
MP 2019-

Sandwich shop owner and the youngest Conservative MP elected in 2019, at the age of 24. Daughter of Peter Britcliffe, who unsuccessfully contested this seat in 1997 and 2001. Aged 22, she took a gap year from university to become the mayoress of Hyndburn; her father was the mayor at the time. She was the youngest person to ever hold the role. Volunteer, Accrington Community Events Team. Member, Homelessness in Hyndburn Group. Cllr, Hyndburn, BC, 2018-. Ed: University of Manchester (BA modern languages).

	Electorate	Share %	Change from 2017 %
	70,910		
S Britcliffe C	20,565	48.50	+8.00
*G Jones Lab	17,614	41.54	-11.82
G Butt Brexit	2,156	5.08	
A Waller-Slack LD	1,226	2.89	+1.07
K Brockbank Green	845	1.99	

CHALLENGERS
Graham Jones (Lab) MP for this seat, 2010-19. Opposition assistant whip, 2010-15; resigned when Jeremy Corbyn was elected leader. Voted against withdrawal agreement four times and for a second referendum. Former graphic designer. **Gregory Butt** (Brexit) Falklands veteran. Appointed MBE in 1998. **Adam Waller-Slack** (LD) Consultant anaesthetist. **Katrina Brockbank** (Green) MSc in chartered management.

CONSTITUENCY PROFILE
Held by the Conservatives from its creation in 1983 until 1992, then won by Labour until 2019. The Labour majority peaked at 11,000 in 1997, but had been in four figures since. The main predecessor seat, Accrington, returned Labour MPs from 1945. Hyndburn is a small collection of Lancashire towns, east of Blackburn. The constituency has a large Asian population and about one in ten residents has Pakistani heritage. Nearly a third of residents are aged under 25. About a sixth of the workforce are in manufacturing and residents receive lower than average pay.

EU REFERENDUM RESULT
65.8% Leave   Remain 34.2%

Ilford North

MAJORITY 5,218 (10.41%)   LABOUR HOLD   TURNOUT 68.70%

WES STREETING
BORN Jan 21, 1983
MP 2015-

Long-time activist interested in education. Former consultant, PwC. President, National Union of Students, 2008-10. Nominated Jess Phillips for leader in 2020. Backed Owen Smith in 2016 and Liz Kendall in 2015. Critical of Jeremy Corbyn, especially on antisemitism. Confronted Ken Livingstone on *Newsnight* over controversial Hitler comments. Remainer; voted against the Brexit withdrawal agreements and for a second referendum. Select cttee: Treasury, 2015-. APPG on antisemitism (vice-chairman). Endorsed in the 2017 election by Sir Ian McKellen.

	Electorate	Share %	Change from 2017 %
	72,963		
*W Streeting Lab	25,323	50.52	-7.26
H Berlin C	20,105	40.11	+0.54
M Johnson LD	2,680	5.35	+3.39
N Anderson Brexit	960	1.92	
D Reynolds Green	845	1.69	
D Akhigbe CPA	210	0.42	

Cllr, Redbridge LBC, 2010-18. Ed: Westminster City Sch; Selwyn Coll, Cambridge (BA history; president, students' union).

CHALLENGERS
Howard Berlin (C) Chartered surveyor. Cllr, Redbridge LBC, 2018-. **Mark Johnson** (LD) Lobbyist, Advertising Association. Former parliamentary assistant. **Neil Anderson** (Brexit) Director, Migration Watch UK. **David**

Reynolds (Green) Contested this seat in the 2015 election.

CONSTITUENCY PROFILE
A marginal seat, changing between Labour and the Conservatives six times since 1945. Wes Streeting gained the seat with a majority of just under 600 in 2015, which increased to more than 9,500 in 2017, the largest majority of any MP for Ilford South since 1987. In northeast London, bordering Essex, Ilford North is a diverse constituency: it has Muslim and Hindu populations in the tens of thousands, a Jewish population of about 6,000 and a Sikh population of about 4,000.

EU REFERENDUM RESULT
53.3% Leave   Remain 46.7%

Ilford South

LABOUR HOLD

TURNOUT 62.95%

SAM TARRY
BORN Aug 27, 1982
MP 2019-

	Electorate	Share %	from 2017 % Change
	84,957		
S Tarry Lab	35,085	65.61	-10.23
A Azeem C	10,984	20.54	-0.41
*M Gapes Change	3,891	7.28	
A Holder LD	1,795	3.36	+2.02
M Sharma Brexit	1,008	1.88	
R Warrington Green	714	1.34	+0.40

President of the Centre for Labour and Social Studies, a left-wing think tank. Officer, TSSA, the transport workers' union. Nominated Rebecca Long Bailey for leader in 2020. Managed Jeremy Corbyn's leadership campaign. Commenting in the aftermath of the 2019 election, he blamed Tony Blair for voters' lack of trust in Labour. Former director, Momentum. First elected chairman of Young Labour. Worked as a campaign organiser for the anti-fascist campaign group Hope not Hate. Cllr, Barking & Dagenham LBC, 2010-18. Ed: UCL (BA history).

CHALLENGERS
Ali Azeem (C) Associate partner, Ipsos Mori. Former policy adviser to George Osborne, the shadow chancellor, 2009. Policy adviser to Matt Hancock's leadership campaign. Voted Leave. **Mike Gapes** (Change) MP for this seat, 1992-2019. Spent 15 years at Labour HQ, including spells as international secretary and national student organiser. Member, Labour national policy forum, 1996-2005. Jeremy

Corbyn critic; self-described "Kinnockite". Quit Labour in protest at antisemitism scandal to co-found The Independent Group (later Change UK).

CONSTITUENCY PROFILE
Labour since 1992, but once marginal, this seat has changed hands between the two main parties six times since 1945. It is denser, younger, and more ethnically diverse than Ilford North, with more than half of its population having Asian heritage. Just over half of residents in the seat were born in the UK. More than a third are Muslim. Levels of private renting are well above average.

EU REFERENDUM RESULT
43.3% Leave   Remain 56.7%

Inverclyde

SNP HOLD

TURNOUT 65.82%

RONNIE COWAN
BORN Sep 6, 1959
MP 2015-

	Electorate	Share %	from 2017 % Change
	60,622		
*R Cowan SNP	19,295	48.35	+9.86
M McCluskey Lab	11,783	29.53	-7.99
H Malik C	6,265	15.70	-5.78
J Stoyle LD	2,560	6.42	+3.91

IT consultant with his own firm. Joined the SNP aged 16; founded Yes Inverclyde, a pro-independence organisation, in 2012. SNP spokesman for infrastructure, 2018-. Select cttees: public administration, 2015-; procedure, 2017-; transport, 2017-. Voted against the withdrawal agreement four times and for a second Brexit referendum. Has campaigned on several causes since entering parliament, including welfare, broadband speed, gambling addiction, employment, and drugs reform. Campaigned to save the Port Glasgow job centre.

Son of the Scottish goalkeeper Jimmy Cowan. Ed: Greenock Academy.

CHALLENGERS
Martin McCluskey (Lab) Policy director, Scottish Labour, 2016-. Parliamentary relations manager, Volunteer Service Overseas, 2010-12. Worked for Equality & Human Rights Commission, 2008-10. Member, GMB. Contested this seat, 2017.
Haroun Malik (C) Criminal defence solicitor. Cadet Sergeant in the Air Training Corps. Voted

Leave. **Jacci Stoyle** (LD) Yoga business owner. Learning and skills manager at various prisons.

CONSTITUENCY PROFILE
Had elected Labour MPs continuously since 1987 until the SNP won it for the first time in 2015. Labour came within 400 votes of taking it back in 2017. Perched on the banks of the Clyde, Inverclyde is to Glasgow's west. Its biggest town, Greenock, was once a centre of Scotland's shipbuilding industry, but the sector has dwindled since the 1980s. About a third of its workers are in routine and semi-routine jobs, which is well above the national average.

EU REFERENDUM RESULT
36.2% Leave   Remain 63.8%

Inverness, Nairn, Badenoch & Strathspey

MAJORITY 10,440 (19.05%)   SNP HOLD   TURNOUT 70.22%

DREW HENDRY
BORN May 21, 1964
MP 2015-

Ousted Danny Alexander, the Lib Dem incumbent, in 2015. SNP spokesman for business, 2017-; transport, 2015-17. Background in retail, manufacturing and new technology. Chairman of terminal illness APPG. Founder, Teclan, the first private sector living wage employer in Inverness. Appointed to the board of Cairngorms National Park Authority, 2007. Cllr, Highland C, 2007-15; leader, 2012-15. Contested European parliament for Scotland, 2009. Ed: Grove Academy, Dundee; Dundee & Angus Coll.

	Electorate	Share %	Change from 2017 %
	78,057		
*D Hendry SNP	26,247	47.89	+8.04
F Fawcett C	15,807	28.84	-1.69
R Rixson LD	5,846	10.67	-1.60
L Whyte Lab	4,123	7.52	-8.67
A Burgess Green	1,709	3.12	
L Durance Brexit	1,078	1.97	

CHALLENGERS
Fiona Fawcett (C) Retired doctor. Breast cancer physician, Jarvis Centre. **Robert Rixson** (LD) Primary and secondary school teacher. Author of several books about Highland history. **Lewis Ian Whyte** (Lab) Hotel receptionist and activities administrator. **Ariane Burgess** (Green) Works in sustainable community development. **Les Durance** (Brexit) Director, Cairngorm Outdoors, 2004-.

CONSTITUENCY PROFILE
The seat was gained by the Lib Dems from its creation in 2005, and held by Danny Alexander, the chief secretary to the Treasury, 2010-15, for ten years until the SNP's 2015 victory. The seat's predecessors were mostly held by Lib Dems and Liberals for 50 years, although Labour won Inverness East, Nairn & Lochaber in 1997 and 2001. A huge, sparse seat in the Highlands, with the Cairngorms in the south and east. Inverness itself is home to about 47,000 people and to Scottish Natural Heritage. Nearly a tenth of residents' jobs are in tourism-related industries.

EU REFERENDUM RESULT
40.1% Leave   Remain 59.9%

Ipswich

MAJORITY 5,479 (11.05%)   CONSERVATIVE GAIN FROM LABOUR   TURNOUT 65.65%

TOM HUNT
BORN Aug 31, 1988
MP 2019-

Accused of making "dog-whistle" comments in a newspaper column after the election, in which he blamed "certain communities" for a "disproportionate number of crimes". Chief of staff to the Cambridgeshire and Peterborough mayor, 2017-19. Head of media at the Countryside Alliance, 2016-17. Parliamentary assistant to Oliver Dowden (Hertsmere), 2015-16. Cllr, East Cambridgeshire DC, 2011-17. Contested: Doncaster Central, 2017. Ed: King's School; Hills Road Sixth Form College; University of Manchester (BA

	Electorate	Share %	Change from 2017 %
	75,525		
T Hunt C	24,952	50.33	+4.58
*S Martin Lab	19,473	39.28	-8.09
A Hyyrylainen-Trett LD	2,439	4.92	+2.60
N Thomas Brexit	1,432	2.89	
B Broom Green	1,283	2.59	+0.95

politics & modern history); University of Oxford (MSc Russian & east European studies).

CHALLENGERS
Sandy Martin (Lab) MP for this seat, 2017-19. Shadow minister for waste and recycling, 2018-19. Local government stalwart and self-described democratic socialist. Cllr, Suffolk CC, 1997-2017. **Adrian Hyyrylainen-Trett** (LD) Development manager. UK's first openly HIV+ candidate

when contesting Vauxhall, 2015. **Nicola Thomas** (Brexit) Teacher and senior leader of primary and secondary schools. **Barry Broom** (Green) IT professional.

CONSTITUENCY PROFILE
Has swung back and forth between Labour and the Conservatives multiple times since its creation in 1918. Labour's 2017 gain was one of several surprising results in that election, although Sandy Martin's majority was a little over 800. Most of the southeast Suffolk town of Ipswich is contained in the seat, although some of its suburban areas are in surrounding constituencies.

EU REFERENDUM RESULT
56.5% Leave   Remain 43.5%

Isle of Wight

MAJORITY 23,737 (31.89%)   CONSERVATIVE HOLD   TURNOUT 65.87%

BOB SEELY
BORN Jun 1, 1966
MP 2017-

Co-authored a 2019 report that recommended banning Huawei from involvement in UK's 5G network. Foreign affairs select cttee, 2018-. PPS to Defra, 2019; resigned to vote against the government on the HS2 rail link. Supported Michael Gove in the 2019 Conservative leadership election. Author and soldier. Started his career as a foreign correspondent in eastern Europe for *The Times* and *The Washington Post*. Served with the TA in Iraq and Afghanistan. Worked as an adviser to Francis Maude and Sir Malcolm Rifkind, and later for MTV Networks

	Electorate	Share %	Change from 2017 %
	113,021		
*B Seely C	41,815	56.17	+4.90
R Quigley Lab	18,078	24.28	+1.30
V Lowthion Green	11,338	15.23	-2.11
C Feeney Network	1,542	2.07	
K Love Ind	874	1.17	
D Pitcher Ind	795	1.07	

International. His great-great-uncle, General Jack Seely, was MP for the Isle of Wight in 1900-06 and 1923-24. Contested Broxtowe, 2005. Ed: Harrow; King's Coll London (war studies).

CHALLENGERS
Richard Quigley (Lab) Works in food and drink logistics. **Vix Lowthion** (Green) History and geology teacher. **Carl Feeney** (Network) Heads campaign for a link tunnel to the Isle of Wight.

CONSTITUENCY PROFILE
Now a safe Conservative seat, the Lib Dems last won Isle of Wight in 1997. They fell to fifth place in 2015 and stood aside for the Greens as part of a "Unite to Remain" pact in 2019. The previous MP, Andrew Turner, stepped down in 2017 after telling schoolchildren that he thought that homosexuality was "wrong" and "dangerous to society". Just south of the Hampshire coast, the seat has the largest electorate of any parliamentary seat. Well over a quarter of its population are aged 65 or older and tourism, health and social care are among the largest industries.

EU REFERENDUM RESULT
61.9% Leave   Remain 38.1%

Islington North

MAJORITY 26,188 (48.67%)   LABOUR HOLD   TURNOUT 71.59%

JEREMY CORBYN
BORN May 26, 1949
MP 1983-

Announced on election night that he would be stepping down as leader of the opposition after leading Labour to its worst result since 1935. Defied the odds to be elected party leader twice, in 2015 and 2016, benefitting from a cult following among the grass roots. Self-identified democratic socialist who rebelled against the New Labour governments many times; he was a perennial backbencher until his sudden elevation to the leadership. Long-time Eurosceptic; voted No in the 1975 EEC referendum and against the Maastricht and Lisbon treaties. Lukewarm

	Electorate	Share %	Change from 2017 %
	75,162		
*J Corbyn Lab	34,603	64.31	-8.67
N Wakeling LD	8,415	15.64	+6.64
J Clark C	5,483	10.19	-2.32
C Russell Green	4,326	8.04	+3.98
Y David Brexit	742	1.38	
N Brick Loony	236	0.44	+0.25

support for Remain in 2016 led to a shadow cabinet revolt. Endorsed holding a referendum on any Brexit deal, in which he would remain neutral. Criticised for the handling of antisemitism cases within Labour, warm words for groups linked to terrorism and a failure in 2018 to condemn the Kremlin for the poisoning of a former Russian military officer in Salisbury. Chaired the Stop the War coalition, 2011-15. Ed: Adams' GS.

CHALLENGERS
Nick Wakeling (LD) Director of financial reporting, Metro Bank, 2015-. **James Clark** (C) Director, Bodewell Homes. **Caroline Russell** (Green) Only non-Labour Islington councillor.

CONSTITUENCY PROFILE
A safe seat that has elected Labour MPs since 1937, mostly with large majorities. Jeremy Corbyn's majority has remained in five figures since the 1992 general election. The smallest constituency in the UK by size, and one of the densest, Islington North is a young and diverse seat where four in ten homes are rented socially.

EU REFERENDUM RESULT
21.6% Leave   Remain 78.4%

Islington South & Finsbury

MAJORITY 17,326 (36.24%)   **LABOUR HOLD**   **TURNOUT 67.83%**

EMILY THORNBERRY
BORN Jul 27, 1960
MP 2005-

First to announce candidacy for Labour leadership, 2020, but did not make it on to the final ballot. Shadow foreign secretary, 2016-; opposed British involvement in Yemen, 2016, and the UK government's response to the murder of the Saudi journalist Jamal Khashoggi, 2018. Re-joined Labour front bench after she was forced to resign as shadow attorney-general, 2011-14, after a controversial tweet about an England flag hung on a house in Rochester. Campaigned to remain in the EU. Shadow secretary of state: Brexit, 2016; defence, 2016. Shadow minister:

	Electorate	Share %	Change from 2017 %
	70,489		
*E Thornberry Lab	26,897	56.25	-6.58
K Pothalingam LD	9,569	20.01	+7.92
J Charalambous C	8,045	16.82	-3.83
T Hussain Green	1,987	4.16	+1.66
P Hannam Brexit	1,136	2.38	
L Sandys of Bunhill Loony	182	0.38	

employment, 2015-16; health, 2010-11; energy, 2010. Barrister; specialised in human rights law. Ed: secondary modern; Kent University (BA law).

CHALLENGERS
Kate Pothalingam (LD) Consultant, International Capital Market Association. **Jason Charalambous** (C) Qualified barrister and practising solicitor-advocate. **Talia Hussain** (Green) Designer and consultant. **Paddy**

Hannam (Brexit) Former Labour member. Contributor, Spiked online magazine.

CONSTITUENCY PROFILE
Has elected only Labour MPs since its creation in 1974, although Emily Thornberry won her first election in 2005 with a majority of only 484 over the Lib Dem candidate. Its previous MP was Chris Smith, who became the first openly gay MP in 1984. A small, dense inner London seat. More than half its residents are aged 16 to 45 and a little under two thirds were born in the UK. Mean income is higher than the national and London averages.

EU REFERENDUM RESULT
28.3% Leave   Remain 71.7%

Islwyn

MAJORITY 5,464 (15.91%)   **LABOUR CO-OP HOLD**   **TURNOUT 61.98%**

CHRIS EVANS
BORN Jul 7, 1977
MP 2010-

Former bookmaker and account manager, Lloyds TSB. Initially rebelled and voted against triggering Article 50, but reversed his position. Critical of Jeremy Corbyn's EU campaigning; publicly called for him to resign. Backed Sir Keir Starmer in 2020, Owen Smith in 2016 and Liz Kendall in 2015. Public accounts select cttee, 2015-. Official, Union of Finance Staff. Marketing executive, University of Glamorgan. Researcher to Don Touhig MP. Contested Cheltenham, 2005. Ed: Porth County CS; Trinity Coll Carmarthen (BA history).

	Electorate	Share %	Change from 2017 %
	55,423		
*C Evans Lab Co-op	15,356	44.70	-14.14
G Chambers C	9,892	28.80	+1.57
J Wells Brexit	4,834	14.07	
Z Hammond PC	2,286	6.66	-0.93
J Watkins LD	1,313	3.82	+1.92
C Linstrum Green	669	1.95	

CHALLENGERS
Gavin Chambers (C) Director, Chambers Academy. Cllr, Epping Forest DC, 2012-. **James Wells** (Brexit) Brexit Party MEP, 2019-20. Head of UK Trade at the ONS, 2013-2019, resigning in 2019 to stand. **Zoe Hammond** (PC) Support worker in the care industry. Cllr, Blackwood TC, 2017-. **Jo Watkins** (LD) Environmentalist. **Catherine Linstrum** (Green) Filmmaker, writer and teacher.

CONSTITUENCY PROFILE
Including its predecessor, Bedwellty, this seat has been represented by Labour for more than a century, and its MP from 1970 until 1995 was Neil Kinnock, the Labour leader in 1983-92. The party's majority fell in 2019, however, to its lowest point since the introduction of universal suffrage. The south Wales constituency consists of several small towns that were once dominated by the coalmining industry. Manufacturing is among the dominant industries in the area now, and nearly two fifths of the workforce are employed in routine and semi-routine jobs.

EU REFERENDUM RESULT
58.9% Leave   Remain 41.1%

Jarrow

MAJORITY 7,120 (17.48%)   **LABOUR HOLD**   TURNOUT 62.57%

KATE OSBORNE
BORN Declined to disclose birth date
MP 2019-

Jeremy Corbyn ally selected as the candidate for Jarrow after Stephen Hepburn, the MP here since 1997, was suspended from the party following an allegation of sexual harassment. Apologised after sharing an image on social media of Theresa May with a gun pointed at her head in 2017; 27 female candidates, citing the murder of Jo Cox, called for her to be banned from standing for helping to incite violence against women in politics. Unite, 1994-. Former foster carer. Cllr, North Tyneside DC, 2017-. Ed: Sudbury Upper School, Suffolk.

	Electorate	Share %	Change from 2017 %
	65,103		
K Osborne Lab	18,363	45.08	-20.05
N Oliver C	11,243	27.60	+2.60
R Monaghan Brexit	4,122	10.12	
J Robertson Ind	2,991	7.34	
D Wilkinson LD	2,360	5.79	+3.09
J Milne Green	831	2.04	+0.31
S Sadler Ind	614	1.51	
M Conway Soc Dem	212	0.52	

CHALLENGERS
Nick Oliver (C) Runs the web channel of his family retail business. Cllr, Northumberland CC, 2017-; cabinet secretary and cabinet member for corporate services. **Richard Monaghan** (Brexit) Management consultant. **John Robertson** (Ind) Contracts manager. In 2011, drove a lorry into council buildings over a contracts row.

CONSTITUENCY PROFILE
Jarrow has elected Labour MPs in all but one election since 1922, that election being in 1931 when Ramsay MacDonald joined the National Government and the seat was won by the Conservatives. Labour's majority in the seat had not, until 2019, fallen below 10,000 at any general election since 1945. On the southern bank of the Tyne, the seat of Jarrow is dominated by manufacturing and consists of the town itself, the eastern edge of Gateshead, and the smaller town of Boldon. The town gave its name to the Jarrow March against unemployment and destitution in 1936.

EU REFERENDUM RESULT
61.8% Leave   Remain 38.2%

Keighley

MAJORITY 2,218 (4.22%)   **CONSERVATIVE GAIN FROM LABOUR**   TURNOUT 72.27%

ROBBIE MOORE
BORN Nov 28, 1984
MP 2019-

Rural chartered surveyor. Set up his own consultancy practice, Brockthorpe Consultancy. Associate and rural surveyor, George F. White, 2009-18. Cllr, Northumberland CC & Alnwick TC, 2017-. Contested a police and crime commissioner election, 2019. From a family of Lincolnshire farmers. Ed: Newcastle University (BA architecture); University College of Estate Management (PG Dip rural surveying).

CHALLENGERS
John Grogan (Lab) MP for this constituency, 2017-19; MP for

	Electorate	Share %	Change from 2017 %
	72,778		
R Moore C	25,298	48.10	+2.05
*J Grogan Lab	23,080	43.88	-2.65
T Franks LD	2,573	4.89	+2.52
W Khan Brexit	850	1.62	
M Barton Yorkshire	667	1.27	
M Rose Soc Dem	132	0.25	

Selby, 1997-2010. Chairman of the Mongolian-British Chambers of Commerce. Former Labour Party press officer. Voted to revoke Article 50 and for a second referendum in the indicative votes. Said after his defeat that Labour needed a new Harold Wilson as leader. Supported English devolution. Contested: Keighley, 2015; Selby, 1992, 1987. **Tom Franks** (LD) Civil engineer. Specialised in irrigation. Cllr, Ilkley TC, 2019-.

CONSTITUENCY PROFILE
Has changed hands between Labour and the Conservatives 11 times since 1945. The 2017 election was the first time since 1979 that Labour had won the seat despite losing nationally, although the margin of Labour's victory was only 239 votes. The former British National Party leader Nick Griffin won more than 4,000 votes in this West Yorkshire seat in 2005. More than 70,000 residents live in the town of Keighley itself. The seat has high home ownership and incomes are slightly higher than the Yorkshire average. It has a large Muslim community of about 13,000.

EU REFERENDUM RESULT
53.3% Leave   Remain 46.7%

Kenilworth & Southam

MAJORITY 20,353 (38.70%)   CONSERVATIVE HOLD   TURNOUT 77.17%

JEREMY WRIGHT
BORN Oct 24, 1972
MP 2005-

Secretary of state for digital, culture, media and sport, 2018-19. Attorney-general, 2014-18. Campaigned for Remain, but led failed government attempt to use royal prerogative to trigger Article 50; defeat gave parliament a veto over when Brexit began. Published an "online harms" white paper to regulate social media companies in 2019. Parly under-sec, justice, 2012-14. Government whip, 2010-12; opposition whip, 2007-10. MP for Rugby & Kenilworth, 2005-10. Ed: Trinity Sch, New York City; University of Exeter (LLB); Inns of Court Sch (BVC).

	Electorate	Share %	Change from 2017 %
	68,156		
*J Wright C	30,351	57.70	-3.11
R Dickson LD	9,998	19.01	+9.42
A Tucker Lab	9,440	17.95	-7.62
A Firth Green	2,351	4.47	+2.26
N Green Loony	457	0.87	

CHALLENGERS
Richard Dickson (LD) Development manager, Rising Global Peace Forum. Cllr: Kenilworth TC, 2017-; Warwick DC, 2019-. Contested this seat in the past two elections. **Antony Tucker** (Lab) Worked in marketing and as a teaching assistant. Co-chairman, LGBT+ Labour West Midlands. **Alison Firth** (Green) Owner and driving instructor, Alison's Driving School, 2009-. Cllr, Kenilworth TC, 2019-.

CONSTITUENCY PROFILE
Has elected a Conservative MP since its creation in 2010, and the Conservatives have never won less than half the votes cast. The predecessor seat, Kenilworth & Rugby, was held by Labour between 1997 and 2005, but otherwise elected Conservatives from its creation in 1983. The Warwickshire seat consists of a rural area to the north, east and west of Warwick. Nearly a quarter of residents are aged 65 or above, more than three quarters of homes are owner-occupied and a large proportion of the workforce are employed in managerial and director-level jobs.

EU REFERENDUM RESULT
46.2% Leave   Remain 53.8%

Kensington

MAJORITY 150 (0.34%)   CONSERVATIVE GAIN FROM LABOUR   TURNOUT 67.73%

FELICITY BUCHAN
BORN Declined to disclose birth date
MP 2019-

Professional career in financial services; worked at JP Morgan and Bank of America. Campaigned for a negotiated Brexit deal. Chairwoman of governors, Bousfield Primary School. Contested Down South, 2015; South Shields, 2017. Ed: Fraserburgh Academy; Christ Church, Oxford (law).

CHALLENGERS
Emma Dent Coad (Lab) MP for this seat, 2017-19. Kensington's first Labour MP, winning in 2017 by 20 votes after three recounts. Blamed local council for the Grenfell fire, which was the

	Electorate	Share %	Change from 2017 %
	64,609		
F Buchan C	16,768	38.32	-3.86
*E Dent Coad Lab	16,618	37.97	-4.26
+S Gyimah LD	9,312	21.28	+9.06
V Lichtenstein Green	535	1.22	-0.76
J Aston Colquhoun Brexit	384	0.88	
R Phillips CPA	70	0.16	
H Gore Touch	47	0.11	
S Dore WRP	28	0.06	

subject of her maiden speech, 2017. Architectural historian. **Sam Gyimah** (LD) Conservative MP for Surrey East, 2010-19. Stood, briefly, for Conservative leader before having the whip removed over a Brexit rebellion and joining the Lib Dems in September 2019. Universities minister, 2018. Investment banker, Goldman Sachs. PPS to David Cameron, 2012-13.

CONSTITUENCY PROFILE
Had never been held by Labour from its creation in 1974 until 2017, in perhaps the most surprising result of that election. The fifth most marginal seat in the 2019 parliament. The predecessor seat of Kensington North elected Labour MPs from 1945 until its abolition in 1974. The west London seat contains both Notting Hill and Grenfell Tower. It has the highest average house prices of any seat, at more than £1.3 million, and an average income of more than £44,000. Child poverty is also, however, above average and the borough of Kensington & Chelsea has a high homelessness rate.

EU REFERENDUM RESULT
31.2% Leave   Remain 68.8%

Kettering

MAJORITY 16,765 (33.96%) **CONSERVATIVE HOLD** **TURNOUT 67.45%**

PHILIP HOLLOBONE
BORN Nov 7, 1964
MP 2005-

Rightwinger and frequent rebel. Said he would refuse to speak to constituents wearing burkas, 2010. Leave campaigner; agreed an electoral pact with Ukip in 2017. Advocated privatising the BBC and NHS. Member of socially conservative Cornerstone Group. Worked as an industry research analyst. Served in TA 1987-95, latterly as a paratrooper; has supported the reintroduction of national service, as well as of capital punishment. Contested: this seat in 2001; Lewisham East, 1997. Ed: Dulwich Coll; LMH, Oxford (BA modern history & economics).

	Electorate	Share %	Change from 2017 %
	73,187		
*P Hollobone C	29,787	60.35	+2.42
C Pavitt Lab	13,022	26.38	-10.16
C Nelson LD	3,367	6.82	+3.55
J Hakewill Ind	1,642	3.33	
J Wildman Green	1,543	3.13	+0.87

CHALLENGERS
Clare Pavitt (Lab) Career in local government for 18 years. Policy and strategy officer specialising in equality and diversity for Kettering borough council. **Chris Nelson** (LD) Science and law teacher. **Jim Hakewill** (Ind) Former Conservative leader of Kettering borough council who contested the seat as an independent after two previous failed attempts to be selected as the Conservative candidate. **Jamie Wildman**

(Green) Postgraduate researcher in environmental science at the University of Northampton.

CONSTITUENCY PROFILE
Although Kettering, in Northamptonshire, was held by Labour between 1945 and 1983, it has mostly returned Conservatives since. Labour held it from 1997 to 2005, although the MP, Phil Sawford, never won by more than a thousand votes. The Conservatives won their largest majority here in postwar history in 2019. Both house prices and incomes are lower than average. Manufacturing and retail are among the largest local industries.

EU REFERENDUM RESULT
61.0% Leave   Remain 39.0%

Kilmarnock & Loudoun

MAJORITY 12,659 (26.58%) **SNP HOLD** **TURNOUT 63.92%**

ALAN BROWN
BORN Aug 12, 1970
MP 2015-

Known for his thick accent, which led Hansard reporters to ask for written translations of his questions. Formerly a civil engineer. SNP spokesman: transport, 2017-; infrastructure and energy, 2017-. European scrutiny select cttee, 2016-. Cllr, East Ayrshire C, 2007-15; cabinet member; chairman, grants cttee; spokesman, housing and strategic planning. Trustee and director roles: Kilmarnock Leisure Centre; Irvine Valley Regeneration Partnership. Enjoys camping. Ed: Loudoun Academy; University of Glasgow (BEng: civil engineering).

	Electorate	Share %	Change from 2017 %
	74,517		
*A Brown SNP	24,216	50.84	+8.50
C Hollins C	11,557	24.26	-2.41
K McGregor Lab	9,009	18.91	-9.94
E Thornley LD	2,444	5.13	+2.99
S Johnstone Libertarian	405	0.85	

CHALLENGERS
Caroline Hollins (C) Maternal health professor, Edinburgh Napier University, 2011-. Spent 11 years as a midwife. Contested Ayrshire Central, 2017. **Kevin McGregor** (Lab) Works in the NHS. Vice-chairman, Ayrshire Health branch of Unison.

CONSTITUENCY PROFILE
A Labour stronghold since 1945, the seat fell to the SNP in their 2015 landslide victory. 2019 was the first time the Conservatives

had come second since 1987. It was held between 1997 and 2010 by Des Browne, a defence secretary under Tony Blair and then Scottish secretary under Gordon Brown. The seat covers the town of Kilmarnock and parts of rural Ayrshire in western Scotland. About half of its constituents live in Kilmarnock itself, a town known for the Johnnie Walker whisky bottled there until 2012, and the scientist Alexander Fleming, who attended Kilmarnock Academy. Like other former industrial towns, the area has suffered from economic decline: incomes are below average and unemployment is relatively high.

EU REFERENDUM RESULT
39.5% Leave   Remain 60.5%

Kingston & Surbiton

MAJORITY 10,489 (17.24%)   LIB DEM HOLD   TURNOUT 74.23%

SIR ED DAVEY
BORN Dec 25, 1965
MP 2017-; 1997-2015

Became acting co-leader of the Liberal Democrats after Jo Swinson lost her seat. Had stood against Ms Swinson in the 2019 leadership election and was subsequently appointed deputy leader. Lib Dem Treasury spokesman, 2019-. Energy secretary, 2012-15. Parly under-sec, business, 2010-12. Various business consulting appointments after losing this seat in 2015. Strongly supports free trade. Chairman of party's 2010 election campaign. Chief of staff to Sir Menzies Campbell, 2006-07. Whip, 1997-2000. Quadrilingual. Ed: Nottingham

	Electorate	Share %	from 2017 %	Change
	81,975			
*E Davey LD	31,103	51.12	+6.39	
A Brandreth C	20,614	33.88	-4.21	
L Werner Lab	6,528	10.73	-4.07	
S Sumner Green	1,038	1.71	+0.84	
S Holman Brexit	788	1.30		
J Giles Ind	458	0.75	+0.59	
C Chinnery Loony	193	0.32	+0.05	
R Glencross UKIP	124	0.20	-0.88	

HS; Jesus Coll, Oxford (BA PPE); Birkbeck Coll, London (MSc economics).

CHALLENGERS
Aphra Brandreth (C) Owner of a local veterinary business. Worked for ten years as an economic adviser for Defra. Cllr, Richmond LBC, 2018-. **Leanne Werner** (Lab) Development manager. Cllr, Southwark LBC,

2018-. **Sharron Sumner** (Green) Defected from Lib Dems to the Green Party in 2018. Career in business development.

CONSTITUENCY PROFILE
Created in 1997 from Kingston and Surbiton, which had both been Conservative seats, but has returned Ed Davey at every election since, with the exception of 2015, when the Tories won it back. A southwest London seat bordering Surrey, it is younger and more diverse than the UK average. More than a sixth of residents are Asian or of Asian descent. House prices are high, but not as high as some other neighbouring seats.

EU REFERENDUM RESULT
40.8% Leave   Remain 59.2%

Kingswood

MAJORITY 11,220 (22.75%)   CONSERVATIVE HOLD   TURNOUT 71.50%

CHRIS SKIDMORE
BORN May 17, 1981
MP 2010-

Minister for universities and science between 2018 and the February 2020 reshuffle. Health minister, 2019. Parly under-sec, Cabinet Office, 2016-18. PPS to George Osborne, 2015-16. Historian; wrote biographies of Edward VI and Richard III, and teaches part-time at Bristol University. Former adviser and researcher for Bristol's bid to become the European Capital City of Culture. Journalist at the *Western Daily Press*. Former adviser to Michael Gove (Surrey Heath) and David Willets. Ed: Bristol GS; Christ Church, Oxford (BA history).

	Electorate	Share %	from 2017 %	Change
	68,972			
*C Skidmore C	27,712	56.19	+1.30	
N Bowden-Jones Lab	16,492	33.44	-6.06	
D Romero LD	3,421	6.94	+3.35	
J Evans Green	1,200	2.43	+0.41	
A Cowell AWP	489	0.99		

CHALLENGERS
Nicola Bowden-Jones (Lab) NHS children's mental health specialist. Previously head of support services at a children's mental health charity. Representative, Unite. Cllr, Bristol City C, 2016-. **Dine Romero** (LD) Background in science and communications. Cllr, Bath & North East Somerset DC, 2003-; leader of the council since 2019. **Joseph Evans** (Green) Environmental planner.

CONSTITUENCY PROFILE
A safe Labour seat from 1992 until 2010 but it has been Conservative since. The Conservative vote share has increased at every election since 2005; in 2019, Chris Skidmore secured his first five-figure majority. Kingswood is a suburban seat just to the east of Bristol. Incomes are slightly lower than the regional average, and lower than in the nearby constituencies of Bristol West and Bristol North West. It has high levels of home ownership and economic activity, and construction and finance are among the most significant sectors.

EU REFERENDUM RESULT
57.1% Leave   Remain 42.9%

Kirkcaldy & Cowdenbeath

MAJORITY 1,243 (2.64%)   **SNP GAIN FROM LABOUR**   **TURNOUT 64.52%**

NEALE HANVEY
BORN Dec 28, 1964
MP 2019-

Won despite being suspended from the SNP, amid allegations of antisemitism related to social media posts he made two years ago, one about the Hungarian Jewish financier George Soros and the other comparing the treatment of Palestinians by Israel to that of Jewish people during the Second World War. Sat as an independent MP while the disciplinary process was being undertaken. Former oncology nurse and divisional nurse director at the Royal Marsden. Cllr, Fife C, 2012-17. Ed: City, University of London (MSc).

	Electorate	Share %	from 2017 % Change
	72,853		
N Hanvey SNP	16,568	35.25	-1.03
*L Laird Lab	15,325	32.60	-4.23
K Leslie C	9,449	20.10	-3.20
G Cole-Hamilton LD	2,903	6.18	+3.76
S Rutherford Green	1,628	3.46	
M William Brexit	1,132	2.41	

CHALLENGERS
Lesley Laird (Lab) MP for this constituency, 2017-19. Narrowly beat Roger Mullin of the SNP in 2017 by 259 votes. Shadow Scotland secretary, 2017-19. Career in human resources. Senior talent manager, RBS, 2009-12. **Kathleen Leslie** (C) Works with young people with additional support needs. **Gill Cole-Hamilton** (LD) Support for learning teacher. **Scott Rutherford** (Green) Researcher

in the Scottish parliament. **Mitch William** (Brexit) Criticised in 2017 for posing in a helmet similar to those worn by SS troops. Ex-soldier, served in Bosnia and Afghanistan.

CONSTITUENCY PROFILE
Formerly a safe Labour seat, held by Gordon Brown from its creation in 2005 to 2015, when it was won by the SNP following his retirement. The seat has since changed hands at each general election, with Labour winning the seat by only 259 votes in 2017. It is a coastal seat along the northern side of the Firth of Forth. Incomes are below the Scottish average.

EU REFERENDUM RESULT
43.3% Leave   Remain 56.7%

Knowsley

MAJORITY 39,942 (72.70%)   **LABOUR HOLD**   **TURNOUT 65.36%**

GEORGE HOWARTH
BORN Jun 29, 1949
MP 1986-

Deputy speaker of the Commons, 2019-. Jeremy Corbyn sceptic. Nominated Jess Phillips for leader, 2020. Opposition spokesman: home affairs, 1994-97; environment, 1989-94. Parly under-sec: Northern Ireland, 1999-2001; home affairs, 1997-99. Select cttees: panel of chairs, 2009-; finance and services, 2012-15; armed forces, 2005-06. Former engineer and teacher. MP for: Knowsley and Sefton East, 1997-2010; Knowsley North, 1986-97. Ed: Huyton Secondary Sch; Kirkby Coll; Liverpool Polytechnic (BA social sciences).

	Electorate	Share %	from 2017 % Change
	84,060		
*G Howarth Lab	44,374	80.77	-4.57
R Millns C	4,432	8.07	-1.19
T McCullough Brexit	3,348	6.09	
P Woodruff Green	1,262	2.30	+1.36
J Slupsky LD	1,117	2.03	-0.11
R Catesby Lib	405	0.74	

CHALLENGERS
Rushi Millns (C) IT professional and teacher. **Tim McCullough** (Brexit) Helps companies to manage financial risk and tackles financial crime. **Paul Woodruff** (Green) First general election campaign after contesting four local elections. **Joe Slupsky** (LD) Lecturer at the University of Liverpool. Leads a group that studies blood cancer. **Ray Catesby** (Lib) Lecturer on crime prevention.

CONSTITUENCY PROFILE
Knowsley is one of the safest seats in the country; Labour received more votes only in Bristol West. It is one of four constituencies, all in Merseyside, where Labour received a majority of at least 70 per cent over the party in second place. The predecessor seat of Huyton was held by Harold Wilson from 1950 until 1983. The seat contains Kirby in the north and Huyton in the south. Knowsley is characterised by council estates, high unemployment and lower than average income. More than a quarter of households are socially rented, well above the national average.

EU REFERENDUM RESULT
52.3% Leave   Remain 47.7%

Lagan Valley

MAJORITY 6,499 (14.31%)   DUP HOLD   TURNOUT 59.95%

SIR JEFFREY DONALDSON
BORN Dec 7, 1962
MP 1997-

	Electorate	Share %	Change from 2017 %
	75,735		
*J Donaldson DUP	19,586	43.14	-16.43
S Eastwood Alliance	13,087	28.82	+17.70
R Butler UUP	8,606	18.95	+2.19
A Haydock SDLP	1,758	3.87	-3.66
G McCleave SF	1,098	2.42	-1.07
G Hynds C	955	2.10	+1.07
A Love Ukip	315	0.69	

Became leader of DUP in the Commons after Nigel Dodds lost his seat at this election. Lifelong political activist who joined the Orange Order in his youth. Later a member, Ulster Young Unionist Council and Ulster Defence Regiment, in which he later became a corporal. Agent to Enoch Powell MP, 1982-84. Northern Ireland assembly member, Down South 1985-86, for the UUP. MLA Lagan Valley 2003-10. Defected to the DUP in 2004. Chief whip, 2015-; party's signatory to confidence and supply pact with Conservatives after the 2017 general election. Campaigned to Leave. DUP spokesman, defence, equality, energy and climate change, 2010-15. First DUP member to be knighted, in 2016 Queen's birthday honours. Ed: Castlereagh Coll.

CHALLENGERS
Sorcha Eastwood (Alliance) Contested Belfast West, 2017. **Robbie Butler** (UUP) Butcher who later became a fire and rescue officer. Contested this seat, 2017. **Ally Haydock** (SDLP) Politics student. **Gary McCleave** (SF) Cllr, Lisburn & Castlereagh City C, 2019-.

CONSTITUENCY PROFILE
Has not elected a nationalist MP since its creation in 1983 and the combined vote share of Sinn Fein and the SDLP has not reached 15 per cent since 1992. The seat is southwest of Belfast and was held by the UUP until Sir Jeffrey defected to the DUP. This was the first time since 2001 that the Alliance had finished second here. Two thirds of residents are Protestant; less than a fifth Roman Catholics.

EU REFERENDUM RESULT
53.1% Leave   Remain 46.9%

Lanark & Hamilton East

MAJORITY 5,187 (9.77%)   SNP HOLD   TURNOUT 68.34%

ANGELA CRAWLEY
BORN Jun 3, 1987
MP 2015-

	Electorate	Share %	Change from 2017 %
	77,659		
*A Crawley SNP	22,243	41.91	+9.33
S Haslam C	17,056	32.14	+0.08
A Hilland Lab	10,736	20.23	-11.64
J Pickard LD	3,037	5.72	+3.32

Once named in *Forbes* magazine's 30 Under 30 list for her work as an MP. Parliamentary assistant to: Bruce Crawford MSP; Clare Adamson MSP. Interned as a legal assistant, Aamer Anwar & Co, solicitors. Former convenor, Young Scots for Independence. Member, SNP national executive committee. Volunteer, Royal Princess Trust for Young Carers. Cllr, South Lanarkshire C, 2012-16. Select cttees: health and social care, 2019-; women and equalities, 2015-. SNP spokeswoman, defence procurement. Ed: John Ogilvie HS; University of Stirling (BA politics); University of Glasgow (LLB law).

CHALLENGERS
Shona Haslam (C) Director of Asthma UK Scotland, 2007-15. Voted Remain but supported Boris Johnson's deal. **Andrew Hilland** (Lab) Director, Inquiry on Protecting Children in Conflict. Policy adviser, Policy and Research Commission. Senior policy adviser to the office of Gordon and Sarah Brown between 2013 and 2015.

Jane Pickard (LD) Mental health counsellor. Worked in financial services.

CONSTITUENCY PROFILE
Was held by Labour from 2005 until 2015, when the SNP won it by more than 10,000. In 2017 only 360 votes separated the SNP from the third-placed Labour candidate. The Conservatives cemented their second-place position at this election. Residents in this southern Scotland seat are older than average and fewer than one in fifty are from an ethnic minority. Home ownership and typical incomes are higher than the Scottish average.

EU REFERENDUM RESULT
36.0% Leave   Remain 64.0%

Lancashire West

MAJORITY 8,336 (15.83%)   LABOUR HOLD   TURNOUT 71.80%

ROSIE COOPER
BORN Sep 5, 1950
MP 2005-

Defected from the Lib Dems in 1999 having been a Liverpool councillor since 1973 and lord mayor of Liverpool, 1992-93. Background in communications, previously at Littlewoods Organisation. Disability advocate; both of her parents were deaf. One of six Labour MPs to vote for Boris Johnson's Brexit deal after the election. Backed Lisa Nandy for leader, 2020. Vice-chairwoman, Liverpool Health Authority; chairwoman, Liverpool Women's Hospital. Target of neo-Nazi murder plot. PPS to: Ben Bradshaw, 2007-10. Contested

	Electorate	Share %	from 2017 %	Change
	73,346			
*R Cooper Lab	27,458	52.14	-6.75	
J Gilmore C	19,122	36.31	-1.09	
S Thomson LD	2,560	4.86	+2.90	
M Stanton Brexit	2,275	4.32		
J Puddifer Green	1,248	2.37	+1.12	

for the Lib Dems: Liverpool Broadgreen, 1992; Knowsley North, 1987; Liverpool Garston, 1983. Ed: Bellerive Convent GS; University of Liverpool.

CHALLENGERS
Jack Gilmore (C) Junior researcher, Daniel Kawczynski (Shrewsbury & Atcham), 2018-. Former contributor, The Bow Group. President, Durham Union Society, 2017-18. Senior member of Students for Britain, 2016. **Simon Thomson** (LD)

Information governance adviser. **Marc Stanton** (Brexit) Former lecturer.

CONSTITUENCY PROFILE
Elected Conservative MPs from its creation in 1983 but gained by Labour in 1992. Since then Labour's smallest majority has been the 4,000 votes by which it held the seat in 2010. North of Liverpool and inland from the coastal seats of Southport and Sefton Central, Lancashire West's biggest towns are Skelmersdale and Ormskirk. The seat contains Edge Hill University and its 7,000 students. It has high home ownership and incomes for the region.

EU REFERENDUM RESULT
55.0% Leave   Remain 45.0%

Lancaster & Fleetwood

MAJORITY 2,380 (5.26%)   LABOUR HOLD   TURNOUT 64.54%

CAT SMITH
BORN Jun 16, 1985
MP 2015-

Background in social work as campaigns and policy officer for the British Association of Social Workers. Led campaigns defending the Royal Lancaster Infirmary and the Fleetwood Hospital. North West regional role on NUS national executive committee. Supported Jeremy Corbyn in 2015 and 2016 and Rebecca Long Bailey in 2020. Shadow minister, voter engagement, 2016-; shadow deputy Commons leader, 2016-17. Contested Wyre & Preston North, 2010. Ed: Barrow Sixth Form Coll; Lancaster University (BA sociology, gender studies).

	Electorate	Share %	from 2017 %	Change
	70,059			
*C Smith Lab	21,184	46.85	-8.26	
L Thistlethwaite C	18,804	41.58	+0.96	
P Jackson LD	2,018	4.46	+1.92	
L Murray Brexit	1,817	4.02		
C Jackson Green	1,396	3.09	+1.36	

CHALLENGERS
Louise Thistlethwaite (C) Leadership support officer, Cumbria CC. Magistrate. Former sub-editor. Law teacher, Lancaster University, 2004-12. Voted Leave. **Peter Jackson** (LD) Businessman; runs a small company selling furnishing trimmings. Was married to Green candidate, Caroline Jackson, for 20 years. **Leanne Murray** (Brexit) Worked in the NHS. **Caroline Jackson** (Green) Cllr, Lancaster City C, 2015-.

CONSTITUENCY PROFILE
This coastal Lancashire seat, created in 2010, was won by the Conservatives on a narrow majority of 333 in that year but was a Labour gain in 2015. Although Labour's majority fell at this election, the margin of victory is still more than a thousand votes higher than it was in 2015. The predecessor seats containing Lancaster mostly elected Conservatives throughout their postwar history, with exceptions in 1966, 1997 and 2001. More than 14,000 students live in the constituency, which contains the University of Lancaster. Levels of private renting are well above average.

EU REFERENDUM RESULT
52.0% Leave   Remain 48.0%

Leeds Central

MAJORITY 19,270 (39.10%)   LABOUR HOLD   TURNOUT 54.18%

HILARY BENN
BORN Nov 26, 1953
MP 1999-

Electorate	Share %	from 2017 %	Change
90,971			
*H Benn Lab	30,413	61.71	-8.46
P Fortune C	11,143	22.61	+2.15
P Thomas Brexit	2,999	6.09	
J Holland LD	2,343	4.75	+2.52
E Carlisle Green	2,105	4.27	+1.78
W Clouston Soc Dem	281	0.57	

Sponsored legislation forcing Boris Johnson to seek a third extension to Brexit, moving the deadline from October 31, 2019 to January 31, 2020. Mr Johnson referred to it as the "surrender act" and called for the general election after it passed. Chairman, Brexit select cttee, 2016-. The fourth generation Benn in parliament; son of the late left-wing firebrand, Tony. Shadow foreign secretary, 2015-16; shadow communities and local government secretary, 2011-15; shadow Commons leader, 2010-11. Sacked from front bench after EU referendum amid rumours he was organising a coup against Jeremy Corbyn. Secretary of state: environment, 2007-10; international development, 2003-07. Ed: University of Sussex (BA Russian and east European studies).

CHALLENGERS
Peter Fortune (C) Training and development manager, Newsquest Media Group. **Paul Thomas** (Brexit) Executive officer, Highways England.

Jack Holland (LD) Associate professor of international relations, University of Leeds. **Ed Carlisle** (Green) Project manager, Leeds-based charity Together for Peace.

CONSTITUENCY PROFILE
Has returned Labour MPs since its re-creation in 1983, and with five-figure majorities at every election since 1987. Its predecessor seat, Leeds South, was held by the Labour leader Hugh Gaitskell and, following his death, by the same party's home secretary Merlyn Rees. The University of Leeds is in the constituency and about 25,000 residents are students.

EU REFERENDUM RESULT
46.0% Leave   Remain 54.0%

Leeds East

MAJORITY 5,531 (14.16%)   LABOUR HOLD   TURNOUT 58.04%

RICHARD BURGON
BORN Sep 19, 1980
MP 2015-

Electorate	Share %	from 2017 %	Change
67,286			
*R Burgon Lab	19,464	49.84	-11.52
J Mortimer C	13,933	35.68	+5.09
S Wass Brexit	2,981	7.63	
D Dresser LD	1,796	4.60	+2.82
S Adris Green	878	2.25	+1.20

Employment rights lawyer and trade union activist. Nominated Jeremy Corbyn for leader in 2015 and emerged as a key ally in aftermath of the shadow cabinet resignations in 2016. Backed Rebecca Long Bailey for leader in 2020 while standing for deputy as a fellow "continuity Corbyn" candidate. Has expressed support for the Venezuelan and Cuban regimes. Campaigned to Remain; later supported official party stance. Shadow Treasury minister, 2015-16; shadow lord chancellor and justice secretary, 2016-. Nephew of Colin Burgon, MP for Elmet, 1997-2010. Ed: Cardinal Heenan RC HS; St John's Coll, Cambridge (BA English literature; chairman, Labour Club).

CHALLENGERS
Jill Mortimer (C) Farmer and trainee barrister. Cllr, Hambleton DC, 2019-. **Sarah Wass** (Brexit) Strategic business consultant. **David Dresser** (LD) Solicitor and photographer. **Shahab Adris** (Green) Lecturer on social justice and inequality, Leeds Beckett University.

CONSTITUENCY PROFILE
Has elected only Labour MPs since its re-creation in 1955 and for much of that time it was the seat of the former defence secretary, chancellor of the exchequer and Labour deputy leader Denis Healey. Labour regularly takes more than half the votes in the seat, the only exceptions being the general elections in 1983, 1987 and 2019. It has the lowest median income of any seat in Yorkshire and the Humber and about a third of households are in the social rented sector. It is a fairly diverse seat: one in ten residents is Muslim. It also has a high rate of long-term unemployment.

EU REFERENDUM RESULT
61.4% Leave   Remain 38.6%

Leeds North East

MAJORITY 17,089 (33.84%)   LABOUR HOLD   TURNOUT 71.55%

FABIAN HAMILTON
BORN Apr 22, 1955
MP 1997-

	Electorate	Share %	Change from 2017 %
	70,580		
*F Hamilton Lab	29,024	57.47	-5.61
A Bashir C	11,935	23.63	-7.40
J Hannah LD	5,665	11.22	+7.53
R Hartshorne Green	1,931	3.82	+2.54
I Iman Brexit	1,769	3.50	
C Foote Green Soc	176	0.35	+0.13

Outspoken critic of all-women Labour shortlists in the 1990s: said that being "kept out of a job just because I'm a man offends me deeply". Supported Emily Thornberry for party leadership, 2020; backed Yvette Cooper, 2015, and Jeremy Corbyn, 2016. Remainer; voted in indicative votes for a second referendum. Rebellions over renewing Trident nuclear deterrent. Shadow Europe minister, 2016; defence, 2016-. APPG: chairman, Tibet. Cllr, Leeds City C, 1989-97. Contested this seat, 1992. Ed: University of York (BA social sciences).

CHALLENGERS
Amjad Bashir (C) Restaurateur. Suspended by the Conservatives for saying British Jews were "brainwashed extremists" when they returned from travelling in Israel; apologised. MEP, 2014-19: initially for Ukip then the Conservatives from 2015. **Jon Hannah** (LD) Teacher, former NHS senior manager. Contested this seat, 2017. **Rachel Hartshorne** (Green) Sustainability architect,

University of Leeds. **Inaya Iman** (Brexit) Project manager, Index on Censorship.

CONSTITUENCY PROFILE
Although this was once the seat of Keith Joseph, a progenitor of Thatcherism, it has been consistently Labour since 1997 and Fabian Hamilton's majority has never fallen below 4,000. Before 1997 Labour had only won the seat once, in 1945. It is one of few seats where Labour's majority increased in this election. The party was no doubt helped by the Conservative candidate's suspension for antisemitism: about one in 20 constituents is Jewish.

EU REFERENDUM RESULT
37.4% Leave   Remain 62.6%

Leeds North West

MAJORITY 10,749 (21.81%)   LABOUR CO-OP HOLD   TURNOUT 72.75%

ALEX SOBEL
BORN Apr 26, 1975
MP 2017-

	Electorate	Share %	Change from 2017 %
	67,741		
*A Sobel Lab Co-op	23,971	48.64	+4.53
S Harper C	13,222	26.83	+7.18
K Hussain LD	9,397	19.07	-15.91
M Hemingway Green	1,389	2.82	+1.56
G Webber Brexit	1,304	2.65	

Former community development worker and general manager at Social Enterprise Yorkshire and the Humber. On the team that lodged bid for Leeds's largest Sure Start scheme. PPS to Emily Thornberry, 2019-; backed her for leadership, 2020. Formed an APPG to find out how to reduce carbon emissions to net zero as early as possible. As a councillor helped to establish first new park in north Leeds in more than 50 years. Contested this seat, 2015. Regional organiser for "Yes" campaign during the 2011 AV referendum and for Ed

Miliband's leadership campaign, 2010. Member: Jewish Labour Movement; Sera, Labour's environmental movement. Born in Leeds. Ed: University of Leeds (BSc information systems).

CHALLENGERS
Stewart Harper (C) Forming consultancy and government business. Voted Leave. **Kamran Hussain** (LD) Senior partner, Whiterose Blackmans solicitors. Speaks Urdu and Punjabi. **Martin Hemingway** (Green)

Teaches geography and law. Former archaeologist. Contested this seat, 2017. **Graeme Webber** (Brexit) Solicitor, former Royal Marine commando.

CONSTITUENCY PROFILE
Returned Conservative MPs from 1950 until 1997. One of few seats where Labour's vote share rose in this election and in fact it had a bigger increase here than in Putney, the only seat that the party gained. The seat contains Leeds Metropolitan University and about 20,000 residents are students. It has the lowest unemployment rate of any Leeds seat and is the most ethnically diverse.

EU REFERENDUM RESULT
35.4% Leave   Remain 64.6%

Leeds West

MAJORITY 10,564 (26.23%)   LABOUR HOLD   TURNOUT 59.48%

RACHEL REEVES
BORN Feb 13, 1979
MP 2010-

Spent ten years as an economist at HBOS, the Bank of England and the British embassy in Washington. Spearheaded Labour's campaign against the bedroom tax. Corbyn sceptic who resigned from the front bench when he was elected leader. Backed Jess Phillips for leader, 2020. Chairwoman, business select cttee, 2017-. Shadow chief secretary to the Treasury, 2011-13; shadow work and pensions secretary, 2013-15. Younger sister, Ellie, is MP for Lewisham West & Penge. Junior chess champion. Contested Bromley & Chislehurst, 2006

	Electorate	Share %	Change from 2017 %
	67,727		
*R Reeves Lab	22,186	55.08	-8.89
M Dormer C	11,622	28.85	+2.69
P Mars Brexit	2,685	6.67	
D Walker LD	1,787	4.44	+2.29
V Smith Green	1,274	3.16	+0.74
I Cowling Yorkshire	650	1.61	+0.72
D Whetstone Soc Dem	46	0.11	
M Davies Green Soc	31	0.08	-0.03

by-election, 2005. Ed: Cator Park Sch, Bromley; New Coll, Oxford (BA PPE); LSE (MSc economics).

CHALLENGERS
Mark Dormer (C) Company director. **Phillip Mars** (Brexit) Junior doctor, former RAF officer. **Dan Walker** (LD) Computer programmer at University of Leeds. **Victoria Smith** (Green) Works for a renewable energy company and in a bicycle shop.

CONSTITUENCY PROFILE
Has been won by Labour at all but one postwar election, when the party lost the seat to a Liberal MP in Margaret Thatcher's 1983 landslide. Labour's majority has fallen below 10,000 only once in the past 30 years, in the 2010 election. This is a young constituency, with almost half of its residents aged between 16 and 45. About half of households are owner-occupied and social renting is higher than the UK average. There is above-average long-term unemployment here.

EU REFERENDUM RESULT
53.3% Leave   Remain 46.7%

Leicester East

MAJORITY 6,019 (12.18%)   LABOUR HOLD   TURNOUT 63.01%

CLAUDIA WEBBE
BORN Mar 8, 1965
MP 2019-

Career politician on the hard left of the party. NEC member, 2016-19; chairwoman of the disputes panel, 2018-19. Senior adviser to Ken Livingstone while mayor of London. Cllr, Islington BC, 2010-; cabinet member for energy, 2014. Founded Operation Trident, an advisory group to tackle the effects of gun crime on black communities. Anti-racism campaigner; former adviser, Kick Racism Out of Football. Voted Remain. Constituency Labour Party chairman resigned over Ms Webbe's selection, calling it "a fix"; a party source dismissed the claim, highlighting

	Electorate	Share %	Change from 2017 %
	78,432		
C Webbe Lab	25,090	50.77	-16.22
B Dave C	19,071	38.59	+14.39
N Dave LD	2,800	5.67	+3.10
T Baldwin Brexit	1,243	2.52	
M Wakley Green	888	1.80	-0.24
S Gogia Ind	329	0.67	-2.68

Ms Webbe's local roots. Ed: De Montfort University (BA social science); Birkbeck, University of London (MSc race relations); Nottingham University (PG socio-legal studies); University of Birmingham, Westhill Coll (community and youth work).

CHALLENGERS
Bhupen Dave (C) Former director of community care. **Nitesh Dave** (LD) Special needs chairman. Contested this seat, 2017. **Tara Baldwin** (Brexit) Worked in litigation and risk management.

CONSTITUENCY PROFILE
Has been won by Labour at every election since 1974, except when a Conservative won the seat by fewer than a thousand votes in 1983. Keith Vaz, the MP here from 1987-2019 and a former chairman of the home affairs select committee, did not stand after years of scandals about his personal conduct. This is the worst-off of Leicester's three constituencies. About half the residents are Indian or of Indian descent, including 35,000 Hindus and 22,000 Muslims.

EU REFERENDUM RESULT
54.0% Leave   Remain 46.0%

Leicester South

LABOUR CO-OP HOLD

JONATHAN ASHWORTH
BORN Oct 14, 1978
MP 2011-

Centre of attention two days before the election after he was recorded saying that Labour could not win due to the unpopularity of Jeremy Corbyn. Shadow health secretary, 2016-; shadow minister without portfolio, 2015-16. NEC deputy chairman, 2013-15. Opposition whip, 2011-13. Remainer. Backed Yvette Cooper's leadership bid in 2015, Mr Corbyn's in 2016 and Lisa Nandy's in 2020. Former Labour staffer: policy officer, 2002-04; political research officer, 2001. Special adviser to Gordon Brown. Married to Emilie Oldknow, a former

	Electorate	Share %	Change from 2017 %
	77,665		
*J Ashworth Lab Co-op	33,606	67.01	-6.54
N Neale C	10,931	21.80	+0.23
C Coghlan LD	2,754	5.49	+2.94
M Lewis Green	1,669	3.33	+1.00
J Potter Brexit	1,187	2.37	

executive director of the Labour Party and the assistant secretary general of Unison. Ed: Philips HS, Whitefield, Manchester; Bury Coll; University of Durham (BA politics and philosophy).

CHALLENGERS
Natalie Neale (C) NHS nurse and midwife for 25 years. **Chris Coghlan** (LD) Former diplomat and soldier; news commentator. **Mags Lewis** (Green) Party spokeswoman, disability. Contested this seat, 2017. **James**

Potter (Brexit) Non-practising solicitor.

CONSTITUENCY PROFILE
Has mostly had Labour MPs but it was won by the Conservatives in 1974 and 1983 and by the Lib Dem Parmjit Singh Gill at a 2004 by-election. Jonathan Ashworth became MP at a by-election in 2011 after Sir Peter Soulsby resigned to become mayor. This constituency contains the city centre and is the most affluent of Leicester's seats. It is home to the university and to more than 20,000 students. There are 33,000 Muslim residents but fewer Hindus than Leicester East.

EU REFERENDUM RESULT
42.4% Leave   Remain 57.6%

Leicester West

LABOUR HOLD

LIZ KENDALL
BORN June 11, 1971
MP 2010-

Contested Labour leadership as the Blairite candidate in 2015; came last with 4 per cent of the vote. Remainer; supported a second referendum. Opposed leadership of Jeremy Corbyn; supported Owen Smith in 2016. Backed Jess Phillips for leader, 2020. Shadow health minister, 2011-15. Primarily interested in early years policy. Associate director, Institute for Public Policy Research. Special adviser to Patricia Hewitt and Harriet Harman in early New Labour years. Later public health researcher, King's Fund. Former director: Ambulance Services

	Electorate	Share %	Change from 2017 %
	64,918		
*L Kendall Lab	17,291	49.72	-11.12
A Wright C	13,079	37.61	+6.25
I Bradwell LD	1,808	5.20	+3.09
J Collier Brexit	1,620	4.66	
A Goddard Green	977	2.81	+1.19

Network; Maternity Alliance. Member: Unite; Fabian Society. Regular panellist, BBC *This Week*. Ed: Watford Girls' GS; Queens' Coll, Cambridge (BA history).

CHALLENGERS
Amanda Wright (C) Solicitor. Cllr, Leicester City C, 2017-. **Ian Bradwell** (LD) Registered blind; disability awareness trainer. Contested this seat, 2017, 2015. **Jack Collier** (Brexit) Entrepreneur and musician. **Ani**

Goddard (Green) Selected as a 17-year-old but turned 18 in time for the election.

CONSTITUENCY PROFILE
Unlike its two neighbours Leicester West has only ever been represented by Labour MPs since its creation in 1974. It is proportionally the least ethnically and religiously diverse of the three Leicester seats, with about 6,000 Muslim and 6,000 Hindu residents. There is also a significant prevalence of routine and semi-routine work compared with the national average and the constituency has the highest proportion of socially rented households in Leicester.

EU REFERENDUM RESULT
50.8% Leave   Remain 49.2%

Leicestershire North West

MAJORITY 20,400 (37.90%)   CONSERVATIVE HOLD   TURNOUT 68.18%

ANDREW BRIDGEN
BORN Oct 28, 1964
MP 2010-

Trained in the Royal Marines, before co-founding and running an agricultural company. Criticised for implying that Jacob Rees-Mogg's comments during the campaign about the victims of the Grenfell fire, in which he appeared to suggest that they lacked "common sense", were correct. Former East Midlands chairman, Institute of Directors. Led campaign to decriminalise non-payment of the TV licence fee. Prominent critic of David Cameron, Theresa May and John Bercow: demanded a vote of confidence in Mr Cameron in 2013 but withdrew it in 2014

	Electorate	Share %	Change from 2017 %
	78,935		
*A Bridgen C	33,811	62.82	+4.64
T Eynon Lab	13,411	24.92	-8.45
G Hudson LD	3,614	6.71	+0.33
C Benfield Green	2,478	4.60	+2.55
E Nudd Ind	367	0.68	
D Liddicott Libertarian	140	0.26	

owing to lack of support. Wrote letter of no confidence in Mrs May in July 2018. Member, ERG. Chairman, Uzbekistan APPG. Ed: The Pingle Sch, Swadlincote; University of Nottingham (BSc biological sciences).

CHALLENGERS
Terri Eynon (Lab) Medical psychotherapist. **Grahame Hudson** (LD) Associate professor in design management, De Montfort University. Former

navy officer, aid monitor in Russia and arms control inspector in eastern Europe. **Carl Benfield** (Green) Chartered engineer.

CONSTITUENCY PROFILE
Has been a bellwether since its creation in 1983. After his victory in 2010 Andrew Bridgen has increased his majority at each successive election. This election marked Labour's lowest vote share since the seat's creation. Incomes are slightly above the UK average and its residents enjoy relatively high levels of home ownership. Prominent industries include manufacturing and transport.

EU REFERENDUM RESULT
60.7% Leave   Remain 39.3%

Leicestershire South

MAJORITY 24,004 (41.77%)   CONSERVATIVE HOLD   TURNOUT 71.37%

ALBERTO COSTA
BORN Nov 13, 1971
MP 2015-

Forced to resign as PPS to the secretary of state for Scotland after tabling an amendment to protect the rights of EU citizens, despite the amendment later being supported by the government and passed unopposed. Lawyer who worked in Whitehall. Consultant, Nicholas Woolf & Co, solicitors. Founded London-based law firm, Costa Carlisle. Grew up in Scotland. Voted to Remain. Loyal backbencher: has never rebelled but has differed from other party members by voting against investigations into the Iraq war and in favour of requiring pub

	Electorate	Share %	Change from 2017 %
	80,520		
*A Costa C	36,791	64.02	+2.64
T Koriya Lab	12,787	22.25	-6.26
P Knowles LD	5,452	9.49	+5.25
N Cox Green	2,439	4.24	+2.32

companies to offer landlords rent-only leases. Served on justice select cttee, 2015-17. Member, Institute of Directors. Freeman of the City of London. Contested Angus, 2010. Ed: University of Glasgow (MA LLB law); University of Strathclyde (PgDip legal practice).

CHALLENGERS
Tristan Koriya (Lab) Business consultant and army reservist. **Phil Knowles** (LD) Cllr, Harborough DC, 2010-. **Nick Cox** (Green) Retired police

officer. Contested Charnwood in the 2017 election.

CONSTITUENCY PROFILE
Has never elected anyone but a Conservative MP and the party's majority has grown at successive elections since its creation in 2010. Its predecessor seat, Blaby, was created in 1974 and also elected only Conservative MPs, including Nigel Lawson, the chancellor of the exchequer under Margaret Thatcher between 1983 and 1989. The seat contains Braunstone Town, a residential area to Leicester's immediate southwest, but beyond commuter towns the seat is mainly rural.

EU REFERENDUM RESULT
58.1% Leave   Remain 41.9%

Leigh

MAJORITY 1,965 (4.18%) CONSERVATIVE GAIN FROM LABOUR CO-OP **TURNOUT 60.68%**

JAMES GRUNDY
BORN Dec 8, 1978
MP 2019-

This constituency's first ever Conservative MP. Cllr, Wigan BC, 2008-; longest serving Conservative councillor in Leigh. Former member of the fire authority and of the Greater Manchester transport authority. Substitute member of the Greater Manchester audit committee. Campaigned for Leigh to have its own council. Regularly attends local residents' association. Voted to Leave the European Union and supported Boris Johnson's deal. Contested this seat, 2017. Ed: University of Central Lancashire (Dip HE criminology).

	Electorate	Share %	Change from 2017 %
	77,417		
J Grundy C	21,266	45.27	+9.44
*J Platt Lab Co-op	19,301	41.08	-15.12
J Melly Brexit	3,161	6.73	
M Clayton LD	2,252	4.79	+2.76
A O'Bern Ind	551	1.17	
L Peters UKIP	448	0.95	-4.98

CHALLENGERS
Joanne Platt (Lab Co-op) MP for Leigh, 2017-19. Won selection after the former Labour leadership contender Andy Burnham's decision to stand down and focus on his successful Greater Manchester mayoral bid; gained Mr Burnham's support after being his election agent in 2015. PPS to Angela Rayner, 2017-19. Voted for Mr Johnson's Brexit deal. Previously worked in marketing and advertising.

James Melly (Brexit) Runs family business. **Mark Clayton** (LD) Former managing director, IT company.

CONSTITUENCY PROFILE
A Red Wall seat in Greater Manchester that had elected Labour MPs at every election since 1922. Leigh was the largest 2017 majority, more than 9,500, to be overturned by another party at this election. It is a working-class area consisting of three former coalmining and mill towns, Leigh, Golborne and Tyldesley, and incomes are lower than in nearby seats such as Warrington North and Bolton West.

EU REFERENDUM RESULT
63.3% Leave   Remain 36.7%

Lewes

MAJORITY 2,457 (4.48%) CONSERVATIVE HOLD **TURNOUT 76.71%**

MARIA CAULFIELD
BORN Aug 6, 1973
MP 2015-

Assistant whip, 2019-. PPS to Grant Shapps, the transport secretary, 2019-. Resigned from role as vice-chairwoman for women in January 2018 in protest at Theresa May's Brexit strategy. Former NHS nurse who led specialist breast cancer research team at Royal Marsden Hospital. Volunteer shepherd, Urban Shepherd. Part-owner and shareholder, Lewes Football Club. Breast Cancer Now ambassador. Co-ordinator of the Sussex No2AV campaign against voting reform, 2011. Non-executive director, BHT Sussex housing charity.

	Electorate	Share %	Change from 2017 %
	71,503		
*M Caulfield C	26,268	47.89	-1.60
O Henman LD	23,811	43.41	+4.08
K Chappell Lab	3,206	5.84	-5.34
J Denis Green	1,453	2.65	
P Cragg ND	113	0.21	

Cllr, Brighton and Hove City C, 2007-11. Contested Caerphilly, 2010. Brexiteer. Daughter of Irish immigrant farmer; grew up on council estate in Wandsworth.

CHALLENGERS
Oli Henman (LD) Environment and human rights campaigner. Cllr, Lewes TC, 2019-. **Kate Chappell** (Lab) Executive member for the environment, Manchester City C, 2013-17. **Johnny Denis** (Green) Had contested three local elections.

CONSTITUENCY PROFILE
Maria Caulfield's majority in this East Sussex seat was cut to less than half its 2017 total. It was held by the Liberal Democrat Norman Baker from 1997 but had otherwise elected Conservatives for well over a century before that. Ms Caulfield ousted Mr Baker in 2015, winning by just over a thousand votes. This is a coastal seat between Brighton and Eastbourne. More than a quarter of residents are aged 65 or over and the seat has high levels of home ownership. There is a high rate of self-employment and constituents are comparatively affluent.

EU REFERENDUM RESULT
47.1% Leave   Remain 52.9%

Lewisham Deptford

LABOUR HOLD

VICKY FOXCROFT
BORN Mar 9, 1977
MP 2015-

Shadow culture minister, 2019-. Sceptical of Jeremy Corbyn and nominated Lisa Nandy for Labour leadership, 2020. Whip, 2015-17. Statutory instruments select committee, 2016-. Union career before parliament: finance sector officer, Unite, 2009-15; political officer, Amicus, 2005-09; research officer, AEEU, 2002-05. Cllr, Lewisham LBC 2010-14; spearheaded successful Save Lewisham Hospital campaign. Led establishment of cross-party youth violence commission, 2016. Ed: De Montfort University, Leicester (BA business studies).

	Electorate	Share %	Change from 2017 %
	80,617		
*V Foxcroft Lab	39,216	70.83	-6.22
G Haran C	6,303	11.38	-2.34
B Dean LD	5,774	10.43	+5.15
A Carey Fuller Green	3,085	5.57	+2.60
M Etienne Brexit	789	1.43	
T Bui Ind	130	0.23	
J Lloyd Green Soc	71	0.13	

CHALLENGERS
Gavin Haran (C) Executive director at JP Morgan. Manager at RBS, 2012-14. Policy adviser on financial stability at the Treasury, 2009-12.
Bobby Dean (LD) PR consultant at youth development charity.
Andrea Carey Fuller (Green) Independent advocate. Former Green housing spokeswoman.
Moses Etienne (Brexit) Local authority worker and magistrate.

CONSTITUENCY PROFILE
Has elected Labour MPs since its creation in 1974, and remained one of the safest seats in the country in 2019 after Labour had won more than three quarters of the votes cast in 2017. At this election, Vicky Foxcroft won the tenth largest vote total of any Labour MP. Deptford has the highest unemployment of the three Lewisham seats, in southeast London. More than two fifths of residents are aged between 25 and 44. Only a third of homes are owner-occupied, one of the lowest rates in the country. More than a third of its residents are black or mixed race.

EU REFERENDUM RESULT
24.4% Leave   Remain 75.6%

Lewisham East

LABOUR HOLD

JANET DABY
BORN Dec 15, 1970
MP 2018-

Selected as the Labour candidate in a 2018 by-election to replace Heidi Alexander, the MP since 2010 who resigned to become the deputy mayor of London for transport. Backed by Unison but not Momentum, and was seen as a centrist option. Nominated Sir Keir Starmer for leader in 2020. Worked in volunteer management and children's social care, acting as a registered fostering manager. Daughter of Windrush migrants from Guyana and Jamaica and grew up on a council estate, where she endured racist abuse. Cllr, Lewisham LBC, 2010-19;

	Electorate	Share %	Change from 2017 %
	67,857		
*J Daby Lab	26,661	59.49	-8.46
S Thurgood C	9,653	21.54	-1.47
A Fatukasi LD	5,039	11.24	+6.82
R Adoo-Kissi-Debrah Green	1,706	3.81	+2.11
W Pollard Brexit	1,234	2.75	
M Martin CPA	277	0.62	+0.14
M Barber Ind	152	0.34	
R Galloway Young	50	0.11	
E Mighton Ind	43	0.10	

deputy mayor. Select cttees: home affairs, 2019-; justice, 2018-19.

CHALLENGERS
Sam Thurgood (C) Advises NHS on property. **Ade Fatukasi** (LD) Management consultant aged 23. **Rosamund Adoo-Kissi-Debrah** (Green) Secondary school teacher who has become a clean-air campaigner following the death of her daughter from asthma.

CONSTITUENCY PROFILE
The Conservatives last gained this seat from Labour in 1983; it returned to Labour in 1992 and has remained so ever since. In the 2018 by-election prompted by Heidi Alexander's resignation, Labour were victorious but the seat produced the largest swing from Labour to the Lib Dems since 2004. Lewisham East is broadly similar to Lewisham Deptford, but with lower incomes and a greater proportion of black and mixed-race residents.

EU REFERENDUM RESULT
35.4% Leave   Remain 64.6%

Lewisham West & Penge

MAJORITY 21,543 (41.35%) LABOUR HOLD TURNOUT 69.83%

ELLIE REEVES
BORN Dec 11, 1980
MP 2017-

Resigned as a PPS to the shadow international development secretary in June 2018 to vote in favour of staying in the single market. Supported Sir Keir Starmer, 2020. Employment law barrister; represented employees against companies such as British Airways and Balfour Beatty. Set up a service to provide legal help to women and families facing workplace discrimination. Younger sister of Rachel Reeves (Leeds West). Justice select committee, 2017-. Married to John Cryer (Leyton & Wanstead). Ed: St Catherine's Coll, Oxford (BA jurisprudence).

	Electorate	Share %	Change from 2017 %
	74,615		
*E Reeves Lab	31,860	61.15	-5.42
A Cuthbert C	10,317	19.80	-3.22
A Feakes LD	6,260	12.02	+5.78
J Braun Green	2,390	4.59	+2.44
T Hambro Brexit	1,060	2.03	
K Hortense CPA	213	0.41	-0.20

CHALLENGERS
Aisha Cuthbert (C) Communications officer for a central London housing association. Represented Great Britain in 2017 swimming competition. Cllr, Bromley LBC, 2018-. Cllr, Lewisham LBC, 2006-14. **Alex Feakes** (LD) Physics teacher in a Bromley secondary school. **James Braun** (Green) Copywriter and netball umpire. **Teixeira Hambro** (Brexit) Businesswoman.

CONSTITUENCY PROFILE
Labour has held this southeast London seat, including its predecessor Lewisham West, since 1992. That election was the first at which Labour won the seat despite being in opposition, and the party has held it in both government and opposition since. Penge, an area of Bromley, was added to the seat in the 2010 boundary changes. Demographically the constituency is similar to the two other in Lewisham seats, but, partly because of Penge's inclusion, it is the most affluent of the three. About three in ten residents are black or mixed race.

EU REFERENDUM RESULT
34.6% Leave   Remain 65.4%

Leyton & Wanstead

MAJORITY 20,808 (46.71%) LABOUR HOLD TURNOUT 68.69%

JOHN CRYER
BORN Apr 11, 1964
MP 2010-;
1997-2005

Regular rebel under Tony Blair. Eurosceptic; voted Leave in 2016 but cautiously announced support for a second referendum in 2019. Hard-left union official and former journalist at *Tribune, Morning Star, Labour Briefing* and *The Guardian*. Did not nominate a leadership candidate in 2015 or 2020. Chairman, parliamentary Labour Party, 2015-. Member, Socialist Campaign Group. MP for Hornchurch, 1997-2005. Son of the former Labour MPs Anne and Bob Cryer. Married to Ellie Reeves (Lewisham West & Penge). Ed: Oakbank Sch,

	Electorate	Share %	Change from 2017 %
	64,852		
*J Cryer Lab	28,836	64.73	-5.08
N Khiljee C	8,028	18.02	-2.83
B Sims LD	4,666	10.47	+4.06
A Gunstock Green	1,805	4.05	+1.13
Z Jannaty Brexit	785	1.76	
H Scott Ind	427	0.96	

Keighley; Hatfield Polytechnic; London College of Printing.

CHALLENGERS
Noshaba Khiljee (C) NHS consultant in Dartford; kidney specialist and GP. **Ben Sims** (LD) Data strategist and tech consultant. Former UN technology and project leader in Africa and Latin America. **Ashley Gunstock** (Green) Former actor on ITV's *The Bill*. **Zulf Jannaty** (Brexit) IT project

manager for Lloyds Banking Group. **Henry Scott** (Ind) Youngest candidate standing; turned 18 a month before the election.

CONSTITUENCY PROFILE
This seat, including its predecessor, Leyton, has elected only Labour MPs since 1966. The party's majority has tended to be in the tens of thousands, with recent exceptions in 2005 and 2010. Almost 40 per cent of residents in this northeast London seat are aged 25 to 44. A little under half the local population is white; a quarter have Asian heritage and a quarter are black or mixed race.

EU REFERENDUM RESULT
34.8% Leave   Remain 65.2%

Lichfield

MAJORITY 23,638 (43.78%)   CONSERVATIVE HOLD   TURNOUT 70.35%

MICHAEL FABRICANT
BORN Jun 12, 1950
MP 1992-

Former broadcaster and economist. Vice-chairman, Conservative Party 2012-14; sacked after publicly opposing HS2. In July 2018 he apologised after he was accused of being Islamophobic for tweeting a degrading image of Sadiq Khan. Also criticised for having an apartheid-era flag of South Africa on the mantelpiece of his parliamentary office. Led campaign to lift ban on gay men giving blood. Government whip, 2010-12; opposition whip, 2005-10. Chartered engineer. Contested South Shields, 1987. Ed: Brighton, Hove and

	Electorate	Share %	Change from 2017 %
	76,751		
*M Fabricant C	34,844	64.53	+0.98
D Robertson Lab	11,206	20.75	-8.09
P Ray LD	5,632	10.43	+5.47
A Muckley Green	1,743	3.23	+0.58
J Madden Ind	568	1.05	

Sussex GS; Loughborough University (BSc economics & law); University of Sussex (MSc operations research).

CHALLENGERS
Dave Robertson (Lab) Organiser for the teachers' trade union. Cllr, Lichfield BC, 2019-. **Paul Ray** (LD) Solicitor. Cllr, Lichfield CC, 2019-. Contested this seat, 2017, 2015. **Andrea Muckley** (Green) International student adviser, Aston University. Cllr, Cannock Chase DC.

CONSTITUENCY PROFILE
Michael Fabricant won this seat by only 238 votes in 1997 but his majority has increased at every election since. The seat's predecessor, Staffordshire Mid, was held by the Conservative Party from 1983 until Labour won it in a 1990 by-election. One fifth of residents are aged 65 or above. In terms of average incomes, the seat is affluent compared with neighbouring seats: three quarters of households in the constituency are owner-occupied. Burntwood, a former mining town, has historically been more Labour-leaning than the constituency's rural villages.

EU REFERENDUM RESULT

57.5% Leave   Remain 42.5%

Lincoln

MAJORITY 3,514 (6.94%)   CONSERVATIVE GAIN FROM LABOUR   TURNOUT 67.71%

KARL MCCARTNEY
BORN Oct 25, 1968
MP 2019-; 2010-17

MP for this constituency, 2010-17. Brexiteer. Former magistrate, director of a communications consultancy and PR manager. Conservative researcher and agent, including for Dame Angela Rumbold. Cleared after an alleged breach of spending rules in 2015. Prosecutors said there was insufficient evidence of dishonesty to proceed. Apologised in campaign for retweeting posts by the far-right campaigner Tommy Robinson. Member, 1922 exec cttee, 2012-17. Contested this seat, 2005. Cllr, Wrothan PC, 1997-2003. Ed: Birkenhead School; University

	Electorate	Share %	Change from 2017 %
	74,778		
K McCartney C	24,267	47.93	+3.19
*K Lee Lab	20,753	40.99	-6.90
C Kenyon LD	2,422	4.78	+2.15
S Horscroft Green	1,195	2.36	+1.16
R Wilkes Brexit	1,079	2.13	
R Bradley Ind	609	1.20	+0.56
C Shaw Lib	304	0.60	

of Wales, Lampeter (BA geography); Kingston Business School (MBA).

CHALLENGERS
Karen Lee (Lab) MP for this seat, 2017-19. Mayor of Lincoln, 2012-13. Helped to form Lincoln's anti-poverty strategy as chairwoman of the council's community leadership scrutiny committee. PPS to John McDonnell, 2017-19. Former nurse. **Caroline Kenyon** (LD) Qualified barrister, magazine editor and entrepreneur. Contested this seat, 2017. **Sally Horscroft** (Green) Retired office administrator. **Reece Wilkes** (Brexit) Lawyer.

CONSTITUENCY PROFILE
From 1974 Lincoln had been a bellwether seat, but Labour's victory in 2017 was the first time the party had won here despite being in opposition since the 1970s. Karl McCartney now has the largest majority any Conservative MP has had in Lincoln since 1987. The east Midlands constituency is home to about 12,000 students.

EU REFERENDUM RESULT

57.4% Leave   Remain 42.6%

Linlithgow & Falkirk East

MAJORITY 11,266 (19.50%) **SNP HOLD** **TURNOUT 66.37%**

MARTYN DAY
BORN Mar 26, 1971
MP 2015-

Claimed the seat in 2015 from Michael Connarty, who had held it for Labour in various incarnations since the 1992 general election. Former personal banking manager at the Bank of Scotland. Member, Chartered Institute of Bankers in Scotland. Community campaigner. Cllr, West Lothian CC, 1999-2015. Select committees: European scrutiny 2018-; public accounts, 2017-18; administration, 2015-17; petitions, 2016-. SNP spokesman, development and transport. Born in Falkirk. Raised in Linlithgow. Ed: Linlithgow Academy.

	Electorate	Share %	from 2017 %	Change
	87,044			
*M Day SNP	25,551	44.23	+7.88	
C Kennedy C	14,285	24.73	-4.35	
W Milne Lab	10,517	18.20	-12.94	
S Pattle LD	4,393	7.60	+4.17	
M Bozza Brexit	1,257	2.18		
G Mackay Green	1,184	2.05		
M Tunnicliff VPP	588	1.02		

CHALLENGERS
Charles Kennedy (C) Quantity surveyor and commercial manager. Led the 2014 West Lothian Better Together campaign. **Wendy Milne** (Lab) Social worker at West Lothian council for 20 years. Joined Labour in 1983 but was thrown out in 1990 for belonging to Militant. Later joined the Scottish Socialist Party and stood against the former Labour

foreign secretary Robin Cook in 2001 in Livingston, losing her deposit. Rejoined Labour in 2006. **Sally Pattle** (LD) Bookseller.

CONSTITUENCY PROFILE
This seat and its predecessors had elected only Labour MPs going back as far as 1945, until the SNP landslide of 2015. The SNP majority fell below 3,000 in 2017. Conservatives overtook Labour in 2019 for the first time in postwar history. On the southern side of the Firth of Forth in eastern Scotland. Residents are older than average, with more than two fifths over the age of 45.

EU REFERENDUM RESULT
42.0% Leave   Remain 58.0%

Liverpool Riverside

MAJORITY 37,043 (70.17%) **LABOUR HOLD** **TURNOUT 65.73%**

KIM JOHNSON
BORN Aug 25, 1966
MP 2019-

Liverpool's first black MP, replacing Louise Ellman, who had represented the seat since 1997. Left-wing former Unison shop steward. Nominated Rebecca Long Bailey for leader, 2020. Worked for many years as a community development officer before joining the city council to work on the successful 2008 Capital of Culture bid; also worked in the adult social care department. Chairwoman, Squash Liverpool, a coffee shop and arts and health initiative in Toxteth. Black members' officer, Liverpool Labour Party. Ed: St Margaret's School.

	Electorate	Share %	from 2017 %	Change
	80,310			
K Johnson Lab	41,170	77.99	-6.56	
S Malkeson C	4,127	7.82	-1.87	
T Crone Green	3,017	5.72	+2.42	
R McAllister-Bell LD	2,696	5.11	+2.64	
D Leach Brexit	1,779	3.37		

CHALLENGERS
Sean Malkeson (C) Lecturer in engineering at Liverpool John Moores University. **Tom Crone** (Green) Energy assessor. Cllr, Liverpool City C, 2014-. **Rob McAllister-Bell** (LD) People manager at Morrisons. **David Leach** (Brexit) Retired hospital laboratory scientist who worked at the Royal Liverpool University.

CONSTITUENCY PROFILE
Has elected only Labour MPs

since its creation in 1983 and is one of the party's safest seats. No other party has received more than 10,000 votes and Labour also held the seat predecessors from 1931. Louise Ellman, the previous MP, resigned from Labour in October 2019, expressing concern over the leadership's failure to tackle antisemitism in the party. Average incomes are higher in this seat than in the other Liverpool constituencies. About 30,000 students live here, as it contains almost all of the university campus buildings in Liverpool. It also contains The Cavern Club, famous for hosting the Beatles in the early 1960s.

EU REFERENDUM RESULT
27.3% Leave   Remain 72.7%

Liverpool Walton

MAJORITY 30,520 (74.83%)   LABOUR HOLD   TURNOUT 65.12%

DAN CARDEN
BORN Oct 28, 1986
MP 2017-

Jeremy Corbyn supporter who was made shadow international development secretary in 2018. Nominated Rebecca Long Bailey for the party leadership in 2020. Accused of singing "Hey Jews" to the tune of *Hey Jude* during a 2018 coach trip, a claim he denied, highlighting his past antiracist campaigning. Beat the Liverpool mayor Joe Anderson in a controversial selection contest that led to the local party secretary quitting in protest. Former aide to the Unite boss Len McCluskey and parliamentary assistant to John Cummings MP. Member,

	Electorate	Share %	from 2017 %	Change
	62,628			
*D Carden Lab	34,538	84.68	-1.05	
A Phillips C	4,018	9.85	+1.26	
T Grant Green	814	2.00	+0.76	
D Newman LD	756	1.85	+0.34	
B Lake Lib	660	1.62		

LGBT Labour. Father was a shop steward sacked during the 1995-98 Liverpool dockers' strike. Ed: St Edward's Coll, Liverpool; London School of Economics (BSc international relations).

CHALLENGERS
Alex Phillips (C) Works in financial services. Cllr, Shropshire DC, 2017-. **Ted Grant** (Green) Vegan Society member. Contested Liverpool Wavertree, 2017. **David Newman** (LD) Career in financial services.

Contested: Bootle, 2017, 2015; Norfolk Mid, 2010.

CONSTITUENCY PROFILE
Has elected only Labour MPs since 1964 and was the party's safest seat in 2019. Previous MPs include the hard-left firebrand Eric Heffer and Steve Rotherham, who was elected mayor of Liverpool City Region in 2017. The seat had the lowest total Conservative votes of any English constituency in 2019. It is the poorest Liverpool seat in terms of average income and has the highest unemployment rate in the city. Contains Anfield and Goodison Park, the stadiums of Liverpool FC and Everton FC.

EU REFERENDUM RESULT
52.2% Leave   Remain 47.8%

Liverpool Wavertree

MAJORITY 27,085 (62.44%)   LABOUR HOLD   TURNOUT 68.36%

PAULA BARKER
BORN May 5, 1972
MP 2019-

Replaced Luciana Berger, the Labour MP since 2010, who defected to The Independent Group in protest at antisemitism before standing in Finchley & Golders Green for the Liberal Democrats in 2019. Gave a speech saying that Labour should not "retreat into soft Brexitism or continue calls for a second referendum", but suggested that her views had changed when seeking selection in this strong Remain seat. Backed by Momentum when seeking Labour nomination; nominated Rebecca Long Bailey for leader, 2020. Local government officer

	Electorate	Share %	from 2017 %	Change
	63,458			
P Barker Lab	31,310	72.18	-7.37	
C Mulhern C	4,225	9.74	-2.29	
R Kemp LD	4,055	9.35	+2.80	
A Heatherington Brexit	1,921	4.43		
K Inckle Green	1,365	3.15	+1.78	
M Coyne Lib	501	1.15		

at Halton council for 17 years, including the most recent ten as a Unison branch secretary. Previously worked for Liverpool city council.

CHALLENGERS
Catherine Mulhern (C) Lawyer and chief executive of a children's welfare charity. Former director, human rights and rule of law organisations in the UK and Africa. **Richard Kemp** (LD) Partner in community business

consultancy. Previously worked on overseas regeneration projects. Cllr, Liverpool City C, 1992-; 1975-84.

CONSTITUENCY PROFILE
Having been re-created in 1997, this seat has only ever elected Labour MPs, although a previous incarnation of the seat elected Conservative MPs at general elections from 1923 until 1983. Labour has not won less than half the votes in Wavertree since 1997. It is home to about 10,000 students and has a significant Northern Irish population, albeit smaller than Liverpool Riverside's. A quarter of households rent privately.

EU REFERENDUM RESULT
35.3% Leave   Remain 64.7%

Liverpool West Derby

MAJORITY 29,984 (68.16%) **LABOUR HOLD** **TURNOUT 67.02%**

IAN BYRNE
BORN May 10, 1960
MP 2019-

Socialist who replaced Stephen Twigg, the MP for this seat since 2010 and a former deputy leader of the Commons, schools minister, shadow education secretary and chairman of the international development select committee. Supported by John McDonnell and Momentum in selection process, which he won by two votes. Apologised after he was criticised for a social media post from 2013 that appeared to make light of domestic violence. Organiser for Unite. Worked as a printer for 24 years; made redundant three times. Co-founded Fans Supporting

	Electorate	Share %	from 2017 % Change
	65,640		
I Byrne Lab	34,117	77.56	-5.19
T Bradley C	4,133	9.40	-0.49
R Pearson Brexit	2,012	4.57	
S Radford Lib	1,826	4.15	-0.61
P Parr LD	1,296	2.95	+1.74
W Ward Green	605	1.38	+0.65

Foodbanks, 2015. Nominated Rebecca Long Bailey for the leadership in 2020.

CHALLENGERS
Tom Bradley (C) Business consultant. Started career working in family's restaurant. **Ray Pearson** (Brexit) Lost his deposit. **Steve Radford** (Lib) Cllr, Liverpool City C, 1984-, 1981-83. Liverpool's first out gay councillor. Contested every election since 1997. **Paul Parr**

(LD) Management consultant. Cllr, Liverpool City C, 2007-11.

CONSTITUENCY PROFILE
Has elected only Labour MPs since the 1964 general election, although before then it mainly elected Conservative MPs. As with the other Liverpool constituencies, it is one of Labour's safest in parliament, and one of seven seats where the party's margin of victory was more than 66 per cent. Slightly more suburban than the other Liverpool seats, and it has a long border with Huyton and Knowsley. Unemployment and social renting are both relatively high.

EU REFERENDUM RESULT
49.8% Leave   Remain 50.2%

Livingston

MAJORITY 13,435 (24.61%) **SNP HOLD** **TURNOUT 66.35%**

HANNAH BARDELL
BORN Jun 1, 1983
MP 2015-

Former producer on GMTV who became Alex Salmond's office manager, 2007-10. SNP spokeswoman for digital, culture, media and sport 2018-. Party's group leader: trade and investment, 2017-18; small business, enterprise and innovation, 2015-17; fair work and employment, 2015. Persuaded by Mr Salmond to work on the SNP's 2007 Holyrood election campaign, producing SNP TV online. Formerly worked for the US State Department in its Edinburgh consulate, managing protocol and press. Held

	Electorate	Share %	from 2017 % Change
	82,285		
*H Bardell SNP	25,617	46.92	+6.86
D Timson C	12,182	22.31	-2.06
C Kane Lab	11,915	21.83	-10.85
C Dundas LD	3,457	6.33	+3.45
C Glasgow Green	1,421	2.60	

communications roles at the manufacturing and engineering firms Stork and Subsea 7. Won Pushkin Prize for writing as a teenager. Ed: Broxburn Academy; University of Stirling (MA film and media; politics and English).

CHALLENGERS
Damian Timson (C) Former RAF serviceman and Scottish rugby panel referee. **Caitlin Kane** (Lab) Communications officer for Neil Findlay MSP.

Charles Dundas (LD) Advocate and policy adviser for an environmental charity.

CONSTITUENCY PROFILE
Held by the New Labour foreign secretary Robin Cook from 1983 until his death in 2005. His successor, Jim Devine, was suspended from the party after he was convicted of false accounting during the expenses scandal. Like most Scottish seats, the SNP won Livingston in 2015. The 2019 election was the first time since the seat's creation that the Conservatives had come second. A West Lothian seat bordering two of the Edinburgh constituencies.

EU REFERENDUM RESULT
43.3% Leave   Remain 56.7%

Llanelli

MAJORITY 4,670 (12.21%) **LABOUR HOLD** TURNOUT 63.18%

NIA GRIFFITH
BORN Dec 4, 1956
MP 2005-

Shadow defence secretary since 2016; clashed with Jeremy Corbyn over Nato and Trident renewal. Nominated Emily Thornberry for leader, 2020. PPS to: Harriet Harman, 2008-10; Hilary Benn, 2007-08. Shadow Wales secretary, 2015-16. Shadow minister: Wales, 2011-15; business, 2010-11. Former language teacher and schools inspector. Cllr, Carmarthen TC, 1987-99; Carmarthen sheriff, 1997-98; deputy mayor, 1998-99. Ed: Newland HS for Girls; Somerville Coll, Oxford (BA modern languages); University of Wales, Bangor (PGCE).

	Electorate	Share %	Change from 2017 %
	60,513		
*N Griffith Lab	16,125	42.18	-11.29
T Reay C	11,455	29.96	+6.30
M Arthur PC	7,048	18.43	+0.21
S Boucher Brexit	3,605	9.43	

CHALLENGERS
Tamara Reay (C) Business career including senior roles at Sainsbury's and Abbey National. Brexiteer. **Mari Arthur** (PC) Director, Sustain Wales charity. Marketing and business strategist. Founder, Mari Arthur Marketing. Board member, Keep Wales Tidy. Contested this seat, 2017. **Susan Boucher** (Brexit) Former Ukip member who planned to sell her house and retire to Spain with her husband. Contested Blaenau Gwent in 2015 for Ukip.

CONSTITUENCY PROFILE
Coastal south Wales seat to the northwest of Swansea that has been held by Labour for almost 100 years. Although it could still be considered a safe seat, Labour's majority has been on a downward trend. The party won the seat with five-figure majorities at every election between 1931 and 1997, but has only managed this feat once since 2001, when Nia Griffith won 12,000 votes more than the Conservative candidate in 2017. Labour's majority in 2019, however, was its lowest since 1924. Llanelli itself, a former mining town, is home to about 50,000 people.

EU REFERENDUM RESULT

56.7% Leave   Remain 43.3%

Londonderry East

MAJORITY 9,607 (24.44%) **DUP HOLD** TURNOUT 56.76%

GREGORY CAMPBELL
BORN Feb 15, 1953
MP 2001-

Staunchly opposed to Irish Language Act and barred for two days from speaking in the Northern Ireland assembly after yawning over a Sinn Fein member speaking Irish. One of 21 MPs who voted against LGBT-inclusive sex and relationship education in English schools in March 2019. DUP spokesman, international development, Cabinet Office. Former civil servant and director of the publisher Causeway Press. MLA for East Londonderry, 1998-2016. Member, Northern Ireland forum for political dialogue, 1996-98. Contested:

	Electorate	Share %	Change from 2017 %
	69,246		
*G Campbell DUP	15,765	40.11	-7.96
C Hunter SDLP	6,158	15.67	+4.89
D Nicholl SF	6,128	15.59	-10.93
C McCaw Alliance	5,921	15.07	+8.88
R Holmes UUP	3,599	9.16	+1.52
S McNicholl Aontu	1,731	4.40	

this seat, 1997; Foyle, 1992, 1987, 1983. Cllr, Londonderry CC, 1981-2011. Ed: Londonderry Tech Coll; Magree Coll (political studies).

CHALLENGERS
Cara Hunter (SDLP) Graduate in journalism aged 24. Cllr, Derry City and Strabane DC, 2019-; deputy mayor. **Dermot Nicholl** (SF) Cllr: Causeway Coast and Glens BC, 2014-; Coleraine BC, 2011-14. **Chris McCaw** (Alliance)

Worked with Invest Northern Ireland. **Richard Holmes** (UUP) Managing director of manufacturing firm based in Antrim. **Sean McNicholl** (Aontu) GP registrar.

CONSTITUENCY PROFILE
This seat has always been held by unionists since its creation in 1983. The Democratic Unionist Party gained it from the Ulster Unionist Party in 2001. The SDLP overtook Sinn Fein for the first time since 2001 in 2019. Mainly a rural constituency in the northwest. It has high rates of economic inactivity for the region, with a large number of over-65s and students.

EU REFERENDUM RESULT

48.0% Leave   Remain 52.0%

Loughborough

MAJORITY 7,169 (13.12%)   CONSERVATIVE HOLD   TURNOUT 68.48%

JANE HUNT
BORN Jun 4, 1966
MP 2019-

Senior caseworker to Nicky Morgan before the culture secretary and former Treasury select committee chairwoman stepped down in 2019 and became Baroness Morgan of Cotes. Worked for seven years in a management role at the Ministry of Justice and in corporate management before that. Has lived in Quorn, Loughborough, since 1995. Contested: Nottingham South, 2017, 2015; Leicester South by-election, 2011; Leicester East, 2010. Ed: Congleton GS; Brunel University (BSc government politics and history).

	Electorate	Share %	from 2017 %	Change
	79,776			
J Hunt C	27,954	51.17	+1.26	
S Brady Lab	20,785	38.05	-3.97	
I Sharpe LD	4,153	7.60	+4.02	
W Walton Green	1,504	2.75	+0.96	
Q Tea Ind	235	0.43		

CHALLENGERS
Stuart Brady (Lab) Barrister at Rope Walk Chambers, Nottingham. Former professional rugby player for Saracens, 2001-03, earning a call-up to the England under-19s. Formerly worked in the European parliament for the Scottish Labour MEP David Martin. **Ian Sharpe** (LD) Retired accountant. **Wes Walton** (Green) Mechanical engineering student at Loughborough University aged 22.

CONSTITUENCY PROFILE
Elected Labour MPs consistently until 1979. Since that election the seat has been won by whichever party has won a plurality of seats in parliament. It consists of the north Leicestershire town of Loughborough and much of the rural area around it, including the smaller towns of Shepsed, Quorn and Barrow upon Soar. The seat contains Loughborough University and about 16,000 of its students. Education and manufacturing are among the overrepresented industries. Unemployement is lower than average and there is less poor public health than nationally.

EU REFERENDUM RESULT
50.1% Leave   Remain 49.9%

Louth & Horncastle

MAJORITY 28,868 (55.16%)   CONSERVATIVE HOLD   TURNOUT 65.70%

VICTORIA ATKINS
BORN Mar 22, 1976
MP 2015-

Junior minister in the Home Office since 2017. Had her responsibility for drug policy removed in 2019 after being criticised over the "political vetting" of candidates for the Advisory Council on the Misuse of Drugs. Minister for women, 2018-20. Former criminal barrister. Serious organised crime specialist, Red Lion Chambers; added to attorney general's regulators panel and Serious Fraud Office's list of specialist fraud prosecutors. Contested Gloucestershire PCC, 2012. Daughter of the former Conservative minister Sir Robert

	Electorate	Share %	from 2017 %	Change
	79,648			
*V Atkins C	38,021	72.65	+8.73	
E Green Lab	9,153	17.49	-9.21	
R Pepper LD	4,114	7.86	+4.09	
T Arty-Pole Loony	1,044	1.99	+1.06	

Atkins. Ed: Corpus Christi Coll, Cambridge (BA law).

CHALLENGERS
Ellie Green (Lab) Accounting assistant, Oxfam. Former library assistant, broadcaster and proofreader. **Ross Pepper** (LD) Project administrator for a marketing and design agency. Contested: Lincoln, 2015; Sleaford & North Hykeham, 2017, 2016 by-election. **The Iconic Arty-Pole** (Loony) Real name Peter Hill. Contested this seat, 2017.

CONSTITUENCY PROFILE
A safe seat. The Conservative majority has grown at every election since its creation in 1997. Louth & Horncastle's previous MP was Sir Peter Tapsell, who was the father of the House during the 2010-15 parliament, having represented this seat and its predecessors from 1966. This is a large and sparsely populated constituency in Lincolnshire, facing out towards the North Sea. More than 30 per cent of the population is aged 65 or above and home ownership, especially outright ownership without a mortgage, is above the national average. The seat retains a small fishing industry.

EU REFERENDUM RESULT
68.9% Leave   Remain 31.1%

Ludlow

MAJORITY 23,648 (47.08%)　　　**CONSERVATIVE HOLD**　　　**TURNOUT 72.23%**

PHILIP DUNNE
BORN Aug 14, 1958
MP 2005-

Privy councillor and health minister, 2016-18. Chairman, environmental audit cttee, 2020-. Faced calls for suspension from the Conservative Party for telling Kuldip Sahota, the Labour candidate, at a hustings in 2019 that he was "talking through his turban". Voted Remain but later embraced Brexit. Managed Jeremy Hunt's leadership campaign, 2019. Defence procurement minister, 2015-16. Other cttees: European statutory instruments, 2018-; Treasury, 2007-08; public accounts, 2006-09; work and pensions, 2005-06. Businessman and

	Electorate	Share %	Change from 2017 %
	69,442		
*P Dunne C	32,185	64.08	+1.18
H Kidd LD	8,537	17.00	+6.32
K Sahota Lab	7,591	15.11	-9.19
H Wendt Green	1,912	3.81	+1.70

banker. Former director, Juvenile Diabetes Research Foundation. Grandson and great-grandson of MPs. Ed: Eton Coll; Keble Coll, Oxford (BA PPE).

CHALLENGERS
Heather Kidd (LD) Cllr, Shropshire C, 2009-. Former teacher. Local campaigner. Contested this seat, 2017, 2015. **Kuldip Sahota** (Lab) Business owner. Cllr, Telford & Wrekin C, 2001-; leader, 2011-16. Contested Telford, 2017. **Hilary Wendt** (Green) Worked in mental

health services. Contested this seat, 2017.

CONSTITUENCY PROFILE
With the exception of the 2001 election, when a Liberal Democrat won the seat, Ludlow has returned Conservative MPs at every election since the First World War. It is a large constituency made up of several small towns and a big area of rural Shropshire, with Birmingham to its east and Wales to its west. Nearly 30 per cent of residents are aged 65 or over and less than a quarter are under the age of 25. Home ownership and the proportion of self-employed residents are high.

EU REFERENDUM RESULT
57.9% Leave　　　Remain 42.1%

Luton North

MAJORITY 9,247 (21.71%)　　　**LABOUR HOLD**　　　**TURNOUT 62.46%**

SARAH OWEN
BORN Jan 11, 1983
MP 2019-

First female MP of Chinese descent. Worked as a political adviser to Lord Sugar. Helped to develop Labour's national small business policy. Nominated Lisa Nandy for the leadership, 2020. Political officer for the GMB. Worked as an NHS care worker and in the London Fire Brigade's emergency planning department. Served on the Labour NEC. Chairwoman, Chinese for Labour. Raised awareness of miscarriage after suffering one in 2018. Contested Hastings & Rye, 2015. Ed: Sussex University (BA international relations and human rights).

	Electorate	Share %	Change from 2017 %
	68,185		
S Owen Lab	23,496	55.17	-8.67
J Bains C	14,249	33.46	+0.42
L Jack LD	2,063	4.84	+3.11
S Sharma Brexit	1,215	2.85	
S Hall Green	771	1.81	+0.42
M Rehman Ind	646	1.52	
S Laidley Women	149	0.35	

CHALLENGERS
Jeet Bains (C) Cllr, Croydon LBC, 2010-. Management consultant. Representative, Addiscombe and Shirley Park Residents' Association. **Linda Jack** (LD) Financial consultant. Cllr, Bedford BC, 2002-07. Contested: Bedfordshire Mid, 2015, 2010; this seat, 2005. **Sudhir Sharma** (Brexit) Property developer. **Simon Hall** (Green) Contested this seat, 2017.

CONSTITUENCY PROFILE
Has elected Labour MPs since 1997, having originally elected a Conservative when the seat was created in 1983. The former Labour MP Kelvin Hopkins, a shadow culture secretary in 2016, was suspended in November 2017 over sexual harassment allegations and did not stand in 2019. Incomes are slightly higher than in Luton South, although both figures are significantly lower than the east of England average. More than a quarter of the constituency's residents are of Asian descent. Transport-related jobs are among the most common sources of work.

EU REFERENDUM RESULT
59.2% Leave　　　Remain 40.8%

Luton South

RACHEL HOPKINS
BORN Mar 30, 1972
MP 2019-

HR professional at the Human Fertilisation and Embryology Authority. Worked as a review manager at the Electoral Commission. Cllr, Luton BC, 2011-. Nominated Rebecca Long Bailey for leader, 2020. Daughter of Kelvin Hopkins, the MP for Luton North, 1997-2019. Ed: Luton Sixth Form Coll; Leicester University (BA French and politics); Bedfordshire University (MSc human resource management).

CHALLENGERS
Parvez Akhtar (C) Engine design specialist. Contested

	Electorate	Share %	from 2017 %	Change
	69,338			
R Hopkins Lab	21,787	51.79	-10.64	
P Akhtar C	13,031	30.98	-1.27	
*G Shuker ND	3,893	9.25		
G Warren Brexit	1,601	3.81		
B Foley Green	995	2.37	+1.41	
M Ashraf Ind	489	1.16	+0.82	
J French Luton	268	0.64		

Bedford mayoral elections, 2009. **Gavin Shuker** (ND) MP for this seat, 2010-19. Lost a motion of confidence by his constituency party, 2018; subsequently resigned from Labour and co-founded Change UK in February 2019 but left that party too in June 2019 to sit as an independent. Shadow international development minister, 2013-15, resigning in opposition to Jeremy Corbyn's

leadership. Church pastor. **Gary Warren** (Brexit) Works in construction. **Ben Foley** (Green) Contested Bedford BC, 2019.

CONSTITUENCY PROFILE
The seat was Conservative from 1983, but has been Labour since 1997. The journalist and presenter Dame Esther Rantzen stood as an independent here in 2010, narrowly losing her deposit. Contains a University of Bedfordshire campus and about 12,000 students live in the constituency. The seat has a large Asian community, about 15,000 of whom are of Pakistani heritage. More than a quarter of households rent privately.

EU REFERENDUM RESULT
54.6% Leave   Remain 45.4%

Macclesfield

DAVID RUTLEY
BORN Mar 7, 1961
MP 2010-

Government whip since 2017 and parliamentary under-secretary for food and animal welfare, 2018-19. Voted Remain but later embraced Brexit. Immigration minister, 2010-12. PPS to: Amber Rudd, 2016-17; Stephen Crabb (Preseli Pembrokeshire), 2016; Sir Iain Duncan Smith (Chingford & Wood Green), 2015-16. Career as a senior executive and marketing director: Barclays, Halifax General Insurance, Asda Stores, Pepsi Co. Special adviser to the Cabinet Office, ministry of agriculture, Treasury, 1994-96. One of three known Mormons

	Electorate	Share %	from 2017 %	Change
	76,216			
*D Rutley C	28,292	52.52	-0.13	
N Puttick Lab	17,581	32.64	-4.17	
N Christian LD	5,684	10.55	+4.38	
J Booth Green	2,310	4.29	+2.05	

in the Commons. Contested St Albans, 1997. Ed: Priory Sch, Lewes; LSE (BSc economics); Harvard University (MBA).

CHALLENGERS
Neil Puttick (Lab) Former youth worker. Cllr, Macclesfield TC, 2015-. Works for an agency supporting digital businesses in the North. Contested this seat, 2017. **Neil Christian** (LD) Barrister working in family, chancery and personal injury. Contested: this seat, 2015; European parliament, 2014.

James Booth (Green) Barrister specialising in personal injury claims. Contested this seat, 2017.

CONSTITUENCY PROFILE
A safe Conservative seat that has been held by the party since 1918. The Conservative majority has never fallen below 5,000 in the past 50 years. A commuter town to Manchester, Macclesfield used to be one of the world's biggest producers of finished silk. There is considerable inequality but low unemployment and high levels of home ownership. It has a thriving manufacturing industry and is home to Astra Zeneca pharmaceuticals.

EU REFERENDUM RESULT
47.2% Leave   Remain 52.8%

Maidenhead

    CONSERVATIVE HOLD

THERESA MAY
BORN Oct 1, 1956
MP 1997-

	Electorate	Share %	from 2017 %	Change
	76,668			
*T May C	32,620	57.74	-7.02	
J Reynolds LD	13,774	24.38	+13.15	
P McDonald Lab	7,882	13.95	-5.38	
E Tomalin Green	2,216	3.92	+2.37	

Prime minister and leader of the Conservative Party, 2016-19. Stayed on as a backbencher after tearful resignation outside Downing Street. Low-profile Remainer in 2016. Promised in first speech as PM to tackle the nation's "burning injustices" but her premiership was consumed by trying to ensure Brexit meant Brexit. Called snap election in 2017 hoping to increase her majority but it resulted in the loss of 13 seats, and with it her majority. Found in contempt of parliament in 2018 for refusing MPs access to Brexit legal advice. Negotiated a withdrawal agreement that suffered three historic defeats in the Commons, culminating in her resignation. Praised for her diligence but mocked for her robotic style. Longest-serving home secretary for 60 years, 2010-16; oversaw cuts to the police, the creation of the National Crime Agency and the "hostile environment" immigration regime. Women and equalities minister, 2010-12. Chairwoman of the Conservative Party, 2002-03; famously said at its 2002 conference that it was seen as the "nasty party".

Contested: Barking, 1994 by-election; Durham North West, 1992. Ed: St Hugh's Coll, Oxford (BA geography).

CHALLENGERS
Joshua Reynolds (LD) Product consultant. **Patrick McDonald** (Lab) Contested this seat, 2017, 2010. **Emily Tomalin** (Green) Solar energy engineer.

CONSTITUENCY PROFILE
A safe Conservative seat since its creation in 1997. Part of the "silicon corridor" along the M4 motorway because of its thriving software industries. Many residents commute to Slough, Reading and London.

EU REFERENDUM RESULT
45.0% Leave   Remain 55.0%

Maidstone & The Weald

    CONSERVATIVE HOLD

HELEN GRANT
BORN Sep 28, 1961
MP 2010-

	Electorate	Share %	from 2017 %	Change
	76,110			
*H Grant C	31,220	60.41	+4.05	
D Wilkinson Lab	9,448	18.28	-3.83	
J Willis LD	8,482	16.41	+0.06	
S Jeffery Green	2,172	4.20	+2.49	
Y Kenward Ind	358	0.69	+0.36	

Vice-chairwoman of the Conservative Party, 2018-19. Minister for sport and tourism, 2013-15. First black woman Conservative MP. Campaigned to Remain; consistently backed Theresa May's withdrawal agreement. Voted for Boris Johnson in 2019 leadership contest. Parly under-sec: equalities, 2012-15; justice, 2012-13. Solicitor, founded firm; specialist in family law. Trustee, Social Mobility Foundation. Sat on reform commission for Centre for Social Justice. Non-executive director, Croydon Primary Care Trust, 2005-07.

Special adviser to Sir Oliver Letwin, 2006-10. Ed: St Aidan's CS, Carlisle; University of Hull (LLB); Coll of Law.

CHALLENGERS
Dan Wilkinson (Lab) Trade union representative and community campaigner. **James Willis** (LD) Small business owner. Cllr, Maidstone BC, 2014-18. Contested Gravesham, 2017. **Stuart Jeffery** (Green) NHS manager. Contested this seat, 2017, 2010.

CONSTITUENCY PROFILE
The seat has elected Conservatives at every election since its creation in 1997. It was held by the right-wing minister and TV personality Ann Widdecombe until 2010. Most of the electorate live in urban Maidstone, which is dominated by the service sector. Many of the residents of this Kent constituency commute to London. Home ownership is above average, with private sector renting also slightly above average. Unemployment is low and a significant proportion of the population work in public administration and defence, as well as construction.

EU REFERENDUM RESULT
55.9% Leave   Remain 44.1%

Makerfield

MAJORITY 4,740 (10.71%)　　　　　LABOUR HOLD　　　　　TURNOUT 59.66%

YVONNE FOVARGUE
BORN Nov 29, 1956
MP 2010-

Resigned as a shadow minister in 2019 to vote against a second Brexit referendum. Voted Remain; later embraced Brexit. Backed Lisa Nandy in the 2020 Labour leadership contest, and Owen Smith in 2016. Shadow minister: housing, communities and local government, 2017-18; business, 2015-16; defence, 2015, 2013-14; education, 2014-15; transport, 2013. Opposition whip, 2011-13. APPGs: consumer protection; debt and personal finance; legal aid. Citizens Advice parliamentarian of the year, 2011. Career as a housing officer in Manchester. Member of Mensa.

	Electorate	Share %	Change from 2017 %
	74,190		
*Y Fovargue Lab	19,954	45.08	-15.10
N King C	15,214	34.37	+3.05
R Wright Brexit	5,817	13.14	
J Skipworth LD	2,108	4.76	+1.95
S Shaw Green	1,166	2.63	

Cllr, Warrington BC, 2004-10. Ed: Sale GS; University of Leeds (BA English).

CHALLENGERS
Nick King (C) Head of business, Centre for Policy Studies. Lead policy adviser to Sajid Javid (Bromsgrove), 2014-17. **Ross Wright** (Brexit) Lifelong Makerfield resident. **John Skipworth** (LD) Retired educational consultant. Contested this seat in the previous two elections.

CONSTITUENCY PROFILE
Makerfield and its predecessor seat, Ince, have been held by the Labour Party since 1906, making it Labour's longest continuously-held constituency. The party's majority in the seat last fell below five figures in 1931. The seat contains a central part of Wigan, the second most populous borough in Greater Manchester. The area is predominantly working class and incomes tend to be lower than average. There are high levels of home ownership and low levels of social renting. Since the decline of coalmining, construction has become a significant industry.

EU REFERENDUM RESULT
64.9% Leave　　　　Remain 35.1%

Maldon

MAJORITY 30,041 (59.60%)　　　　CONSERVATIVE HOLD　　　　TURNOUT 69.39%

JOHN WHITTINGDALE
BORN Oct 16, 1959
MP 1992-

Minister for media and data, 2020-. Veteran backbencher who served as Margaret Thatcher's political secretary in 1988-90. Brexiteer; opposed Theresa May's withdrawal agreement and supported no-deal. Backed Boris Johnson in the 2019 leadership election. Culture secretary, 2015-16, having been chairman of the culture select committee, 2005-15, and played a central role in its inquiries into the phone hacking scandal. Vice-chairman, 1922 cttee, 2010-15. Shadow secretary: culture, 2004-05, 2002-03; environment, 2003-04; trade and industry, 2001-02. Brexit select

	Electorate	Share %	Change from 2017 %
	72,641		
*J Whittingdale C	36,304	72.02	+4.07
S Capper Lab	6,263	12.42	-8.85
C Baldy LD	5,990	11.88	+7.54
J Band Green	1,851	3.67	+1.53

cttee, 2016-. PPS to William Hague, 1999-2001. Worked for NM Rothschilds. Awarded an OBE in 1990 resignation honours. Ed: Winchester Coll; UCL (BSc economics).

CHALLENGERS
Stephen Capper (Lab) Director, Core Education UK, 2012-. Former head teacher. Trustee, the Museum of Power, 2017-. **Colin Baldy** (LD) Professional opera singer and visiting music professor. Inspired to stand after the death of his husband,

citing John Whittingdale's mixed record on equality.

CONSTITUENCY PROFILE
This Essex constituency is a Conservative stronghold, last held by the Labour Party between 1945 and 1955, and by only Conservative MPs ever since. The seat has a mostly middle class and affluent demographic, with generally high-skilled jobs in the largely rural area. Maldon has a high proportion of older residents, high levels of home ownership and extremely low levels of social renting and unemployment. Maldon sea salt is produced in the area.

EU REFERENDUM RESULT
61.0% Leave　　　　Remain 39.0%

Manchester Central

MAJORITY 29,089 (55.63%)   **LABOUR CO-OP HOLD**   **TURNOUT 55.48%**

LUCY POWELL
BORN Oct 10, 1974
MP 2012-

Shadow education secretary, 2015-16, who resigned in protest at Jeremy Corbyn's leadership. Did not nominate anyone in 2020 leadership contest but supported Owen Smith in 2016 and Andy Burnham in 2015. Voted Remain and for a second referendum. Manchester's first female Labour MP. Vice-chairwoman, Labour general election campaign, 2015. Shadow minister: Cabinet Office, 2014-15; education, 2013-14. Select cttees: education, 2017-; transport, 2012-13. APPGs: families in early years (chairwoman); miscarriages of justice (vice-chairwoman). Chief

	Electorate	Share %	Change from 2017 %
	94,247		
*L Powell Lab Co-op	36,823	70.42	-6.99
S Jaradat C	7,734	14.79	+0.62
J Bridges LD	3,420	6.54	+3.17
S Chadwick Brexit	2,335	4.47	
M Horrocks Green	1,870	3.58	+1.87
D Leech Soc Eq	107	0.20	

of staff to Ed Miliband, 2010-12; managed his 2010 leadership campaign. Ed: Xaverian Coll, Manchester; Somerville Coll, Oxford (BSc chemistry); King's Coll London (MSc chemistry).

CHALLENGERS
Shahden Jaradat (C) Research strategy co-ordinator of science and engineering, University of Manchester. Contested Manchester Gorton, 2017. **John Bridges** (LD) Cllr, Manchester

City C, 1993-2010, 1987-88. Political officer, Association of Liberal Democrat Councillors. Contested this seat, 2017.

CONSTITUENCY PROFILE
A safe Labour seat, held continuously by the party since 1935, if predecessors are included. The seat contains the University of Manchester and approximately three in ten residents are students. The seat has an ethnically diverse population that is 15 per cent Asian and Asian British. Levels of social renting are among the highest in the country; unemployment and child poverty are also high.

EU REFERENDUM RESULT
36.4% Leave   Remain 63.6%

Manchester Gorton

MAJORITY 30,339 (68.11%)   **LABOUR HOLD**   **TURNOUT 58.29%**

AFZAL KHAN
BORN Apr 5, 1958
MP 2017-

Made shadow immigration minister in 2017, three weeks after first being elected. Voted Remain and supported a second referendum. Nominated Emily Thornberry for leader, 2020. APPGs: British-Pakistan trade and tourism (chairman); adult social care (vice-chairman); British Muslims; immigration detention. Former Greater Manchester police officer who retrained as a solicitor and became a partner at Mellor & Jackson. MEP for the North West, 2014-17. Cllr, Manchester City C, 2000-14. Awarded a CBE in 2008 for work in local

	Electorate	Share %	Change from 2017 %
	76,419		
*A Khan Lab	34,583	77.64	+1.29
S Lowe C	4,244	9.53	+2.23
J Pearcey LD	2,448	5.50	-0.16
E Tyrrell Green	1,697	3.81	+1.55
L Kaya Brexit	1,573	3.53	

government and community cohesion. Manchester's first Muslim lord mayor, 2005-06. Born in Pakistan; moved to Britain aged 11. Ed: Manchester Polytechnic (BA law).

CHALLENGERS
Sebastian Lowe (C) Cllr, Rugby BC, 2017-. Practice leader, Laing O'Rourke PLC, a multinational construction company. **Jackie Pearcey** (LD) Works in IT. Cllr, Manchester City C, 1991-2012. Contested this seat, 2017. **Eliza**

Tyrrell (Green) Business analyst. Contested Manchester City C, 2019.

CONSTITUENCY PROFILE
Labour's biggest majority by percentage in any seat outside Merseyside and a safe seat for the party since the 1930s. It was held by Sir Gerald Kaufman, the "Father of the House" in the 2015-17 parliament, for 34 years until his death in February 2017. Has a large student population and is one of the most diverse seats in the country: 30 per cent of residents are Asian or Asian British and a further 15 per cent are black or mixed race. Nearly half of children live in poverty.

EU REFERENDUM RESULT
38.2% Leave   Remain 61.8%

Manchester Withington

MAJORITY 27,905 (52.66%)   **LABOUR HOLD**   TURNOUT 69.25%

JEFF SMITH
BORN Jan 26, 1963
MP 2015-

	Electorate	Share %	Change from 2017 %
	76,530		
*J Smith Lab	35,902	67.75	-3.94
J Leech LD	7,997	15.09	-0.86
S Zhi C	5,820	10.98	+0.67
L Bannister Green	1,968	3.71	+2.10
S Ward Brexit	1,308	2.47	

An opposition whip since 2015 who defied his own party lines to vote against triggering Article 50. Voted Remain and for a second referendum in the indicative votes. Nominated Sir Keir Starmer for the leadership, 2020, Owen Smith, 2016, and Andy Burnham, 2015. Environmental audit select cttee, 2015. APPGs: drug policy reform (vice-chairman); mental health; humanist (co-chairman). Former DJ and nightclub promoter. Cllr, Manchester City C, 1997-2015. Member: Unite; Socialist Education Association; Friends of the Earth; Withington Civic Society. Ed: Manchester GS; University of Manchester (BA politics and economics).

CHALLENGERS
John Leech (LD) MP for this constituency, 2005-15. Shadow transport spokesman, 2006-10. Serial rebel during coalition years: voted against raising tuition fees, welfare and legal aid cuts. Cllr, Manchester City C, 2016-, 1998-2008. **Shengke Zhi** (C) Worked as a nuclear engineer. Manager for a company facilitating Chinese-British nuclear collaboration.

CONSTITUENCY PROFILE
A Conservative seat from its creation in 1931 until it turned Labour in 1987. It was gained by the Liberal Democrats in 2005, in part due to protest votes against the Iraq War, but was won back in 2015. Large influx of young professionals in the area and about one fifth of the population are students. Ethnically diverse seat, with 12 per cent of residents coming from an Asian background. Home ownership is lower than average, with a third of residents renting privately.

EU REFERENDUM RESULT
24.9% Leave   Remain 75.1%

Mansfield

MAJORITY 16,306 (33.09%)   **CONSERVATIVE HOLD**   TURNOUT 63.88%

BEN BRADLEY
BORN Dec 11, 1989
MP 2017-

	Electorate	Share %	Change from 2017 %
	77,131		
*B Bradley C	31,484	63.90	+17.26
S Ward Lab	15,178	30.80	-13.73
S Brown LD	1,626	3.30	+1.91
S Pepper Ind	527	1.07	-1.08
S Harvey ND	458	0.93	

Became the first Conservative to be returned for Mansfield in its 134-year history in 2017. Served as vice-chairman of the Conservative Party in 2018. Criticised for blogs written in 2011-12 that appeared to advocate police brutality and vasectomies for the unemployed; he apologised for them in 2018. Remainer who embraced Brexit. Backed Esther McVey, then Boris Johnson, in the 2019 leadership contest. Select cttees: education, 2018-; regulatory, 2018-. Office manager for Mark Spencer (Sherwood), 2015-17. Previously worked in customer service and as a recruitment manager. Won parliamentary beard of the year award in December 2018 after Jeremy Corbyn, a seven-time winner, was not allowed to compete. Ed: Derby GS; Nottingham Trent University (BA politics).

CHALLENGERS
Sonya Ward (Lab) Cllr, Mansfield DC, 2011-. Associate lecturer, the Open University. **Sarah Brown** (LD) Works in higher education. Contested Stockton North, 2017. **Sid Pepper** (Ind) Entrepreneur. Contested this seat, 2017, 2015.

CONSTITUENCY PROFILE
A portent for the collapse of Labour's Red Wall in 2019. After being held by Labour since 1923, the seat was gained by the Conservatives in 2017, with a thin majority of just over 1,000. Ben Bradley's majority in 2019, however, was larger than any Mansfield MP has had since 1997. A former mining town in Nottinghamshire, the mines closed long ago and unemployment has been made worse by the closure of other local industries.

EU REFERENDUM RESULT
70.9% Leave   Remain 29.1%

Meon Valley

MAJORITY 23,555 (42.96%) **CONSERVATIVE HOLD** **TURNOUT 72.39%**

FLICK DRUMMOND
BORN Jun 16, 1962
MP 2019-; 2015-17

MP for Portsmouth South, 2015-17. Women and equalities select cttee, 2015-17. Director, Conservative Policy Forum, 2018-. Board member, National Citizens Service, 2018-. Director of corporate affairs, Conservative Middle East Council, 2010-11. Cllr, Winchester City C, 1996-2000. Career as an insurance broker, Ofsted inspector and TA intelligence officer. APPG chairwoman, women and work. Contested Portsmouth South, 2017, 2010. Ed: University of Hull (BA Southeast Asian studies); Southampton (MA international relations).

	Electorate	Share %	Change from 2017 %
	75,737		
F Drummond C	35,271	64.33	-1.41
L North LD	11,716	21.37	+10.48
M Bunday Lab	5,644	10.29	-8.03
M Wallace Green	2,198	4.01	+1.61

CHALLENGERS
Lewis North (LD) Government relations adviser, Environmental Agency. Environmental policy adviser, Catherine Bearder MEP, 2015-19. **Matthew Bunday** (Lab) Cllr, Southampton City C, 2019-. Lecturer in event management at University of West London. Member: Fabian Society; UCU. **Malcolm Wallace** (Green) Engineer and business owner.

CONSTITUENCY PROFILE
This south Hampshire constituency, created in 2010,

is a Conservative safe seat. The party's vote share has not fallen below 60 per cent in the past three general elections. The second-placed party has changed at each successive election since the seat was created, from the Liberal Democrats to Ukip to Labour in 2010, 2015 and 2017 respectively. The seat's largest town is Waterlooville, although its population is split between Meon Valley and Havant. It is a relatively affluent area and has very low levels of unemployment. It is characterised by high levels of home ownership and very low levels of social renting.

EU REFERENDUM RESULT
51.9% Leave Remain 48.1%

Meriden

MAJORITY 22,836 (42.16%) **CONSERVATIVE HOLD** **TURNOUT 63.44%**

SAQIB BHATTI
BORN Jun 18, 1985
MP 2019-

Chartered accountant; qualified at Deloitte. Director of family accountancy firm since 2011. Youngest ever president of the Greater Birmingham Chambers of Commerce, representing more than 3,000 businesses in the West Midlands. Former president, the Asian Business Chambers of Commerce. On the national board of the Vote Leave campaign. Deputy chairman, Andy Street's 2020 mayoral campaign. Board member, West Midlands Reserve Forces and Cadets Association. Guest lecturer, Birmingham City University; Warwick University;

	Electorate	Share %	Change from 2017 %
	85,368		
S Bhatti C	34,358	63.44	+1.45
T Beddis Lab	11,522	21.27	-5.58
L McCarthy LD	5,614	10.37	+5.49
S Caudwell Green	2,667	4.92	+2.33

University College Birmingham. Raised £27,000 for Prostate Cancer UK, 2019. Ed: King Edward VI Boys School; LSE (LLB law).

CHALLENGERS
Teresa Beddis (Lab) Former teacher. Member, Labour National Policy Forum. Women's officer and political education officer, Meriden CLP. **Laura McCarthy** (LD) Cllr, Solihull MBC, 2018-. Small business owner. Founder and volunteer, Elmdon Park Litter Pickers.

CONSTITUENCY PROFILE
Last won by Labour in 1974, the Conservatives gained Meriden in 1979 and have not lost it since. Labour came within 600 votes of winning the West Midlands seat in 1997, but the Conservative majority has grown at every subsequent election. Its previous MP, Dame Caroline Spelman, was an environment secretary under David Cameron and, in 2019, put her name to an amendment ruling out a no-deal Brexit. The seat has Solihull to its west and Coventry to its east. There are high levels of inequality and unemployment, although wages are higher than the regional average.

EU REFERENDUM RESULT
58.8% Leave Remain 41.2%

Merthyr Tydfil & Rhymney

MAJORITY 10,606 (32.89%)   **LABOUR HOLD**   **TURNOUT 57.25%**

GERALD JONES
BORN Aug 21, 1970
MP 2015-

Shadow defence minister, 2017-. Voted Remain and supported a second referendum. Attracted controversy in 2015 for hiring his partner as his senior parliamentary assistant. Listed as neutral towards Jeremy Corbyn in a leaked party document in 2016; nominated Emily Thornberry for leader in 2020. Shadow Wales minister, 2016-17. Select cttees: public admin and constitutional affairs, 2015-17; Welsh affairs, 2015-16. Activist who said he was politicised by 1984-85 miners' strike. Former development officer, Gwent Association of Voluntary

	Electorate	Share %	from 2017 % Change
	56,322		
*G Jones Lab	16,913	52.45	-14.35
S Jones C	6,307	19.56	+1.45
C Jones Brexit	3,604	11.18	
M Evans PC	2,446	7.59	-0.58
D Hughes Ind	1,860	5.77	
B D'Cruz LD	1,116	3.46	+0.95

Organisations. Ed: Bedwelty Comp Sch; Ystrad Mynach Coll.

CHALLENGERS
Sara Jones (C) Non-executive director, Farmers' Union of Wales. Head of the Welsh Retail Consortium. Cllr, Monmouthshire CC, 2012-. **Colin Jones** (Brexit) Born and raised in Merthyr Tydfil. **Mark Evans** (PC) Football coach; worked with Ryan Giggs in managing the Wales national team.

CONSTITUENCY PROFILE
Centred on the town of Merthyr Tydfil in Glamorgan, south Wales, this has consistently been a solid Labour seat since the 1950s, except when an independent candidate won in 1970. In 2019 Labour's majority fell to its lowest level since 2010, when the Liberal Democrats came in second place. At one time the greatest iron-producing centre in Britain, as well as a mining and railway hub, now manufacturing is a significant industry in the region. Income is significantly below the regional average, unemployment is very high and more than a fifth of households are socially rented.

EU REFERENDUM RESULT
58.4% Leave   Remain 41.6%

Middlesbrough

MAJORITY 8,390 (24.62%)   **LABOUR HOLD**   **TURNOUT 52.90%**

ANDY MCDONALD
BORN Mar 8, 1958
MP 2012-

Lawyer specialising in serious injuries; advised defence select committee on armed forces compensation. Elected in a by-election after the death of Sir Stuart Bell, the MP since 1983. Appointed shadow transport minister in 2016 following Jonathan Reynolds' resignation, and shadow transport secretary five months later after Lilian Greenwood's resignation. Jeremy Corbyn loyalist; nominated Rebecca Long Bailey for the leadership, 2020. Voted Remain and for a second referendum. Justice select cttee, 2012-16. Cllr, Middlesbrough BC, 1995-99. Ed:

	Electorate	Share %	from 2017 % Change
	60,759		
*A McDonald Lab	17,202	53.52	-12.15
R Betson C	8,812	27.42	+0.67
A High Ind	4,548	14.15	+12.38
T Crawford LD	816	2.54	+1.51
H Alberti Green	546	1.70	+1.00
F Clements Brexit	216	0.67	

St George's SS; St Mary's Sixth Form Coll; Leeds Polytechnic (LLB).

CHALLENGERS
Ruth Betson (C) Cllr, South Cambridgeshire DC, 2017-. Communications manager, Institute of Chartered Accountants in England and Wales, 2018-. **Antony High** (Ind) Cllr, Middlesbrough BC, 2019-. **Thomas Crawford** (LD) University student.

CONSTITUENCY PROFILE
Middlesbrough is a safe Labour seat, held by the party since its creation in 1974. Its majority fell in 2019, however, to its lowest point in percentage terms since 1983. Middlesbrough is a large industrial town to the south of the River Tees. The constituency, a former centre for steel production, has one of the highest unemployment rates in the country. Household income is lower than in the rest of the North East and the seat has a high child poverty rate, at 37 per cent. The seat also includes the University of Teesside and has a relatively high proportion of 16 to 24-year-olds.

EU REFERENDUM RESULT
66.1% Leave   Remain 33.9%

Middlesbrough South & Cleveland East

MAJORITY 11,626 (24.31%)   CONSERVATIVE HOLD   TURNOUT 66.10%

SIMON CLARKE
BORN Sep 28, 1984
MP 2017-

	Electorate	Share %	Change from 2017 %
	72,339		
*S Clarke C	28,135	58.84	+9.19
L Dingsdale Lab	16,509	34.53	-12.98
J Joy LD	1,953	4.08	+1.24
S Brown Green	1,220	2.55	

Minister of state in the Ministry of Housing, Communities and Local Government since 2020. A former Slaughter and May solicitor, elected in 2017 as this constituency's first Conservative MP. Exchequer secretary to the Treasury, 2019-20. Policy adviser and head of media for Graham Stuart (Beverley & Holderness), 2013-; parliamentary assistant to Dominic Raab (Esher & Walton), 2010-13. Brexiteer; supporter of Leave Means Leave. Submitted vote of no confidence in Theresa May's leadership, 2018. Contested Middlesbrough, 2015. Ed: University Coll, Oxford (BA modern history); Oxford Brookes (GD law); BPP Law Sch (LPC).

CHALLENGERS
Lauren Dingsdale (Lab) A commerical solicitor with Slaughter and May. Links to the Flemish aristocracy; also goes by Lauren De Thibault de Boesinghe. Once appeared on *Who Wants to be a Millionaire?*. **Jemma Joy** (LD) Accounts manager, Astra Zeneca. Contested Guisborough BC, 2019. **Sophie Brown** (Green) History teacher.

CONSTITUENCY PROFILE
Created in 1997, this seat had been held by Labour until 2017. Its previous MP, Tom Blenkinsop, declined to stand in 2017, after criticising Jeremy Corbyn's leadership. The seat's predecessors were held by the Conservatives between 1974 and 1997, including by the Thatcher-era home secretary Leon Brittan, but Cleveland had been Labour except after the 1959 election. The seat contains the southern outskirts of Middlesbrough and extends east to the coast. Has one of the highest proportions of residents employed in mining and the decline of this sector has hit the area hard.

EU REFERENDUM RESULT
65.3% Leave   Remain 34.7%

Midlothian

MAJORITY 5,705 (11.83%)   SNP GAIN FROM LABOUR   TURNOUT 68.36%

OWEN THOMPSON
BORN Mar 17, 1978
MP 2019-; 2015-17

	Electorate	Share %	Change from 2017 %
	70,544		
O Thompson SNP	20,033	41.54	+7.15
*D Rowley Lab	14,328	29.71	-6.64
R Fraser C	10,467	21.71	-3.74
S Arrundale LD	3,393	7.04	+3.23

Deputy party whip, 2015-17. Chief of staff to Peter Grant (Glenrothes), 2017-18. Lost seat in 2017 Labour resurgence. Director, consultancy firm. Cllr, Midlothian C, 2005-15; leader, 2013-15. Parliamentary assistant to: Clare Adamson MSP, 2011-15; Rob Gibson MSP, 2007-11. Ed: Beeslack HS, Napier University (BA accounting and finance).

CHALLENGERS
Danielle Rowley (Lab) MP for this seat, 2017-19; Labour's youngest MP at the time. Campaigns officer for the homelessness charity Shelter Scotland, 2016-17. Constituency media manager for Gordon Brown, 2014-15. Daughter of the Scottish Labour deputy leader Alex Rowley. **Rebecca Fraser** (C) Former hotelier; managed several boutique properties in the region. Contested Scottish Borders Council, 2017, as an independent. **Steve Arrundale** (LD) IT delivery programmes manager.

CONSTITUENCY PROFILE
In 2017 Labour won back this seat in its former heartlands from the SNP with a slim 885-vote majority. Labour had previously held Midlothian continuously from 1950 until 2015. In 2019 the SNP's majority stood at 4,000 below its 2015 peak. In the 19th century the seat was represented by the Liberal prime minister William Ewart Gladstone. A rural seat to the south of Edinburgh, the largest town is Dalkeith, which is the only settlement of more than 10,000 people. Also contains the former mining villages of Gorebridge and Newtongrange, which are both now home to Edinburgh commuters. A relatively high proportion of households are socially rented.

EU REFERENDUM RESULT
37.9% Leave   Remain 62.1%

Milton Keynes North

MAJORITY 6,255 (10.00%) CONSERVATIVE HOLD TURNOUT 68.33%

BEN EVERITT
BORN Nov 22, 1979
MP 2019-

Head of strategy for the Institute of Chartered Accountants since 2015. Previously a consultant with Deloitte. Policy adviser to John Prescott, the Labour deputy prime minister, 2004-06. Cllr, Aylesbury Vale DC, 2015-. Chairman, Streatham Conservatives, 2011-13. Chairman, St Leonard's Safer Neighbourhoods Panel. Called for Milton Keynes to become the country's first town with only electric buses, 2020. Brexiteer. Ed: King Grantham Sch; Durham University (BSc education; chairman, Ambassador's Society).

	Electorate	Share %	Change from 2017 %
	91,535		
B Everitt C	30,938	49.47	+2.01
C Pullen Lab	24,683	39.47	-4.99
A Mir LD	4,991	7.98	+4.07
C Rose Green	1,931	3.09	+1.35

CHALLENGERS
Charlynne Pullen (Lab) Head of data and evaluation, the Education and Training Foundation, 2014-. Contested this seat, 2017; Bedfordshire Mid, 2015. School governor, Milton Keynes Coll. Cllr, Islington LBC, 2010-14; chairwoman, education cttee, 2013-14. **Aisha Mir** (LD) Managing director, Concept Deals UK. Contested Edinburgh South West, 2017, 2015. **Catherine Rose** (Green) Arts education manager. Member, Olney Sustainable Futures.

CONSTITUENCY PROFILE
This seat has been Conservative since its creation in 2010. Labour reduced the Tory majority from almost 10,000 to below 2,000 in 2017 but it crept back up in 2019. Its predecessor seat, Milton Keynes North East, was held by Labour 1997-2005, but by the Conservatives either side of that period. The seat contains the northern part of Milton Keynes, the biggest planned new town in Britain, and many of the Buckinghamshire villages to its north. It has an ethnically diverse population: about one in ten residents is Asian or Asian British and a further one in ten is black or mixed race.

EU REFERENDUM RESULT
49.7% Leave Remain 50.3%

Milton Keynes South

MAJORITY 6,944 (10.85%) CONSERVATIVE HOLD TURNOUT 66.44%

IAIN STEWART
BORN Sep 18, 1972
MP 2010-

Government whip since 2019; assistant whip, 2018-19. Scottish-born accountant. Former board member at the headhunters Odgers, Ray & Berndtson. Ran a research unit in Westminster analysing legislation for clients. Voted for Jeremy Hunt in the leadership contest, 2019. PPS to: Liam Fox (North Somerset), 2016-17; David Mundell (Dumfriesshire, Clydesdale & Tweeddale), 2015-16; Sir Patrick McLoughlin, 2013-15. Transport select cttee, 2010-17. Champion for Oxford-MK-Cambridge corridor. Deputy chairman, LGBT Conservatives, 2009-11.

	Electorate	Share %	Change from 2017 %
	96,343		
*I Stewart C	32,011	50.01	+2.48
H O'Neill Lab	25,067	39.16	-5.69
S Ahsan LD	4,688	7.32	+4.39
A Francis Green	1,495	2.34	+0.51
S Fulton Ind	539	0.84	
A Ogba CPA	207	0.32	

Brexiteer. Contested this seat, 2005, 2001. Ed: Hutchesons' GS, Glasgow; University of Exeter (BA politics).

CHALLENGERS
Hannah O'Neill (Lab) Cllr, Milton Keynes BC, 2008-; cabinet member, health and wellbeing; deputy leader, 2014-. Contested this seat, 2017. Experience in housing policy. **Saleyha Ahsan** (LD) A&E doctor, former army officer.

CONSTITUENCY PROFILE
A similar history to that of its neighbour to the north. The 2015 Tory majority of almost 9,000 fell to below 2,000 in 2017 but recovered in 2019. Unlike Milton Keynes North, Labour held this seat's predecessor in 2005. More densely populated and slightly more ethnically diverse than its neighbour: roughly one in four residents is from an ethnic minority. Home ownership is below average, but shared ownership is high in both seats: the town is the UK's shared-ownership capital. An Amazon distribution centre here means that a lot of residents are employed in the retail sector.

EU REFERENDUM RESULT
53.1% Leave Remain 46.9%

Mitcham & Morden

MAJORITY 16,482 (36.03%) **LABOUR HOLD** **TURNOUT 65.33%**

SIOBHAIN
MCDONAGH
BORN Feb 20, 1960
MP 1997-

Committed backbencher not afraid to stand out from the crowd; first MP to publicly call Gordon Brown's leadership into question in 2008. Voted Remain. Supported Jess Phillips, 2020; Owen Smith, 2016; Liz Kendall, 2015; David Miliband, 2010. Voted for 2015 Syria airstrikes. Labour party's youngest councillor, 1982. Assistant whip, 2007-08. Select cttees: women and equalities, 2015-16; education, 2012-15. Lives with her sister, Baroness (Margaret) McDonagh, Labour general-secretary, 1998-2001. Ed: Essex University (BA politics).

	Electorate	Share %	Change from 2017 %
	70,014		
*S McDonagh Lab	27,964	61.14	-7.53
T Williams C	11,482	25.10	+0.86
L Taylor LD	3,717	8.13	+5.02
J Maddocks Brexit	1,202	2.63	
P Maslin Green	1,160	2.54	+1.20
D Coke CPA	216	0.47	+0.01

CHALLENGERS
Toby Williams (C) Head of press, GLA Conservatives, 2018-. National Police Chiefs' Council communications officer, 2017-18. Parliamentary assistant to Cheryl Gillan and Hugo Swire, 2014-17. **Luke Taylor** (LD) Project manager and aviation consultant. **Jeremy Maddocks** (Brexit) IT broadcast technology: Irdeto; Cisco. **Pippa Maslin** (Green) Visiting media arts tutor, Royal Holloway.

CONSTITUENCY PROFILE
Although this suburban, densely populated south London constituency is now a safe one for Labour, it was held by the Tories from 1982 to 1997. Like several other formerly marginal London seats, Labour's majority is greater now than it was under the last Labour government. The area is diverse, with large Asian, black and European migrant communities. The seat is home to a young working population, many of whom commute into central London, with significant proportions employed in the retail and service sectors. Income is below the London average.

EU REFERENDUM RESULT
44.7% Leave   Remain 55.3%

Mole Valley

MAJORITY 12,041 (21.08%) **CONSERVATIVE HOLD** **TURNOUT 76.49%**

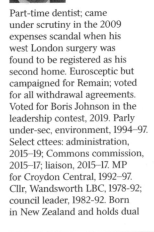

SIR PAUL
BERESFORD
BORN Apr 6, 1946
MP 1992-

Part-time dentist; came under scrutiny in the 2009 expenses scandal when his west London surgery was found to be registered as his second home. Eurosceptic but campaigned for Remain; voted for all withdrawal agreements. Voted for Boris Johnson in the leadership contest, 2019. Parly under-sec, environment, 1994-97. Select cttees: administration, 2015-19; Commons commission, 2015-17; liaison, 2015-17. MP for Croydon Central, 1992-97. Cllr, Wandsworth LBC, 1978-92; council leader, 1982-92. Born in New Zealand and holds dual

	Electorate	Share %	Change from 2017 %
	74,665		
*P Beresford C	31,656	55.43	-6.43
P Kennedy LD	19,615	34.35	+15.03
B Bostock Lab	2,965	5.19	-8.67
L Scott-Conte Green	1,874	3.28	+0.70
R Horsley Ind	536	0.94	
G Cox Ukip	464	0.81	-1.57

citizenship. Knighted in 1990 for parliamentary and political service. Ed: University of Otago, New Zealand (dentistry).

CHALLENGERS
Paul Kennedy (LD) Former actuary. Cllr, Mole Valley DC, 2016-. Contested this seat, 2017. **Brian Bostock** (Lab) Clinical lead, Continuing Healthcare, Kent. **Lisa Scott-Conte** (Green) Spearheaded Community Speed Watch project.

CONSTITUENCY PROFILE
A rural seat in Surrey bordering Guildford that has been continuously held by the Conservatives since its creation in 1983. Its original MP was the cabinet minister Kenneth Baker. Alhough the Lib Dems, and before them the Liberals, have consistently come second, they have never managed to cut the Tory majority to less than five figures. The seat consists primarily of affluent commuter towns and villages. It is home to a cluster of technology and research businesses and a higher than average proportion of residents are in professional or technical occupations.

EU REFERENDUM RESULT
47.3% Leave   Remain 52.7%

Monmouth

MAJORITY 9,982 (19.88%)　　CONSERVATIVE HOLD　　TURNOUT 74.85%

DAVID DAVIES
BORN Jul 27, 1970
MP 2005-

Parliamentary under-secretary for Wales, 2019-. Former TA member who worked for British Steel. Nightclub promoter and rickshaw driver in Australia, before returning to work as a lorry driver. Initially supported Dominic Raab in the leadership contest before voting for Boris Johnson, 2019. Nine years as special constable with British Transport Police. Brexiteer; climate change sceptic. Outspoken critic of gender self-identification. Suggested refugee children should have their age verified using dental records, 2016. Select cttees:

	Electorate	Share %	Change from 2017 %
	67,094		
*D Davies C	26,160	52.09	-1.01
Y Murphy Lab	16,178	32.22	-4.39
A Willott LD	4,909	9.78	+5.63
I Chandler Green	1,353	2.69	+0.78
H Kocan PC	1,182	2.35	-0.34
M Ford Ind	435	0.87	

national policy statements, 2017-; liaison, 2010-. Representative on UK delegation to assembly of Council of Europe, 2012. Learnt Welsh when elected to Welsh assembly. Former president, the Welsh Amateur Boxing Association. Ed: Bassaleg Comp.

CHALLENGERS
Yvonne Murphy (Lab) Theatre director and arts consultant. **Alison Willott** (LD) School teacher. Magistrate.

Chairwoman, Monmouth branch of Gwent Wildlife Trust.

CONSTITUENCY PROFILE
Labour has won this seat only in 2001, 1997, 1966, and in a 1991 by-election. David Davies's majority peaked at almost 11,000 in 2015. This rural, sparsely populated seat in southeast Wales borders Gloucestershire and Herefordshire. One of the lowest proportions of Welsh speakers of any Welsh seat; a third of the seat's population were born in England. Incomes are well above average, compared to Wales as a whole and the seat has a large retired population.

EU REFERENDUM RESULT
48.1% Leave　　　　Remain 51.9%

Montgomeryshire

MAJORITY 12,138 (35.48%)　　CONSERVATIVE HOLD　　TURNOUT 69.83%

CRAIG WILLIAMS
BORN Jun 7, 1985
MP 2019-; 2015-17

Replaced Glyn Davies, who held the seat for nine years. MP for Cardiff North, 2015-17. Remainer in 2016; voted consistently with party whip, including against investigations into the Iraq war. PPS to David Gauke, 2016-17. Select cttees: Welsh affairs, 2016-17; Scottish affairs, 2016-17; work and pensions, 2015-16. Lost Cardiff North seat to Labour candidate Anna McMorrin in 2017. Special adviser to Stephen Barclay, the Brexit secretary (Cambridgeshire North East), 2019. Cllr, Cardiff C, 2008-15. Ed: Watford Coll; University of Birmingham.

	Electorate	Share %	Change from 2017 %
	48,997		
C Williams C	20,020	58.51	+6.71
K Devani LD	7,882	23.04	-2.16
K Duerden Lab	5,585	16.32	+0.44
G Evans Gwlad	727	2.12	

CHALLENGERS
Kishan Devani (LD) Son of Ugandan Asian refugees. Chief adviser to World Youth Organisation, ambassador for the Religious Education Council. FRSA. **Kait Duerden** (Lab) Mentor, Women's Equality Network Wales, 2019-. Accounts manager at Computer Sciences Corporation, 2003-17. Board director and charity trustee, domestic violence charity. Member, Institute of Directors. **Gwyn Evans** (Gwlad) Leader, new pro-independence party.

CONSTITUENCY PROFILE
This central Wales seat has the largest Conservative majority of any Welsh constituency, although it has been in Conservative hands only since 2010. It was held by Liberals and Liberal Democrats almost all of the 20th century, including by the postwar Liberal leader Clement Davies and from 1997 by Lembit Öpik, famous for his appearances on reality TV shows. Rural and sparsely populated it includes the town of Welshpool. Contains a significant proportion of self-employed people and unemployment is low. Earnings are slightly below Welsh and UK averages

EU REFERENDUM RESULT
55.8% Leave　　　　Remain 44.2%

Moray

MAJORITY 513 (1.05%) CONSERVATIVE HOLD TURNOUT 68.73%

DOUGLAS ROSS
BORN Apr 9, 1983
MP 2017-

Junior Scotland minister since 2019. Home affairs select committee, 2017-19. Highlands & Islands MSP, 2016-17. Initially supported Mark Harper then voted for Boris Johnson in the Conservative leadership contest, 2019. PPS to Mary Scanlon MSP. Member, Scottish Senior Football Referee Association. Cllr, Moray C, 2012-. Contested this seat, 2015 and 2010. Criticised by Amnesty International for wanting tougher enforcement against Traveller communities. Ed: Alves Primary & Forres Academy; Scottish Agricultural Coll.

	Electorate	Share %	from 2017 Change %
	71,035		
*D Ross C	22,112	45.29	-2.26
L Mitchell SNP	21,599	44.24	+5.42
J Kirby Lab	2,432	4.98	-5.96
F Campbell Trevor LD	2,269	4.65	+2.38
R Scorer Ukip	413	0.85	

CHALLENGERS
Laura Mitchell (SNP) Communications manager for Richard Lochhead MSP, 2013-. Contested Scottish parliament, 2016. Organised 500-mile "tartan march" from Oslo to Glasgow. **Jo Kirby** (Lab) Teacher. Lead anti-poverty officer for Northern Alliance. **Fiona Campbell Trevor** (LD) Worked for the Social Democratic Party leader David Owen. Cllr, East Dunbartonshire C, 2003-08; vice-convenor, social services.

CONSTITUENCY PROFILE
For most of the past 30 years, this seat has been held by the SNP, who won it from the Conservatives in 1987. Its previous MP, the SNP's former Westminster leader Angus Robertson, lost to Douglas Ross in 2017 by a little over 4,000 votes. It is now the fifth most marginal Tory seat in parliament and the third most marginal seat in Scotland. A large rural seat in northeast Scotland in which agriculture, fishing, tourism and whisky distilling are important industries. Defence also provides many jobs, with the RAF Lossiemouth base located in the seat.

EU REFERENDUM RESULT
49.9% Leave Remain 50.1%

Morecambe & Lunesdale

MAJORITY 6,354 (14.02%) CONSERVATIVE HOLD TURNOUT 67.23%

DAVID MORRIS
BORN Jan 3, 1966
MP 2010-

Founder of a hairdressing business. Accomplished guitarist who once played in a band with Rick Astley. PPS to Stephen Crabb, 2014-15. Voted Remain; supported Theresa May's withdrawal agreement. Voted for Jeremy Hunt in the leadership contest, 2019. Select cttees: public administration and constitutional affairs, 2017-; political and constitutional reform, 2014-15, science and tech, 2010-14. APPGs: space, coastal and marines, classic rock and blues, self-employment. Member: Institute of Directors, National Hairdressing Council.

	Electorate	Share %	from 2017 Change %
	67,397		
*D Morris C	23,925	52.80	+5.11
L Collinge Lab	17,571	38.78	-5.84
O Lambert LD	2,328	5.14	+1.42
C Buckley Green	938	2.07	+1.02
D Clifford Ind	548	1.21	

Contested Carmarthen West & South Pembrokeshire, 2005. Ed: St Andrews Nassau, Bahamas; Lowton Sch, Lancashire.

CHALLENGERS
Lizzi Collinge (Lab) Mental health worker and programme management officer. Cllr, Lancashire CC, 2016-. Member, Unison. **Owen Lambert** (LD) Teacher. Contested Lancashire CC, 2019. **Chloe Buckley** (Green) Lecturer, Manchester Metropolitan University.

CONSTITUENCY PROFILE
The constituents of this seat had elected Conservative candidates to represent them in parliament since its creation in 1950 until Labour won it in 1997, holding it for the duration of the New Labour years. David Morris's majority is the largest any MP for the seat has won since 1992. Consists of the seaside town of Morecambe and an area that stretches into the Pennines in the east. It is characterised by high levels of home ownership and fairly low unemployment. The average earnings in the seat are lower than the regional average. A fifth of residents are aged 65 or over.

EU REFERENDUM RESULT
58.2% Leave Remain 41.8%

Morley & Outwood

MAJORITY 11,267 (21.70%)   **CONSERVATIVE HOLD**   **TURNOUT 65.90%**

ANDREA JENKYNS
BORN Jun 16, 1974
MP 2015-

	Electorate	Share %	Change from 2017 %
	78,803		
*A Jenkyns C	29,424	56.66	+5.95
D Ferguson Lab	18,157	34.96	-11.73
C Dobson LD	2,285	4.40	+1.80
C Bell Green	1,107	2.13	
D Woodlock Yorkshire	957	1.84	

Varied career as an international business development manager, music teacher, shop manager and soprano singer. Became a trustee of MRSA Action UK after father died of the superbug in 2011. Initially supported Dominic Raab in the leadership contest before voting for Boris Johnson, 2019. Cllr, Lincolnshire CC, 2009-13. Select cttees: Speaker's cttee on the Electoral Commission, 2018-; Brexit, 2016-; health and social care, 2015-17. Brexiteer; signed letter of no confidence in Theresa May and voted against her withdrawal agreement. Reached final of the

Miss UK beauty pageant aged 18. Married to Jack Lopresti (Filton & Bradley Stoke). Ed: Open University (Dip economics); University of Lincoln (BA international relations and politics).

CHALLENGERS
Deanne Ferguson (Lab) Trade unionist; GMB regional organiser, 2001-. **Craig Dobson** (LD) GP and medical adviser. Medical technologies appraisal committee.

CONSTITUENCY PROFILE
Created in 2010 from the west Yorkshire seats of Morley and Rothwell & Normanton, this seat was initially held by Ed Balls, the shadow chancellor from that year until his defeat became a symbol of Labour's failure in the 2015 election. The Tories' majority has grown since, increasing from 422 in 2015 to 2,104 in 2017. This seat, south of Leeds, is dominated by the former textiles and coalmining town of Morley, which has a population of 44,000. It is less ethnically diverse than much of West Yorkshire. More than 70 per cent of households are owner-occupied.

EU REFERENDUM RESULT
59.8% Leave   **Remain 40.2%**

Motherwell & Wishaw

MAJORITY 6,268 (14.11%)   **SNP HOLD**   **TURNOUT 64.51%**

MARION FELLOWS
BORN May 5, 1949
MP 2015-

	Electorate	Share %	Change from 2017 %
	68,856		
*M Fellows SNP	20,622	46.43	+7.90
A Feeney Lab	14,354	32.31	-5.45
M Gallacher C	7,150	16.10	-4.15
C Wilson LD	1,675	3.77	+1.58
N Wilson Ukip	619	1.39	+0.12

Former business studies teacher and education trade union member. Campaigned for Remain. SNP small business spokeswoman, 2017-. Party whip, 2015-17. Select cttees: education, 2015-; administration, 2018-. Senior figure in the Yes campaign during 2014 Scottish independence referendum, winning a majority for the campaign in Motherwell & Wishaw. Offices were vandalised during election campaign. Cllr, Wishaw C, 2012-15. Member, SNP trade union group. Ed: Heriot-Watt University (BA accountancy and finance).

CHALLENGERS
Angela Feeney (Lab) Cllr, North Lanarkshire C, 2017-. NHS Podiatrist. Member: Unison, Campaign for Socialism. Set up Wishaw to Calais refugee appeal 2015. Contested: this seat, 2017 and the Scottish parliament, 2016. **Meghan Gallacher** (C) Complaints handler at John Lewis. Cllr, North Lanarkshire C, 2017-. Contested: this seat, 2017, 2015; Scottish parliament, 2016. **Christopher Wilson** (LD) University of Glasgow student.

CONSTITUENCY PROFILE
Once a safe Labour seat, with the party winning five-figure majorities at every election from its creation in 1997 until the SNP won an 11,000-strong majority of its own in 2015. The SNP majority was reduced to 318 votes in 2017. It is a small seat in North Lanarkshire, just to the southeast of Glasgow. There are high levels of unemployment and a higher-than-average proportion of adults have relatively low levels of educational attainment. A significantly high proportion of households are rented socially, and residents' earnings tend to be below the Scottish average.

EU REFERENDUM RESULT
37.7% Leave   **Remain 62.3%**

Na h-Eileanan an Iar

MAJORITY 2,438 (16.84%)　　　　SNP HOLD　　　　TURNOUT 68.59%

ANGUS MACNEIL
BORN Jul 21, 1970
MP 2005-

Electorate	Share %	Change from 2017 %
21,106		
*A MacNeil SNP	6,531 45.11	+4.53
A MacCorquodale Lab	4,093 28.27	-5.51
J Ross C	3,216 22.21	+5.74
N Mitchison LD	637 4.40	+2.71

Former BBC Radio Scotland reporter and primary school teacher. One of the "Super Six" SNP MPs elected in 2005. Criticised in connection with London hotel expenses claimed while reportedly having an affair; the SNP denied any claims of financial impropriety. First MP to call for investigation into "cash for honours" in 2006. Locked himself in Commons lavatory to avoid voting on whether to hold the EU referendum, after he had walked into the wrong lobby. Voted against Article 50. Rarely rebels. SNP spokesman: environment, 2017-18, 2005-10;

international trade, 2017-19; national security, 2015-19. Contested Inverness East, Nairn & Lochaber, 2001. Ed: The Nicolson Institute, Stornoway; University of Strathclyde (BEng civil engineering); Jordanhill Coll (PGCE).

CHALLENGERS
Alison MacCorquodale (Lab) Economic development officer for local government, 2000-. **Jennifer Ross** (C) Internet entrepreneur. Previously worked in rural tourism and marketing.

CONSTITUENCY PROFILE
Gaelic for "Western Isles", Na h-Eileanan an Iar is the smallest seat in parliament by electorate, with about 21,000 voters – one fifth of the electorate in the most populous constituency, the Isle of Wight. The seat first elected a Labour MP in 1935 and has since switched between Labour and the SNP, typically being held by each party for a long period. Labour last held the seat from the 1987 general election until Angus MacNeil's victory in 2005. More than a quarter of the population is over 65, home ownership is high and the seat has a below-average private renting rate.

EU REFERENDUM RESULT
43.9% Leave　　　　Remain 56.1%

Neath

MAJORITY 5,637 (15.34%)　　　　LABOUR CO-OP HOLD　　　　TURNOUT 65.15%

CHRISTINA REES
BORN Feb 21, 1954
MP 2015-

Electorate	Share %	Change from 2017 %
56,416		
*C Rees Lab Co-op	15,920 43.31	-13.40
J Burns C	10,283 27.98	+4.25
D Williams PC	4,495 12.23	-1.72
S Briscoe Brexit	3,184 8.66	
A Kingston-Jones LD	1,485 4.04	+2.13
M Lloyd Green	728 1.98	
P Rogers Ind	594 1.62	
C Williams Soc Dem	67 0.18	

Former barrister, justice of the peace and squash professional. Voted Remain. Resigned from Jeremy Corbyn's shadow cabinet following the vote of no confidence in his leadership but returned to front bench. Supported Sir Keir Starmer in 2020, Owen Smith in 2016 and Andy Burnham in 2015. Cllr, Bridgend BC, 2012-15. Member: Unite; GMB. Shadow Welsh secretary, 2017-. Shadow justice minister, 2016-17. Select cttees: justice, 2016-17, 2015; Welsh affairs, 2015-16. Contested European parliament, 2014. Ed: Cynffig Comp Sch; Ystrad

Mynach Coll; University of Wales (LLB law).

CHALLENGERS
Jon Burns (C) Former Conservative campaign director. Cllr, Cardiff CC, 2004-. Worked for the Home Office. **Daniel Williams** (PC) Professor of English, Swansea University. **Simon Briscoe** (Brexit) Statistician and economist.

CONSTITUENCY PROFILE
This south Wales seat has elected Labour MPs since 1922; its former MP was the cabinet minister and anti-apartheid campaigner Peter Hain. Labour's majority in 2019 was the smallest in almost 100 years. The town of Neath is northeast of Swansea and has a population of about 19,000. The seat also has a rural area up to the edge of the Brecon Beacons. The workforce is skewed towards routine and semi-routine occupations and incomes are slightly below the Welsh average. Home ownership in Neath is above average and private sector renting is comparatively rare.

EU REFERENDUM RESULT
54.0% Leave　　　　Remain 46.0%

New Forest East

CONSERVATIVE HOLD

JULIAN LEWIS
BORN Sep 26, 1951
MP 1997-

Former deputy director, Conservative research department. Royal Navy reservist. Defence consultant and political researcher. Author. Visiting lecturer, King's College London. Infiltrated Labour in 1970s to oust "Trotskyite" leftwingers. Vigorous rightwinger and leading Eurosceptic. Voted against LGBT inclusive sex education in schools. One of the 28 "Spartans" to vote against Theresa May's withdrawal agreement three times. Chairman, defence select cttee, 2015-19. Select cttees: arms export controls, 2016-17, 2014-15;

	Electorate	Share %	Change from 2017 %
	73,552		
*J Lewis C	32,769	64.52	+1.91
J Hope Lab	7,518	14.80	-4.99
B Johnston LD	7,390	14.55	-0.61
N Jolly Green	2,434	4.79	+2.36
A Knight AWP	675	1.33	

national security, 2015-19. Ed: Dynevor GS, Swansea; Balliol Coll, Oxford (MA philosophy and politics); St Antony's Coll, Oxford (DPhil strategic studies).

CHALLENGERS
Julie Hope (Lab) Former maths teacher. Contested this seat, 2017. Anti-racism campaigner, worked with indigenous Australian communities. **Bob Johnston** (LD) Retired biology lecturer, Oxford Brookes. Cllr, Oxfordshire CC, 2013-. **Nicola**

Jolly (Green) PhD graduate working in education.

CONSTITUENCY PROFILE
This Hampshire seat has elected Tories since its 1997 creation, as its predecessors did going as far back as 1910. The Lib Dems reduced the Conservative majority to less than 4,000 in 2001, but the Tories' grip has since strengthened. The seat's largest town is Totton, with about 28,000 people. The seat contains most of the national park. A quarter of residents are aged 65 or above and home ownership is well above average, with about three quarters of households owner-occupied.

EU REFERENDUM RESULT
60.2% Leave   Remain 39.8%

New Forest West

CONSERVATIVE HOLD

SIR DESMOND
SWAYNE
BORN Aug 20, 1956
MP 1997-

Director of a property development company. Former teacher and manager at RBS. Army officer in reserves for nearly 40 years. Served in Iraq, 2003. Knighted in 2016 for political service. Brexiteer. Defended historic use of blackface at *Blues Brothers*-themed party, saying he wanted his costume to be "as authentic as possible". Supported Boris Johnson in the leadership contest, 2019. International development minister, 2014-16. Whip, 2012-14. Select cttees: Northern Ireland, 2019; ecclesiastical, 2017-19; 2005-10;

	Electorate	Share %	Change from 2017 %
	70,867		
*D Swayne C	32,113	63.84	-3.00
J Davies LD	7,710	15.33	+5.69
J Graham Lab	6,595	13.11	-6.51
N Bubb Green	3,888	7.73	+4.80

international trade, 2016-17. PPS to: David Cameron, 2005-12; Michael Howard, 2004-05. Ed: Bedford Sch; University of St Andrews (MA theology).

CHALLENGERS
Jack Davies (LD) Cllr, New Forest DC, 2018-; Lib Dem housing spokesman. **Jo Graham** (Lab) Primary school teacher. Ran interactive galleries at Science Museum. Contested this seat, 2017. **Nick Bubb** (Green) Director of a wildlife conservation organisation. Cllr,

Lymington & Pennington TC, 2015-.

CONSTITUENCY PROFILE
Contains less of the New Forest than its easterly neighbour but like its neighbour has been a safe Conservative seat since its creation in 1997. The Tory majority has never fallen below five figures. The biggest settlements are the coastal towns of New Milton and Ringwood. A third of residents are aged 65 or over and about three quarters of households are owner-occupied. Incomes are in line with the average for Hampshire, although median income here is slightly higher than in New Forest East.

EU REFERENDUM RESULT
55.3% Leave   Remain 44.7%

Newark

CONSERVATIVE HOLD

TURNOUT 72.14%

ROBERT JENRICK
BORN Jan 9, 1982
MP 2014-

	Electorate	Share %	Change from 2017 %
	75,855		
*R Jenrick C	34,650	63.32	+0.65
J Baggaley Lab	12,814	23.42	-6.28
D Watts LD	5,308	9.70	+4.64
J Henderson Green	1,950	3.56	

Appointed secretary of state for housing, communities and local government in 2019. Career as a solicitor and international managing director of Christie's. Elected in 2014 by-election after Patrick Mercer's resignation during the "cash for questions" furore. Vocal campaigner for flood defences. Supported Remain but voted for no-deal in 2019; backed Boris Johnson for leader, 2019. Attended President Trump's inauguration, 2017. PPS to: Amber Rudd, 2017-18, 2014-15; Liz Truss, 2016-17; Michael Gove, 2015-16. In June 2019, he represented the government at the Israel-Palestine peace initiative, led by Jared Kushner, senior adviser to Mr Trump. Contested Newcastle-under-Lyme, 2010. Ed: Wolverhampton GS; St John's Coll, Cambridge (BA history); University of Pennsylvania (Thouron fellow); Coll of Law (Grad Dip law); BPP Law Sch (LPC).

CHALLENGERS
James Baggaley (Lab) Policy and engagement manager, King's Coll, London. Cllr, Newark TC.
David Watts (LD) Solicitor and lecturer. Cllr, Broxtowe BC, 1995-2015; leader, 2010-11. Contested: this seat, 2017, 2014; Broxtowe, 2010, 2005, 2001. **Jay Henderson** (Green) Cllr, Newark TC.

CONSTITUENCY PROFILE
This Nottinghamshire seat was represented by Labour in 1950-79 and 1997-2001, but has otherwise elected Conservatives for the past 100 years, including at the 2014 by-election, in which Ukip won a quarter of the vote. A large seat on the county border with Lincolnshire, Newark has an ageing population, with just over a fifth of residents aged 65 or above.

EU REFERENDUM RESULT
55.7% Leave   Remain 44.3%

Newbury

CONSERVATIVE HOLD

TURNOUT 71.93%

LAURA FARRIS
BORN Jun 13, 1978
MP 2019-

	Electorate	Share %	Change from 2017 %
	83,414		
L Farris C	34,431	57.39	-4.08
L Dillon LD	18,384	30.64	+9.25
J Wilder Lab	4,404	7.34	-6.79
S Masters Green	2,454	4.09	+1.57
B Holden-Crowther Ind	325	0.54	

Barrister specialising in employment and public law, Littleton Chambers, 2010-. Appointed junior counsel to the Crown, 2015; counsel to the Independent Inquiry on Child Sexual Abuse, 2017; counsel to the Equality and Human Rights Commission, 2019. Former freelance journalist for Reuters and the BBC, 2004-05. Daughter of Michael McNair-Wilson, MP for this seat, 1974-92. Voted Remain but backed Boris Johnson's deal. Contested Leyton & Wanstead, 2017. Ed: Lady Margaret Hall, University of Oxford (BA PPE); BPP Law School (Bar vocational course); City, University of London (GDL).

CHALLENGERS
Lee Dillon (LD) Works for Sovereign housing association. Former mayor of Thatcham. Cllr, West Berkshire CC. Contested Islwyn, 2005. **James Wilder** (Lab) History and politics teacher. **Stephen Masters** (Green) Aircraft engineer in the RAF for 20 years. Homeless for ten months in 2009, but has since moved on to a houseboat. Arrested in November 2019 at a climate rally outside parliament. Cllr, West Berkshire CC.

CONSTITUENCY PROFILE
Seat in Berkshire that has returned a Conservative MP in every election since 1924, with the exception of 1993-2005, when it was held by the Liberal Democrats. The Conservative majority has not fallen below 10,000 at the past four elections. Richard Benyon, the seat's MP from 2005 to 2019, was one of the 21 Conservative MPs who had the whip withdrawn for voting against the Johnson government on Brexit.

EU REFERENDUM RESULT
47.8% Leave   Remain 52.2%

Newcastle-under-Lyme

MAJORITY 7,446 (16.64%)   CONSERVATIVE GAIN FROM LABOUR   TURNOUT 65.59%

AARON BELL
BORN Feb 25, 1980
MP 2019-

Senior trading performance analyst at Bet365 for 13 years and co-owner of Divide Buy, a financial technology business. Worked at Ladbrokes, 2003-06. Successful in TV game shows: part of the *University Challenge* team for St John's College, Oxford, that were runners up in the 2000-01 series; also won £25,000 on *Deal or No Deal*. Brexiteer. Contested Don Valley, 2017. Ed: St Olave's Grammar School; St John's, Oxford (MA PPE).

CHALLENGERS
Carl Greatbach (Lab) Assistant

	Electorate	Share %	from 2017 %	Change
	68,211			
A Bell C	23,485	52.49	+4.38	
C Greatbatch Lab	16,039	35.85	-12.33	
N Jones LD	2,361	5.28	+1.57	
J Cooper Brexit	1,921	4.29		
C Johnson Green	933	2.09		

branch secretary, Manchester Unison, 2013-. Socialist. Member: Momentum and Open Labour. Left school at 16 to work in the Stoke potteries. **Nigel Jones** (LD) MP for Cheltenham, 1992-2005. Made a life peer upon standing down from the seat in 2005. Former computer industry worker. **Jason Cooper** (Brexit) Consultant, University Hospitals of North Midlands; specialist in obstetrics and gynaecology. **Carl Johnson** (Green) Haulage company owner.

CONSTITUENCY PROFILE
Had been represented by Labour MPs for 100 years, since Josiah Wedgewood defected to Labour from the Liberals in 1919. The Conservatives' victory looked increasingly likely: Labour's majority fell from 1,552 in 2010 to 650 in 2015, to 30 in 2017. The constituency is part of the same metropolitan area as Stoke-on-Trent, and the town of Newcastle-under-Lyme is home to about 75,000 people. It extends west into a more rural area that contains Keele University, with about 9,000 students living in the constituency. Incomes are below the regional average.

EU REFERENDUM RESULT
61.6% Leave   Remain 38.4%

Newcastle upon Tyne Central

MAJORITY 12,278 (32.76%)   LABOUR HOLD   TURNOUT 64.78%

CHI ONWURAH
BORN Apr 12, 1965
MP 2010-

Chartered engineer. Former head of telecoms technology, Ofcom. Originally from the North East, but spent two years living in Nigeria with her mother before fleeing during the country's civil war. Nominated Emily Thornberry in the 2020 leadership election and backed Owen Smith in 2016, despite nominating Jeremy Corbyn in 2015. Claimed that Mr Corbyn discriminated against her and another ethnic minority MP, 2016, a claim that Mr Corbyn denied. Voted Remain. Shadow minister: industrial strategy, 2016-; business, 2015-16, 2010-

	Electorate	Share %	from 2017 %	Change
	57,845			
*C Onwurah Lab	21,568	57.55	-7.34	
E Payne C	9,290	24.79	+0.17	
A Avaei LD	2,709	7.23	+2.34	
M Griffin Brexit	2,542	6.78		
T Pitman Green	1,365	3.64	+2.04	

13; culture, 2015-16; Cabinet Office, 2013-15. Former national executive, Anti-Apartheid Movement. Ed: Kenton Comp; Imperial Coll, London (BEng electrical engineering); Manchester Business Sch (MBA).

CHALLENGERS
Emily Payne (C) Worked for BAE Systems. Volunteered in northern Iraq in 2004 and worked subsequently as a political risk analyst. Cllr, Westminster CC, 2018-. **Ali**

Avaei (LD) Area manager for a pharmacy chain. Cllr, Newcastle City C, 2019-. **Mark Griffin** (Brexit) Originally planned to stand in Hexham. **Tay Pitman** (Green) Senior analyst, Care Quality Commission.

CONSTITUENCY PROFILE
First seat to declare on election night. Has been held by Labour at every postwar election other than the 1983 Conservative landslide. Sizeable student population of 13,000, which constitutes about a seventh of the overall population. The seat is home to about 13,000 Muslims and is the most diverse of the three Newcastle seats.

EU REFERENDUM RESULT
48.0% Leave   Remain 52.0%

Newcastle upon Tyne East

MAJORITY 15,463 (35.66%)   LABOUR HOLD   TURNOUT 67.97%

NICHOLAS BROWN
BORN Jun 13, 1950
MP 1983-

Tough enforcer who has spent three stints as chief whip under different leaders. Spent years trying to get Jeremy Corbyn to toe the New Labour party line before being asked by him to return to the role in 2016. Previously worked in advertising for Proctor & Gamble and for a dry-cleaning company. Said he would campaign for Remain in a second EU referendum. Backed Sir Keir Starmer for leader in 2020 and Yvette Cooper in 2015. Close to Gordon Brown. Minister: North East, 2007-10; work and pensions, 2001-03; agriculture, fisheries and food,

	Electorate	Share %	Change from 2017 %
	63,796		
*N Brown Lab	26,049	60.07	-7.48
R Gwynn C	10,586	24.41	+3.12
W Taylor LD	4,535	10.46	+4.28
N Hartley Green	2,195	5.06	+3.25

1998-2001. Shadow deputy Commons leader, 1992-94. Shadow solicitor-general, 1985-92. Multiple shadow spokesman roles. Cllr, Newcastle City C, 1980-84. Awarded freedom of Newcastle, 2001. Ed: Tunbridge Wells Tech HS; Manchester University.

CHALLENGERS
Robin Gwynn (C) Civil servant with a long career at the Foreign Office, including senior posts in Africa. Voted Leave. Contested Jarrow, 2017. **Wendy**

Taylor (LD) Breast cancer consultant, Freeman Hospital. Cllr, Newcastle City C, 1988-. Has contested this seat at every election since 2010.

CONSTITUENCY PROFILE
Has elected only Labour MPs since 1945, with the sole exception of the 1959 election, when the Conservatives won. In 1983 Nicholas Brown unseated his predecessor, Mike Thomas, who had defected to the Social Democratic Party two years earlier. This is the smallest, densest and most urban Newcastle seat. It is home to 24,000 students, who make up about a quarter of constituents.

EU REFERENDUM RESULT
41.1% Leave   Remain 58.9%

Newcastle upon Tyne North

MAJORITY 5,765 (12.27%)   LABOUR HOLD   TURNOUT 68.63%

CATHERINE
MCKINNELL
BORN Jun 8, 1976
MP 2010-

Chairwoman of the petitions select cttee, 2020-. Co-chairwoman, antisemitism APPG. Employment solicitor born and raised in Newcastle. First shadow cabinet member to quit over Jeremy Corbyn's leadership in 2016. Nominated Jess Phillips for leader in 2020 and Yvette Cooper in 2015. Voted Remain. Shadow attorney-general, 2015-16. Shadow cabinet: secretary to the Treasury, 2013-15; minister for children, 2011-13; solicitor general, 2010-11. Ed: University of Edinburgh (MA politics and history); Northumbria University (law).

	Electorate	Share %	Change from 2017 %
	68,486		
*C McKinnell Lab	21,354	45.44	-9.92
M Lehain C	15,589	33.17	-0.75
N Cott LD	4,357	9.27	+4.02
R Ogden Brexit	4,331	9.22	
A Ford Green	1,368	2.91	+1.85

CHALLENGERS
Mark Lehain (C) Former maths teacher. Founded and led one of the first free schools, Bedford Free School, 2012-17. Head of the Parents and Teachers for Excellence group, which campaigns for stricter discipline and more facts in the curriculum. **Nicholas Cott** (LD) Associate lecturer in history, the Open University. Cllr, Newcastle City C, 2000-. **Richard Ogden** (Brexit) Runs a local dog home business. Voted Remain in 2016

but now supports Brexit. **Alistair Ford** (Green) Climate scientist, Newcastle University. Contested this seat, 2017.

CONSTITUENCY PROFILE
Represented by Conservative MPs from 1918 to 1983 before becoming one of few Labour gains in that election, it has elected Labour MPs at every election since. This was caused partly by significant boundary changes. The least urban of the city's three seats, this constituency stretches beyond the city of Newcastle and contains a large portion of the city's northern and western suburbs.

EU REFERENDUM RESULT
56.8% Leave   Remain 43.2%

Newport East

MAJORITY 1,992 (5.49%)　　　　　LABOUR HOLD　　　　　TURNOUT 61.96%

JESSICA MORDEN
BORN May 29, 1968
MP 2005-

Chairwoman, statutory
instruments select cttee, 2018-.
General secretary, Welsh
Labour. Previously worked
for GMB and as a researcher
for the MPs Huw Edwards
and Llew Smith. Nominated
Sir Keir Starmer for leader in
2020; backed Owen Smith in
2016 and Liz Kendall in 2015.
Remainer who voted for a
second referendum in indicative
votes. Opposition whip, 2015-.
PPS to: Owen Smith, 2015-16;
Peter Hain, 2009-10, 2007-08;
Paul Murphy, 2008-09. Ed:
Croesyceiliog School; University
of Birmingham (BA history).

	Electorate	Share %	Change from 2017 %
	58,554		
*J Morden Lab	16,125	44.44	-12.06
M Brown C	14,133	38.95	+4.19
J Price Brexit	2,454	6.76	
M Hamilton LD	2,121	5.85	+3.22
C Wixcey PC	872	2.40	+0.01
P Varley Green	577	1.59	

CHALLENGERS
Mark Brown (C) Co-ordinator
for Vote Leave during the EU
referendum. Previously lived
in South Africa, where he was
a member of Conservatives
Abroad and ran his own
business. Spent several months
based in Jerusalem as an
intern with *The Times of Israel*.
Wales co-ordinator, LGBT+
Conservatives. **Julie Price**
(Brexit) Former Ukip member.
Mike Hamilton (LD) Former

university lecturer. **Cameron
Wixcey** (PC) Contested this seat
in 2017.

CONSTITUENCY PROFILE
This seat has returned Labour
MPs at every election since its
creation in 1983, and the same
was true of its predecessor seat
since 1945. The party's majority
has only once been lower than
in 2019, having fallen to 1,650
in 2010. Divided from Newport
West by the River Usk, this seat
is larger and more rural than
its neighbour, expanding out
towards Wales's border with
England. The seat contains the
Llanwern steelworks, which
employs about 1,600 people.

EU REFERENDUM RESULT
59.3% Leave　　　　　Remain 40.7%

Newport West

MAJORITY 902 (2.08%)　　　　　LABOUR HOLD　　　　　TURNOUT 65.16%

RUTH JONES
BORN Apr 23, 1962
MP 2019-

Senior negotiating officer
for the Chartered Society of
Physiotherapy. First elected
in an April 2019 by-election
triggered by the death of
Paul Flynn, the Labour MP
for this seat since 1987. NHS
physiotherapist from 1983.
President of the Wales TUC,
2017-19. Joined Labour when
Tony Blair was leader and has
declared herself a "socialist"
but is not openly factional.
Voted Remain and argued for
a cross-party consensus on
Brexit and a second referendum.
Environmental audit select cttee,
2019-. Contested Monmouth,

	Electorate	Share %	Change from 2017 %
	66,657		
*R Jones Lab	18,977	43.69	-8.62
M Evans C	18,075	41.62	+2.33
R Jones LD	2,565	5.91	+3.66
C Edwards Brexit	1,727	3.98	
J Clark PC	1,187	2.73	+0.25
A Womack Green	902	2.08	+0.93

2017, 2015. Ed: Duffryn High
School; Cardiff University.

CHALLENGERS
Matthew Evans (C) Proprietor
of a corporate catering business.
Cllr, Newport City C, 1999-2019;
counil leader, 2008-12; mayor
of Newport, 2014-15. Contested
April 2019 by-election. **Ryan
Jones** (LD) Owner of a local
construction company. Also
contested the 2019 by-election.
Cameron Edwards (Brexit)

Digital marketing executive.
Jonathan Clark (PC) MPhil in
Roman archaeology at Cardiff
University. Contested the April
2019 by-election.

CONSTITUENCY PROFILE
Has only been won by the
Conservatives once, in 1983,
when the constituency was
created. Labour's majority since
had never previously been below
1,000. In 2019 the seat had the
third-smallest majority in Wales.
It contains Newport Docks and
stretches across the south Wales
coast towards Cardiff. It also
includes the University of South
Wales and its 5,000 full-time
students.

EU REFERENDUM RESULT
53.7% Leave　　　　　Remain 46.3%

Newry & Armagh

MAJORITY 9,287 (18.29%)   SINN FEIN HOLD   TURNOUT 62.52%

MICKEY BRADY
BORN Oct 7, 1950
MP 2015-

Former welfare rights officer, working as a benefits and housing campaigner. Member of the Northern Ireland assembly, Newry & Armagh, 2007-15. Sinn Fein spokesman for welfare and older people. Served as deputy chairman, Northern Ireland assembly social development committee. Campaigned to Remain, fighting the case for designated special status within the EU for Northern Ireland. Faced death threats and a bomb alert at his home in 2015. Enjoys the sport hurling. Ed: Abbey Christian Brothers' Grammar School; University of Liverpool.

	Electorate	Share %	Change from 2017 %
	81,226		
*M Brady SF	20,287	39.95	-7.95
W Irwin DUP	11,000	21.66	-2.93
P Byrne SDLP	9,449	18.61	+1.71
J Coade Alliance	4,211	8.29	+5.95
S Nicholson UUP	4,204	8.28	+0.02
M Kelly Aontu	1,628	3.21	

CHALLENGERS
William Irwin (DUP) Dairy farmer who got involved in politics after his son drowned. Orangeman. MLA, Newry & Armagh, 2007-. Cllr, Armagh City and DC, 2005-14. Contested this seat, 2017. **Pete Byrne** (SDLP) Runs Granite Memorial business. LGBT+ campaigner. Cllr, Newry, Mourne & Down Council DC. **Jackie Coade** (Alliance) Social worker. Contested this seat, 2017. **Sam**

Nicholson (UUP) Chartered architect. Orangeman. Contested this seat, 2017. **Martin Kelly** (Aontu) Funeral director.

CONSTITUENCY PROFILE
On the border with the Republic of Ireland. Ulster Unionist Party MPs were elected here between 1922 and 1983, with the Social Democratic and Labour Party taking the seat at a 1986 by-election. The seat has been held by nationalists since, with Sinn Fein first gaining the seat from the SDLP in 2005. Sinn Fein's majority was cut to just over 4,000 in 2015, when the Democratic Unionist Party did not field a candidate.

EU REFERENDUM RESULT
37.1% Leave   Remain 62.9%

Newton Abbot

MAJORITY 17,501 (33.30%)   CONSERVATIVE HOLD   TURNOUT 72.46%

ANNE MARIE MORRIS
BORN Jul 5, 1957
MP 2010-

Briefly suspended from the Conservative Party after describing the prospect of leaving the EU without a deal as a "real n***er in the woodpile" in July 2017. Corporate lawyer, later marketing director: PWC; Ernst & Young. Set up a consultancy mentoring small businesses in the South West. Publicly criticised the chancellor for proposed rise in national insurance, 2016. Brexiteer. Supported Dominic Raab, then Boris Johnson, in the 2019 leadership contest. One of 30 Tory rebels against Isis airstrikes, 2013. Submitted a letter of no

	Electorate	Share %	Change from 2017 %
	72,533		
*A Morris C	29,190	55.54	+0.09
M Wrigley LD	11,689	22.24	+1.71
J Osben Lab	9,329	17.75	-4.47
M Debenham Green	1,508	2.87	+1.08
D Halpin Ind	840	1.60	

confidence in Theresa May's leadership in November 2018. PPS to Jo Johnson, 2015-16. Cllr, West Sussex DC, 2005-07. Ed: Hertford Coll, Oxford (BA jurisprudence); Coll of Law, London; Open University (MBA).

CHALLENGERS
Martin Wrigley (LD) Software and management consultant. Cllr, Teignbridge DC. **James Osben** (Lab) Mental health nurse. Chairman, Newton Abbot

CLP. Contested this seat in 2017. **Megan Debenham** (Green) Former social worker and Open University tutor.

CONSTITUENCY PROFILE
Teignbridge, the predecessor seat, was held by the Liberal Democrats, 2001-10, but the Conservatives won by 523 votes in the newly reconfigured seat in 2010. The Conservative vote had grown while the Lib Dem vote had been receding in general elections until 2019, when it increased marginally. The town of Newton Abbot is home to about 26,000 people. Other large towns include Teignmouth and Dawlish, both on the coast.

EU REFERENDUM RESULT
56.0% Leave   Remain 44.0%

Norfolk Mid

GEORGE FREEMAN
BORN Jul 12, 1967
MP 2010-

Transport minister, 2019-20. Venture capitalist who founded 4D Biomedical, a consultancy, and was managing director, 2003-10. Campaigned to Remain but later embraced Brexit. Backed Matt Hancock for leader, 2019. Was the first ever minister for life sciences, 2014-16. Adviser to David Willets, 2011-13. PPS to Greg Barker, 2010-12. Co-founder, 2020 group of Conservative MPs. Parliamentary under-secretary, business and health, 2014-16. Said benefits should only go to "really disabled" people in 2017. In September 2018, he called

	Electorate	Share %	from 2017 %	Change
	81,975			
*G Freeman C	35,051	62.38	+3.41	
A Heald Lab	12,457	22.17	-7.90	
S Aquarone LD	7,739	13.77	+8.66	
P O'Gorman Ind	939	1.67		

for Theresa May's resignation once a Brexit deal was passed. Contested Stevenage, 2005. Ed: Radley Coll; Girton Coll, Cambridge (BA geography).

CHALLENGERS
Adrian Heald (Lab) Consultant physician in diabetes and endocrinology at Leighton and Macclesfield Hospitals. Approved clinician in psychiatry. Research fellow, Manchester University, and visiting tutor, St Peter's Coll, Oxford. **Steffan Aquarone** (LD) Film and technology

entrepreneur. Cllr, Norwich City C, 2017-.

CONSTITUENCY PROFILE
A safe Conservative seat that has not been held by another party since its creation in 1983. Labour came close to winning it in 1997, finishing 1,336 votes behind the Conservatives. It is a rural seat to the west of Norwich, containing a mixture of villages and market towns. A significant number of people move here to retire and the proportion of residents aged over 65 is well above the national average. The median income is slightly lower than in the rest of the region.

EU REFERENDUM RESULT
60.6% Leave   Remain 39.4%

Norfolk North

DUNCAN BAKER
BORN Nov 15, 1979
MP 2019-

Finance and IT director at CT Baker Group, a North Norfolk builders' merchants, since 2008. Former mayor of Holt and Conservative leader on North Norfolk DC. Chartered accountant who worked as an auditor at Baker Tilly International, 2002-06, and Grant Thornton LLP, 2006-07. Finance manager, Archant, 2007-08. Chairman of the Holt 1940s weekend and Owl Trail project. Cllr, North Norfolk DC, 2019-. Born in Norfolk. Ed: Gresham's School; Nottingham Trent University (BA business studies).

	Electorate	Share %	from 2017 %	Change
	70,729			
D Baker C	29,792	58.62	+16.95	
K Ward LD	15,397	30.30	-18.11	
E Corlett Lab	3,895	7.66	-2.26	
H Gwynne Brexit	1,739	3.42		

CHALLENGERS
Karen Ward (LD) Ran Aditi Unlimited, a business advisory firm. Author of two business books. Previously a senior civil servant. Cllr, North Norfolk DC, 2016-. **Emma Corlett** (Lab) Mental health nurse for 20 years. Former trade union representative. Cllr, Norfolk City C, 2013-. **Harry Gwynne** (Brexit) Worked as a consultant and researcher for Vote Leave and founded 3rd Chamber, a social network promoting direct democracy.

CONSTITUENCY PROFILE
In 2001 Norman Lamb won this seat for the Liberal Democrats, becoming the first Liberal to represent the seat since 1918. For most of the 20th century the seat had flipped between Labour and the Conservatives, including continuous Tory wins from 1970. Mr Lamb, a minister for health and employment during the 2010-15 coalition government, stood down at this election. A rural and coastal seat made up of small towns and fishing villages, it has one of the highest proportions of older people in the UK, and, as a result of this, 45 per cent of households have no adult in employment.

EU REFERENDUM RESULT
58.4% Leave   Remain 41.6%

Norfolk North West

JAMES WILD
BORN Jan 5, 1977
MP 2019-

Special adviser to Boris Johnson from July to November 2019. Chief of staff to David Lidington, chancellor of the Duchy of Lancaster, 2018-19. Adviser to Sir Michael Fallon during his time as an MP. Worked in the Conservative research department, 2000-01. Worked as a lobbyist for T-Mobile, 2005-09, and Hanover Communications. Married to Baroness Evans of Bowes Park. Brexiteer. Contested Norfolk North, 2017. Blamed 2017 defeat on the manifesto. Ed: Norwich School; Queen Mary, University of London (BA politics).

	Electorate	Share %	from 2017 %	Change
	72,080			
J Wild C	30,627	65.72	+5.47	
J Rust Lab	10,705	22.97	-9.03	
R Colwell LD	3,625	7.78	+4.92	
A De Whalley Green	1,645	3.53	+1.79	

CHALLENGERS
Jo Rust (Lab) Early years and child development officer, Norfolk CC. Secondment as Norfolk campaigns organiser for Unison. Contested this seat, 2017. **Rob Colwell** (LD) Solicitor in King's Lynn. Led the West Norfolk Remain campaign in the 2016 EU referendum. **Andrew De Whalley** (Green) Self-employed IT consultant. Served in Iraq with the Royal Auxiliary Air Force in 2003. Started the successful King's Lynn Without Incineration campaign.

Contested this seat in the 2017, 2015 and 2010 general elections.

CONSTITUENCY PROFILE
Although this is a fairly safe Conservative seat, Labour held it for one term after the 1997 landslide. Sir Henry Bellingham stood down as the MP in 2019, having represented it for all but four years since 1983. The constituency stretches from the East Anglian coast to the regional centre of King's Lynn, and contains the surrounding farmland and villages, as well as the royal estate of Sandringham. It is a popular location to retire to and almost a quarter of residents are over 65.

EU REFERENDUM RESULT
65.8% Leave   Remain 34.2%

Norfolk South

RICHARD BACON
BORN Dec 3, 1962
MP 2001-

Investment banker, financial journalist and associate partner of Brunswick PR consultancy. Set up his own business advising companies on communications. Supported Michael Gove for the leadership in 2019. Select cttees: public accounts, 2001-; European scrutiny, 2001-07. Trenchant critic of financial mismanagement and fraud in the EU; tried to introduce a bill to repeal the Human Rights Act in 2012. Campaigned to Leave the EU. Co-author of *Conundrum: Why Every Government Gets Things Wrong and What We Can Do About It.* Consistently

	Electorate	Share %	from 2017 %	Change
	86,214			
*R Bacon C	36,258	58.03	-0.19	
B Jones Lab	14,983	23.98	-6.95	
C Brown LD	8,744	13.99	+5.69	
B Price Green	2,499	4.00	+1.45	

rebelled against military action in Middle East, including the 2003 invasion of Iraq. Contested Vauxhall, 1997. Ed: King's Sch; Worcester; LSE (BSc politics and economics).

CHALLENGERS
Beth Jones (Lab) Mental health nurse. Former care assistant. Cllr, Norwich City C, 2016-. **Christopher Brown** (LD) PR professional and business owner. Trustee of a local homelessness charity. Cllr, South Norfolk DC, 2019-. **Ben Price** (Green)

Gardener. Cllr, Norwich City C, 2012-.

CONSTITUENCY PROFILE
Safe Conservative seat, with Labour having last won it in 1945. The Liberals and Liberal Democrats had come second in the seat from 1983, but since 2015 Labour has replaced them as the runner-up. Situated just south of Norwich, this largely rural area includes the market towns of Diss and Harleston and several villages. There is a significant retired population, with almost 20 per cent of residents aged 65 or above, and there are very high levels of home ownership.

EU REFERENDUM RESULT
50.9% Leave   Remain 49.1%

Norfolk South West

ELIZABETH TRUSS
BORN Jul 26, 1975
MP 2010-

	Electorate	Share %	Change from 2017 %
	78,455		
*E Truss C	35,507	68.99	+6.24
E Blake Lab	9,312	18.09	-9.73
J Ratcliffe LD	4,166	8.09	+3.58
P Devulapalli Green	1,645	3.20	
E Of Outwell Loony	836	1.62	

Appointed secretary of state for international trade and minister for women and equalities by Boris Johnson in 2019, having backed him in the leadership contest. Had been chief secretary to the Treasury since a post-2017 election reshuffle, in what was seen as a demotion. Justice secretary, 2016-17; criticised by some in legal community for not defending judicial independence after Supreme Court verdict on Article 50. Environment secretary, 2014-16. Education minister, 2012-14; youngest-ever female cabinet minister upon appointment. Former economics director, Cable & Wireless, and commerical analyst, Shell. Director, Reform think tank, 2008-09. Founder, Free Enterprise Group. Cllr, Greenwich BC, 2006-10. Contested: Calder Valley, 2005; Hemsworth, 2001. Ed: Roundhay Sch, Leeds; Merton Coll, Oxford (BA PPE).

CHALLENGERS
Emily Blake (Lab) Broadcaster and award-winning plus-size model. **Josie Ratcliffe** (LD) Cllr,

King's Lynn & West Norfolk BC, 2019-.

CONSTITUENCY PROFILE
This is a safe seat for the Conservatives, the party having won five-figure majorities here since 2005, although Tony Blair's Labour Party did reduce the Tory majority to less than 2,500 votes in 1997. This is a sparsely populated and rural constituency with significant employment in public administration and defence, since the seat includes the army's Stanford training area. Levels of home ownership are high and the unemployment rate is lower than the national average.

EU REFERENDUM RESULT
66.7% Leave   Remain 33.3%

Normanton, Pontefract & Castleford

YVETTE COOPER
BORN Mar 20, 1969
MP 1997-

	Electorate	Share %	Change from 2017 %
	84,527		
*Y Cooper Lab	18,297	37.91	-21.58
A Lee C	17,021	35.27	+5.25
D Florence-Jukes Brexit	8,032	16.64	
T Gordon LD	3,147	6.52	+5.11
L Walker Yorkshire	1,762	3.65	+0.74

Unsuccessfully stood to be Labour leader in 2015. Was expected to stand again in 2020 but did not receive enough support. Considered a Brownite and hostile to Jeremy Corbyn. Campaigned to Remain and scrutinised Brexit policy as chairwoman of the home affairs select cttee, 2016-. Married to Ed Balls, the shadow chancellor, 2011-15; first married couple to sit in cabinet together. Shadow home secretary, 2011-15; shadow foreign secretary, 2010-11. Held a range of ministerial positions under New Labour and was work and pensions secretary, 2009-10. Chief economics correspondent, *The Independent*, 1995-97. Research associate, Centre for Economic Performance, 1994. Policy adviser to Harriet Harman (Camberwell & Peckham), 1992. Researcher for John Smith, 1990-92. Labour Friends of Israel supporter. Ed: Balliol Coll, Oxford (BA PPE); LSE (MSc economics); Harvard (Kennedy scholar).

CHALLENGERS
Andrew Lee (C) Cllr, North Yorkshire CC. Voted Leave. Contested this seat, 2017. **Deneice Florence-Jukes** (Brexit) Served in RAF and Metropolitan Police. Cllr, East Staffordshire BC, 2017-. **Thomas Gordon** (LD) Caseworker and researcher, Shaffaq Mohammed MEP. Cllr, Wakefield DC, 2019-.

CONSTITUENCY PROFILE
This seat and its predecessors have voted Labour since 1935, but the party's majority has never been as low as in 2019; the last time it fell below five figures was in 1945. A former coalmining area, the main industries now include manufacturing and retail, and wages are below average.

EU REFERENDUM RESULT
69.3% Leave   Remain 30.7%

Northampton North

MICHAEL ELLIS
BORN Oct 13, 1967
MP 2010-

Solicitor-general since Boris Johnson became prime minister, before which he was a transport minister for three months in 2019. PPS to the culture department, 2018-19. Assistant whip and deputy Commons leader, 2016-18. Criminal barrister and QC; worked on legal aid cases. Regular contributor to broadcast media on constitutional issues. Campaigned for extra funds to reduce potholes, which were granted in 2014 budget. Member, Society of Conservative Lawyers. Cllr, Northamptonshire CC, 1997-2001. Ed: Wellingborough

	Electorate	Share %	from 2017 %	Change
	59,265			
*M Ellis C	21,031	53.19	+5.97	
S Keeble Lab	15,524	39.26	-5.96	
M Sawyer LD	2,031	5.14	+2.62	
K Pate Green	953	2.41	+0.84	

Sch; University of Buckingham (LLB); City, University of London (BVC).

CHALLENGERS
Sally Keeble (Lab) MP for this constituency, 1997-2010. Jeremy Corbyn critic. Supporter of a second Brexit referendum. Parliamentary under-secretary: international development, 2002-03; transport, 2001-02. PPS to Hilary Armstrong, 1999-2001. Former journalist and communications director. Contested this seat in 2017.

Martin Sawyer (LD) Local businessman. **Katherine Pate** (Green) Education publisher.

CONSTITUENCY PROFILE
Bellwether since its creation in 1974, held by whichever party won most seats. Labour came within about 800 votes of winning in 2017 but in 2019 the Conservative majority was at its largest since 1987. The seat is more densely populated than its southern neighbour, containing most of the campuses of the University of Northampton and about 7,000 students. Income is below both the East Midlands and national averages. Home ownership in the area is low.

EU REFERENDUM RESULT
60.3% Leave   Remain 39.7%

Northampton South

ANDREW LEWER
BORN Jul 18, 1971
MP 2017-

Campaigned for Brexit on the basis that David Cameron's renegotiation was not good enough. ERG member. Backed Boris Johnson in the 2019 Tory leadership election. Worked in publishing before entering politics. MEP, 2014-17; spokesman on education and culture. Cllr, Derbyshire CC, 2005-15; council leader 2009-13. Awarded an MBE for services to local government in 2014. Governor, University of Derby. Director, Derbyshire Historic Buildings Trust. Vice-chairman, Millbank Club. Ed: QE Grammar School; Newcastle University

	Electorate	Share %	from 2017 %	Change
	62,712			
*A Lewer C	20,914	51.22	+4.35	
G Eales Lab	16,217	39.71	-4.33	
J Hope LD	2,482	6.08	+2.65	
S Mabbutt Green	1,222	2.99	+1.30	

(BA history); Downing Coll, Cambridge (MA history).

CHALLENGERS
Gareth Eales (Lab) Full-time trade union official for the Communication Workers Union for more than 20 years. **Jill Hope** (LD) Corporate banker. Instrumental in team that relocated Barclaycard from London to Northampton. **Scott Mabbutt** (Green) Doctor at Northampton General Hospital in the Barratt Maternity Unit. Contested this seat in 2017.

CONSTITUENCY PROFILE
It has mainly been held by the Conservatives since its creation in 1974. The seat has been won by Labour only in 1997 and 2001, both times with a majority of less than a thousand. The subsequent Conservative majorities peaked at a little over six thousand in 2010 but, as in Northampton North, Labour came fairly close in 2017, losing by fewer than 1,200 votes. The seat, which contains the city centre, has a small proportion of older residents: only a third are over the age of 45. Home ownership is below average, and more than a fifth of households are privately rented.

EU REFERENDUM RESULT
59.0% Leave   Remain 41.0%

Northamptonshire South

MAJORITY 27,761 (41.49%)   CONSERVATIVE HOLD   TURNOUT 73.65%

ANDREA LEADSOM
BORN May 13, 1963
MP 2010-

Leading Brexiteer who reached the final two in the 2016 Tory leadership contest but dropped out after implying in an interview with *The Times* that being a mother would make her a better prime minister than Theresa May. Also unsuccessfully stood for leader in 2019. Sacked as business secretary in the February 2020 reshuffle after six months in the role. Leader of the House of Commons, 2017-19; resigned in protest at Mrs May's Brexit strategy. Environment secretary, 2016-17; energy minister, 2015-16; economic secretary to the

	Electorate	Share %	Change from 2017 %
	90,840		
*A Leadsom C	41,755	62.41	-0.06
G Kitchen Lab	13,994	20.92	-6.41
C Lofts LD	7,891	11.79	+6.22
D Donaldson Green	2,634	3.94	+1.85
J Phillips Ind	463	0.69	+0.24
S McCutcheon ND	171	0.26	

Treasury, 2014-15. Career in the City, including at Barclays and Invesco Perpetual. Contested Knowsley South, 2005. Ed: Tonbridge Girls' GS; University of Warwick (BA political science).

CHALLENGERS
Gen Kitchen (Lab) Fundraising officer, Sarcoma UK. Cllr, Newham LBC, 2018-. **Chris Lofts** (LD) Former deputy chief executive at South

Northamptonshire county council. **Denise Donaldson** (Green) Nurse.

CONSTITUENCY PROFILE
Since this seat was re-created in 2010 the Conservative Party has not received less than half of the vote. Andrea Leadsom's vote total has grown at every successive election. A sprawling rural seat, Northamptonshire South's biggest settlements are the market towns of Brackley and Towcester, although its largest population centre comes from Northampton's southern suburbs. Home ownership and the median income in the seat are both well above average.

EU REFERENDUM RESULT
53.3% Leave   Remain 46.7%

Norwich North

MAJORITY 4,738 (10.24%)   CONSERVATIVE HOLD   TURNOUT 68.91%

CHLOE SMITH
BORN May 17, 1982
MP 2009-

Minister of state for the constitution and devolution, 2020-. Former management consultant at Deloitte, who was seconded to the Conservatives' implementation unit. Gained the seat in a 2009 by-election to become the youngest ever Conservative woman in the Commons and the youngest MP. Career stalled after a disastrous *Newsnight* interview with Jeremy Paxman about a U-turn on fuel duty, 2012. Parliamentary secretary, Cabinet Office, 2018-20, 2012-13; assistant whip, 2017-18; parliamentary under-secretary, Northern Ireland,

	Electorate	Share %	Change from 2017 %
	67,172		
*C Smith C	23,397	50.55	+2.83
K Davis Lab	18,659	40.31	-6.30
D Thomas LD	2,663	5.75	+2.53
A Holmes Green	1,078	2.33	+0.63
D Moreland Ukip	488	1.05	

2017; economic secretary to the Treasury, 2011-12; whip, 2010-11. Supported Boris Johnson for leadership in 2019. Ed: Swaffham Sixth Form Coll; University of York (BA English literature).

CHALLENGERS
Karen Davis (Lab) Teacher. Worked in bars and lived in a squat. Cllr, Norwich City C, 2016-; cabinet member for social inclusion. **Dave Thomas** (LD) Manager and trainer at Tax Assist Accountants. Cllr,

Broadland DC, 2019-.

CONSTITUENCY PROFILE
Held by Labour from its creation in 1950 until the Conservatives won in 1983. Has been a bellwether since. Labour won in 1997 and held the seat until the 2009 by-election prompted by the resignation of Ian Gibson after he was caught up in the expenses scandal. The Tories have held it since, but with a majority of only 507 in 2017. Norwich North is sparser and more residential than its southern neighbour. Just over a fifth of residents are 65 or older and the median income is lower than in Norwich South.

EU REFERENDUM RESULT
56.7% Leave   Remain 43.3%

Norwich South

MAJORITY 12,760 (24.69%) LABOUR HOLD TURNOUT 66.38%

CLIVE LEWIS
BORN Sep 11, 1971
MP 2015-

Stood for the Labour leadership in 2020 but withdrew after failing to receive the required number of nominations from MPs and MEPs. Jeremy Corbyn ally and self-described "proud socialist". Shadow Treasury minister, 2018-; shadow business secretary, 2016-17; shadow defence secretary, 2016. Campaigned against Brexit and resigned from shadow cabinet to vote against triggering Article 50. Criticised for using offensive language at the 2017 Labour Party conference, at which he was also accused of groping a woman, which he denied. He was

	Electorate	Share %	from 2017 % Change
	77,845		
*C Lewis Lab	27,766	53.73	-7.23
M Spencer C	15,006	29.04	-1.56
J Wright LD	4,776	9.24	+3.71
C Rowett Green	2,469	4.78	+1.87
S Gilchrist Brexit	1,656	3.20	

cleared after an investigation by the Labour Party. Former NUS vice-president, BBC reporter and army reservist. Ed: University of Bradford (BA economics; SU president).

CHALLENGERS
Mike Spencer (C) Consultant psychiatrist. **James Wright** (LD) Worked in the IT industry for 20 years, including for the BBC. **Catherine Rowett** (Green) Philosophy professor, UEA. MEP for East of England, 2019-20.

CONSTITUENCY PROFILE
The only time Labour failed to win over the past 30 years was in 2010, when the Liberal Democrats gained a majority of 310, beating the former home secretary Charles Clarke. Norwich South is denser and more urban than its neighbour, containing the medieval city centre and Carrow Road stadium. The University of East Anglia and Norwich University of the Arts are based in the seat, which is home to more than 18,000 16 to 24-year-olds. Aviva, formerly Norwich Union, is still an important employer in the city, which is a stronghold for the Green Party at council level.

EU REFERENDUM RESULT
40.5% Leave Remain 59.5%

Nottingham East

MAJORITY 17,393 (43.48%) LABOUR HOLD TURNOUT 60.37%

NADIA WHITTOME
BORN Aug 29, 1996
MP 2019-

Elected at the age of 23, making her the baby of the House. Pledged to take the UK average full-time wage of £35,000 per year if elected an MP, donating the rest to local causes. Nominated Clive Lewis for the leadership before backing Emily Thornberry once he had pulled out of the contest. Worked as a carer and on a project tackling hate crime. Member of Momentum and organiser of the Labour Campaign for Free Movement. Helped to organise Nottingham's first Deliveroo workers' strike. Ed: West Bridgford School; New College

	Electorate	Share %	from 2017 % Change
	66,262		
N Whittome Lab	25,735	64.33	-7.13
V Stapleton C	8,342	20.85	-0.79
R Swift LD	1,954	4.88	+2.33
*C Leslie Change	1,447	3.62	
D Smith Brexit	1,343	3.36	
M Vacciana Green	1,183	2.96	+1.18

Nottingham (access to law); University of Nottingham (LLB).

CHALLENGERS
Victoria Stapleton (C) Caseworker for Craig Tracey (North Warwickshire). **Robert Swift** (LD) Worked for 17 years in telecommunications. **Chris Leslie** (Change) Labour MP for Shipley, 1997-2005 and this seat, 2010-19. Left the party in February 2019 in protest at Jeremy Corbyn's leadership;

co-founded The Independent Group. Shadow chancellor, 2015.

CONSTITUENCY PROFILE
A safe Labour seat held by the party since 1992, with the 2019 majority slightly lower than the record of more than 19,500 achieved in 2017. The seat has a young electorate, owing in large part to a high student population. It is much more ethnically diverse than the rest of the East Midlands: one in six residents is of Asian heritage and one in ten is black. There are very low levels of home ownership and the seat has a high child poverty rate of almost 40 per cent.

EU REFERENDUM RESULT
42.9% Leave Remain 57.1%

Nottingham North

MAJORITY 4,490 (12.71%)   **LABOUR CO-OP HOLD**   **TURNOUT 53.12%**

ALEX NORRIS
BORN Feb 4, 1984
MP 2017-

	Electorate	Share %	Change from 2017 %
	66,495		
*A Norris Lab Co-op	17,337	49.09	-11.11
S Bestwick C	12,847	36.37	+5.30
J Carter Brexit	2,686	7.60	
C Morgan-Danvers LD	1,582	4.48	+2.72
A Jones Green	868	2.46	+1.05

Acting shadow international development minister, 2019-. Close ally of the former Nottingham North MP Graham Allen, who stepped down in 2017 citing ill health. Signed a letter calling on Jeremy Corbyn to step down. Backed Lisa Nandy for leader. Former trade union organiser for Unison. GMB member. Called for a debate on the introduction of safe standing in football stadiums. Cllr, Nottingham City C, 2011-17; held adults and health portfolio. Chairman of governors, Rosslyn Park Primary Sch. Ed: Manchester GS; University of

Nottingham (BA politics).

CHALLENGERS
Stuart Bestwick (C) Business owner. Former director of Oakwood Archer Limited. Contested Sherwood in 2017 for Ukip. **Julian Carter** (Brexit) Nuclear inspector. Worked internationally for Oxfam and the United Nations High Commissioner for Refugees. **Christina Morgan-Danvers** (LD) Customer operative for a non-profit energy company.

CONSTITUENCY PROFILE
Has elected Labour MPs since the constituency's creation in 1955, with the sole exception of 1983, when it elected a Conservative with a majority of 362 votes. Alex Norris's 2019 majority was the smallest Labour had won in the constituency since 1987. Containing a significant proportion of urban Nottingham, this is a young area in which more than three fifths are aged under 45 and nearly a quarter under 16. About a quarter of residents are from an ethnic minority. It has the highest median income of the three Nottingham seats.

EU REFERENDUM RESULT
63.8% Leave   Remain 36.2%

Nottingham South

MAJORITY 12,568 (26.11%)   **LABOUR HOLD**   **TURNOUT 60.56%**

LILIAN GREENWOOD
BORN Mar 26, 1966
MP 2010-

	Electorate	Share %	Change from 2017 %
	79,485		
*L Greenwood Lab	26,586	55.23	-7.13
M Nykolyszyn C	14,018	29.12	-1.73
B Holliday LD	3,935	8.18	+4.93
J Lawson Brexit	2,012	4.18	
C Sutherland Green	1,583	3.29	+2.05

Shadow transport secretary, 2015-16, but resigned from the front bench after feeling ignored and undermined by Jeremy Corbyn and lacking confidence in his leadership. Nominated Lisa Nandy for the leadership in 2020. Remainer; voted against triggering Article 50. Career as a Unison regional organiser, manager and officer. Chairwoman, transport select cttee, 2017-20. Member: Fabian Society; Fawcett Society. Ed: Canon Slade Sch, Bolton; St. Catherine's Coll, Cambridge (BA economics, social and political science); Southbank Polytechnic

(MSc sociology & social policy).

CHALLENGERS
Marc Nykolyszyn (C) Fundraising manager for the NGO Oceana. Previously worked in New York for The Boys' Club of New York and the Kaufman Music Center. **Barry Holliday** (LD) Runs a charity-based service helping adults with learning disabilities. Remain campaign spokesman. **John Lawson** (Brexit) Former finance director.

CONSTITUENCY PROFILE
Over the past 30 years Nottingham South has been the most marginal of the three Nottingham seats, although in 2017 and 2019 Nottingham North had slimmer majorities. The seat has been held by Labour since 1992, having returned a Conservative MP in 1983 and 1987. This ethnically diverse constituency includes some of the most affluent and most deprived areas of the city. It contains the University of Nottingham campus and one site of Nottingham Trent University, and has one of the largest student populations of any seat in the country.

EU REFERENDUM RESULT
46.5% Leave   Remain 53.5%

Nuneaton

MAJORITY 13,144 (29.09%)   CONSERVATIVE HOLD   TURNOUT 64.35%

MARCUS JONES
BORN Apr 5, 1974
MP 2010-

Government whip, 2020-, and assistant whip, 2019-20. Remainer, but voted to keep a no-deal Brexit on the table. One of 24 MPs not to declare expenses for a battlebus in 2015 election, but the Crown Prosecution Service took no action. Vice-chairman of the Conservative Party, 2018-19. Parliamentary under-secretary, communities, 2015-. PPS to Sajid Javid, 2013-15. Entrepreneur who ran a string of small businesses. Interested in local government and housing. Campaigned against fuel duty increases and to scrap the beer duty escalator.

	Electorate	Share %	from 2017 Change %
	70,226		
*M Jones C	27,390	60.61	+9.04
Z Mayou Lab	14,246	31.52	-9.75
R Brighton-Knight LD	1,862	4.12	+2.14
K Kondakor Green	1,692	3.74	+2.09

Cllr, Nuneaton and Bedworth BC, 2005-10; leader, 2008-09. Ed: St Thomas More RC School, Nuneaton; King Edward VI Coll.

CHALLENGERS
Zoe Mayou (Lab) Union official, Unite, and former speech therapist. **Richard Brighton-Knight** (LD) Doctor based in Harley Street. **Keith Kondakor** (Green) Environmental campaigner. Cllr, Warwickshire CC, 2013-. Contested Warwickshire North in the 2017 election.

CONSTITUENCY PROFILE
Nuneaton has been a bellwether seat since 1983, although it was held by Labour for the whole of its postwar history before that. As the first key marginal to declare in 2015, it was a notable portent for Labour's defeat. The 2019 Conservative majority in Nuneaton was the largest, in percentage terms, of any since 1974, and the biggest that the party has achieved. This north Warwickshire seat, located just north of Coventry, has relatively high levels of home ownership, but lower than average earnings. The town of Nuneaton itself is relatively large and was home to the author George Eliot.

EU REFERENDUM RESULT

64.5% Leave	Remain 35.5%

Ochil & Perthshire South

MAJORITY 4,498 (7.78%)   SNP GAIN FROM CONSERVATIVE   TURNOUT 73.39%

JOHN NICOLSON
BORN Jun 23, 1961
MP 2019-; 2015-17

Criticised for seeming to forget which seat he was standing in during the 2019 campaign. MP for Dunbartonshire East, 2015-17, losing his seat to Jo Swinson, who lost it back to the SNP in 2019 while leader of the Liberal Democrats. SNP spokesman, culture, 2015-17. Select cttees: culture, 2015-17; Speaker's advisory on works of art, 2015-17. BBC journalist who presented live coverage of the 9/11 terrorist attacks on New York. Vocal opponent of Brexit. Ed: Hutchesons' Grammar School; University of Glasgow (MA English literature and politics).

	Electorate	Share %	from 2017 Change %
	78,776		
J Nicolson SNP	26,882	46.50	+11.22
*L Graham C	22,384	38.72	-2.76
L Robertson Lab	4,961	8.58	-11.44
I Stefanov LD	3,204	5.54	+2.33
S Martin Ukip	382	0.66	

CHALLENGERS
Luke Graham (C) MP for this constituency, 2017-19. PPS to the Cabinet Office, 2018-19. Was finance director of Britain Stronger In Europe, the official Remain campaign. Select cttees: public accounts, 2017-18; finance, 2018-19. Chartered accountant. Contested this seat, 2015. **Lorna Robertson** (Lab) NHS worker. Unite representative. **Iliyan Stefanov** (LD) Led student support services at Queen Margaret University.

CONSTITUENCY PROFILE
Created in 2005, this rural seat has been won by four different MPs from three different parties in the past four elections. Labour held it from 2005 until the SNP's landslide victory in 2015. The Conservative Party's Luke Graham defeated the SNP's Tasmina Ahmed-Sheikh in 2017. The SNP majority in 2019 was less than half the size it was in 2015. The largest town in the seat is Alloa, home to about 19,000 people, which sits in the far south of the constituency. The median income is slightly above the Scottish average, as are the levels of home ownership.

EU REFERENDUM RESULT

39.5% Leave	Remain 60.5%

Ogmore

LABOUR HOLD TURNOUT 61.46%

CHRIS ELMORE
BORN Dec 23, 1983
MP 2016-

Former butcher's apprentice who won a by-election in May 2016 that was prompted by Huw Irranca-Davies's resignation to seek election to the Welsh assembly. Worked in further education. Supported Owen Smith in 2016 Labour leadership election. Opposition whip, 2016-. Vice-chairman, APPG for the coalfield communities. Cllr, Vale of Glamorgan CC, 2008-17. Member of Barry Communities First and Barry YMCA Hub. Contested Vale of Glamorgan in 2015. Ed: Cardiff Metropolitan University (BA history and culture).

	Electorate	Share %	Change from 2017 %
	57,581		
*C Elmore Lab	17,602	49.74	-12.69
S Vidal C	9,797	27.68	+2.54
C Roach Brexit	2,991	8.45	
L Fletcher PC	2,919	8.25	+0.73
A Davies LD	1,460	4.13	+2.53
T Muller Green	621	1.75	

CHALLENGERS
Sadie Vidal (C) Media officer at the British Medical Association. Cllr, Bridgend BC, 2017-. **Christine Roach** (Brexit) NHS worker, supporting people with long-term health conditions. **Luke Fletcher** (PC) 24-year-old economic and financial researcher. Cllr, Pencoed TC, 2019-. **Anita Davies** (LD) Works for the Cardiff Institute for the Blind as a locality development manager. Partially sighted.

CONSTITUENCY PROFILE
A rural south Wales seat located between Swansea and Cardiff that has returned a Labour MP at every election since its creation in 1918. The 2019 election was the first time, however, that Labour won less than 50 per cent of the votes cast. It was also the first time that Labour's majority had fallen below 10,000 since 1922. Its largest town is Pencoed, which has fewer than 10,000 residents. Home ownership is well above average, mainly at the expense of privately rented accommodation. The manufacturing industry provides a high proportion of jobs.

EU REFERENDUM RESULT
58.9% Leave   Remain 41.1%

Old Bexley & Sidcup

CONSERVATIVE HOLD TURNOUT 69.81%

JAMES BROKENSHIRE
BORN Jan 8, 1968
MP 2005-

Minister of state at the Home Office, 2020-. Secretary of state for housing, communities and local government, 2018-19, and for Northern Ireland, 2016-18, when he was criticised for failing to broker the restoration of the power-sharing executive at Stormont; he resigned before an operation to treat early stage lung cancer. Immigration minister, 2014-16; negotiated Abu Qatada's deportation in 2012. Lawyer and former partner, Jones Day Gouldens. MP for Hornchurch from 2005 unil 2010, when the constituency was dissolved. Worked on the

	Electorate	Share %	Change from 2017 %
	66,104		
*J Brokenshire C	29,786	64.55	+3.05
D Tingle Lab	10,834	23.48	-5.83
S Reynolds LD	3,822	8.28	+5.01
M Browne Green	1,477	3.20	+1.49
C Valinejad CPA	226	0.49	+0.32

Conservatives' 1996 European election campaign. Former vice-chairman, Young Conservatives. Ed: Cambridge Centre for Sixth Form Studies; University of Exeter (LLB).

CHALLENGERS
David Tingle (Lab) Runs own tuition centre. Former maths teacher. **Simone Reynolds** (LD) Works in mental health for a local authority in southeast London. **Matt Browne** (Green) Green Party's policy manager.

CONSTITUENCY PROFILE
A safe Conservative seat, which before 2001 was held by the former Conservative leader Edward Heath, prime minister from 1970 to 1974. Labour came within about 3,500 of winning it in 1997 and 2001, but the Conservatives have won five-figure majorities here since the party returned to government in 2010. It is a southeast London seat, bordering the county of Kent. About one in five residents is aged 65 or over, compared to the London average of one in ten. Home ownership is well above average, with nearly four fifths of households owner-occupied.

EU REFERENDUM RESULT
62.4% Leave   Remain 37.6%

Oldham East & Saddleworth

MAJORITY 1,499 (3.25%)   LABOUR HOLD   TURNOUT 63.96%

DEBBIE ABRAHAMS
BORN Sep 15, 1960
MP 2011-

Former public health consultant. Shadow work and pensions secretary, 2016-18; sacked after a Labour Party investigation into allegations that she had bullied staff, which she denied. Shadow minister, disabled people, 2015-16. PPS, 2011-15, to Andy Burnham, whom she nominated for leader before supporting Jeremy Corbyn in 2016 and Sir Keir Starmer in 2020. Chairwoman of Labour health committee; organised inquiry into the effectiveness of international health systems. Chairwoman, Rochdale primary care trust, 2002-07;

	Electorate	Share %	Change from 2017 %
	72,173		
*D Abrahams Lab	20,088	43.51	-10.97
T Lord C	18,589	40.27	+3.18
P Brierley Brexit	2,980	6.46	
S Al-Hamdani LD	2,423	5.25	+1.67
P Errock Oldham	1,073	2.32	
W Olsen Green	778	1.69	
A Lindo Ind	233	0.50	

resigned over the use of private health companies in the NHS. Contested Colne Valley, 2010. Ed: University of Salford (BSc biochemistry and physiology); University of Liverpool (MEd public health).

CHALLENGERS
Tom Lord (C) Barrister. Works with disadvantaged children in primary education. **Paul Brierley** (Brexit) Company

director. Started career as an apprentice joiner.

CONSTITUENCY PROFILE
Created in 1997, this seat has elected only Labour MPs, as had its predecessor seats since 1959. The Liberal Democrats came within 103 votes of unseating Labour in 2010, in a result that was declared void when the MP Phil Woolas was found to have falsely portrayed his rival on campaign leaflets. This led to the January 2011 by-election in which Debbie Abrahams was first elected. On the eastern edge of Greater Manchester it is more rural, affluent and ethnically homogenous than Oldham West.

EU REFERENDUM RESULT
59.9% Leave   Remain 40.1%

Oldham West & Royton

MAJORITY 11,127 (25.04%)   LABOUR CO-OP HOLD   TURNOUT 60.82%

JIM MCMAHON
BORN Jul 7, 1980
MP 2015-

Centre-left Remain supporter elected in a December 2015 by-election after the death of Michael Meacher. PPS to Tom Watson, 2016. Shadow minister: communities, 2018-; devolution, 2016-18. Supported Sir Keir Starmer for the leadership in 2020 and Owen Smith in 2016. Appointed OBE in 2015 for leading regeneration of Oldham. Extensive local government experience, including involvement in devolution negotiations for Greater Manchester. Varied career as a town centre manager, a technician at the University

	Electorate	Share %	Change from 2017 %
	73,063		
*J McMahon Lab Co-op	24,579	55.32	-9.87
K Finlayson C	13,452	30.27	+2.65
H Formby Brexit	3,316	7.46	
G Harkness LD	1,484	3.34	+1.25
D Jerrome Green	681	1.53	+0.57
D Cole Oldham	533	1.20	
A Prince Ukip	389	0.88	-3.27

of Manchester and a delivery driver. Cllr, Oldham MBC, 2003-16; leader, 2011-16.

CHALLENGERS
Kirsty Finlayson (C) Director of communications for the British Conservation Alliance. Previously a trainee solicitor at Weightmans. Contested East Ham, 2017. **Helen Formby** (Brexit) Runs bookbinding business in Ramsbottom,

repairing antique books. **Garth Harkness** (LD) Maths and special needs teacher.

CONSTITUENCY PROFILE
Has elected Labour MPs since it was created in 1997, with five-figure majorities in every election other than 2010. Nick Griffin stood in the seat in 2001 for the British National Party, coming third with a sixth of the vote. Its predecessor seats elected Labour MPs at every general election since 1945. More than a quarter of the population is Asian or of Asian heritage. It is a less affluent seat than the regional average and a quarter of households are socially rented.

EU REFERENDUM RESULT
61.3% Leave   Remain 38.7%

Orkney & Shetland

MAJORITY 2,507 (10.82%) LIB DEM HOLD TURNOUT 67.70%

ALISTAIR CARMICHAEL
BORN Jul 15, 1965
MP 2001-

Liberal Democrat chief whip since 2015 and spokesman on Northern Ireland, 2017-19. Scotland secretary in coalition, 2013-15. Deputy leader of the Scottish Lib Dems, 2012-. Quit the party front bench to vote for a referendum on EU membership in 2008, but campaigned to Remain in 2016. Admitted leaking a memo in the 2015 election that contained inaccurate information about Nicola Sturgeon. He said he thought that the memo had been true and that he did not intend to smear her. Career began in the hotel industry. Studied law

	Electorate	Share %	from 2017 %	Change
	34,211			
*A Carmichael LD	10,381	44.82	-3.77	
R Leslie SNP	7,874	34.00	+5.00	
J Fairbairn C	2,287	9.87	+1.18	
C Drake Lab	1,550	6.69	-4.75	
R Smith Brexit	900	3.89		
D Barnard Ind	168	0.73	-0.33	

and practised as a solicitor. Ed: Islay HS; University of Aberdeen (Scots law LLB, Dip LP).

CHALLENGERS
Robert Leslie (SNP) Energy officer at Orkney Housing Association. Former news editor of the *Orcadian* and *Orkney Today* newspapers. Author of a recently published history of Orkney rugby club. **Jennifer Fairbairn** (C) Retired; volunteers at the Salvation Army shop in

Kirkwall. **Coilla Drake** (Lab) Works at the Bakehouse and part-time as a lifeguard.

CONSTITUENCY PROFILE
With the exception of 1935, variants of the Liberal Party have held the seat since the foundation of the Liberals in 1859. It was the only seat in Scotland that the Lib Dems won at the 2015 election. Represented by only three people for the past 70 years, its MP from 1950 until 1983 was the Liberal leader Jo Grimond. The second smallest parliamentary seat by population, consisting of a pair of archipelagos off the northwest coast of Scotland.

EU REFERENDUM RESULT
40.3% Leave Remain 59.7%

Orpington

MAJORITY 22,378 (45.93%) CONSERVATIVE HOLD TURNOUT 70.73%

GARETH BACON
BORN Apr 7, 1972
MP 2019-

Former leader of the Conservative group in the Greater Lonon Authority. Elected to the London assembly in May 2016 for the constituency of Bexley & Bromley. Chaired the assembly's budget and performance committee and the budget monitoring sub-committee. Elected deputy leader of Bexley council after the local elections of 2014, leaving in 2015 after being appointed by Boris Johnson, the mayor of London, as chairman of the London Fire and Emergency Planning Authority, succeeding James Cleverly. Elected to

	Electorate	Share %	from 2017 %	Change
	68,884			
G Bacon C	30,882	63.39	+0.44	
S Jeal Lab	8,504	17.45	-6.92	
A Tweddle LD	7,552	15.50	+8.93	
K Wheller Green	1,783	3.66	+1.56	

Bexley LBC in 1998, 2002 and 2006. Born in Hong Kong. Ed: University of Kent (BA politics & government; MA European studies).

CHALLENGERS
Simon Jeal (Lab) Compliance consultant at Northern Trust Management Services. **Allan Tweddle** (LD) Chartered accountant. Volunteer speaker for the Guide Dogs for the Blind Association. **Karen Wheller** (Green) Volunteer zookeeper at Beaver Water World in Tatsfield.

CONSTITUENCY PROFILE
The previous MP, Jo Johnson, the pro-EU brother of Boris, stood down in 2019, having represented the seat since 2010. It has elected Conservative MPs since 1945, except for a period of eight years between 1962 and 1970, when it was held by the Liberals. The 2017 election was the first time that Labour finished second in the seat since 1959. The Liberal Democrats almost took control in 2001, losing by 269 votes. Orpington is in southeast London, within the borough of Bromley. The median income is well above the national average. Four in five households are owner-occupied.

EU REFERENDUM RESULT
57.5% Leave Remain 42.5%

Oxford East

LABOUR CO-OP HOLD

ANNELIESE DODDS
BORN Mar 16, 1978
MP 2017-

Former senior lecturer in public policy at Aston University. Took over in 2017 from Andrew Smith, who had been the seat's MP for 30 years. Shadow Treasury minister, 2017-. Backed Sir Keir Starmer for leader, 2020. Voted for every anti-Brexit option in indicative votes. South East MEP, 2014-17; member: conference of delegation chairs; economic and monetary affairs cttee. Delivered a speech in the European parliament on tax avoidance while cradling young daughter, in solidarity with working mothers. Former acting director, National Institute for

	Electorate	Share %	from 2017 %	Change
	77,947			
*A Dodds Lab Co-op	28,135	57.00	-8.16	
L Staite C	10,303	20.87	-1.08	
A Fernie LD	6,884	13.95	+4.85	
D Williams Green	2,392	4.85	+1.53	
R Carter Brexit	1,146	2.32		
D Henwood Ind	238	0.48		
C Artwell Ind	143	0.29		
P Taylor Ind	118	0.24		

Health Research Patient Safety Centre, King's College London. Previously an invited professor at Kosovan universities. Scottish. Ed: St Hilda's Coll, Oxford (BA PPE); University of Edinburgh (MA social policy); LSE (PhD government).

CHALLENGERS
Louise Staite (C) Executive assistant, Vision Capital, international investment group, 2012-. PA to Lord Ashcroft, 2007-10; diary secretary to David Cameron, 2006-07. **Alistair Fernie** (LD) Former senior adviser, McKinsey. **David Williams** (Green) Former lecturer.

CONSTITUENCY PROFILE
Although the seat was won by the Conservatives when it was created in 1983, it has elected only Labour MPs since 1987. It contains most of Oxford itself, including the city centre, many of Oxford University's colleges and Oxford Brookes University. More than a quarter of residents are students.

EU REFERENDUM RESULT
32.5% Leave   Remain 67.5%

Oxford West & Abingdon

LIB DEM HOLD

LAYLA MORAN
BORN Sep 12, 1982
MP 2017-

Former maths and physics teacher. Among the early favourites to replace Jo Swinson as party leader, having unexpectedly declined to stand in 2019. Won this seat from the Conservatives in 2017 and retained it with an increased majority. Party spokeswoman, culture, 2019-; education, 2017-19. Initially defended the party's policy of revoking Article 50, but confirmed two weeks before the election that she had "gone back to plan A" of a second referendum. Admitted to slapping her then boyfriend at a party conference in 2013, leading

	Electorate	Share %	from 2017 %	Change
	76,953			
*L Moran LD	31,340	53.28	+9.53	
J Fredrickson C	22,397	38.07	-4.31	
R Sourbut Lab	4,258	7.24	-5.38	
A Wild Brexit	829	1.41		

to them both being arrested. No further action was taken. First MP of Palestinian descent. First out pansexual MP. Contested: this seat, 2015; Battersea, 2010. Ed: Imperial Coll, London (BSc physics); Brunel University (MA comparative education).

CHALLENGERS
James Fredrickson (C) Head of policy and regulation, Gigaclear, a digital technology company. **Rosie Sourbut** (Lab) English student. **Allison Wild** (Brexit) Software engineer.

CONSTITUENCY PROFILE
Layla Moran overturned a Conservative majority of 9,500 to win the seat by just over 800 votes in 2017. In 2019 she achieved the biggest swing to the Lib Dems in any of the 11 seats that the party won. The seat was created in 1983 and initially elected a Conservative MP before it was gained in 1997 by a Lib Dem and held by the party for 13 years. Abingdon, a predecessor seat, had returned mostly Conservatives for almost a century after this seat was created. It is a more rural seat than Oxford East, containing the north of Oxford and some of the countryside to its west.

EU REFERENDUM RESULT
38.0% Leave   Remain 62.0%

Paisley & Renfrewshire North

MAJORITY 11,902 (23.96%)   **SNP HOLD**   **TURNOUT 69.00%**

GAVIN NEWLANDS
BORN Feb 2, 1980
MP 2015-

Career in restaurant
management. Joined SNP
youth wing in 1992, aged 12.
Campaigned for Remain and
voted in favour of a second
referendum. Had previously
demonstrated support on social
media for Jeremy Corbyn. Party
spokesman: sports, Wales and
Northern Ireland. Backbench
business select cttee, 2015-17. Cllr,
Renfrewshire C, 2011-15. APPG
chairman: white ribbon; Scottish
sports. Had to defend having
claimed £15,000 in expenses for
business class flights to and from
London in 2016. Ed: Trinity HS;
James Watt Coll.

	Electorate	Share %	from 2017 %	Change
	72,007			
*G Newlands SNP	23,353	47.00	+9.56	
A Taylor Lab	11,451	23.05	-8.79	
J Pirone C	11,217	22.58	-4.97	
R Stalker LD	3,661	7.37	+4.20	

CHALLENGERS
Alison Taylor (Lab) Senior
managing director of Avison
Young, property advisers. Fellow,
Royal Institution of Chartered
Surveyors. Contested this seat
in 2017. Former chairwoman,
Scottish Labour business
forum. Joined party in 1997,
having campaigned in favour
of devolution. Remainer. **Julie
Pirone** (C) Communications
manager, Royal Mail. Former
journalist. **Ross Stalker** (LD)
Campaign organiser and
customer service adviser.

CONSTITUENCY PROFILE
A Labour stronghold from its
creation in 2005 until the SNP's
landslide in 2015. Its predecessor
seats had elected mostly Labour
MPs since 1945. Although the
SNP's majority fell to just over
2,500 in 2017, the Labour vote
has continued to slide and
the party won only 234 votes
more than the Conservatives
at this election. This is a varied
constituency, taking in Glasgow
airport, former industrial
shipping and tannery areas and
some of the more leafy and
affluent districts on the edges
of Glasgow. Home ownership
is above average and private
renting is relatively rare.

EU REFERENDUM RESULT
35.5% Leave   Remain 64.5%

Paisley & Renfrewshire South

MAJORITY 10,679 (24.79%)   **SNP HOLD**   **TURNOUT 66.92%**

MHAIRI BLACK
BORN Sep 12, 1994
MP 2015-

Became the country's youngest
MP since 1832 when she was
first elected as a 20-year-old
undergraduate. Described
Westminster as a defunct "old
boys' club". Party spokeswoman:
children and families, 2018-;
pensions, youth affairs, 2017-.
Deputy spokeswoman, equalities
and disabilities, 2018-. Work and
pensions select cttee. 2015-17.
Supported same-sex marriage in
Northern Ireland. Has described
herself as a socialist and
endorsed Jeremy Corbyn's anti-
austerity politics. Voted Remain
but said she had had to "hold her
nose" while doing so. Labelled

	Electorate	Share %	from 2017 %	Change
	64,385			
*M Black SNP	21,637	50.22	+9.55	
M Ramage Lab	10,958	25.43	-9.14	
M Dougan C	7,571	17.57	-1.90	
J Clark LD	2,918	6.77	+3.59	

a "champagne nationalist" in
2016 for expensing business class
flights to London worth about
£13,500. She said that the tickets
did not provide premium seating
and were economical because
they were flexible. Ed: University
of Glasgow (BA politics and
public policy).

CHALLENGERS
Moira Ramage (Lab) Contested
Scottish parliament, 2016. **Mark
Dougan** (C) PhD student. **Jack
Clark** (LD) Politics
undergraduate.

CONSTITUENCY PROFILE
This seat, and its Paisley South
predecessor, had elected only
Labour MPs for more than 30
years until Mhairi Black's victory
in 2015 over Labour's shadow
foreign secretary Douglas
Alexander. Her majority fell
to just over 2,500 in 2017 but,
although she won fewer votes in
2019, Labour's continued slide
meant her majority was bigger
after this election than it was in
2015. There are high levels of
unemployment in the seat and a
significant number of long-term
sick and disabled people. Social
renting is well above average,
making up almost three in ten
households.

EU REFERENDUM RESULT
34.8% Leave   Remain 65.2%

Pendle

MAJORITY 6,186 (11.91%) CONSERVATIVE HOLD TURNOUT 68.10%

ANDREW STEPHENSON
BORN Feb 17, 1981
MP 2010-

Junior minister with experience as a parliamentary private secretary to four ministers, including Boris Johnson. Minister: rail, 2020-; Africa and international development, 2019-20. Parliamentary under-secretary, industry, 2019. Whip, 2018. Campaigned to leave the EU and supported Theresa May's Brexit deal in the first vote, serving as a teller in the second and third. Campaigned against hospital cuts. National deputy chairman, Conservative Future, 2001-02. Cllr, Macclesfield BC, 2003-07. Career in insurance. Ed: Poynton County HS; Royal

	Electorate	Share %	Change from 2017 %
	65,289		
*A Stephenson C	24,076	54.15	+5.14
A Ali Lab	17,890	40.24	-5.93
G Lishman LD	1,548	3.48	+1.38
C Hales Green	678	1.52	+0.41
J Richardson Ind	268	0.60	

Holloway, University of London (BSc business management).

CHALLENGERS
Azhar Ali (Lab) Senior adviser to Blair and Brown governments, 2005-10. Twenty years of experience in local government. Said that Jeremy Corbyn would be a disaster for the country in 2015, but supported him in the 2016 leadership contest. **Gordon Lishman** (LD) Eighth time standing in a general election. Cllr, Burnley BC, 2018-.

CONSTITUENCY PROFILE
This Lancashire seat, created in 1983, elected a Labour MP between 1992 and 2010 but has otherwise been represented by the Conservatives. The Conservative vote share has grown at successive elections, although Labour reduced the majority to fewer than 1,300 votes in 2017, helped by a decline among the smaller parties. Andrew Stephenson's 2019 majority is the largest his party has achieved in the seat since 1983. Lancashire's easternmost constituency, the old textile industry that once thrived in the area is long gone, leaving small commuter and tourist towns.

EU REFERENDUM RESULT
63.2% Leave   Remain 36.8%

Penistone & Stocksbridge

MAJORITY 7,210 (14.56%) CONSERVATIVE GAIN FROM LABOUR TURNOUT 69.82%

MIRIAM CATES
BORN Aug 23, 1982
MP 2019-

Software finance director. Ran a smartphone app called Foodbank with her husband. It allowed food banks to request the donation of items of which they were short, but charged users £180 to subscribe. She denied profiting from food banks and said that the fee covered the cost of running the app. Science teacher, Tapton School. Finance director, Redemption Media, 2006-. Chairwoman of school parent teacher association. Ed: King Edward VII School; Cambridge University (BA genetics); Sheffield Hallam University (PGCE).

	Electorate	Share %	Change from 2017 %
	70,925		
M Cates C	23,688	47.84	+4.68
F Johnson Lab	16,478	33.28	-12.53
H Kitching LD	5,054	10.21	+6.10
J Booker Brexit	4,300	8.68	

CHALLENGERS
Francyne Johnson (Lab) Youth and community worker. Cllr, Sheffield CC, 2018-. **Hannah Kitching** (LD) Runs a manufacturing company. Cllr, Barnsley MBC, 2018-. **John Booker** (Brexit) Former Ukip councillor. Shared a social media post that said the US was cutting its own throat by not "fighting back" against Islam.

CONSTITUENCY PROFILE
Created in 2010, Penistone & Stocksbridge elected a

Conservative MP for the first time in 2019. The old Penistone seat, which was abolished in 1983, was held only by Labour MPs from 1935. Angela Smith, MP for this seat from 2010-19, resigned from the Labour Party in protest at Jeremy Corbyn's leadership in February 2019. Ms Smith, who apologised after she appeared to refer to ethnic minorities as having a "funny tinge" in a TV interview, joined the Liberal Democrats after a spell in Change UK. This seat is occupied mostly by commuters to Sheffield, Leeds and Manchester. The Peak District is in the west. A fifth of residents are retired.

EU REFERENDUM RESULT
60.7% Leave   Remain 39.3%

Penrith & The Border

MAJORITY 18,519 (38.72%) **CONSERVATIVE HOLD** **TURNOUT 70.79%**

NEIL HUDSON
BORN Declined to disclose birth date
MP 2019-

Equine vet and university lecturer selected to replace Rory Stewart, the former international development secretary, prisons minister, Conservative leadership candidate and MP for this seat, 2010-19. Former director of undergraduate admissions at the University of Edinburgh. Principal fellow, Higher Education Academy, 2019-. Inspector during the foot and mouth crisis. Member, Cambridge Footlights; appeared at the Edinburgh Fringe Festival four times. Ed: University of Sydney (Dip clinical studies);

	Electorate	Share %	Change from 2017 %
	67,555		
N Hudson C	28,875	60.38	-0.04
S Williams Lab Co-op	10,356	21.65	-4.53
M Severn LD	5,364	11.22	+3.38
A Ross Green	2,159	4.51	+2.30
J Davies Cumbria	1,070	2.24	

University of Cambridge Veterinary School (VetMIB); University of Edinburgh (PhD).

CHALLENGERS
Sarah Williams (Lab Co-op) Freelance musician and music teacher who has performed on the West End in *Les Miserables* and *The Phantom of the Opera*. **Matthew Severn** (LD) Bookshop manager. Cllr, South Lakeland DC, 2014-. **Ali Ross** (Green) Cllr, Eden DC, 2019-. **Jonathan Davies** (Cumbria) Party founder.

CONSTITUENCY PROFILE
The Conservatives have held this seat at every election since it was created in 1950 and the party's majority has increased in every one since 2010. It was represented by Rory Stewart as an independent in the final months before the election after he had the Conservative whip removed over Brexit. Mr Stewart stood down with the intention of standing for London mayor in 2020. This large, rural seat in northern Cumbria is mostly farmland with a few small towns. More than 3,000 residents work in agriculture or forestry and more than 70 per cent of homes are owner-occupied.

EU REFERENDUM RESULT
55.2% Leave   Remain 44.8%

Perth & Perthshire North

MAJORITY 7,550 (13.96%) **SNP HOLD** **TURNOUT 74.48%**

PETE WISHART
BORN Mar 9, 1962
MP 2001-

Claims to be the first MP to appear on *Top of the Pops*: he played the keyboard in Runrig from the late 1980s until his election in 2001. Formerly a trained community worker and columnist for the *Scots Independent* newspaper. Scottish affairs cttee chairman, 2015-. Resolute that Scotland would leave the EU with the rest of the Union, although has made the case for re-entry if independence is achieved. Generally toes party line but was against renewing Trident and opposed UK air strikes in Iraq. Musicians' Union. Member of the parliamentary

	Electorate	Share %	Change from 2017 %
	72,600		
*P Wishart SNP	27,362	50.60	+8.28
A Forbes C	19,812	36.64	-5.64
P Barrett LD	3,780	6.99	+1.97
A Bretherton Lab	2,471	4.57	-5.81
S Powell Brexit	651	1.20	

rock band MP4. Ed: Queen Anne HS, Dunfermline; Moray House Coll of Education (Dip CommEd).

CHALLENGERS
Angus Forbes (C) Self-employed photographer. Voted Remain and supported Jeremy Hunt for the Conservative leadership, 2019. Cllr, Perth & Kinross, 2017-. **Peter Barrett** (LD) Cllr, Perth & Kinross, 2012-. **Angela Bretherton** (Lab) Stood for European parliament, 2019.

CONSTITUENCY PROFILE
This seat, created in 2005, has consistently elected an SNP MP and its predecessor, Tayside North, elected SNP MPs from 1997. The Conservatives have been the second-placed party in the seat throughout that time and reduced Pete Wishart's majority to 21 in 2017, the second smallest majority in Scotland. The seat covers a huge swathe of remote Scottish mountains, forests and moorlands as well as the city of Perth itself, where most of the electorate lives. It is an affluent area with earnings above the national average, although there are pockets of deprivation.

EU REFERENDUM RESULT
39.9% Leave   Remain 60.1%

Peterborough

MAJORITY 2,580 (5.40%)   **CONSERVATIVE GAIN FROM LABOUR**   TURNOUT 65.88%

PAUL BRISTOW
BORN Mar 27, 1979
MP 2019-

	Electorate	Share %	Change from 2017 %
	72,560		
P Bristow C	22,334	46.72	-0.08
*L Forbes Lab	19,754	41.33	-6.75
B Sellick LD	2,334	4.88	+1.54
M Greene Brexit	2,127	4.45	
J Wells Green	728	1.52	-0.25
L Ferguson Ind	260	0.54	
T Rogers CPA	151	0.32	
Very Raving Mr P Loony	113	0.24	

Managing director of a public affairs consultancy. Fourth MP in three years for this constituency. Stood in the June 2019 by-election and was pushed into third place by the Brexit Party candidate. The by-election was triggered when the seat's Labour MP, Fiona Onasanya, was removed by a recall petition six months after she was jailed for perverting the course of justice. Chairman, Association of Professional Political Consultants, 2017-. Cllr, Hammersmith and Fulham LBC; cabinet member for residents' services, 2007-10. Grew up in neighbouring Whittlesey, and educated at a state school. Contested Middlesbrough South & Cleveland East, 2010.

CHALLENGERS
Lisa Forbes (Lab) Peterborough's MP for less than six months after winning the June 2019 by-election. Former Thomas Cook employee; unsuccessfully called for a government bailout of the firm, which employed a thousand people in this seat. Contested Peterborough in 2015. **Beki Sellick** (LD) Former engineering manager, British Rail. **Mike Greene** (Brexit) Was expected to win the by-election; lost to Ms Forbes by 683 votes.

CONSTITUENCY PROFILE
A swing seat. Labour had reclaimed it from the Conservatives in 2017, having last held it between 1997 and 2005. Peterborough has a sizeable Asian population, with about one in six residents having Asian heritage, mostly Pakistani. The city itself is a strong retail and services centre.

EU REFERENDUM RESULT
61.3% Leave   Remain 38.7%

Plymouth Moor View

MAJORITY 12,897 (29.15%)   **CONSERVATIVE HOLD**   TURNOUT 63.72%

JOHNNY MERCER
BORN Aug 17, 1981
MP 2015-

	Electorate	Share %	Change from 2017 %
	69,430		
*J Mercer C	26,831	60.65	+8.76
C Holloway Lab Co-op	13,934	31.50	-9.34
S Martin LD	2,301	5.20	+3.18
E Melling Flavell Green	1,173	2.65	+1.47

Eccentric former army captain and Afghanistan veteran. Entered politics with a view to improving veterans' physical and mental healthcare. Minister for veterans, jointly with Cabinet Office, 2019-. Critical of Iraq Historic Allegations Team and announced in 2019 that he would no longer support the government until it ended prosecution of historical allegations against British soldiers in Northern Ireland. Voted Remain but backed Theresa May's Brexit withdrawal agreement every time and supported no-deal in indicative votes. Select cttees: defence, 2015-; health and social care, 2017-19. Attracted media attention after a radio interview in which he said that "you don't put diesel in a Ferrari" when asked if he had taken drugs. Backed Boris Johnson for leader, 2019. Sleeps on a boat in east London to avoid "obscene" house prices in capital. Ed: Eastbourne Coll; RMA Sandhurst.

CHALLENGERS
Charlotte Holloway (Lab Co-op) Backed by the big trade unions.

Sarah Martin (LD) Background in NHS marketing and communications. Cllr, Saltash TC, 2018-. **Ewan Melling Flavell** (Green) Computer science teacher and private tutor.

CONSTITUENCY PROFILE
The Conservatives gained this south Devon seat, created in 2010, from Labour in 2015. Johnny Mercer's majority has increased at both subsequent elections. MPs here have included the Labour foreign secretary and Social Democratic Party leader David Owen, 1974-92, and Michael Foot, who later became Labour leader, for ten years from 1945.

EU REFERENDUM RESULT
66.4% Leave   Remain 33.6%

Plymouth Sutton & Devonport

MAJORITY 4,757 (8.95%)   LABOUR CO-OP HOLD   TURNOUT 68.30%

LUKE POLLARD
BORN Apr 10, 1980
MP 2017-

Former head of public affairs for the travel association Abta. Shadow environment secretary, 2020-; shadow minister, flooding and coastal communities, 2018-2020. PPS to Sue Hayman, shadow environment secretary, 2017-18. Campaigned to stop the sale of British warships; wants to increase Britain's naval capacity. Transport select cttee, 2017-19. Born and raised in Plymouth; son of a Royal Navy submariner. Member, GMB and Unite. Contested: this seat, 2015; Devon South West, 2010. Ed: Tavistock Coll, Christleton HS; University of Exeter (BA politics).

	Electorate	Share %	Change from 2017 %
	77,852		
*L Pollard Lab Co-op	25,461	47.88	-5.40
R Smith C	20,704	38.93	-1.05
A Widdecombe Brexit	2,909	5.47	
G Reed LD	2,545	4.79	+2.36
J Ellwood Green	1,557	2.93	+1.75

CHALLENGERS
Rebecca Smith (C) Communications manager for Johnny Mercer (Plymouth Moor View) and Sir Gary Streeter (Devon South West), 2016-. Cllr, Plymouth City C, 2018-. **Ann Widdecombe** (Brexit) Conservative MP for Maidstone and Maidstone & The Weald, 1987-2010; government minister and roles in shadow cabinet. Brexit Party MEP, South West, 2019-20. Known for her socially conservative views

and appearances on television programmes such as *Strictly Come Dancing* and *Celebrity Big Brother*. **Graham Reed** (LD) Glassblower and business owner.

CONSTITUENCY PROFILE
This seat was created in 2010. It was won by the Conservatives that year and in 2015, with small majorities both times. The constituency's predecessor, Plymouth Sutton, was held by Labour only at elections when the party won a substantial national majority. The seat contains Devonport naval base, which is home to seven nuclear submarines. About 17,000 residents are students.

EU REFERENDUM RESULT
54.4% Leave   Remain 45.6%

Pontypridd

MAJORITY 5,887 (15.07%)   LABOUR HOLD   TURNOUT 64.75%

ALEX DAVIES-JONES
BORN Apr 15, 1989
MP 2019-

Replaced Owen Smith, the challenger for the Labour leadership against Jeremy Corbyn in 2016, who had been the MP here since 2010 but stood down before this election for "personal and political reasons". Communications manager, Welsh Water, 2015-. Cllr, Tonyrefail West C, 2017-. Research and policy officer, Welsh assembly, 2012-13. Unite committee, 2014-. Voted Remain; supported second referendum. In favour of greater devolution. Singer and darts player. Ed: Tonyrefail School, Cardiff University (LLB).

	Electorate	Share %	Change from 2017 %
	60,327		
A Davies-Jones Lab	17,381	44.50	-10.91
S Trask C	11,494	29.43	+2.72
F Elin PC	4,990	12.78	+2.49
S Bayliss Brexit	2,917	7.47	
M Powell Ind	1,792	4.59	
S Prior Ind	337	0.86	
J Bishop ND	149	0.38	

CHALLENGERS
Sam Trask (C) Aircraft engineer and magistrate. **Fflur Elin** (PC) Former partner, Darwin Gray law firm. Head of parliamentary affairs for Plaid Cymru in Westminster. Contested this seat, 2017. **Steve Bayliss** (Brexit) Staff support worker. **Mike Powell** (Ind) Cllr, Rhondda Cynon Taf, 1999-. Had been asked to stand aside as part of the Unite to Remain pact.

CONSTITUENCY PROFILE
This seat in south Wales has voted for Labour MPs since 1922. The party's majority, however, has fallen precipitously in recent years: all its winning margins from 1945 until 2010 were in five figures but they have been below 10,000 at three of the last four elections. The seat covers the Taf and Ely valleys and is home to a large middle-class population, a strong service sector and the University of South Wales. There are high levels of home ownership and median wages are above the Welsh average. The seat's longest serving MP was Arthur Pearson, who represented it from 1938-70.

EU REFERENDUM RESULT
46.5% Leave   Remain 53.5%

Poole

CONSERVATIVE HOLD

SIR ROBERT SYMS
BORN Aug 15, 1956
MP 1997-

Former managing director of a plant hire firm. Campaigned to Leave the EU. Government whip, 2016-17; assistant whip, 2012-13. Shadow minister: communities and local government, 2005-07; office of the deputy prime minister, 2003-05. Opposition whip, 2003. Vice-chairman, Conservative Party, 2001-02. Shadow spokesman, environment, transport and the regions, 1999-2001. Select cttees include: finance, 2017-; statutory instruments, 2017-; administration, 2016-17; HS2 2014-16; health, 2007-10; 1997-2000. Contested Walsall North,

	Electorate	Share %	Change from 2017 %
	73,992		
*R Syms C	29,599	58.67	+0.72
S Aitkenhead Lab Co-op	10,483	20.78	-8.67
V Collins LD	7,819	15.50	+6.61
B Harding-Rathbone Green	1,702	3.37	+0.77
D Young Ind	848	1.68	

1992. Criticised in 2009 expenses scandal for claiming £2,000 for furniture for his London home that was delivered to his parent's address in Wiltshire. He said that transporting it himself was easier than waiting in for it in London. Ed: Colston's Sch, Bristol.

CHALLENGERS
Sue Aitkenhead (Lab Co-op) Owns local chiropractic clinic. **Victoria Collins** (LD) Tech entrepreneur. **Barry Harding-Rathbone** (Green) Antiques

dealer and presenter of paranormal TV programmes. **David Young** (Ind) Former Brexit Party candidate.

CONSTITUENCY PROFILE
A safe Conservative seat on the south coast of England. Sir Robert Syms has the largest majority that any MP here has had since the 1979 election. The Labour and Lib Dem vote was too evenly split at elections between 1997 and 2005 for either party to come close to providing a credible challenge. The area covers the Sandbanks peninsula, which has one of the largest concentrations of expensive properties outside of London.

EU REFERENDUM RESULT
57.4% Leave   Remain 42.6%

Poplar & Limehouse

LABOUR HOLD

APSANA BEGUM
BORN May 25, 1990
MP 2019-

Replaced the retiring Jim Fitzpatrick, MP for this seat since 1997; he was one of the few Labour MPs to vote for the Brexit deals. Grew up locally; has Bangladeshi heritage. Apologised after sharing a social media post in 2017 that said Saudi Arabia's leaders were "inspired by their Zionist masters". Accused of jumping a housing queue, but denied this, saying her "particular circumstances" explained why she was assessed as in need of a council flat. Former administrator for the Tower Hamlets mayor Lutfur Rahman, who was found guilty

	Electorate	Share %	Change from 2017 %
	91,760		
A Begum Lab	38,660	63.09	4.17
S Oke C	9,756	15.92	4.22
A Cregan LD	8,832	14.41	+7.68
N Jameson Green	2,159	3.52	+1.84
C Cui Brexit	1,493	2.44	
A Erlam Ind	376	0.61	-1.90

of corruption in 2015. Endorsed Rebecca Long Bailey for leader, 2020. Member of Momentum. Backed by Unite. Ed: Mulberry Sch for Girls; Queen Mary, University of London.

CHALLENGERS
Sheun Oke (C) Leadership coach. Migrated to Britain from Nigeria aged nine. **Andrew Cregan** (LD) Policy adviser, British Retail Consortium, 2016-. **Neil Jameson** (Green) Executive

director, Citizens UK. **Catherine Cui** (Brexit) Previously at Bank of England.

CONSTITUENCY PROFILE
Labour's majority in Poplar & Limehouse rose from 6,000 in 2010 to almost 30,000 in 2019. From 1922 until its abolition in 1950, the predecessor seat of Limehouse was held by Clement Attlee, Labour leader from 1935 to 1955 and prime minister from 1945 to 1951. It is an unequal seat, where overall earnings are well above the national average, but 37 per cent of children live in poverty. Four in ten residents are Asian, predominantly Bangladeshi.

EU REFERENDUM RESULT
34.2% Leave   Remain 65.8%

Portsmouth North

MAJORITY 15,780 (34.37%)   CONSERVATIVE HOLD   TURNOUT 64.39%

PENNY MORDAUNT
BORN Mar 4, 1973
MP 2010-

Former magician's assistant from a military family who pursued a career in business and communications. Briefly served as the first female defence secretary between Gavin Williamson's sacking in May 2019 and her unexpected removal in Boris Johnson's July 2019 reshuffle. Appointed paymaster general in February 2020. International development secretary, 2017-19. Minister for: women and equalities, 2016-17; disabilities, 2016-17; armed forces, 2015-16. Brexiteer. Known to court publicity, most notably by participating in a series of the

	Electorate	Share %	from 2017 %	Change
	71,299			
*P Mordaunt C	28,172	61.36	+6.59	
A Martin Lab	12,392	26.99	-6.68	
A Harrison LD	3,419	7.45	+1.92	
L Day Green	1,304	2.84	+1.16	
G Madgwick ND	623	1.36		

ITV diving programme *Splash!* in 2014. Accused of trivialising the Commons when she made a speech on poultry using rude language as a dare in 2013. Royal Navy reservist. Ed: Oaklands RC Comp; University of Reading (BA philosophy).

CHALLENGERS
Amanda Martin (Lab) Primary school teacher. First sole president of the National Education Union after the merger of the National Union of

Teachers and the Association of Teachers and Lecturers. **Antonia Harrison** (LD) Therapist. **Lloyd Day** (Green) Paramedic.

CONSTITUENCY PROFILE
A bellwether seat since its creation in 1974. In 2019 Penny Mordaunt secured the largest majority any Portsmouth North MP has had since the 1980s. The constituency contains the Navy Command Headquarters on Whale Island and almost one in ten working residents is employed in public administration and defence. As in much of the southeast, home ownership is slightly higher than the national average.

EU REFERENDUM RESULT
63.7% Leave   Remain 36.3%

Portsmouth South

MAJORITY 5,363 (11.31%)   LABOUR HOLD   TURNOUT 63.93%

STEPHEN MORGAN
BORN Jan 17, 1981
MP 2017-

The only Labour MP for Portsmouth South in the seat's 101-year history. Former charity chief executive. Previously worked for the Royal Borough of Kensington & Chelsea and Basingstoke Voluntary Action, commuting from Portsmouth. Shadow minister, communities and local government, 2019-. PPS to Andrew Gwynne, 2017-. Campaigns on veterans issues. Early supporter of a second referendum on Brexit. APPGs: key cities, cycling. Member: Labour Friends of Israel; LGBT Labour. Called for Jeremy Corbyn to stand down in June

	Electorate	Share %	from 2017 %	Change
	74,186			
*S Morgan Lab	23,068	48.64	+7.60	
D Jones C	17,705	37.33	-0.22	
G Vernon-Jackson LD	5,418	11.42	-5.85	
J Kennedy Brexit	994	2.10		
S George JACP	240	0.51		

2016; backed Sir Keir Starmer in the 2020 leadership contest. Ed: Priory Sch, Southsea; Portsmouth Coll; University of Bristol (BSc politics & sociology); Goldsmiths, University of London (MA politics).

CHALLENGERS
Donna Jones (C) Cllr, Portsmouth City C, 2008-; group leader, 2014-18. Magistrate; once youngest member of judiciary in England and Wales. **Gerald Vernon-Jackson** (LD) Cllr,

Portsmouth City C, 2018-; group leader, 2004-14. **John Kennedy** (Brexit) Former royal aide.

CONSTITUENCY PROFILE
Having gained the seat in 2017 for the first time in a century, Labour increased its vote in Portsmouth South more than almost anywhere else in the country. The constituency contains Portsmouth's docks, shipyards, and the university; it has 20,000 student residents, making it the most student-heavy of the two Portsmouth seats. It is more diverse than Portsmouth North, with roughly one in six residents from an ethnic minority.

EU REFERENDUM RESULT
51.8% Leave   Remain 48.2%

Preseli Pembrokeshire

MAJORITY 5,062 (11.93%) CONSERVATIVE HOLD TURNOUT 71.19%

STEPHEN CRABB
BORN Jan 20, 1973
MP 2005-

Stood for the leadership in 2016 but was derailed by a sexting scandal and was not reappointed to cabinet afterwards. Nominated Sajid Javid for leader, 2019. Chairman, Welsh affairs select cttee, 2020-. Work and pensions secretary, 2016; Welsh secretary, 2014-16. Whip and parly under-sec for Wales, 2012-14. Former marketing consultant and policy manager at the London Chamber of Commerce. Interested in energy policy and human rights; election observer in Bosnia-Herzegovina, 1998. Select cttees: Treasury, 2008-09; Welsh affairs, 2005-07.

	Electorate	Share %	from 2017 %	Change
	59,586			
*S Crabb C	21,381	50.40	+7.03	
P Thompson Lab	16,319	38.47	-4.16	
C Tomos PC	2,776	6.54	+0.12	
T Hughes LD	1,943	4.58	+1.96	

Leader of Project Umubano, the Conservatives' social action project in Rwanda and Sierra Leone. Raised by a single mother in a council house. Contested this seat, 2001. Ed: Tasker Milward Sch, Haverfordwest; University of Bristol (BSc politics); London Business School (MBA).

CHALLENGERS
Philippa Thompson (Lab) Foreign Office, deputy team leader. Contested this seat, 2017. Cris Tomos (PC) Contested

Pembrokeshire CC, 2017. Tom Hughes (LD) Military historian. Royal Navy reservist.

CONSTITUENCY PROFILE
Initially held by Labour after being created in 1997 before it was gained by the Conservatives in 2005. Stephen Crabb's majority had fallen to 314 votes in 2017. The predecessor seat, Pembrokeshire, was won by Labour from 1950 through to 1966, and again in 1992, but was Conservative-held throughout the 1970s and 1980s. Most westerly Welsh seat, at the tip of the Pembrokeshire peninsula, containing Milford Haven port, key to Britain's energy network.

EU REFERENDUM RESULT
55.3% Leave Remain 44.7%

Preston

MAJORITY 12,146 (35.94%) LABOUR CO-OP HOLD TURNOUT 56.63%

SIR MARK HENDRICK
BORN Nov 2, 1958
MP 2000-

Knighted in 2018 for parliamentary and political service. Interested in foreign affairs and defence. Select committees: international trade, 2018-; foreign affairs, 2012-17; international development, 2009-10; European scrutiny, 2001-04. Supported leadership campaigns of: Lisa Nandy, 2020, Owen Smith, 2016, Liz Kendall, 2015, and David Miliband, 2010. PPS to: Ivan Lewis, 2009-10; Jack Straw, 2007-08; Dame Margaret Beckett, 2003-07. Engineer and college lecturer. MEP for Central Lancashire, 1994-99. Cllr, Salford CC, 1987-95. Ed: Salford GS;

	Electorate	Share %	from 2017 %	Change
	59,672			
*M Hendrick Lab Co-op	20,870	61.76	-6.25	
M Scott C	8,724	25.82	+1.98	
R Sherratt Brexit	1,799	5.32		
N Darby LD	1,737	5.14	+1.76	
M Welton Green	660	1.95	+0.98	

Liverpool Poly (BSc electrical and electronic engineering); University of Manchester (MSc computer science, Cert Ed).

CHALLENGERS
Michele Scott (C) Cllr, Blackpool Council, 2019-. Rob Sherratt (Brexit) Retired chartered engineer for BAE systems. Neil Darby (LD) Marketing co-ordinator. Caseworker for Gordon Birtwistle, 2010-13. Cllr, Preston City C, 2014-. Contested this seat, 2017.

CONSTITUENCY PROFILE
Since Preston became a single seat in 1983 it has consistently returned Labour MPs. Before this, it consisted of two marginal constituencies, both of which flipped several times between 1950 and 1983. Preston contains the centre, east and west of the city, with its northern area included in the Wyre & Preston North constituency. The administrative centre for Lancashire, its major industries include retail, distribution, call centres and defence. About one in five residents is Asian or Asian British. Home to the University of Central Lancashire, and 12,000 of its students.

EU REFERENDUM RESULT
55.7% Leave Remain 44.3%

Pudsey

MAJORITY 3,517 (6.49%) **CONSERVATIVE HOLD** **TURNOUT 74.05%**

STUART ANDREW
BORN Nov 25, 1971
MP 2010-

Deputy chief whip, 2020-. Junior government whip, 2019-20. Defence procurement minister and parly under-sec, Wales, 2018-19. Assistant Treasury whip, 2017-18. PPS to: Patrick McLoughlin, 2015-17; Francis Maude, 2012-15. Vice-chairman of the Conservative Party, 2016-. Contested Wrexham in 1997; defected to Labour in 1998 after becoming disillusioned with the Conservatives, but rejoined in 2000. Charity fundraiser, including at the British Heart Foundation. Cllr, Leeds City C, 2003-10. Ed: Ysgol David Hughes, Anglesey.

	Electorate	Share %	from 2017 % Change
	73,212		
*S Andrew C	26,453	48.79	+1.44
J Aitchison Lab	22,936	42.31	-4.43
I Dowling LD	3,088	5.70	+2.43
Q Daley Green	894	1.65	
B Buxton Yorkshire	844	1.56	-0.55

CHALLENGERS
Jane Aitchison (Lab) President, Leeds TUC. Gained media attention after pausing for 12 seconds when asked in a radio interview whether Zarah Sultana (Coventry South) should continue to stand despite saying in 2015 that she would celebrate the death of Tony Blair. **Ian Dowling** (LD) Chartered management accountant. Contested Leeds City C, 2019, 2015, 2016. **Quinn Daley** (Green) Software developer.

CONSTITUENCY PROFILE
This West Yorkshire seat has mostly been held by the Conservatives since its creation in 1950, but often by narrow margins. No party has ever won a five-figure majority. Labour won it for the first time in 1997 but it was regained by the Conservatives in 2010. Only 331 votes separated the two parties in the 2017 election. Encompassing the area between Leeds and Bradford, Pudsey is mostly an affluent residential area for commuters to these cities. Almost three quarters of households are owner-occupied, which is well above average, and social renting is low.

EU REFERENDUM RESULT
48.6% Leave Remain 51.4%

Putney

MAJORITY 4,774 (9.46%) **LABOUR GAIN FROM CONSERVATIVE** **TURNOUT 77.00%**

FLEUR ANDERSON
BORN Feb 6, 1971
MP 2019-

Manager of a local community centre in Battersea. Worked in Bosnia during the war in the 1990s, rebuilding villages. Supported Sir Keir Starmer for leader, 2020. Led a campaign for a 20mph limit. Cllr, Wandsworth LBC, 2014-; deputy leader of Wandsworth Labour, 2016-18; Labour spokeswoman for community services and the environment, 2015-18. Co-founded Wandsworth Welcomes Refugees. Ed: University of York (BA politics; president of students' union); Open University (development management).

	Electorate	Share %	from 2017 % Change
	65,542		
F Anderson Lab	22,780	45.14	+4.35
W Sweet C	18,006	35.68	-8.42
S Wixley LD	8,548	16.94	+5.32
F McEntee Green	1,133	2.25	-0.12

CHALLENGERS
Will Sweet (C) Former civil servant in the Foreign Office. Cllr, Wandsworth LBC, 2014-; cabinet member for education and children's services; planning chairman. **Sue Wixley** (LD) Contested Wandsworth LBC, 2018. Co-founded South African Campaign to Ban Landmines. Served on board of Consortium for Street Children. **Fergal McEntee** (Green) Extinction Rebellion spokesman. Director of renewable energy firm. Stood for Wandsworth LBC, 2018.

CONSTITUENCY PROFILE
The only seat that Labour gained at the 2019 election, and the first time since 1970 that the party had won it despite being in opposition. Created in 1918, it was held by the Conservatives for most of its history, with spells of Labour dominance from 1964 to 1979 and 1997 to 2005. Its previous MP, the former education secretary Justine Greening, stood down in 2019 after having the Tory whip removed over Brexit. A mostly affluent seat on the south bank of the Thames. Three in ten homes are privately rented and a quarter of residents are from an ethnic minority.

EU REFERENDUM RESULT
27.8% Leave Remain 72.2%

Rayleigh & Wickford

MAJORITY 31,000 (56.47%)   CONSERVATIVE HOLD   TURNOUT 69.53%

MARK FRANCOIS
BORN Aug 14, 1965
MP 2001-

Bellicose deputy chairman and de facto whip of the ERG, 2018-. Consistent critic of Theresa May, voting against her Brexit deals and submitting a letter of no confidence in her leadership. Minister, communities, 2015-16; defence, 2012-15. Will remain an EU citizen after Brexit because he has an Italian mother. Supported Boris Johnson for leader, 2019. Notably pro-armed forces. Served as a territorial army infantry officer with local Royal Anglican Regiment. Worked as a self-employed consultant. Contested Brent East, 1997. Cllr, Basildon DC,

	Electorate	Share %	from 2017 % Change
	78,959		
*M Francois C	39,864	72.61	+5.89
D Flack Lab	8,864	16.15	-8.19
R Tindall LD	4,171	7.60	+4.78
P Thorogood Green	2,002	3.65	+1.73

1991-95. Ed: University of Bristol (BA history); King's Coll London (MA war studies).

CHALLENGERS
David Flack (Lab) Retired head teacher. Former Cllr, Essex CC. Former Cllr and group leader, Rochford DC. **Ron Tindall** (LD) Former trade union organiser. Cllr, Dacroum BC, 2013-; leader of the opposition. Cllr, Hertfordshire CC, 2009-. **Paul Thorogood** (Green) Former news reporter. Cllr, Braintree DC, 2019-.

CONSTITUENCY PROFILE
Created from Rayleigh in 2010, this is a safe Conservative seat in rural Essex. It was among the party's biggest ten majorities and where it won its fifth highest number of votes. The towns of Rayleigh and Wickford are both home to about 30,000 people. Wickford is undergoing regeneration through the Thames Gateway project. The seat is relatively affluent with low levels of unemployment and income higher than the regional average. Five in six houses are owner-occupied, one of the highest rates in the country. Ukip came second in 2015 in this heavily Brexit-supporting area.

EU REFERENDUM RESULT
67.7% Leave   Remain 32.3%

Reading East

MAJORITY 5,924 (10.59%)   LABOUR HOLD   TURNOUT 72.18%

MATT RODDA
BORN Dec 15, 1966
MP 2017-

Education specialist. Worked on the academies programmes as a civil servant at the Department for Education. Shadow transport minister, 2018-. Emily Thornberry supporter, 2020. Former journalist, including at the *Coventry Telegraph* and *The Independent*. Project manager and consultant for the voluntary sector. Cllr, Reading BC, 2011-18; campaigned to prevent closure of a centre for disabled adults. Contested: this seat, 2015; Surrey East, 2010. Became involved in public service after surviving 1999 Ladbroke Grove rail crash. Ed: University of Sussex.

	Electorate	Share %	from 2017 % Change
	77,465		
*M Rodda Lab	27,102	48.47	-0.58
C Morley C	21,178	37.87	-4.39
I Shepherd-DuBey LD	5,035	9.00	+2.89
D McElroy Green	1,549	2.77	+0.79
M Feierstein Brexit	852	1.52	
Y Awolola CPA	202	0.36	

CHALLENGERS
Craig Morley (C) Diplomat for more than eight years. China and Hong Kong specialist. Youth coach at Bicester rugby club. **Imogen Shepherd-DuBey** (LD) Works in IT. Cllr, Wokingham TC, 2018-. Contested: Milton Keynes North, 2017; New Forest West, 2015. **David McElroy** (Green) Engineer, gardener and personal assistant. **Mitchell Feierstein** (Brexit) Banker and newspaper columnist.

CONSTITUENCY PROFILE
Labour increased its majority in Reading East in 2019 by winning nine votes more than in 2017. Created in 1983, the seat was initially held by the Conservatives, with Labour winning the seat in 1997 and 2001. Reading itself is an affluent commercial centre and commuter town in Berkshire. Home to technology and service industries, a significant proportion of its residents work in information and communication. Reading East is ethnically diverse with a large number of Indian and Pakistani residents. The seat contains the University of Reading.

EU REFERENDUM RESULT
38.3% Leave   Remain 61.7%

Reading West

CONSERVATIVE HOLD

TURNOUT 67.53%

ALOK SHARMA
BORN Sep 6, 1967
MP 2010-

Appointed business secretary and minister for the Cop26 UN climate conference in February 2020 reshuffle. International development secretary, 2019-20. Minister: employment, 2018-19; housing, 2017-18, when he was responsible for the government's response to the Grenfell Tower fire. Parly under-sec for Asia and the Pacific, 2016-17. Chartered accountant, Coopers & Lybrand Deloitte. Later went into banking. Former Conservative vice-chairman for BME communities. Vocal supporter of Crossrail, HS2 and Heathrow expansion. PPS to:

	Electorate %	Share %	from 2017 % Change
	74,623		
*A Sharma C	24,393	48.41	-0.49
R Eden Lab Co-op	20,276	40.24	-3.10
M O'Connell LD	4,460	8.85	+2.98
J Whitham Green	1,263	2.51	+0.62

Sir Oliver Letwin, 2015-16; Mark Hoban, 2010-12. Served as David Cameron's infrastructure envoy to India. Ed: Reading Blue Coat Sch; University of Salford (BSc applied physics with electronics).

CHALLENGERS
Rachel Eden (Lab Co-op) Chartered accountant. Director of a small consultantancy. Cllr, Reading BC, 2010-. Contested Wantage, 2017. **Meri O'Connell** (LD) Gum and candy taster. Cllr, Reading BC, 2012-. Contested this seat, 2017, 2015.

CONSTITUENCY PROFILE
A bellwether constituency since its creation in 1983, this seat had been held by the Conservatives until the Labour landslide of 1997. It was then won back by the Conservatives in 2010. The Conservative majority peaked at almost 17,000 in 1987 but Labour cut the party's lead in half in 2017, from more than 6,000 to less than 3,000. It is slightly less affluent than its neighbour, Reading East and has some areas of deprivation, but the median earnings are above the regional and national averages. The seat has benefited from regeneration of the town centre and investment.

EU REFERENDUM RESULT
51.5% Leave   Remain 48.5%

Redcar

CONSERVATIVE GAIN

TURNOUT 62.02%

JACOB YOUNG
BORN Feb 2, 1993
MP 2019-

Brexit campaigner who worked as the lead technician for a petrochemicals company. Cllr, Middlesbrough C, 2017-; first Conservative to represent the area since Middlesbrough council became a unitary authority. Part of the team that set up Middlesbrough food bank in 2012. Contested: Middlesbrough, 2017; this seat, 2015. Ed: Redcar & Cleveland College; Teeside University (HMC chemical engineering).

CHALLENGERS
Anna Turley (Lab Co-op) MP for this seat, 2015-19. Blamed

	Electorate %	Share %	from 2017 % Change
	65,855		
J Young C	18,811	46.06	+12.84
*A Turley Lab Co-op	15,284	37.42	-18.08
J Cummins Brexit	2,915	7.14	
K King LD	2,018	4.94	-1.75
F Wales Ind	1,323	3.24	
R McLaughlin Green	491	1.20	

Jeremy Corbyn for her defeat. Won a libel claim against Unite and the blogger Stephen Walker, editor of The Skwawkbox, over an article accusing her of dishonesty. Long-time civil servant; worked in the Cabinet Office and the Department for Work and Pensions. **Jacqui Cummins** (Brexit) Stopped actively contesting the seat to help Jacob Young. **Karen King** (LD) Cllr, Redcar and Cleveland BC, 2015-. Mayor, 2017.

CONSTITUENCY PROFILE
First Conservative victory here since 1959, when they won the predecessor constituency, Cleveland. Only one seat gained by the Conservatives from Labour in 2019, Leigh, had a bigger Labour majority in 2017 than Redcar. Before the 2019 election it had been held by Labour in all but one parliament since its creation in 1974, when the closure of the steelworks in 2009 presaged a huge swing to the Lib Dems a year later. Mo Mowlam, the Northern Ireland secretary during the Good Friday Agreement, was its MP, 1987-2001. It is an industrial seat on the south of the Tees estuary.

EU REFERENDUM RESULT
67.7% Leave   Remain 32.3%

Redditch

RACHEL MACLEAN
BORN Oct 3, 1965
MP 2017-

Parliamentary under-secretary at the Department for Transport, 2020-. Technology entrepreneur and sales manager who founded small businesses specialising in publishing IT content and HR software. PPS to Sajid Javid, 2019-. Business select cttee, 2017-18. Chairwoman, carers APPG. Co-chairwoman of the successful West Midlands mayoral campaign of Andy Street, the former John Lewis chief executive. Regional council member, CBI. Supported Michael Gove in the Conservative leadership contest, 2019. Founder and

Electorate	Share %	Change from 2017 %
65,391		
*R Maclean C	27,907	63.33 +11.00
R Jenkins Lab	11,871	26.94 -9.10
B Horton LD	2,905	6.59 +4.00
C Davies Green	1,384	3.14 +2.30

director of Skilled and Ready, an employment charity. Contested Birmingham Northfield, 2015. Born in Chennai, India. Ed: St Hugh's Coll, Oxford (BSc psychology); Aston University (MSc work and organisational psychology); Stanford GSB (EPGC cert).

CHALLENGERS
Rebecca Jenkins (Lab) History and religious studies teacher.
Bruce Horton (LD) Director of environmental consultancy.
Claire Davies (Green) Social

worker. Contested Redditch BC, 2019, 2018.

CONSTITUENCY PROFILE
Redditch was held by Jacqui Smith for 13 years from its creation in 1997, including during her time as home secretary. Her loss to the Conservatives in 2010 was a symbolic moment marking the end of the New Labour years. The Tory majority has increased at every election since, more than doubling in 2019 from 7,363 in 2017. The east Worcestershire town of Redditch expanded after its creation in the 1960s as the population surrounding nearby Birmingham grew.

EU REFERENDUM RESULT
61.0% Leave   Remain 39.0%

Reigate

CRISPIN BLUNT
BORN Jul 15, 1960
MP 1997-

Army officer, 1979-90; resigned commission as captain to stand for parliament. Worked as a political consultant and as special adviser to Sir Malcolm Rifkind, 1993-97. Chairman, foreign affairs select committee, 2015-17. Opposed to Trident; a public critic and rebel on the issue. Parly under-sec, prisons and youth justice, 2010-12. Former chairman, Conservative Middle East Council. Announced his use of the party drug poppers during a Commons debate in 2016. Humanist who opposes parliamentary prayers. Uncle of the actress Emily Blunt.

Electorate	Share %	Change from 2017 %
74,842		
*C Blunt C	28,665	53.93 -3.48
S Gregory Lab	10,355	19.48 -5.20
J Vincent LD	10,320	19.41 +8.47
J Essex Green	3,169	5.96 +1.85
J Searle Ukip	647	1.22 -1.65

Contested West Bromwich East, 1991. Ed: Wellington College; Sandhurst; Durham University (BA politics); Cranfield University School of Management (MBA).

CHALLENGERS
Susan Gregory (Lab) Senior area manager, Nested estate agency.
John Vincent (LD) Aviation safety expert. Contested: Runnymede & Weybridge, 2017, 2015; Crawley, 2010; European parliament, 2019, 2014. **Jonathan**

Essex (Green) Chartered civil engineer. Cllr, Reigate and Banstead BC, 2010-.

CONSTITUENCY PROFILE
Won by the Conservatives at every election since 1910. Labour reduced the Conservative majority to less than 8,000 in 1997, but it grew back to more than 22,000 in 2015. This Surrey seat, on the southern border of Greater London, is characterised by high levels of economic activity and home ownership. Reigate itself has a little over 20,000 residents and the area has transport links to London and the south coast, making it popular with commuters.

EU REFERENDUM RESULT
48.0% Leave   Remain 52.0%

Renfrewshire East

SNP GAIN FROM CONSERVATIVE

TURNOUT 76.64%

KIRSTEN OSWALD
BORN Dec 21, 1972
MP 2019-; 2015-17

Scottish National Party's spokeswoman for armed forces and veterans, 2015-17. Chairman and business convenor of the party, 2018-. Head of human resources, South Lanarkshire College; previously worked in human resources for Motherwell College. Member of a local Women for Independence group, where she was responsible for food bank collections. Ed: Carnoustie HS; Glasgow University (MA history).

CHALLENGERS
Paul Masterton (C) MP for this constituency, 2017-19. PPS to the

	Electorate	Share %	from 2017 %	Change
	72,232			
K Oswald SNP	24,877	44.94	+13.71	
*P Masterton C	19,451	35.14	-4.86	
C Davidson Lab	6,855	12.38	-14.31	
A McGlynn LD	4,174	7.54	+5.47	

Home Office, 2018-19, resigning to vote in favour of ruling out a no-deal Brexit. Former solicitor specialising in pensions law; worked for McGregors and then Pinsent Masons. Introduced a ten-minute rule bill on pensions while in parliament that was subsequently adopted as government policy. **Carolann Davidson** (Lab) Claimed Labour did not deserve votes because of its failure to tackle antisemitism. Cllr, Renfrewshire C, 2017. **Andrew McGlynn** (LD) Policy officer, Scottish Young Liberals.

CONSTITUENCY PROFILE
The Conservatives won their first victory in the seat for a quarter of a century in 2017. The seat had elected Conservative or Unionist MPs at every election from 1924 until Labour won in 1997. Its MP for the subsequent 18 years was Jim Murphy, a New Labour cabinet minister who served from 2014 to 2015 as the leader of the Scottish Labour Party, resigning after the 2015 election at which he and all but one of his Scottish Labour colleagues lost their seats. Located to the south of Glasgow, the seat has the largest Jewish population of any seat in Scotland.

EU REFERENDUM RESULT
25.7% Leave   Remain 74.3%

Rhondda

LABOUR HOLD

TURNOUT 58.97%

CHRIS BRYANT
BORN Jan 11, 1962
MP 2001-

Runner-up in the contest to replace John Bercow as Speaker in 2019. Shadow leader of the Commons, 2015-16; resigned in protest at Jeremy Corbyn's leadership, warning the leader that he would be remembered as the man who broke the Labour Party. Nominated Jess Phillips in 2020. Former clergyman; stopped being a vicar when he realised he was gay, aged 25. Author of several political biographies and a book about Christian socialism. Head of European affairs at the BBC, 1998-2000. PPS to: Harriet Harman (Camberwell

	Electorate	Share %	from 2017 %	Change
	50,262			
*C Bryant Lab	16,115	54.37	-9.69	
H Jarvis C	4,675	15.77	+5.65	
B Cennard PC	4,069	13.73	-8.59	
J Watkins Brexit	3,733	12.59		
S Berman LD	612	2.06	+1.22	
S Thomas Green	438	1.48		

& Peckham), 2007-08; Lord Falconer, 2005-06. Contested Wycombe, 1997. Cllr, Hackney BC, 1993-98. Ed: Cheltenham Coll; Mansfield Coll, Oxford (BA English); Ripon Coll, Cuddesdon (MA theology).

CHALLENGERS
Hannah Jarvis (C) Served with Royal Welsh Regiment. **Branwen Cennard** (PC) Local company director and TV producer, including for the BBC.

CONSTITUENCY PROFILE
A safe Labour seat in south Wales, held by the party at every election since 1910. Third lowest turnout of any Welsh seat. Of every mainland seat in Britain, Rhondda was the one in which Conservatives won the fewest votes in the 2017 election; 2019, however, was the first election at which the Conservatives had come second here since 1979. The Rhondda is a former coalmining area that suffered economic deprivation after the closure of the mines. Home ownership is relatively high in the constituency but median pay is £80 a week below the Welsh average.

EU REFERENDUM RESULT
60.4% Leave   Remain 39.6%

Ribble Valley

NIGEL EVANS
BORN Nov 10, 1957
MP 1992-

Deputy speaker, 2020-. Welsh Brexiteer who owned a corner shop. Spent one year as an independent backbencher after being charged with rape and sexual assault; he was acquitted in 2014. He lost his life savings defending himself in court, which led him to criticise cuts to legal aid that he had voted for in 2012. Involved in the LGBT group ParliOut. Worked on three US presidential campaigns in the 1980s and led the Conservative general election campaign in Wales in the 2001 election. Shadow Wales secretary, 2001-03. Vice-chairman of the

	Electorate	Share %	Change from 2017 %
	79,247		
*N Evans C	33,346	60.32	+2.49
G Bridge Lab	14,907	26.96	-6.95
C Seddon LD	4,776	8.64	+2.76
P Yates Green	1,704	3.08	+0.70
T Johnson Ind	551	1.00	

Conservative Party, 1999-2001. Contested: this seat, 1991 by-election; Pontypridd, 1989 by-election; Swansea West, 1987. Cllr, West Glamorgan CC, 1985-91. Ed: University Coll, Swansea (BA politics).

CHALLENGERS
Giles Bridge (Lab) Barrister working on criminal and regulatory cases. Police officer, 1991-99. **Chantelle Seddon** (LD) Project manager with background in education.

CONSTITUENCY PROFILE
Ribble Valley has been won by the Conservative Party at every general election since 1983, although the Liberal Democrats held it briefly after their victory in a 1991 by-election. The majority in the seat in 2019 was its biggest since 1987, when it was held by former home secretary David Waddington. A predominantly rural Lancashire seat, mostly to the northeast of Preston, Ribble Valley is home to a significant population of commuters and retirees. The seat is characterised by very high levels of property ownership and low unemployment.

EU REFERENDUM RESULT
58.7% Leave   Remain 41.3%

Richmond (Yorks)

RISHI SUNAK
BORN May 12, 1980
MP 2015-

Rising star unexpectedly made chancellor in February 2020 reshuffle. Chief secretary to the Treasury, 2019-20; stood in for Boris Johnson in an ITV election debate. Parly under-sec, housing, 2018-19. Leave campaigner. Member of David Cameron's secret "A-list", 2015. Environment select cttee, 2015-17. Director, Catamaran Ventures; co-founded an investment firm. Worked for Goldman Sachs and the charity hedge fund The Children's Investment. Was head of the BME Research Unit. Son-in-law of the Indian billionaire Nagavara Murthy.

	Electorate	Share %	Change from 2017 %
	82,601		
*R Sunak C	36,693	63.59	-0.36
T Kirkwood Lab	9,483	16.43	-6.98
P Knowles LD	6,989	12.11	+6.22
J Yorke Green	2,500	4.33	+1.28
L Waterhouse Yorkshire	1,077	1.87	-1.83
N Jardine Ind	961	1.67	

Ed: Winchester College; Lincoln Coll; Oxford (BA PPE); Stanford University (MBA, Fulbright scholar).

CHALLENGERS
Thom Kirkwood (Lab) English teacher. First ever openly non-binary candidate in a general election. **Philip Knowles** (LD) Associate lecturer, Manchester Metropolitan University, specialising in marketing. Chairman, South Yorkshire

branch of Chartered Institute of Marketing. **John Yorke** (Green) Worked as a mental health nurse for 30 years.

CONSTITUENCY PROFILE
One of the safest Conservative seats in the country, represented continually by the party since 1910. The MP from 1989 to 2015 was William Hague, who led the Conservative Party between 1997 and 2001, was foreign secretary under David Cameron and now sits in the House of Lords. Vast seat that covers several villages and hamlets in rural North Yorkshire. About a fifth of constituents are aged 65 or above.

EU REFERENDUM RESULT
54.7% Leave   Remain 45.3%

Richmond Park

MAJORITY 7,766 (11.94%)   LIB DEM GAIN FROM CONSERVATIVE   TURNOUT 78.68%

SARAH OLNEY
BORN Jan 11, 1977
MP 2019-; 2016-17

Victory over Zac Goldsmith was the only highlight of a disappointing election night for the Liberal Democrats. MP for this seat, 2016-17, having joined the party the previous year. Firmly against government plans for a third runway at Heathrow. Lib Dem spokeswoman: business, 2020-; international trade, 2020-; education, 2017. Qualified accountant. Previously worked at Barclays. Finance manager at National Physical Laboratory. Chief of staff to Sir Vince Cable, 2017-19. Ed: All Hallows Catholic Sch; King's College, London (BA English).

	Electorate	Share %	from 2017 %	Change
	82,696			
S Olney LD	34,559	53.11	+8.04	
*Z Goldsmith C	26,793	41.18	-3.96	
S Keen Lab	3,407	5.24	-3.88	
C Shah Ind	247	0.38		
J Usher Ind	61	0.09		

CHALLENGERS
Zac Goldsmith (C) Maintained position as an environment minister despite his election defeat by being made a life peer by Boris Johnson. Left the Conservatives over plans for Heathrow runway, losing at the resulting by-election as an independent in 2016. Re-elected as a Conservative in 2017. Stood for London mayor in 2016, losing to the Labour candidate Sadiq Khan. **Sandra Keen** (Lab) Disability benefits adviser.

CONSTITUENCY PROFILE
Richmond Park had the highest turnout of any seat in England. Created in 1997, it was held by the Lib Dems until Zac Goldsmith's first victory in 2010. The Lib Dems won the by-election caused by his resignation but 2019 was the first general election the party had won here since 2005, the Green Party having stood aside as part of a deal to promote Remain-voting candidates. An affluent suburban seat in southwest London. A high proportion of residents are in managerial or professional positions, and are likely to have university degrees. Self-employment is common.

EU REFERENDUM RESULT
28.7% Leave   Remain 71.3%

Rochdale

MAJORITY 9,668 (20.38%)   LABOUR HOLD   TURNOUT 60.13%

TONY LLOYD
BORN Feb 25, 1950
MP 2017-;
1983-2012

Labour stalwart. Was the MP for Stretford, 1983-97 and Manchester Central, 1997-2012, before becoming Greater Manchester's police and crime commissioner in 2012. Acted as Manchester's interim mayor 2015-17. Leadership nominations have included Neil Kinnock in 1983, John Prescott in 1994 and Lisa Nandy in 2020. Stood in this seat after its MP Simon Danczuk was barred for having sent explicit texts to a 17-year-old. Shadow Northern Ireland secretary, 2018-; shadow Scotland secretary, 2019-. Shadow housing minister, 2017-

	Electorate	Share %	from 2017 %	Change
	78,909			
*T Lloyd Lab	24,475	51.58	-6.44	
A Shah C	14,807	31.21	+2.80	
C Green Brexit	3,867	8.15		
A Kelly LD	3,312	6.98	-1.07	
S Croke Green	986	2.08		

18. Cllr, Trafford BC, 1979-84. Chairman, PLP, 2006-10. Ed: University of Nottingham (BSc mathematics); Manchester Business School (MBA).

CHALLENGERS
Atifa Shah (C) Entrepreneur. Former Labour member who was also once described as a "Lib Dem rising star"; said she could not recall having been a Lib Dem member. **Chris Green** (Brexit) Worked in the oil industry. **Andy Kelly** (LD) Cllr

Rochdale BC, 2019-. Contested Rochdale, 2017, 2015. Claims to hold the UK record for TV game show appearances.

CONSTITUENCY PROFILE
This seat, in the northwest of Greater Manchester, has flipped between Labour and the Lib Dems, or the Liberals before 1988, for 60 years. For 20 years from 1972 its MP was Cyril Smith, a Liberal MP who in 2012 was revealed to have been a serial sexual abuser of children. Labour gained it in 1997, holding it until 2005, the last election at which the Lib Dems won Rochdale. One in four residents is Asian or Asian British.

EU REFERENDUM RESULT
57.5% Leave   Remain 42.5%

Rochester & Strood

MAJORITY 17,072 (32.88%)   CONSERVATIVE HOLD   TURNOUT 63.26%

KELLY TOLHURST
BORN Aug 23, 1978
MP 2015-

Parliamentary under-secretary, Department for Transport, since 2020. Vocal critic of the Israeli government. Voted Remain but for no-deal in indicative vote. Backed Boris Johnson, 2019. Contested the 2014 by-election in this seat caused by the MP Mark Reckless's defection to Ukip; lost by 3,000 votes before beating him by 7,000 in 2015. Parly under-sec, business, 2018-. Assistant whip, 2018. Cttees: business, 2015-17; European scrutiny, 2015-16. Cllr, Medway BC, 2011-18. Director of a marine surveyors and consultancy business. Ed: Old Chapter HS.

	Electorate	Share %	from 2017 % Change
	82,056		
*K Tolhurst C	31,151	59.99	+5.63
T Murray Lab	14,079	27.11	-8.93
G Colley LD	3,717	7.16	+4.95
S Hyner Green	1,312	2.53	+1.07
R Freshwater Ukip	1,080	2.08	-3.30
C Spalding Ind	587	1.13	+0.89

CHALLENGERS
Teresa Murray (Lab) Former teacher and deputy head of education, Maidstone Prison. Member, UCU. Cllr, Medway BC, 2007-; deputy leader, Labour group; party spokeswoman for health and adult social care. Contested this seat, 2017, 2010. **Graham Colley** (LD) Solicitor. President of Lib Dem Lawyers Association. Contested Mid-Kent, 1992, 1987; EU parliament, 2019. **Sonia Hyner** (Green)

Contested this seat, 2017. **Roy Freshwater** (Ukip) Cllr, Medway BC, 2015-19.

CONSTITUENCY PROFILE
Rochester & Strood, in northern Kent, was created in 2010. Emily Thornberry resigned from Ed Miliband's shadow cabinet in 2014 after appearing to mock a Rochester resident's house flying an England flag. Kelly Tolhurst's majority has increased at every election since she defeated Mark Reckless in 2015. Part of the London commuter belt, one in nine workers is employed in the construction sector and median wages are £50 a week above the national average.

EU REFERENDUM RESULT
63.7% Leave   Remain 36.3%

Rochford & Southend East

MAJORITY 12,286 (26.63%)   CONSERVATIVE HOLD   TURNOUT 61.01%

JAMES DUDDRIDGE
BORN Aug 26, 1971
MP 2005-

Junior minister in the Foreign Office and Department for International Development, 2020-. One of the MPs to submit a letter of no confidence in Theresa May, 2018. Tabled a motion of no confidence in John Bercow, 2017. Backed Boris Johnson for leader, 2019. Parly under-sec, Brexit, 2019-20; Foreign Office, 2014-16. Whip, 2010-12; opposition whip, 2008-10. Select cttees: high speed rail, 2018-; international development, 2017-18, 2006-08; procedure, 2016-17; draft deregulation bill, 2013; liaison, 2012-14; regulatory reform,

	Electorate	Share %	from 2017 % Change
	75,624		
*J Duddridge C	27,063	58.66	+9.95
A Dalton Lab	14,777	32.03	-4.94
K Miller LD	2,822	6.12	+3.44
N Kumar Ind	1,107	2.40	-3.79
J Pilley PFP	367	0.80	

2012-14; environment, 2005-07. Barclays banker, 1993-2003; ran operations in Botswana. Founder member, YouGov. Contested Rother Valley in 2001. Ed: Essex University (BA government).

CHALLENGERS
Ashley Dalton (Lab) Sustainable travel adviser. Manager, South Essex Active Travel programme, 2017-. Project manager, Southend BC, 2016-. Member, Unison. Contested this seat, 2017. **Keith Miller** (LD)

Former medical representative. Contested Stafford, 2017; Tonbridge & Malling, 2015; Middlesbrough, 2001; Houghton & Washington East, 1997.

CONSTITUENCY PROFILE
Rochford & Southend East has been held by the Conservatives since its creation in 1997, and James Duddridge has the biggest majority any MP for the seat has enjoyed in that time. The predecesor constituencies also elected Conservative MPs for several decades. As with many seaside towns, tourism remains a major source of jobs, and Southend Airport is also located here. One of only a

EU REFERENDUM RESULT
60.9% Leave   Remain 39.1%

Romford

ANDREW ROSINDELL
BORN Mar 17, 1966
MP 2001-

On the hard right of his party. Criticised for questioning the ability of Rachel Reeves (Leeds West) to combine her motherhood with being a shadow minister, 2015. Tabled an early day motion in 2016 calling for the national anthem to be played daily on BBC One to celebrate Brexit. Referred to burgundy passports as source of humiliation. Expressed admiration for the Chilean dictator Augusto Pinochet. Supported Boris Johnson for the leadership, 2019. Death penalty advocate. Shadow home affairs minister, 2007-10; opposition

	Electorate	Share %	Change from 2017 %
	72,350		
*A Rosindell C	30,494	64.56	+5.15
A Leatherbarrow Lab	12,601	26.68	-5.14
I Sanderson LD	2,708	5.73	+3.30
D Hughes Green	1,428	3.02	+1.39

whip, 2005-07; party vice-chairman, 2004-05. Contested: Glasgow Provan, 1992; Thurrock, 1997. Member, Conservative Christian Fellowship. Cllr, Havering BC, 1990-2002. Ed: Marshalls Park CS, Romford.

CHALLENGERS
Angelina Leatherbarrow (Lab) Chairwoman, Romford CLP, 2018-. **Ian Sanderson** (LD) Former computer engineer and associate lecturer, Open University. Contested this seat, 2017, 2015; London Assembly,

2016. **David Hughes** (Green) Contested this seat, 2017.

CONSTITUENCY PROFILE
Labour held this seat for 20 of the 25 years after the Second World War, with the exception of 1950-55, but that dominance has switched. The Conservatives gained the seat in 1974, and Labour has won it back only once since then, in 1997, losing it to Andrew Rosindell at the following election. Historically a part of Essex, now of Greater London. A big office and retail centre for east London. Home ownership is above the national average, and considerably higher than the London average.

EU REFERENDUM RESULT
69.3% Leave   Remain 30.7%

Romsey & Southampton North

CAROLINE NOKES
BORN Jun 26, 1972
MP 2010-

Got her first taste of politics working as a policy adviser to her father, the Conservative politician Roy Perry. Rebelled to vote for an EU referendum, 2011, but supported Remain in 2016. Had the whip removed after voting against the Johnson government on Brexit; later restored. Immigration minister, 2018-19; found out she had been sacked by Boris Johnson from a journalist's tweet. Supported the leadership campaign of Sajid Javid, 2019. Parly under-sec: Cabinet Office, 2017-18; work and pensions, 2016-17. Cllr, Test Valley BC, 1999-2011. Contested:

	Electorate	Share %	Change from 2017 %
	68,228		
*C Nokes C	27,862	54.22	-2.93
C Fletcher LD	16,990	33.06	+11.81
C Ransom Lab	5,898	11.48	-7.69
G Bentley Ukip	640	1.25	

Romsey, 2005; Southampton Itchen, 2001. Ed: Peter Symonds Coll, Winchester; University of Sussex (BA politics and international relations).

CHALLENGERS
Craig Fletcher (LD) Founded Multiplay, a gaming website, and sold it for £20 million. Contested New Forest local election, 2018. **Claire Ransom** (Lab) Public service worker and Unison activist. **Geoff Bentley** (Ukip) Tree surgeon. Contested East Hampshire local election, 2019.

CONSTITUENCY PROFILE
The Conservatives have held Romsey & Southampton North since its creation in 2010, but the predecessor seat of Romsey was held by Sandra Gidley of the Liberal Democrats for the ten years before that, following a by-election in 2000. The Conservative majority peaked at more than 18,000 in 2017. An affluent Hampshire seat, it mostly consists of the towns and villages of the Test Valley, stretching north from Southampton. About one in six residents is aged 16-24, well above average, due to Southampton University's student population.

EU REFERENDUM RESULT
46.1% Leave   Remain 53.9%

Ross, Skye & Lochaber

MAJORITY 9,443 (23.69%)   SNP HOLD   **TURNOUT 73.52%**

IAN BLACKFORD
BORN May 14, 1961
MP 2015-

SNP Westminster leader, 2017-.
Voted Remain. SNP pensions
spokesman, 2015-. Ejected
from PMQs by John Bercow in
2018 for refusing to sit down,
leading to a mass SNP walk out.
Tabled early day motion of no
confidence in the government
after Theresa May pulled a
Brexit vote in December 2018.
Select cttees: intelligence and
security, 2017-; petitions, 2015-16.
Former managing director,
Deutsche Bank; First Seer
investor relations consultancy.
Contested: Paisley South by-
election, 1997; Ayr, 1997. Ed:
Royal HS, Edinburgh.

		Electorate	Share %	from 2017 % Change
		54,229		
*I Blackford	SNP	19,263	48.32	+8.06
C Harrow	LD	9,820	24.63	+3.72
G Berkenheger	C	6,900	17.31	-7.56
J Erskine	Lab	2,448	6.14	-6.07
K Brownlie	Brexit	710	1.78	
D Boyd	SCP	460	1.15	
R Lucas	Scot Family	268	0.67	

CHALLENGERS
Craig Harrow (LD) Strategic
communications adviser. Lib
Dem vice-president, 2010-16.
Founding board member, Better
Together. **Gavin Berkenheger**
(C) Geologist. Forced to deny
claims he entered into a
Lab-Lib Dem unionist pact.
Contested Highland local
election, 2018. **John Erskine**
(Lab) Parliamentary researcher
in Holyrood; private secretary

to Kezia Dugdale, leader
of Scottish Labour, 2016-17.
Contested Caithness, Sutherland
& Easter Ross, 2015.

CONSTITUENCY PROFILE
Charles Kennedy, the Lib
Dem leader 1999-2006, held
variations of this seat between
1983 and 2015, when it was
won by the SNP. A vast, rural
seat, geographically the largest
in the UK. Its largest town,
Fort William, is home to about
11,000 residents; otherwise
the constituency is sparsely
populated. Ben Nevis is within
its boundaries. Tourism and
agriculture are key industries,
and there is low unemployment.

EU REFERENDUM RESULT

43.5% Leave	Remain 56.5%

Rossendale & Darwen

MAJORITY 9,522 (19.50%)   CONSERVATIVE HOLD   **TURNOUT 67.09%**

JAKE BERRY
BORN Dec 29, 1978
MP 2010-

Minister for the northern
powerhouse and local growth,
2017-20. Stood down in February
2020 reshuffle, saying he had
been offered a different role
involving more travel but turned
it down to spend more time
with his family. Backed Boris
Johnson, 2019. Parly under-sec,
communities, 2017-18. Advised
David Cameron on housing,
regional growth and local
government as a member of No
10 policy unit. Voted Remain.
Agent to Amber Rudd, 2005.
Finance select cttee, 2015-17.
Solicitor specialising in property
and development law: City Law

		Electorate	Share %	from 2017 % Change
		72,771		
*J Berry	C	27,570	56.47	+5.63
A Barnes	Lab	18,048	36.97	-7.46
P Valentine	LD	2,011	4.12	+1.03
S Hall	Green	1,193	2.44	+0.80

Partnership; DWF; Halliwells.
Interested in social housing and
manufacturing. Ed: Liverpool
Coll; Sheffield University (LLB);
Coll of Law, Chester.

CHALLENGERS
Alyson Barnes (Lab) Works
in the rehabilitation of ex-
offenders. Cllr, Rossendale BC,
1999-; council leader, 2011-.
Contested this constituency, 2017.
Paul Valentine (LD) Insolvency
practitioner. Former civil
servant. Contested: South Ribble
BC, 2019; Lancashire CC, 2017.

Sarah Hall (Green) Cllr, Burnley
BC, 2019-.

CONSTITUENCY PROFILE
Gained by Labour in 1992,
Rossendale & Darwen came
back to the Conservatives in
2005. Will Straw, the son of
the Labour foreign secretary,
Jack, and the director of Britain
Stronger in Europe, the official
Remain campaign, was Labour's
candidate in 2015. Jake Berry's
majority in 2019 was the largest
that the Conservatives had
won in the seat since 1983.
The constituency contains the
West Pennine Moors south of
Blackburn, and the towns of
Rawtenstall, Bacup and Darwen.

EU REFERENDUM RESULT

58.9% Leave	Remain 41.1%

Rother Valley

ALEXANDER STAFFORD
BORN Jul 19, 1987
MP 2019-

Rother Valley's first Tory MP. External relations adviser at Shell before entering politics; previously head of media at the wildlife charity WWF UK. Senior researcher for Owen Paterson (Shropshire North) and Andrew Rosindell (Romford), 2008-12. Voted Leave. Opposed HS2. Cllr, Ealing BC, 2014-. Former regional chairman of Conservative Future. Won the Diana Memorial Award for youth achievement as a teenager. Ed: St Benedict's Sch; St Benet's Hall, Oxford (BA history; president, Conservative Association).

	Electorate	Share %	from 2017 %	Change
	74,802			
A Stafford C	21,970	45.11	+4.82	
S Wilson Lab	15,652	32.14	-15.99	
A Cowles Brexit	6,264	12.86		
C Taylor LD	2,553	5.24	+2.91	
E West Green	1,219	2.50	+0.75	
N Short Ind	1,040	2.14		

CHALLENGERS
Sophie Wilson (Lab) Born in 1996, 13 years after the retiring Labour MP Kevin Barron was first elected to parliament. South Yorkshire Fire & Rescue. Cllr, Sheffield CC, 2017-. **Allen Cowles** (Brexit) Retired IT manager. Cllr, Rotherham MBC, 2014-. Defected from Ukip in 2019. Criticised Environment Agency following 2019 Yorkshire floods. Contested Rotherham, 2017 (for Ukip). **Colin Taylor**

(LD) Former IT manager. Cllr, Sheffield CC, 2009-12.

CONSTITUENCY PROFILE
Before 2019 Rother Valley had been held by Labour for more than a century, since its creation in 1918. The party's majority had fallen to less than 4,000 in 2017, the lowest it had ever been. Kevin Barron, one of the few Labour MPs to have voted for Theresa May's withdrawal agreement, served as the MP here from 1983, standing down in 2019. Towns and villages in this south Yorkshire seat flourished with the expansion of coalmining, though the area's last coalmine closed in 2013.

EU REFERENDUM RESULT
66.7% Leave   Remain 33.3%

Rotherham

SARAH CHAMPION
BORN Jul 10, 1969
MP 2012-

Rotherham's first female MP, succeeding Denis MacShane, who stood down during the expenses scandal. Shadow women and equalities secretary, 2016-17; apologised and resigned over an article she wrote for *The Sun* saying that Britain had "a problem with British Pakistani men raping and exploiting white girls". Shadow minister for preventing abuse, 2015-16. Chairwoman, victims and witnesses APPG, 2014-15. Select cttees: women and equalities, 2018-; administration, 2017-; environment, 2015; transport, 2012-15. Admitted in 2014

	Electorate	Share %	from 2017 %	Change
	61,688			
*S Champion Lab	14,736	41.33	-15.11	
G Hickton C	11,615	32.58	+6.17	
P Hague Brexit	6,125	17.18		
A Carter LD	2,090	5.86	+1.24	
D Bannan Yorkshire	1,085	3.04	-0.73	

that she rarely attends PMQs. Arrested and cautioned by police in 2007 after assaulting her then-husband. Ed: Prince William CS, Oundle; University of Sheffield (BA psychology).

CHALLENGERS
Gerri Hickton (C) Driving instructor. Cllr, Erewash BC, 2013-. **Paul Hague** (Brexit) Cllr, Rotherham MBC, 2015-. Defected from Ukip. **Adam Carter** (LD) Junior doctor. Cllr, Rotherham MBC, 2017-.

CONSTITUENCY PROFILE
The Labour Party has won this south Yorkshire seat at every election since 1933, although Sarah Champion's 2019 majority was the smallest in all of that time. In the early 2010s, child sexual abuse dating back to the 1980s and involving an estimated 1,400 children was found to have been covered up or ignored by the local authorities, with the scandal leading to multiple inquiries, trials and convictions. Three in ten households are socially rented and one in ten residents is Asian or Asian British. There is higher than average unemployment after years of industrial decline.

EU REFERENDUM RESULT
68.3% Leave   Remain 31.7%

Rugby

CONSERVATIVE HOLD

MARK PAWSEY
BORN Jan 16, 1957
MP 2010-

	Electorate	Share %	Change from 2017 %
	72,340		
*M Pawsey C	29,255	57.57	+3.28
D Bannigan Lab	15,808	31.11	-7.19
R Das-Gupta LD	4,207	8.28	+2.73
B Stevenson Green	1,544	3.04	+1.18

Successful businessman who started a multimillion-pound catering supply business with his brother. Relatively quiet backbencher, interested in land issues and agriculture. Voted Remain but later embraced Brexit. Supported repealing the ban on fox hunting. Member, 1922 exec cttee. PPS to: Damian Green (Ashford), 2016-; Anna Soubry, 2014-16. Founder and chairman of vaping APPG; spoke in parliament about the alleged benefits of e-cigarettes and has campaigned against regulation of the tobacco industry. Cllr, Rugby BC, 2002-07. Contested Nuneaton, 2005. Plays for Lords & Commons rugby club. Son of the former Tory MP James Pawsey, who held this seat 1979-97. Ed: University of Reading (BSc estate management).

CHALLENGERS
Debbie Bannigan (Lab) Former CEO of Swanswell, a drug and alcohol abuse charity. Accountant. Member, Unite. **Rana Das-Gupta** (LD) Consultant plastic surgeon. Refugee from Burma; arrived in the UK aged two. **Becca**

Stevenson (Green) Farmer. Midlands co-ordinator, Land Workers' Alliance. Contested Rugby BC, 2019.

CONSTITUENCY PROFILE
Rugby has been in Conservative hands since its re-creation in 2010, with the party's vote share growing at each successive election. Its predecessor seat, Kenilworth & Rugby, was narrowly won by Labour in 1997 and 2001. Rugby is an engineering and industrial town, home to about 70,000 people. The seat also encompasses countryside to the north and west of Rugby and many affluent commuter villages.

EU REFERENDUM RESULT
58.6% Leave   Remain 41.4%

Ruislip, Northwood & Pinner

CONSERVATIVE HOLD

DAVID SIMMONDS
BORN Feb 22, 1976
MP 2019-

	Electorate	Share %	Change from 2017 %
	73,191		
D Simmonds C	29,391	55.56	-1.68
P Assad Lab	12,997	24.57	-6.48
J Banks LD	7,986	15.10	+7.95
S Green Green	1,646	3.11	+0.74
F Amin AWP	325	0.61	
T Blackwell Ind	295	0.56	
J Wilson Ind	264	0.50	

Chartered insurer who worked in financial services for Lloyds TSB and HSBC. Cllr, Hillingdon LBC, 1998-; deputy council leader, 2002-19. London's youngest councillor when first elected. Member, LGA executive. Vice-chairman, National Employers Organisation for School Teachers. Led efforts to persuade councils to house 20,000 Syrian refugees. Awarded CBE for services to children, families and local government, 2015. Magistrate; NHS trust non-executive director; trustee, Early Intervention Foundation. Ed: Durham University (BA politics, economics and management); University of London (PG Cert elected member development).

CHALLENGERS
Peymana Assad (Lab) Charity sector worker. Cllr, Harrow LBC, 2018-. Born in Kabul, lived in a refugee camp, moved to the UK aged 3. Fluent in Dari and Pashto. **Jonathan Banks** (LD) Sales and marketing consultant. Worked with UNFAO and WEF

on sustainability issues. **Sarah Green** (Green) Operates Grand Union Canal passenger boat business. Arrested for protesting against HS2 in 2018.

CONSTITUENCY PROFILE
Created in 2010, Ruislip, Northwood & Pinner is a safe Conservative seat, which the party has won with five-figure majorities in all four elections in that time. Its predecessor, Ruislip-Northwood, also elected Conservative MPs, often with large margins, at every election since 1950. It is the most northwesterly seat in Greater London, and is an affluent, suburban commuter area.

EU REFERENDUM RESULT
49.5% Leave   Remain 50.5%

Runnymede & Weybridge

MAJORITY 18,270 (34.28%) CONSERVATIVE HOLD TURNOUT 69.03%

BEN SPENCER
BORN Dec 11, 1981
MP 2019-

NHS consultant psychiatrist. Vice-chairman, Conservative Mental Health special interest group, 2017-. Chairman, South East London Conservatives, 2017-. Member, Tory Reform Group. Voted Remain. Governor, NHS Foundation Trust. Volunteer, London Street Rescue. Contested Camberwell & Peckham, 2017. Ed: Queen Mary's GS; UCL (BSc neuroscience with basic medical sciences); UCL & Royal Free Medical School (medicine); University of Northumbria (LLM mental health law); KCL (PhD psychological medicine).

	Electorate	Share %	Change from 2017 %
	77,196		
B Spencer C	29,262	54.91	-6.00
R King Lab	10,992	20.63	-5.31
R O'Carroll LD	9,236	17.33	+10.04
B Smith Green	1,876	3.52	+0.91
S Mackay Ind	777	1.46	
L Rowland Ind	670	1.26	
N Wood Ukip	476	0.89	-2.35

CHALLENGERS
Robert King (Lab) Born in 1995. Economics postgraduate, Royal Holloway. Cllr, Runnymede BC, 2019-. Chairman, Runnymede & Weybridge CLP. Member: UCU; Unite. Youth Parliament, 2008-10. **Rob O'Carroll** (LD) Former archaeologist. Cllr, Richmond LBC, 2018-. **Benjamin Smith** (Green) Former deputy leader, Welsh Greens. Contested Cardiff Central, 2017.

CONSTITUENCY PROFILE
Created in 1997, this north Surrey seat has always returned Conservative candidates to parliament, with the party winning more than half the vote in every election since 2005. Philip Hammond, the chancellor of the exchequer under Theresa May, stood down in 2019, having lost the Conservative whip for voting against the government on Brexit. An affluent seat with strong London transport links, many residents work in transport. About one in eight residents are students at Royal Holloway, University of London, and Brooklands College.

EU REFERENDUM RESULT
49.8% Leave   Remain 50.2%

Rushcliffe

MAJORITY 7,643 (12.63%) CONSERVATIVE HOLD TURNOUT 78.52%

RUTH EDWARDS
BORN May 11, 1984
MP 2019-

Cybersecurity expert; head of community and public policy at BT Security. Previous roles at Deloitte, Policy Exchange and Tech UK. Produced reports on border enforcement for the home affairs select cttee. Winner, ISG Paragon "women in technology" award. Supports 50:50 parliament campaign. Researcher for Crispin Blunt (Reigate), 2009-10. Has volunteered for Water Aid and Thames Reach. Qualified scuba diver. Keeps alpacas, chickens, bees, and a tortoise named Geoffrey. Ed: London School of Theology (BA theology);

	Electorate	Share %	Change from 2017 %
	77,055		
R Edwards C	28,765	47.54	-4.29
C Pidgeon Lab	21,122	34.91	-3.18
J Billin LD	9,600	15.87	+11.13
M Faithfull Ukip	591	0.98	-1.58
J Kirby Ind	427	0.71	

University of Bristol (MA international development and security).

CHALLENGERS
Cheryl Pidgeon (Lab) Unite regional officer; former TUC regional secretary. Contested Erewash, 2010; Derbyshire South, 2015. **Jason Billin** (LD) Established own publishing house. Endorsed by Green and Reform parties under Unite to Remain pact. **Matthew Faithfull** (Ukip) Contested this seat, 2017.

CONSTITUENCY PROFILE
Rushcliffe is a safe Conservative seat, held continually by the party for half a century. Ken Clarke, father of the House, 2017-19, a chancellor under John Major, and a pro-EU "big beast", stood down in 2019 after serving as Rushcliffe's MP since 1970. A mostly rural area in Nottinghamshire, its major population centre, West Bridgford, is immediately south of Nottingham and home to 47,000 people. More than three quarters of households are owner-occupied, two in five residents are educated to degree level, and many residents work in the education sector.

EU REFERENDUM RESULT
41.5% Leave   Remain 58.5%

Rutherglen & Hamilton West

MAJORITY 5,230 (9.72%) SNP GAIN FROM LABOUR CO-OP TURNOUT 66.48%

MARGARET
FERRIER
BORN Sep 10, 1960
MP 2019-; 2015-17

Won back seat after two years
away from parliament. Shadow
SNP spokeswoman for Scotland
office; member of scottish
affairs select cttee, 2015-17.
Member: Amnesty International;
Scottish CND. Opposes Trident.
Animal rights campaigner.
Trained teacher; worked as
a sales manager in blue chip
manufacturing construction
company in Motherwell before
being elected. Ed: Holyrood
Catholic Secondary School.

CHALLENGERS
Ged Killen (Lab Co-op) MP for
this seat, 2017-19. PPS to Nia

	Electorate	Share %	Change from 2017 %
	80,918		
M Ferrier SNP	23,775	44.20	+7.17
*G Killen Lab Co-op	18,545	34.47	-3.07
L Nailon C	8,054	14.97	-4.57
M McGeever LD	2,791	5.19	+0.95
J Mackay Ukip	629	1.17	+0.26

Griffith (Llanelli); resigned in
2018 to defy the whip and vote
in favour of the UK joining the
EEA. LGBT campaigner. Cllr,
South Lanarkshire C, 2013-.
Lynne Nailon (C) Works in
local government. Formerly
in the civil service and NHS.
Cllr, South Lanarkshire DC,
2017-. **Mark McGeever** (LD)
Defected from the Conservatives
the day after Boris Johnson
became leader. Former media
officer, Scottish Fire and Rescue.
Cllr, South Lanarkshire DC,

2017-. Contested East Kilbride,
Strathaven and Lesmahagow,
2017 (for the Conservatives).

CONSTITUENCY PROFILE
Created in 2005, this seat
initially elected a Labour MP,
but in 2015 the SNP overturned
a 21,000-strong majority to
win the seat by almost 10,000
votes. Its predecessor seats,
Rutherglen and Hamilton, had
both been held by Labour for
35 years by the time the seat
was created. The seat has since
swung between the two parties.
A suburban area dominated by
high-density housing, the seat
has high levels of social housing
and below-average wages.

EU REFERENDUM RESULT
37.6% Leave Remain 62.4%

Rutland & Melton

MAJORITY 26,924 (46.17%) CONSERVATIVE HOLD TURNOUT 70.50%

ALICIA KEARNS
BORN Nov 11, 1987
MP 2019-

Counter-terrorism consultant
and crisis management expert.
Director, Global Influence.
Adviser to the Foreign Office,
leading on interventions in
Iraq and Syria. Worked with
70 foreign governments in the
fight against Isis. Previously:
MoD, MoJ. Former deputy
chairwoman, Cambridge
Conservatives. Contested
Mitcham & Morden, 2017. Spent
three months volunteering for
the Lighthouse Relief charity on
Lesbos, Greece. Ed: Impington
International Sixth Form;
Fitzwilliam Coll, Cambridge (BA
social and political sciences).

	Electorate	Share %	Change from 2017 %
	82,711		
A Kearns C	36,507	62.61	-0.22
A Thomas Lab	9,583	16.43	-6.26
C Weaver LD	7,970	13.67	+5.49
A McQuillan Green	2,875	4.93	+1.88
M King UKIP	917	1.57	-1.67
A Watchorn Ind	458	0.79	

CHALLENGERS
Andy Thomas (Lab) Academic
researching international space
programmes. Cllr, Manchester
City C, 1980-82. Contested
Harborough, 2017. **Carol Weaver**
(LD) International peacekeeping
adviser. Chaired the Leicester &
Rutland cross-party European
movement. Executive member of
Liberal Democrats International.
Alastair McQuillan (Green)
Works in a pub. Former
biological researcher. Contested

this constituency in the 2015 and
2017 general elections.

CONSTITUENCY PROFILE
The largest and most rural seat
in Leicestershire, Rutland, in a
few different forms, has elected
only Conservative MPs for more
than 150 years. The outgoing
MP Sir Alan Duncan, a former
minister and the first openly
gay Conservative MP, had
represented the seat since 1992.
The constituency's largest town
is Melton Mowbray. More than
three quarters of households are
owner occupied. Almost half of
the population is aged 45 or over.
Manufacturing and education
are the big employment sectors.

EU REFERENDUM RESULT
53.9% Leave Remain 46.1%

Saffron Walden

MAJORITY 27,594 (43.74%)   **CONSERVATIVE HOLD**   **TURNOUT 72.50%**

KEMI BADENOCH
BORN Jan 2, 1980
MP 2017-

Electorate	Share %	from 2017 %	Change
87,017			
*K Badenoch C	39,714	62.95	+1.18
M Hibbs LD	12,120	19.21	+5.21
T Van De Bilt Lab	8,305	13.16	-7.62
C Wing Green	2,947	4.67	

Appointed exchequer secretary to the Treasury and junior international trade minister in February 2020. Assisted Zac Goldsmith's unsuccessful 2016 London mayoral campaign. Parly under-sec, children and families, 2019-20. 1922 exec cttee, 2017-. Select cttees: justice, 2017-; standing orders, 2017-. Party vice-chairwoman for candidates, 2018-19. Passionate about education access, particularly for ethnic minorities. Voted Leave. Apologised in 2018 for hacking into the website of Harriet Harman MP a decade previously. Business analyst at RBS;

vice-president, Coutts. Later head of digital, *The Spectator*. Deputy leader, Conservative London Assembly group, 2016-17. Contested Dulwich & West Norwood, 2010. Ed: Birkbeck Coll, University of London (LLB); University of Sussex (MEng engineering).

CHALLENGERS
Mike Hibbs (LD) Architect. Cllr, Saffron Walden TC, 1987-; mayor, 2008-09. Contested this seat, 2017, 2015; Basildon & Billericay, 2010. **Thomas**

Van De Bilt (Lab) IT engineer. **Coby Wing** (Green) Health and education worker. Was homeless as a child.

CONSTITUENCY PROFILE
Conservative for almost a century, the seat has returned MPs with majorities of more than 10,000 at every election since 1977. Represented between 1929 and 1965 by Rab Butler, who held three of the great offices of state in the 1950s and 1960s and succeeded Winston Churchill as father of the House in 1964. A large, rural seat in Essex containing the historic market towns of Saffron Walden and Great Dunmow.

EU REFERENDUM RESULT
51.2% Leave   **Remain 48.8%**

St Albans

MAJORITY 6,293 (10.93%)   **LIB DEM GAIN FROM CONSERVATIVE**   **TURNOUT 78.13%**

DAISY COOPER
BORN Oct 29, 1981
MP 2019-

Electorate	Share %	from 2017 %	Change
73,721			
D Cooper LD	28,867	50.12	+17.73
*A Main C	22,574	39.19	-3.92
R Lury Lab	5,000	8.68	-14.37
S Grover Green	1,004	1.74	+0.29
J Sherrington ND	154	0.27	

Former joint executive director, Hacked Off, the press regulation advocacy group. Executive director, More United, 2017-19. Ran Jo Swinson's leadership campaign, 2019, and Norman Baker's 2015 general election campaign. Seen as a likely leadership candidate, 2020. Justice and culture spokeswoman. Spent more than a decade specialising in Commonwealth affairs. Commonwealth Secretariat, 2006-10. Former campaigns director, Commonwealth Advisory Bureau. Cllr, Lewes DC. Leader, St Albans

Commuter and Passenger Action Group. Contested: this seat, 2017; Sussex Mid, 2015; Suffolk Coastal, 2010. Ed: University of Nottingham (LLM); University of Leeds (LLB).

CHALLENGERS
Anne Main (C) MP for this seat, 2005-19. Brexiteer in 2016 referendum. **Rebecca Lury** (Lab) Partner, Pagefield. Cllr, Southwark LBC, 2012-; council deputy leader, 2018-. Contested Ruislip, Northwood & Pinner,

2017. **Simon Grover** (Green) Children's TV scriptwriter. Played a Death Eater in *Harry Potter*. Cllr, St Albans DC, 2011-.

CONSTITUENCY PROFILE
Daisy Cooper's victory in St Albans came 113 years after the Liberals last held the seat; the party lost it in 1906 to the Conservatives. Labour broke the Conservative dominance in this Hertfordshire constituency only in 1945, 1997 and 2001. An affluent seat consisting of the eponymous cathedral city and its surrounding countryside. It has a younger than average population, with three in five residents under the age of 45.

EU REFERENDUM RESULT
37.8% Leave   **Remain 62.2%**

St Austell & Newquay

MAJORITY 16,526 (29.63%)   CONSERVATIVE HOLD   TURNOUT 69.78%

STEVE DOUBLE
BORN Dec 19, 1966
MP 2015-

Former pastor and evangelical Christian. Noted for having an affair with one of his married caseworkers in 2016, despite having made traditional family values a key issue in his 2015 campaign; publicly apologised and reconciled with his wife. Brexiteer. Supported vote of no confidence in Theresa May, 2018, although relucantly supported her Brexit withdrawal agreemeent, calling it "the best turd we've got". Supported Mark Harper in the 2019 leadership contest. APPG chairman: hospitality, ocean conservation. Select cttees: transport, 2017-;

	Electorate	Share %	Change from 2017 %
	79,930		
*S Double C	31,273	56.07	+6.53
F Owen Lab	14,747	26.44	-2.55
T Styles LD	5,861	10.51	-10.97
D Cole Kernow	1,660	2.98	
C Harker Green	1,609	2.88	
R Byrne Lib	626	1.12	

petitions, 2017-; European scrutiny, 2017-. Former director, Phoenix Corporate, an events company. Cllr, St Austell C, 2009-15; mayor, 2013-14. Cllr, Cornwall CC, 2009-13. Ed: Poltair Sch; Cornwall Coll (Btec business studies).

CHALLENGERS
Felicity Owen (Lab) NHS worker of 40 years. Member, Royal College of Nursing. **Tim Styles** (LD) Barrister specialising

in employment law. Mayor of St Austell, 2019-.

CONSTITUENCY PROFILE
The old Truro seat, with boundaries relatively similar to those of St Austell & Newquay, returned Liberal and Liberal Democrat MPs at every election from 1974. The Lib Dems held on to the new seat when it was created in 2010, but only by a little over 1,300. The party was relegated to third place in 2017. This constituency combines the south Cornwall market town of St Austell and the seaside town of Newquay, each home to about 20,000 people. It also contains the Eden Project.

EU REFERENDUM RESULT
64.1% Leave   Remain 35.9%

St Helens North

MAJORITY 12,209 (25.67%)   LABOUR HOLD   TURNOUT 62.92%

CONNOR MCGINN
BORN Jul 31, 1984
MP 2015-

Former voluntary sector worker specialising in mental health and prison work. Northern Irish; assisted introduction of same-sex marriage legislation. Father was a Sinn Fein councillor and mayor. Vehemently anti-Jeremy Corbyn, calling him "out of touch with the concerns of ordinary people" after the 2019 election defeat. Supported Sir Keir Starmer, 2020. Voted Remain. Select cttees: foreign affairs, 2019; consolidation bills, 2017-19; regulatory reform, 2017-19; Northern Ireland affairs, 2017-19. Chairman of APPGs on: Ireland; Irish in Britain; coalfield

	Electorate	Share %	Change from 2017 %
	75,593		
*C McGinn Lab	24,870	52.29	-11.45
J Charles C	12,661	26.62	-0.47
M Webster Brexit	5,396	11.35	
P Moloney LD	2,668	5.61	+3.05
D Van Der Burg Green	1,966	4.13	+1.70

communities; darts. Opposition whip, 2015-16; stood down after sacking of Dame Rosie Winterton. Socialist society representative. Vice-chairman, Fabian Society, 2011-12. Ed: St Pauls HS, Bessbrook; London Metropolitan University (BA history and politics).

CHALLENGERS
Joel Charles (C) National charity director. Cllr, Harlow DC, 2014-, 2008-12; first elected aged 22. **Malcolm Webster**

(Brexit) Part-time driving instructor, retired police officer. **Pat Moloney** (LD) Director, Stanhope Pension Trust. Has contested five elections in three seats.

CONSTITUENCY PROFILE
Staunchly Labour, St Helens North in Merseyside has been held by the party since its creation in 1983, as had the predecessor seat since 1935. Labour's majority in the 2019 election was the lowest since 1983, which was the only time it fell below 10,000. The unemployment rate is above average, and the weekly wage is £50 less than the UK average.

EU REFERENDUM RESULT
58.4% Leave   Remain 41.6%

St Helens South & Whiston

MAJORITY 19,122 (38.01%)   **LABOUR HOLD**   **TURNOUT 63.64%**

MARIE RIMMER
BORN Apr 27, 1947
MP 2015-

	Electorate	Share %	Change from 2017 %
	79,058		
*M Rimmer Lab	29,457	58.55	-9.29
R Short C	10,335	20.54	-1.27
D Oxley Brexit	5,353	10.64	
B Spencer LD	2,886	5.74	+1.76
K Taylor Green	2,282	4.54	+1.86

A Pilkington's glass factory worker, who rose up the ranks into staff procurement. Cllr, St Helens MBC, 1978-2016, and leader for almost 20 years; awarded CBE in 2005 for services to local government. Registered as disabled owing to deafness. Supported Sir Keir Starmer in 2020, having backed Owen Smith in 2016 and Yvette Cooper in 2015. Told a PLP meeting that it "wasn't easy" to vote Labour in the 2019 European election because of the party's lack of support for a second referendum. Shadow minister for disabled people,

2017. Arrested and charged with assault while campaigning against Scottish independence at a Glasgow polling station in 2014; later cleared of charges. Ed: Lowe House Girls Sch.

CHALLENGERS
Richard Short (C) Deputy director, Conservative Workers and Trade Unionists. Contested Warrington North, 2015. **Daniel Oxley** (Brexit) Tour operator. Former chairman, Newham Ukip. Contested East Ham for

Ukip, 2017, 2015. **Brian Spencer** (LD) Electrician. Contested this seat, 2017, 2015, 2010.

CONSTITUENCY PROFILE
Like its neighbour to the north, St Helens South has been held by Labour since the two seats were created in 1983. Whiston, a part of Knowsley, was added to the seat in 2010. Its previous MP was Shaun Woodward, who defected from the Conservatives to Labour in 1999 and held the constituency from 2001 to 2015, serving as Northern Ireland secretary in 2007-10. The area is known for its glass production, with Pilkington, and formerly Ravenhead, based in the seat.

EU REFERENDUM RESULT
56.1% Leave   Remain 43.9%

St Ives

MAJORITY 5,284 (8.32%)   **CONSERVATIVE HOLD**   **TURNOUT 74.71%**

DEREK THOMAS
BORN Jul 20, 1972
MP 2015-

	Electorate	Share %	Change from 2017 %
	68,795		
*D Thomas C	25,365	49.35	+6.17
A George LD	21,081	41.01	-1.56
A Bates Lab	3,553	6.91	-7.33
I Flindall Green	954	1.86	
R Smith Lib	314	0.61	
J Harris People	132	0.26	

Former development manager for Mustard Seed, a Cornwall-based voluntary organisation. Brexiteer and ERG member. Voted to leave the EU with no-deal, although he eventually supported Theresa May's withdrawal agreement. Backed Jeremy Hunt in the 2019 leadership race. Signed up to the Make Votes Matter alliance, a pressure group pushing for proportional representation. Select cttees: health and social care, 2018-19; work and pensions, 2018-19; environmental audit, 2019. Chairman of APPGs: axial spondyloarthritis; brain tumours;

vascular and venous disease. Contested this seat, 2010. School governor. Born to missionary parents. Grew up in West Cornwall; took apprenticeship to qualify as a mason in the construction industry.

CHALLENGERS
Andrew George (LD) MP for this seat, 1997-2015. Shadow international development secretary, 2005-06. Shadow minister: rural affairs, 2002-05;

disabilities, 2000-01; fisheries, 1997-2001. First MP to speak Cornish in parliament. **Alana Bates** (Lab) Cllr, Penzance TC, 2018-.

CONSTITUENCY PROFILE
St Ives returned Conservative MPs from 1970 until 1997, when the Liberal Democrats gained the seat. It was reclaimed by the Tories in 2015, although the Lib Dems reduced the party's majority to 312 in 2017. The seat covers the southwestern tip of England, including Penzance, Land's End and the Isles of Scilly. The dominant industries were once tin-mining and fishing, but tourism now dominates.

EU REFERENDUM RESULT
54.8% Leave   Remain 45.2%

Salford & Eccles

MAJORITY 16,327 (32.25%) LABOUR HOLD TURNOUT 61.59%

REBECCA
LONG BAILEY
BORN Sep 22, 1979
MP 2015-

	Electorate	Share %	from 2017 %	Change
	82,202			
*R Long Bailey Lab	28,755	56.79	-8.66	
A Choudhary C	12,428	24.55	-0.73	
M Mickler Brexit	4,290	8.47		
J Overend LD	3,099	6.12	+3.42	
B Blears Green	2,060	4.07	+2.37	

Labour leadership contender in 2020 characterised as the continuity Corbyn candidate, having rated his leadership "ten out of ten" despite the party's crushing defeat in the 2019 election. Shadow: business secretary, 2017-; chief secretary to the Treasury, 2016-17; Treasury minister, 2015-16. Former solicitor specialising in NHS procurement contracts. Worked in call centres, a furniture factory and as a postwoman. Responsible for Labour's 2019 "Green Industrial Revolution" policy framework. Advocated abolishing the House of Lords. Replaced Hilary Benn on Labour NEC, September 2015. Rebelled to vote against renewing Trident in 2016, but said she would be prepared to use it as PM. Ed: Chester Catholic HS; Manchester Metropolitan University (BA politics and sociology).

CHALLENGERS
Attika Choudhary (C) BBC journalist, 2009-. Cllr, Rushmoor BC, 2010-14; mayoress, 2017-18; deputy mayoress, 2016-17. Matt

Mickler (Brexit) Recruitment manager. Jake Overend (LD) Presenter, Salford City Radio.

CONSTITUENCY PROFILE
Combined in 2010, the seats of Salford and Eccles had both returned Labour MPs at every election since 1945. Labour's majority grew from 6,000 in 2010 to more than 19,000 in 2017. Its previous MP, Hazel Blears, was a cabinet minister during the New Labour years. The Greater Manchester seat covers Ellesmere Park, Salford and Pendlebury. The University of Salford campus is within its boundaries and about one in eight residents is a student.

EU REFERENDUM RESULT
53.6% Leave Remain 46.4%

Salisbury

MAJORITY 19,736 (36.73%) CONSERVATIVE HOLD TURNOUT 72.06%

JOHN GLEN
BORN Apr 1, 1974
MP 2010-

	Electorate	Share %	from 2017 %	Change
	74,560			
*J Glen C	30,280	56.36	-1.70	
V Charleston LD	10,544	19.62	+8.40	
T Corbin Lab	9,675	18.01	-7.54	
R Page Green	2,486	4.63	+2.47	
K Pendragon Ind	745	1.39	+0.61	

An anti-immigration Eurosceptic who ultimately backed Remain in the 2016 referendum. Economic secretary to the Treasury, 2018-; parly under-sec, culture, 2017-18. Parliamentary chairman of the Conservative Christian Fellowship. Voted for Sajid Javid in the 2019 leadership race, before supporting Boris Johnson in the final round. Stints at Conservative research department: head of political section under William Hague; director, 2004-06. PPS to: Philip Hammond, 2016-17; Sajid Javid, 2015-16. Contested Plymouth Devonport, 2001. Ed: King Edward's Sch, Bath; Mansfield Coll, Oxford (BA history) King's Coll, London (MA international security and strategy).

CHALLENGERS
Victoria Charleston (LD) Policy and development manager, Suzy Lamplugh Trust, a personal safety charity. Former chief of staff to Tessa Munt MP. Tom Corbin (Lab) Train driver and Aslef union rep. Cllr, Salisbury City C, 2013-. Contested this seat, 2017, 2015.

CONSTITUENCY PROFILE
Salisbury has returned a Conservative MP at every election since 1924 and the seat has been held by Liberal MPs for only five years since 1886. The Conservative majority over the Liberal Democrats was less than 6,000 in 2010, but the Lib Dems then finished fourth in 2015. Located in Wiltshire, it is home to Stonehenge amd Salisbury Cathedral. It became the centre of global attention following the poisoning of Sergei and Yulia Skripal in March 2018. The number of people in full-time work is high. The MoD is a key employer here, with several military bases located near by.

EU REFERENDUM RESULT
49.9% Leave Remain 50.1%

Scarborough & Whitby

MAJORITY 10,270 (20.65%)   CONSERVATIVE HOLD   TURNOUT 66.84%

ROBERT
GOODWILL
BORN Dec 31, 1956
MP 2005-

Long-time Eurosceptic but eventually supported Remain in 2016. NFU member; has 250-acre family farm. Minister: agriculture, 2019; children and families, 2017-18; immigration, 2016-17. Parly under-sec, transport, 2013-16. Shadow minister, transport, 2007-10. Supported Jeremy Hunt in the 2019 leadership race. MEP for Yorkshire and the Humber, 1999-2004; environment spokesman, 2001-04. Select cttees: environmental audit, 2018-; Northern Ireland affairs, 2018-. Has served in several whip roles. Member, Cornerstone Group.

	Electorate	Share %	Change from 2017 %
	74,393		
*R Goodwill C	27,593	55.49	+7.12
H Fearnley Lab	17,323	34.84	-6.72
R Lockwood LD	3,038	6.11	+3.43
L Derrick Yorkshire	1,770	3.56	+2.83

Contested: Leicestershire North West, 1997; Redcar, 1992. Ed: Bootham Sch, York; Newcastle University (BSc agriculture).

CHALLENGERS
Hugo Fearnley (Lab) Development director for a natural medicines start up. Vice-chairman, Scarborough and Whitby CLP. Former HR administrator. Contested: Scarborough BC, 2017. **Robert Lockwood** (LD) Self-employed businessman. Contested this constituency in 2017.

CONSTITUENCY PROFILE
Scarborough & Whitby has elected a Conservative MP at almost every election since 1918. The only exceptions were the Labour landslides of 1997 and 2001, meaning that the seat has had a Labour MP for only eight years in more than a century. Located on the coast of North Yorkshire, a little to the south of Middlesbrough, the constituency has a large number of retirees, accounting for almost a quarter of residents. Home ownership is slightly higher than average, but wages are significantly lower than national levels. A large number of local jobs are linked to the tourism sector.

EU REFERENDUM RESULT
61.3% Leave   Remain 38.7%

Scunthorpe

MAJORITY 6,451 (17.09%)   CONSERVATIVE GAIN FROM LABOUR   TURNOUT 60.93%

HOLLY
MUMBY-CROFT
BORN Jul 1983
MP 2019-

Daughter of a Scunthorpe steelworker. Emphasised the protection of British Steel during her campaign. Cllr, North Lincolnshire DC, 2015-; health scrutiny committee chairwoman; Broughton TC, 2010-; mayor, 2013-15. Youngest ever elected mayor. Earned a reputation for holding hospital managers to account over waiting lists and ambulance delays. Has campaigned against wind farms. Contested Scunthorpe, 2017.

CHALLENGERS
Nic Dakin (Lab) MP for this constituency, 2010-19.

	Electorate	Share %	Change from 2017 %
	61,955		
H Mumby-Croft C	20,306	53.79	+10.30
*N Dakin Lab	13,855	36.70	-15.33
J Gorman Brexit	2,044	5.41	
R Downes LD	875	2.32	+0.94
P Dennington Green	670	1.77	

Shadow minister for schools, 2015-16; resigned in protest at the party's leadership and supported Owen Smith in his challenge to Jeremy Corbyn, 2016. Opposition whip, 2011-15; shadow deputy Commons leader, 2015-16. **Jerry Gorman** (Brexit) Retired steelworker of 50 years. Scunthorpe steelworks executive, 1989-91. **Ryk Downes** (LD) Trustee, Citizens' Advice Bureau. Cllr, Leeds City C, 2018-. Contested: this seat, 2017; Pudsey, 2015.

CONSTITUENCY PROFILE
One of Labour's nine losses in the Yorkshire and the Humber region. The party had held the north Lincolnshire seat of Scunthorpe and its predecessors for all but eight years from 1935 – the Conservatives gained the Brigg & Scunthorpe seat in 1979 and held it until Labour won Glanford & Scunthorpe in 1987. Labour's majority declined from a peak of more than 14,000 in 1997 and was between 2,500 and 3,500 at each of the three previous elections. A leading source of employment in the area is British Steel, which provides work for several thousand people.

EU REFERENDUM RESULT
68.7% Leave   Remain 31.3%

Sedgefield

MAJORITY 4,513 (10.86%) **CONSERVATIVE GAIN FROM LABOUR** **TURNOUT 64.62%**

PAUL HOWELL
BORN Jan 10, 1960
MP 2019-

Accountant who became a financial and logistics director. Voted Remain in 2016. Wants better broadband in rural areas and improved road connectivity and public transport throughout the region. Cllr, Durham City C, 2017-; economy and environment committee. Cllr, Darlington BC, 2019-. Treasurer, Friends of Darlington Library. Former deputy chairman of the South Durham Conservatives. School governor. State educated. Golfer and private pilot. Contested Houghton & Sunderland South, 2017. Ed: Durham University (MBA).

	Electorate	Share %	from 2017 %	Change
	64,325			
P Howell C	19,609	47.18	+8.36	
*P Wilson Lab	15,096	36.32	-17.06	
D Bull Brexit	3,518	8.46		
D Welsh LD	1,955	4.70	+2.79	
J Furness Green	994	2.39	+0.74	
M Joyce Ind	394	0.95		

CHALLENGERS
Phil Wilson (Lab) MP for this seat, 2007-19. Former aide to Tony Blair. Co-author of a parliamentary amendment to pass a Brexit deal provided it was put to a referendum. Opposition assistant whip, 2010-15. PPS to: Andy Burnham, 2009-10; Vernon Coaker, 2008-09. **David Bull** (Brexit) MEP for North West England, 2019-20. Television doctor. Former Conservative member.

CONSTITUENCY PROFILE
Sedgefield was for many years a safe Labour seat, held by the Labour Party continuously since 1935, and by Tony Blair between 1983 and 2007. Labour's majority peaked in 1997, at more than 25,000, but Mr Blair's successor Phil Wilson had seen his majority fall at successive general elections to just over 6,000 in 2017. A former mining seat in the North East where earnings are in line with the national average. Two thirds of households are owner-occupied, which is just above average. A significant proportion of jobs are routine and in the manufacturing sector.

EU REFERENDUM RESULT
59.4% Leave   Remain 40.6%

Sefton Central

MAJORITY 15,122 (29.72%) **LABOUR HOLD** **TURNOUT 72.94%**

BILL ESTERSON
BORN Oct 27, 1966
MP 2010-

Small business advocate. Shadow minister: international trade, 2016-; business, 2016-; small business, 2015-16. Backed Sir Keir Starmer for leader, 2020. Introduced bill to improve labelled drinking guidelines for pregnant women, 2015. Voted against military intervention in Syria, 2014. Cites the former Bolsover MP Dennis Skinner as his political hero. PPS to Stephen Twigg, 2011-13. Cllr, Medway C, 1995-2010. Director of training consultancy firm. Ed: Rochester Mathematical Sch; University of Leeds (BSc maths and philosophy).

	Electorate	Share %	from 2017 %	Change
	69,760			
*B Esterson Lab	29,254	57.50	-5.54	
W Mughal C	14,132	27.78	-5.27	
K Cawdron LD	3,386	6.65	+4.00	
P Lomas Brexit	2,425	4.77		
A Gibbon Green	1,261	2.48	+1.22	
A Preston Lib	285	0.56		
C Burns Renew	137	0.27		

CHALLENGERS
Wazz Mughal (C) Works in research and development for a renewable energy company. Former IT engineer. Contested European parliament, 2019. **Keith Cawdron** (LD) NHS hospice chief executive. Anglican church reader. Trustee, Age Concern. **Paul Lomas** (Brexit) Former banker and businessman. Founder of Stonker, a mobile business card app.

CONSTITUENCY PROFILE
A safe Labour seat on the coast between Liverpool and Southport. Its predecessor seat was held by the Conservatives from its creation in 1950 until Labour's landslide in 1997. Part of Knowsley was added in 2010, when Sefton Central was created, making the boundaries more favourable to Labour. Well over half its residents are aged over 45. Eight-five per cent of households are owner-occupied, one of the highest rates in the country, and child poverty is half the national and regional average. The constituency is home to Aintree racecourse and the Grand National.

EU REFERENDUM RESULT
44.1% Leave   Remain 55.9%

Selby & Ainsty

MAJORITY 20,137 (35.69%)   CONSERVATIVE HOLD   TURNOUT 71.67%

NIGEL ADAMS
BORN Nov 30, 1966
MP 2010-

Minister in the Foreign Office and Department for International Development, 2020-. Culture minister, 2019-20. Parly under-sec: Wales, 2018-19; housing, 2018. Assistant whip, 2018-19. Chairman of the biomass APPG; was criticised for accepting £50,000 in political donations and trips from the biomass industry, 2017. Pro-Brexit; quit his post as parly under-sec for Wales following Theresa May's decision to negotiate with Jeremy Corbyn to find a Brexit compromise. Backed Boris Johnson, 2019. Member of No

	Electorate	Share %	Change from 2017 %
	78,715		
*N Adams C	33,995	60.26	+1.55
M Rofidi Lab	13,858	24.56	-9.59
K Macy LD	4,842	8.58	+4.49
M Jordan Yorkshire	1,900	3.37	
A Warneken Green	1,823	3.23	

10 Policy Board; responsible for economic affairs before 2015. PPS to: Lord Hill, 2013-14; Lord Strathclyde, 2010-13. Played for Lords and Commons Cricket Club. Contested Rossendale & Darwen, 2005. Started a telecoms business. Ed: Selby HS.

CHALLENGERS
Malik Rofidi (Lab) Mayor of Selby, 2019-20. Cllr, Selby TC, 2018-. CAD technician. **Katharine Macy** (LD) Graduate student at York University.

CONSTITUENCY PROFILE
This constituency, created in 2010, has elected its Conservative MP with larger majorities at every successive election. Its predecessor, Selby, was a bellwether from its creation in 1983, gained for Labour by John Grogan, later the MP for Keighley, in 1997. The seat is a large, rural area in North Yorkshire between York and Leeds. Much of its economy is related to agriculture. As an affluent part of Yorkshire and the Humber region, child poverty levels are low, as is unemployment, and more than three quarters of households are owner-occupied.

EU REFERENDUM RESULT
57.7% Leave   Remain 42.3%

Sevenoaks

MAJORITY 20,818 (40.85%)   CONSERVATIVE HOLD   TURNOUT 70.99%

LAURA TROTT
BORN Dec 7, 1984
MP 2019-

Former head of strategic communications under David Cameron, 2015-16; he made her an MBE in his resignation honours list. No 10 policy unit, 2012-15; co-authored the 2015 manifesto. Cabinet Office special adviser, 2010-12. Voted Remain but backed Boris Johnson in the 2019 Tory leadership race. Ambassador, Sutton Trust. Fought off a challenge from the former Peterborough MP Stewart Jackson to be selected for this seat. Grew up in Oxted, Surrey. First in her family to go to university. Has climbed Mount Kilimanjaro. Ed:

	Electorate	Share %	Change from 2017 %
	71,777		
L Trott C	30,932	60.70	-3.03
G Willis LD	10,114	19.85	+11.49
S McCauley Lab	6,946	13.63	-7.31
P Wharton Green	1,974	3.87	+0.61
P Furse Ind	695	1.36	
S Finch Libertarian	295	0.58	

Pembroke Coll, Oxford (history and economics).

CHALLENGERS
Gareth Willis (LD) Geography teacher and house master, Sevenoaks School. Contested Sevenoaks DC, 2019. **Seamus McCauley** (Lab) Editor of a travel website. Established several local news websites with Northcliffe Newspapers. Chairman of the Sevenoaks constituency Labour Party.

CONSTITUENCY PROFILE
Sevenoaks has been held by the Conservatives since its creation in 1885, with the sole exception of 1923, when it was won by a Liberal. Sir Michael Fallon, the defence secretary from 2014 to 2017, stood down from this seat in 2019 after 22 years. It is a commuter area bordering London's southeastern edges, covering many Kent villages and large areas of the green belt. Sevenoaks itself is a historic market town with a population of about 30,000. The seat has high levels of home ownership and self-employment and residents are likely to be working in managerial-level positions.

EU REFERENDUM RESULT
54.0% Leave   Remain 46.0%

Sheffield Brightside & Hillsborough

MAJORITY 12,274 (30.99%)   **LABOUR HOLD**   **TURNOUT 57.12%**

GILL FURNISS
BORN Mar 14, 1957
MP 2016-

First shadow minister for steel, postal affairs and consumer protection, 2016-, who was elected in a 2016 by-election to replace her late husband, Harry Harpham, the MP since the 2015 general election. Former library assistant and hospital administrator who left school aged 16. Daughter of a steel worker. Shop steward for Nalgo, then later Unison. Supported Remain in 2016. Backed Lisa Nandy for the Labour leadership in 2020. Chairwoman, post offices APPG. Women and equalities select cttee, 2016. Contested Sheffield Hallam,

	Electorate	Share %	Change from 2017 %
	69,333		
*G Furniss Lab	22,369	56.49	-10.85
H Westropp C	10,095	25.49	+3.88
J Johnson Brexit	3,855	9.73	
S Porter LD	1,517	3.83	+1.30
C Gilligan Kubo Green	1,179	2.98	+1.22
S Harper Ukip	585	1.48	-4.84

2001. Cllr, Sheffield City C, 1999-2016. Ed: Chaucer Comp, Sheffield; Leeds Metropolitan University (BA library and information studies).

CHALLENGERS
Hannah Westropp (C) Cllr, South Kesteven DC, 2015-. Head of business development in the private wealth division of Irwin Mitchell, a legal services firm. **Johnny Johnson** (Brexit) Lived 157 miles away in Harrow,

London. **Stephen Porter** (LD) Contested Sheffield City C, 2019.

CONSTITUENCY PROFILE
This Yorkshire seat has returned Labour MPs with five-figure majorities at every general election. Its predecessors, Brightside and Hillsborough, were both held by Labour continuously from 1935. David Blunkett, a former home secretary, represented the seat and its predecessor for 28 years. Nearly two fifths of households are socially rented, and the child poverty rate is nearly 40 per cent. Contains Hillsborough stadium, site of the 1989 disaster in which 96 football fans died.

EU REFERENDUM RESULT
60.0% Leave   Remain 40.0%

Sheffield Central

MAJORITY 27,273 (53.57%)   **LABOUR HOLD**   **TURNOUT 56.57%**

PAUL BLOMFIELD
BORN Aug 25, 1953
MP 2010-

Advocate of education reform and long-time opponent of tuition fees. Shadow minister for Brexit, 2016-. PPS to Hilary Benn (Leeds Central), 2010-16. Anti-apartheid campaigner. Made an impassioned plea for legalising assisted dying on the anniversary of the suicide of his father, who had had lung cancer diagnosed. Chairman: Sheffield Labour Party, 1993-2009; Sheffield City Trust, 1997-2008. Chairman, APPGs: students; international students. Member: Unison; Unite; GMB; Co-op Party. Married to the former Labour MEP Linda McAvan. Ed:

	Electorate	Share %	Change from 2017 %
	89,849		
*P Blomfield Lab	33,968	66.72	-4.22
J Silvester-Hall C	6,695	13.15	+0.17
A Teal Green	4,570	8.98	+0.94
C Ross LD	3,237	6.36	+1.21
P Ward Brexit	1,969	3.87	
J Carrington Yorkshire	416	0.82	+0.41
B James Ind	30	0.06	
C Marsden Soc Eq	28	0.05	

Tadcaster GS; University of York (BA theology).

CHALLENGERS
Janice Silvester-Hall (C) Cllr, Lichfield DC, 2019-. **Alison Teal** (Green) Cllr, Sheffield City C, 2016-. Family therapist and psychologist. **Colin Ross** (LD) Taught geology in Sheffield and Rotherham for 34 years.

CONSTITUENCY PROFILE
Although Sheffield Central is a strongly Labour seat, the Liberal Democrats came within 165 votes of winning it in 2010 and the Green Party won the most votes here in the European parliament elections. Covering the University of Sheffield and Sheffield Hallam University campuses, as many as two in five residents are students, one of the highest proportions in the country. The seat includes the city centre and has a significant ethnic minority population, almost three in ten. The proportion of households that are privately rented is well above average, at more than a third.

EU REFERENDUM RESULT
31.9% Leave   Remain 68.1%

Sheffield Hallam

MAJORITY 712 (1.25%)   LABOUR HOLD   TURNOUT 78.18%

OLIVIA BLAKE
BORN Mar 10, 1990
MP 2019-

Prominent local politician. Cllr, Sheffield City C, 2014-; deputy leader, 2017-19. Worked to bring outsourced services back in-house, including HR and cleaning contracts. Resigned from her position to support a petition to change the council's governance structure. Member: GMB; Acorn; Momentum; Labour for a Green New Deal; the Co-op Party. Campaign focused on rebuilding public services and remaining in the EU. Grew up in Leeds with four siblings and a single mother. Ed: Sheffield University (BSc biomedical sciences).

	Electorate	Share %	from 2017 Change %
	72,763		
O Blake Lab	19,709	34.65	-3.73
L Gordon LD	18,997	33.40	-1.25
I Walker C	14,696	25.83	+2.05
N Thomas Green	1,630	2.87	+1.42
T McHale Brexit	1,562	2.75	
M Virgo UKIP	168	0.30	-1.33
E Aspden Ind	123	0.22	

CHALLENGERS
Laura Gordon (LD) Former humanitarian aid worker with Oxfam and Save the Children; worked in Russia, Mali and Sudan. Member, Liberal Democrat Women. Ian Walker (C) Chartered engineer. Member, Conservative Christian Fellowship. Trustee, Sheffield Church Burgesses Trust. Contested this constituency in the previous two elections.

CONSTITUENCY PROFILE
The most marginal seat in Sheffield. It was gained by Labour in 2017 for the first time after 20 years of Lib Dem representation, having elected Conservatives for most of the the previous century. Jared O'Mara, the MP since 2017, resigned the Labour whip in 2018 and stood down after being arrested in August 2019 on suspicion of fraud. His predecessor was Nick Clegg, the Lib Dem leader from 2007 until 2015 and deputy prime minister in the coalition government, 2010-15. The seat covers a rural area stretching from Sheffield's west into the Peak District.

EU REFERENDUM RESULT
34.0% Leave   Remain 66.0%

Sheffield Heeley

MAJORITY 8,520 (19.96%)   LABOUR HOLD   TURNOUT 63.78%

LOUISE HAIGH
BORN Jul 22, 1987
MP 2015-

Shadow minister: policing, 2017-; digital economy, 2016-17; Cabinet Office, 2015-16. Former political researcher to Lisa Nandy (Wigan), whom she backed for leader in 2020, having supported Owen Smith in 2016 and nominated Jeremy Corbyn in 2015. Named hardest working of 2015's new MPs by independent House of Commons Library Research, 2016. Unite shop steward. Set up APPG on international corporate responsibility. Chairwoman of the social care APPG. Attempted to pass a private member's bill that would have removed the

	Electorate	Share %	from 2017 Change %
	66,940		
*L Haigh Lab	21,475	50.30	-9.68
G Gregory C	12,955	30.34	+1.64
T Knowles Brexit	3,538	8.29	
S Clement-Jones LD	2,916	6.83	+2.26
P Turpin Green	1,811	4.24	+2.11

parental rights of fathers who conceived their child through rape. Sheffield HS; University of Nottingham (BA politics).

CHALLENGERS
Gordon Gregory (C) NHS doctor. Cllr, Boston BC, 2015-19. Tracy Knowles (Brexit) Contested: Norfolk Mid, for Ukip, 2017; EU parliament, 2019. Simon Clement-Jones (LD) Managing director of CDE Systems, a database design company.

CONSTITUENCY PROFILE
Sheffield Heeley has been held by the Labour Party since 1974, mostly by relatively comfortable majorities. The party's smallest winning margin in the previous 35 years came in 2010, when its majority over the Liberal Democrats slipped a little below 6,000. Only twice in the same time period — in 2010 and 2015 — has Labour won fewer than half the votes cast. The constituency mostly covers the city's middle-class suburbs and postwar inner-city estates. Three in ten households are socially rented and the median weekly wage is about £70 below the UK average.

EU REFERENDUM RESULT
57.2% Leave   Remain 42.8%

Sheffield South East

MAJORITY 4,289 (10.21%)　　　　**LABOUR HOLD**　　　　**TURNOUT 61.91%**

CLIVE BETTS
BORN Jan 13, 1950
MP 1992-

Backbencher who served as an opposition and government whip under Tony Blair. Remainer; supported a second referendum. Nominated Sir Keir Starmer for leader, 2020; Owen Smith, 2016; and Andy Burnham, 2015. Government whip, 1998-2001; assistant whip, 1997-98; opposition whip, 1996-97. Select cttees: panel of chairs, 2008-; housing, communities and local government, 2006-, (chairman, 2010-); finance, 2005-. Former economist for the TUC and local government. Cllr, Sheffield City C, 1976-92; council leader, 1987-92. Ed: King Edward VII

	Electorate	Share %	from 2017 %	Change
	67,832			
*C Betts Lab	19,359	46.10	-12.44	
M Bayliss C	15,070	35.88	+4.41	
K Kus Brexit	4,478	10.66		
R Chowdhury LD	2,125	5.06	+1.78	
A Martin Yorkshire	966	2.30		

Sch, Sheffield; Pembroke Coll, Cambridge (BA economics and politics).

CHALLENGERS
Marc Bayliss (C) Cllr, Worcester City C, 2015-; council leader, 2019-. Cllr, Worcestershire CC, 2013-17. **Kirk Kus** (Brexit) Cllr, Derby City C, 2019-. Contested Derby City C, 2016. Working-class Polish background. **Rajin Chowdhury** (LD) Anaesthetic and intensive care doctor. Joined the party in 2015.

CONSTITUENCY PROFILE
Labour has held this seat since it was created in 2010 from Sheffield Attercliffe, which the party had held since 1935. In the 2019 election Labour's majority here fell to its lowest level in that time. A formerly industrial area of Sheffield, incorporating old mining villages and some of the city's southern and eastern suburbs. The constituency includes the vast Meadowhall shopping centre and the main local employment is in retail, health and social work, and manufacturing. About one in seven constituents is from an ethnic minority; one in ten is Muslim.

EU REFERENDUM RESULT
66.3% Leave　　　　Remain 33.7%

Sherwood

MAJORITY 16,186 (30.71%)　　　　**CONSERVATIVE HOLD**　　　　**TURNOUT 67.62%**

MARK SPENCER
BORN Jan 20, 1970
MP 2010-

Appointed chief whip by Boris Johnson in 2019 and before that served as deputy leader of the Commons. Remainer who has embraced Brexit. Government whip, 2017-19; assistant whip, 2016-17. Controversially defended sanctioning of jobseeker four minutes late for Jobcentre appointment, saying he should learn timekeeping, 2015. Select cttees: selection, 2017-; backbench business, 2013; environment, food and rural affairs, 2013-15; environmental audit, 2010-15. Farmer and businessman. Trustee, Core Centre Calverton adult

	Electorate	Share %	from 2017 %	Change
	77,948			
*M Spencer C	32,049	60.80	+9.29	
J Hague Lab	15,863	30.10	-11.68	
T Ball LD	2,883	5.47	+3.38	
E Cropper Green	1,214	2.30	+1.06	
S Rood Ind	700	1.33		

education centre. Former chairman, National Federation of Young Farmers' Clubs. Cllr, Nottinghamshire CC, 2005-13, 2001-03. Cllr, Gedling BC, 2003-11. Ed: Colonel Frank Seely Sch; Shuttlesworth Agricultural Coll.

CHALLENGERS
Jerry Hague (Lab) Personal injury solicitor who advises asbestos victims. Member, GMB; Unite Community. **Timothy Ball** (LD) Contested Nottingham North, 2010.

CONSTITUENCY PROFILE
There was a big swing in the 2019 election to the Conservatives, who had never before won a five-figure majority in Sherwood. The seat, created in 1983, was gained by Labour in 1992 and held until the Conservatives won it back in 2010 by 214 votes. The party's majority has risen at every subsequent election. The area itself is primarily residential, sitting to the north of Nottingham and including Sherwood Forest. The largest town, Hucknall, is home to about 32,000 people. Strong coalmining tradition, although the last mine closed in 2015.

EU REFERENDUM RESULT
63.7% Leave　　　　Remain 36.3%

Shipley

MAJORITY 6,242 (11.56%)   CONSERVATIVE HOLD   TURNOUT 72.95%

PHILIP DAVIES
BORN Jan 5, 1972
MP 2005-

The first MP to publicly call for Britain to leave the EU. Supported Theresa May's withdrawal agreement. In 2018 he defended stop-and-search powers by saying that black people were more likely to be murderers. Backed Boris Johnson's leadership bid, 2019. One of 21 MPs who voted against LGBT-inclusive sex and relationship education. Parliamentary spokesman, Campaign Against Political Correctness. Men's rights campaigner; organised the first International Men's Day debate, 2015. Organiser, Taxpayers'

	Electorate	Share %	Change from 2017 %
	74,029		
*P Davies C	27,437	50.81	-0.54
J Pike Lab	21,195	39.25	-3.33
C Jones LD	3,188	5.90	+1.78
C Hickson Green	1,301	2.41	
D Longhorn Yorkshire	883	1.64	

Alliance. Member, The Freedom Association governing council. Select cttees: culture, 2019, 2006-15; panel of chairs, 2017-; women and equalities, 2016-; justice, 2015-17. Former marketing manager, Asda. Partner is Esther McVey (Tatton). Ed: University of Huddersfield (BA history and political studies).

CHALLENGERS
Jo Pike (Lab) Former lecturer in childhood and education, Leeds Beckett University. Working on

a cross-party parliamentary inquiry on children's food insecurity. **Caroline Jones** (LD) Former councillor. Contested this seat, 2017.

CONSTITUENCY PROFILE
Won by Labour with narrow majorities in 1997 and 2001, but has otherwise elected Conservatives at every election since 1950. In 2005, it was the only seat out of 23 in West Yorkshire to elect a Conservative MP. Sits to the north and west of Bradford and is largely residential, containing the towns of Bingley and Shipley as well as the small villages around them. Home ownership is fairly high.

EU REFERENDUM RESULT
52.2% Leave   Remain 47.8%

Shrewsbury & Atcham

MAJORITY 11,217 (18.99%)   CONSERVATIVE HOLD   TURNOUT 71.82%

DANIEL KAWCZYNSKI
BORN Jan 24, 1972
MP 2005-

Polish-born Brexiteer who claimed that he formally asked the Polish government to veto any requests to extend Article 50. Former ERG member, who left expressing anger at the inability of the group to compromise. Warned in a 2020 parliamentary debate against using the term "Nazis" as it excused the German people as a whole for the Holocaust; said in 2019 that he had consulted lawyers about prosecuting the German government on behalf of members of his family killed in the Second World War. Foreign affairs

	Electorate	Share %	Change from 2017 %
	82,237		
*D Kawczynski C	31,021	52.52	+2.57
J Buckley Lab	19,804	33.53	-5.04
N Green LD	5,906	10.00	+2.69
J Dean Green	1,762	2.98	+1.15
H Locke Ind	572	0.97	

select cttee, 2015-17. Worked in telecommunications. Ed: Stirling University (BA business studies with French and Spanish).

CHALLENGERS
Julia Buckley (Lab) Cllr, Bridgnorth TC, 2017-. Inspired to stand for parliament by her friend, Jo Cox, the Labour MP for Batley & Spen who was murdered during the 2016 referendum. Contested Ludlow, 2017. **Nat Green** (LD) Contested Cannock Chase, 2017.

CONSTITUENCY PROFILE
Shrewsbury, the predecessor constituency to this one, elected only Conservative MPs from 1924 until its abolition in 1983. It has elected mostly Conservatives since, although Labour won narrow victories here in 1997 and 2001. Paul Marsden, elected twice as a Labour MP, defected to the Lib Dems in 2001 but returned to Labour in 2005. He stood down as an MP before the 2010 election. This seat, on the border with Wales, is centred on Shrewsbury, a historic market town that is home to about 70,000 people. The seat also includes the surrounding rural area.

EU REFERENDUM RESULT
52.9% Leave   Remain 47.1%

Shropshire North

OWEN PATERSON
BORN Jun 24, 1956
MP 1997-

Environment secretary, 2012-14, in which role he expressed scepticism about climate change. He was subsequently criticised for making cuts to flood defence and heckled by locals on a visit to flooded Somerset Levels, 2014. First cabinet member to publicly oppose the same-sex marriage bill, 2012. Shadow Northern Ireland secretary, 2007-10. Shadow minister: transport, 2006-07; environment, 2005-06. Opposition whip, 2000-01. Founder and chairman, UK2020. Member, Leave Means Leave political advisory board. Countryside businessman who

	Electorate	Share %	from 2017 %	Change
	83,257			
*O Paterson C	35,444	62.72	+2.21	
G Currie Lab	12,495	22.11	-8.98	
H Morgan LD	5,643	9.99	+4.68	
J Adams Green	1,790	3.17	+0.07	
R Jones Salop	1,141	2.02		

spent 20 years working in the leather industry. Supported Boris Johnson's leadership bid, 2019. Contested Wrexham, 1992. Ed: Radley Coll; Corpus Christi Coll, Cambridge (BA history); National Leathersellers College, Northampton.

CHALLENGERS
Graeme Currie (Lab) Runs an independent social work business across West Midlands. Cllr, Oldham BC, 1994-2003. Contested this seat in 2017

and 2015. **Helen Morgan** (LD) Chartered accountant. Worked in the energy industry. **John Adams** (Green) Works in higher education.

CONSTITUENCY PROFILE
Including the predecessor seat of Oswestry, the Conservatives have held the area since 1906. Although Owen Paterson's margin of victory in 1997 was just over 2,000, his majority has increased to more than ten times that. Immediately north of Shrewsbury & Atcham, this is a rural seat on the Welsh border made up of small market towns and villages. Seven in ten households are owner-occupied.

EU REFERENDUM RESULT
59.8% Leave   Remain 40.2%

Sittingbourne & Sheppey

GORDON HENDERSON
BORN Jan 27, 1948
MP 2010-

Working-class Eurosceptic. Grew up on a council estate. ERG member who backed Theresa May's withdrawal agreement in the third meaningful vote. Outspoken on Facebook: called those who defaced his campaign posters scum. Was criticised the day after the 2017 London Bridge attack for saying that terrorists find sanctuary in the midst of British Muslims. Mixed employment history: director, Swale Community Action Project; operations manager, Beams UK; director, Unwins Wine Group; manager, Woolworths. Children's book and

	Electorate	Share %	from 2017 %	Change
	83,917			
*G Henderson C	34,742	67.60	+7.45	
C Johnson Lab	10,263	19.97	-10.58	
B Martin LD	3,213	6.25	+3.54	
M Bonney Ind	1,257	2.45		
S Collins Green	1,188	2.31	+1.23	
M Young Loony	404	0.79	+0.00	
L McCall Ind	327	0.64		

short story author. Contested Sittingbourne, 2010, 2005; Luton South, 2001. Ed: Fort Luton HS, Chatham.

CHALLENGERS
Clive Johnson (Lab) Cllr, Medway C, 2015-. Business development manager, Citizens Advice. **Ben Martin** (LD) Cllr, Swale BC, 2019-. Member, Faversham Community Land Trust.

CONSTITUENCY PROFILE
A coastal seat in north Kent, Sittingbourne & Sheppey was created in 1997. Held by Labour during the Blair years, by only 79 votes in 2005, but gained by the Conservatives in 2010. Every Conservative majority has been in five figures. The seat covers the Isle of Sheppey, which is separated from the mainland by the Swale, and the town of Sittingbourne. It features nature reserves, caravan parks and three prisons. Compared to many seats in the region, it is not particularly affluent, with home ownership a little above the regional average but median wages a little below.

EU REFERENDUM RESULT
65.4% Leave   Remain 34.6%

Skipton & Ripon

MAJORITY 23,694 (40.35%)　　　CONSERVATIVE HOLD　　　TURNOUT 74.64%

JULIAN SMITH
BORN Aug 30, 1971
MP 2010-

Unexpectedly sacked as
Northern Ireland secretary
after six months in February
2020, despite being named as
the *Spectator*'s minister of the
year, 2019, for his work restoring
devolved power-sharing. Chief
whip, 2017-19, who resisted calls
to resign after allegations that
he had instructed five MPs
to break pairing agreements.
Deputy chief whip, 2017; whip,
2016-17; asst whip, 2015-16. Select
cttees: selection, 2015-17; Scottish
affairs, 2010. Pushed for changes
to the EU as a co-chairman of
the APPG on European reform.
PPS to: Justine Greening,

	Electorate	Share %	Change from 2017 %
	78,673		
*J Smith C	34,919	59.46	-3.19
B McDaid Lab	11,225	19.11	-9.16
A Murday LD	8,701	14.82	
A Brown Green	2,748	4.68	-1.74
J Render Yorkshire	1,131	1.93	-0.72

2012-15; Alan Duncan, 2010-12.
Junior international squash
player turned entrepreneur. Ed:
University of Southampton (BA
English and history).

CHALLENGERS
Brian McDaid (Lab) Works in
the finance sector. Assistant
general secretary of the finance
union Aegis. Contested Craven
DC, 2019, 2018. **Andrew Murday**
(LD) Cardiothoracic surgeon.
Has worked as a palliative care
doctor in a hospice. Left the

Labour Party in 2016 in protest
at Jeremy Corbyn's leadership.

CONSTITUENCY PROFILE
Skipton & Ripon, created
in 1983, has always elected
Conservative MPs, typically
with well over half the vote.
Its predecessors, the separate
seats of Skipton and Ripon,
also elected Conservatives at
every election since the First
World War. One of the most
sparsely populated and rural
constituencies in England,
covering large areas of the
Yorkshire Dales and two of the
Yorkshire Three Peaks. Skipton
is a former mill town; Ripon is a
small cathedral city.

EU REFERENDUM RESULT
53.2% Leave　　　Remain 46.8%

Sleaford & North Hykeham

MAJORITY 32,565 (48.93%)　　　CONSERVATIVE HOLD　　　TURNOUT 70.23%

**CAROLINE
JOHNSON**
BORN Dec 31, 1977
MP 2016-

Consultant paediatrician
who continues to work at
Peterborough City Hospital.
Campaigned to leave the EU.
ERG member who voted for
Theresa May's withdrawal
agreement on all three
occasions. Voted for Boris
Johnson in the leadership
election. Member, 1922 cttee.
Select cttees: environment,
food and rural affairs, 2017-;
health and social care, 2017-.
Chairs APPGs on rural crime;
children needing palliative care.
Contested Scunthorpe, 2010. Ed:
Gordonstoun Sch; Newcastle
University (MBChB).

	Electorate	Share %	Change from 2017 %
	94,761		
*C Johnson C	44,683	67.14	+2.93
L Edwards-Shea Lab	12,118	18.21	-7.64
O Craven LD	5,355	8.05	+3.91
M Overton Lincs	1,999	3.00	
S Tooke Green	1,742	2.62	+1.15
C Coram Ind	657	0.99	-0.38

CHALLENGERS
Linda Edwards-Shea (Lab)
Self-employed actor and private
tutor. Worked as a physicist for
British Aerospace, GEC and
London South Bank University.
Contested: North Kesteven DC,
2019; Lincolnshire CC, 2017.
Oliver Craven (LD) 19-year-
old bartender. Contested
City of Lincoln C, 2019.
Marianne Overton (Lincs) Cllr,
Lincolnshire CC, 2001-. Leader
of Lincolnshire Independents.

CONSTITUENCY PROFILE
The Conservatives' largest
majority in the country. In 1997,
when the seat was created, the
party had a majority of just over
5,000 but it has grown at each
successive election. Caroline
Johnson won a 2016 by-election
caused by the resignation of
Stephen Phillips, who stood
down citing irreconcilable
differences with the government
over Brexit. A mostly rural area
to the south of Lincoln, with the
two towns in its name home
to fewer than 20,000 people
each. There is a large retired
population in this seat and about
half its residents are aged 45 or
older.

EU REFERENDUM RESULT
61.6% Leave　　　Remain 38.4%

Slough

MAJORITY 13,640 (26.73%) LABOUR HOLD TURNOUT 58.24%

TAN DHESI
BORN Aug 17, 1978
MP 2017-

Jeremy Corbyn's PPS, 2020. First Sikh MP to wear a turban in parliament. Remainer, supported a second referendum. Nominated Lisa Nandy for leader, 2020. Housing, communities and local government select cttee, 2018-. APPGs: British-Pakistan trade and tourism; British Muslims; FGM; Sikhs; religion in the media. Cllr, Gravesham BC, 2007-19; mayor, 2011. Ed: UCL (BSc mathematics with management studies); Keble Coll, Oxford (MSc applied stats); Fitzwilliam Coll, Cambridge (MPhil history and politics of South Asia).

	Electorate	Share %	Change from 2017 %
	87,632		
*T Dhesi Lab	29,421	57.65	-5.29
K Toor Gill C	15,781	30.92	-0.71
A Chahal LD	3,357	6.58	+4.17
D Gray-Fisk Brexit	1,432	2.81	
J Edmonds Green	1,047	2.05	

CHALLENGERS
Kanwal Toor Gill (C) Entrepreneur who has worked in finance, modelling and as a Bollywood actress. Miss India finalist in 2001. Founder, Collective for Women and Children. **Aaron Chahal** (LD) Finance assistant, British Airways Pensions. Studying to be a certified chartered accountant. **Delphine Gray-Fisk** (Brexit) Contested Beaconsfield, 2010, for Ukip. Previously Conservative member. Former airline pilot.

CONSTITUENCY PROFILE
Although this seat voted for Conservatives from its creation in 1983, it was gained by Labour in the 1997 landslide and has been held by the party since. Slough is a large commuter town and business hub to the southwest of London and has the largest industrial estate in Europe. Mars and Lego have head offices in the constituency, and it was home to Blackberry and Nintendo. The area is ethnically diverse, with a Sikh community of more than 14,000 and a Muslim community of 32,000. Retail, transport and health are among its residents' main sources of employment.

EU REFERENDUM RESULT
54.1% Leave Remain 45.9%

Solihull

MAJORITY 21,273 (38.44%) CONSERVATIVE HOLD TURNOUT 70.27%

JULIAN KNIGHT
BORN Jan 5, 1972
MP 2015-

Parliamentary private secretary to the Treasury, 2019-. Prime ministerial trade envoy to Mongolia. Remainer; supported Theresa May's withdrawal agreement. Nominated James Cleverly for leader, 2019. PPS: department of work and pensions, 2018-; ministry of justice, 2018. Chairman of culture select committee, 2020. Select cttees: public accounts, 2017-; culture, 2016-; communities and local government, 2015-17. Former BBC News journalist who is now a critic of the licence fee. Author of books including *British*

	Electorate	Share %	Change from 2017 %
	78,760		
*J Knight C	32,309	58.38	+0.25
N Stephens Lab Co-op	11,036	19.94	-1.93
A Adeyemo LD	9,977	18.03	+2.34
R Sexton Green	2,022	3.65	+1.61

Politics for Dummies; *Cricket for Dummies*; and *Wills, Probate & Inheritance Tax for Dummies*, which was criticised for tax avoidance advice. Ed: University of Hull (BA history).

CHALLENGERS
Nick Stephens (Lab Co-op) Cllr, Solihull MBC, 2010-14, 1983-2006. Retired bank officer. Member, Unite. **Ade Adeyemo** (LD) Cllr, Solihull MBC, 2016-. Works in engineering and risk management. Contested: this seat, 2017; Meriden, 2015.

CONSTITUENCY PROFILE
The Conservatives had held Solihull at every postwar election until 2005, when Lorely Burt, a Liberal Democrat, won it with a majority of 279, and repeated the feat in 2010, with a winning margin of 175. It was reclaimed decisively by the Conservatives in the 2015 election. A commuter town for Birmingham's middle class, Solihull has a large retired population, with one in five residents aged 65 or above. It has one of the UK's highest proportions of home ownership. Home to a Jaguar Land Rover factory and Birmingham airport is located just outside the constituency.

EU REFERENDUM RESULT
53.3% Leave Remain 46.7%

Somerset North

MAJORITY 17,536 (28.26%)   **CONSERVATIVE HOLD**   **TURNOUT 77.38%**

LIAM FOX
BORN Sept 2, 1961
MP 1992-

Scottish GP and army doctor exiled to the backbenches in disgrace before making a comeback as the first secretary of state for international trade, 2016-19. Had resigned as defence secretary, 2010-11, after it was revealed he had given a friend inappropriate access to the MoD and taken him on official overseas trips. Two failed leadership bids in 2005 and 2016. Brexiteer. MP for Woodspring, 1992-2010. Co-chairman, Conservative Party, 2003-05. Shadow secretary of state: defence, 2005-10; foreign, 2005; health, 1999-2003. PPS

	Electorate	Share %	Change from 2017 %
	80,194		
*L Fox C	32,801	52.86	-1.35
H Young Lab	15,265	24.60	-2.02
A Cartman LD	11,051	17.81	+8.16
P Neve Green	2,938	4.73	+1.55

to Michael Howard, 1993-94. Patron, Mencap. Ed: St Bride's HS; University of Glasgow (MB; ChB medicine).

CHALLENGERS
Hannah Young (Lab) Cllr, Clevedon TC, 2019-. Runs a social consultancy. Worked in police, health, and mental health services. **Ashley Cartman** (LD) Qualified accountant. Cllr, North Somerset PC, 2019-. **Phil Neve** (Green) Scientist, business owner and energy consultant. Cllr, North Somerset PC, 2019-.

CONSTITUENCY PROFILE
This seat, including its predecessor Woodspring, has been held by the Conservatives since 1950. Labour almost won it in 1950 and 1966, and the Liberal Democrats reduced the Conservative majority to less than 8,000 in 1997, 2005 and 2010. Located between Bristol and Weston-Super-Mare, the seat contains Bristol airport and the redeveloped port town of Portishead. The Victorian seaside town of Clevedon and the inland Nailsea are the area's other big towns. Four in five households are owner-occupied and median wages are above the regional average.

EU REFERENDUM RESULT
47.6% Leave   Remain 52.4%

Somerset North East

MAJORITY 14,729 (26.16%)   **CONSERVATIVE HOLD**   **TURNOUT 76.44%**

JACOB REES-MOGG
BORN May 24, 1969
MP 2010-

Eccentric lord president of the council and leader of the Commons, 2019-. Submitted a letter of no confidence in Theresa May for her Brexit proposal, but voted for it in the third meaningful vote. Ardent Brexiteer; chairman of the ERG, 2018-19. Backed Boris Johnson. 2019. Apologised and disappeared from 2019 general election campaign after saying it would have been "common sense" for Grenfell Tower residents to have ignored official advice and fled the fire. Select cttees: public accounts, 2019-; Brexit, 2017-; European scrutiny,

	Electorate	Share %	Change from 2017 %
	73,665		
*J Rees-Mogg C	28,360	50.37	-3.28
M Huband Lab	13,631	24.21	-10.50
N Coates LD	12,422	22.06	+13.81
F Whitfield Green	1,423	2.53	+0.22
S Hughes Ind	472	0.84	-0.25

2015-17. Contested Treasury select cttee chairmanship, 2017, but lost to Nicky Morgan. Former stockbroker and businessman: Rothschild analyst; founder, Somerset Capital Management. Son of William Rees-Mogg, the late editor of *The Times*. Ed: Eton Coll; Trinity Coll, Oxford (BA history).

CHALLENGERS
Mark Huband (Lab) Director, Livingstone & Co. Former parliamentary and foreign

correspondent for *The Guardian* and *Financial Times*. Contested Cotswolds, 2017. **Nick Coates** (LD) Chartered accountant.

CONSTITUENCY PROFILE
The immediate predecessor to this seat, Wandsyke, was held by Labour from 1997 until 2010, but it has otherwise been Conservative. The party won in 2010 by just less than 5,000 votes; its majority has since tripled. The seat surrounds Bath and has Bristol to its north. It is an affluent seat, the north of which is a commuter area. One in five residents is over 65 and three quarters of households are owner-occupied.

EU REFERENDUM RESULT
51.6% Leave   Remain 48.4%

Somerton & Frome

MAJORITY 19,213 (29.61%)   **CONSERVATIVE HOLD**   **TURNOUT 75.58%**

DAVID WARBURTON
BORN Oct 28, 1965
MP 2015-

Parliamentary private secretary to the Department for Education, 2018-. Brexiteer who supported no-deal. Voted for Boris Johnson in the 2019 leadership election. European scrutiny select cttee, 2016-. APPG chairman, music. One of five Conservative MPs to rebel in support of the so-called Dubs amendment, calling on the government to accept vulnerable child refugees. Worked in entertainment, telecoms and property development. Founder and chairman, The Pulse Youth orchestra. Advocate, Age UK Somerset. Former music teacher

	Electorate	Share %	from 2017 %	Change
	85,866			
*D Warburton C	36,230	55.83	-1.15	
A Boyden LD	17,017	26.22	+5.27	
S Dromgoole Lab	8,354	12.87	-4.42	
A Dexter Green	3,295	5.08	+1.86	

and composer. RSA fellow. Ed: Reading Sch; Waingels Coll; Royal Coll of Music (Dip RCM; M Mus); King's Coll London (PhD music composition).

CHALLENGERS
Adam Boyden (LD) Cllr: Mendip DC, 2011-; Frome TC, 2013-15. Environmental consultant. Anti-fracking campaigner. Contested: Kingswood, 2015. **Sean Dromgoole** (Lab) Works in market research. Contested: this seat, 2017; South Somerset DC, 2019; Somerset CC, 2017.

CONSTITUENCY PROFILE
The Liberal Democrats held this seat from 1997, with majorities of less than 1,000 for three successive elections during that period. The Lib Dem vote collapsed in 2015 and the Conservatives gained the seat, having also held it before 1997. The Somerset constituency is mostly rural, and contains the market towns of Frome, Somerton and Langport. Residents are generally older than average and levels of home ownership are high. Residents are more likely to be self-employed and median pay is slightly above the regional average.

EU REFERENDUM RESULT
50.3% Leave   Remain 49.7%

South Holland & The Deepings

MAJORITY 30,838 (62.71%)   **CONSERVATIVE HOLD**   **TURNOUT 64.72%**

SIR JOHN HAYES
BORN Jun 23, 1958
MP 1997-

Socially conservative Eurosceptic who was an adviser to David Cameron. Transport minister, 2016-18. Member, ERG. Supported Theresa May's withdrawal agreement and backed Michael Gove's 2019 leadership bid. Minister: Home Office, 2015-16; transport, 2014-15; energy, 2012-13. Shadow minister: education, 2009-10, 2001; communities and local government, 2003-05. Vice-chairman, Conservative Party, 1999-2000. Co-founder and chairman, Cornerstone. Knighted in 2018. Former sales director. Cllr, Nottinghamshire

	Electorate	Share %	from 2017 %	Change
	75,990			
*J Hayes C	37,338	75.92	+6.01	
M Popple Lab	6,500	13.22	-7.22	
D Kirby LD	3,225	6.56	+3.71	
M Blake Green	1,613	3.28	+1.50	
R Stringer Ind	503	1.02	+0.34	

CC, 1985-97. Sustained serious head injury in a car crash when younger; suffers slight disabilities from this. Ed: Colfe's GS; University of Nottingham (BA politics; PGCE history and English).

CHALLENGERS
Mark Popple (Lab) Conveyancer. Former customer assistant at Tesco. **Davina Kirby** (LD) Solicitor. Director, Chesham Youth Club. Volunteer, Chesham Fridge Food Bank.

CONSTITUENCY PROFILE
One of the safest Conservative seats in the country: the party received its third highest vote share and gained its third largest majority here in 2019. Ukip won a fifth of the vote in the 2015 election, but with the exception of that election the Conservatives have increased their majority at every election since the creation of the South Holland & The Deepings constituency in 1997. It covers the East Midlands towns of Spalding and Market Deeping. Agriculture and farming are a significant part of the local economy; many local residents work in retail.

EU REFERENDUM RESULT
71.1% Leave   Remain 28.9%

South Ribble

CONSERVATIVE HOLD

TURNOUT 71.38%

KATHERINE FLETCHER
BORN Feb 18, 1976
MP 2019-

Owner of an antique and vintage furniture company called British Originals. Managing consultant with the global consultancy firm Capgemini before moving to South Africa to work as a safari ranger in an unfenced camp. Worked as a director of a small business transformation consultancy; later became head of strategy for Lloyds Bank. Contested Ellesmere Port & Neston, 2015. Advisory partner of a GP practice, 2010-11. Ed: Altrincham GS; University of Nottingham (BSc biological anthropology).

	Electorate	Share %	from 2017 % Change
	75,344		
K Fletcher C	30,028	55.83	+2.98
K Snape Lab	18,829	35.01	-4.31
J Barton LD	3,720	6.92	+3.14
A Fewings Green	1,207	2.24	+1.34

CHALLENGERS
Kim Snape (Lab) Cllr, Lancashire CC, 2017-; Chorley BC, 2016-. Works for the Royal Voluntary Service. **Jo Barton** (LD) Cllr, Sefton MBC, 2014-; member, licensing and regulatory cttee. Cllr, Barnstable TC, 2007-11. Contested Lancashire West, 2017; Preston, 2015. **Andy Fewings** (Green) Managing director, Redwings Renewables, a project management consultancy for renewable energy projects. Cllr, Burnley BC, 2018-.

CONSTITUENCY PROFILE
South Ribble was held by Labour from 1997 until 2010, but had voted for the Conservatives before that. The party has won increased majorities at each successive election since winning the seat back in 2010. Its previous MP, Seema Kennedy, quit parliament, having served as a PPS to Theresa May, 2017-19. The seat is a mostly rural one; its major population centres are Leyland and the Preston suburb of Penwortham. Nearly three quarters of households are owner-occupied. The predominant local industries are manufacturing and defence.

EU REFERENDUM RESULT
56.6% Leave   Remain 43.4%

South Shields

LABOUR HOLD

TURNOUT 60.33%

EMMA LEWELL-BUCK
BORN Nov 8, 1978
MP 2013-

Shadow minister for children and families, 2016-. Resigned as shadow minister for communities and local government in 2016, criticising the state of the party; backed Owen Smith in the 2016 leadership contest. Nominated Lisa Nandy for leader in 2020. Remainer; voted for a second referendum. South Shields' first female MP. Member, Co-op Party. PPS to Ivan Lewis, 2013. Select cttees: work and pensions, 2015-16; environment, 2013-15. Child protection social worker. Cllr, South Tyneside BC, 2004-13. Ed: Northumbria University (BA politics and media studies);

	Electorate	Share %	from 2017 % Change
	62,793		
*E Lewell-Buck Lab	17,273	45.60	-15.91
O Oviri C	7,688	20.29	-5.63
G Thompson Brexit	6,446	17.02	
G Thompson Ind	3,658	9.66	
W Shepherd LD	1,514	4.00	+2.33
S McKeown Green	1,303	3.44	-0.08

Durham University (MA social work).

CHALLENGERS
Oni Oviri (C) Cllr, Croydon LBC, 2018-. Business consultant, Encompass Development. **Glenn Thompson** (Brexit) Cllr, South Tyneside C, 2019-; elected to the council as a pro-Brexit independent.

CONSTITUENCY PROFILE
South Shields has elected Labour MPs continuously since 1935, and was formerly the seat of David Miliband, Labour's last foreign secretary who lost to his brother, Ed, in the 2010 Labour leadership election. It is one of the seats to have gone the longest without ever electing a Conservative MP, having done so most recently in 1837. The south Tyneside seaside town, to the east of Newcastle and north of Sunderland, has suffered economic decline after the closure of the mines and decline of the shipyards. Almost one third of households are in socially rented accommodation and median wages are slightly below average.

EU REFERENDUM RESULT
62.1% Leave   Remain 37.9%

Southampton Itchen

ROYSTON SMITH
BORN May 13, 1964
MP 2015-

Engineer who spent ten years in the RAF and 16 years as an aeronautical engineer for British Airways. Brexiteer; voted to leave the EU without a deal. Supported Jeremy Hunt in the 2019 Tory leadership contest. Dubbed the "least active" new MP by *The Independent* in 2016. Awarded George Medal for bravery after tackling and disarming a gunman who had indiscriminately opened fire and shot dead a navy serviceman on board HMS *Astere* in 2011. Select cttees: foreign affairs, 2017-18; work and pensions, 2016-17. Cllr, Southampton City C, 2000-16;

	Electorate	Share %	Change from 2017 %
	72,293		
*R Smith C	23,952	50.51	+3.97
S Letts Lab	19,454	41.02	-5.45
L Jarvis LD	2,503	5.28	+2.24
O Sen-Chadun Green	1,040	2.19	+0.64
K Rose Ukip	472	1.00	-1.40

leader, 2010-12. Contested this seat, 2010. Ed: Bitterne Park Sch.

CHALLENGERS
Simon Letts (Lab) Science teacher and business owner. Cllr, Southampton City C, 2006-18; leader, 2013-18. Contested this constituency in 2017. **Liz Jarvis** (LD) Journalist specialising in travel and lifestyle. Initally a Labour Party member, but joined the Lib Dems in 2018 after criticising Jeremy Corbyn's leadership.

CONSTITUENCY PROFILE
The Labour Party held Southampton Itchen from 1950 until 1983, and again between 1992 and 2015; the party cut the Conservative majority in this constituency to 31 votes in the 2017 election. The seat contains the city centre of Southampton and a number of postwar council and private housing estates in the east of the city. The busiest marinas of the port fall within the boundaries of the constituency, as does Southampton Solent University. Nearly a quarter of households are socially rented and more than one in eight residents is a student.

EU REFERENDUM RESULT
60.3% Leave   Remain 39.7%

Southampton Test

ALAN WHITEHEAD
BORN Sep 15, 1950
MP 1997-

Charity director and former professor of public policy at Southampton Institute. Shadow minister for energy and climate change, 2016-. Backed Sir Keir Starmer in 2020 leadership election. Remainer; supported a second referendum. Won this constituency in 1997 after it had been held by the Conservatives for 18 years. Vice-chairman, APPGs on: food waste; environment; fuel poverty and energy efficiency. Expert in energy policy and local government. Sells electricity produced from solar panels on his home back to the National

	Electorate	Share %	Change from 2017 %
	70,113		
*A Whitehead Lab	22,256	49.46	-9.19
S Galton C	16,043	35.66	+1.53
J Richards LD	3,449	7.67	+3.63
P Crook Brexit	1,591	3.54	
K Barbour Green	1,433	3.18	
K Barry ND	222	0.49	

Grid. Cllr, Southampton City C, 1980-92; leader, 1984-92. Ed: Isleworth GS; University of Southampton (BA politics and philosophy; PhD political science).

CHALLENGERS
Steve Galton (C) Self-employed web designer. Cllr, Southampton City C, 2018-, 2014-2016. Member, Crohns & Colitis UK. **Joe Richards** (LD) Co-founder, Economy, an education charity.

Contested: Hackney North & Stoke Newington, 2017; Hackney LBC, 2018. **Philip Crook** (Brexit) Retired lieutenant-colonel.

CONSTITUENCY PROFILE
From 1955 the seat was close to being a bellwether, falling to Labour in 1966 and October 1974, but otherwise electing Conservatives until Labour took the seat in 1997. Labour has held it since then, its majority falling to a low of 2,413 in 2010. This is the larger of the two Southampton seats and includes the University of Southampton, as well as the more affluent suburbs of the city. Home ownership levels are low.

EU REFERENDUM RESULT
49.4% Leave   Remain 50.6%

Southend West

MAJORITY 14,459 (31.07%) **CONSERVATIVE HOLD** **TURNOUT 67.40%**

SIR DAVID AMESS
BORN Mar 26, 1952
MP 1983-

	Electorate	Share %	from 2017 %	Change
	69,043			
*D Amess C		27,555	59.21	+4.02
A Line Lab		13,096	28.14	-5.86
N Stimson LD		5,312	11.41	+6.94
S Joseph Ind		574	1.23	+0.84

Socially conservative staunch patriot and monarchist. Veteran backbencher who was famously tricked into condemning a fake drug, "cake", in a 1997 *Brass Eye* sting. Brexiteer and ERG member; supported Dominic Raab for the leadership, 2019. Described sexual misconduct allegations against Harvey Weinstein as "dubious"; retracted the statement, which he said was issued without his approval, and apologised. Backed a prohibition of abortion bill, 2005. Sparked security alert on a health cttee trip, 2007, by telling officials that his bag had been packed by Osama Bin Laden. MP for Basildon, 1983-97. PPS to: Michael Portillo, 1988-97; Lord Skelmersdale, 1988; Edwina Currie, 1987-88. Select cttees: administration, 2015-; panel of chairs, 2001-. Knighted in 2015. Ed: Bournemouth College of Technology (BSc economics and government).

CHALLENGERS
Aston Line (Lab) Business manager. Environmental activist. **Nina Stimson** (LD) Executive vice-president of an international consumer healthcare company. Contested this seat, 1997, 1992.

CONSTITUENCY PROFILE
Held by the Conservatives at every election since its creation in 1950. The Tory majority in the seat fell below 3,000 in 1997 but has otherwise mostly been in five figures. Southend and then Southend West were represented by five members of the aristocratic Guinness family between 1918 and 1997. The Essex seat has one of the highest proportions of workers in finance and insurance, partly owing to the proximity of a large HMRC office.

EU REFERENDUM RESULT
55.1% Leave **Remain 44.9%**

Southport

MAJORITY 4,147 (8.61%) **CONSERVATIVE HOLD** **TURNOUT 68.02%**

DAMIEN MOORE
BORN Apr 26, 1980
MP 2017-

	Electorate	Share %	from 2017 %	Change
	70,837			
*D Moore C		22,914	47.56	+8.90
L Savage Lab		18,767	38.95	+6.37
J Wright LD		6,499	13.49	-12.91

Worked as a retail manager at Asda. Quiet backbencher who voted for Boris Johnson in leadership contest. Introduced a private member's bill for voluntary regulation of online news platforms. Campaigned to improve Southport's rail links and boost local businesses. Select cttees: science and technology, 2018-; petitions, 2017-. Vice-chairman, coastal communities APPG. Contested this seat in 2015, missing out by about a thousand votes. Cllr, Preston City C, 2012-; deputy leader of the Conservative group. Former chairman, Preston Conservative Association. Ed: University of Central Lancashire (BA history).

CHALLENGERS
Liz Savage (Lab) Teacher. Cllr, West Lancashire BC, 2011-19. Gave speech on education at 2014 Labour conference. Supported by Southport firefighters. Contested this seat in the previous two elections. **John Wright** (LD) Retired teacher; taught in prisons and colleges. Contested South Ribble in the 2017 general election and Lancashire CC in the local elections of the same year.

CONSTITUENCY PROFILE
The Liberals and Lib Dems held the seat for 25 of the previous 30 years. The most recent Lib Dem MP, John Pugh, was first elected in 2001 and stood down in 2017. The Conservatives gained the seat in that year and Labour pushed the Lib Dems into third place. The seat, at the northern tip of Merseyside, has been the only one in Merseyside not to return a Labour MP in every election since 2015. The seaside town of Southport itself is a popular home for those commuting to Liverpool or Preston. It has a considerable retired population, as well as high levels of home ownership.

EU REFERENDUM RESULT
46.3% Leave **Remain 53.7%**

Spelthorne

MAJORITY 18,393 (37.15%)   CONSERVATIVE HOLD   TURNOUT 69.80%

KWASI KWARTENG
BORN May 26, 1975
MP 2010-

Minister of state for the
Department of Business, Energy
and Industrial Strategy, 2019-.
Brexiteer; voted for no-deal.
Supported Boris Johnson in
the 2019 leadership election.
Criticised for saying "many
people believe judges are biased"
after a Scottish court ruled that
Mr Johnson's prorogation of
parliament was illegal. Select
cttees: public accounts, 2016-17;
finance, 2015-17; work and
pensions, 2013-15; transport,
2010-13. Chairman, Bow Group,
2005-06. Financial analyst:
WestLB; JP Morgan Cazenove;
Odey Asset Management.

	Electorate	Share %	from 2017 % Change
	70,929		
*K Kwarteng C	29,141	58.86	+1.61
P Mann Lab	10,748	21.71	-8.76
D Campanale LD	7,499	15.15	+9.65
P Jacobs Green	2,122	4.29	+2.08

Journalist and author. Born
in UK to Ghanaian parents.
Ed: Eton Coll (King's scholar;
Newcastle scholar); Trinity Coll,
Cambridge (BA classics and
history, MA; PhD economic
history; on winning *University
Challenge* team, 1995); Harvard
(Kennedy Scholar).

CHALLENGERS
Pavitar Mann (Lab) Cllr, Slough
BC, 2010-. Worked in public
affairs. Campaigns organiser for
Andy Slaughter (Hammersmith)
and Fiona Mactagart. **David**

Campanale (LD) Cllr, Slough
BC, 2010-.

CONSTITUENCY PROFILE
Spelthorne has been held
by the Conservatives since
1950, Labour having won
the seat just once, in its 1945
landslide. Labour reduced the
Conservative majority to less
than 4,000 in 1997 and 2001 but
the winning margin returned
to five figures in 2010. The
commuter-heavy Surrey seat
has Heathrow to the north and
the Thames to the south, and a
significant portion of it is made
up of reservoirs. The principal
town of Staines-upon-Thames
houses about 18,000 people.

EU REFERENDUM RESULT
60.3% Leave   Remain 39.7%

Stafford

MAJORITY 14,377 (28.11%)   CONSERVATIVE HOLD   TURNOUT 70.48%

**THEODORA
CLARKE**
BORN Aug 4, 1985
MP 2019-

Entrepreneur, art historian,
lecturer and critic. Chief
executive, Coalition for Global
Prosperity, 2017-19. Board
member, Africa House London,
2017-19. Co-founder, Association
of Women in the Arts, 2016-19.
Director, Conservative Friends
of International Development,
2016-17. Founder and editor,
Russian Art & Culture magazine,
2011-16. Campaigner for Rory
Stewart. Contested Bristol
East in 2017 and 2015. Ed:
Downe House Sch; University
of Newcastle (BA combined
studies); Courtauld Institute of
Art (MA history of art).

	Electorate	Share %	from 2017 % Change
	72,572		
T Clarke C	29,992	58.64	+3.89
J Still Lab	15,615	30.53	-9.33
A Wagner LD	3,175	6.21	+3.24
E Carter Green	2,367	4.63	+2.19

CHALLENGERS
Joyce Still (Lab) Worked as
a nurse and midwife. Trade
unionist. Contested: Hart DC,
2018, 2016; Hampshire CC, 2017.
Alex Wagner (LD) Campaigner
aged 18 who was the youngest
Liberal Democrat candidate
in the country. Pro-European.
Emma Carter (Green) Self-
employed accountant. Liason
officer, Ellie Chowns MEP, 2019-
20. Trustee, People and Planet.
Contested: Leeds North East,
2015; Leeds City C, 2018, 2016;
Stafford BC, 2019.

CONSTITUENCY PROFILE
Stafford has elected mostly
Conservative MPs for more
than a century, with exceptions
in 1945 and then at the three
elections won by New Labour
under Tony Blair. David
Cameron was the Conservative
candidate in the seat in 1997. The
constituency is made up of the
town of Stafford, home to about
70,000 people, and its rural
surroundings. A commuter town
feeding into nearby Birmingham
and Stoke, the decline of
shoe-making has led the way
for electrical engineering to
dominate the town's industry.
The town is considered a
potential HS2 hub.

EU REFERENDUM RESULT
57.5% Leave   Remain 42.5%

Staffordshire Moorlands

MAJORITY 16,428 (37.63%) **CONSERVATIVE HOLD** **TURNOUT 66.67%**

KAREN BRADLEY
BORN Mar 12, 1970
MP 2010-

Chairwoman, procedure select cttee, 2020-. Secretary of state for Northern Ireland, 2018-19; criticised by all sides in March 2019 for invoking the Nuremberg defence to excuse the actions of UK forces "acting under orders" during the Troubles. Admitted that she had not understood Northern Irish politics before her appointment. Voted for Michael Gove in the 2019 leadership election. Culture secretary, 2016-18. Parly under-sec, Home Office, 2014-16. Government whip, 2013-14; assistant whip, 2012-13. Select cttees: administration, 2012-14; procedure, 2011-12; work

	Electorate	Share %	Change from 2017 %
	65,485		
*K Bradley C	28,192	64.58	+6.44
D Price Lab	11,764	26.95	-6.94
A Gant LD	2,469	5.66	+2.31
D Rouxel Green	1,231	2.82	+1.61

and pensions, 2010-12. Chartered accountant. Seconded from KPMG to Michael Howard's shadow Treasury team. Ed: Buxton Girls' Sch; Imperial Coll, London (BSc mathematics).

CHALLENGERS
Darren Price (Lab) Architect. Cllr, Staffordshire Moorlands DC, 2017-. **Andrew Gant** (LD) Lecturer in music, University of Oxford. Cllr, Summertown CC, 2014-. **Douglas Rouxel** (Green) Contested Stoke-on-Trent North, 2017.

CONSTITUENCY PROFILE
Labour held this seat during its most recent 13 years in government, and also held the predecessor constituency from 1935 until 1970. The seat has otherwise, in its postwar history, elected Conservatives. It combines several commuter villages just east of Stoke, the town of Leek, home to a little over 20,000 people, and a southwestern area of the Peak District. It contains multiple nature reserves and Alton Towers, in the south of the seat, provides jobs in the tourism industry. The seat has one of England's highest proportions of owner-occupied households.

EU REFERENDUM RESULT
64.7% Leave Remain 35.3%

Staffordshire South

MAJORITY 28,250 (56.49%) **CONSERVATIVE HOLD** **TURNOUT 67.86%**

GAVIN WILLIAMSON
BORN Jun 25, 1976
MP 2010-

Secretary of state for education, 2019-, who was dismissed as defence secretary, 2017-19, after a leak from the National Security Council about the Chinese company Huawei; he denied leaking the information. Voted Remain but embraced Brexit; backed Boris Johnson for leader, 2019. Chief whip, 2016-17. PPS to: David Cameron, 2013-15; Patrick McLoughlin, 2012-13; Owen Paterson (Shropshire North), 2012; Hugo Swire, 2012. Chairman, motor neurone disease APPG. Worked as a managing director of an architectural design practice.

	Electorate	Share %	Change from 2017 %
	73,692		
*G Williamson C	36,520	73.03	+3.27
A Freeman Lab	8,270	16.54	-8.75
C Fewtrell LD	3,280	6.56	+3.92
C McIlvenna Green	1,935	3.87	+1.56

Contested Blackpool North & Fleetwood, 2005. Ed: Raincliffe Sch; Scarborough Coll; Bradford University (BA social sciences).

CHALLENGERS
Adam Freeman (Lab) Cllr, Pattingham & Patshull PC, 2019-. Contested: this seat, 2017; South Staffordshire DC, 2019; South Staffordshire CC, 2017. **Chris Fewtrell** (LD) Screenwriter and former journalist for the BBC. Has written scripts for *Home from Home*, *Coronation Street* and *Rosemary and Thyme*.

CONSTITUENCY PROFILE
This seat has been held by the Conservatives since its creation in 1983. It is on the western flank of the West Midlands, stretching south along the western border of Cannock, Birmingham, Wolverhampton and Stourbridge. It is made up of rural and commuter villages and is relatively affluent. More than three quarters of households are owner-occupied and median wages are about £60 a week above the national average. Industry is fairly dependent on retail, manufacturing and construction. Jaguar Land Rover recently built a large engine plant in the area.

EU REFERENDUM RESULT
65.2% Leave Remain 34.8%

Stalybridge & Hyde

JONATHAN REYNOLDS
BORN Aug 28, 1980
MP 2010-

Shadow economic secretary to the Treasury, 2016-. Remainer, but believed after the referendum that Labour had to end support for free movement to become electorally credible. Supported leadership campaigns of: Sir Keir Starmer, 2020; Liz Kendall, 2015. Defied whip to vote in favour of a more proportional electoral system. Shadow minister: transport, 2015-16; energy and climate change, 2013-15. Opposition assistant whip, 2010-11. Select cttees: ecclesiastical, 2017-19; business, energy and industrial strategy,

	Electorate	Share %	from 2017 % Change
	73,873		
*J Reynolds Lab Co-op	19,025	44.90	-12.28
T Amjad C	16,079	37.95	-0.19
J Newton Brexit	3,591	8.48	
J Dwan LD	1,827	4.31	+1.97
J Wood Green	1,411	3.33	+1.00
J Edge Lib	435	1.03	

2016. Solicitor. Ed: Houghton Kepier Comp; Sunderland City Coll; Manchester University (BA politics and modern history); BPP (GDL; LPC).

CHALLENGERS
Tayub Amjad (C) Restaurateur. Son of Amjad Bashir, a former Ukip MEP who defected to the Conservatives in 2015 and was selected for Leeds North East in 2019 before being suspended for allegedly antisemitic comments.

Julian Newton (Brexit)Ejected from a Morrisons supermarket for forcing campaign leaflets on customers.

CONSTITUENCY PROFILE
This Greater Manchester seat has elected a Labour MP at every election since 1945, but only in 1997 did Labour win the seat with a five-figure majority. The previous MP was James Purnell, who resigned as culture secretary in protest at Gordon Brown's leadership in 2009. One of three seats in the Tameside area, the eastern edge of Greater Manchester, with the Pennines situated to its east. Incomes are below average.

EU REFERENDUM RESULT
59.3% Leave   Remain 40.7%

Stevenage

STEPHEN MCPARTLAND
BORN Aug 9, 1976
MP 2010-

Busy backbencher who has chaired several APPGs focusing on healthcare, education and technology. Voted for Boris Johnson in the 2019 leadership contest. Criticised in 2015 for having a number of second jobs, despite telling voters in 2010 that Stevenage needed an MP who "treats it as a full-time job". PPS to Lord Livingston of Parkhead, 2014-15. Select cttees: finance, 2017-; liaison, 2017-; regulatory reform, 2017. Worked as a campaign manager for local, parliamentary and European elections. Ed: Liverpool Coll; University of Liverpool (BA

	Electorate	Share %	from 2017 % Change
	71,562		
*S McPartland C	25,328	53.12	+2.85
J Borcherds Lab	16,766	35.16	-8.25
L Nash LD	4,132	8.67	+4.55
V Snelling Green	1,457	3.06	+0.86

history); Liverpool John Moores University (MSc technology management).

CHALLENGERS
Jill Borcherds (Lab) Maths teacher for 23 years. Former Sainsbury's retail manager. **Lisa Nash** (LD) Senior midwifery lecturer at University of Middlesex. Cllr, North Hertfordshire DC, 2018-. Volunteer at St John Ambulance service. **Victoria Snelling** (Green) Contested this constituency, 2017.

CONSTITUENCY PROFILE
Created in 1983, Stevenage has been a bellwether seat, having been won by Labour from 1997 until 2010, when it was won back by the Conservatives. The Conservative majority in 2019 was significantly larger than in the 1980s but smaller than Labour's 1997 majority. The seat consists of the postwar new town of Stevenage, home to 88,000 people, and the rural area to its southwest, including Knebworth House, which is associated with major concerts by the likes of Oasis and The Rolling Stones. Social renting is well above average and incomes are slightly below the regional average.

EU REFERENDUM RESULT
57.0% Leave   Remain 43.0%

Stirling

MAJORITY 9,254 (17.59%) **SNP GAIN FROM CONSERVATIVE** **TURNOUT 76.85%**

ALYN SMITH
BORN Sep 15, 1973
MP 2019-

MEP for Scotland, 2004-19.
President of the European
Free Alliance Group, 2019, and
member of the EU agriculture
committee, 2004 to 2012.
Worked as a solicitor for Clifford
Chance. Member, Scottish
National Party's NEC. Honorary
vice-president, Scottish Society
for the Prevention of Cruelty
to Animals. Won the *Scottish
Farmer* magazine's award for
Outstanding Contribution to
Scottish Agriculture at the
Highland Show, 2009. Ed: Leeds
University (LLB); Nottingham
Trent University; College of
Europe.

	Electorate	Share %	Change from 2017 %
	68,473		
A Smith SNP	26,895	51.11	+14.35
*S Kerr C	17,641	33.53	-3.53
M Ross Lab	4,275	8.12	-13.96
F Rehman LD	2,867	5.45	+2.04
B Quinn Green	942	1.79	

CHALLENGERS
Stephen Kerr (C) MP for this
seat, 2017-19. Ardent Brexiteer
who supported no-deal. Voted
for Michael Gove in 2019
leadership election. Called Alyn
Smith "sweetcheeks" during
a hustings. **Mary Ross** (Lab)
Student, aged 19. Daughter of a
former Labour councillor in her
hometown of Motherwell.

CONSTITUENCY PROFILE
This Highlands seat was held by
the Conservative Party from its

creation in 1983 until 1997, when
Labour won it. Like all but three
seats in Scotland, it was won by
the Scottish National Party in
2015, but the Conservatives won
it back in 2017 by a margin of
only 148 votes. The seat is home
to the University of Stirling,
and to 9,000 students. A vast
and predominantly rural seat,
it stretches northwest from the
city of Stirling and nearby towns
Doune and Dunblane, taking in
part of Loch Lomond. Stirling
is a more affluent constituency
than most in Scotland, with
home ownership slightly above
average and the median wage
£70 a week higher than the UK
or Scottish average.

EU REFERENDUM RESULT
32.2% Leave   Remain 67.8%

Stockport

MAJORITY 10,039 (24.07%) **LABOUR HOLD** **TURNOUT 63.73%**

NAVENDU MISHRA
BORN Aug 22, 1989
MP 2019-

Appointed parliamentary
private secretary to Angela
Rayner, 2019. Former trade
union organiser for Unison in
the North West; also worked for
John Lewis. CLP representative,
Labour NEC, 2018-19. Founder,
Momentum Stockport. Member:
Unite; USDAW; Labour Socialist
Campaign group. Backed
Jeremy Corbyn in the 2015
and 2016 leadership elections,
and nominated Rebecca Long
Bailey for leader in 2020. Grew
up in India; came to the UK in
2003. Contested: Hazel Grove,
2017; Stockport MBC, 2018.
Ed: University of Hull (BA

	Electorate	Share %	Change from 2017 %
	65,457		
N Mishra Lab	21,695	52.01	-11.26
I Imarni C	11,656	27.94	-0.47
W Meikle LD	5,043	12.09	+7.81
L Montague-Trenchard			
Brexit	1,918	4.60	
H Mellish Green	1,403	3.36	+1.94

economics and marketing); Keele
University (union leadership and
industrial relations).

CHALLENGERS
Isy Imarni (C) Cllr, Dacorum
BC, 2015-. Freelance designer
and businesswoman. Ran a
youth club for ten years as a
volunteer. **Wendy Meikle** (LD)
Cllr, Stockport MBC, 2004-;
mayor of Stockport, 2012. As
mayor she raised £31,000 for
local charities The Tree House

in Stepping Hill and Stockport
Without Abuse.

CONSTITUENCY PROFILE
Stockport was recreated in 1983
and held by the Conservatives
until 1992, but it has elected only
Labour MPs since. Its previous
MP, Ann Coffey, left Labour
in February 2019, and went on
to set up Change UK. She did
not stand in 2019. The seat is
located in the south of Greater
Manchester and incomes are
slightly above the UK average
but home ownership is below
average. The predecessor seat
was once held by Richard
Cobden, a Radical and supporter
of free trade in the 19th century.

EU REFERENDUM RESULT
46.8% Leave   Remain 53.2%

Stockton North

MAJORITY 1,027 (2.50%)   LABOUR HOLD   TURNOUT 61.73%

ALEX CUNNINGHAM
BORN May 1, 1955
MP 2010-

Shadow housing minister, 2019-. Previously led campaign supporting a ban on smoking in cars. Nominated Sir Keir Starmer for leader, 2020; Owen Smith, 2016; Andy Burnham, 2015; David Miliband, 2010. Remainer; supported a second referendum. Voted no confidence in Jeremy Corbyn in 2016. Shadow minister: pensions, 2016-17; environment, 2015-16. Select cttees: environmental audit, 2019; education, 2011-15. Chairman, carbon capture and storage APPG. Journalism background; worked in newspapers and radio. Runs own

	Electorate	Share %	Change from 2017 %
	66,676		
*A Cunningham Lab	17,728	43.08	-13.80
S Jackson C	16,701	40.58	+4.10
M Walker Brexit	3,907	9.49	
A King LD	1,631	3.96	+2.45
M Burdon NE Party	1,189	2.89	

PR and web design consultancy. Cllr, Stockton-on-Tees BC, 1999-2010. Ed: Branksome Comp; Queen Elizabeth Sixth Form Coll; Coll of Technology, Darlington.

CHALLENGERS
Steven Jackson (C) Cllr, Harrogate BC, 2011-. Engineer who works on regenerating brownfield sites. Contested Wentworth & Dearne, 2017. **Martin Walker** (Brexit) Has worked in retail and marketing.

CONSTITUENCY PROFILE
Unlike its neighbour to the south, Stockton North has elected only Labour MPs since its creation in 1983. The predecessor constituency, Stockton-on-Tees, elected Labour MPs from 1945, one of whom, Bill Rodgers, was one of the "Gang of Four" who defected to found the Social Democratic Party in 1981. The seat contains the north of Stockton and the former chemical manufacturing base of Billingham. The seat's residents have lower incomes and lower home ownership, both compared to the UK average and also to Stockton South.

EU REFERENDUM RESULT
66.3% Leave   Remain 33.7%

Stockton South

MAJORITY 5,260 (9.60%)   CONSERVATIVE GAIN FROM LABOUR   TURNOUT 71.27%

MATT VICKERS
BORN Sep 24, 1983
MP 2019-

Trainee solicitor, Coles Solicitors. Has worked as a customer assistant, bartender and bricklayer. Cllr, Stockton-on-Tees BC, 2015-19; leader of the Conservative group. Claimed he was physically assualted while canvassing in the constituency. Worked as a constituency agent in Richmond (Yorks) for William Hague and his successor in the seat, Rishi Sunak. Contested, police and crime commissioner elections, 2016. Ed: Teesside University (BA business management; LLB law; LLM law); University of Law (LLM law and business; LPC).

	Electorate	Share %	Change from 2017 %
	76,895		
M Vickers C	27,764	50.66	+3.82
*P Williams Lab	22,504	41.06	-7.43
B Devlin LD	2,338	4.27	+2.50
J Prescott Brexit	2,196	4.01	

CHALLENGERS
Paul Williams (Lab) MP for this constituency, 2017-19. Practising GP and public health doctor. Remainer who voted for a second referendum and to revoke Article 50. Led a hospital and community health programme in Uganda for five years, implementing a health insurance scheme for 60,000 locals. Patron, Stockton-based charity Justice First. **Brendan Devlin** (LD) Co-ordinates offshore wind investments in the North Sea. Chairs UN

committees on methane and climate change. **John Prescott** (Brexit) IT consultant.

CONSTITUENCY PROFILE
Stockton South has swing between the two major parties at recent elections. Held by the Social Democratic Party in the early 1980s, it was gained by the Conservatives in 1987, becoming a bellwether until Labour bucked the national trend by winning it in 2017. This is the more affluent of the two constituencies covering Stockton-on-Tees; it has higher average incomes and almost three quarters of households are owned by their inhabitants.

EU REFERENDUM RESULT
57.8% Leave   Remain 42.2%

Stoke-on-Trent Central

MAJORITY 670 (2.09%)   CONSERVATIVE GAIN FROM LABOUR CO-OP   TURNOUT 57.86%

JO GIDEON
BORN Nov 7, 1952
MP 2019-

Chief executive, The Knowledge Hive, a business consultancy. Former aide to Damian Green (Ashford). Director of fundraising, the Ella Foundation, 2009-11. Co-founder, Futures for Heroes. Founding member, Women 2 Win. Cllr: Ashford BC, 2019-; Thanet DC, 2003-15. Contested: Greater Grimsby, 2017; Scunthorpe, 2015. Was a full-time carer to her father, a D-Day veteran. Ed: University of Birmingham (BA German).

CHALLENGERS
Gareth Snell (Lab Co-op) MP for this constituency, 2017-19;

	Electorate	Share %	from 2017 % Change
	55,424		
J Gideon C	14,557	45.39	+5.61
*G Snell Lab Co-op	13,887	43.30	-8.24
T Mahmood Brexit	1,691	5.27	
S Pritchard LD	1,116	3.48	+1.43
A Colclough Green	819	2.55	+1.41

gained the seat in a by-election prompted by the resignation of Tristram Hunt, a former shadow education secretary for Labour. Voted Remain but opposed a second referendum in the indicative votes and voted for Boris Johnson's withdrawal agreement. Worked as a union official and community campaigner. **Tariq Mahmood** (Brexit) Barrister specialising in judicial review. Contested Stoke-on-Trent South in the 2015 election for Ukip.

CONSTITUENCY PROFILE
Stoke-on-Trent Central was held by Labour from the creation of the seat in 1950 until this election. The Labour majority had, however, declined at every election since 1997, and 2017 was the first general election at which the party's majority dipped below 4,000. It contains the University of Staffordshire and more than 8,000 students live in the constituency. One in ten residents is Asian or Asian British. It has the lowest home ownership of the three Stoke constituencies, with more than a quarter of households in the social rented sector. High child poverty rate.

EU REFERENDUM RESULT
64.8% Leave   Remain 35.2%

Stoke-on-Trent North

MAJORITY 6,286 (15.66%)   CONSERVATIVE GAIN FROM LABOUR   TURNOUT 47.58%

JONATHAN GULLIS
BORN Jan 9, 1990
MP 2019-

Humanities teacher. Trade union representative, NASUWT. Cllr, Stratford DC, 2011-12. Member, Conservative Education Society. Volunteer at the Leamington & Stratford-upon-Avon food bank. Brexiteer and ERG member. Voted for Boris Johnson in the 2019 Conservative leadership contest; had initially volunteered for Dominic Raab's campaign. Contested: Washington & Sunderland West, 2017; Warwickshire CC, 2017. Ed: Princethorpe Coll; Oxford Brookes (BA international relations and law); UCL Institute of Education (PGCE).

	Electorate	Share %	from 2017 % Change
	84,357		
J Gullis C	20,974	52.26	+7.00
*R Smeeth Lab	14,688	36.60	-14.31
R Watkin Brexit	2,374	5.92	
P Andras LD	1,268	3.16	+0.97
A Borgars Green	508	1.27	-0.37
M Dilworth Ind	322	0.80	

CHALLENGERS
Ruth Smeeth (Lab) MP for this constituency, 2015-19. Lifelong trade unionist. Remainer, but resigned as PPS to Tom Watson to vote against a second referendum, and voted for Boris Johnson's Brexit deal. Parliamentary chairwoman, Jewish Labour Movement, 2019. Left an antisemitism event in tears after an audience member accused her of being part of a media conspiracy. **Richard**

Watkin (Brexit) Replaced a candidate who was deselected over controversial social media posts about immigration.

CONSTITUENCY PROFILE
Like Stoke Central, this seat had been held by the Labour Party without interruption since it was created in 1950, and the party's majority had decreased at every general election since the 1997 landslide. Stoke-on-Trent North, which also contains Kidsgrove, is the least affluent seat in Stoke, with residents earning slightly less than those in nearby constituencies. Residents are more likely than the national average to have routine jobs.

EU REFERENDUM RESULT
72.1% Leave   Remain 27.9%

Stoke-on-Trent South

MAJORITY 11,271 (15.66%)   CONSERVATIVE HOLD   TURNOUT 61.40%

JACK BRERETON
BORN 13 May, 1991
MP 2017-

Youngest of the Conservative intake in 2017, when he became the first member of the party to ever win this seat. Brexiteer who voted for no-deal in indicative votes. Select cttees: work and pensions, 2017-; public accounts, 2017-19; transport, 2018-19. Contested the 2017 Stoke-on-Trent Central by-election, coming third behind Labour's Gareth Snell, and Paul Nuttall of Ukip. Cllr, Stoke-on-Trent City C, 2011-17; aged 19 when elected, later deputy leader of the Conservative group. Ed: Keele University (BA politics and international relations); UCL.

	Electorate	Share %	Change from 2017 %
	64,499		
*J Brereton C	24,632	62.20	+13.14
M McDonald Lab	13,361	33.74	-13.73
R Gordon LD	1,611	4.07	+2.13

CHALLENGERS
Mark McDonald (Lab) Born in Birmingham and left school aged 16 to join a metalworking factory. Worked in NHS for 14 years, starting off as a porter and training as an operating department assistant. Took A levels as a mature student and became an international human rights and criminal defence lawyer. Founding member, Labour Friends of Palestine and the Middle East. **Rosalyn Gordon** (LD) Lost her deposit after failing to win more than 5 per cent of the vote.

CONSTITUENCY PROFILE
The 2017 result in this seat presaged what would happen in the rest of the Potteries two and a half years later. Jack Brereton's slim majority of 633 at that election marked the first time that Labour had lost the seat since the constituency had been created 76 years earlier. It is the least diverse of the three Stoke seats, with about 7,000 ethnic minority residents. It is also the most affluent: two thirds of households are owner-occupied and median wages are higher than in its two neighbours, although still below the national average. It is home to Stoke City FC's Bet365 stadium.

EU REFERENDUM RESULT
71.1% Leave   Remain 28.9%

Stone

MAJORITY 19,945 (40.02%)   CONSERVATIVE HOLD   TURNOUT 71.84%

SIR BILL CASH
BORN May 10, 1940
MP 1984-

Ardent Eurosceptic and founder of the Maastricht Referendum Campaign in the 1990s. Voted for no-deal in the Brexit indicative votes. Select cttee: European scrutiny, 2010-. Shadow secretary of state, constitutional affairs, 2003. Shadow attorney general, 2001-03. Introduced a bill forcing government to consider impact of foreign aid on reducing gender inequality, 2013. Had to repay £15,000 after being caught in the expenses scandal claiming to pay his daughter's rent. Distant cousin of Johnny Cash. Wrote a biography of the Victorian liberal John

	Electorate	Share %	Change from 2017 %
	69,378		
*B Cash C	31,687	63.57	+0.39
M Stubbs Lab	11,742	23.56	-4.66
A Sandiford LD	4,412	8.85	+4.41
T Adamson Green	2,002	4.02	+2.60

Bright. Appointed a knight in 2014. Solicitor. Ed: Stoneyhurst Coll; Lincoln Coll, Oxford (BA history).

CHALLENGERS
Mike Stubbs (Lab) Cllr, Newcastle-under-Lyme BC, 2018-, 2012-16; previously leader and deputy leader. Former chief executive, renewable energy company. Served as volunteer RAF reservist. **Alec Sandiford** (LD) Professional chef. Carer. **Tom Adamson** (Green) Former aircraft engineer in the navy.

CONSTITUENCY PROFILE
Stone and its predecessor seat Stafford & Stone have been held by the Conservatives at every election since 1918. Labour came within 3,000 votes of winning it in 1997 but it has otherwise been a relatively safe seat. It is a large and mostly rural Staffordshire constituency, predominantly to the south of Stoke-on-Trent. More than half the residents are aged 45 or over; a quarter are 65 or over. Nearly four in five households in the constituency are owner-occupied and average incomes are higher in the seat than they are in most constituencies in the West Midlands region.

EU REFERENDUM RESULT
57.5% Leave   Remain 42.5%

Stourbridge

MAJORITY 13,571 (29.70%)   CONSERVATIVE HOLD   TURNOUT 65.37%

SUZANNE WEBB
BORN Feb 4, 1966
MP 2019-

Replaced Margot James, the MP for Stourbridge since 2010 who had the whip removed for rebelling over Brexit. It was later restored, but Ms James declined to stand for election again. Regional chairwoman, West Midlands Conservatives, 2019-; vice-chairwoman, 2017-19. Cllr, Birmingham City C, 2018-. Brexiteer, but voted Remain in 2016 as she was living in Germany. Supported Boris Johnson for leadership. Describes herself as a "green Conservative". Twenty years at a logistics firm. Ed: York St John University (BA history).

	Electorate	Share %	from 2017 % Change
	69,891		
S Webb C	27,534	60.26	+5.73
P Lowe Lab	13,963	30.56	-7.74
C Bramall LD	2,523	5.52	+3.22
A Mohr Green	1,048	2.29	+1.25
A Hudson Ind	621	1.36	

CHALLENGERS
Pete Lowe (Lab) Cllr, Dudley MBC, 2003-; former leader. Contested this seat in the previous two elections. **Chris Bramall** (LD) Solicitor. Pursuing a degree in international studies with the Open University. Contested this seat in previous three general elections. Cllr, Dudley MBC, 1995-2004. **Andi Mohr** (Green) Campaign manager, London mayoral and assembly elections, 2019-. **Aaron Hudson** (Ind) Bodybuilder who

was previously the Brexit Party candidate.

CONSTITUENCY PROFILE
Created in 1997, Stourbridge was held by Labour until 2010 but the Conservatives have increased their majority at every election since. An urban West Midlands seat to the south of Dudley, Stourbridge has relatively high levels of home ownership, mainly at the expense of private renting. Incomes are higher than in neighbouring seats such as Dudley or Halesowen & Rowley Regis. The town itself was the centre of glass-making during the industrial revolution.

EU REFERENDUM RESULT
63.7% Leave   Remain 36.3%

Strangford

MAJORITY 7,071 (18.86%)   DUP HOLD   TURNOUT 56.01%

JIM SHANNON
BORN Apr 21, 1964
MP 2010-

Countryside enthusiast. Served in Ulster Defence Regiment, 1974-77; Royal Artillery, 1977-78. Member, Northern Ireland assembly, 1998-; forum for political dialogue, 1996-98. Select cttees: Northern Ireland affairs, 2016-17; defence sub-committee, 2015-16. Member of parliament with the highest total for expenses claims out of all 650 in the 2018 calendar year: £205,798 for staff, travel, office costs and accommodation. Voted against LGBT-inclusive sex and relationship education in English schools. Ed: Coleraine Academical Inst.

	Electorate	Share %	from 2017 % Change
	66,928		
*J Shannon DUP	17,705	47.23	-14.80
K Armstrong Alliance	10,634	28.37	+13.68
P Smith UUP	4,023	10.73	-0.67
J Boyle SDLP	1,994	5.32	-0.88
G Abraham C	1,476	3.94	+2.63
M Macartney Green	790	2.11	+0.54
R Carlin SF	555	1.48	-1.31
R Stephenson Ukip	308	0.82	

CHALLENGERS
Kellie Armstrong (Alliance) MLA, Strangford, 2016-. **Philip Smith** (UUP) MLA, Ards & North Down, 2016-. **Joe Boyle** (SDLP) Ards & North Down, 2005-. Portaferry businessman. **Grant Abraham** (C) Barrister and solicitor. Previously lived and worked in Asia, Africa and the Middle East.

CONSTITUENCY PROFILE
Held by the Ulster Unionist Party from its creation in 1983, Strangford has never elected a nationalist MP and the combined vote share of the unionist parties has always significantly outstripped that of the nationalists. The UUP lost the seat to the DUP in 2001, when Iris Robinson, wife of the former first minister Peter, became the MP. At the 2011 census, 17 per cent of Strangford's residents were listed as Catholic and 73 per cent were Protestant. A large seat to the southwest of Belfast, it is named after Strangford Lough, the largest sea loch in the British Isles.

EU REFERENDUM RESULT
55.5% Leave   Remain 44.5%

Stratford-on-Avon

MAJORITY 19,972 (36.28%)   CONSERVATIVE HOLD   TURNOUT 74.35%

NADHIM ZAHAWI
BORN Jun 2, 1967
MP 2010-

Founder of the polling company YouGov and the second highest earning MP. Former chief strategy officer, Gulf Keystone Petroleum. At the age of nine he fled Saddam Hussein's regime in Iraq with his family. Won £200,000 in libel damages in 2017 after false reports that he had bought crude oil from Islamic State. Campaigned to leave the EU; backed Dominic Raab then Boris Johnson, 2019. Parly under-sec: industry, 2019-; education, 2018-19. First Kurdish Iraqi MP; criticised President Trump's Muslim travel ban, 2017. Co-author, *Masters of Nothing*,

	Electorate	Share %	Change from 2017 %
	74,038		
*N Zahawi C	33,343	60.57	-1.60
D Skinner LD	13,371	24.29	+12.19
F Ling Lab	6,222	11.30	-10.97
D Passingham Green	2,112	3.84	+1.28

a book about the 2008 crash. Foreign affairs select cttee, 2012-. Reported as attending Presidents Club dinner; faced calls to resign from government position; promised never to attend another men-only event. Ed: UCL (BSc chemical engineering).

CHALLENGERS
Dominic Skinner (LD) Lecturer in sustainable architecture. Featured on the BBC show *DIY SOS*. Cllr, Warwick CC, 2018-. **Felix Ling** (Lab) Organising assistant, National Education

Union. **Dave Passingham** (Green) Has contested local elections.

CONSTITUENCY PROFILE
Has elected a Tory MP at every election since its creation in 1950. The MP from that election until 1963 was John Profumo, the Conservative war minister forced to resign in a sex scandal. It was briefly represented by Labour when the MP Alan Howarth defected in 1995. A large rural seat in Warwickshire, based around the historic town after which it is named, a quarter of residents are aged over 65. A more affluent constituency than the West Midlands average.

EU REFERENDUM RESULT
51.0% Leave   Remain 49.0%

Streatham

MAJORITY 17,690 (31.30%)   LABOUR HOLD   TURNOUT 66.65%

BELL RIBEIRO-ADDY
BORN Mar 1, 1985
MP 2019-

Replaced Chuka Umunna, the MP for Streatham since 2010. Chief of staff and adviser to Diane Abbott, 2016-19. Organiser, Society of Black Lawyers, and African Caribbean Alumni Network. Backed by Momentum and beat the more moderate candidate Jennifer Brathwaite to become candidate. Backed Rebecca Long Bailey for leader, 2020. Black students' officer and co-convenor on anti-racism and anti-fascism, National Union of Students. Ed: University of Bradford (BSc biomedical sciences), Queen Mary (MA medical law and

	Electorate	Share %	Change from 2017 %
	84,788		
B Ribeiro-Addy Lab	30,976	54.81	-13.67
H Thompson LD	13,286	23.51	+17.04
R O'Broin C	9,060	16.03	-5.34
S Ainslie Green	2,567	4.54	+1.50
P Becker Brexit	624	1.10	

ethics), BPP Law School (GDL).

CHALLENGERS
Helen Thompson (LD) Head of humanitarian programmes, Care International UK, 2018-. Former civil servant at the department for international development, including work in Afghanistan. **Rory O'Broin** (C) Business counsel for AIG, 2015-. Former associate, Pinsent Masons, 2006-14. **Scott Ainslie** (Green) MEP, 2019-20. Appeared in several independent zombie films.

CONSTITUENCY PROFILE
Created in 1918, Streatham elected Conservative MPs until 1992 but has been safely Labour since. Chuka Umunna, the former MP, resigned from the Labour Party in February 2019 and later joined the Liberal Democrats, standing as their candidate in the Cities of London & Westminster. Streatham, a dense, urban constituency in south London, is a diverse seat, where two in five residents are from an ethnic minority, mostly black and mixed race. Fewer than two in five households are owner-occupied and the seat has high youth unemployment.

EU REFERENDUM RESULT
20.5% Leave   Remain 79.5%

Stretford & Urmston

MAJORITY 16,417 (32.79%)   LABOUR HOLD   TURNOUT 69.20%

KATE GREEN
BORN May 2, 1960
MP 2010-

Chairwoman, select committee on standards and privileges 2018-. Shadow minister: women and equalities, 2015-16; disabled people, 2013-15. Resigned from Jeremy Corbyn's front bench and was the chairwoman of Owen Smith's leadership campaign against him in 2016. Chairwoman of the Women's Parliamentary Labour Party and of the Fabian Society. City of London magistrate, 1993-2009, and chief executive, Child Poverty Action Group, 2004-09. Greater Manchester ambassador for the LGBT homelessness charity the Albert Kennedy

Electorate	Share %	from 2017 %	Change %
72,356			
*K Green Lab	30,195	60.31	-6.47
M Mirza C	13,778	27.52	-0.00
A Fryer LD	2,969	5.93	+3.94
G Powell Brexit	1,768	3.53	
J Leicester Green	1,357	2.71	+1.43

Trust, 2013-. Member, GMB, Unite, Fawcett Society. Ed: Edinburgh University (LLB).

CHALLENGERS
Mussadak Mizra (C) Personal injury barrister for 15 years. Chairman, Saltrincham & Sale West Conservative Party. Member, Conservative Muslim Forum. **Anna Fryer** (LD) Mental health doctor. **Gary Powell** (Brexit) Could not replicate Ukip's success in coming third in this seat in 2017.

CONSTITUENCY PROFILE
Safe Labour seat which the party has held since the constituency's predecessor of Stretford was created in 1983. Before that, Labour had won only in 1945 and 1966, elections in which it won national majorities. The seat has become more favourable to the left over recent elections and the Labour majority in 2019 exceeded even that in 1997. It stretches southwest from central Manchester through Trafford, Stretford and the more suburban area of Urmston. It contains the Old Trafford football and cricket grounds. More than a fifth of households are socially renting.

EU REFERENDUM RESULT
48.9% Leave   Remain 51.1%

Stroud

MAJORITY 3,840 (5.82%)   CONSERVATIVE GAIN FROM LABOUR CO-OP   TURNOUT 77.99%

SIOBHAN BAILLIE
BORN Aug 28, 1981
MP 2019-

Stroud's first female MP. Born in Yorkshire and left home aged 15. Became a legal assistant and, from 2010, a family law solicitor. Legal 500 ranking recommended solicitor. Head of policy and communications at One Plus One, a relationship science charity. Cllr, Camden LBC, 2014-18; chaired a review of mental health provision for young people. Unsuccessfully stood for the London Assembly, 2015. Contested Bermondsey & Old Southwark in 2017, having unsuccessfully sought to become the candidate for Hampstead & Kilburn, but came third.

Electorate	Share %	from 2017 %	Change %
84,534			
S Baillie C	31,582	47.90	+1.98
*D Drew Lab Co-op	27,742	42.08	-4.92
M Scott Cato Green	4,954	7.51	+5.28
D Latimer Brexit	1,085	1.65	
G Gogerly Libertarian	567	0.86	

CHALLENGERS
David Drew (Lab Co-op) MP for Stroud, 1997-2010, 2017-19. On the left of the party. Serial rebel, particularly against the Iraq war and terrorism legislation. Staunch Eurosceptic but did not vote for Brexit because of the framing of the Leave campaign. Shadow minister, environment, 2017-19. Supported John McDonnell's leadership bid, 2007. Friend of Jeremy Corbyn. Former teacher. **Molly Scott Cato** (Green) South West

England MEP, 2014-20. Former lecturer in green economics. **Desi Latimer** (Brexit) Renewable energy project developer.

CONSTITUENCY PROFILE
Before 1997, Labour had only won Stroud in 1945. The party's narrow victory at the 2017 election was the first time Labour had won the seat despite losing nationally. It is a mostly rural area in Gloucestershire. The town of Stroud itself is home to about 13,000 people. Levels of home ownership are above average, with nearly three quarters owner occupied, but the median wage is slightly below average.

EU REFERENDUM RESULT
45.9% Leave   Remain 54.1%

Suffolk Central & Ipswich North

MAJORITY 23,391 (41.58%)   CONSERVATIVE HOLD   TURNOUT 73.82%

DAN POULTER
BORN Oct 30, 1978
MP 2010-

NHS doctor who worked in mental health services. Voted Remain, but consistently voted along party lines to allow no-deal and to suspend parliament. As parliamentary under-secretary for health, 2012-15, he introduced language checks for overseas health staff to ensure they spoke adequate levels of English. He also sought to improve NHS procurement processes and reduce bureaucracy. Critical of Jeremy Hunt's junior doctor contracts in 2015 and has not held a government role since that year. APPG chairman: global

	Electorate	Share %	from 2017 % Change
	76,201		
*D Poulter C	35,253	62.67	+2.53
E Bonner-Morgan Lab	11,862	21.09	-8.65
J Sandbach LD	6,485	11.53	+7.23
D Pratt Green	2,650	4.71	+1.78

health; public administration and constitutional affairs. Ed: University of Bristol (LLB), King's College London (MBBS, AKC).

CHALLENGERS
Emma Bonner-Morgan (Lab) Local singer and pianist. **James Sandbach** (LD) Director of policy and external affairs at a pro bono law charity. Contested: Suffolk Coastal, 2017, 2015; Putney, 2010; Castle Point, 2005. **Daniel Pratt** (Green) Geography teacher.

CONSTITUENCY PROFILE
This is a safe Conservative seat. It was created in 1997 and Conservative majorities over Labour were initially a little over 3,000, but its predecessor seats had returned Conservative MPs since the 1950s. It contains residential suburbs to the north of Ipswich and a large area of rural Suffolk, stretching north to the border with Norfolk. The area is relatively affluent and levels of home ownership and earnings are above the national average. The area also has a large proportion, more than a fifth, of residents over the age of 65. An overwhelming majority are white British.

EU REFERENDUM RESULT
54.9% Leave   Remain 45.1%

Suffolk Coastal

MAJORITY 20,533 (35.21%)   CONSERVATIVE HOLD   TURNOUT 71.19%

THÉRÈSE COFFEY
BORN Nov 18, 1971
MP 2010-

Work and pensions secretary, 2019-. Environment minister, 2016-19. Deputy leader of the Commons, 2015-16. Assistant whip, 2014-15. Tabled motion to hide the identities of MPs who had been arrested, 2016. Ardent Liverpool fan; backed a 2016 early day motion requesting a knighthood for Kenny Dalglish. Former finance manager, BBC. Stood for the European parliament, 2009, 2004. Contested Wrexham, 2005. Ed: St Edward's Coll, Liverpool; Somerville Coll, Oxford (BSc chemistry); University College London (PhD chemistry).

	Electorate	Share %	from 2017 % Change
	81,910		
*T Coffey C	32,958	56.52	-1.53
C Matthews Lab	12,425	21.31	-9.17
J Ewart LD	8,719	14.95	+7.98
R Smith-Lyte Green	2,713	4.65	+1.55
T Love Ind	1,493	2.56	+1.17

CHALLENGERS
Cameron Matthews (Lab) Firefighter. Critical of the Conservative government's handling of the fire at Grenfell Tower and the treatment of firefighters. **Jules Ewart** (LD) Worked for Persell Ewart & Co, a financial management firm. Mature student studying for a PhD at the University of East Anglia. Former Conservative Party member. **Rachel Smith-Lyte** (Green) Cllr, East Suffolk DC, 2019-.

CONSTITUENCY PROFILE
A fairly safe Conservative seat, having elected Conservatives since its creation in 1983. The party's majority dipped below 5,000 in 1997 and 2001, when the MP was John Gummer, who was agriculture minister during the mad cow disease epidemic and is the father of the former Ipswich MP Ben Gummer. Covering most of Suffolk's coastline, the constituency includes Felixstowe, which processes about a third of the container cargo going in and out of the country and is the UK's biggest container port. More than a quarter of the population is aged 65 or over and home ownership is common.

EU REFERENDUM RESULT
55.2% Leave   Remain 44.8%

Suffolk South

MAJORITY 22,903 (42.81%) CONSERVATIVE HOLD TURNOUT 70.20%

JAMES CARTLIDGE
BORN Apr 30, 1974
MP 2015-

Entrepreneur, mortgage broker and founder of Share to Buy, the online property portal. Host of the London Home Show. Former volunteer business adviser for the homelessness charity St Mungo's Broadway. Voted against the 2017 Queen's Speech amendment to give emergency and public service workers a pay rise. PPS to: Jeremy Hunt, 2018-19; Ben Wallace, 2019-. One of 73 MPs to vote against marriage equality in Northern Ireland, 2019. Select cttees: work and pensions, 2016-17; public accounts, 2015-17. Chairman, APPG on housing and planning.

	Electorate	Share %	from 2017 %	Change
	76,201			
*J Cartlidge C	33,276	62.20	+1.67	
E Hughes Lab	10,373	19.39	-8.41	
D Beavan LD	6,702	12.53	+6.71	
R Lindsay Green	3,144	5.88	+2.70	

Son-in-law of the former Conservative defence minister Gerald Howarth. Ed: Manchester University (BSc economics).

CHALLENGERS
Elizabeth Hughes (Lab) Quality assurance technician in manufacturing. Cllr, Ipswich BC, 2018-. GMB member. Contested: Norfolk Mid, 2010; Essex North, 2005. **David Beavan** (LD) Cllr, East Sussex CC, 2019-. Boat restorer. **Robert Lindsay** (Green) Cllr, Suffolk CC, 2017-. Contested this seat, 2017, 2015.

CONSTITUENCY PROFILE
Held by the party since the constituency was created in 1983. The Conservative majority has grown at every election after reaching a low of just over 4,000 in 1997. Stretching from Suffolk's border with Essex to the peninsula south of Ipswich, the area is mostly rural but also covers the market towns of Sudbury and Hadleigh and several suburbs of Ipswich. Sudbury has a population of 13,000, the only settlement in the seat with more than 10,000 residents. More than one in five residents is aged 65 or over, and seven in ten households are owner-occupied.

EU REFERENDUM RESULT
54.0% Leave   Remain 46.0%

Suffolk West

MAJORITY 23,194 (45.09%) CONSERVATIVE HOLD TURNOUT 64.14%

MATT HANCOCK
BORN Oct 2, 1978
MP 2010-

Stood in the Conservative leadership election in 2019, during which he criticised the suggestion that parliament could be suspended. He withdrew after winning only 20 votes in the first ballot of MPs and endorsed Boris Johnson. Secretary of state for: health and social care, 2018-; culture, 2018. Minister for: culture, 2016-18; Cabinet Office, 2015-16; business, energy 2014-15; skills, 2013-14. Chief of staff to George Osborne, shadow chancellor, 2005-10. Campaigned to Remain in the EU. Select cttees: public accounts; standards and privileges, 2010-12. Worked

	Electorate	Share %	from 2017 %	Change
	80,192			
*M Hancock C	33,842	65.79	+4.63	
C Unwin Lab	10,648	20.70	-7.49	
E Tealby-Watson LD	4,685	9.11	+4.90	
D Allwright Green	2,262	4.40	+2.59	

as a Bank of England economist after graduating. Took paternity leave before the birth of his third child, 2013. Ed: Exeter Coll, Oxford (BA PPE); Christ's Coll, Cambridge (MPhil economics).

CHALLENGERS
Claire Unwin (Lab) Vice-chairwoman, West Sussex Labour. Youth worker. **Elfreda Tealby-Watson** (LD) Owner of a small property business. Contested Saffron Walden, 2005, 2001. **Donald Allwright** (Green) Software engineer in Cambridge.

CONSTITUENCY PROFILE
Although Labour came within 2,000 votes of winning Suffolk West in 1997, the Conservatives have increased their majority in every election since, making it a safe Conservative seat. It is mainly rural but also contains Haverhill, an industrial manufacturing town near to the Essex and Cambridgeshire border. The constituency is also home to Newmarket, famous for horse racing, and to two large US Air Force bases. It is not particularly affluent. Home ownership is below average, unusually for such a rural seat, and the median weekly wage is £50 below average.

EU REFERENDUM RESULT
63.2% Leave   Remain 36.8%

Sunderland Central

MAJORITY 2,964 (6.82%) **LABOUR HOLD** **TURNOUT 59.82%**

JULIE ELLIOTT
BORN Jul 29, 1963
MP 2010-

Born and raised in Sunderland. Policy, media and research officer, GMB. Remainer who voted for a second referendum in indicative votes. Regarded as hostile to Jeremy Corbyn in a leaked list of MPs, 2016. Nominated Jess Phillips for leader in 2020, Owen Smith in 2016 and Liz Kendall, 2015. Shadow energy minister, 2013-15. PPS to Caroline Flint, 2010-13. Select cttees: culture, 2017-19, 2015-17; regulatory reform, 2017-19; business, 2011-13; European scrutiny, 2010-15. APPGs: chairwoman, rugby union; vice-chairwoman, state

	Electorate	Share %	Change from 2017 %
	72,677		
*J Elliott Lab	18,336	42.17	-13.37
T D'Silva C	15,372	35.36	+1.98
V Parikh Brexit	5,047	11.61	
N Hodson LD	3,025	6.96	+3.02
R Featherstone Green	1,212	2.79	+1.22
D Mckenzie Ind	484	1.11	+0.44

pension inequality. Supporter, Labour Friends of Palestine and the Middle East. Ed: Seaham Northlea Comp; Newcastle Polytechnic (government and public policy).

CHALLENGERS
Tom D'Silva (C) Recent graduate. Worked in schools and colleges office of London Conservative Future. **Viral Parikh** (Brexit) Pharmacist from Mumbai. Studied at Sunderland

University. **Niall Hodson** (LD) Trained as an art historian and works as a museum curator. Cllr, Sunderland City C, 2016-.

CONSTITUENCY PROFILE
Has been a Labour seat since its creation in 2010, although the party's majority in 2019 was less than half the size of at any other time since then. The city is a former shipbuilding and coal-mining area, although both industries have all but disappeared. Despite some regeneration, wages remain fairly low and unemployment exceeds the national average. More than a quarter of children live in poverty.

EU REFERENDUM RESULT
59.9% Leave   Remain 40.1%

Surrey East

MAJORITY 24,040 (40.27%) **CONSERVATIVE HOLD** **TURNOUT 71.79%**

CLAIRE COUTINHO
BORN Jul 8, 1985
MP 2019-

Replaced Sam Gyimah, the Conservative MP for this seat since 2010, who had the whip removed for rebelling on Brexit and stood for the Liberal Democrats in Kensington at the 2019 election. Special adviser at the Treasury, 2019-; adviser to Rishi Sunak. Former corporate responsibility manager, KPMG, 2017-18. Also worked as a programme director for the Housing and Financial Institute. Policy lead for the Centre for Social Justice. Voted Leave. Indian heritage; daugher of two doctors. Ed: Exeter Coll, Oxford (BA maths and philosophy).

	Electorate	Share %	Change from 2017 %
	83,148		
C Coutinho C	35,624	59.68	+0.04
A Ehmann LD	11,584	19.41	+8.94
F Rehal Lab	8,247	13.82	-5.43
J Booton Green	2,340	3.92	+2.06
H Windsor Ind	1,374	2.30	-2.72
M Hogbin Loony	521	0.87	

CHALLENGERS
Alex Ehmann (LD) Director of UK public affairs, Tata Group, 2014-. Cllr, Richmond upon Thames LBC, 2014-18. **Frances Rehal** (Lab) Originally from Galway. Trained as a nurse at King's College London. **Joseph Booton** (Green) Insurance worker. Punch and Judy performer. **Helena Windsor** (Ind) Ran a specialist microbiology laboratory. Campaigner, Rural England.

CONSTITUENCY PROFILE
The Conservative candidate has won more than half of the votes cast in this seat at every election since 1918. The highest vote share ever achieved by a non-Conservative candidate was 34 per cent, by Labour in 1974. Between 1974 and 1992 it was represented by Geoffrey Howe, the former chancellor, foreign secretary and deputy prime minister who became Lord Howe of Aberavon. Bordering Kent, West Sussex and south London, the seat comprises several affluent commuter towns and villages. Gatwick Airport, a significant employer, is in neighbouring Crawley.

EU REFERENDUM RESULT
54.2% Leave   Remain 45.8%

Surrey Heath

MAJORITY 18,349 (31.28%)   CONSERVATIVE HOLD   **TURNOUT 72.10%**

MICHAEL GOVE
BORN Aug 26, 1967
MP 2005-

Chancellor of the Duchy of Lancaster, 2019-; Cabinet Office minister, 2020-. Co-convened the Vote Leave campaign in 2016. Sabotaged Boris Johnson's first bid for the Conservative leadership by standing himself. He came third, as he did when he stood again in 2019 and his campaign was derailed by the admission that he had used cocaine. Environment secretary, 2017-19; justice secretary, 2015-16; chief whip, 2014-15; education secretary, 2010-14. Known for bringing reformist zeal to government departments. Former journalist, including

	Electorate	Share %	Change from 2017 %
	81,349		
*M Gove C	34,358	58.58	-5.62
A Pinkerton LD	16,009	27.29	+16.45
B Mohanty Lab	5,407	9.22	-11.84
S Galliford Green	2,252	3.84	-0.07
D Roe Ukip	628	1.07	

at *The Times*, where he rose from leader writer to assistant editor. Married to the *Daily Mail* columnist Sarah Vine. Ed: Lady Margaret Hall, Oxford (BA English).

CHALLENGERS
Alasdair Pinkerton (LD) Associate professor of geopolitics at Royal Holloway, University of London. **Brahma Mohanty** (Lab) MSc, English local history, Kellogg Coll, Oxford. Previously prominent in student politics.

CONSTITUENCY PROFILE
Created in 1997, this is a safe Conservative seat. The party's candidate has won more than 50 per cent of the vote at every election other than in 2001. Its predecessors were also held continuously by the Conservatives from 1910. Its largest town, Camberley, is next to Farnborough, in the neighbouring seat of Aldershot. The seat has high levels of home ownership, with three quarters of households owner-occupied. Many residents work in managerial roles and median wages are more than £100 a week higher than the national average.

EU REFERENDUM RESULT
51.9% Leave   Remain 48.1%

Surrey South West

MAJORITY 8,817 (14.61%)   CONSERVATIVE HOLD   **TURNOUT 76.26%**

JEREMY HUNT
BORN Nov 1, 1966
MP 2005-

Came second to Boris Johnson in the 2019 Conservative leadership contest, winning about a third of the final vote. Chairman, health and social care select cttee, 2020-. Foreign secretary, 2017-19; oversaw the arrest of the Wikileaks founder Julian Assange. Longest-serving health secretary in history, 2012-17; faced down strikes over changes to junior doctors' contracts. Culture secretary, 2010-12; supervised planning of the London Olympics. Voted Remain and was not as firm in setting a no-deal Brexit deadline as Mr Johnson during their leadership

	Electorate	Share %	Change from 2017 %
	79,129		
*J Hunt C	32,191	53.35	-2.39
P Follows LD	23,374	38.74	+28.86
T Corry Lab	4,775	7.91	-4.67

race. Shadow culture secretary, 2007-10; shadow minister for disabled people, 2005-07. Former management consultant. Co-founded £35 million education publishing business, Hotcourses, in 1996. Spent two years in Japan teaching English. Ed: Charterhouse; Magdalen Coll, Oxford (BA PPE; president of the Conservative Association).

CHALLENGERS
Paul Follows (LD) Consultant, BAE systems. Cllr, Godalming TC, 2017-; leader 2019-. **Tim Corry** (Lab) Military aviation

specialist. Former RAF officer and Chinook helicopter pilot.

CONSTITUENCY PROFILE
This seat and its predecessors have been held by Conservative MPs since 1910. Its three most recent MPs have all been cabinet ministers: Maurice Macmillan, employment secretary under Ted Heath and son of the former prime minister Harold Macmillan; Virginia Bottomley, health secretary under John Major; and Jeremy Hunt. It is an affluent area on the border with Sussex and Hampshire. A significant proportion of residents are managers or directors.

EU REFERENDUM RESULT
40.7% Leave   Remain 59.3%

Sussex Mid

MAJORITY 18,197 (28.99%)   CONSERVATIVE HOLD   TURNOUT 73.72%

MIMS DAVIES
BORN Jun 2, 1975
MP 2019-; 2015-19

	Electorate	Share %	Change from 2017 %
	85,141		
+M Davies C	33,455	53.30	-3.62
R Eggleston LD	15,258	24.31	+11.57
G Bolton Lab	11,218	17.87	-7.13
D Nicholson Green	2,234	3.56	+1.01
B Von Thunderclap Loony	550	0.88	+0.12
B Mortensen Advance	47	0.07	

Announced she was standing down as the MP for Eastleigh to spend more time with her children, but was selected for this safe seat shortly after. Backed Sajid Javid for leader, then Boris Johnson, in 2019. Parly under-sec: work and pensions, 2019-; Wales, 2018. Sport minister and assistant whip, 2018-19. PPS to Matt Hancock (Suffolk West), 2016-17. Women and equalities select cttee, 2015-16. Media, events and communications background, including as a radio producer and journalist for West Sussex Today and the BBC. First in family to go to university. Ed: Royal Russell Sch; Swansea University (BA politics with international relations).

CHALLENGERS
Robert Eggleston (LD) Head of credit and commercial legal counsel. Cllr, Mid Sussex DC and leader of Burgess Hill TC. **Gemma Bolton** (Lab) Local social worker. Member of pro-Corbyn Campaign for Labour Party Democracy. **Deanna** Nicholson (Green) Maths and physics sixth form teacher.

CONSTITUENCY PROFILE
Created in 1974, this seat has always been won by the Conservatives, with the Lib Dems typically finishing second. Sir Nicholas Soames, the grandson of Winston Churchill, stood down at this election after losing the whip in September 2019 for voting against the government's Brexit plan. It is an affluent constituency comprising three towns – Haywards Heath, East Grinstead and Burgess Hill – and many small villages. Three quarters of households are owner-occupied.

EU REFERENDUM RESULT
46.4% Leave   Remain 53.6%

Sutton & Cheam

MAJORITY 8,351 (16.54%)   CONSERVATIVE HOLD   TURNOUT 70.36%

PAUL SCULLY
BORN Apr 29, 1968
MP 2015-

	Electorate	Share %	Change from 2017 %
	71,760		
*P Scully C	25,235	49.98	-1.14
H Bokhari LD	16,884	33.44	+6.76
B Craven Lab	7,200	14.26	-6.26
C Jackson-Prior Green	1,168	2.31	+0.64

Appointed a parliamentary under-secretary in the business department and the minister for London, February 2020. Founding partner of the Nudge Factory consultancy. Deputy chairman of the Conservative Party, 2019-. PPS to: Alok Sharma (Reading West), 2010-12; Shailesh Vara (Cambridgeshire North West), 2007-09. Voted for the Referendum Party, the single-issue Eurosceptic party, in 1997; expressed regret for helping to allow a Lib Dem to win in Sutton and joined the Conservatives two weeks later. Cllr, Sutton BC, 2006-10. Rarely rebels. Controversy after being one of 24 Tory MPs to use Conservative HQ's battle buses in the 2015 election and not declare it in expenses; CPS took no action. Burmese heritage. Ed: Bedford Sch; University of Reading (BSc chemistry and food science).

CHALLENGERS
Hina Bokhari (LD) Teacher and founder of two charities. Cllr, Merton BC, 2018-. **Bonnie Craven** (Lab) Trade union officer. Associate director, Incisive Health, 2015-16. **Claire Jackson-Prior** (Green) Administrator in Leatherhead.

CONSTITUENCY PROFILE
Held by the Liberal Democrats from 1997 until 2015. The seat had otherwise been held by the Tories since its creation in 1945, although the Liberals won a 1972 by-election. The Conservative majority, although reduced, is still twice the size of Mr Scully's first in 2015. This southwest London seat is less ethnically diverse than London as a whole but considerably more so than the rest of the country. Just over a fifth of residents were born outside the UK.

EU REFERENDUM RESULT
51.3% Leave   Remain 48.7%

Sutton Coldfield

MAJORITY 19,272 (36.83%) CONSERVATIVE HOLD TURNOUT 69.18%

ANDREW MITCHELL
BORN Mar 23, 1956
MP 2001-; 1987-97

	Electorate	Share %	Change from 2017 %
	75,638		
*A Mitchell C	31,604	60.40	-0.56
D Knowles Lab	12,332	23.57	-8.38
J Wilkinson LD	6,358	12.15	+7.80
B Auton Green	2,031	3.88	+2.06

Resigned as chief whip a month after being appointed in 2012 over a row with a Downing Street police officer in an incident that became known as "plebgate". Backed Boris Johnson for leader in 2019. Said that by supporting the Saudi coalition in Yemen, Britain was complicit in creating a famine. MP for Gedling, 1987-97. International development secretary, 2010-12; shadow international develpment secretary, 2005-10. Vocal on the importance of access to female contraception. Founder of Project Umubano, a Conservative project in central and West Africa. Served in the army before a career in finance. Son of the Tory MP Sir David Mitchell. Contested Sunderland South, 1983. Ed: Rugby Sch; Jesus Coll, Cambridge (BA history; president, Cambridge Union).

CHALLENGERS
David Knowles (Lab) Head of campaigns for an organisation representing GPs. **Jenny Wilkinson** (LD) Forensic accountant. **Ben Auton** (Green) Contractor in the construction sector.

CONSTITUENCY PROFILE
This is a safe Conservative seat, held by the party since its creation in 1945. The majority has been in five figures at every election since 1950, falling to its lowest level, about 10,000, in 2001. Sutton Coldfield is an affluent constituency situated to the northeast of Birmingham. There are high levels of home ownership, with almost four in five households owner-occupied. Average wages outstrip the regional average by more than £150 a week. There are six universities in Birmingham near by and a significant proportion of residents work in higher education.

EU REFERENDUM RESULT
51.7% Leave   Remain 48.3%

Swansea East

MAJORITY 7,970 (23.74%) LABOUR HOLD TURNOUT 57.45%

CAROLYN HARRIS
BORN Sep 18, 1960
MP 2015-

	Electorate	Share %	Change from 2017 %
	58,450		
*C Harris Lab	17,405	51.83	-11.61
D Howard C	9,435	28.10	+2.10
T Willicombe Brexit	2,842	8.46	
G Havard PC	1,905	5.67	+0.87
C Hutchinson LD	1,409	4.20	+2.42
C Evans Green	583	1.74	+0.72

Led successful campaigns to introduce a children's funeral fund and a £2 maximum stake on fixed-odds betting terminals. Campaigns against unsafe electrical goods. Shadow minister: women and equalities, 2017-; home affairs, 2016-17. Deputy leader of Welsh Labour, 2018-. Backed Sir Keir Starmer for leader in 2020. Supported Owen Smith in 2016 and Andy Burnham in 2015. Rebelled to vote against renewing Trident. Former barmaid, dinner lady and charity worker; regional manager for a children's cancer charity. Worked as parliamentary assistant to Sian James, MP, 2005-15. Ed: Llwyn y bryn GS; Brynhfrd Junior (BSc primary education); Swansea University (BSc social history and social policy).

CHALLENGERS
Denise Howard (C) Former producer at ITV. Regional press officer for the Conservative Party in Wales. **Tony Willicombe** (Brexit) Former head of finance. **Geraint Havard** (PC) Doctor of materials engineering. **Chloe Hutchinson** (LD) Education officer for Swansea University Students' Union.

CONSTITUENCY PROFILE
Safe seat held by Labour since 1922. The 2019 election, however, was the first time that the party's majority had fallen below 10,000 since 1931, although its vote share was slightly lower in 2010. Covering the large council estates, docks and industrial estates along the River Tawe, Swansea East is less affluent and less ethnically diverse than its western neighbour. Local employment is dominated by the retail and defence sectors.

EU REFERENDUM RESULT
61.8% Leave   Remain 38.2%

Swansea West

GERAINT DAVIES
BORN May 3, 1960
MP 2010-;
1997-2005

Introduced a clean air bill in 2017 and has campaigned against revenge porn and a lack of regulation in psychotherapy. Remain campaigner; voted against the Labour whip and in favour of a second referendum. Former group product manager for Unilever and marketing manager for Colgate-Palmolive. Businessman. Founder: Pure Crete; Equity Creative. Appointed to Environment Agency Wales in 2005 to lead a team protecting Wales from flood risks. Nominated Sir Keir Starmer for leader, 2020; supported Owen Smith, Yvette

	Electorate	Share %	Change from 2017 %
	57,078		
*G Davies Lab Co-op	18,493	51.61	-8.14
J Price C	10,377	28.96	-2.37
M O'Carroll LD	2,993	8.35	+4.95
G Williams PC	1,984	5.54	+1.44
P Hopkins Brexit	1,983	5.53	

Cooper and Ed Miliband in previous contests. MP for Croydon Central, 1997-2005. Ed: Llanishen CS, Cardiff; Jesus Coll, Oxford (BA PPE).

CHALLENGERS
James Price (C) Special adviser to the leader of the Lords, Baroness Evans of Bowes Park. Campaign manager at the Taxpayers' Alliance. Worked on the 2015 Tory election campaign. **Michael O'Carroll** (LD) Commercial development

manager at Swansea University. **Gwyn Williams** (PC) Eye surgeon.

CONSTITUENCY PROFILE
Held by Labour since 1964. Alan Williams, the Father of the House from 2005, represented the constituency for 46 years until 2010. The Conservatives have held it only once, in 1959-64, and the Lib Dems came 504 votes short of winning in 2010. Previously an industrial area, it contains Swansea University and a large student population, with about 15,000 students. Median income is about £100 per week higher than its eastern neighbour.

EU REFERENDUM RESULT
43.4% Leave   Remain 56.6%

Swindon North

JUSTIN TOMLINSON
BORN Nov 5, 1976
MP 2010-

Minister for disabled people since 2019; parly under-sec, work and pensions, 2018-19; parly under-sec, disabled people, 2015-16. PPS to Ed Vaizey, 2014-15. Suspended and faced calls to resign in 2015 when it was revealed that he had leaked public accounts committee information to the payday lender Wonga; he apologised. Suggested that people affected by universal credit changes should "take in a lodger" to avoid penury. Voted to leave the EU in 2016; backed Boris Johnson, 2019. Marketing executive and businessman: owned and ran TB

	Electorate	Share %	Change from 2017 %
	82,441		
*J Tomlinson C	32,584	59.12	+5.52
K Linnegar Lab	16,413	29.78	-8.64
K Critchlow LD	4,408	8.00	+4.42
A Bentley Green	1,710	3.10	+1.54

Marketing, a print supplier for local Conservative parties. Cllr, Swindon BC, 2000-10. Contested this seat, 2005. Ed: Harry Cheshire HS, Kidderminster; Oxford Brookes University (BA business and marketing).

CHALLENGERS
Kate Linnegar (Lab) Criticised for sharing posts on Facebook that called allegations of antisemitism in Labour "smears". **Katie Critchlow** (LD) Parliamentary adviser at Big Green Change.

CONSTITUENCY PROFILE
Swindon North has been a bellwether since its creation in 1997. The Conservatives have won bigger majorities since they gained the seat in 2010 than Labour did from 1997. It stretches north from Swindon town centre to the surrounding suburban area and the market town of Highworth. The manufacturing, retail, transport and financial services sectors are all key employers but the local Honda plant employing 3,500 people was due to close in 2021. The seat has higher than average levels of property ownership, but slightly lower median pay than Swindon South.

EU REFERENDUM RESULT
57.3% Leave   Remain 42.7%

Swindon South

MAJORITY 6,625 (13.06%)   CONSERVATIVE HOLD   TURNOUT 69.40%

ROBERT BUCKLAND
BORN Sep 22, 1968
MP 2010-

Barrister and QC interested in criminal justice policy and planning. Lord chancellor and justice secretary, 2019-. Prisons minister, May to July 2019. Solicitor-general, 2014-19. Centrist; warned against a Conservative shift to the right. Supported Boris Johnson for leader, 2019. Member: Conservative Group for Europe; Tory Reform Group. Interested in disability and chaired the autism APPG. Won Grassroots Diplomat Policy Driver award for campaigning on SEN. Contested: this seat, 2005; Preseli Pembrokeshire, 1997;

	Electorate	Share %	from 2017 %	Change
	73,118			
*R Buckland C	26,536	52.29	+3.90	
S Church Lab Co-op	19,911	39.24	-4.35	
S Pajak LD	4,299	8.47	+4.42	

Islwyn, 1995 by-election. Crown court recorder. Co-ordinator, Swindon SEN Network. Ed: St Michael's Sch, Bryn; Hatfield Coll, Durham (BA law).

CHALLENGERS
Sarah Church (Lab Co-op) Head of policy and risk at Recycling Technologies, a plastic waste treatment firm. Former army major. Awarded Commander in Chief's Commendation for service on operations in Baghdad, 2004-05, including fundraising more than $10,000 for an Iraqi charity. **Stan Pajak**

(LD) Cllr, Swindon BC, 1985-; mayor, 2002-03.

CONSTITUENCY PROFILE
Like its neighbour, Swindon South was held by Labour from 1997 until 2010 but has been Conservative since. The old Swindon seat elected Labour MPs from 1945 until 1983, when it was won by the Conservatives. The Tories held the seat until it was split up in 1997. It covers half of the town of Swindon, which is between Bristol and Reading, and surrounding rural areas. A former centre for railway manufacturing, the seat hosts several large companies including Nationwide.

EU REFERENDUM RESULT
51.7% Leave   Remain 48.3%

Tamworth

MAJORITY 19,634 (42.6%)   CONSERVATIVE HOLD   TURNOUT 64.34%

CHRISTOPHER PINCHER
BORN Sep 24, 1969
MP 2010-

Britain's tenth minister of state for housing in ten years, appointed in the 2020 reshuffle. Minister for Europe and the Americas, 2019-20. Deputy chief whip, 2018-19. Resigned from role as an assistant whip, 2016-17, after Alex Story, a fellow Conservative politician, accused him of inappropriate sexual conduct; he rejoined the government after being cleared by the Conservative Party in 2017. Former IT management consultant. Vehemently opposed to the HS2 rail link development. PPS to Philip Hammond, 2015-16. Worked in

	Electorate	Share %	from 2017 %	Change
	71,580			
*C Pincher C	30,542	66.31	+5.29	
C Bain Lab Co-op	10,908	23.68	-11.13	
R Wheway LD	2,426	5.27	+1.10	
A Tilley Green	935	2.03		
R Bilcliff Ukip	814	1.77		
J Wright Ind	431	0.94		

consultancy as a manager at Accenture. Contested: this seat, 2005; Warley, 1997. Ed: Ounsdale Sch, Wolverhampton; LSE (BA history).

CHALLENGERS
Christopher Bain (Lab Co-op) Chief executive, Healthwatch Warwickshire. Worked for Age Concern England, 1997-2007. **Rob Wheway** (LD) Director of the Children's Play Advisory Service. Became Coventry's

first elected Liberal councillor in 59 years in November 1985. **Andrew Tilley** (Green) Works at a local high school.

CONSTITUENCY PROFILE
Tamworth elected a Labour MP from its creation in 1997 until 2010, when it was won by the Conservatives. The area is historically associated with Sir Robert Peel, a founder of the modern Conservative Party and Tamworth's MP from 1830 until 1850. This Staffordshire seat, which spreads from Tamworth and borders Lichfield, is dominated by family households, and home ownership is slightly above average.

EU REFERENDUM RESULT
66.0% Leave   Remain 34.0%

Tatton

MAJORITY 17,387 (35.51%)   CONSERVATIVE HOLD   TURNOUT 70.95%

ESTHER MCVEY
BORN Oct 24, 1967
MP 2017-; 2010-15

	Electorate	Share %	Change from 2017 %
	69,018		
*E McVey C	28,277	57.75	-0.82
J Weinberg Lab	10,890	22.24	-6.22
J Smith LD	7,712	15.75	+6.73
N Hennerley Green	2,088	4.26	+2.18

Finished last in the 2019 party leadership election. The ITV presenter Lorraine Kelly, a former colleague, went viral during the 2019 general election campaign when she appeared to snub her on air. Ninth housing minister in less than ten years; sacked during the February 2020 reshuffle, having been in the role for only six months. Work and pensions secretary, 2018; forced to apologise to the Commons after misleading parliament over universal credit and later resigned in protest at Theresa May's Brexit strategy. Deputy chief whip, 2017-18.

Work and pensions minister, 2013-15. MP for Wirral West, 2010-15; parachuted into Tatton to replace George Osborne after losing her seat. Contested Wirral West, 2005. Former TV presenter. Partner of Philip Davies (Shipley). Ed: Queen Mary (LLB law); City University (MA radio journalism); Liverpool John Moores University (MSc corporate governance).

CHALLENGERS
James Weinberg (Lab) Politics lecturer, University of Sheffield.

Jonathan Smith (LD) Former director of social services.

CONSTITUENCY PROFILE
Though the seat has elected mostly Conservative MPs, it was gained by an independent candidate, Martin Bell, in 1997 after the incumbent Neil Hamilton was embroiled in a cash-for-questions scandal, and the Labour and Liberal Democrat candidates stood aside. George Osborne, chancellor under David Cameron, won it in 2001 when Mr Bell did not stand. It is a semi-rural Cheshire seat consisting largely of small towns and affluent villages.

EU REFERENDUM RESULT
45.6% Leave   Remain 54.4%

Taunton Deane

MAJORITY 11,700 (18.36%)   CONSERVATIVE HOLD   TURNOUT 71.87%

REBECCA POW
BORN Oct 10, 1960
MP 2015-

	Electorate	Share %	Change from 2017 %
	88,675		
*R Pow C	34,164	53.60	+0.74
G Amos LD	22,464	35.25	+7.58
L Canham Lab	4,715	7.40	-7.97
J Hunt Ind	2,390	3.75	

Career centred on agriculture and the environment and has championed these interests in parliament. Parly under-sec: environment and rural opportunities, 2019-; arts, tourism and heritage, May to September 2019. Formerly a PPS to: Esther McVey, Gavin Barwell. Grew up on a farm and worked for the National Farmers' Union. Worked as a journalist on environment and farming issues for the BBC, ITV and Channel 4. Ran the Taste of Somerset, an organisation supporting local food and drink producers. Set up Pow

Productions, a communications and PR agency. Ed: La Sainte Union Convent, Bath; Wye Coll, London University (BSc rural environmental science).

CHALLENGERS
Gideon Amos (LD) Chartered architect. Chief executive for Town and Country Planning Association; awarded OBE for work reinventing the garden city concept. **Liam Canham** (Lab) Works in the public sector on social housing and local authority service.

CONSTITUENCY PROFILE
Created in 2010, Taunton Deane was initially claimed by the Lib Dems but the Conservatives won the seat emphatically, with majorities of more than 15,000, in 2015 and 2017. The forerunner seat, Taunton, elected Lib Dems in 2005 and 1997, and a Labour MP in 1945, but the seat had otherwise elected Conservatives since 1924. The seat covers the Somerset town of Taunton, its smaller neighbour, Wellington, and the surrounding villages and farmland. A fifth of the seat's residents are aged 65 and over. The seat also contains Musgrove Park Hospital, one of the largest hospitals in the southwest.

EU REFERENDUM RESULT
52.9% Leave   Remain 47.1%

Telford

MAJORITY 10,941 (25.55%) **CONSERVATIVE HOLD** **TURNOUT 62.14%**

LUCY ALLAN
BORN Oct 2, 1964
MP 2015-

	Electorate	Share %	Change from 2017 %
	68,921		
*L Allan C	25,546	59.65	+10.92
K Gilman Lab	14,605	34.10	-13.02
S Roberts LD	2,674	6.24	+4.11

Has campaigned to reduce the number of children taken into care after her own experience of being labelled a danger to her son when she sought help for depression in 2010. Founded Family First Group to improve child protection system. Accused of bullying her staff, a charge that she has denied. Cllr, Wandsworth BC, 2006-12. Started career as a chartered accountant at PwC before moving on to investment management. Former director: UBS Warburg; Gartmore Investment; First State Investments. Set up the employment law consultancy Workplace Law for Women, which specialised in discrimination and maternity issues. Ed: Durham University (BA anthropology); Kingston Law School (MA employment law).

CHALLENGERS
Katrina Gilman (Lab) Worked in the public sector in criminal justice for just under two decades. **Shana Roberts** (LD) Chairwoman of the national lottery-funded group Brookside Big Local.

CONSTITUENCY PROFILE
Telford, created in 1997, was initially won by Labour. Lucy Allan gained the seat for the Conservatives with majorities of less than 800 in 2015 and 2017, before beating Labour by more than 10,000 votes at the 2019 election. The seat consists of several old industrial towns and rapidly growing new town developments. A petition to prevent the closure of the Princess Royal Hospital's A&E has more than 12,000 signatures from residents. The constituency is home to a large number of families with children, although home ownership is lower than average.

EU REFERENDUM RESULT
66.2% Leave   **Remain 33.8%**

Tewkesbury

MAJORITY 22,410 (36.65%) **CONSERVATIVE HOLD** **TURNOUT 72.82%**

LAURENCE ROBERTSON
BORN Mar 29, 1958
MP 1997-

	Electorate	Share %	Change from 2017 %
	83,958		
*L Robertson C	35,728	58.44	-1.56
A Hegenbarth LD	13,318	21.78	+8.27
L Chaplin Lab	9,310	15.23	-6.56
C Cody Green	2,784	4.55	+1.89

Right-wing social conservative from a working-class Labour background. Career in industry, manufacturing and consultancy. Faced "cash for access" allegations when he gave a Commons pass to a lobbyist after receiving funds; denied any wrongdoing. Advanced a private member's bill in 2005 to try to outlaw abortion. Pro-Brexit; active in the Better Off Out pressure group. Submitted letter of no confidence in Theresa May as prime minister. Chairman of the Northern Ireland select cttee from 2010 to 2015. Contested: Ashfield, 1992; Makerfield, 1987.

Ed: St James' CofE Secondary Sch; Farnworth GS; Bolton Higher Education Inst (Dip management service).

CHALLENGERS
Alex Hegenbarth (LD) Engagement officer for the National Trust. **Lara Chaplin** (Lab) Lecturer at the University of Coventry. Previously manager of a cinema chain. Involved with regeneration projects. **Cate Cody** (Green) Career as an independent environmental consultant.

CONSTITUENCY PROFILE
Has been represented by Conservative MPs for well over a century, with an exception from 1951 until 1959, when the Cirencester & Tewkesbury MP William Morrison was Speaker. Tewkesbury became an individual seat again in 1997, the Conservative majority falling to a low of just over 6,000 in 2010. It is a mostly rural constituency that includes the outskirts of Cheltenham and Gloucester. A fifth of residents are aged 65 or older and a further quarter are aged 45 to 64. The area's residents are fairly affluent, and more than three quarters of households are owner-occupied.

EU REFERENDUM RESULT
53.6% Leave   **Remain 46.4%**

Thanet North

MAJORITY 17,189 (35.68%)   CONSERVATIVE HOLD   TURNOUT 66.17%

SIR ROGER GALE
BORN Aug 20, 1943
MP 1983-

Former broadcaster and producer at Radio Caroline, Radio 270, Radio London and BBC Radio 4, who became BBC director of children's television. Accused of sexism when he referred to employed family members as "girls" on BBC Radio 4. Former pirate radio DJ. Vice-chairman, Conservative Party, 2001-03. Supported Jeremy Hunt in 2019. Select cttees: ecclesiastical, 2015-17; procedure, 2007-15; panel of chairs, 1997-2017; home affairs, 1987-92. Contested Birmingham Northfield, 1982. Ed: Guildhall School of Music and Drama.

	Electorate	Share %	from 2017 %	Change
	72,811			
*R Gale C		30,066	62.41	+6.20
C Jones Lab		12,877	26.73	-7.26
A Curwen LD		3,439	7.14	+3.86
R Edwards Green		1,796	3.73	+2.02

CHALLENGERS
Coral Jones (Lab) GP. Vice-chairwoman of Doctors in Unite; member of Save Our NHS Kent. **Angie Curwen** (LD) Works at Quex Park as assistant to the estate manager. Worked at Pfizer in the Drug Safety Department. **Rob Edwards** (Green) Sports club manager.

CONSTITUENCY PROFILE
A safe Conservative seat, held by the party since its creation in 1983, when Cherie Blair stood for Labour, coming third behind the Tory and Social Democratic Party candidates. Sir Roger Gale's majorities in Thanet North have always exceeded 10,000, except during the three elections won nationally by Tony Blair. Ukip came second in 2015, winning more than a quarter of the vote. The seat consists of the northeastern coast of Kent, made up of the seaside towns of Herne Bay and Margate, and the rural area between them. The seat has a significant population of over-65s, and more than half its residents are aged 45 or older. Construction and health are among the predominant local sectors.

EU REFERENDUM RESULT
65.2% Leave   Remain 34.8%

Thanet South

MAJORITY 10,587 (21.94%)   CONSERVATIVE HOLD   TURNOUT 65.83%

CRAIG MACKINLAY
BORN Oct 7, 1966
MP 2015-

Firm rightwinger and founder of the Anti-Federalist League, which later became Ukip. Founding treasurer and vice-chairman of Ukip, 1993-97; briefly party leader in 1997 but demoted to deputy leader, 1997-2000. Defected to the Tories in 2005. Charged by CPS for overspending during 2015 election campaign; acquitted of all charges, 2019. Chartered accountant and tax specialist. Cllr, Medway BC, 2007-. Contested: Gillingham, 2005, 1997, (both for Ukip), 1992 (as Ind); Totnes 2001 (for Ukip). Ed: Rainham Mark GS; University

	Electorate	Share %	from 2017 %	Change
	73,302			
*C Mackinlay C		27,084	56.12	+5.35
R Gordon-Nesbitt Lab		16,497	34.19	-3.75
M Pennington LD		2,727	5.65	+2.61
B Wing Green		1,949	4.04	+2.41

of Birmingham (BSc zoology & comparative physiology); ICAEW (accountancy); CIOT (tax advisory).

CHALLENGERS
Rebecca Gordon-Nesbitt (Lab) Academic at King's College London's Cultural Institute working in the arts. Previously a researcher at Manchester Metropolitan University. **Martyn Pennington** (LD) Worked in international development. **Becky Wing** (Green) Former teacher.

CONSTITUENCY PROFILE
This seat, created in 1983, was initially won by the Conservative cabinet minister Jonathan Aitken, but gained by Labour in 1997. Alhough the Conservatives won it back in 2010, the party almost lost it to Nigel Farage, who was then the Ukip leader and came within 3,000 votes of gaining the seat in 2015. The comedian and satirist Al Murray also stood in 2015, winning 318 votes. Tourism is important in this coastal Kent seat, which is dominated by Ramsgate, Sandwich and Broadstairs. More than a fifth of residents are aged 65 or over and home ownership is below the regional average.

EU REFERENDUM RESULT
61.7% Leave   Remain 38.3%

Thirsk & Malton

MAJORITY 25,154 (44.45%) CONSERVATIVE HOLD TURNOUT 69.88%

KEVIN
HOLLINRAKE
BORN Sep 28, 1963
MP 2015-

Supported Remain before
the referendum and voiced
concern over Boris Johnson's
"do or die" Brexit policy. Backed
Michael Gove for leader in 2019.
Pro-fracking; resigned as vice-
chairman of the unconventional
oil and gas APPG in 2016
because of complaints by
constituents about the group's
funding. Communities and local
government select cttee, 2015-17.
PPS to Sir David Lidington,
2016-17. Businessman; worked
in property. Managing director
and co-founder, Hunters Estate
Agents. Ed: Easingwold Sch;
Sheffield Hallam University (BSc

	Electorate	Share %	Change from 2017 %
	80,979		
*K Hollinrake C	35,634	62.97	+2.94
D Yellen Lab	10,480	18.52	-7.53
D Keal LD	6,774	11.97	+5.07
M Brampton Green	2,263	4.00	+2.03
J Hall Yorkshire	881	1.56	
S Mullins Ind	245	0.43	-0.54
G Johnson ND	184	0.33	
M Taylor Soc Dem	127	0.22	

physics, but never completed).

CHALLENGERS
David Yellen (Lab) Worked
at North Yorkshire CC as a
manager in children's services for
more than 30 years. Dinah Keal
(LD) Media and communications
manager at Alzheimer's Society.
Cllr, Ryedale DC, 2012-, 2003-11.
Martin Brampton (Green) IT
worker.

CONSTITUENCY PROFILE
Thirsk & Malton, created in
2010, has elected Conservative
MPs with five-figure majorities
in all four elections in that time,
the majority rising from an
initial 11,000 to well over double
that in 2019. Its predecessors
returned Conservative MPs
since the 19th century, apart
from a one-year Liberal
Democrat stint after a by-
election in 1986. An affluent,
rural area in North Yorkshire
with a high rate of owner-
occupation, its population is
disproportionately made up of
residents aged 45 and over. The
local economy is largely based
on tourism and agriculture.

EU REFERENDUM RESULT
56.4% Leave   Remain 43.6%

Thornbury & Yate

MAJORITY 12,369 (23.68%) CONSERVATIVE HOLD TURNOUT 75.18%

LUKE HALL
BORN Jul 8, 1986
MP 2015-

Minister for local government
and homelessness since 2019.
Career in retail, which began
as a sales assistant at Lidl aged
18 and led to him becoming the
southwest regional manager for
Farmfoods. Voted Remain, but
backed the government's Brexit
policy. One of seven MPs to
support Mark Harper for leader,
2019; he later switched to Sajid
Javid. Has campaigned to protect
the green belt and improve
transport services in South
Gloucestershire. Select cttees:
environmental audit, 2015-17;
work and pensions, 2016-17;
petitions, 2016-17. Chairman of

	Electorate	Share %	Change from 2017 %
	69,492		
*L Hall C	30,202	57.81	+2.56
C Young LD	17,833	34.13	+2.69
R Logan Lab	4,208	8.05	-4.00

the APPG on retail. Ed: John
Cabot Academy.

CHALLENGERS
Claire Young (LD) Former
software engineer who
worked for IBM. Cllr, South
Gloucestershire CC, 2007-;
deputy leader of the Lib Dem
group, 2011-. Contested this seat
in the 2017 general election.
Rob Logan (Lab) Director of
procurement at the University
of Bristol since 2018. Worked
for Bristol council in a variety of
roles for 11 years between 2007
and 2018.

CONSTITUENCY PROFILE
The seat's predecessor,
Northavon, was narrowly won
from the Conservatives in
1997 by the Liberal Democrat
Steve Webb, who continued
to hold it after the minor
boundary changes that created
Thornbury & Yate in 2010. The
Conservatives narrowly regained
it in 2015, boosting their majority
to more than 12,000 when Mr
Webb did not stand in 2017.
The seat is made up of affluent
commuter towns and villages
to the north of Bristol. A third
of workers are in managerial,
administrative or professional
occupations and median pay is
above the regional average.

EU REFERENDUM RESULT
52.2% Leave   Remain 47.8%

Thurrock

MAJORITY 11,482 (24.19%)   CONSERVATIVE HOLD   TURNOUT 59.59%

JACKIE
DOYLE-PRICE
BORN Aug 5, 1969
MP 2010-

Worked as a consumer advocate for the Financial Services Authority. Co-sponsored a private member's bill backing an EU referendum, but voted to Remain. Backed Mark Harper for the Conservative leadership in 2019, before transferring her support to Jeremy Hunt. Parliamentary under-secretary, health, 2017-19. Assistant whip, 2015-17. Select cttees: selection, 2015-17; public accounts, 2010-14. School food APPG. Assistant private secretary, Lord Mayor of City of London, 2000-05. Contested Sheffield Hillsborough, 2005. Ed: Notre Dame RC Sch, Sheffield; University of Durham (BA economics and politics).

	Electorate	Share %	Change from 2017 %
	79,655		
*J Doyle-Price C	27,795	58.56	+19.05
J Kent Lab	16,313	34.37	-4.45
S Stone LD	1,510	3.18	+1.60
J Woollard Ind	1,042	2.20	
B Harvey Green	807	1.70	

Dame RC Sch, Sheffield; University of Durham (BA economics and politics).

CHALLENGERS
John Kent (Lab) Cllr, Thurrock C, 1993-; former council leader. Left school at 16 to pursue an apprenticeship. Member, Unite. Voted to Remain in the EU. Contested this constituency, 2017. **Stewart Stone** (LD) Director, Enhancing Potential, a talent and change management consultancy.

CONSTITUENCY PROFILE
Thurrock was won by Labour at every election from 1945 to 2010, except for a narrow Conservative victory in 1987. The Tories gained it with a majority of 92 in 2010, and in 2015 there was a three-way battle in which the Conservatives won 34 per cent of the vote, Labour 33 per cent and Ukip 32 per cent. In 2017, it was the only seat in which Ukip received more than 10,000 votes. The seat is on the north of the Thames Estuary. About one in six residents is from an ethnic minority, most of them black or mixed race. Tilbury remains a major port.

EU REFERENDUM RESULT
70.3% Leave   Remain 29.7%

Tiverton & Honiton

MAJORITY 24,239 (40.66%)   CONSERVATIVE HOLD   TURNOUT 71.86%

NEIL PARISH
BORN May 26, 1956
MP 2010-

Somerset farmer who still lives on family farm. MEP for South West England, 1999-2009. PPS to John Hayes (South Holland & The Deepings), 2014-15. Backed continued membership of the single market in indicative votes on Brexit. Supported Michael Gove for leader in 2019, before switching to Boris Johnson. Chairman, environment select cttee, 2015-. APPGs: beef and lamb; eggs, pigs and poultry; dairy. Tabled an urgent question on air quality and transport emissions. African politics expert; barred from entering Zimbabwe by Robert Mugabe

	Electorate	Share %	Change from 2017 %
	82,953		
*N Parish C	35,893	60.21	-1.14
L Pole Lab	11,654	19.55	-7.55
J Timperley LD	8,807	14.77	+6.75
C Reed Green	2,291	3.84	+0.32
M Dennis UKIP	968	1.62	

after campaigning for the British government to reject the legitimacy of the tyrant's party, 2008. Left school at 16 to run family farm. Contested Torfaen, 1997. Ed: Brymore Sch.

CHALLENGERS
Liz Pole (Lab) Chairwoman, Tiverton & Honiton CLP. Dual UK-US citizen. Runs software company. **John Timperley** (LD) Consultant orthopaedic surgeon. **Colin Reed** (Green) Studies law at the Open University.

CONSTITUENCY PROFILE
Created in 1997, this seat has always elected Tory MPs. The party has recently won large majorities, but initially the Tory majority over the Lib Dems was less than 2,000. Its predecessor seats, Tiverton and Honiton, both elected Tory MPs almost exclusively since the late 19th century. About a quarter of residents are aged 65 or more, one of the highest proportions in the country. Home ownership is slightly above average, but median pay is £70 a week below the UK median. A significant proportion of residents are self-employed and much of the workforce is in agriculture.

EU REFERENDUM RESULT
57.8% Leave   Remain 42.2%

Tonbridge & Malling

MAJORITY 26,941 (47.26%) **CONSERVATIVE HOLD** **TURNOUT 73.67%**

TOM TUGENDHAT
BORN Jun 27, 1973
MP 2015-

Served in the army from 2003 to 2013, including in Iraq and Afghanistan; in 2005-07 he helped to set up the new administration in Helmand, Afghanistan. Later worked as a management consultant and energy analyst. Chairman, foreign affairs select cttee, 2017-. Said that the Salisbury novichok attack on a Russian former spy was "a warlike act". Chairman, genocide and crimes against humanity APPG. Remainer in 2016. Son of the judge Sir Michael Tugendhat and nephew of Lord Christopher Tugendhat, the British EU Commissioner,

	Electorate	Share %	Change from 2017 %
	77,380		
*T Tugendhat C	35,784	62.78	-0.87
R Morris LD	8,843	15.51	+8.86
D Jones Lab	8,286	14.54	-7.80
A Clark Green	4,090	7.18	+3.07

1977-85. Dual British-French national. Ed: St Paul's Sch; University of Bristol (BA theology); Gonville & Caius Coll, Cambridge (MA Islamics).

CHALLENGERS
Richard Morris (LD) Chairman, Yehudi Menuhin School, 2011-. Former lawyer, banker, publisher and chief executive. **Dylan Jones** (Lab) Distribution manager, Royal Mail. Member: CWU; Unite. Contested: this seat, 2017; Ashford BC, 2018 by-election. **April Clark** (Green) Cllr,

Tonbridge & Malling BC, 2019-. Contested: this seat, 2017; Kent CC, 2017.

CONSTITUENCY PROFILE
This is a relatively safe Conservative seat, with the party winning by more than 10,000 votes at all but two elections since the seat's 1974 creation. With the exception of 2017, the Tory majority has grown at every election since 2001. Although a rural Kent seat, many of its residents commute into London. A large proportion of them work in finance, science and technology, and property. Median wages are £100 a week higher than the national average.

EU REFERENDUM RESULT
52.9% Leave **Remain 47.1%**

Tooting

MAJORITY 14,307 (24.47%) **LABOUR HOLD** **TURNOUT 76.01%**

ROSENA
ALLIN-KHAN
BORN May 10, 1977
MP 2016-

Accident and emergency doctor who has also worked delivering humanitarian aid. Working-class background, with Polish and Pakistani heritage. Stood for Labour deputy leadership, 2020. Noted for 2019 election campaign video parodying *Love Actually*. Cllr, Wandsworth LBC, 2014-18. Remainer; voted against triggering Article 50 and later voted in indicative votes to revoke it to avert a no-deal departure. Shadow sports minister, 2016-. Member, genocide and crimes against humanity APPG. Tabled an urgent question on racism in

	Electorate	Share %	Change from 2017 %
	76,933		
*R Allin-Khan Lab	30,811	52.69	-6.95
K Briscoe C	16,504	28.22	-4.84
O Glover LD	8,305	14.20	+8.95
G Goodwin Green	2,314	3.96	+2.50
A Shakir Brexit	462	0.79	
R Hubley Soc Dem	77	0.13	

football. Amateur boxer. Ed: Trinity St Mary Sch; Brunel University (BSc medical biochemistry); Lucy Cavendish Coll, Cambridge (medicine).

CHALLENGERS
Kerry Briscoe (C) Public speaker and businesswoman. Educational charity trustee, giving young people career advice. **Olly Glover** (LD) Operations development executive at a railway company

developing rail links in southeast England. Contested Wandsworth LBC, 2018.

CONSTITUENCY PROFILE
Sadiq Khan was the MP here from 2005 until he became the mayor of London in 2016. Labour has held the seat since its creation in 1974, but the Conservatives reduced Mr Khan's majority in 2010 and 2015 to less than 3,000. It is an urban, densely populated seat with a large black and Asian population. A high proportion of residents work in finance, information and communication, and property. More than two fifths of residents are aged 25-44.

EU REFERENDUM RESULT
25.6% Leave **Remain 74.4%**

Torbay

MAJORITY 17,749 (35.20%)   CONSERVATIVE HOLD   TURNOUT 67.19%

KEVIN FOSTER
BORN Dec 31, 1978
MP 2015-

Criminal defence paralegal.
Parly under-sec: Wales, 2019-;
Home Office, 2019-; assistant
government whip, 2019-. PPS
to Sir David Lidington, 2018-
19. Ecclesiastical select cttee,
2017-. Voted both for continued
single market membership
and for leaving with no-deal
in the Brexit indicative votes.
Nominated Sajid Javid for
Conservative leader, 2019, before
endorsing Boris Johnson in
the later stages of the election.
Worked for Coventry city
council, including as deputy
leader, 2011-13. Contested
Coventry South, 2010. Ed: Hele's

	Electorate	Share %	Change from 2017 %
	75,054		
*K Foster C	29,863	59.22	+6.18
L Howgate LD	12,114	24.02	-1.10
M Middleditch Lab	6,562	13.01	-5.18
S Moss Green	1,239	2.46	+1.18
J Channer Ind	648	1.29	

Sch; Warwick University (LLB;
international economic law).

CHALLENGERS
Lee Howgate (LD) Cllr, Torbay
C, 2019-; overview and scrutiny
co-ordinator. Member, Devon
and Cornwall Police and Crime
Panel. Assistant head teacher.
Michele Middleditch (Lab)
Secretary of Torbay constituency
Labour party. Retired dance
and drama teacher. **Sam Moss**
(Green) Former Royal Marine.
Member, CND.

CONSTITUENCY PROFILE
Created in 1974, the Lib Dems
took the seat from the Tories
in 1997, holding it until the
party's national collapse in 2015.
The Lib Dem MP for those 18
years, Adrian Sanders, had a
majority of 12 when he was first
elected in 1997. Kevin Foster
has increased his majority at
successive elections. Made up
of Torquay and Paignton, this is
a coastal seat where tourism is
an important sector, alongside
retail. It has a large population
of residents aged 65 and over.
Private renting is much higher
than average, and median
weekly wages are £50 a week
less than the national average.

EU REFERENDUM RESULT
62.5% Leave   Remain 37.5%

Torfaen

MAJORITY 3,742 (10.07%)   LABOUR HOLD   TURNOUT 60.21%

NICK
THOMAS-SYMONDS
BORN May 26, 1980
MP 2015-

Former politics tutor at St
Edmund Hall, Oxford. Later a
practising barrister in civil and
public law, Chambers Civitas
Law. Author: *Attlee: A Life in
Politics* and *Nye: The Political
Life of Aneurin Bevan*. Quit
front bench protesting Jeremy
Corbyn's leadership, 2016.
Supported Sir Keir Starmer in
2020 leadership election. APPGs:
legal and constitutional affairs;
archives and history; industrial
heritage; chairman, off-patent
drugs. Shadow minister: home
affairs, 2017-; solicitor general,
2016-17; work and pensions,
2015-16. Justice select cttee, 2015.

	Electorate	Share %	Change from 2017 %
	61,743		
*N Thomas-Symonds Lab	15,546	41.82	-15.78
G Smith C	11,804	31.75	+0.80
D Thomas Brexit	5,742	15.45	
J Miller LD	1,831	4.93	+2.71
M Bowler-Brown PC	1,441	3.88	-1.48
A Heygate-Browne Green	812	2.18	

Ed: St Alban's RC HS, Pontypool;
St Edmund Hall, Oxford (BA
PPE).

CHALLENGERS
Graham Smith (C) Engineer.
Cllr, Torfaen CBC, 2008-17;
group leader. Cllr, Pontypool
CC, 2012-17. Contested this
seat, 2017, 2015. **David Thomas**
(Brexit) Cllr, Torfaen CBC, 2017-;
elected as a Labour candidate,
but resigned from the party over
its decision to raise council tax.

John Miller (LD) Chairman,
Newport and Severnside Lib
Dems.

CONSTITUENCY PROFILE
Torfaen, along with its
predecessor, Pontypool, has been
Labour since 1918. Leo Abse, a
pioneer of gay rights legislation,
was the MP, 1951-87. The Labour
majority has steadily declined
from its 1997 peak, and the
party's winning margin in 2019
was its smallest in 95 years. The
seat sits to the north of Newport.
A high proportion of housing is
socially rented. The area once
had big coal and iron industries,
but these have been replaced by
manufacturing and retail.

EU REFERENDUM RESULT
60.8% Leave   Remain 39.2%

Totnes

CONSERVATIVE HOLD

ANTHONY MANGNALL
BORN Aug 12, 1989
MP 2019-

Worked for William Hague in the Foreign Office, 2010-12, before joining shipbroking firms in Singapore and London, 2012-16. After the former foreign secretary was given a peerage, Mr Mangnall returned to work for him, 2016-18. Special adviser to Alun Cairns (Vale of Glamorgan), 2018-19. Voted Leave. Campaigned for better digital connectivity in rural communities. Son of a soldier. Grew up in Northern Ireland and Zimbabwe, but spent time in Devon. Former chairman, South West Wiltshire Conservative Association. Kite surfer and wild

	Electorate	Share %	Change from 2017 %
	69,863		
A Mangnall C	27,751	53.18	-0.47
*S Wollaston LD	15,027	28.80	+15.93
L Webberley Lab	8,860	16.98	-9.87
J Kitson ND	544	1.04	

swimmer. Contested Warley, 2017. Ed: Shrewsbury Sch; Exeter University (BA history, politics and sociology).

CHALLENGERS
Sarah Wollaston (LD) MP for this seat, 2010-19. Initially a Tory but defected to The Independent Group in February 2019, before joining the Lib Dems later that year. Chairwoman, health select cttee, 2010-19; member, liaison cttee, 2017-19. NHS doctor. First MP selected as a candidate for a major party through a postal

open primary. Remainer. **Louise Webberley** (Lab) Social worker. Cllr, Totnes TC. Campaigner, Plastic Free Totnes.

CONSTITUENCY PROFILE
This affluent, picturesque south Devon seat has been won by the Tories in every election since 1924, although from 1997 to 2010 the Lib Dems were close contenders. The Greens stood down in 2019 as part of the "Unite to Remain" alliance. Tourism, farming and fishing are major industries. The level of home ownership is very high and the proportion of people aged 65 or over is among the highest in the country.

EU REFERENDUM RESULT
53.9% Leave   Remain 46.1%

Tottenham

LABOUR HOLD

DAVID LAMMY
BORN Jul 19, 1972
MP 2000-

Active backbencher, having been a junior minister towards the end of the New Labour years. Authored an influential eponymous review into the treatment of ethnic minorities in the criminal justice system, 2017. Remain campaigner; criticised for comparing the ERG to the Nazis. Prominent critic of the government on the Windrush scandal and hostile environment policy. Supported Sir Keir Starmer for leader, 2020. Nominated Jeremy Corbyn in 2015 but was not a diehard supporter. Minister: higher education, 2008-10; culture,

	Electorate	Share %	Change from 2017 %
	75,740		
*D Lammy Lab	35,621	76.02	-5.55
J Newhall C	5,446	11.62	+0.14
T Palmer LD	3,168	6.76	+3.34
E Chan Green	1,873	4.00	+1.41
A Turay Brexit	527	1.12	
A Bence Soc Dem	91	0.19	
F Sweeney WRP	88	0.19	
J Silberman Comm Lge	42	0.09	

2005-07. Select cttees: Speaker's advisory, works of art, 2017-; ecclesiastical, 2017-. Chairman, race and community APPG. First black Briton to study a masters in law at Harvard. Admitted to the Bar in 1994. Born and raised in Tottenham. Ed: Soas (law); Harvard (MA law).

CHALLENGERS
James Newhall (C) Adviser to

John Penrose (Weston-Super-Mare). London campaign director of the Brexit group Grassroots Out. **Tammy Palmer** (LD) Cllr, Haringey, LBC 2018-.

CONSTITUENCY PROFILE
This north London seat has been Labour since it was created in 1950. Densely populated and diverse: a quarter of residents are black, and there are significant Asian, Cypriot, Turkish, Irish, eastern European, Muslim and Jewish communities. Social and private renting is common, and home ownership is low. In 2011 and 1985 there were riots in this seat, which is undergoing significant urban regeneration.

EU REFERENDUM RESULT
23.8% Leave   Remain 76.2%

Truro & Falmouth

MAJORITY 4,561 (7.71%)   CONSERVATIVE HOLD   TURNOUT 77.15%

CHERILYN MACKRORY
BORN Jun 5, 1976
MP 2019-

Yorkshire-born IT project manager. Worked for Steve Double (St Austell & Newquay) and Scott Mann (Cornwall North). Replaced Sarah Newton, the MP from 2010 to 2019, after she decided not to stand for re-election. Has campaigned for greater investment in the NHS, schools and policing, and against climate change. Voted to leave the EU in 2016. Cllr, Cornwall CC, 2017-. APPGs: fisheries; broadband and digital communications.

CHALLENGERS
Jennifer Forbes (Lab) Trade

	Electorate	Share %	Change from 2017 %
	76,719		
C Mackrory C	27,237	46.02	+1.67
J Forbes Lab	22,676	38.31	+0.65
R Gripper LD	7,150	12.08	-2.86
T Scott Green	1,714	2.90	+1.43
P Nicholson Lib	413	0.70	

union lecturer. Trained as an engineer with BT. Ran an outdoor parent and toddler group. Member, CWU and UCU. Former secretary, Truro & Falmouth CLP. Director, Community Heart, a charity combating homelessness. Voted Remain. **Ruth Gripper** (LD) Knowledge exchange officer at University of Exeter, 2019-. Parliamentary researcher to Norman Lamb (Norfolk North), 2010-13. Contested Southwark LBC, 2018.

CONSTITUENCY PROFILE
From 1974, the predecessor seat of Truro was a strong Liberal Democrat one; the Conservatives pipped the Lib Dems to win this seat in 2010 after boundary changes, and then clung onto it in 2017 despite a large swing to Labour. It is on the coast and popular with tourists, with tourism-related industries and retail the largest employers. The number of retired residents is above average and, with the University of Falmouth and a campus of the University of Exeter in the seat, the number of full-time students is also high, at roughly one in ten residents.

EU REFERENDUM RESULT
45.9% Leave   Remain 54.1%

Tunbridge Wells

MAJORITY 14,645 (26.80%)   CONSERVATIVE HOLD   TURNOUT 73.05%

GREG CLARK
BORN Aug 28, 1967
MP 2005-

On the moderate wing of the Conservative Party. Business secretary, 2016-19. Universities minister, 2014-15. Financial secretary to the Treasury, 2012-13; communities minister, 2010-12. Chairman, science and technology select cttee, 2020-. Had the party whip removed in September 2019 for voting to prevent a no-deal Brexit; it was restored in October. Director, Conservative policy, 2001-05. Worked for the Boston Consulting Group in the US, Mexico, South America and Iceland. Spad to the trade and industry secretary Ian

	Electorate	Share %	Change from 2017 %
	74,816		
*G Clark C	30,119	55.11	-1.81
B Chapelard LD	15,474	28.31	+18.44
A Weiss Lab	8,098	14.82	-11.73
C Camp Ind	488	0.89	
N Peacock Ind	471	0.86	

Lang, 1996-97. BBC controller, commercial policy. Voted Remain in the 2016 referendum. Backed Jeremy Hunt for the leadership in 2019. Ed: Magdalene Coll, Cambridge (economics); LSE (PhD).

CHALLENGERS
Ben Chapelard (LD) Teacher. Cllr, Tunbridge Wells BC, 2010-; leader of Lib Dem group. **Antonio Weiss** (Lab) Cllr, Harrow LBC, 2014-. Best-selling author of *101 Business Ideas That*

Will Change the Way You Work.

CONSTITUENCY PROFILE
Held by the Tories, often with large majorities, since it was created in 1974. Including its predecessors, the constituency has been held by the Tories for more than a century. Includes the affluent town of Royal Tunbridge Wells, home to about 60,000 people, and a swathe of rural Kent. Median wages are more than £100 a week higher than average, and a greater proportion of residents hold managerial-level jobs. Home ownership, however, is relatively low for a rural seat in the South East.

EU REFERENDUM RESULT
44.6% Leave   Remain 55.4%

Twickenham

MUNIRA WILSON
BORN Apr 26, 1978
MP 2019-

Corporate affairs director, Merck Group, a pharmaceutical company, 2016-19. Strategic account manager, NHS Digital, 2015-16. Head of government affairs, Novartis, 2009-15. Public affairs officer at Save the Children, 2006-08. Political assistant to Nick Clegg, 2006. Cllr, Richmond LBC, 2006-10. Campaign focused on Brexit, public service funding and opposition to Heathrow expansion. Contested Feltham & Heston, 2010. Ed: Grammar school; St Catharine's Coll, University of Cambridge (BA French and German).

	Electorate	Share %	from 2017 %	Change
	84,901			
M Wilson LD	36,166	56.07	+3.32	
I Grant C	22,045	34.18	-3.85	
R Walia Lab	5,476	8.49	-0.73	
S Wells Brexit	816	1.27		

CHALLENGERS
Isobel Grant (C) Associate and civil engineer at Arup. Featured in the *Telegraph*'s Top 50 Women in Engineering, 2018. Trustee, RedR UK, a disaster relief charity. Campaigned to bring Crossrail 2 to Twickenham. Cllr, Ealing LBC, 2010-14. **Ranjeev Walia** (Lab) Area sales manager, Bayer, a pharmaceuticals company. Re-joined Labour in 2015 to vote for Jeremy Corbyn in the leadership election that year. Election agent, 2017. Contested Richmond LBC, 2018.

CONSTITUENCY PROFILE
The safest Liberal Democrat seat in the country, both by size of majority and vote share. The party's former leader, Sir Vince Cable, who served as business secretary during the coalition government, retired as an MP at the 2019 election. Sir Vince had led the Lib Dems to second place in the 2019 European parliament elections. Twickenham, home to the England rugby team, is an affluent area on the banks of the Thames. It has good rail links to London and the average annual salary of residents is more than £42,000. The seat also has a higher rate of home ownership than the London average.

EU REFERENDUM RESULT
33.3% Leave   Remain 66.7%

Tynemouth

SIR ALAN
CAMPBELL
BORN Jul 8, 1957
MP 1997-

History teacher turned MP. Supported Remain. Considered hostile towards Jeremy Corbyn's leadership; defied him to vote for Syria airstrikes, but otherwise has rarely rebelled during his time in parliament. Deputy chief whip, 2010-. Parly under-sec, Home Office, 2008-10. Whip, 2006-08; assistant whip, 2005. PPS: Adam Ingram, 2003-05; Gus McDonald, 2001-03. Select cttees: selection, 2010-19, 2006-08; armed forces bill, 2005-06; public accounts, 1997-2001. Ed: Blackfyne SS, Consett; Lancaster (BA politics); Leeds (PGCE); Newcastle Poly (MA history).

	Electorate	Share %	from 2017 %	Change
	77,261			
*A Campbell Lab	26,928	48.06	-8.92	
L Bartoli C	22,071	39.39	+2.93	
J Appleby LD	3,791	6.77	+3.73	
E Punchard Brexit	1,963	3.50		
J Erskine Green	1,281	2.29	+1.18	

CHALLENGERS
Lewis Bartoli (C) Cllr, North Tyneside MBC, 2019-. Member, Tynemouth Volunteer Life Brigade. Local magistrate of 15 years. Supported Leaving the EU; backed Boris Johnson for leader. **John Appleby** (LD) Head of mechanical engineering at Newcastle University. Contested this constituency in the 2017 and 2010 elections, and Tyneside North in the 2015 election. **Ed Punchard** (Brexit) Runs a documentary-making business.

CONSTITUENCY PROFILE
Labour gained Tynemouth from the Tories in 1997, having won the seat only once before, in 1945. Sir Alan Campbell's majority has fluctuated, but in 2019 it was at its lowest ever in percentage terms; it was slightly lower numerically in 2005. This coastal area, just north of South Shields and east of Newcastle-upon-Tyne, is dominated by Tynemouth and Whitley Bay. Moderately affluent; seven in ten households are owner-occupied and the median wage is slightly above the UK average. Regeneration projects are taking place in areas once dominated by coalmining and shipbuilding.

EU REFERENDUM RESULT
47.6% Leave   Remain 52.4%

Tyneside North

MAJORITY 9,561 (18.96%)   LABOUR HOLD   TURNOUT 63.91%

MARY GLINDON
BORN Jan 13, 1957
MP 2010-

Former civic mayor. Supported Remain. Resigned over Jeremy Corbyn's leadership in 2016 but joined shadow cabinet after his re-election. Shadow farming and rural communities minister, 2016-. PPS: shadow transport team, 2014-16; Mary Creagh, 2013-14. Select cttees: transport, 2015-16; communities, 2013-15; environment, 2010-15. Backed Sir Keir Starmer for leader, 2020. Chairwoman, APPGs on Parkinson's and healthy homes and buildings. Member of APPGs on: Kurdistan; Hadrian's Wall; muscular dystrophy. Cllr, North Tyneside C, 1995-2010.

	Electorate	Share %	Change from 2017 %
	78,902		
*M Glindon Lab	25,051	49.68	-14.80
D Carroll C	15,490	30.72	+3.41
A Husband Brexit	5,254	10.42	
C Boyle LD	3,241	6.43	+3.55
J Buttery Green	1,393	2.76	+1.47

Admin officer, CSA, DWP, 2008-10. Ran North Shield's People's Centre. Ed: Newcastle Polytechnic (BSc sociology).

CHALLENGERS
Dean Carroll (C) Director, PR agency. Cllr, Shropshire CC, 2013-. Cllr, Shrewsbury TC, 2009-13. Vote Leave campaign sub-agent. **Andrew Husband** (Brexit) Chief executive, United Hygiene and Catering. **Chris Boyle** (LD) Legal aid lawyer. Cllr, Newcastle City C, 2003-12.

Contested Houghton & Sunderland South, 2010.

CONSTITUENCY PROFILE
This seat has been held by Labour since its 1997 creation. The 2019 election was the first time that Labour's majority had fallen below 10,000. Its previous MP was Stephen Byers, a Labour cabinet minister who retired after the expenses scandal and a lobbying sting. The seat includes Wallsend, Newcastle's eastern and northern suburbs and some former mining communities. The mining and shipbuilding communities declined over the past few decades, but defence remains a major industry.

EU REFERENDUM RESULT
59.5% Leave   Remain 40.5%

Tyrone West

MAJORITY 7,478 (18.16%)   SINN FEIN HOLD   TURNOUT 62.16%

ORFHLAITH
BEGLEY
BORN Dec 19, 1991
MP 2018-

Solicitor in civil and criminal law. Won the seat in a May 2018 by-election prompted by the resignation of the sitting Sinn Fein MP, Barry McElduff. Native of Carrickmore, County Tyrone. First female MP since the consituency's 1997 creation. Member, Carrickmore Gaelic Athletic Club; played football for the club. Keen supporter of the Éire Óg hurling club. Ed: Queen's, Belfast (law).

CHALLENGERS
Thomas Buchanan (DUP) MLA, Tyrone West, 2003-. Cllr, Omagh DC, 1993-2013. Promoted

	Electorate	Share %	Change from 2017 %
	66,259		
*O Begley SF	16,544	40.17	-10.56
T Buchanan DUP	9,066	22.01	-4.93
D McCrossan SDLP	7,330	17.80	+4.84
S Donnelly Alliance	3,979	9.66	+7.36
A McKane UUP	2,774	6.74	+1.55
J Hope Aontu	972	2.36	
S Glass Green	521	1.26	+0.28

teaching of creationism in schools and told children at a public event that homosexuality was "an abomination". Contested this seat in 2018 by-election, 2017, 2015 and 2010. **Daniel McCrossan** (SDLP) Party's Brexit spokesman. MLA, Tyrone West, 2016-. Member, SDLP national executive, 2012-15. Contested this seat in the 2018 by-election and the 2017 and 2015 general elections.

CONSTITUENCY PROFILE
This seat, created in 1997, initially elected an Ulster Unionist, but has elected Sinn Fein MPs since 2001. It has one of the largest Catholic populations of any seat in Northern Ireland. Omagh, in this seat, was the scene of an IRA car bomb that killed 29 people in 1998. Barry McElduff, the MP elected in 2017 whose resignation prompted the 2018 by-election won by Orfhlaith Begley, stood down after tweeting a video of himself with a loaf of Kingsmill on his head 42 years to the day after the Kingsmill massacre, in which the Provisional IRA killed ten Protestants.

EU REFERENDUM RESULT
33.2% Leave   Remain 66.8%

Ulster Mid

MAJORITY 9,537 (21.37%)   SINN FEIN HOLD   TURNOUT 63.34%

FRANCIE MOLLOY
BORN Dec 16, 1950
MP 2013-

Veteran republican who cut his teeth in 1960s civil rights campaign. MLA, Ulster Mid, 1998-2013; principal speaker, 2011-13. Stood in European elections, 1994. Elected to Northern Ireland Forum, 1996. Temporarily suspended from Sinn Fein after criticising party policy on BBC radio. Described British airstrikes on Syria as "Brits back to what they do best, murder", and said David Cameron was "the real terrorist" in 2015. Marched with Jeremy Corbyn during Bloody Sunday protest in the 1980s. Ed: St Patrick's, Dungannon; Felden

	Electorate	Share %	from 2017 %	Change
	70,449			
*F Molloy SF	20,473	45.88	-8.63	
K Buchanan DUP	10,936	24.51	-2.40	
D Johnston SDLP	6,384	14.31	+4.54	
M Boyle Alliance	3,526	7.90	+5.56	
N Richardson UUP	2,611	5.85	-0.61	
C Rafferty Ind	690	1.55		

government training centre (engineering); Ulster University; Newry FE Coll (foundation studies humanities).

CHALLENGERS
Keith Buchanan (DUP) MLA, Mid Ulster, 2016-. Worked for a food processing company. Involved with the Loyal Orders. Contested Mid Ulster DC, 2014. Contested this seat, 2017. **Denise Johnston** (SDLP) Justice and reconciliation campaigner.

Contested Mid Ulster DC, 2019. **Mel Boyle** (Alliance) Founder, Stormont parkrun. Contested Mid Ulster DC, 2019.

CONSTITUENCY PROFILE
This safe Sinn Fein seat was held by Martin McGuinnes, the late deputy first minister, from 1997 to 2013. The seat had been held mostly by Unionist MPs from 1955, except for 1969-74, when it was held by a "Unity" Irish nationalist and socialist candidate. The area is primarily Catholic, and the local economy is dominated by construction, manufacturing and retail. It also has an above-average percentage of the workforce in agriculture.

EU REFERENDUM RESULT
39.6% Leave   Remain 60.4%

Upper Bann

MAJORITY 8,210 (16.41%)   DUP HOLD   TURNOUT 60.38%

CARLA LOCKHART
BORN Feb 28, 1985
MP 2019-

Worked in the Lurgan DUP advice centre. MLA, Upper Bann, 2016-19. Cllr, Craigavon BC, 2007-16; Craigavon's youngest ever mayor. Member, Royal British Legion. School governor. Campaign focused on securing a perinatal palliative care hospice, maternal mental health unit, and better childcare facilities for the constituency. Replaced David Simpson, MP 2005-19, who decided not to stand in the wake of the revelation of an extramarital affair. Anti-abortion. Farming background. Ed: Armagh Tech; University of Ulster (MBA).

	Electorate	Share %	from 2017 %	Change
	82,887			
C Lockhart DUP	20,501	40.97	-2.57	
J O'Dowd SF	12,291	24.56	-3.39	
E Tennyson Alliance	6,433	12.85	+8.33	
D Beattie UUP	6,197	12.38	-3.03	
D Kelly SDLP	4,623	9.24	+0.66	

CHALLENGERS
John O'Dowd (SF) Education minister at Stormont, 2011-16. MLA, Upper Bann, 2003-. Unsuccessful bid to challenge the party vice-president Michelle O'Neill, 2019. Contested this seat in 2017, 2010 and 2005. **Eoin Tennyson** (Alliance) Cllr, Armagh City, Banbridge & Craigavon BC, 2019-. **Doug Beattie** (UUP) Royal Irish Regiment officer. Completed 28 years of service in Bosnia, Kosovo, Iraq and Northern

Ireland. Cllr, Armagh City, Banbridge & Craigavon BC, 2014-19. MLA, Upper Bann, 2016-. Contested this seat, 2017.

CONSTITUENCY PROFILE
David Trimble, the UUP leader, 1995-2005, and the first minister, 1998-2002, represented this seat from 1990 until 2005, when he was beaten by David Simpson, who held the seat for the DUP until 2019. About half of residents are Protestant, while about 40 per cent are Catholic. The seat is home to a strong manufacturing sector, but also contains some of the most deprived wards in Northern Ireland.

EU REFERENDUM RESULT
52.6% Leave   Remain 47.4%

Uxbridge & Ruislip South

MAJORITY 7,210 (14.96%)   CONSERVATIVE HOLD   TURNOUT 68.48%

BORIS JOHNSON
BORN Jun 19, 1964
MP 2015-; 2001-08

The prime minister and leader of the Conservative Party since July 2019, who led the Tories to their biggest election victory since 1987. Advised the Queen to prorogue parliament in an attempt to avoid scrutiny of his Brexit bill, August 2019; advice declared unlawful by the Supreme Court. Foreign secretary, 2016-18; resigned in protest at Theresa May's Brexit strategy. Figurehead, Vote Leave campaign. Accused of racism for comments made in columns in *The Daily Telegraph*, for which he had been Brussels correspondent in the early 1990s. Mayor of

	Electorate	Share %	Change from 2017 %
	70,369		
*B Johnson C	25,351	52.61	+1.82
A Milani Lab	18,141	37.65	-2.36
J Humphreys LD	3,026	6.28	+2.35
M Keir Green	1,090	2.26	+0.37
G Courtenay Ukip	283	0.59	-2.79
L Buckethead Loony	125	0.26	
C Binface Ind	69	0.14	
A Utting Ind	44	0.09	
Y Yogenstein ND	23	0.05	
N Burke Ind	22	0.05	
B Smith ND	8	0.02	
W Tobin ND	5	0.01	

London, 2008-16. MP for Henley, 2001-08. Sacked as shadow arts minister by Michael Howard in 2004 after lying about an affair. Editor of *The Spectator*, 1999-2005. Fired from *The Times* for fabricating a quote, 1988. Ed:

Eton Coll; Balliol Coll, Oxford (BA classics; president, Oxford Union; Bullingdon Club).

CHALLENGERS
Ali Milani (Lab) Cllr, Hillingdon LBC, 2018-. Vice-president of the NUS, 2017-19. **Jo Humphreys** (LD) Refused calls to stand aside for Ali Milani.

CONSTITUENCY PROFILE
An ethnically diverse commuter-belt seat on London's western edge, bordering Berkshire. It is relatively affluent and home to both Buckinghamshire New University and Brunel University. The seat is also close to Heathrow airport.

EU REFERENDUM RESULT
57.2% Leave   Remain 42.8%

Vale of Clwyd

MAJORITY 1,827 (4.91%)   CONSERVATIVE GAIN FROM LABOUR   TURNOUT 65.69%

JAMES DAVIES
BORN Feb 27, 1980
MP 2019-; 2015-17

MP for this constituency, 2015-17. Known for holding surgeries in supermarkets and pubs. GP and dementia clinical champion. Select cttees: Welsh affairs, 2015-17; health, 2015-17. Cllr: Denbighshire CC, 2004-15; Prestayn TC, 2008-15. Member of the BMA. Trustee, local environmental association. Traces heritage in the constituency back seven generations. Ed: King's Sch; Christ's Coll, Cambridge (medicine).

CHALLENGERS
Chris Ruane (Lab) MP for this

	Electorate	Share %	Change from 2017 %
	56,649		
J Davies C	17,270	46.41	+2.35
*C Ruane Lab	15,443	41.50	-8.71
G Swingler PC	1,552	4.17	+0.16
P Dain Brexit	1,477	3.97	
G Scott LD	1,471	3.95	+2.23

seat, 2017-19, 1997-2015. Defeated by James Davies in 2019 for a second time. Shadow minister for Wales, 2017-19. Opposition whip, 2011-13. PPS to: David Miliband, 2009-10; Caroline Flint, 2007-08; Peter Hain, 2003-07. Consistently voted for more EU integration. Trustee, Oxford Mindfulness Centre. Set up mindfulness APPG; produced Mindful Nation report 2015. **Glenn Swingler** (PC) Adult mental health support worker. Cllr, Denbigh TC, 2017-.

CONSTITUENCY PROFILE
Created in 1997, the Vale of Clwyd was held by the Labour MP Chris Ruane until 2015, when James Davies won it by 237 votes. The marginal constituency swapped between Mr Ruane and Mr Davies in the 2017 and 2019 general elections. Positioned on the north coast of Wales, the Vale of Clwyd is sparsely populated and contains the seaside towns of Rhyl and Prestatyn. The former is one of the most deprived areas in the United Kingdom. Much of the employment along the coast is related either to healthcare and social work or to the tourism industry.

EU REFERENDUM RESULT
56.6% Leave   Remain 43.4%

Vale of Glamorgan

MAJORITY 3,562 (6.50%)   CONSERVATIVE HOLD   TURNOUT 71.64%

ALUN CAIRNS
BORN Jul 30, 1970
MP 2010-

Resigned as Welsh secretary at
the start of the 2019 election
campaign over claims that he
had known about a former
aide's role in the "sabotage" of
a rape trial, although he was
later cleared of breaching the
ministerial code. Voted Remain;
backed Boris Johnson in 2019.
Suspended from the party in
2008 for referring to Italians
as "greasy wops" on live radio,
for which he apologised. Parly
under-sec, Wales, 2014-16. Select
cttees: public administration,
2011-14; Welsh affairs, 2010-11.
Member of Welsh assembly,
1999-2011. Consultant and field

	Electorate	Share %	Change from 2017 %
	76,508		
*A Cairns C	27,305	49.82	+2.35
B Loveluck-Edwards Lab	23,743	43.32	-0.07
A Slaughter Green	3,251	5.93	+5.15
L Williams Gwlad	508	0.93	

manager, Lloyds Banking Group.
Ed: Ysgol Gyfun Ystalyfera;
University of Wales, Newport
(MBA).

CHALLENGERS
Belinda Loveluck-Edwards
(Lab) NASUWT regional officer,
2016-. **Anthony Slaughter**
(Green) Garden designer.
Contested Cardiff South &
Penarth, 2017 and 2015.

CONSTITUENCY PROFILE
The southernmost seat in Wales,
the Vale of Glamorgan has been
a bellwether and a marginal
since it was created in 1983.
Only in the landslides of 1983
and 1997 have the Conservatives
and Labour, respectively, won
five-figure majorities in the
seat. The constituency covers
the countryside along the south
Wales coast to the southwest of
Cardiff. The main population
centre is the large resort and
industrial port of Barry. Cardiff
airport is a big employer and
many constituents commute
into the Welsh capital. Residents
earn a higher median income,
and are more likely to own their
homes, than the Welsh average.
The economy is based largely on
agriculture.

EU REFERENDUM RESULT
52.6% Leave   Remain 47.4%

Vauxhall

MAJORITY 19,612 (34.81%)   LABOUR CO-OP HOLD   TURNOUT 63.55%

FLORENCE
ESHALOMI
BORN Sep 18, 1980
MP 2019-

Worked as a public affairs
manager for the Runnymede
Trust and Four Communications.
Ardent Remainer in the
2016 referendum. Member:
Momentum; GMB; Unison.
Nominated Sir Keir Starmer
in the 2020 leadership contest,
supported Liz Kendall in 2015
and did not vote in 2016 in
protest at the lack of a female
candidate. GLA member, 2016-;
Cllr, Lambeth LBC, 2006-18.
Promotes diversity in the arts
and was formerly a member
of the Arts Council. Ed: St
Francis Xavier Sixth Form
Coll; Middlesex University

	Electorate	Share %	Change from 2017 %
	88,647		
F Eshalomi Lab Co-op	31,615	56.12	-1.25
S Lewis LD	12,003	21.31	+0.73
S Bool C	9,422	16.73	-1.95
J Bond Green	2,516	4.47	+2.37
A McGuinness Brexit	641	1.14	
S Faissal Ind	136	0.24	

(BA politics and international
development with law).

CHALLENGERS
Sarah Lewis (LD) Worked as a
global development and health
campaigner at the Bill & Melinda
Gates Foundation. Campaigning
to prevent estate demolition
in Lambeth. **Sarah Bool** (C)
Property solicitor. Executive
member, Society of Conservative
Lawyers. **Jacqueline Bond**
(Green) Private tutor.

CONSTITUENCY PROFILE
Vauxhall has been held by
Labour MPs since its creation in
1983. Kate Hoey, an outspoken
Brexiteer, represented it from
1989 to 2019. It is an inner-
city south London seat, facing
Westminster across the Thames.
The constituency has an
ethnically diverse population,
with large Jamaican and
Ghanaian communities. It is
unequal; median pay is slightly
above the London average but
the area contains pockets of
deprivation. The seat is densely
populated, with one of the lowest
levels of home ownership in
the country and above-average
house prices.

EU REFERENDUM RESULT
22.4% Leave   Remain 77.6%

Wakefield

MAJORITY 3,358 (7.46%) CONSERVATIVE GAIN FROM LABOUR TURNOUT 64.15%

IMRAN AHMAD-KHAN
BORN Sep 6, 1973
MP 2019-

	Electorate	Share %	Change from 2017 %
	70,192		
I Ahmad-Khan C	21,283	47.27	+2.30
*M Creagh Lab	17,925	39.81	-9.86
P Wiltshire Brexit	2,725	6.05	
J Needle LD	1,772	3.94	+1.90
R Kett Yorkshire	868	1.93	-0.61
S Whyte Ind	454	1.01	+0.22

Launched campaign by skydiving into Wakefield in a retort to claims that he was a "parachute" candidate. Replaced Antony Calvert, a prospective candidate who stood down over past offensive social media posts. Worked on overseas security and peacebuilding operations for the government and the UN. Established a counter-terrorism NGO, the Trans-national Crisis Project. LGBT Conservatives issued a correction after he was included on a list of openly gay Tory MPs, explaining that his campaign team had mistakenly applied for their LGBT Conservative Candidates Fund. Ed: CIFE, Nice (PG Dip international relations); King's College London (BA war studies; AKC); Pushkin Institute, Moscow (Russian).

CHALLENGERS
Mary Creagh (Lab) MP for this seat, 2005-19. Confronted Jeremy Corbyn after election defeat and demanded that he apologise. Voted Remain. Shadow secretary: international development, 2014-15; transport, 2013-14; environment, 2010-13. Opposition assistant whip, 2010. Former lecturer in entrepreneurship. **Peter Wiltshire** (Brexit) Contested European parliament, 2019.

CONSTITUENCY PROFILE
Had returned a Labour MP at every election since 1932. The River Calder flows through this Yorkshire seat and it contains the city of Wakefield, the town of Horbury and a smattering of neighbouring villages. Predominantly white with a significant Pakistani community, the area has high unemployment and low home ownership.

EU REFERENDUM RESULT
62.8% Leave   Remain 37.2%

Wallasey

MAJORITY 18,322 (39.41%) LABOUR HOLD TURNOUT 70.11%

ANGELA EAGLE
BORN Feb 17, 1961
MP 1992-

	Electorate	Share %	Change from 2017 %
	66,310		
*A Eagle Lab	29,901	64.31	-7.14
J Baker C	11,579	24.91	+1.68
M York Brexit	2,037	4.38	
V Downie LD	1,843	3.96	+2.37
L Clough Green	1,132	2.43	+1.12

Former shadow cabinet member who launched an abortive leadership campaign in July 2016, withdrawing after losing to Owen Smith in a vote among Labour MPs. Accused Jeremy Corbyn of allowing an environment to flourish in which MPs opposed to his leadership faced abuse, 2016. Shadow cabinet: business secretary, 2015-16; leader of the Commons, 2011-15; chief secretary to the Treasury, 2010-11. Minister for pensions, 2009-10. Select cttees: Palace of Westminster, 2015; House of Commons commission, 2015. Whip, 1996-97. Told to "calm down, dear" by David Cameron at PMQs in 2011, sparking accusations of sexism. Twin sister of Maria Eagle (Garston & Halewood). Ed: Formby Comp; St John's Coll, Oxford (BA, PPE).

CHALLENGERS
James Baker (C) Comms adviser and former barrister. Member, LGBT Conservatives. Trustee for charity working to improve social mobility in PR industry. Sits on Tory Reform Group board. **Martin York** (Brexit) Worked as an RAF officer and a sales and marketing adviser.

CONSTITUENCY PROFILE
Angela Eagle won the seat from the Tories in 1992, who had held it continuously since 1918; by 2019 it had become a Labour stronghold. A diverse coastal Merseyside seat that suffers from severe deprivation. Unemployment is high, particularly among young people, and a large number of residents are in poor health. A £60 million regeneration project is under way in New Brighton and it has brought a new cinema, casino and hotel to the area.

EU REFERENDUM RESULT
49.9% Leave   Remain 50.1%

Walsall North

MAJORITY 11,965 (32.73%)   CONSERVATIVE HOLD   TURNOUT 54.42%

EDDIE HUGHES
BORN Oct 3, 1968
MP 2017-

Assistant whip, 2020-. PPS to Dominic Raab (Esher & Walton), 2018-19; supported his leadership campaign in 2019 before backing Boris Johnson. Works with the libertarian Conservative think tank Freer UK, jointly releasing a report advising the UK government to appoint a chief blockchain officer. Chaired excellence in the built environment APPG's inquiry into the need for a new homes ombudsman, announced by the government in October 2018. Select cttees: women and equalities, 2017-; consolidation bills, 2017-. Chairman, Walsall

	Electorate	Share %	from 2017 % Change
	67,177		
*E Hughes C	23,334	63.83	+14.20
G Ogilvie Lab	11,369	31.10	-11.71
J Gray LD	1,236	3.38	+1.84
M Wilson Green	617	1.69	

Housing Group. Deputy chief executive, YMCA Birmingham. Cllr, Walsall BC, 1999-2017. Ed: Handsworth GS; University of Glamorgan (civil engineering).

CHALLENGERS
Gill Ogilvie (Lab) Regional organiser, GMB. Led campaigns to protect children's services and lollipop wardens in the West Midlands. Spoke at counter-protest against the far-right English Defence League in Walsall, 2018. **Jennifer Gray** (LD) Director, Streetly Sports

and Community Association. Former teacher.

CONSTITUENCY PROFILE
Created in 1955, the seat had returned only Labour MPs until the election of Eddie Hughes. This West Midlands seat contains areas of severe deprivation. Wages are low and the number of people who own their own home is significantly smaller than regional and national levels. In addition, a considerable number of residents are unemployed and more than 34 per cent of the children living in the area are in poverty — 14 per cent higher than the national average.

EU REFERENDUM RESULT
74.2% Leave   Remain 25.8%

Walsall South

MAJORITY 3,456 (8.14%)   LABOUR HOLD   TURNOUT 62.44%

VALERIE VAZ
BORN Dec 7, 1954
MP 2010-

Privy councillor since 2019 and shadow leader of the Commons, 2016-. Leadership nominations: Sir Keir Starmer, 2020, Jeremy Corbyn, 2016, Andy Burnham, 2015, and Ed Miliband, 2010. Select cttees: environment, food and rural affairs, 2016; science and technology, 2015-16; regulatory reform, 2010-15; health, 2010-15. Solicitor and local government lawyer; set up community law firm, Townsend Vaz. Deputy district judge; joined government legal service in 2001, working in the Treasury and the Ministry of Justice. Presenter, BBC TV Network

	Electorate	Share %	from 2017 % Change
	68,024		
*V Vaz Lab	20,872	49.14	-8.23
G Bains C	17,416	41.01	+3.81
G Hughes Brexit	1,660	3.91	
P Harris LD	1,602	3.77	+2.44
J Macefield Green	634	1.49	
A Mehboob Ind	288	0.68	

East, 1987. Cllr, Ealing LBC, 1986-90. Sister of Keith Vaz, MP for Leicester East between 1987 and 2019. Ed: Twickenham County GS; Bedford Coll, University of London (BSc biochemistry).

CHALLENGERS
Gurjit Bains (C) Lobbyist. Cllr, Gravesham BC, 2015-. Worked for Vote Leave and Theresa May's leadership campaign. Parliamentary researcher for Priti Patel (Witham), 2014-15.

Gary Hughes (Brexit) Worked as a police officer, IT consultant and private investigator.

CONSTITUENCY PROFILE
This seat has elected Labour MPs since 1974, although the Conservatives came within 2,000 votes of gaining it in 2010. The seat covers the town centre and suburbs of Walsall in the West Midlands. Nearly a third of residents are Asian or Asian British, and about 3,500 are black. As with many former industrial towns, the local economy is relatively dependent on the retail and services sector. The constituency has a child poverty rate of 40 per cent.

EU REFERENDUM RESULT
61.6% Leave   Remain 38.4%

Walthamstow

MAJORITY 30,862 (63.85%)   LABOUR CO-OP HOLD   TURNOUT 68.79%

STELLA CREASY
BORN Apr 5, 1977
MP 2010-

	Electorate	Share %	Change from 2017 %
	70,268		
*S Creasy Lab Co-op	36,784	76.10	-4.48
S Adoh C	5,922	12.25	-1.82
M Chadha LD	2,874	5.95	+3.07
A Johns Green	1,733	3.59	+1.11
P Campbell Brexit	768	1.59	
D Longe CPA	254	0.53	

Vocal critic of Jeremy Corbyn; described the culture of the Labour movement as "toxic" in June 2019. Campaigned against unregulated payday lending. Tabled amendment to 2017 Queen's Speech to allow Northern Irish women to access free NHS abortions in England and Wales, resulting in the government's adoption of the policy. Nominated Lisa Nandy in the 2020 Labour leadership contest, having previously supported Owen Smith in 2016 and David Miliband in 2010. Came second in Labour deputy leadership contest in

2015. Voted Remain and for a second referendum. Shadow minister: business, 2013-15; Home Office, 2011-13. Former lobbyist, and researcher and speechwriter for Labour MPs. Cllr, Waltham Forest BC, 2002-06; mayor, 2003. Ed: Colchester HS; Magdalene Coll, Oxford (BA psychology); LSE (PhD psychology).

CHALLENGERS
Shade Adoh (C) Nurse. Cllr,

Wycombe DC, 2011-. Contested Doncaster North, 2017.

CONSTITUENCY PROFILE
A safe Labour constituency; the Conservatives last won it in 1987. This east London seat is densely populated, diverse and in parts deprived. Nearly a quarter of residents are Asian or Asian British and other ethnic minorities represent nearly 30 per cent of the population. There is also a large number of immigrants from the European Union. Income and earnings are much lower than the London average and there are low levels of home ownership; many residents live in social housing.

EU REFERENDUM RESULT
33.5% Leave   Remain 66.5%

Wansbeck

MAJORITY 814 (2.01%)   LABOUR HOLD   TURNOUT 63.96%

IAN LAVERY
BORN Jan 6, 1963
MP 2010-

	Electorate	Share %	Change from 2017 %
	63,339		
*I Lavery Lab	17,124	42.27	-15.06
J Gebhard C	16,310	40.26	+7.51
E Webley Brexit	3,141	7.75	
S Psallidas LD	2,539	6.27	+1.52
S Leyland Green	1,217	3.00	+1.32
M Flynn CPA	178	0.44	

Chairman of the Labour Party, 2017-, and shadow minister for the Cabinet Office, 2016-. Nominated Rebecca Long Bailey in the 2020 leadership contest, having supported Jeremy Corbyn, Andy Burnham and Ed Miliband in previous ballots. Select cttees: energy, 2010-15; Northern Irish affairs, 2010-11. Worked at Lynemouth and Ellington collieries. General secretary, National Union of Mineworkers, Northumberland Area, 1992-2010; president of the NUM, 2002-10. Cleared of wrongdoing after allegations that £75,000 from the union's

benevolent fund went on his mortgage. Apologised to the Commons after failing to declare the union's share in his home, 2013. Took an £89,887 redundancy payment from the union after leaving to become an MP. Ed: Youth Training Scheme (construction industry).

CHALLENGERS
Jack Gebhard (C) Cllr, Morpeth TC, 2017-; mayor, 2018-19. Spelt own middle name wrong on

nomination papers. Royal Navy reservist. Former teacher. Eden Webley (Brexit) Contested Northumbria University students' union presidential election. Stephen Psallidas (LD) Railway engineer.

CONSTITUENCY PROFILE
North of Newcastle, the constituency covers the towns of Ashington, Morpeth and Newbiggin. A former mining area; the final deep coalmine ceased operations in 2005. The three MPs elected since the seat's creation in 1983 have been former miners. A safe Labour seat until 2019, with majorities usually in five figures.

EU REFERENDUM RESULT
56.3% Leave   Remain 43.7%

Wantage

MAJORITY 12,653 (18.84%)   CONSERVATIVE HOLD   TURNOUT 73.92%

DAVID JOHNSTON
BORN Nov 27, 1981
MP 2019-

Chief executive of the Social
Mobility Foundation, 2009-
19; received OBE in 2018 for
services to social mobility
and education. Created Social
Mobility Employer Index,
ranking leading UK employers.
Director of Future, an education
and youth charity, 2006-09.
Brexiteer who opposed no-deal.
Former co-ordinator, Oxford
Access Scheme, 2003-06.
Commissioner, parliament's
Social Mobility Commission
2012-17. First in his family to
attend university. Ed: Oxford
University (BA modern history
and politics).

	Electorate	Share %	Change from 2017 %
	90,875		
D Johnston C	34,085	50.74	-3.44
R Benwell LD	21,432	31.91	+17.39
J Roberts Lab	10,181	15.16	-11.70
M Gray Ind	1,475	2.20	

CHALLENGERS
Richard Benwell (LD)
Chief executive, Wildlife &
Countryside Link. Environment
and sustainability expert.
Worked at Defra, 2018-19, as
a policy adviser to Michael
Gove (Surrey Heath). Lobbyist
for WWT and RSPB. **Jonny
Roberts** (Lab) Head of forward
planning and political research,
Westminster Forum Projects.
Member: GMB; Scientists for
Labour; Labour Campaign for
International Development;
Co-op. Contested Newbury, 2015.

CONSTITUENCY PROFILE
Wantage has been a
Conservative seat since its
creation in 1983 apart from
a brief spell when the Tory
MP Robert Jackson defected
to Labour in January 2005.
This rural Oxfordshire seat
encompasses Didcot, called "the
most normal town in England"
by statisticians, Faringdon and
Wantage. Wages exceed the
regional average, and there are
high levels of home ownership
and low unemployment. The
economy is centred on high-
tech industry; the constituency
contains the Diamond Light
Source synchrotron facility and
the Williams F1 team.

EU REFERENDUM RESULT

46.5% Leave   Remain 53.5%

Warley

MAJORITY 11,511 (30.91%)   LABOUR HOLD   TURNOUT 59.66%

JOHN SPELLAR
BORN Aug 5, 1947
MP 1992-; 1982-83

Shadow Foreign Office minister,
2010-15. Opposed Jeremy
Corbyn and his "band of Trots".
Only Labour MP to vote against
LGBT-inclusive education, 2019.
Did not declare Brexit stance;
voted against the withdrawal
agreements and against a second
referendum. MP for Birmingham
Northfield, 1982-83, winning
a by-election but losing at the
subsequent general election. Did
not publicise choice of leader,
2020. Assistant chief whip,
2008-10. Minister: Northern
Ireland, 2003-05; transport,
2001-03; armed forces, 1999-
2001. Defence select cttee,

	Electorate	Share %	Change from 2017 %
	62,421		
*J Spellar Lab	21,901	58.81	-8.35
C Kanneganti C	10,390	27.90	+1.73
M Cooper Brexit	2,469	6.63	
B Manley-Green LD	1,588	4.26	+2.33
K Downs Green	891	2.39	+1.01

2015-. Political officer of the
electricians' and plumbers'
union, 1969-92, a role in which
he fought against Bennism. Ed:
Dulwich Coll; St Edmund Hall,
Oxford (BA, PPE).

CHALLENGERS
Chandra Kanneganti (C) Cllr,
Stoke-on-Trent City C, 2019-.
GP. *Pulse* magazine's top 50
most influential GPs. National
chairman, British International
Doctors Association. **Michael
Cooper** (Brexit) Small business

owner. **Bryan Manley-Green**
(LD) Translator. Member, Black
Country Chamber of Commerce.

CONSTITUENCY PROFILE
The Tories won the predecessor
seat, Smethwick, in 1964 in a
campaign remembered for its
racism. Otherwise Warley has
been held by Labour since the
Second World War. Situated
to Birmingham's west, the area
suffers economic deprivation.
Earnings fall below the regional
average and unemployment is
more than double the national
rate. A quarter of residents
are Asian or Asian British and
there are large Muslim and Sikh
communities.

EU REFERENDUM RESULT

61.6% Leave   Remain 38.4%

Warrington North

MAJORITY 1,509 (3.23%)   LABOUR HOLD   TURNOUT 64.60%

CHARLOTTE NICHOLS
BORN Apr 5, 1991
MP 2019-

	Electorate	Share %	Change from 2017 %
	72,235		
C Nichols Lab	20,611	44.17	-12.22
W Maisey C	19,102	40.93	+4.30
D Crowther LD	3,071	6.58	+4.09
E Babade Brexit	2,626	5.63	
L McAteer Green	1,257	2.69	+1.42

GMB national research and policy officer. Research officer at the union of shopworkers, 2013-15. Worked on Jeremy Corbyn's leadership campaigns, 2016, 2015; nominated Emily Thornberry for leader in 2020. Visited Srebrenica as a Jewish faith representative as part of the 21st anniversary commemorations of the Bosnian genocide. Member, Unite. Former secretariat, adult social care APPG. Involved in Labour's Thirty by 2030 climate report. Jewish convert; attended Seder hosted by the radical leftist, anti-Zionist group Jewdas with Mr Corbyn in 2018, for which he received criticism. Ed: University of Liverpool (BA politics).

CHALLENGERS
Wendy Maisey (C) Founder and director of an IT company. Co-founder, Women Inspiring Women. Co-ordinated local Back Boris campaign. Contested European parliament, 2019. **David Crowther** (LD) Contested: Makerfield, 2019; Crewe & Nantwich, 2017. **Elizabeth Babade** (Brexit) Lawyer.

CONSTITUENCY PROFILE
Labour has held Warrington North since its creation in 1983 and the predecessor seat since 1945. Warrington is a former industrial town between Manchester and Liverpool. It has a buoyant economy: wages are relatively high and more than two thirds of residents are homeowners. The unemployment rate is below the national average. The constituency includes the large village of Culcheth and business parks in Birchwood that employ about 5,000 people. United Utilities, the UK's largest water company, is based in Warrington.

EU REFERENDUM RESULT

58.1% Leave   Remain 41.9%

Warrington South

MAJORITY 2,010 (3.25%)   CONSERVATIVE GAIN FROM LABOUR   TURNOUT 71.96%

ANDY CARTER
BORN Jan 25, 1974
MP 2019-

	Electorate	Share %	Change from 2017 %
	86,015		
A Carter C	28,187	45.54	+1.27
*F Rashid Lab	26,177	42.29	-6.09
R Bate LD	5,732	9.26	+3.87
C Aspinall Brexit	1,635	2.64	
K Hickson Soc Dem	168	0.27	

Radio journalist and brand consultant. Group managing director of Guardian Media Group radio, based in Manchester, 2010-14. Chairman of a regional advisory board on alternative provision in education. Magistrate, Merseyside Bench. Deputy chairman, Warrington Conservatives. Ed: Wharton Business School, University of Pennsylvania; University of Leicester (BSc economics).

CHALLENGERS
Faisal Rashid (Lab) MP for this seat, 2017-19. Criticised in 2018 for going on five overseas trips worth £10,000 paid for by NGOs, companies or overseas governments. Select cttees: arms export controls, 2017-19; international development, 2017-19. Former bank manager. Cllr, Warrington BC, 2011-17; mayor, 2016-17. Member, Unite. Trustee, St Rocco's Hospice. **Ryan Bate** (LD) Secondary school teacher. Cllr, Warrington BC, 2016-. Worked as a financial analyst. Fellow, Royal Geographical Society. Contested Halton, 2017.

CONSTITUENCY PROFILE
Covering most of Warrington and the large village of Lymm, this is a fairly affluent constituency. More than 75 per cent of constituents are homeowners, 95 per cent are white and earnings are well above the national average. Constituents are typically well educated. Although it is a marginal seat, it is not quite a bellwether: between 1992 and 2010 it was held by Labour, before being secured by David Cameron's Conservatives in two consecutive elections. In 2017, however, Warrington South was reclaimed by Labour with a 4.4 per cent swing.

EU REFERENDUM RESULT

51.1% Leave   Remain 48.9%

Warwick & Leamington

MAJORITY 789 (1.46%)   LABOUR HOLD   TURNOUT 70.97%

MATT WESTERN
BORN Nov 11, 1962
MP 2017-

Quiet backbencher. Nominated Emily Thornberry for the Labour Party leadership in the 2020 contest. Select committees: international trade, 2017-; housing, communities and local government, 2018-. Chairman, Parliamentary Campaign for Council Housing. Spent 24 years working in various management positions at Peugeot before becoming an MP. Founded Oxygency, a branding, marketing and business development consultancy. Cllr, Warwickshire CC, 2013-18. Ed: St Albans Sch; University of Bristol (BSc geography).

	Electorate	Share %	Change from 2017 %
	76,373		
*M Western Lab	23,718	43.76	-2.91
J Rankin C	22,929	42.30	-2.14
L Adam LD	4,995	9.22	+4.02
J Chilvers Green	1,536	2.83	+0.62
T Griffiths Brexit	807	1.49	
B Dhillon Ind	153	0.28	
X Bennett Soc Dem	67	0.12	

CHALLENGERS
Jack Rankin (C) Worked as a financial and business development analyst for Centrica. Cllr, Windsor & Maidenhead BC, 2015-. Contested Ashton-under-Lyne, 2017. **Louis Adam** (LD) Cllr, Stratford DC, 2019-. **Jonathan Chilvers** (Green) Cllr, Warwickshire CC, 2013-. Contested this seat, 2017. **Tim Griffiths** (Brexit) Party co-

ordinator for Coventry and Warwickshire. Said he joined Ukip after watching Nigel Farage on *Question Time*.

CONSTITUENCY PROFILE
Having elected Conservatives for more than 90 years, this seat was held by Labour from 1997 to 2010. The 2019 election was the first time Labour had held it while in opposition. The neighbouring towns of Warwick and Royal Leamington Spa account for more than four fifths of the population. More than 9,000 students live in the area, which contains the University of Warwick. Residents tend to have high incomes.

EU REFERENDUM RESULT
41.6% Leave   Remain 58.4%

Warwickshire North

MAJORITY 17,956 (39.11%)   CONSERVATIVE HOLD   TURNOUT 65.34%

CRAIG TRACEY
BORN Aug 21, 1974
MP 2015-

Hard-headed former insurance broker. Brexiteer. Select cttees: business and energy, 2016-; education, 2015-16; business and innovation, 2015-16. Co-chairman, insurance and financial services APPG. Board member, Southern Staffordshire Employment and Skills Board. West Midlands co-ordinator, Conservative Voice, 2012-15. Senior partner, Dunelm Insurance Brokers. Worked as a director of Politically Correct, a political consultancy. Trustee, Lichfield Garrick Theatre, 2012-16. Chairman, North Warwickshire

	Electorate	Share %	Change from 2017 %
	70,271		
*C Tracey C	30,249	65.88	+8.95
C Breeze Lab Co-op	12,293	26.77	-12.12
R Whelan LD	2,069	4.51	+2.33
J Platt Green	1,303	2.84	+0.85

Conservative Association, 2012-14. Family comes from a mining background near Durham. Ed: Framwellgate Moor Sch.

CHALLENGERS
Claire Breeze (Lab Co-op) Unison regional organiser. Cllr, Coleshill TC, 2016-19. **Richard Whelan** (LD) Lib Dem campaigner since the age of 14. Born with cerebral palsy; spent six months as a child receiving physical therapy at the Peto Institute, Budapest. **James Platt** (Green) Postgraduate student.

CONSTITUENCY PROFILE
A Labour-Conservative marginal to the northeast of Birmingham. It was won by Labour in 1992 but since 2010 has returned Conservative MPs. The seat encompasses the towns of Atherstone and Bedworth. Given its proximity to the second largest city in the UK, the constituency is a haven for commuters. It is relatively affluent: nearly three quarters of constituents are homeowners and comparatively few live in social housing. There is a considerable number — somewhere in the region of 10,000 — of residents who are aged 65 or above.

EU REFERENDUM RESULT
67.8% Leave   Remain 32.2%

Washington & Sunderland West

MAJORITY 3,723 (9.92%)   LABOUR HOLD   TURNOUT 56.60%

SHARON HODGSON
BORN Apr 1, 1966
MP 2005-

Northern Rock accountant turned Labour organiser. Submitted a private member's bill in 2008 that became the SEN Act. Shadow minister: public health, 2016-; education, 2015-16, 2010-13; equalities, 2013-15. Resigned from shadow cabinet in 2016 over Jeremy Corbyn's leadership. Supported Lisa Nandy, 2020. Opposition whip, 2010; assistant whip, 2009-10. PPS to: Dawn Primarolo, 2008-09; Bob Ainsworth, 2007-08; Liam Byrne, 2006-07. Passionate about women's issues and health; chairwoman, ovarian cancer APPG. Ed: Heathfield

	Electorate	Share %	Change from 2017 %
	66,278		
*S Hodgson Lab	15,941	42.49	-18.23
V Allen C	12,218	32.57	+3.74
H Brown Brexit	5,439	14.50	
C West LD	2,071	5.52	+3.15
M Chantkowski Green	1,005	2.68	+1.41
K Jenkins Ukip	839	2.24	-4.57

Senior HS, Gateshead; Newcastle Coll (HEFC English); Trade Union Congress Academy (TUC Dip Labour Party organising).

CHALLENGERS
Valerie Allen (C)
Businesswoman. Received an MBE in 2015 for services to the community and business. Contested: Warrington North, 2017; Sefton Central, 2015; St Helens South & Whiston, 2010. **Howard Brown** (Brexit)

Teacher. Regional NUT leader for 20 years. **Carlton West** (LD) Member, Friends of the Earth.

CONSTITUENCY PROFILE
Created in 2010, this has been a safe Labour seat for the past decade. Labour's dominance in the area is longstanding: the seat's various predecessors have mostly returned Labour MPs since the Second World War, although Sunderland South had a Conservative MP in 1953-64. Comprising Washington and Sunderland's western suburbs, this was a mining area, but the Japanese car company Nissan is now a significant employer and has a factory in the seat.

EU REFERENDUM RESULT
61.9% Leave   Remain 38.1%

Watford

MAJORITY 4,433 (7.63%)   CONSERVATIVE HOLD   TURNOUT 69.66%

DEAN RUSSELL
BORN Aug 8, 1976
MP 2019-

Founder of the leadership and pitch consultancy firm Win That Pitch. Previous senior roles advising global brands, chief executives, governments and philanthropists. Writes for publications including the *Health Service Journal* and *Third Sector* magazine. Author of *How To Win: The Ultimate Profession Pitch Guide* and four children's books. Former cllr, St Albans DC; chairman, health and wellbeing partnership. Contested: Luton South, 2017; Luton North, 2015. Ed: De Montfort University (BSc physics and business studies; MPhil physics).

	Electorate	Share %	Change from 2017 %
	83,359		
D Russell C	26,421	45.50	-0.11
C Ostrowski Lab	21,988	37.87	-4.17
I Stotesbury LD	9,323	16.06	+6.95
M McGetrick Soc Dem	333	0.57	

CHALLENGERS
Chris Ostrowski (Lab)
Businessman; runs an English language training company. Grandson of a Polish airman who fought with the RAF in the Second World War. Contested: this seat, 2017; European parliament elections in 2014. **Ian Stotesbury** (LD) Engineer working in spacecraft design. Environmentalist. Cllr, Watford BC, 2018-. Contested this seat, 2017. **Michael McGetrick** (Soc Dem) IT and software solutions consultant, working with public

and private sector clients. Party is Eurosceptic and centrist.

CONSTITUENCY PROFILE
A bellwether since 1979, Watford returned a Conservative MP throughout the 1980s until Labour won the seat in 1997. Its former MP, Richard Harrington, had the Conservative whip removed in September 2019 after he voted against Boris Johnson's government over Brexit. Part of the Hertfordshire commuter belt, the seat also consists of several villages. Watford is home to several large business headquarters, such as JD Wetherspoon, and wages exceed the regional average.

EU REFERENDUM RESULT
51.2% Leave   Remain 48.8%

Waveney

MAJORITY 18,002 (35.20%) **CONSERVATIVE HOLD** **TURNOUT 61.76%**

PETER ALDOUS
BORN Aug 26, 1961
MP 2010-

Suffolk born and raised, from a farming background. Worked on the family farm and as a chartered surveyor. Backed Michael Gove for leader in 2019. Select cttees: draft reg bill, 2019; environmental audit, 2010-17. Campaigner for business rates reform. Member: Countryside Alliance; Royal Institute of Chartered Surveyors; Farmers' Club. Contested this seat, 2005. Cllr: Suffolk CC, 2001-05; deputy leader of the Conservative group; Waveney DC, 1999-2002. Squash player, Ipswich Town FC season ticket holder. Ed: Harrow; Reading (BSc land management).

	Electorate	Share %	from 2017 %	Change
	82,791			
*P Aldous C	31,778	62.15	+7.77	
S Barker Lab	13,776	26.94	-9.94	
E Brambley-Crawshaw Green	2,727	5.33	+2.80	
H Korfanty LD	2,603	5.09	+3.17	

CHALLENGERS
Sonia Barker (Lab) Supply teacher. Cllr, Waveney DC, 2013-; Labour group leader; opposition spokeswoman for education and skills. Cllr, East Suffolk C, 2011-18. Contested this seat, 2017.
Elfrede Brambley-Crawshaw (Green) Beccles town mayor, 2018-19. Cllr: Beccles TC, 2015-; Suffolk CC, 2017-. Chairwoman of local neighbourhood plan.
Helen Korfanty (LD) Solicitor. Contested Bury St Edmunds in the 2017 election.

CONSTITUENCY PROFILE
Created in 1983, Waveney is a bellwether seat. Since regaining the constituency from Labour in 2010, however, the Conservatives have increased their majority from an initial 769 to more than 9,000 in 2017, and almost double that in the 2019 election. Situated in the northeast of Suffolk, it includes the coastal town of Lowestoft, which was once a fishing port and home to Shell's southern operations but is now the UK's renewable energy capital. The constituency has lower wages than elsewhere in the region. Almost a quarter of its residents are aged 65 or above.

EU REFERENDUM RESULT
63.4% Leave   Remain 36.6%

Wealden

MAJORITY 25,655 (42.12%) **CONSERVATIVE HOLD** **TURNOUT 73.35%**

NUSRAT GHANI
BORN Sep 1, 1972
MP 2015-

First female Muslim minister to speak from the House of Commons dispatch box. Parly under-sec, transport, between 2018 and her surprise sacking in the February 2020 reshuffle. Proposed legislation to ban the term "honour killing". Government whip, 2019-20; assistant whip, 2018-19. Selected by 400 members of the public in an open primary before the 2015 election. Backed Jeremy Hunt for leader, 2019. Worked in communications and fundraising for the BBC World Service. Contested Birmingham Ladywood, 2010. Ed: Bordesley

	Electorate	Share %	from 2017 %	Change
	83,038			
*N Ghani C	37,043	60.82	-0.42	
C Bowers LD	11,388	18.70	+8.31	
A Smith Lab	9,377	15.40	-6.76	
G Taylor Green	3,099	5.09	+1.85	

Green Girls' Sch; Leeds University (MA international relations).

CHALLENGERS
Chris Bowers (LD) Tennis commentator. Co-editor of a cross-party book, *The Alternative*, with Lisa Nandy (Wigan) and Caroline Lucas (Brighton Pavilion). Founder, Environmental Transport Association. Contested: this seat, 2017, 2010; Brighton Pavilion, 2015; European parliament, 2019. **Angela Smith** (Lab) Cllr,

Uckfield TC, 2019-. Domestic violence campaigner. Jo Cox Women in Leadership graduate.

CONSTITUENCY PROFILE
A safe Conservative seat since its creation in 1983, returning MPs with majorities of well over 10,000 votes. Situated in East Sussex, the seat covers the towns of Uckfield, Crowborough and Hailsham. These are commuter centres, although there is a sizeable retired community. Residents are more likely than average to have been educated to degree level, home ownership rates are above average, and earnings are much higher than elsewhere in the country.

EU REFERENDUM RESULT
52.8% Leave   Remain 47.2%

Weaver Vale

MAJORITY 562 (1.11%)   **LABOUR HOLD**   TURNOUT 71.88%

MIKE AMESBURY
BORN May 6, 1969
MP 2017-

	Electorate	Share %	from 2017 % Change
	70,551		
*M Amesbury Lab	22,772	44.90	-6.60
A Wordsworth C	22,210	43.80	+0.06
D Parker LD	3,300	6.51	+3.30
N Goulding Brexit	1,380	2.72	
P Bowers Green	1,051	2.07	+0.52

Adviser to Andy Burnham and Angela Rayner before entering parliament himself. Shadow employment minister, 2018-. Nominated Sir Keir Starmer, 2020. Director, City South Manchester Housing Trust, 2010-17. Cllr, Manchester City C, 2006-17. Labour National Policy Forum elected representative, 2010-15. Former convenor for Unison, working for careers services in Manchester. Apologised in 2019 for sharing an antisemitic caricature on Facebook in 2013. Ed: University of Bradford (BA sociology, psychology, politics, economics);

University of Central England (Dip careers guidance).

CHALLENGERS
Adam Wordsworth (C) Greater Manchester police officer for nine years, leaving in 2017 to enter politics. Served as parliamentary adviser to William Wragg (Hazel Grove). Cllr, Frodsham TC. **Daniela Parker** (LD) Spent 13 years working in prison rehabilitation services. Area manager for a national charity supporting victims and

witnesses in criminal court.
Nicholas Goulding (Brexit) Founded local taxi business in Knutsford. Territorial Army veteran.

CONSTITUENCY PROFILE
A marginal seat in the North West created in 1997 and held by Labour until the Conservatives won it in 2010 and 2015 by less than a thousand votes. Labour won it back in 2017. The seat consists of part of Runcorn as well as Frodsham and Northwich. It was home until 2014 to a large Tata-owned chemical plant. Residents are mostly middle class and earnings outstrip the UK average.

EU REFERENDUM RESULT
50.6% Leave   Remain 49.4%

Wellingborough

MAJORITY 18,540 (35.71%)   **CONSERVATIVE HOLD**   TURNOUT 64.28%

PETER BONE
BORN Oct 19, 1952
MP 2005-

	Electorate	Share %	from 2017 % Change
	80,764		
*P Bone C	32,277	62.18	+4.74
A Watts Lab	13,737	26.46	-7.57
S Austin LD	4,078	7.86	+4.51
M Turner-Hawes Green	1,821	3.51	+1.71

Right-winger and frequent rebel known for quoting to David Cameron at PMQs the breakfast-table remarks of his wife. Hardline Brexiteer involved in Leave Means Leave campaign. Supported Boris Johnson for leader, 2019. Select cttees: panel of chairs, 2010-17; backbench business, 2015-16, 2010-12; health, 2007-10; statutory instruments, 2005-10; trade and industry, 2005-07. Investigated by the police for an alleged £100,000 benefit fraud concerning care home fees for his mother-in-law in February 2014. No charges were brought and the case was

dropped because, prosecutors said, "no element of dishonesty could be proved". Cricketer and marathon runner. Ed: Westcliff-on-Sea GS.

CHALLENGERS
Andrea Watts (Lab) Works for a major logistics company. Cllr, Wellingborough BC, 2011-. Trade unionist. Dedicated supporter of equal rights as a member of the LGBT community and a carer for her disabled brother. **Suzanna Austin** (LD) Small business owner. Contested:

Kettering, 2017; European parliament, 2019. Helped to uncover a waiting-list scandal at Kettering General Hospital.

CONSTITUENCY PROFILE
Alhough it produced a large Conservative majority in 2019, Labour held this constituency between 1997 and 2005, having also won it in several successive elections after the Second World War, and in 1964 and 1966. Peter Bone's majorities have all been in five figures since 2010. The Nottinghamshire seat includes the towns of Wellingborough and Rushden. Once famous for its shoemaking, it is now a retailing centre.

EU REFERENDUM RESULT
63.0% Leave   Remain 37.0%

Wells

MAJORITY 9,991 (16.21%)   **CONSERVATIVE HOLD**   **TURNOUT 72.86%**

JAMES HEAPPEY
BORN Jan 30, 1981
MP 2015-

Defence procurment minister since 2019. Parliamentary private secretary to Boris Johnson, whom he had backed for leader. Previously held the same role for Chris Grayling (Epsom & Ewell). Army major, serving with The Rifles in Afghanistan, Northern Ireland and Kenya; MoD civil servant; researcher for Liam Fox (Somerset North). Apologised for telling a schoolgirl to "f*** off back to Scotland" after she said she would vote for Scottish independence in a second referendum. Voted Remain but backed the Brexit deals.

	Electorate	Share %	Change from 2017 %
	84,124		
*J Heappey C	33,336	54.39	+4.28
T Munt LD	23,345	38.09	+0.44
K McKenzie Lab	4,034	6.58	-5.14
D Dobbs Ind	373	0.61	
S Quatermass Motherworld	207	0.34	

Vice-president, Association for Decentralised Energy. Ed: University of Birmingham (BA politics); RMA Sandhurst.

CHALLENGERS
Tessa Munt (LD) MP for this seat, 2010-15. PPS to Vince Cable, 2012-15; quit to vote against fracking. Contested: this seat, 2005; Suffolk South, 2001; Ipswich by-election, 2001. Revealed in 2014 that she was a survivor of child sexual abuse. Cllr, Somerset CC, 2017-. **Kama**

McKenzie (Lab) Had been working in young person and family services for the past 15 years.

CONSTITUENCY PROFILE
Since the 1970s Wells has been a marginal seat contested closely by the Conservatives and the Liberal Party, then after 1988 the Liberal Democrats. Tessa Munt finally won for the Lib Dems in 2010. A rural Somerset constituency containing England's smallest city, Wells, the coastal resort of Burnham-on-Sea and Glastonbury. Home to several landmarks, notably Cheddar Gorge and Glastonbury Tor; tourism is a vital industry.

EU REFERENDUM RESULT
53.6% Leave   Remain 46.4%

Welwyn Hatfield

MAJORITY 10,955 (21.05%)   **CONSERVATIVE HOLD**   **TURNOUT 69.50%**

GRANT SHAPPS
BORN Sep 14, 1968
MP 2005-

Transport secretary, 2019-. Backed Boris Johnson for leader, 2019. Resigned as international development minister in November 2015 over his appointment of Mark Clarke, who was at the centre of a Conservative Party bullying scandal. Mr Clarke has denied all the allegations against him. Revealed, in 2015, to have done business under the name Michael Green while an MP. Minister: international development, 2015; without portfolio, Cabinet Office, 2012-15; housing, 2010-12. Shadow housing and planning minister,

	Electorate	Share %	Change from 2017 %
	74,892		
*G Shapps C	27,394	52.63	+1.58
R Newbigging Lab	16,439	31.58	-5.20
P Zukowskyj LD	6,602	12.68	+5.26
O Sayers Green	1,618	3.11	+1.49

2007-10. Cousin of Mick Jones, the lead guitarist in the Clash. Ed: Cassio Coll, Watford; Manchester Polytechnic (HND business and finance).

CHALLENGERS
Rosie Newbigging (Lab) Works in youth services. Campaigned to stop the closure of the New QE2 urgent care centre. **Paul Zukowskyj** (LD) Cllr: Welwyn Hatfield BC, 2016-; Hertfordshire CC, 2013-, shadow deputy leader. Contested this constituency in the 2010 general election.

CONSTITUENCY PROFILE
Labour held this seat from its creation in 1974 until 1979 and again between 1997 and 2005, but it has otherwise been Conservative. Located in Hertfordshire and bordering Enfield, Welwyn Hatfield is home to many commuters into London. It also contains the University of Hertfordshire and a significant student population. Welwyn Garden City, one of only two garden cities in the country, is in the centre of the constituency and houses about 50,000 people. An extremely high proportion of residents live in social housing, with low levels of owner occupation.

EU REFERENDUM RESULT
52.8% Leave   Remain 47.2%

Wentworth & Dearne

MAJORITY 2,165 (5.21%)   LABOUR HOLD   TURNOUT 55.75%

JOHN HEALEY
BORN Feb 13, 1960
MP 1997-

	Electorate	Share %	Change from 2017 %
	74,536		
*J Healey Lab	16,742	40.29	-24.67
E Barley C	14,577	35.08	+3.80
S Cavell Brexit	7,019	16.89	
J Middleton LD	1,705	4.10	+0.33
L Brown Yorkshire	1,201	2.89	
D Bettney Soc Dem	313	0.75	

A Brownite, popular in the parliamentary party, who despite supporting the failed attempt to oust Jeremy Corbyn in 2016, has served as shadow housing secretary from 2016 and as a shadow housing minister, 2015-16. Supported Sir Keir Starmer's leadership bid, 2020. Shadow health secretary, 2010-11. Only rebels on procedure. Voted Remain. Minister: housing, 2009-10; local government, 2007-09. Treasury: financial secretary, 2005-07; economic secretary, 2002-05. PPS to Gordon Brown, 1999-2001. Edited *The House* magazine. GMB member;

former TUC campaigns director. Contested Ryedale, 1992. Ed: Lady Lumley's CS, Pickering; St Peter's Sch, York; Christ's Coll, Cambridge (BA social and political science).

CHALLENGERS
Emily Barley (C) Communications consultant. Chairwoman, Conservatives for Liberty. Co-authored the Due Process report into Human Rights abuses in European

Arrest Warrant member states, campaigning for reform of the European Arrest Warrant. Stephen Cavell (Brexit) Private equity executive. Janice Middleton (LD) Head teacher.

CONSTITUENCY PROFILE
Including its predecessor seats, Wentworth & Dearne has been held by Labour for more than a century. The party's majority in 2019, however, was almost a seventh of what it was in 2017. Formerly a significant coalmining region but since the industry's decline in the 1980s manufacturing, construction, processing and retail have become the dominant sectors.

EU REFERENDUM RESULT
70.3% Leave   Remain 29.7%

West Bromwich East

MAJORITY 1,593 (4.43%)   CONSERVATIVE GAIN FROM LABOUR   TURNOUT 57.92%

NICOLA RICHARDS
BORN Dec 19, 1994
MP 2019-

	Electorate	Share %	Change from 2017 %
	62,111		
N Richards C	16,804	46.71	+8.47
I Dogus Lab	15,211	42.28	-15.69
C Lucas Brexit	1,475	4.10	
A Graham LD	1,313	3.65	+2.05
M Redding Green	627	1.74	+0.38
G Galloway Ind	489	1.36	+0.53
C Rankine Yeshua	56	0.16	

Specialist in adult social care, health and children's services. Worked for Chris Kelly, Mike Wood (Dudley South) and Margot James, 2013-17. Midlands manager, Jewish Leadership Council, 2017. Chairwoman, Young Conservatives, 2015-19; deputy chairwoman, Dudley South group, 2018-19. Content creator for West Midlands mayor, 2018-19. Cllr, Dudley MBC, 2015-; overview and scrutiny management committee chairwoman, 2019-. Born and bred in the Black Country. Ed: University of Birmingham (BA political science).

CHALLENGERS
Ibrahim Dogus (Lab) Selected after the former Labour deputy leader Tom Watson, MP for West Bromwich East since 2001, stood down. Cllr, Lambeth LBC, 2018-; mayor of Lambeth, 2019-. Restaurateur; founder, British Kebab Awards. Gained media attention for providing food free of charge for emergency workers during 2017 Westminster Bridge attack. Targeted by the

far right after printing "Brexit is bad. Immigrants make Britain great" on his customer receipts. Contested Cities of London & Westminster, 2017.

CONSTITUENCY PROFILE
The fifth biggest Labour majority to be overturned by the Conservatives at this election. Tom Watson, Labour's deputy leader in 2015-19, had held it by more than 7,000 votes in 2017. He stepped down at the 2019 election. Labour had also represented the seat since its creation in 1974, and the precedessor seat of West Bromwich since 1935. One in five residents is of Asian descent.

EU REFERENDUM RESULT
68.2% Leave   Remain 31.8%

West Bromwich West

MAJORITY 3,799 (11.02%)　　　CONSERVATIVE GAIN FROM LABOUR　　　TURNOUT 53.36%

SHAUN BAILEY
BORN Jul 22, 1992
MP 2019-

Trainee solicitor at Barclays, 2019-. Born and raised in the West Midlands in a single parent family. Worked in a number of paralegal roles. French speaker and self-taught Welsh speaker. Signatory, Stand Up for Brexit. Cllr, Chetwynd, Aston & Woodcote PC, 2019-. Contested Gloucestershire CC, 2017. Ed: Aberystwyth University (BA law with French); University of the West of England (LLM legal practice course).

CHALLENGERS
James Cunningham (Lab)
Labour community organiser

	Electorate	Share %	from 2017 %	Change
	64,576			
S Bailey C	17,419	50.55	+10.85	
J Cunningham Lab	13,620	39.53	-12.53	
F D'Aulerio Brexit	1,841	5.34		
F Clucas LD	915	2.66	+1.73	
K Williams Green	664	1.93	+1.03	

and alleged former member of the Alliance for Workers Liberty, a Trotskyist group that aimed to end capitalism. Previously a Momentum activist in south Birmingham. Subject of a number of outstanding complaints made to the party relating to allegations of bullying. **Franco D'Aulerio** (Brexit) Son of Italian immigrants. Career in banking; leading global treasury specialist. **Flo Clucas** (LD) Councillor in Liverpool for more than 25 years,

1986-2012. Received OBE in 2005 for community services to the people of Merseyside.

CONSTITUENCY PROFILE
A Labour seat since its creation in 1974 until falling to the Conservatives at the 2019 election. Its first MP, Betty Boothroyd, served as the first and only female Speaker from 1992 until 2000. Made up of Tipton, Wednesbury and Oldbury, towns famed for coal mines, iron foundries and steel mills. About 15 per cent of residents are Asian or Asian British. Home ownership is low and the median income is lower than in West Bromwich East.

EU REFERENDUM RESULT
68.7% Leave　　　Remain 31.3%

West Ham

MAJORITY 32,388 (53.80%)　　　LABOUR HOLD　　　TURNOUT 61.46%

LYN BROWN
BORN Apr 13, 1960
MP 2005-

Acting shadow home secretary for a single day in 2017, when Diane Abbott stood aside on the eve of the election due to ill health. Shadow minister: Treasury, 2018-; policing, 2016-17; Home Office, 2015-17; communities, 2013-15. Opposition whip, 2010-13; assistant government whip, 2009-10. Former social worker. Member: Co-op Party; Fabian Society. Cllr, Newham LBC, 1988-2005. Married her husband in the Commons chapel in 2008, presided over by the former vicar Chris Bryant (Rhondda). Contested Wanstead &

	Electorate	Share %	from 2017 %	Change
	97,942			
*L Brown Lab	42,181	70.07	-6.68	
S Kumar C	9,793	16.27	+0.06	
E O'Casey LD	4,161	6.91	+3.89	
D Keeling Green	1,780	2.96	+1.38	
E Stockdale Brexit	1,679	2.79		
P Jobson CPA	463	0.77	+0.19	
H Kamran Communities	143	0.24		

Woodford, 1992. Ed: Plashet CS; Whitelands Coll, Roehampton (BA English and religion; president, students' union).

CHALLENGERS
Sara Kumar (C) Events manager at the Centre for Social Justice, 2018-. **Eimear O'Casey** (LD) Magistrate. Advocate for criminal justice reform. Analyst on the former Soviet Union for a political risk consultancy.

CONSTITUENCY PROFILE
Labour representation in this east London seat has been continual since 1922, when the party gained the predecessor seat of Stratford from the Conservatives. One of the most diverse places in the country; more than a third of residents are Asian and nearly a quarter are black. Three quarters of its population are aged 45 or under. Suffered from the collapse of the dockers' industry in the East End but the 2012 London Olympics brought signficant investment, with the Olympic Park built in the seat. The Olympic Stadium is now the home of West Ham United Football Club.

EU REFERENDUM RESULT
48.0% Leave　　　Remain 52.0%

Westminster North

MAJORITY 10,759 (25.07%)   **LABOUR HOLD**   TURNOUT 65.49%

KAREN BUCK
BORN Aug 30, 1958
MP 1997-

Electorate	Share %	Change from 2017 %
65,519		
*K Buck Lab	23,240 54.16	-5.74
J Macfarlane C	12,481 29.09	4.23
G Lee LD	5,593 13.03	+7.83
H Robinson Green	1,064 2.48	+1.11
C Parvin Brexit	418 0.97	
G Fajardo Palacios CPA	115 0.27	

Private member's bill came into force as the Homes (Fitness for Human Habitation) Act in March 2019. Supported Sir Keir Starmer, 2020. Not afraid to rebel against party leadership; voted against the Iraq War, renewal of Trident and the triggering of Article 50. Declined to take up role in whips' office after being appointed without consultation in 2001. PPS to Ed Miliband (Doncaster North), 2013-15. Shadow minister: education, 2011-13; work and pensions, 2010-11. Parly undersec, transport, 2005-06. Named Child Poverty Action Group's

MP of the year, 2009. Disability and public health worker. Cllr, Westminster City C, 1990-97. Ed: Chelmsford County HS; LSE (BSc economics).

CHALLENGERS
Jamie Macfarlane (C)
Entrepreneur helping students to start their own businesses. Studied at Stanford Business school and worked in Silicon Valley. Democracy activist and senior adviser to the Cambodian

opposition leader Sam Rainsy during elections in 2013. Environmentalist and animal welfare campaigner. **George Lee** (LD) Former chief inspector at the Metropolitan Police.

CONSTITUENCY PROFILE
A marginal seat re-created in 2010 that swung significantly to Labour in 2017. The most densely populated seat in the Commons. Ethnically diverse. More than a third of households rent privately. Residents are more likely than average to have highly skilled jobs, and by median income Westminster North constituents are among the best paid in the country.

EU REFERENDUM RESULT
33.7% Leave   Remain 66.3%

Westmorland & Lonsdale

MAJORITY 1,934 (3.67%)   **LIB DEM HOLD**   TURNOUT 77.76%

TIM FARRON
BORN May 27, 1970
MP 2005-

Electorate	Share %	Change from 2017 %
67,789		
*T Farron LD	25,795 48.94	+3.11
J Airey C	23,861 45.27	+0.94
P Black Lab	2,293 4.35	-4.90
S Bolton Brexit	763 1.45	

Leader of the Liberal Democrats, 2015-17. Coalition critic who did not hold a ministerial brief during his party's time in government. Rebelled to vote against tuition fee rise and the bedroom tax. Leadership during the 2017 election was dogged by questions about his Christian beliefs and attitudes towards gay sex and abortion. Lib Dem spokesman: work and pensions, communities and local government, housing and planning, northern powerhouse, 2019-. Worked in higher education before entering politics. Contested: this

seat, 2001; South Ribble, 1997; Durham North West, 1992. Lib Dem party president, 2011-14. Ed: Lostock Hall HS; Runshaw Coll; Newcastle University (BA politics).

CHALLENGERS
James Airey (C) Prize-winning sheep farmer. Cllr, Cumbria CC, 2009-. Contested: this seat in 2017; Morecambe & Lunesdale, 2005; Barrow & Furness, 2001. Amateur clay pigeon shooter. **Phillip Black** (Lab) Self-employed professional

photographer. Cllr, Lancaster City C, 2019-.

CONSTITUENCY PROFILE
Situated in the south of Cumbria, Westmorland & Lonsdale was a Conservative seat from its creation in 1983 until Tim Farron narrowly gained it for the Liberal Democrats in 2005. Having subsequently won majorities close to 10,000, Mr Farron held the seat by only 777 votes in 2017. Almost a quarter of residents are aged 65 or above and less than a quarter are under the age of 25. The constituency contains a chunk of the Lake District and the local economy benefits from tourism.

EU REFERENDUM RESULT
47.1% Leave   Remain 52.9%

Weston-Super-Mare

MAJORITY 17,121 (30.78%)   CONSERVATIVE HOLD   TURNOUT 67.39%

JOHN PENROSE
BORN Jun 22, 1964
MP 2005-

Millionaire publisher. Involved in planning for the Olympics and Queen's Diamond Jubilee as tourism and heritage minister, 2010-12. Minister: Northern Ireland, 2018-19; constitutional reform, 2015-16. Government whip, 2013-15. Former Logotron chairman. Outspoken advocate of an energy price cap. Voted Remain but has loyally supported government Brexit policy since. Backed Jeremy Hunt for leader, 2019. Contested this seat, 2001; Ealing Southall, 1997. Ed: Ipswich Sch; Downing Coll, Cambridge (BA law); Columbia University (MBA).

	Electorate	Share %	Change from 2017 %
	82,526		
*J Penrose C	31,983	57.51	+4.36
T Taylor Lab	14,862	26.72	-5.96
P Keating LD	6,935	12.47	+3.30
S Basu Green	1,834	3.30	+1.72

CHALLENGERS
Tim Taylor (Lab) Human resources manager, Lloyds Banking Group. Cllr, Weston TC, 2011-15, 2003-07; finance and personnel committee; leader of Labour group. Contested this seat in the previous two general elections. **Patrick Keating** (LD) Cllr, North Somerset DC, 2019-. Manager, Honda Motor Europe, 2016-. School governor and charity trustee. **Suneil Basu** (Green) Computer science teacher. Artist and keen triathlete.

CONSTITUENCY PROFILE
Conservative-held for most of the 20th century, Weston-Super-Mare was gained by the Liberal Democrats in 1997 and the party represented the seat for eight years before the Conservatives won it back. In 2019 the Conservatives secured their largest majority in the seat since 1979. The Somerset town, home to about 76,000 people, has been a popular seaside resort since the early 19th century, although tourism declined significantly in the second half of the 20th century. Median wages are well below average: £50 less per week than the figure for the South West as a whole.

EU REFERENDUM RESULT
57.2% Leave   Remain 42.8%

Wigan

MAJORITY 6,728 (14.94%)   LABOUR HOLD   TURNOUT 59.52%

LISA NANDY
BORN Aug 9, 1979
MP 2010-

Labour leadership candidate who was encouraged to stand by some soft-left members in both the 2015 and 2016 elections, before eventually putting her name on the ballot for the 2020 contest. Shadow energy secretary, 2016. Shadow minister: Cabinet Office, 2013-15; education, 2013. Set up a think tank called Centre for Towns, 2018. Career in third sector before entering parliament. Parliamentary researcher to Neil Gerrard (Walthamstow, 1992-2010). Cllr, Hammersmith & Fulham LBC, 2006-10. Remainer but voted for Boris Johnson's

	Electorate	Share %	Change from 2017 %
	75,680		
*L Nandy Lab	21,042	46.72	-15.49
A Williams C	14,314	31.78	+3.28
W Malloy Brexit	5,959	13.23	
S Thomas LD	2,428	5.39	+3.46
P Jacobs Green	1,299	2.88	+1.30

Brexit deal. Father was a Marxist academic from Calcutta and her grandfather, Frank Byers, was a Liberal MP. Ed: Parrs Wood Comp, Manchester; Newcastle upon Tyne (BA politics); Birkbeck Coll, London (MSc politics and government).

CHALLENGERS
Ashley Williams (C) Cllr, Lincolnshire CC, 2017-. Chaired local party of Sir Edward Leigh (Gainsborough). Fundraising and development manager, St Mark

Universal Care, a healthcare charity. **William Malloy** (Brexit) Public sector accountant.

CONSTITUENCY PROFILE
Continually held by Labour since 1918, but the party's majority fell to its lowest since 1931 in the 2019 election. In Greater Manchester, it was once an important mill town and coalmining district, its working conditions the subject of George Orwell's *The Road to Wigan Pier*, but these industries declined in the later 20th century. Food manufacturing has replaced some of those lost jobs, but median wages remain lower than the national average.

EU REFERENDUM RESULT
63.0% Leave   Remain 37.0%

Wiltshire North

MAJORITY 17,626 (32.19%)   CONSERVATIVE HOLD   TURNOUT 74.72%

JAMES GRAY
BORN Nov 7, 1954
MP 1997-

	Electorate	Share %	from 2017 % Change
	73,283		
*J Gray C	32,373	59.12	-1.20
B Mathew LD	14,747	26.93	+9.20
J Fisher Lab	5,699	10.41	-7.09
B Jackson Green	1,939	3.54	+1.42

Jackson (Green) Former corporate legal executive.

Career in shipping and trading. Spent seven years in the Territorial Army. Advocate of the pro-Brexit lobby group Leave Means Leave. Survived two deselection attempts in 2006-07 after admitting having an affair while his wife was undergoing cancer treatment. Said MPs should spend less time on constituency casework because it diverts from holding government to account. Was one of 21 MPs who voted against LGBT-inclusive sex and relationship education in English schools, 2019. Caught up in the expenses scandal over the redecoration

of his second home. Shadow Scotland secretary for 11 days in 2005; resigned after saying that the Scottish parliament should be abolished. Contested Ross, Cromarty & Skye, 1992. Ed: High Sch of Glasgow; University of Glasgow (MA history); Christ Church, Oxford (MA history).

CHALLENGERS
Brian Mathew (LD) Worker with Water Aid in Africa. Contested this seat in 2017 and 2015. **Jon Fisher** (Lab) Community worker. **Bonnie**

CONSTITUENCY PROFILE
A safe Conservative seat. The party's majority fell below 4,000 in 1997 and 2001, when the Liberal Democrats made a strong showing. The Tory majority returned to five figures after the coalition government years, in 2015. Affluent and predominantly rural, the constituency has high levels of home ownership; nearly three quarters of households are owner-occupied. Residents are more likely than average to be employed in managerial roles, and median wages are high.

EU REFERENDUM RESULT
50.3% Leave   Remain 49.7%

Wiltshire South West

MAJORITY 21,630 (39.40%)   CONSERVATIVE HOLD   TURNOUT 70.41%

ANDREW
MURRISON
BORN Apr 24, 1961
MP 2001-

	Electorate	Share %	from 2017 % Change
	77,970		
*A Murrison C	33,038	60.18	+0.20
E Pomroy-Smith Lab	11,408	20.78	-5.73
E Nicholson LD	8,015	14.60	+4.81
J Phillips Green	2,434	4.43	+1.79

Minister of state for international development and the Middle East, 2019-20. Trade envoy to Morocco and Tunisia, 2016-. Special representative for Great War centenary commemorations, 2011-18. Parliamentary under-secretary: Northern Ireland, 2014-15; defence, 2012-14. PPS to Andrew Lansley, 2010-12. Backed Boris Johnson for leader in 2019. Spent 18 years as a Royal Navy medical officer and surgeon commander; recalled for six-month tour in Iraq, 2003. Locum consultant and GP. Former research assistant

to Lord Freeman. Member, Bow Group. Ed: Harwich HS; Britannia Royal Naval Coll, Dartmouth; University of Bristol (MD, MBChB); Hughes Hall, Cambridge (DPH).

CHALLENGERS
Emily Pomroy-Smith (Lab) Has a business designing and making clothing for children. **Ellen Nicholson** (LD) Nursing lecturer and former primary care nurse. **Julie Phillips** (Green) Manager in the care and education sectors.

CONSTITUENCY PROFILE
The Conservatives have always won this seat, created in 2010, with majorities in five figures. Including its predecessor, Westbury, the seat has consistently returned Conservative MPs to parliament since 1924. Sparsely populated and mostly rural, the largest towns are Trowbridge, Westbury and Warminster. More than a fifth of residents are aged over 65 and levels of home ownership are slightly above average. Defence and security are over-represented industries as the area, bordering Devizes and Salisbury, houses several military facilities.

EU REFERENDUM RESULT
56.9% Leave   Remain 43.1%

Wimbledon

MAJORITY 628 (1.18%)　　　CONSERVATIVE HOLD　　　TURNOUT 77.72%

STEPHEN HAMMOND
BORN Feb 4, 1962
MP 2005-

Had the Conservative whip removed in September 2019 for voting to rule out a no-deal Brexit, but it was restored a month later. Sacked as vice-chairman of the Conservative Party for voting in favour of giving MPs a meaningful vote on any Brexit deal in December 2017. Health minister, 2018-19. Parly under-sec, transport, 2012-14; joined the transport firm Inmarsat in an £800-per-hour advisory role months after he was removed from government in a reshuffle. Supported Matt Hancock in the 2019 leadership election. Former investment

	Electorate	Share %	Change from 2017 %
	68,232		
*S Hammond C	20,373	38.42	-8.05
P Kohler LD	19,745	37.24	+22.73
J Schneider Lab	12,543	23.65	-11.91
G Hadley Ind	366	0.69	

banker. Contested: this seat, 2001; Warwickshire North, 1997. Ed: King Edward VI Sch, Southampton; Richard Hale Sch, Hertford; Queen Mary Coll, London (BSc economics).

CHALLENGERS
Paul Kohler (LD) Head of law at Soas, University of London. Led successful legal challenge against proposed closure of Wimbledon police station. An attack by burglars in 2014 left him with severe facial injuries. Cllr, Merton LBC, 2018-. **Jackie**

Schneider (Lab) Primary school music teacher.

CONSTITUENCY PROFILE
The southwest London seat that is home to the famous All England Lawn Tennis and Croquet Club. Has been held mostly by Conservative MPs but also claimed by Labour in years when it won big majorities. The Conservatives won in 2019 with the lowest ever vote share of a winning party in Wimbledon. It is a commuter-heavy area in which a large proportion of the population works in managerial-level jobs. Median pay is the highest of any seat in the country.

EU REFERENDUM RESULT
29.4% Leave　　　Remain 70.6%

Winchester

MAJORITY 985 (1.67%)　　　CONSERVATIVE HOLD　　　TURNOUT 77.92%

STEVEN BRINE
BORN Jan 28, 1974
MP 2010-

Remainer who had the whip temporarily removed in 2019 for voting to block a no-deal Brexit. Voted for single market and customs union membership during indicative votes, resigning from his ministerial post two days before. Parly under-sec, health, 2017-19. Supported Jeremy Hunt in the 2019 Conservative Party leadership election. Opposed legalising gay marriage in 2013. Assistant whip, 2016-17. PPS to: Jeremy Hunt, 2015-16; Mike Penning, 2013-15. Former radio journalist for BBC Radio Five Live and WGN Radio in the United States.

	Electorate	Share %	Change from 2017 %
	75,582		
*S Brine C	28,430	48.28	-3.74
P Ferguson LD	27,445	46.60	+12.08
G Baker Lab	2,723	4.62	-5.89
T Skelton JACP	292	0.50	+0.24

Businessman and consultant for The Azalea Group public relations agency. Ed: Bohunt Comp; Highbury College; Liverpool Hope University Coll (BA history).

CHALLENGERS
Paula Ferguson (LD) Works with children who have learning difficulties. Previously worked in corporate banking, data analysis and management consultancy but retrained in psychology. **George Baker** (Lab) Founded a support agency.

CONSTITUENCY PROFILE
Held by the Conservatives for most of the 20th century, the Liberal Democrats gained the seat in 1997, holding it throughout New Labour's time in government. Mark Oaten, an MP during that period, quit frontline politics in 2006 after a sex scandal. Labour has not come second since 1979. This wealthy borough is a key Hampshire tourist destination. The University of Winchester is located here and there is a student population of more than 9,000. Incomes are significantly higher than the southeast average. IBM has a large research site in the seat.

EU REFERENDUM RESULT
39.6% Leave　　　Remain 60.4%

Windsor

ADAM AFRIYIE
BORN Aug 4, 1965
MP 2005-

First mixed-race Conservative MP. Pro-Brexit and anti-immigration. In the shadow cabinet before 2010, but on the back benches since then. Has rarely rebelled except on Europe. Shadow science and innovation minister, 2007-10. Members' expenses select cttee, 2011-15. Entrepreneur who founded the IT company Connect Support Services. A stake in Axonn Media, the marketing agency, helped to make him worth up to £100 million, but the firm went into administration in November 2019. Born in Wimbledon to a Ghanaian father. Ed:

	Electorate	Share %	Change from 2017 %
	75,038		
*A Afriyie C	31,501	58.61	-5.78
J Tisi LD	11,422	21.25	+11.17
P Shearman Lab	8,147	15.16	-7.72
F McKeown Green	1,796	3.34	+0.68
D Buckley Ind	508	0.95	
W Da Costa Ind	376	0.70	

Imperial Coll (BSc agricultural economics).

CHALLENGERS
Julian Tisi (LD) Chartered accountant who previously worked at PwC. **Peter Shearman** (Lab) Technology developer for Cisco. Previously worked on government policy for the Broadband Stakeholder Group. **Fintan McKeown** (Green) Actor, best known for his performances at the National Theatre and in

Star Trek and *Game of Thrones*.

CONSTITUENCY PROFILE
A safe seat held by the Conservatives for well over a century. The Liberal Democrats returned to second place in 2019, having been the Conservatives' main rival for two decades until the party's national collapse in 2015. An affluent seat in the east of Berkshire, the median income is more than £100 a week higher than the national average. The seat includes villages along the River Thames and contains Eton College and Windsor Castle. A significant proportion of residents works in managerial and professional roles.

EU REFERENDUM RESULT
46.7% Leave   Remain 53.3%

Wirral South

ALISON MCGOVERN
BORN Dec 30, 1980
MP 2010-

Gave emotional speech during emergency debate on Aleppo, urging parliament to intervene in Syria. Nominated Jess Phillips for leader in 2020. Backed Owen Smith in 2016 and Liz Kendall in 2015, and was a prominent critic of Jeremy Corbyn. Shadow minister: Treasury, 2015; education, 2014-15; international development, 2013-14. Opposition whip, 2013. Select cttees: Speaker's advisory on works of art, 2010-17; international development, 2010-13. Former public affairs manager: Network Rail; The Art Fund. Cllr, Southwark LBC,

	Electorate	Share %	Change from 2017 %
	57,280		
*A McGovern Lab	22,284	51.17	-6.07
S Gardiner C	16,179	37.15	-1.67
C Carubia LD	2,917	6.70	+3.77
M Waring Brexit	1,219	2.80	
H Gorman Green	948	2.18	+1.17

2006-10. Commons researcher, 2002-06. Chairwoman of Progress, 2015-. Ed: Wirral GS for Girls; UCL (BA philosophy); Birkbeck Coll (PG Cert economics).

CHALLENGERS
Stewart Gardiner (C) Town planner. Cllr; Knutsford TC, 2008-; mayor, 2011-12; Cheshire East C, 2011-. Contested Birkenhead, 2017. **Christopher Carubia** (LD) IT professional. **Martin Waring** (Brexit) Chief

operating officer for a financial services start-up.

CONSTITUENCY PROFILE
Although Wirral South, like most Merseyside seats, now seems like a relatively safe one for Labour, the party gained the seat from the Conservatives only in 1997. The Conservatives came close to wresting back control in 2010, losing by 531 votes, but Labour has won more decisive majorities since then. Situated on the Wirral peninsula, the constituency contains the towns of Bebington and Heswall. It is an affluent area and the median wage is higher than the national average.

EU REFERENDUM RESULT
46.5% Leave   Remain 53.5%

Wirral West

LABOUR HOLD

TURNOUT 77.26%

MARGARET GREENWOOD
BORN Mar 14, 1959
MP 2015-

Shadow work and pensions secretary, 2018-; shadow minister in same department, 2016-18. Backed Rebecca Long Bailey for leader in 2020. Supported Jeremy Corbyn in 2016 and Andy Burnham in 2015. PPS to: Debbie Abrahams; Owen Smith. Environment audit select cttee, 2015-16. Web consultant. Former English teacher in secondary schools, lecturer in further education and an adult education tutor. Also worked as a travel writer and web editor. Committed campaigner on the NHS and environmental issues. Launched the Save Hilbre

	Electorate	Share %	Change from 2017 %
	55,550		
*M Greenwood Lab	20,695	48.22	-6.08
L Evans C	17,692	41.22	-0.87
A Corkhill LD	2,706	6.31	+3.68
J Coyne Green	965	2.25	+1.27
J Kelly Brexit	860	2.00	

and Dee Estuary campaigns. Founding member of Defend our NHS, a Merseyside-based campaign group.

CHALLENGERS
Laura Evans (C) Works in marketing and development. **Andy Corkhill** (LD) Runs a pasta-making business. **John Coyne** (Green) Liberal Democrat until 2006, when he defected to the Greens over Liverpool council's support of the Pathfinder housing programme.

John Kelly (Brexit) Left-wing former supporter of a "United States of Europe".

CONSTITUENCY PROFILE
Wirral West, created in 1983, was a bellwether seat until Margaret Greenwood bucked the trend by gaining it from the Conservatives in 2015. Its Conservative MP from 2010 to 2015 was Esther McVey, who later became the MP for Tatton, a housing minister and Conservative leadership candidate. The seat covers an affluent and prosperous part of the Wirral peninsula, encompassing West Kirby and the seaside town of Hoylake.

EU REFERENDUM RESULT

44.7% Leave	Remain 55.3%

Witham

CONSERVATIVE HOLD

TURNOUT 70.09%

PRITI PATEL
BORN Mar 29, 1972
MP 2010-

Home secretary since 2019. Extremely pro-Leave and one of the six rebel ministers who led the charge for Brexit. Criticised for advocating threatening Ireland with food shortages during Brexit negotiations. Sacked as international development secretary, 2016-17, after apologising for holding unauthorised meetings with the Israeli government. Thatcherite who voted against same-sex marriage and once said she supported the reintroduction of the death penalty. Work and pensions minister, 2015-16; exchequer secretary to the

	Electorate	Share %	Change from 2017 %
	70,402		
*P Patel C	32,876	66.63	+2.31
M Edobor Lab	8,794	17.82	-8.63
S North LD	4,584	9.29	+3.78
J Abbott Green	3,090	6.26	+2.54

Treasury, 2014-15. Worked as a lobbyist for British American Tobacco early in her career. Criticised for previously employing her husband part-time when he had two other jobs. Contested Nottingham North, 2005. Ed: Westfield Girls' Sch, Watford; Keele University (BA economics); Essex University (MSc British government).

CHALLENGERS
Martin Edobor (Lab) GP. **Sam North** (LD) Runs a small

business. **James Abbott** (Green) Runs a gardening business.

CONSTITUENCY PROFILE
Safe Conservative seat to the northeast of Chelmsford, stretching up to the outskirts of Colchester. The Conservative vote total and share has increased at every election since the seat's creation in 2010. Construction and finance are over-represented employers here. Witham itself is a former spa and wool town and the seat also includes Stanway, a suburb of Colchester. It is an affluent area with high median earnings and high levels of home ownership.

EU REFERENDUM RESULT

60.5% Leave	Remain 39.5%

Witney

CONSERVATIVE HOLD

TURNOUT 73.12%

ROBERT COURTS
BORN Oct 21, 1978
MP 2016-

Replaced David Cameron in a 2016 by-election prompted by the former prime minister's decision to leave parliament. He beat Natasha Witmill, an aide to Mr Cameron, to be selected as the party's candidate. Known for his small-state, libertarian leanings and identifies with the Austrian School of Economics. PPS to Theresa Villiers (Chipping Barnet). ERG member. Trading standards and personal injury barrister. Called to Bar, 2003, Lincoln's Inn. Worked for New Zealand government's Crown Law Office, 2008. Campaigned for Brexit;

	Electorate	Share %	from 2017 %	Change
	83,845			
*R Courts C		33,856	55.23	-0.31
C Hoagland LD		18,679	30.47	+10.02
R Bolger Lab Co-op		8,770	14.31	-6.37

supported Boris Johnson for leader, 2019. Cllr, West Oxford DC, 2014-17. Ed: University of Sheffield (LLB).

CHALLENGERS
Charlotte Hoagland (LD) Worked for fellow Liberal Democrats Lord Thurso, in Westminster, and Liam McArthur and Jim Hume in the Scottish parliament. **Rosa Bolger** (Lab Co-op) TV producer, including at Disney between 2011 and 2014. Leader of Witney TC. Cllr, West Oxfordshire DC, 2018-.

CONSTITUENCY PROFILE
Witney, in Oxfordshire, is a safe Conservative seat. It was represented by David Cameron from 2001 until 2016. The previous MP, Shaun Woodward, defected to Labour in 1999. The Liberal Democrats came within 6,000 votes of the Conservatives at the 2016 by-election caused by Mr Cameron's decision to leave parliament. A large and affluent rural seat that includes part of the Cotswolds and the towns of Witney, Carterton and Chipping Norton. There is an RAF base at Brize Norton, and the economy benefits from tourists attracted to the Cotswolds and Blenheim Palace.

EU REFERENDUM RESULT
46.3% Leave   Remain 53.7%

Woking

CONSERVATIVE HOLD

TURNOUT 71.48%

JONATHAN LORD
BORN Sep 17, 1962
MP 2010-

Quiet backbencher who has not yet held a committee seat or frontbench position. Brexiteer; supported Dominic Raab in the 2019 leadership election. Chairman, Guildford Conservative Association, 2013-17. Managed Anne Milton's 2005 general election campaign in Guildford. Marketing consultant. Former director, Saatchi & Saatchi. Cllr, Surrey CC, 2009-10. Contested Oldham West & Royton, 1997. Ed: Shrewsbury Sch; Kent Sch, Connecticut; Merton Coll, Oxford (BA modern history; president, Conservative Association).

	Electorate	Share %	from 2017 %	Change
	75,455			
*J Lord C		26,396	48.94	-5.19
W Forster LD		16,629	30.83	+13.25
G Mitchell Lab		8,827	16.37	-7.49
E Walding Green		1,485	2.75	+0.78
T De Leon Ukip		600	1.11	-0.99

CHALLENGERS
Will Forster (LD) Worked for Catherine Bearder, MEP. Cllr: Woking BC, 2011-; Surrey CC, 2009-. Contested this seat in 2017. **Gerry Mitchell** (Lab) Social policy researcher. **Ella Walding** (Green) Senior service designer, the Innovation Unit. **Troy De Leon** (Ukip) Business analyst.

CONSTITUENCY PROFILE
Woking has been held by the Conservative Party since the seat was created in 1950. The Liberal

Democrats' recovery here caused Jonathan Lord's majority to fall from 17,000 in 2017. The Lib Dems had been the primary rival to the Conservatives in the seat for two decades until the party's 2015 national collapse. Woking is the largest town in Surrey and is an affluent area; many of its residents commute into London. More residents are in work than the national average, earnings are relatively high and more than two thirds of households are occupied by their owners. About 7 per cent of the seat's residents are Muslim and Woking is home to the first purpose-built mosque in Britain, the Shah Jahan Mosque.

EU REFERENDUM RESULT
44.3% Leave   Remain 55.7%

Wokingham

MAJORITY 7,383 (11.91%)   CONSERVATIVE HOLD   TURNOUT 73.84%

SIR JOHN REDWOOD
BORN Jun 15, 1951
MP 1987-

One of John Major's "Bastards"; contested the Tory leadership in 1997 and 1995. Memorably failed to mime the Welsh national anthem while Welsh secretary in 1993. Long-term Eurosceptic. Backbencher since 2005. Extensive work outside parliament: chairman of Investment Committee at CS Pan Asset Capital Management. Author, including of *Superpower Struggles*, about the EU, China and the United States. Head, Downing Street policy unit, 1983-85. Fellow, All Souls. Ed: Kent Coll; Magdalen Coll, Oxford (MA modern history);

	Electorate	Share %	from 2017 %	Change
	83,957			
*J Redwood C	30,734	49.57	-7.06	
+P Lee LD	23,351	37.66	+21.73	
A Medhurst Lab	6,450	10.40	-14.74	
K Johannessen Green	1,382	2.23	-0.06	
A Mullin Advance	80	0.13		

St Antony's Coll, Oxford (DPhil modern history).

CHALLENGERS
Phillip Lee (LD) MP for the neighbouring seat of Bracknell, 2010-19. Crossed the floor on September 3, 2019, to join the Lib Dems in protest at his party's position on Brexit, leaving the Conservatives with no working majority. Parly under-sec, justice, 2016-18. **Annette Medhurst** (Lab) Doctor working in cancer research. **Kizzi Johannessen**

(Green) Mental health worker.

CONSTITUENCY PROFILE
Has returned Conservative MPs at every election since its creation in 1950. In percentage terms the Conservative majority fell to its lowest level since 1950 in 2019, although numerically it was slightly lower in 2001 and 2005. Situated in Berkshire, the seat contains the town of Wokingham itself and the south Reading suburbs of Earley and Winnersh. The area is relatively affluent. Wages are higher than elsewhere in the southeast, a majority of households are owner-occupied and residents are likely to have degrees.

EU REFERENDUM RESULT
42.7% Leave   Remain 57.3%

Wolverhampton North East

MAJORITY 4,080 (11.90%)   CONSERVATIVE GAIN FROM LABOUR   TURNOUT 55.44%

JANE STEVENSON
BORN Feb 18, 1971
MP 2019-

Classical singer for more than 20 years who became a singing teacher. Sang in more than 40 countries, as well as at the Royal Albert Hall. Campaigned for Leave in Wolverhampton during the 2016 referendum. Conservative deputy chairwoman in the Black Country. Cllr, Wolverhampton CC, 2018-. Grew up in Merry Hill. Ed: Warstones; Wolverhampton Girls' HS; Guildhall School of Music & Drama (PG opera).

CHALLENGERS
Emma Reynolds (Lab) MP

	Electorate	Share %	from 2017 %	Change
	61,829			
J Stevenson C	17,722	51.70	+11.44	
*E Reynolds Lab	13,642	39.79	-13.02	
V Khatri Brexit	1,354	3.95		
R Maxwell LD	960	2.80	+1.24	
A Cantrill Green	603	1.76	+0.44	

for this constituency, 2010-19. Remain campaigner. Shadow communities secretary, 2015. Shadow minister: housing, 2013-15; Foreign Office, 2010-13. Select cttees: Brexit, 2016-17; health, 2015-16; foreign affairs, 2010-13. Special adviser to Geoff Hoon MP. Political adviser to Robin Cook as president of Party of European Socialists in Brussels. **Vishal Khatri** (Brexit) Aviation professional and sports agent. **Richard Maxwell** (LD) Engineer and community activist.

CONSTITUENCY PROFILE
Wolverhampton North East, created in 1950, had chosen to elect a non-Labour MP only once before 2019, in 1987, when the Conservatives won the seat by 214 votes. Labour's share of the vote in the seat had never been lower than two fifths until this election. The seat covers the northeast corner of Wolverhampton, Wednesfield, a residential suburb, as well as the large Low Hill housing estate. It is slightly less ethnically diverse than the other Wolverhampton constituencies. About a third of residents live in social housing and median wages are £100 a week below the national average.

EU REFERENDUM RESULT
67.7% Leave   Remain 32.3%

Wolverhampton South East

PAT MCFADDEN
BORN Mar 26, 1965
MP 2005-

From the party's moderate wing. Speechwriter for John Smith, adviser to Tony Blair and researcher to Donald Dewar, the first Scottish first minister. Nominated Jess Phillips for leader in 2020, having previously backed David Miliband, Liz Kendall and Owen Smith. Shadow Europe minister, 2014-16; alleged he was sacked because of comments after the Paris terrorist attacks that served to undermine Jeremy Corbyn's leadership. Part of Open Britain, a pro-European campaign group. Shadow business secretary, 2010. Business minister, 2007-10.

	Electorate	Share %	Change from 2017 %
	63,006		
*P McFadden Lab	15,522	46.41	-11.81
A Ejaz C	14,287	42.72	+7.95
R Chaggar Brexit	2,094	6.26	
R Coleman-Taylor LD	1,019	3.05	+1.81
K Gilbert Green	521	1.56	+0.40

Parliamentary under-secretary, Cabinet Office, 2006-07. Ed: Holyrood Secondary Sch, Glasgow; University of Edinburgh (MA politics).

CHALLENGERS
Ahmed Ejaz (C) Dudley optometrist. Raj Chaggar (Brexit) Runs own accounting practice. Moved to England from Uganda in 1968. Ruth Coleman-Taylor (LD) Former teacher. Kathryn Gilbert (Green) Teacher of management.

CONSTITUENCY PROFILE
Labour's majority fell in 2019 to its lowest point since the seat was created in 1974. The seat had the lowest turnout of any constituency in the West Midlands, and the eighth lowest in the country. It contains Bilston, a part of Wolverhampton that was an old steel town, and Coseley, a town once dominated by car manufacturing. The area is diverse: 18,000 residents are of Asian descent and 10,000 are black or mixed race. Almost a third of households are socially rented and the seat has the lowest pay of the Wolverhampton seats.

EU REFERENDUM RESULT
68.1% Leave   Remain 31.9%

Wolverhampton South West

STUART
ANDERSON
BORN Jul 17, 1976
MP 2019-

Founder and chief executive of E Travel Safety, a security company. Former sniper in the army. Shot in the foot at the age of 17 but returned to full service despite initially being told that it would have to be amputated. He serving for eight years in the Royal Green Jackets, including in Kosovo and Northern Ireland. After leaving the army he worked in the defence and security industry, including as a bodyguard for a former prime minister of Qatar. Cllr, Herefordshire CC, 2017-19. Ed: University of Leicester (MSc security and risk management).

	Electorate	Share %	Change from 2017 %
	60,895		
S Anderson C	19,864	48.29	+4.10
*E Smith Lab	18,203	44.25	-5.10
B Ricketts LD	2,041	4.96	+3.11
L Grandison Brexit	1,028	2.50	

CHALLENGERS
Eleanor Smith (Lab) First black MP for this seat, 2017-19. Jeremy Corbyn supporter. Parents arrived as part of the Windrush generation. Spent more than 30 years as a theatre nurse. First black female president of Unison, 2011-12. Commissioned an outside agency to produce a review into BAME blood, organ and stem cell donation. Public administration and constitutional affairs select cttee. Bart Ricketts (LD) Chartered waste manager.

CONSTITUENCY PROFILE
From 1950 to 1974 this seat was held by Enoch Powell, whose infamous 1968 "rivers of blood" speech, making a dire prediction about the future of race relations, made him one of the most divisive political figures of his generation. It was taken by Labour in 1997, won back by the Tories in 2010, and narrowly returned to Labour in 2015. It is the most affluent of the three Wolverhampton seats by median income and contains the Wolverhampton University campus and Molineux stadium, home of Wolverhampton Wanderers FC. There is a large Sikh population.

EU REFERENDUM RESULT
54.4% Leave   Remain 45.6%

Worcester

ROBIN WALKER
BORN Apr 12, 1978
MP 2010-

Entrepreneur who set up an internet business. Later became a partner at the lobbying and PR firm Finsbury. Northern Ireland minister, 2020-. Parly undersec: Scotland and Northern Ireland, 2019-20; Brexit, 2016-19. Campaigned to Remain in 2016. PPS to: Liz Truss (Norfolk South West), 2014-15; Andrew Robathan, 2013-14. Press officer to Oliver Letwin MP, 2005; assistant to Richard Adams, PPC for Worcester, 2001; PA to and driver for Stephen Dorrell MP, 1997. Member, Tory Reform Group. Son of Peter Walker, who held this seat for the

	Electorate	Share %	Change from 2017 %
	73,475		
*R Walker C	25,856	50.80	+2.71
L Denham Lab	19,098	37.52	-5.69
S Kearney LD	3,666	7.20	+3.79
L Stephen Green	1,694	3.33	+0.97
M Potter Ind	584	1.15	+0.94

Conservatives from 1961 to 1992. Ed: St Paul's Sch; Balliol Coll, Oxford (BA ancient and modern history).

CHALLENGERS
Lynn Denham (Lab) Worked as a hospital pharmacist and senior NHS manager. Cllr, Worcester City C, 2012-. **Stephen Kearney** (LD) Chief executive, Regenerate community charity. Founding director, UK Youth Parliament. **Louis Stephen** (Green) Engineer. **Martin Potter** (Ind) Finance

worker. Brexit Party candidate until Nigel Farage's decision to withdraw the party from Conservative seats.

CONSTITUENCY PROFILE
Held by the Conservatives from 1923 until 1997, when Labour gained the seat for the first time. The Conservatives won it back in 2010, and although a Labour surge cut the party's numerical majority in 2017, its vote share has increased in every election since. Southwest of Birmingham, the city of Worcester has a population of just over 100,000, and was once an industrial centre and the home of the glove industry.

EU REFERENDUM RESULT
53.7% Leave   Remain 46.3%

Worcestershire Mid

NIGEL HUDDLESTON
BORN Oct 13, 1970
MP 2015-

Parliamentary under-secretary, culture department, 2020-; particular interest in tourism and technology. Assistant whip, 2019-. Opposed Brexit in 2016 referendum. Backed Sajid Javid for the leadership, 2019. Member, Tory Reform Group. Former management consultant for Arthur Andersen and Deloitte. Industry head of travel, Google, 2011-15. Cllr, St Albans DC, 2011-14. Contested Luton South, 2010. Freeman of the City of Lincoln. Culture select cttee, 2015-17. Ed: Robert Pattinson CS; Oxford (BA PPE); UCLA (MBA entertainment management).

	Electorate	Share %	Change from 2017 %
	78,221		
*N Huddleston C	37,426	66.69	+1.40
H Russell Lab	9,408	16.76	-6.18
M Rowley LD	6,474	11.54	+5.27
S Howarth Green	2,177	3.88	+1.39
B Brockman Loony	638	1.14	

CHALLENGERS
Helen Russell (Lab) Trade union training officer for the Chartered Society of Physiotherapy. Has been crowned a world champion in the quadrathlon and duathlon. **Margaret Rowley** (LD) Former senior manager in the NHS. Cllr, Wychavon DC, 1995-. Author of canal guides. Fifth time contesting this seat. **Sue Howarth** (Green) Biologist. Chairwoman of the West Midlands branch of the Royal Society of Biology.

CONSTITUENCY PROFILE
The Conservative majority fell to a little under 10,000 in the 1990s but has increased at every successive election and in 2019 was one of the Conservatives' ten biggest majorities. To the south of Birmingham, and made up of a stretch of the countryside to the north and east of Worcester, its major towns are Droitwich Spa and Evesham, each home to about 24,000 people. More than a fifth of residents are aged 65 or above. The local economy includes fruit growing, farming and tourism. Earnings are slightly above the West Midlands average and home ownership is well above average.

EU REFERENDUM RESULT
59.4% Leave   Remain 40.6%

Worcestershire West

MAJORITY 24,499 (42.58%)   CONSERVATIVE HOLD   TURNOUT 75.43%

HARRIET BALDWIN
BORN May 2, 1960
MP 2010-

Background in finance, specialising in currency markets for pension funds. Africa and international development minister, 2018-19; sacked by Boris Johnson in July 2019. Remainer who supported Theresa May's withdrawal agreement. Defence procurement minister, 2016-18; economic secretary to the Treasury, 2015-16; whip, 2014-15. Voted in favour of same-sex marriage in Northern Ireland. Supported Jeremy Hunt in the 2019 leadership race. Represented the UK in Nato parliamentary assembly. Contested Stockton North, 2005.

	Electorate	Share %	from 2017 %	Change
	76,267			
*H Baldwin C	34,909	60.68	-0.77	
B Nielsen LD	10,410	18.09	+8.70	
S Charles Lab	9,496	16.51	-7.18	
M Allen Green	2,715	4.72	+1.88	

Ed: Lady Margaret Hall, Oxford (BA French and Russian); McGill University, Canada (MBA).

CHALLENGERS
Beverley Nielsen (LD) Cllr, Malvern Hills DC, 2019-; cabinet member for economic development and tourism. Founded a promotions company. Associate fellow, University of Warwick. **Samantha Charles** (Lab) Sexual offences forensic examiner. Co-founder, People in Motion, a refugee charity. Political education officer,

Malvern Hills DC, 2018-. Contested this seat in 2017.

CONSTITUENCY PROFILE
Created in 1997, Worcestershire West has always elected Conservative MPs. Its predecessor constituency, Worcestershire South, elected Tory MPs without interruption from 1950 until 1997. This rural seat sits to the north of Tewkesbury and is split by the Severn and Avon rivers. About a quarter of residents are aged 65 or above and seven in ten households are owned by their occupiers. The local economy is dominated by the agricultural sector.

EU REFERENDUM RESULT
52.5% Leave   Remain 47.5%

Workington

MAJORITY 4,176 (10.04%)   CONSERVATIVE GAIN FROM LABOUR   TURNOUT 67.78%

MARK JENKINSON
BORN Jan 28, 1982
MP 2019-

Describes himself as a working-class Tory. His victory embodied the Conservative Party's election campaign strategy. Trained nuclear technical officer, but an electrician by trade. Cllr, Allerdale BC, 2019-; Conservative group leader. Contested this seat for Ukip in 2015 as a founding member of the party's West Cumbria branch, and was personally congratulated by Nigel Farage on his election victory in 2019. Board of directors: Workington Heritage Group; Seaton Rangers Rugby Club. Ed: state school and electrical apprenticeship.

	Electorate	Share %	from 2017 %	Change
	61,370			
M Jenkinson C	20,488	49.25	+7.52	
*S Hayman Lab	16,312	39.21	-11.94	
D Walker Brexit	1,749	4.20		
N Hughes LD	1,525	3.67	+0.95	
N Cockburn Ind	842	2.02	+1.36	
J Perry Green	596	1.43		
R Ivinson ND	87	0.21		

CHALLENGERS
Sue Hayman (Lab) Cumbria's first female MP, 2015-19. Shadow environment secretary, 2017-19. APPGs: nuclear energy (co-chairwoman); rural business (vice-chairwoman). Supported Remain in 2016. **David Walker** (Brexit) Retired dentist and property developer. **Neil Hughes** (LD) Cllr, Cumbria CC, 2013-. Contested: Penrith & The Border, 2017; Carlisle, 2015.

CONSTITUENCY PROFILE
The source of the term "Workington Man", a frequent refrain in the 2019 election used to refer to the idea of a traditional Labour voter who voted for Brexit and was likely to switch to the Tories for the first time. This Cumbria seat had been won by Labour at every general election since 1918 and the Conservatives overturned a Labour majority of almost 4,000 to win. A sparse seat, with an older than average population. More than two fifths of workers are employed in manufacturing, construction or retail, the area having declined with the fall of the coal and steel industries.

EU REFERENDUM RESULT
61.0% Leave   Remain 39.0%

Worsley & Eccles South

MAJORITY 3,101 (7.20%)   LABOUR HOLD   TURNOUT 59.59%

BARBARA KEELEY
BORN Mar 26, 1952
MP 2005-

	Electorate	Share %	from 2017 % Change
	75,219		
*B Keeley Lab	20,446	45.73	-11.33
A Saunders C	17,227	38.53	-0.17
S Martin Brexit	3,224	7.21	
J Johnson-Tod LD	2,510	5.61	+3.23
D Towers Green	1,300	2.91	+1.06

Early career as an IBM programmer. Resigned from Jeremy Corbyn's shadow cabinet in June 2016 and supported Owen Smith's leadership challenge, but rejoined the front bench in October of the same year. Backed Sir Keir Starmer, 2020. Underwent treatment for breast cancer during the 2019 election campaign. Shadow minister: mental health and social care, 2016-; health, 2016-17, 2010; Treasury, 2015; communities, 2010-11. Deputy leader of the Commons, 2009-10; shadow deputy leader, 2010. Assistant whip, 2008-09.

Chairwoman, Waspi APPG, 2016-. PPS to: Harriet Harman, 2007-08 (Camberwell & Peckham); Jim Murphy, 2006-07. Cllr, Trafford BC, 1995-2004. GMB member. Ed: Mount St Mary's RC Coll, Leeds; Salford University (BA politics and contemporary history).

CHALLENGERS
Arnie Saunders (C) Rabbi for a local care home and hospital. Cllr, Salford City C, 2017-; first Conservative councillor for 25

years. Voted Remain. **Seamus Martin** (Brexit) Previously Ukip co-chairman for Greater Manchester. **Joe Johnson-Tod** (LD) University of Salford student.

CONSTITUENCY PROFILE
This seat and its predecessor, Worsley, have elected Labour MPs since 1983. The party's majority, however, was at its lowest in 2019 since the seat's creation. To the west of Manchester city centre, Worsley & Eccles South covers the relatively affluent and residential area of Worsley, along with former mining towns and green belt farmland to the southwest.

EU REFERENDUM RESULT
59.8% Leave   Remain 40.2%

Worthing East & Shoreham

MAJORITY 7,441 (14.07%)   CONSERVATIVE HOLD   TURNOUT 70.69%

TIM LOUGHTON
BORN May 30, 1962
MP 1997-

	Electorate	Share %	from 2017 % Change
	75,195		
*T Loughton C	27,104	50.99	+2.06
L O'Connor Lab	19,663	36.99	-2.32
A Ridley LD	4,127	7.76	+3.01
L Groves Williams Green	2,006	3.77	+1.38
S Cook ND	255	0.48	

City fund manager who worked at Montagu Loebl Stanley. Later director, Fleming Private Asset Management. Recruited Andrea Leadsom (Northamptonshire South) to the Conservative Party at 1981 Warwick University freshers' fair and ran her 2016 leadership campaign. Nominated her in 2019 before supporting Boris Johnson. Admitted in 2017 that he meditated in the bath for one hour every morning; expensed £662 in water bills over two years. Minister for children, 2010-12. Shadow minister: children, 2003-10; health, 2001-03. Select cttees: home affairs,

2014-17; draft mental health bill, 2004-05; environmental audit, 1997-2001. Contested Sheffield Brightside, 1992. Ed: Warwick University (BA classical civilisation); Clare Coll, Cambridge (MA Mesopotamian archaeology).

CHALLENGERS
Lavinia O' Connor (Lab) Civil servant. Cllr, Adur & Worthing DC, 2018-; audit licensing committee. In the Labour movement for 38 years. **Ashley**

Ridley (LD) Eighteen-year-old football coach. **Leslie Groves Williams** (Green) UN senior ethics adviser. Fluent in French and Spanish.

CONSTITUENCY PROFILE
A coastal constituency in West Sussex held by the Conservatives since its 1997 creation, although Labour reduced the Tory majority in the seat by about 10,000 votes in 2017. Has a significant population of older voters and almost three quarters of households owner-occupied. Incomes are considerably lower than the regional average and the constituency is less affluent than Hove, its eastern neighbour.

EU REFERENDUM RESULT
53.7% Leave   Remain 46.3%

Worthing West

MAJORITY 14,823 (27.12%)   CONSERVATIVE HOLD   TURNOUT 69.54%

SIR PETER BOTTOMLEY
BORN Jul 30, 1944
MP 1975-

Electorate	Share %	Change from 2017 %
78,587		
*P Bottomley C	30,475	55.77 +0.39
B Cooper Lab	15,652	28.64 -4.55
J Bennett LD	6,024	11.02 +5.55
J Paul Green	2,008	3.67 +0.71
D Aherne Ind	489	0.89

Became father of the House, the longest-serving MP in parliament, in 2019 after Ken Clarke stood down and Dennis Skinner lost his seat. Vocal supporter of gay marriage and signed Queen's Speech amendment calling for legal abortions in Northern Ireland, 2017. One of two Tories to support early day motion on Palestinian membership of the UN, 2011. PPS to: Northern Ireland office, 1989-90; transport, 1986-89; employment, 1984-86. Supported Jeremy Hunt, 2019. Co-chairman, haemophilia and contaminated blood APPG.

Trustee, Christian Aid. Knighted in 2011. Contested Woolwich West in both 1974 elections. Ed: Westminster Sch; Trinity Coll, Cambridge (BA economics).

CHALLENGERS
Beccy Cooper (Lab) Public health consultant and doctor. Cllr, Worthing BC, 2017-; Labour group leader. First Labour councillor elected to the borough in 41 years. Contested this seat, 2017. **Jamie Bennett** (LD) General manager, Kaplan. Cllr:

Arun DC, 2019-; Rustington PC, 2009-. **Jo Paul** (Green) Senior lecturer in history. **David Aherne** (Ind) Contested this seat for the Greens, 2015, 2010.

CONSTITUENCY PROFILE
The seat that confirmed the Conservative majority on election night in 2019, Worthing West has been held by Sir Peter Bottomley since its creation in 1997. Including its predecessor seat, Worthing, the constituency has been represented by only three different MPs since 1945. Sandwiched between Shoreham and Littlehampton on the south coast. More than a quarter of its residents are aged over 65.

EU REFERENDUM RESULT
56.0% Leave   Remain 44.0%

Wrekin, The

MAJORITY 18,726 (38.30%)   CONSERVATIVE HOLD   TURNOUT 69.16%

MARK PRITCHARD
BORN Nov 22, 1966
MP 2005-

Electorate	Share %	Change from 2017 %
70,693		
*M Pritchard C	31,029	63.47 +8.04
D Harrison Lab	12,303	25.16 -10.95
T Janke LD	4,067	8.32 +5.60
T Dawes Green	1,491	3.05 +1.43

Backbencher with an interest in defence and foreign policy. Arrested after being accused of rape in 2014; called for a review of anonymity laws after the investigation was dropped. Eurosceptic, but campaigned for Remain. Voted for Boris Johnson, 2019. Campaigned for reduced abortion term limits. UK representative to the Nato parliamentary assembly, 2005-10. Led UK's delegation to the OSCE. Trade envoy to Georgia and Armenia. Select cttees: international development, 2012-13; national security strategy, 2010-15; human rights, 2015-17;

transport, 2008-10; work and pensions, 2006-09; Wales, 2007-10; environmental audit, 2005-15. Grew up in an orphanage and later in foster care. Ed: Regents Theological College (BA theology); London Guildhall University (MA marketing and management); Buckingham University (MA international diplomacy).

CHALLENGERS
Dylan Harrison (Lab) Social work team manager. Contested: this seat, 2017; Telford & Wrekin

BC, 2015. **Thomas Janke** (LD) Iraq War veteran, Queen's Royal Lancers. Works with PTSD charities.

CONSTITUENCY PROFILE
The Wrekin, in Shropshire, was held by Labour from 1987 until 2005. The seat contains the town of Telford and a number of small, commuter villages. RAF and military bases contribute significantly to local employment. Harper Adams University, the country's only agricultural-specialist university, is located here. A petition to prevent the overnight closure of Princess Royal Hospital's A&E collected 12,000 signatures.

EU REFERENDUM RESULT
59.3% Leave   Remain 40.7%

Wrexham

MAJORITY 2,131 (6.36%)   CONSERVATIVE GAIN FROM LABOUR   TURNOUT 67.42%

SARAH ATHERTON
BORN Nov 15, 1967
MP 2019-

First female Conservative MP to be elected in Wales. Left school aged 16 and joined the Intelligence Corps. Retrained as a nurse at local Maelor Hospital. Social worker, specialising in mental health and older people. Voted to Leave. Supporter of tougher sentencing for antisocial behaviour. Favours brownfield construction. Learnt Welsh, but was criticised for lack of Welsh language campaign material. The previous Tory candidate, Andrew Atkinson, publicly refused to support her candidacy on *Politics Live*. Gresford community councillor. Contested Alyn &

	Electorate	Share %	Change from 2017 %
	49,734		
S Atherton C	15,199	45.33	+1.67
M Wimbury Lab Co-op	13,068	38.97	-9.91
C Harper PC	2,151	6.41	+1.42
T Sly LD	1,447	4.32	+1.85
I Berkeley-Hurst Brexit	1,222	3.64	
D Rees Green	445	1.33	

Deeside for the Welsh assembly, 2018. Ed: Bangor University (nursing).

CHALLENGERS
Mary Wimbury (Lab Co-op) Chief executive, Care Forum Wales, 2017-. Member, GMB. Campaigned with People's Vote. On the moderate wing of the Labour Party. Contested: EU parliament, 2019; Aberconwy, 2015. **Carrie Harper** (PC) Cllr: Wrexham BC, 2017-; 2008-12.

Tim Sly (LD) Founded a technology company. **Ian Berkeley-Hurst** (Brexit) Flower seller turned solicitor.

CONSTITUENCY PROFILE
In the northeast of Wales, on the English border, this seat was a Labour stronghold that the party had won in every election since 1935. The 2019 election was the first time that the Tories had ever won the seat since its creation in 1918. The outgoing MP, Ian Lucas, 2001-19, was a junior minister under Gordon Brown. Home ownership is below average for Wales. Manufacturing is a significant source of local jobs.

EU REFERENDUM RESULT
57.6% Leave   Remain 42.4%

Wycombe

MAJORITY 4,214 (7.70%)   CONSERVATIVE HOLD   TURNOUT 70.12%

STEVE BAKER
BORN Jun 6, 1971
MP 2010-

Prominent among the 28 Brexit "Spartans". Conducted parliamentary guerilla campaign as a member of the ERG. Submitted letter of no confidence in Theresa May, voted against her withdrawal agreement on three occasions. Later voted for Boris Johnson as leader and called for Brexiteers to back his deal. Parly under-sec, Brexit, 2017-18. Treasury cttee, 2018-19, 2014-17, 2010-13. Aerospace engineer for the RAF. Centre for Social Justice associate consultant. Member, Cornerstone Group. Evangelical Christian. Voted against gay

	Electorate	Share %	Change from 2017 %
	78,094		
*S Baker C	24,766	45.23	-4.81
K Ahmed Lab	20,552	37.53	-0.21
T Brodelle LD	6,543	11.95	+4.20
P Sims Green	1,454	2.66	+0.45
J Wassell Wycombe	926	1.69	
V Srao Ukip	324	0.59	-1.67
E Gemmell Ind	191	0.35	

marriage in 2013. Ed: St Austell Sixth Form Coll; Southampton University (BEng aerospace systems engineering); St Cross Coll, Oxford (MSc computation).

CHALLENGERS
Khalil Ahmed (Lab) Cllr, Wycombe DC, 2011-; mayor, 2014-15. IT manager. Unison. **Toni Brodelle** (LD) Founder of Incredible Me, a wellbeing group. Member, Council for Christian-

Muslim relations. **Peter Sims** (Green) Author; specialist in electronic engineering.

CONSTITUENCY PROFILE
Wycombe has been a Conservative seat for almost 70 years, having been claimed by the Labour Party only once, in 1945. The 2019 Conservative majority decreased almost 15,000 since 2015 and was its lowest since 2001. An affluent part of Buckinghamshire consisting of High Wycombe and its surrounding villages, the area is more ethnically diverse than the rest of the region. The median weekly income is slightly above the southeast average.

EU REFERENDUM RESULT
48.5% Leave   Remain 51.5%

Wyre & Preston North

MAJORITY 16,781 (31.70%)   CONSERVATIVE HOLD   TURNOUT 70.41%

BEN WALLACE
BORN May 15, 1970
MP 2005-

Defence secretary since 2019. Longstanding ally of Boris Johnson, and was set to manage his aborted 2016 leadership bid. Security minister, 2016-19; parly under-sec, Northern Ireland, 2015-16; assistant whip, 2014-15. PPS to Ken Clarke, 2010-14. *The Spectator* campaigner of the year, 2008, for pushing for transparency on MPs' expenses. Voted to Remain in the EU in 2016, but supported no-deal in indicative votes. Commissioned into the Scots Guards aged 20, serving in Germany, Cyprus and Northern Ireland between 1990 and 1998. Left the army to

Electorate	Share %	from 2017 %	Change
	75,168		
*B Wallace C	31,589	59.69	+1.40
J Ainscough Lab	14,808	27.98	-7.04
J Potter LD	4,463	8.43	+3.59
R Norbury Green	1,729	3.27	+1.42
D Ragozzino Ind	335	0.63	

work in the aerospace industry; overseas director, Qinetiq, 2003-05. MSP for Northeast Scotland, 1999-2003. Qualified skiing instructor. Ed: Millfield Sch, Somerset; RMA Sandhurst.

CHALLENGERS
Joanne Ainscough (Lab) Software developer. Women's officer, Morecambe & Lunesdale Labour, 2019-. **John Potter** (LD) Cllr, Lancashire CC, 2017-. Leader, Preston Liberal Democrats. **Ruth Norbury**

(Green) Teacher. Campaigner, Frack Free Lancashire.

CONSTITUENCY PROFILE
Despite Ben Wallace's majority falling slightly in 2015 and 2017, his winning margin in 2019 was the biggest his party had won here since the seat was created in 2010. This predominantly rural seat contains much of the farmland north of Preston and east of Blackpool. It is a wealthy area with one of the lowest child poverty rates in the country and wages above the regional average. Home ownership is very high and the proportion of residents in social housing is one of the lowest in the country.

EU REFERENDUM RESULT
54.2% Leave   Remain 45.8%

Wyre Forest

MAJORITY 21,413 (42.35%)   CONSERVATIVE HOLD   TURNOUT 64.76%

MARK GARNIER
BORN Feb 26, 1963
MP 2010-

Junior trade minister, 2016-18. Admitted asking an assistant to buy sex toys; an investigation cleared him of breaking the ministerial code but he was sacked in a reshuffle two months later. Secretly recorded in 2014 dismissing "dog-end voters" in the "outlying regions" of Britain. Warned in 2015 that holding an EU referendum would cost Britain investment. Campaigned to Remain; voted for the withdrawal agreement on every occasion. Supported Jeremy Hunt for Conservative leader in 2019. Select cttees: Treasury, 2010-16; finance, 2015-

Electorate	Share %	from 2017 %	Change
	78,079		
*M Garnier C	32,960	65.19	+6.79
R Lunn Lab	11,547	22.84	-9.48
S Miah LD	4,081	8.07	+4.27
J Davis Green	1,973	3.90	+1.90

16. Voted against gay marriage in 2013. Hedge fund manager and investment banker. Cllr, Forest of Dean DC, 2003-07. Freeman of the City of London. Contested this seat in 2005. Ed: Dulwich Coll; Charterhouse Sch.

CHALLENGERS
Robin Lunn (Lab) Director, Eastmills Ltd, a financial advisory company, 2014-. Cllr, Worcester City C, 2013-; Labour group leader. **Shazu Miah** (LD) Principal, SM Lawson Solicitors. Cllr, Wyre Forest DC, 2016-.

CONSTITUENCY PROFILE
The Conservative majority here has increased at every election since Mark Garnier gained the seat in 2010. Before that it was represented by Richard Taylor, an independent MP, 2001-10, and it elected a Labour MP in 1997, which was the only time it had voted Labour since the seat's creation in 1983. The Worcestershire seat contains Kidderminster, with a population of 56,000, the smaller towns of Bewdley and Stourport-on-Severn, and a cluster of villages. Seven in ten households are owner occupied. Median income is £30 per week below the national average.

EU REFERENDUM RESULT
63.1% Leave   Remain 36.9%

Wythenshawe & Sale East

MAJORITY 10,396 (23.23%)   LABOUR HOLD   TURNOUT 58.65%

MIKE KANE
BORN Jan 9, 1969
MP 2014-

Self-described Blairite elected in a by-election after the death of Paul Goggins, MP 1997-2014. Introduced bill to help mesothelioma sufferers. Remainer; voted to trigger Article 50. Shadow minister: schools, 2016-19; international development, 2015-16. Resigned from shadow front bench after 2016 referendum. Nominated Lisa Nandy for the leadership in 2020, Owen Smith, 2016, Liz Kendall, 2015. Primary school teacher. Later chief executive, Movement for Change, a grassroots campaigning group. Cllr, Manchester City C, 1991-

	Electorate	Share %	Change from 2017 %
	76,313		
*M Kane Lab	23,855	53.30	-8.92
P Harrop C	13,459	30.07	+0.45
S Lepori LD	3,111	6.95	+3.67
J Fousert Brexit	2,717	6.07	
R Nunney Green	1,559	3.48	+2.23
C Bellamy Comm Lge	58	0.13	

2008. Worked for Jonathan Reynolds (Stalybridge & Hyde) and James Purnell, 2008-11. Young carer for MS-suffering mother. Ed: Manchester Metropolitan University (BA social sciences); University of Manchester (PGCE).

CHALLENGERS
Peter Harrop (C) Operations manager for Verastar, Yodel and other companies. Armed forces veteran. **Simon Lepori**

(LD) LGBT Liberal Democrats. Contested Trafford MBC, 2018.

CONSTITUENCY PROFILE
Labour has won this seat at every election since its creation in 1997. Its predecessor, Manchester Wythenshawe, had elected Labour MPs since 1964. A varied constituency south of Manchester, containing the interwar Wythenshawe council estate, one of the largest in the country, as well as the suburban area of Sale. Home to Manchester airport, a major employer, and Wythenshawe hospital. A third of households are socially rented, nearly double the national average.

EU REFERENDUM RESULT
49.6% Leave   Remain 50.4%

Yeovil

MAJORITY 16,181 (27.31%)   CONSERVATIVE HOLD   TURNOUT 71.86%

MARCUS FYSH
BORN Nov 8, 1970
MP 2015-

Australian-born businessman who ran agriculture and healthcare start-ups. Investment manager, Mercury Asset Management; director, London Wessex. Cleared by the CPS over 2015 expenses rule breach. "Spartan" Brexiteer who voted against Theresa May's withdrawal agreement every time, but voted for Boris Johnson's in October 2019. Supported Mr Johnson in the 2019 Tory leadership contest. Voted against LGBT-inclusive sex and relationship education in schools, 2019. Select cttees: international trade, 2016-19;

	Electorate	Share %	Change from 2017 %
	82,468		
*M Fysh C	34,588	58.37	+3.88
M Clark LD	18,407	31.06	+1.36
T Ledlie Lab	3,761	6.35	-6.14
D Wood Green	1,629	2.75	+0.98
T Capozzoli Ind	689	1.16	-0.38
T Fox Constitution	186	0.31	

public administration, 2016-19; European scrutiny, 2017-19. Cllr: South Somerset DC, 2011-15; Somerset CC, 2013-15. Ed: Winchester Coll; Corpus Christi Coll, Oxford (BA English language and literature).

CHALLENGERS
Mick Clark (LD) NHS worker and RAF serviceman. Amateur cider brewer. Known locally for coming to the aid of a woman after a freak accident at South

Somerset carnival. **Terry Ledlie** (Lab) Postman, Royal Mail. Somerset Labour chairman.

CONSTITUENCY PROFILE
This Somerset seat has been won by Conservatives except for the period between 1983 and 2015, during which time the seat was held by the Liberals and then the Lib Dems. Its MP for most of that time was Paddy Ashdown, the Lib Dem leader, 1988-99. The town of Yeovil is home to about 45,000 people, and the area's local economy is weighted towards manufacturing and defence. About a fifth of residents are aged 65 or above and home ownership is common.

EU REFERENDUM RESULT
59.9% Leave   Remain 40.1%

Ynys Mon

MAJORITY 1,968 (5.38%)   **CONSERVATIVE GAIN FROM LABOUR**   TURNOUT 70.39%

VIRGINIA CROSBIE
BORN Dec 8, 1966
MP 2019-

Pharmaceutical analyst turned maths teacher. Senior roles at HSBC, Glaxo Wellcome and UBS. Mentor, Into University, a charity that aims to get students from disadvantaged backgrounds into higher education. Director, Women 2 Win, 2017-. A dolphin trainer in her youth; appeared on the BBC children's show *Animal Magic*. Contested Rhondda, 2017. Ed: Colchester Grammar School for Girls, Queen Mary University (BSc microbiology and immunology); University of Westminster (PgDip management studies); LSE (corporate finance programme).

	Electorate	Share %	from 2017 % Change
	51,925		
V Crosbie C	12,959	35.45	+7.66
M Roberts Lab	10,991	30.07	-11.79
A Ap Dafydd PC	10,418	28.50	+1.11
H Jenner Brexit	2,184	5.98	

CHALLENGERS
Mary Roberts (Lab) Researcher for Albert Owen, the MP for this seat, 2001-19. Campaign staff with Women's Institute. Member, Unite. Backed Yvette Cooper for the leadership, then Owen Smith. Voted to remain in the EU. Welsh speaker. **Aled Ap Dafydd** (PC) Sports and political reporter for the BBC; worked for the Welsh language channel S4C. First time running for elected office. **Helen Jenner** (Brexit) Teacher and writer. Supports Wylfa nuclear plant.

CONSTITUENCY PROFILE
Ynys Mon, the Welsh name for the Isle of Anglesey, had been held by Labour since 2001, when Albert Jones gained the seat from Ieuan Wyn Jones, PC leader, 2000-12. The Conservatives held it from 1979 to 1987, Labour having held it before that, from 1951. The island seat, located off the northwest of Wales, is home to Four Mile Bridge, Holy Island, Newlands Park, Llangefni and a collection of villages. Almost a quarter of residents are aged 65 or above, and almost seven in ten households are owner occupied. There are two RAF stations on the island.

EU REFERENDUM RESULT
50.9% Leave   Remain 49.1%

York Central

MAJORITY 13,545 (27.36%)   **LABOUR CO-OP HOLD**   TURNOUT 66.10%

RACHAEL MASKELL
BORN Jul 5, 1972
MP 2015-

Care worker and senior NHS physiotherapist. Head of health, Unite. Backed Clive Lewis (Norwich South) for leader, 2020; Jeremy Corbyn, 2016; Andy Burnham, 2015. Voted Remain; resigned from shadow cabinet to vote against triggering Article 50. Shadow: transport minister, 2017-; environment secretary, 2016-17; defence minister, 2015-16. Select cttees: ecclesiastical, 2015-19; health and social care, 2015. Chairwoman, ageing APPG; also a member of flood prevention APPG. Labour NEC, 2011-15. Niece of the prison reformer Terence Morris.

	Electorate	Share %	from 2017 % Change
	74,899		
*R Maskell Lab Co-op	27,312	55.17	-9.99
F Tate C	13,767	27.81	-2.37
J Blanchard LD	4,149	8.38	+3.72
T Franklin Green	2,107	4.26	
N Szkiler Brexit	1,479	2.99	
A Snedden Yorkshire	557	1.13	
A Dunn Soc Dem	134	0.27	

Ed: University of East Anglia (physiotherapy).

CHALLENGERS
Fabia Tate (C) Business development manager, Labman, an automation company. Campaign manager for Zac Goldsmith, 2014-16. **James Blanchard** (LD) NHS engagement support manager. Contested York Outer, 2017, 2015. Cllr: Kirklees DC, 2011-15;

Islington LBC, 2002-06. **Tom Franklin** (Green) Treasurer, Yorkshire & the Humber Greens.

CONSTITUENCY PROFILE
This densely populated seat has been Labour since its creation. In 2010 its predecessor, City of York, was divided into two, with York Outer entirely surrounding York Central. Labour's majority in 2019, though reduced, was still more than double what it was in 2010 or 2015. With the University of York just to the south, the seat has a large student population. Home ownership is very low and a high proportion of its residents rent their homes privately.

EU REFERENDUM RESULT
38.8% Leave   Remain 61.2%

York Outer

MAJORITY 9,985 (18.04%)   **CONSERVATIVE HOLD**   **TURNOUT 74.12%**

JULIAN STURDY
BORN Jun 3, 1971
MP 2010-

Farmer. Supported leaving the EU in 2016. Voted against Theresa May's withdrawal agreement in the first Commons vote, but supported it thereafter. Backed Boris Johnson for leader, 2019. Has fought to protect the Yorkshire green belt. Introduced a bill granting owners of horses more freedom in disposing of them, which became the Control of Horses Act, 2015. Select cttees: environment, 2017-; consolidation bills, 2015-; energy, 2015-16; transport, 2010-12. APPG chairman: science and technology in agriculture. Contested Scunthorpe, 2005.

	Electorate	Share %	from 2017 %	Change %
	74,673			
*J Sturdy C	27,324	49.37	-1.75	
A Perrett Lab	17,339	31.33	-5.36	
K Aspden LD	9,992	18.05	+7.76	
S Marmion Ind	692	1.25		

Cllr, Harrogate BC, 2002-07. Ed: Ashville Coll; Harper Adams Agricultural Coll.

CHALLENGERS
Anna Perrett (Lab) Owner of Active Outcomes, a consultancy and communications firm. Charity worker. Helped to establish the York Women's Forum. Backed by Momentum. **Keith Aspden** (LD) Secondary school history teacher. Cllr, York City C, 2003-; leader of the Lib Dem group, 2013-. Became Fulford councillor at the age of 21. **Scott Marmion** (Ind) Physicist and historian.

CONSTITUENCY PROFILE
Has been held by the Conservatives since its creation in 2010. The Lib Dems initially came a strong second, but in the past three elections the Tories have won majorities of about 10,000 votes over Labour. York Outer covers the city's suburbs, including the historic villages of Fulford, Osbaldwick and Skelton, and forms a ring around York Central. It encompasses the University of York campus, and is home to about 8,000 students. More than a fifth of residents are aged 65 or above.

EU REFERENDUM RESULT
44.7% Leave   Remain 55.3%

Yorkshire East

MAJORITY 22,787 (43.18%)   **CONSERVATIVE HOLD**   **TURNOUT 65.25%**

SIR GREG KNIGHT
BORN Apr 4, 1949
MP 2001-; 1983-97

Qualified solicitor. MP for Derby North from 1983 until Tony Blair's 1997 landslide. Went viral during 2017 election for a video urging people to "get it right, vote for Greg Knight". Drummer and founding member of MP4, the parliamentary rock band; released charity single with other musicians to support the launch of the Jo Cox Foundation, 2016. Brexiteer who voted for no-deal and for Boris Johnson, 2019. Backed the withdrawal agreement all but the first time. Author of six books. Whip, 2012-13. Shadow minister: transport, 2005; environment, 2003-05;

	Electorate	Share %	from 2017 %	Change %
	80,871			
*G Knight C	33,988	64.41	+6.14	
C Minnis Lab	11,201	21.23	-9.24	
D Needham LD	4,219	8.00	+4.04	
T Norman Yorkshire	1,686	3.20	+1.31	
M Jackson Green	1,675	3.17	+1.43	

culture, 2003. Ed: Alderman Newton's (Grammar); Guildford College of Law.

CHALLENGERS
Catherine Minnis (Lab) Secondary school teacher. Contested East Riding C, 2019. **Dale Needham** (LD) Contested East Riding C, 2019. **Tim Norman** (Yorkshire) Hotelier. East Riding councillor. **Mike Jackson** (Green) Scientist with a physics PhD. Plays in several local bands.

CONSTITUENCY PROFILE
The Conservatives have always held this seat, initially winning a majority of a little more than 3,000 over Labour in 1997, with the party's majority increasing at every subsequent general election. The Conservatives also held the predecessor seat, Bridlington, at every election since it was created in 1950. The constituency stretches from the eastern fringes of York to the coastal town of Bridlington, and includes the market town of Driffield and several small villages. A quarter of residents are aged 65 or above. More than seven in ten households are owner-occupied.

EU REFERENDUM RESULT
63.7% Leave   Remain 36.3%

Index to candidates